HARDPRESS.NET
HOME OF HARD-TO-FIND BOOKS

The Works of the Right Reverend John Stark Ravenscroft ...
by John Stark Ravenscroft

Address:
HardPress
8345 NW 66TH ST #2561
MIAMI FL 33166-2626
USA
Email: info@hardpress.net

Sarah Anne

RIGHT REV. JOHN STARK RAVENSCROFT, D.D.

Bishop of the Protestant Episcopal Church

IN THE DIOCESE OF NORTH CAROLINA.

ENGRAVED BY J.H. DIMIER AND PAINTED BY J. RICHOLTZ.   Printed by J. Neale

ENGRAVED BY J. H. DIMDER AND PAINTED BY J. EICHOLTZ.

Printed by J. Neale

THE

WORKS

OF

THE RIGHT REVEREND

JOHN STARK RAVENSCROFT, D. D.,

BISHOP OF THE PROTESTANT EPISCOPAL CHURCH IN THE
DIOCESE OF NORTH-CAROLINA.

CONTAINING HIS

SERMONS, CHARGES, AND CONTROVERSIAL TRACTS;

TO WHICH IS PREFIXED,

A MEMOIR OF HIS LIFE:

DEVISED BY THE AUTHOR TO THE " EPISCOPAL BIBLE, PRAYER BOOK, TRACT, AND
MISSIONARY SOCIETY OF NORTH-CAROLINA," AND NOW
PUBLISHED FOR THEIR BENEFIT.

IN TWO VOLUMES.

VOL. I.

NEW-YORK:

PROTESTANT EPISCOPAL PRESS.

MDCCCXXX.

PREFACE.

THE name of the first Bishop of North Carolina is familiarly known throughout the Church in these United States of America; and his memory will now be as extensively cherished and revered by all who delight to behold her distinctive principles firmly and fearlessly maintained in union with an ardent, pure, and unaffected piety. Nor will it be confined within the limits of our own Church, or to the present generation. The bold features of his strong and decided character, the remarkable circumstance of his conversion to the faith of CHRIST, and his engaging in the Gospel ministry at a comparatively advanced period of life, the zeal, courage, and self-denial with which he fulfilled the responsible duties of his sacred calling, and the prominent station which he occupied when advanced to the highest order of the Priesthood, as the Apostle of a new Diocese, will all combine to render him distinguished in the annals of this period of our ecclesiastical history. Sustained by these alone, his memory would long have flourished. But we have reason for gratitude to the Fountain of all wisdom, the Giver of every good and perfect gift, that he was permitted to provide for himself the materials of a more durable monument. In these volumes it is now set up, and will stand conspicuous amongst those on which are engraven the wisdom and piety, the faithful labours and profitable instructions of the great and good men to whom we look back, extending in bright succession even to the Apostles' days, and whom we regard with affectionate veneration as Fathers in the Christian Church.

Looking to the Church of England, what a host of names recur to our minds, of her mitred worthies, who have zealously and effectively occupied every department of knowledge which could illustrate the records of revealed truth, defend its doctrines, enforce its precepts, or was in any way connected with the moral and religious improvement of man. Descended from such a parent, the American Church will not be found a degenerate daughter. The period of her separate existence is but half a century, and the whole number of her Bishops has been but twenty-four; and amongst those whose earthly labour has been finished, and who have gone to their reward, leaving us precious memorials of their wisdom and piety, in works which already take their place with the standard writers of the Church, we can enumerate with proud satisfaction, Seabury, Moore, Dehon, and Hobart. * We have now a farther and

---

* The first Bishop of Connecticut, a man for strength of mind, firmness of purpose, moral courage, and the decided character of his Church principles, very much resembling him whose works are now published, is the author of two volumes of Sermons, which for lucid statements and conclusive arguments, upon the principal doctrines and the primitive order of the Church, have seldom been equalled. Two volumes of interesting and instructive Sermons, by the Rt. Rev. Bishop Moore, of New-York, have been published. They are distinguished for their sedate and rational exhibitions of the temper and principles of true piety, while they are not deficient in earnestness; and their style of diction is eminently chaste and classical. Bishop Dehon, of South Carolina, has also left us two volumes of Sermons, which have embodied the graces of his pure and amiable piety, and exhibit the distinctive principles and the holy rites and observances of our Church in a most impressive and attractive manner.

We have as yet but two volumes of Sermons by Bishop Hobart, together with various single productions. Every thing which fell from the pen of this revered and distinguished prelate was marked by his vigorous and ardent mind, and we rejoice in the anticipation of having his whole works collected and arranged, and given to the Christian community. They will be an invaluable inheritance left to the Church which he so dearly loved, for which he so faithfully and so successfully laboured, and in whose cause his life was consumed.

To several of our living Bishops the Church is indebted for valuable publications, and more especially to the venerable and beloved presiding Bishop, and to the excellent Bishop of the Eastern Diocese. Long may they continue to bless the Church with the mild influence of their pious examples. When also called to their reward, a grateful and merited tribute will be paid to their memory.

most valuable accession to our stores of theological knowledge and practical exhortation to godliness, in the collected works of BISHOP RAVENSCROFT.

These volumes comprise a republication of what had before been issued from the press under the Bishop's own inspection, together with sixty-one* sermons, selected by him during his last illness, for posthumous publication. The whole was left by him as a legacy to the "Episcopal Bible, Prayer Book, Tract, and Missionary Society of North Carolina."

The discourses contained in the first volume, (with the exception of those which follow the Charges,) the controversial tract in vindication of the "Doctrines of the Church," and in defence of "the Integrity of Revealed Religion," and the three Charges, are the parts which have already appeared before the public. In presenting them again no alteration has been made, save the correcting the errors of the press, and the omission of a few sentences of a local or personal character, but of no importance to the chief matter.

It may be wished by many readers that these omissions had been carried to a greater extent in the tract entitled "A Vindication of the Church." As regards this piece, it is marked by several passages of a merely temporary interest, and which contain personal allusions, such as are unhappily too often found in controversial tracts, and are, perhaps, hardly separable from them, when discussions are carried on by men of ardent temperaments, and who are clear and decided in their views of sacred truth. It must not be disguised, that in the judgment of those gentlemen connected with the New-York Protestant Episcopal Press, who have superintended the present publication, this tract would have appeared better, and perhaps have been more universally acceptable and useful, had it been freed

---

* See note, page 656, Vol. I.

from these peculiarities, and the close and conclusive argument of the Bishop left to work its way by its own irresistible force, and no portion of his powerful and eloquent language been suffered to draw the reader's attention towards an adversary who, however well he might have merited the severe chastisement inflicted upon him, was yet unimportant in reference to the great question in dispute. In justice to the Bishop it should be stated, that on his death-bed he gave full permission to the editors of his works, " to alter the form of the Vindication, and to change some expressions in it." After " due deliberation, however, it was thought best, at least for the present, to republish this tract substantially as it first came from the press; that the reader might be able to form an unbiassed judgment of its original character." The friends of the Church will acquiesce in this decision ; and while reading the portion of his works alluded to, if they object to the severity of any expressions contained in it, they will remember that the heart of its author was as free from malice as his tongue from guile, and that it was not in his generous and honourable nature, even if his Christian profession did not prohibit it, to harbour resentment against a human being.

The fifteen Sermons which follow the Charges, in the first volume, together with the whole of those contained in the second volume, were such as the Bishop had written in the ordinary course of his ministrations, and had all of them been preached on several occasions. They were not originally intended for publication, having been composed under the pressure of a variety of labours, growing out of the double character in which he officiated—that of Parish Priest, and Bishop ; or in effect, " chief Missionary" of the Diocese—in the latter of which he was employed at least six months in the year ; and it was only at the earnest request of some of his clergy that he consented to mark a few of his manuscripts for preservation. In publishing them, the alterations from the manuscripts have been very few, and those unimportant. Such changes only were ventured upon as had perhaps escaped his notice while looking over them in those intervals of relief from pain and distressing weakness which he obtained during his last illness; and such as would, in all probability, have met his entire approbation. In no instance has a sentiment been changed or modified; and very rarely a form of expression, and then only when an epithet has been substituted for another more definite, or when the extreme length of a sentence or its involved construction required, as the case might be, a subdivision or a slight simplification. The paragraphs even, with very few exceptions, are printed as they were found in the manuscripts.

The arrangement of the Sermons is not at present exactly what would have been preferred, or what would have been adopted, had it been originally designed to comprise the whole works in two volumes. The publication having commenced with what was to be the second of three volumes, the best arrangement was afterwards made which the circumstances of the case permitted. In the first volume, after the very interesting Memoir and the letter upon the character of the Bishop, prepared by friends who well knew and warmly loved him, and who have written with equal candour and discrimination, and with a deep felt interest in their subject, the works proceed in the following order :—First, the sermons already printed are republished in chronological order—next, the controversial tract, "The doctrines of the Church vindicated, &c." to which has been added a note containing extracts and references on the important subject of the authority of the primitive fathers in matters of controversy, which may be useful to those who have not the means of examining for themselves—

and three Charges, in the order in which they were delivered. The publication of the posthumous works of the Bishop then proceeds with fifteen Sermons, upon the sacraments, the principal ordinances, and the festivals of the Church. With these the first volume concludes; and it will be found to contain a mass of most impressive argument, instruction, and exhortation, concerning the distinctive principles of the Church.

The second volume comprises Sermons upon the general grounds of revealed religion, and the most important doctrines and duties of Christianity. They have been arranged, as nearly as the subjects of them would permit, in systematical order.

These volumes are now sent forth under the full conviction that they will prove to be a rich source of edification and comfort, not only to those who enjoyed the living ministrations of their revered author, and who must receive them with a peculiar interest, but also to the whole Church of which he was so distinguished a member. Although there may arise a difference of opinion as regards some few points of doctrine, and also some diversity of sentiment as to the manner in which particular questions have been stated and defended, yet it is believed that in very few volumes of theology in our language will there be found more full and clear views of the fundamental doctrines of the Gospel, more powerful and conclusive arguments to enforce them, or more cogent and eloquent appeals to the consciences of men to receive and obey the truth as it is in JESUS.

CONTENTS TO VOL. I.

PAGE.

Memoir, - - - - - - - - - - - - - - - 1

A Farewell Discourse ; preached in St. James' Church, Mecklenburg County,
Virginia, - - - - - - - - - - - - - 71

A Sermon on the Church ; delivered before the Annual Convention of the
Protestant Episcopal Church of North-Carolina, - - - - - 95

A Sermon on the Christian Ministry ; delivered in St. Peter's Church,
Washington, N. C., at an ordination, - - - - - - - 121

Revelation the Foundation of Faith ; a Sermon preached in St. Luke's
Church, Salisbury, N. C., at an ordination, - - - - - 145

A Sermon preached before the Bible Society of North-Carolina, - - - 163

A Sermon on the Study and Interpretation of the Scriptures ; delivered in the
Episcopal Chapel, Raleigh, - - - - - - - - - 181

A Sermon preached at the consecration of Christ Church, Raleigh, N. C., - 197

The Doctrines of the Church vindicated from the misrepresentations of Dr.
John Rice ; and Revealed Religion defended against the "No Comment"
Principle of promiscuous Bible Societies, - - - - - - 213

An Episcopal Charge, delivered to the Convention of the Protestant Episcopal
Church, assembled in Washington, N. C., in April, 1825, - - - 425

An Episcopal Charge, delivered to the Convention of the Protestant Episcopal
Church, assembled in Hillsborough, N. C., in May, 1826, - - - 437

An Episcopal Charge, delivered to the Convention of the Protestant Episcopal
Church, assembled in Fayetteville, N. C., in May, 1828, - - - 447

VOL. I.—A.

SERMONS ON VARIOUS SUBJECTS.

SERMON I.

BAPTISM.

JOHN iii. 5.—JESUS answered, Verily, Verily, I say unto thee, Except a man be born of water, and of the SPIRIT, he cannot enter into the kingdom of GOD. - - - - - - - - - - - - 471

SERMON II.

CONFIRMATION.

ACTS xv. 41.—And he went through Syria and Cilicia, confirming the churches. 489

SERMON III.

NATURE AND DESIGN OF THE HOLY COMMUNION.

LUKE xxii. 19, *last clause.*—This do, in remembrance of me. - - - 503

SERMON IV.

THE OBLIGATION TO PARTAKE OF THE LORD'S SUPPER.

1 CORINTHIANS xi. 26.—For as often as ye eat this bread, and drink this cup, ye do show the LORD's death till he come. - - - - 516

SERMON V.

COMMUNION OF SAINTS.

1 CORINTHIANS x. 17.—For we being many, are one bread, and one body; for we are all partakers of that one bread. - - - - - 528

SERMON VI.

UNITY OF THE CHURCH.

EPHESIANS iv. 4.—There is one body. - - - - - - - 541

SERMON VII.

CHRISTMAS.

MATTHEW xi. 28.—Come unto me, all ye that labour, and are heavy laden, and I will give you rest. - - - - - - - - 558

SERMON VIII.

NEW-YEAR'S DAY.

PSALM xxxi. 15, *first clause.*—My times are in thy hand. - - - - 571

SERMON IX.

NEW-YEAR'S DAY.

HEBREWS i. 12, *last clause.*—But thou art the same, and thy years shall not fail. - - - - - - - - - - - - 585

SERMON X.

ASCENSION OF CHRIST.

JOHN vi. 62.—What and if ye shall see the Son of Man ascend up, where he was before ? - - - - - - - - - - - 597

SERMON XI.

TRINITY SUNDAY.

1 TIMOTHY iii. 16.—And without controversy, great is the mystery of godliness ; GOD was manifest in the flesh, justified in the SPIRIT, seen of angels, preached unto the Gentiles, believed on in the world, received up into glory. - - - - - - - - - 607

SERMON XII.

ORDINATION, OR INSTITUTION.

1 THESSALONIANS v. 25.—Brethren, pray for us. - - - - 619

SERMON XIII.

ORDINATION SERMON.

2 CORINTHIANS iv. 5.—For we preach not ourselves, but CHRIST JESUS the LORD, and ourselves your servants, for JESUS' sake. - - - 631

SERMON XIV.

CONSECRATION.

PSALM xciii. 5, *last clause.*—Holiness becometh thine house, O LORD, for ever. 645

SERMON XV.

THE OLD PATHS :—A CONSECRATION SERMON ; PREACHED IN VIRGINIA AND NORTH-CAROLINA.

JEREMIAH vi. 16.—Thus saith the LORD, Stand ye in the ways, and see, and ask for the old paths, where is the good way, and walk therein, and ye shall find rest for your souls. - - - - - - 656

MEMOIR.

JOHN STARK RAVENSCROFT, D. D., late Bishop of the diocese of North-Carolina, was born in the year 1772, at an estate near Blandford, in the county of Prince George, Virginia, which had long been in the possession of his family. He was the only child of Dr. John Ravenscroft, a gentleman of fortune, who had been educated for the practice of medicine.

Dr. Ravenscroft's ample possessions and small family soon induced him to relinquish the practice of his laborious profession, and within two months after the birth of his son, he removed to Great-Britain, where he ultimately purchased a small landed estate in the south of Scotland, to the improvement of which he devoted the rest of his life.

The mother of the subject of our memoir, was the daughter of Mr. Hugh Miller, a Scotch gentleman who resided in the same county, and both she and her husband, Dr. Ravenscroft, were descended maternally from the extensive and respectable family of the Bollings.

It is not known, certainly, what were the chief inducements with Dr. Ravenscroft to remove to Europe. Though of Scotch descent and married into a Scottish family, it is not probable that the dissentions between the colonies and the mother country had any influence upon his determination, for it will be recollected that, although great excitement had prevailed in the country for some years previous, the year 1772 and the early part of '73 was a season of remarkable tranquillity, and the opinion was generally entertained that the conciliatory measures of the British government would ultimately subdue the spirit of disaffection in her colonies. Be that as it may, however, it is certain that he regarded his removal as final, having previously to his departure empowered an attorney to dispose of the whole of his patrimonial and other property. The sale was effected, but owing to the unsettled state of the country at that period, and the subsequent very great depreciation in the value of the current money of the time, the doctor during his life time derived but very little benefit from it, and having in the purchase that he made in Scotland, relied upon the funds which he expected from Virginia, he was in consequence somewhat embarrassed during his whole life. He notwithstanding so far arranged his affairs before his death, as to leave his widow, who is still living, in easy circumstances. He died about the close of the year 1780.

Mrs. Ravenscroft availed herself of the excellent opportunity which Scotland afforded, at that time as now, of giving her son a very complete and thorough classical education ; and after he had finished his course at one of the most respectable grammar schools in that country, she placed him at a seminary of somewhat higher grade in the north of England, where, besides continuing his classical studies, he was instructed in mathematics, natural philosophy, and other sciences.

Soon after Mr. Ravenscroft had entered his seventeenth year, his friends thought it expedient that he should return to Virginia, for the purpose of looking after the remains of his father's property, which, from causes already mentioned, still remained in a very precarious condition. He accordingly left his friends in Scotland at the beginning of the winter of 1788—9, and reached Virginia in the January following. He was here so far successful in recovering some remnants of his father's large property, as to be subsequently in easy, if not affluent circumstances. Intending to devote himself to the profession of the law, he entered William and Mary college, at Williamsburg, in Virginia, with a view to the prosecution of that study, and to the acquisition of a more perfect acquaintance with the sciences. Mr. Wythe was at that period professor of law at Williamsburg, and of course the advantages for students in that department were unusually great ; but owing to the extreme relaxation of discipline in the college, joined to the large pecuniary allowance made to Mr. Ravenscroft by his guardian, and which induced habits of extravagance and dissipation, he did not derive that instruction from the lectures of this eminent lawyer which his friends might have expected. It is not necessary here to dwell upon the time wasted, and the evil courses pursued, by Mr. Ravenscroft during this dangerous period of his life : the reader will find in a subsequent part of this narrative, the candid account which that most ingenuous of men himself gives of it. It is to be remarked, however, that his conviction of sin was so strong in the latter part of his life, and his self-accusations so severe in respect to his misspent youth, that the picture which he has drawn of it, is, probably, too highly coloured to convey *a just* idea of his character and conduct. Those who knew him at this and at a somewhat latter period of life, are not aware of his addiction to any vices, in the *popular* sense of that term, except profane swearing and a general contempt for religion. It is true that these vices go very far towards making a depraved character, but some palliation may be found for them, in the peculiar circumstances in which Mr. Ravenscroft was placed. Separated by an ocean from his family—supplied by a too indulgent guardian with almost unlimited means of gratifying his inclination—and placed at the early age of seventeen at a seminary notorious at that period for its total want of discipline, it is not to be wondered at, that he should have indulged in excesses and contracted habits, which, in after years, appeared to his self-abhorring spirit to be of the most vicious kind. At the same time, it is very certain that those habits and excesses were not of that nature, which is usually thought to be degrading to the youthful character.

As might have been expected, however, his studies did not result in any very considerable acquaintance with the principles of the profession to which he had proposed devoting his chief attention, and though he remained for some time a member of the college, with the ostensible object of preparing himself for the practice of law, it does not appear that he ever procured a license to practice, or if he did it is certain that he never availed himself of it. Before Mr. Ravenscroft left Williamsburg, an event took place which seems to have been, in the hand of GOD, the means of arresting him in that career of youthful dissipation, which, as he advanced towards manhood, was assuming the more alarming character of habitual vice. He formed an acquaintance with the lady who afterwards became his wife, and whose lovely character appears from that time to have exerted an influence over his wayward disposition, sufficiently powerful to counteract the adverse influence of his former bad habits and want of religious principle, and to make him the estimable and respectable man he afterwards became, till the more powerful operations of God's grace brought him to the foot of the cross.

This lady was the daughter of Lewis Burwell, Esq., of Mecklenburg County, and was on a visit to her friends in Williamsburg, at the time of her first acquaintance with Mr. Ravenscroft. She is represented as having been remarkable for her personal beauty, and for what was of far greater value, especially in the particular station assigned her by Providence, a gentleness of disposition peculiarly adapted to a collision with the ardent temperament of her husband, and at the same time a firmness of character, and correctness of principle, which, while it enabled her to mould his less established character, preserved her from the contagion of his evil example.

About the year 1792, Mr. Ravenscroft re-visited Scotland for the last time, with the view of converting the property which he had inherited from his father in that country, into money, preparatory to his final establishment in Virginia. This addition to his already competent estate rendered his situation such as justified him in marrying, notwithstanding that he had now abandoned all thoughts of prosecuting the profession of law. Accordingly, soon after his return from Scotland, and a short time previous to his coming of age, he was married to Miss Burwell. Not having purchased any property prior to his marriage, and having no near relations residing in the vicinity of his birth place, to make it a desirable residence for himself, he was easily induced to yield to the wishes of his wife in purchasing an estate in the more healthy district of country where his father-in-law lived. He settled in Lunenburgh County, not far from Mr. Burwell, and henceforward devoted himself to the usual pursuits of a country life, until it pleased God to call him to be a labourer in his vineyard. During a period of eighteen years,

Mr. Ravenscroft here continued to sustain his several relations towards his family and neighbours, in a manner that gave him a high and honourable reputation among men. The remark already made, respecting the hateful terms in which he was wont in after years to refer to this wasted period of life—wasted as to *the chief purpose* of life, may here be repeated, and the impression very generally entertained, in consequence, respecting his character and conduct at this time, be corrected. As a husband, a master, a member of society—a husband to the widow, and in a peculiar sense, a father to the orphan, Mr. Ravenscroft was every thing that was estimable ; and the absurd stories of his fondness for gaming and other low vices, are utterly groundless. It is true that his good qualities were all obscured by a more than ordinary neglect, and perhaps contempt, of, religious obligations. And it is this that led him when his eyes became open, to loathe himself to the degree which was so remarkable a trait of his religious character. But, doubtless, many a mere moralist has built his claims for acceptance with his GOD upon a foundation more slender than the morality which Mr. Ravenscroft practised for years, though without any reference to his accountability.

Mr. Ravenscroft was never blessed with children of his own, but towards five orphan children, who were placed under his care while infants, he for many years discharged the duties of an affectionate and conscientious parent. The survivors of these objects of his parental affection bear testimony, in the warmest terms, to the undeviating kindness and judicious care which marked the conduct of their adopted father towards them, from their earliest recollection to the day of his death ; and the filial respect uniformly manifested on their part, has afforded to all who witnessed it, a pleasing evidence of the sincerity of their gratitude.

It is not consistent with the chief purposes of this memoir to dwell at much length upon this portion of Mr. Ravenscroft's life. That he lived utterly *without* GOD *in the world,* he himself was ever most ready to acknowledge, and the mere details of an ordinary irreligious life, passed in the obscurity of the country, would possess neither novelty nor instruction. That he did not suffer his mind to languish or his early advantages to remain unimproved, is obvious from the large fund of acquired information which he carried with him into the ministry, and those habits of close and logical reasoning which formed so striking a characteristic of his pulpit oratory. Although he interested himself with his usual ardour in the politics of the day and in the various objects of local interest which successively presented themselves, he was never induced to leave the retirement of private life or to seek that kind of popularity which seems almost the natural food of tempers as active as his. In the bosom of his family, and in the diligent discharge of the numerous charities of life, he sought and found that happiness which this world can give. Though blessed with a wife, who seems to have found her own happiness in promoting his, with an estate that was equal to his utmost wishes, and with the respect and affection of a large circle of friends, he yet experienced that truth which enters so largely into the experience of every man, that the happiness of this world is empty and unsatisfying—and his well informed mind was gradually brought, though after a long night of delusion, to the conviction that " here was not his rest."

We are henceforth to consider the character of Mr. Ravenscroft in a new aspect. So heartily and earnestly did he co-operate with the grace of GOD, when it had once broken down the vain opposition of his sinful and long cherished lusts, that the change in his views, his feelings, and his pursuits, though far from being instantaneous or even very rapid, soon became marked and decisive. Some groundless stories respecting the immediate causes and manner of his conversion, have been related and even published ; and it is well for the cause of truth, as also for Mr. Ravenscroft's own reputation, that he was prevailed upon to commit to writing during his last confinement, an authentic and detailed account of the rise and progress in his heart of that great change by which *he put off, concerning the former conversation, the old man,* and *put on the new man, which after* GOD *is created in righteousness and true holiness.*

The stories referred to, very seriously implicated his private and domestic character, and if true, would have presented him in the odious light of a persecutor of religion in *the persons* of its professors, as well as in its *principles*. That there was no foundation for these stories, either in the character of Mr. Ravenscroft, or in any circumstances connected with his conversion, was well known to all who knew him, or who had access to correct information on the subject; but the public have remained long deceived, and Mr. Ravenscroft, who always acted with a motive, was induced by a conscientious apprehension of doing harm to the cause of religion, to refrain from undeceiving them during his life. As he says himself in a letter to a friend, who had requested information from him in relation to the great change in his heart and life, "It is a subject I have never been fond of stirring, because I was averse to putting myself forward, and because the peculiar circumstances of my case might have been used and perverted to strengthen the despisers of the means of grace, in their neglect of all the outward appointments of God's wisdom and goodness, to beget consideration in their hearts, and lead them to repentance. Therefore it was, that when some person, both unknown to me, and ignorant of me, undertook to publish what was totally without foundation; I cared not to contradict it otherwise than in conversation to the few friends who questioned me on the subject."

This same disregard of his own reputation when brought into collision with the interests of his fellow men, or with the glory of his God, continued to actuate all Mr. Ravenscroft's motions until the day of his death. He was induced, however, towards the close of his life, to believe, or rather to yield to the opinions of his friends, that a narrative of his religious life, and of his life and character before he became a convert, would be useful: and the reader is here presented with the last records of that pen which has done so much for the sacred cause of religion. Although the hand of death arrested its author in his progress towards its completion, yet enough has been told in this memoir to vindicate him from the calumnies, which, in connexion with the fictitious story of his conversion, were circulated much more widely than his verbal contradictions of them.

" IN fulfilment of a promise made to several of my friends, who judged—whether rightly or not must be proved by the event—that advantage might be derived to the cause of true religion, and the interests of the Church promoted, from the circumstances attending my entering upon a religious course of life authentically communicated ; and that as a public man I owed it to the public, and particularly to the communion of which I am a minister, to record the leading events of my religious life, I commit to writing what the memoranda I have preserved enable me to give of my personal history, so far as that is connected with edification to the members of the Church, and to all other serious and unprejudiced persons.   In performing this promise, I rather yield to the reasonings of others than to the conviction of my own mind, having long been of opinion that effects which have not followed the *living* services of any uninspired minister of CHRIST, are hardly to be expected from *posthumous* endeavours.   GOD, however, can give effect to whatever means seem good to him, and if it shall be his will to work by this for the salvation of even a single sinner, or to remove a single prejudice against his Church, to his holy and merciful name be all the glory both now and for ever.

" JOHN S. RAVENSCROFT."

———

" THOUGH a native of Virginia, being born in the county of Prince George, in the year 1772, of which state my progenitors, as far back as I have been able to trace them, with the exception of my maternal grandfather, were also natives—my first recollections are of Scotland, my parents having removed from Virginia the same year in which I was born ; and, after an interval of about two years spent in the north of England, purchased and settled finally in the south of Scotland, where my mother and two sisters still reside.   Here I received the rudiments of my education ; and I feel bound to record, that I owe much to the custom there established of making the Scriptures a school book—a custom, I am grieved to say it, not only abandoned in the schools and academies among us, but denounced as improper, if not injurious. Although I was unconscious, at the time, of any power or influence over my thoughts or actions thence derived, yet what mere memory retained of their life-giving truths, proved of unspeakable advantage, when I became awakened on the subject of religion; and I am constrained to believe, that what was thus unconsciously sown in my heart, though smothered and choked by the levity of youth, and abused and perverted by the negligence and sinfulness of my riper years, was nevertheless a preparation of Heaven's foresight and mercy, for grace to quicken me—a mighty help to my amazed and confounded soul, when brought to a just view of my actual condition as a sinner, both by nature and by practice. Without this help, I might, like thousands of others, have wandered in a bewildered state, the prey of many delusions—engendered by the anxieties of a disturbed and ignorant mind, or by the fanaticism of those many well meaning, perhaps, but certainly most ignorant men, who yet venture to become teachers of religion. For this reason it is that I have been earnest, during my ministry, in pressing upon parents, and upon those who have the care of youth, the great duty of furnishing their tender and pliant minds with the treasures of divine knowledge and saving truth, contained in GOD's revealed word. No matter what specious arguments may be brought against the practice, we can reply, that it is a means of grace of GOD's own appointment, and one too which he has promised to bless and make effectual. No matter though it be objected, as it often is objected by the vain disputers of this world—that the minds of children can not comprehend such deep and unsearchable wonders— GOD, we know, is able to open their understandings, and *out of the mouths of babes and sucklings to perfect his praise.* No matter, though it be argued, that it is in vain, if not actually wrong, to force their minds to religion, and thus give them a distaste, and even an antipathy against it. Alas! what a flimsy subterfuge of unbelief and opposition to GOD; and yet what numbers are swayed by it! For, is it thought wrong, or even improper, *to force* their minds, if we must use the words, to any other branch of learning? and yet the danger of distaste, and even of antipathy, to human sciences, must be equally great. Besides, is not this distaste, and even antipathy, to divine things, the *natural* state of fallen creatures : and religion, the love of GOD, and goodness, a *forced*, that is, an unnatural state, to us spiritually dead and undone creatures, and therefore to be counteracted by every possible means ? Let no parent, then, be led away by this infidel sophistry, to withhold religious instruction from the earliest years of his children, or to trust them in a school where the Bible is excluded as a class book.

" Having lost my father in my ninth year, it became necessary to return to Virginia, to look after the wreck of his property. In my seventeenth year, accordingly, I was separated from all I had ever known, and that was dear to me, and landed in Virginia on New Year's day, 1789—a stranger to all around me, and in great part my own master—at least without any control I had been accustomed to respect. That under such circumstances I should quickly overcome those habits which the restraints of education had imposed, and wander after the lusts of my sinful heart, and the desires of my darkened eyes, is hardly to be wondered at. Wander indeed I did, not even waiting for temptation, but madly seeking it, and soon lost every early good impression, and even those fears and misgivings about futurity, of which all men are conscious occasionally.

" In looking back upon this period of my life, I think it may be profitable to advert to a circumstance which had great influence in confirming me in the sinful course I was pursuing. It being determined by my friends that I should turn my attention to the profession of the law, as presenting the fairest prospects of honour and emolument, I entered the college of William and Mary, that I might attend the law lectures of the celebrated Mr. Wythe, together with the other courses of scientific acquirement there taught. The plan was doubtless good, and might have been of the greatest advantage to my prospects in life ; but by throwing me still more upon my own guidance, and increasing my means of self indulgence, by the liberal allowance for my expenses, it increased in an equal degree the power of temptation, and I have to look back on the time spent in college as more marked by proficiency in extravagance, and juvenile vice, than in scientific attainment. Yet the means of improvement were fully within my reach, and that I did not profit more, is wholly my own fault. The professors in the different departments were able men, and the regulations of the institution good in themselves, but they were not enforced with the vigilance and precision necessary to make them efficient, in that moral discipline so supremely important at this period of life. Except at the hours appropriated to the lectures, my time was at my own disposal; and though expected to attend prayers every morning in the college chapel, absence was not strictly noticed, and very slight excuses were admitted. Attendance at church, on Sunday, was entirely optional, and the great subject of religion wholly unattended to. The students were required to board in college; but from the small number—not exceeding fifteen—from the low price of board, and the constant altercations with the steward—the public table was given up, and the students permitted to board in the taverns, or elsewhere, as suited them. This every way injurious, and most unwise permission, presented facilities for dissipation which would not otherwise have been found; and encouraged as they were by the readiness with which credit was obtained from persons whose calculations were formed on the heedlessness and improvidence of youth, temptation was divested of all present impediment to its power. This last is an evil which I believe attends all seminaries of learning, and forms one of the greatest obstacles to their real usefulness, and one of the most fruitful nurseries of vice. As such, it ought to be met and resisted by the whole power of the community, and by the arm of the law inflicting severe pecuniary penalty, independent of the loss of the debt contracted—and even imprisonment of the person convicted of giving credit to a student at any college, or other public seminary of learning. Some such provision, it appears to me, is essential to the public usefulness of such institutions; and if enforced with due vigilance by the professors, in whose name, and at whose instance, the prosecution should be carried on, would go far to counteract this increasing mischief. And when it is considered that the practice of giving credit to minors under such circumstances, is a stab at the very vitals of society, hardly any penalty can be considered too severe.

" While I thus *walked according to the course of this world, fulfilling the desires of the flesh and of the mind,* the customs and manners of genteel society imposed some degree of restraint upon my outward deportment ; and the respect I really entertained for some excellent persons, who favoured me with their notice and regard, preserved me from open debauchery. Strange creatures ! we can submit to some restraint, and command ourselves to some self denial, for the praise of *man that is a worm,* while we madly defy the omnipotent GOD ! We can be influenced by the fear of a fellow creature, while there is *no fear of* GOD *before our eyes.* What other proof do we need to convince us that we are fallen creatures, spiritually dead, and must continue such, unless quickened into life by GOD the HOLY GHOST ?

" These restraints, however, could not have continued to operate for any length of time against the natural tendency of vice to wax worse and worse ; and that I became not totally and irrecoverably sunk in its ruinous depths, I owe, under GOD, to a most excellent woman, who consented to become my wife in my 21st year. This event gave a new direction to the course of my life. I abandoned the study of law and embraced a country life, devoting myself to agricultural pursuits. Thus removed from the temptations and facilities to vice, which our cities and towns present so readily, with regular and pleasant occupation on my farm, and my domestic happiness studied and promoted by the affectionate partner of my life—my years rolled on as happily—were the present life alone to be provided for—as could reasonably be desired. The personal regard I entertained for my wife, increased to the highest esteem, and even veneration, as the virtues of her character opened upon me, while the prudence and discretion of her conduct won me gradually from my previous dissipated habits. She was a woman of high principle and of a very independent character : what she did not approve of, she would not smile upon ; yet she never gave me a cross word, or an illnatured look in her life, and in the twenty-three years it pleased GOD to spare her to me, such was her discretion, that though I often acted otherwise than she could have wished me to do, and though she was faithful to reprove me, there never was a quarrel or temporary estrangement between us. *She opened her mouth with wisdom, and in her tongue was the law of kindness.* So that when she left me for a better world, it was an exceeding comfort to me that I could look back upon so little to reproach myself with, respecting her ; only this, that but for the last five years of our union, had I any sense of her real value, or of GOD's goodness in giving her to me, or any communion with her in the love of that Saviour, who had been her hope and trust through life, (though she was not formally a professor——the Church in which she was baptized having been cast down before she came to years of discretion)——and who was her stay and support in the hour of death. "O how good it is" would she say to me as I watched by her dying bed, "to have a Saviour, and *such* a Saviour !

"But though my marriage certainly produced a great change in my outward conduct, I was nevertheless as far from GOD as ever ; without even a thought of religion, or once opening the Bible for eighteen years, to learn what GOD the LORD should say, or once bending my knees in prayer to him, on whom my all depended ; and though twice in this time brought to the gates of death by sickness, yet no uneasy thought of hereafter disturbed my mind. So true is the expression of the Psalmist that *the wicked hath no bands in death.* So great was my neglect, in fact disrespect, of even the outward forms of religion, that from the year 1792 to the year 1810, I was not present at any place of public worship more than six or seven times, and then not from choice, but from some accidental accommodation to propriety, in surrendering to the opinions of others.

"Indeed the kind of preaching I had in my power to hear, was not of a description to engage the attention of any informed mind. I soon found that I knew more of the Scriptures from memory than the preachers, and was vain enough to think that I understood them better and could apply them more correctly, than the well-meaning perhaps, but certainly most ignorant, unqualified, and of course injurious men, who appeared around in the character of ministers of religion. But as I had no spiritual senses as yet quickened in me, the preaching of the cross, even from an angel, would have been to me as to the Greeks of old—foolishness. Oh what a miracle of long suffering, that in all this time GOD was not provoked to cut me off! What a miracle of grace, that I am permitted to think and speak of it, and to adore the riches of his mercy, in bringing me to a better mind!

"It was in the year 1810 that it pleased GOD to set my mind at work, and gradually to bring me to doubt the dark security of my unawakened state. But I am not conscious of any peculiar incident or circumstance, that first led me to considerations of the kind.

"As I was the manager of my own estate, which comprised a set of mills, as well as a plantation, about two miles distant from each other, I was of course much alone, at least in that kind of solitude which gives the mind opportunity to commune with itself. It was in my rides from one to the other, and while superintending the labors of my people, that a train of thought, to which I was previously altogether unaccustomed, began to occupy my attention, and though dismissed once and again would still return, and with every return would interest me more and more. That the train of thought thus suggested, concerned my condition as an accountable creature, will be readily imagined, as also, that on the review I found it bad enough. This it was no difficult thing for me to feel and to admit, nor as yet did there appear much difficulty in reforming what I could not justify.

"An impatient and passionate temper, with a most sinful and hateful habit of profane swearing, in which I was a great proficient, were my most open and besetting sins. These, however, I considered as within my own control, and as such, set forthwith about amending them, but without any reliance upon GOD for help, or without much if any impression that it was at all needful. In this endeavour at reformation, which it pleased GOD thus to permit me to make, I went on prosperously for a season, and began to pride myself in that self-command I seemed to possess. But my own weakness was yet to be showed me, and when temptation again assailed me, all my boasted self-command was but as a rush against the wall. I surrendered to passion, and from passion to blasphemy. When I came to reflect upon this, then it was that, for the first time in my life, I was sensible of something like concern—some consciousness of wrong beyond what was apparent. But without waiting to examine farther, I hastily concluded to exert myself more heartily, and yet to command myself thoroughly.

"During these my endeavours, however, the Scriptures were more and more the object of my attention, and from them I began gradually to discover (what I was very loth to admit) the true state and condition of human nature. What little I had lately come to know of myself, however, and all that I knew of the world, seemed to rise up as strong proofs that the doctrine of our natural depravity was true. Willing, however, to escape from it, I resorted to the subterfuge of too many among us—that what we find in the Scriptures is *figuratively* expressed, and is, therefore, not to be taken in the strictness of the letter. But my own experience was to be the expositor of the word. Again and again were my self-righteous endeavours foiled and defeated, much as at the first ; and humbled and confounded, I became alarmed at what must be the issue—if I was thus to remain the sport of passions I could not command, the prey of sin I could not conquer. Something like prayer would flow from my lips, but it was the prayer of a heart that yet knew not aright, its own plague. One more effort was to be made, and with great circumspection did I watch over myself for some weeks. Still did I continue, however, my search in and meditation upon the Scriptures : and here it was that I found the benefit of my early acquaintance with them. I had not to look afar off for their doctrines, they were familiar to my memory from a child ; I had known them thus far, though now it was that their living proof was to be experienced. The whole, I believe, was to be made to depend, on my acquiescence in the turning point of all religion—that we are lost and undone, spiritually dead and helpless in ourselves—and so I found it.

"Again and dreadfully did I fall from my own steadfastness— temptation like *a mighty man that shouteth by reason of wine*, swept my strength before it, carried away my resolutions as Sampson did the gates of Gaza. I returned to the house convinced of my own helplessness, of my native depravity, and that to spiritual things I was incompetent. I now found of a truth that *in me dwelt no good thing.* I threw myself upon my bed in my private room—I wept—I prayed. Then was showed unto me my folly in trusting to an arm of flesh. Then did it please the LORD to point my bewildered view to him who is *the* LORD *our righteousness.* Then was I enabled in another strength to commit myself unto his way. From that moment my besetting sin of profane swearing was overcome, and to this moment has troubled me no more. But much was yet to be done, which the same gracious friend of poor sinners continued to supply ; and to lead me step by step, to proclaim his saving name, and declare his mighty power openly to the world.

" In making an outward profession of religion, I acted as multitudes, alas, do, without considering that any thing depended on my being a member of the Church of CHRIST, or that any difficulty existed as to what was and what was not truly such. In choosing between the different denominations into which the Christian world is split up, I considered nothing more to be necessary than agreement in points of faith and practical religion, with such a system of discipline as was calculated to promote the peace and edification of the society. This I thought I found in a body of Christians called *Republican Methodists ;* and influenced in no small degree by personal friendship for one of their preachers, Mr. John Robinson, of Charlotte county, my wife and myself took membership with them. At this time, however, they had no church organized within reach of my dwelling, only a monthly appointment for preaching at one of the old churches, eight miles distant.

" It was not very long, however, before this want was supplied in the gathering together of a sufficient number to constitute a church according to their rule, in which I was appointed a lay elder, and laboured for the benefit of the members by meeting them on the vacant Sundays, and reading to them such printed discourses as I thought calculated to instruct and impress them ; and these meetings were well attended, considering the prevalent delusion on the subject of preaching, and the wide and deep objection to prepared sermons.

When I had been engaged in this way about three years, increasing in knowledge myself, as I endeavoured to impart it to others, I gradually began to be exercised on the subject of the ministry, and to entertain the frequently returning thought, that I might be more useful to the souls of my fellow sinners than as I then was, and that I owed it to God. To this step, however, there appeared objections insurmountable, from my worldly condition, and from my want of public qualifications. Yet I could not conceal from myself, that if the men with whom I occasionally associated, and those of whom I had obtained any acquaintance as ministers of religion, were qualified to fill the station, I was behind none, and superior to most of them, in acquired knowledge, if not in Christian attainment. My objections were, therefore, chiefly from my personal interests, and personal accommodation, cloaked under the want of the necessary qualifications for a public speaker, and some obscure views of the great responsibility of the office. I felt that I dreaded it, and, therefore, did not encourage either the private exercises of my own mind, or the open intimations of my brethren. Yet I could not escape from the often returning meditation of the spiritual wants of all around me, of the never to be paid obligation I was under to the divine mercy, and of the duty I owed to give myself in any and in every way to God's disposal.

"Of this I entertained no dispute; yet the toils and privations, the sacrifices of worldly interest, and the contempt for the calling itself, manifested by the wealthier and better informed classes of society, which I once felt myself, and now witnessed in others, were a severe stumbling-block; and I was willing to resort to any subterfuge to escape encountering it. Yet I would sometimes think, that a great part of this was more owing to the men than to the office."

Thus abruptly terminates this interesting narrative, to the composition of which Mr. Ravenscroft devoted the intervals of strength and leisure that he enjoyed during his last illness. Among the memoranda to which he referred in the preparation of it, is found one written by himself, in the year 1819, which is here subjoined, as a continuation of the history of his motives and views in entering the ministry of the Protestant Episcopal Church, and the causes of his dissatisfaction with the communion to which he had first attached himself.

"In the year 1815, being much exercised on the subject of the ministry, and believing myself called to a public station in the church, as well as pressed by the solicitations of my brethren, I began to revolve the question of orders in my mind, and to seek for information on a subject which I felt was of the last consequence to my comfort, and I may say usefulness as a minister of CHRIST, viz. the *authority* by which I should be commissioned to perform the duties of the ministry. To rest it upon the assurance I felt, that I was called of GOD to the work, was personal to myself, but could not weigh with others beyond my own opinion ; and something more than that was essential to prevent me from feeling myself an intruder into the sacred office.

"On mentioning my difficulty to the pastor of the congregation to which I belonged, an able and sensible, though not a learned man, I found that it was a question he could not entertain, being, like Dissenters in general, little if at all impressed with the importance (not to themselves alone, but to those under their charge,) of valid and authorized ministrations in the Church. Being thus left to my own resources, and the word of GOD, I became fully convinced that the awful deposit of the Word, by which we shall all be judged, could never be thrown out into the world to be scrambled for, and picked up by whosoever pleased to take hold of it ; and though this objection might in some sort be met by the manifestation of an internal call, yet as that *internal call* could not now be demonstrated to others, something more was needed, which could only be found in the *outward* delegation of authority, from that source to which it was originally committed. Of the necessity of this verifiable authority to the comfort and assurance of Christians in the present day, the Sacrament of Baptism presented itself to me as demonstrative truth. Being the only possible mode by which fallen creatures can become interested in the covenant of grace, and entitled to the benefit of CHRIST's gracious undertaking for the salvation of sinners, it must be of the last importance to parents and children to be satisfied and assured that such unspeakable blessings should be authoritatively conveyed. And as the authority of CHRIST is the very essence of Baptism, in the assurance of its pledges to those to whom it is administered, and as this assurance can only be such by the verification of the requisite power and authority to administer the rite, it appeared clear to me, that no assumption of that power by any man, or body of men, neither any consequent delegation of it, could by any possibility answer the intention and purpose of the Author and Finisher of our faith, in making Baptism the door of admission into his Church.

"In this view of the subject, I was compelled to lay before the district meeting of the Republican Methodist Church, so called, my reasons for requiring an authority to minister in the Church of CHRIST, which they had not to give, and to request a letter of dismission from their communion. This was granted me by the congregation of which I was a member, in the most friendly and affectionate manner. The other dissenting denominations among us I found in the same situation; all of them, according to my view, acting upon usurped authority; though I paused a while on the *Presbyterian* claim to apostolic succession—but as that claim could date no farther back than the era of the Reformation, and in its first lines labours under the dispute whether it has actually the authority which *mere Presbyters* can bestow, (for it does not appear satisfactorily that Calvin ever had orders *of any* kind,) I had to turn my attention to the Protestant Episcopal Church for that deposit of apostolic succession, in which alone verifiable power to minister in sacred things was to be found in these United States.

"I presented myself accordingly to Bishop Moore, in the city of Richmond, together with my credentials, and was by him received as a candidate for holy orders. The canons of the Church requiring that persons applying for orders shall have their names inscribed in the books, as candidates for one year previous to their ordination, I was furnished by Bishop Moore with letters of licence as a lay-reader in the Church, which are dated the 17th of February, 1816. Having laboured during the year in the parishes of Cumberland, in Lunenburg county, and of St. James, in the county of Mecklenburg, with acceptance, and, by the blessing of GOD, with effect, particularly in St. James' parish, I was most earnestly invited to take charge of the latter congregation, as their minister. This invitation I accepted; and having received the necessary testimonials from the Standing Committee of the Diocese, and passed the requisite trials, I was admitted to the office of Deacon in the Church, on Friday, the 25th day of April, 1817, in the Monumental Church, in the city of Richmond; and for reasons satisfactory to the Bishop and Standing Committee of the Diocese, by virtue of the canon in such case made and provided, I was admitted to the order of Priest; and ordained thereto in the church in the town of Fredericksburg, on Tuesday, the 6th day of May following, during the session of the Convention in that place. On returning to my parish, deeply impressed with the awful commission intrusted to me, and with the laborious task of rescuing from inveterate prejudice the doctrines, discipline, and worship of the Church, and of reviving among the people that regard for it, to which it is truly entitled, I commenced my ministerial labours, as the only real business I now had in life, relying on GOD's mercy and goodness, through the LORD JESUS CHRIST, for fruit to his praise."

The most obvious reflection which occurs on the reading of this history of the motions of Mr. Ravenscroft's mind, when he was about to assume the character of a minister in the Church, is, that he was brought to the result he mentions, contrary to established prejudices, and without any extraneous influence. The simple fact of his having first joined a body of Christians, the fundamental principle of whose society is the rejection of all order and all creeds, shows how far removed in attachment he was from that Church which subsequently became so dear to him. Having become so far bound to that society as to be a prominent leader in it, and entertaining the warmest personal regard for many of those with whom he was in communion, it is probable that his inclinations, so far from according with the dictates of his reason and judgment, on the important subject of Orders, would have rather prompted him to resist them, and that the conclusion to which he ultimately came, in favour of the Church, was *forced* upon his conscience, by the *pressure of truth alone*, unaided by any adventitious circumstances.

The clergyman of the parish in whose bounds he resided, died about the same time when he seems to have been first exercised on the subject of the ministry, and though Mr. Ravenscroft felt for that gentleman the sincerest attachment, and on many occasions sought his aid and counsel in his religious course, yet his death deprived him of the assistance he might have otherwise looked for from that quarter, in his more enlarged enquiries. He was thus left, to use his own expression, "to his own resources and the word of God," and guided alone by the light of the latter, he attained that perfect conviction of the exclusive Divine right, appertaining to Episcopal ministrations, which he asserted so unwaveringly in his after life.

A reference to these circumstances has been here made, as they account, in some measure, for the inflexibility of Mr. Ravenscroft on the subject of Episcopacy ever afterwards. Had be been trained up from a child to love and to venerate the Church, or had he been led by the mere force of education or of expediency to become a member and a minister of it, it is possible that his feelings in relation to it might have been somewhat different from what they were. An ingenuous mind like his, would have made some allowances for the prejudices of education, even in regard to its own reasonings, and still more for the bias given by inclination or accidental circumstances. Conscious of the general effect of these causes, it might have sometimes faltered in urging the exclusive truth of opinions formed under their influence, and have occasional misgivings that its conclusions were not necessarily correct. But there were no such sources of indecision to operate upon Mr. Ravenscroft's conduct. He had arrived at a conclusion adverse to established opinions, and contrary, as may be presumed, to his own wishes.   He had to make the painful and often humiliating sacrifice of sentiments already avowed and acted upon—to separate himself from a Society to which he was warmly attached, and which had evidenced its attachment to him, by an appointment to a responsible station ; and on the other hand, was drawn by the word of GOD to a Church, whose principles, (so far, at least, as regards the necessity of government and established creeds) were as much opposed to those of the society to which he belonged, as two communions professing to worship the same GOD, could be.   It is very apparent, that under circumstances like these, Mr. Ravenscroft must have been actuated by the most assured conviction that the opinions he embraced were in strict and *exclusive* accordance with the Bible, and that he was not justifiable in holding, and still less in preaching, any others.   And when once the veil of prejudice was removed from his eyes, his vigorous mind clearly discerned that these opinions, if true, and if taught by GOD himself, were not to be covered up and kept out of view, because they differed from the vain imaginations of men.   As a faithful servant, he paid more regard to the injunctions of his Master, than to the clamours of those whose errors he denounced ; and believing the opinions referred to, to be, without question, distinctly revealed, he shrunk not from what he conceived to be his imperative duty, in preaching them.   From the hour that he connected himself with the Church, his opinions respecting its character, its doctrine, and its discipline, were decidedly and avowedly of that kind known by the appellation of *High Church* principles, and as he progressed in Christian experience, and in the knowledge of the word of GOD, and of the writings of those fathers who are considered its best interpreters, his opinions only became the more clear and confirmed.

In preaching in public, and advocating in private, these opinions which he regarded as essential to the validity of the ministrations that he exercised, Mr. Ravenscroft still retained that earnestness of manner and ardour of expression, which, besides being constitutional, had been habitual with him for near forty years ; and many who had no opportunities of knowing the kindliness of his nature and the warmth of his Christian benevolence, were disposed to regard him as over-bearing and uncharitable ; but in his case, as in many others, the character of the *Christian* was modified, without being spoiled by the constitution of the *man ;* and his earnestness and ardour were certainly unaccompanied with the defilements of malice or of bigotry. The circumstances already mentioned, attending his union with the Church, made him repose unusual confidence in the conclusions at which he had arrived, and the ardent gratitude to God, for his long forbearance towards himself, which was unquestionably the distinguishing trait of his Christian character, prompted him to the most devoted zeal in His service. These combined causes might make him at times appear positive and importunate ; but whoever had an opportunity of contemplating him in his private intercourse with his flock, and of witnessing his gentle and paternal deportment towards them, knew that these outward indications of harshness had no correspondent feelings in his bosom.

Mr. Ravenscroft's character as a Christian was fully appreciated by the little flock over which he was now the overseer, and his labours as a minister were attended with very gratifying success. At the time that he first connected himself as a lay reader with it, the Liturgy of the Church was entirely unknown, except in one family ; and in fifteen months afterwards he had a large congregation of "attentive hearers and devout worshippers," who erected for their use a commodious place of public worship. To some, however, his preaching was very offensive, and brought upon him that reproach to which the faithful minister of Christ has been liable in every period of the world. To the rich and worldly-minded, especially, to whom he had been so long allied in feeling and in practice, he now addressed his most heart-searching appeals, and familiar as he was with all their shifts and evasions, he exposed them to themselves with a fidelity and truth of colouring which they could not tolerate. Preaching of this kind, which they knew not how to resist, they affected to despise, and this faithful minister, though never deterred for a moment from revealing the whole of God's will, was

much and often grieved at the deadness and coldness of this class
of his hearers. To those, too, from whom he differed in opinion
respecting the constitution of the Church, he often gave serious
offence ; and in one of the congregations which he served he
met from this source with many painful impediments. But with
a remarkable self-devotion and decision of character, he pursued
the tenor of his way, alike undismayed by the reproaches of his
adversaries, and unchanged by the admiration of his friends.
He seems to have been actuated by an unbounded sense of
God's mercy towards himself and to have thought the dedication to his service of all the energies of his body and mind, far
from being an adequate acknowledgement of the divine bounty :
doubtless the recollection of the many years, during which his
talent had been buried, added to his diligence in preparing for
the coming of his Lord.

Having lost his first wife in the year 1814, Mr. Ravenscroft
was married to his second wife in the year 1818. This lady, to
whom he was ever a most affectionate husband, and whose consistent Christian character was at once a comfort and an aid to
him during their union, was Miss Buford, of Lunenburg county,
the daughter of one of his oldest friends. In the ensuing winter
he sustained a severe loss by fire, having had his dwelling house,
and all it contained, burnt during his absence from home. This
loss, joined to his profuse generosity, and probably his diminished attention to his secular affairs after he entered the ministry,
reduced considerably the value of his estate, and after this
period he was, in part, dependent upon the support which he
derived from his connexion with his parish.

His attention to the duties of his calling, which he suffered
nothing to divert, was indeed remarkable. His punctuality as
a minister, for instance, was so exact, that during the whole
time he officiated as deacon and priest, he was never known to
fail in keeping an appointment. Relying, with a confidence
which ultimately became fatal, upon the vigour and stability of
his constitution, he set at naught all kinds of weather, while
engaged in duties that called him from home. Even when the
weather was so inclement that he would not permit his servant,
who acted as the sexton to his churches, to accompany him, he

would himself take the keys and ride off alone five or ten miles to the regular place of worship, without, perhaps, the slightest expectation of meeting an individual, and sometimes, as he used to express himself, " would ride around the Church when the snow was a foot deep, and *leave his track as a testimony against his people.*" This seemingly supererogatory exposure of himself he found necessary for some members of his congregation. " If," said he, " they could say with any sort of plausibility—the weather is bad to-day, and Mr. Ravenscroft will not turn out, the consequence would be that the slightest inclemency would avail them as an excuse for staying at home ; but I put a stop to all such evasions, by being always at Church, let the weather be what it may, and they can always calculate with certainty upon meeting *me* if they choose to turn out themselves."

All this diligence and devotion did not fail to be attended with their usual and natural results. By the blessing of GOD upon his labours, the seed which he sowed with so much industry and fidelity, and watered with fervent and unceasing prayers, brought forth a large and rapid increase, not only in his own parish, but wherever he had thrown it by the way-side. An eminent member of the diocese of Virginia, himself an active labourer in his LORD's vineyard, the late Dr. Wilmer, writes to Mr. Ravenscroft about this period, to the following effect. " The LORD of the vineyard seems to be granting you the rare favour, that as you have entered late into his service you should have the honour and reward of doing much in a short space—while we who have been longer at the work hardly begin to enter upon the fruits, you at once seem to have reaped a glorious harvest. You get even more than your ' penny.' "

Neither were Mr. Ravenscroft's influence and usefulness circumscribed within the sphere of his parochial duties. Though young in the ministry, his powerful talents and evident single ness of purpose in his ministerial labours acquired for him a degree of consideration amongst his brethren, which he did not fail to use for the good of the Church and the glory of GOD. Besides the active and efficient part which he took in the councils of the Church, and of the several societies under its control, he hesitated not to stimulate his fellow labourers, by the most

VOL. I.—4

affectionate appeals, to constant diligence and faithfulness, and amongst his papers are found letters thanking him for his "friendly smitings." One of his correspondents says in reply : " I concur with you on the importance and necessity of our bringing before the people more faithfully the distinctive principles and features of the Church. There has been a lamentable deficiency among many of us—at least I speak for myself. It appears to me that the best mode is to do it gradually, by private instruction, by tracts and books, and especially by forming the rising generation upon the primitive model. This I shall endeavour to do, by the grace of God." That this labour of love on his part, was not regarded as obtrusive or unkindly performed, appears abundantly from other parts of this correspondence. " Happy am I," says his correspondent, " in the belief that we agree in the main point, and that no difference of opinion will be sufficient to interrupt that brotherly love, which, it is a great part of my happiness to believe, subsists between us."

In the years 1820 and 1821 the subject of baptism underwent a very extensive examination in the Theological Repertory, a periodical under the patronage of the Virginia Convention, and edited by some of its ablest ministers. Although the views held by the Editors in relation to that sacrament, were opposed to the sentiments of Mr. Ravenscroft, and it was a subject, too, in which he took a very great interest, he did not (contrary to the received opinion of his fondness for controversy) enter into the lists with them as a public opponent. Circumstances, however, ultimately brought him into collision with the principal writer in the Repertory, and a long and interesting private correspondence ensued between them, begun, continued, and ended, with the most Christian temper and brotherly love. The circumstances referred to, are these : A lady of Fairfax county, in the immediate vicinity of which the Repertory was published, distracted probably by the opposite views of baptism, which she found in the pages of that work, (for the Editors candidly admitted contributions from able men on both sides of the question,) applied to Mr. Ravenscroft by letter for counsel and instruction. This he did not hesitate or delay to give, and as the subject is one of universal and paramount interest, his letter in reply is here inserted.

To Mrs. Robinson, Fairfax County, Virginia.

Makeshift, 11th *July*, 1820.

DEAR MADAM.

Your favour of the 22d June was received on Saturday, and it is with pleasure that I take the first spare hour I have to reply to it.

Whatever difficulty yourself and many others may labour under upon this subject, proceeds altogether from confounding two subjects altogether distinct, viz. *Regeneration* and *Conversion :* both to be sure essential to us as sinners, but in a manner distinct from each other.

A right view of our situation as fallen creatures, spiritually dead, points to some means or other to do away the disability consequent on original transgression, and render us capable of profiting by the gracious means GOD hath provided in his Son and made known by the gospel. This is the starting place to us on every thing that relates to religion. Without this, it would be as absurd to expect any motions of spiritual life, or any capacity of spiritual improvement, as for a body really dead to move and act. *Regeneration,* then, is a grace imparted to us by Almighty GOD, restoring, to some extent, not precisely designated in Scripture, that capacity for spiritual improvement lost by the fall ; which puts us once more upon trial as it were, with better hopes, more effectual means, and surer promises ratified in the blood of GOD's dear and only Son. In this work of GOD upon the soul we are purely passive. It is a *grace,* or rather *grace* imparted, a power communicated, if we may so speak, (for language is very poor in many things relating to the mystery of our redemption) the first effect of CHRIST's gracious undertaking to bear the penalty of our sins, that he might bring us to GOD.

This is the first and highest sense in which the word regeneration is used, and may with sufficient propriety be called *a being born again,* but more properly in the words of the apostle Peter, *a being begotten again.*

But there is another sense in which the word regeneration is used, which it is proper to notice ; and that is in its application to the change of outward condition, which takes place when we become openly and visibly parties to the new covenant made with GOD in CHRIST.

By our natural birth we are parties to nothing but the curse entailed upon sin—our birthright is only that of *strangers to the covenants of promise,* " having no hope and without GOD in the world." And would we have this destitute state removed, we must, in that manner which the wisdom of GOD hath seen fit to appoint, personally subscribe to the terms and conditions on which the benefits purchased for us by the sufferings and death of JESUS CHRIST are promised and assured. In the Old Testament Church, GOD was pleased to appoint the rite of circumcision for this purpose ; by which every descendant of Abraham became a party to all the hopes which the promised seed of the woman was in the fulness of time to bring to them and all nations—and in this sense it is that our Saviour, speaking of Jewish children, calls them " those little ones which believe in him," styling them *believers,* because they were, by circumcision, parties to the covenant made with him as the representative of the human race.

In the New Testament Church, the ordinance of baptism is the appointed and only means to change our condition by nature, and bring us into relation with GOD as heirs of the promise. By the water of baptism, and by that only, (to the exclusion of all other modes and means according to revelation) can we obtain an interest in CHRIST, by being admitted into that Church, which he " purchased with his own most precious blood." *Except a man be born of water and of the spirit, he cannot enter into the kingdom of* GOD.

In both these senses the word *regeneration* is used in our baptismal service—first as an expression of an effect produced in bestowing spiritual grace : secondly to denote a change of condition—that those rightly baptized are *no more strangers and foreigners, but fellow citizens with the saints and of the household of* GOD.

A careful examination of the office for Baptism, will show you that such is the meaning which the Church attaches to the word *regeneration* : and if attended to as it ought to be, would not only prevent the confusion of mind consequent on confounding regeneration and conversion, but restore the ordinance itself to that respect in the eyes of Christians to which it is so highly entitled.

In the sense above explained, I used the expression "Laver of regeneration," respecting baptism—a phrase taken from the brazen laver mentioned in the thirtieth chapter of Exodus, verse 18th, &c., in which the priests were to wash before they presented any offering to the LORD ; the whole being an emblem of that purity which should accompany those who are dedicated to the service of GOD, which children certainly are in baptism. The expression I think warranted by what is spoken of this ordinance and its effects in the epistles. In that to Titus, third chapter and 5th verse, St. Paul says, *Not by works of righteousness which we have done, but according to his mercy he saved us by the washing of regeneration, and renewing of the* HOLY GHOST. In his first Epistle to the Corinthians, the sixth chapter, and 11th verse, speaking of the effect of baptism on the members of that Church—*And such were some of you, but ye are washed, but ye are sanctified, but ye are justified, in the name of the* LORD JESUS, *and by the* SPIRIT *of our* GOD. And to the Ephesians, fifth chapter, and 26th verse, speaking of the love of CHRIST to his Church, and his purpose in giving himself for it, *that he might sanctify and cleanse it with the washing of water, by the word.* There are many more passages in the New Testament which apply to this ordinance, and if duly considered, could not fail to impress Christians with a more reverential sense of the right itself, and of the blessings and obligations growing out of it. But in the divisions among us, and from seeing it administered by any and every person who chooses to assume the ministerial character, yea, moreover, to hear it decried and derided by some in its application to infants of believing parents, we have gradually lost sight of its high purpose in the Church—the solemn obligations it imposes are lost sight of, and the mighty benefits of which it is the seal, have dwindled down to a mere ceremony for giving a name. A more solemn sense of it, I trust, is entertained by yourself and your husband, both as regards yourselves and your children, and in fulfilling that solemn vow under which it laid you, you may fully expect GOD's promised blessing on your faithful endeavour to "train them up in the nurture and admonition of the LORD."

Conversion, on the other hand, is the consequence of repentance on the part of the sinner—an additional grace or favour of GOD, known only to the gospel—a provision of mercy through the mediation of CHRIST, by which those who have abused the grace conferred in regeneration, and by personal sin have again departed from GOD, on sincere repentance and renewed obedience, are once more received into a state of favour.

In this, however, we are not passive, inasmuch as the warnings of the word, and the admonitions of the HOLY SPIRIT, are to be attended to and improved, seeing it is a matter of choice on the part of the sinner whether he will be moved by considerations of religion to cease from the error of his ways—to turn to the means of grace provided for his good and in obedience to the convincing power of the HOLY SPIRIT, by hearty repentance and true faith flee to the cross of CHRIST for pardon and acceptance, and for renewed power to love GOD and to keep his commandments. Of this every converted sinner must have the experience, for such cannot but be sensible how often during their career of folly and rebellion, the good SPIRIT OF GOD interposed to stop them, and turn them from the broad and beaten road of destruction, to the strait and narrow, but safe way that leadeth unto life ; but they would not, putting away from them his gracious checks and admonitions, and stifling and quenching his good motions within them. Oh, what miracles of grace, what patient long-suffering on the part of GOD is treasured up in CHRIST JESUS—especially for us gospel sinners ! Surely GOD "is not willing that any should perish, but that all should come to repentance."

This letter having fallen into the hands of one of the parties to the controversy already mentioned, occasioned a further correspondence, which it is not proposed to insert here at length. An extract from one of the letters of Mr. Ravenscroft, will, perhaps, suffice to complete the view of his opinions on this momentous subject.

" As it contributes greatly to a right understanding of each other in discussions of this kind, to explain the sense and meaning in which a leading word or phrase is made use of, I shall take that mode, convinced that by so doing little or no difference will be found between us, and if there should, that it will be the readiest way to attain to desired and desirable uniformity— for I think I can truly say I desire to know the truth.

By the *Sacrament of Baptism*, I understand a mystery ordained by CHRIST himself in his Church, of perpetual obligation and essential in its nature, inasmuch as the wilful rejection of it, is a bar to the salvation of the gospel. I believe it to be the only revealed means, by which a child of Adam can enter into covenant with GOD in CHRIST, and become entitled to all the benefits which his satisfaction hath procured for sinners. I believe it a seal or ratification of the new covenant ; on the part of GOD, a visible and authentic assurance transacted by his commissioned servant, his ambassador, that the promises made in that covenant *are* and *will be* performed on his part : on the part of man, an open understanding and thankful acceptance of the conditions of that covenant as declared in CHRIST the Mediator, with a solemn and public promise to keep and fulfil them.

By *Regeneration*, I understand an act or operation of Almighty GOD in behalf of, and upon, the creature, for the communication of spiritual power, to render fallen man capable of religion ; the production of a new principle which was not previously in man, neither could be attained by the application of any power left to him ; the restoring to an extent not precisely declared in Scripture, nor needful to be known—the spiritual power, or qualification, or whatever it may be called, lost by the sin of Adam, and required to put him once more in a state of trial ; the germ of any and every religious attainment.

This seems to me to be the original scriptural ground, on which the Church connects regeneration with baptism—not *in the judgment of charity*, as you contend, but absolutely and virtually flowing from the promise, as connected with the ordinance. For the promise of the new covenant is *A new heart also will I give you, and I will put my spirit within you.* Now the question is, when is this done? The Church assumes, on the sure ground of Scripture, that this blessing is conferred *in baptism ;* and the 27th Article and the Office for baptism are framed accordingly. They harmonize completely. Nor is there the smallest need for the exercise of charity, to enable us to believe that a gracious GOD having been pleased to connect his promise with a sensible sign, to be administered only by the authority of CHRIST in his Church, does most surely fulfil it.

To this it is objected—that we do not find the fact verified by experience—all baptized persons, even those baptized in the Church, do not show by any difference from others that they are regenerate. To this I reply, that the objection is founded on the mistaken, though popular, meaning attached to the word *regeneration ;* and, therefore, is not a good one : or it is founded on the Calvinistical notion of indefectible grace, which is not the doctrine of the Church—as is evident from the 16th article, not yet the doctrine of the gospel. The Church declares the grace given in baptism to be an " inward," and, therefore, " invisible, spiritual grace :" but it is not on that account the less real. Neither is it any argument against the fact, that the majority of baptized persons are found sinners in practice even as others. The Church is aware of this melancholy possibility, and guards by every means against it ; and when she delivers back the regenerate infant to those who have undertaken the charge of its spiritual growth, she takes from them the most solemn obligation accountable creatures can enter into, to foster and cherish the seed of divine grace in the heart, and *train up the child in the nurture and admonition of the* LORD. When this shall be done in the spirit of the institution, and the same unhappy result attend the administration of the ordinance—then will the objection be a good one, but not till then.

I, therefore, understand the Church, in the Office for baptism, to mean what the words convey—that she does not pretend to confer an uncertain or conjectural benefit in the baptism which she administers by the authority of CHRIST ; that she does not return thanks for a visionary or problematical blessing conferred on the infant baptized, depending on the judgment of charity for comfort and assurance to those interested ; nor yet by the words " they that receive baptism rightly," made use of in the 27th Article, do I understand any allusion to the state of the parties baptized, as worthy or unworthy, but the lawful authority to administer it, on which its efficiency altogether depends."

The interest that Mr. Ravenscroft took in this subject, " with which he believed the whole frame and polity of the Church to be connected," was so great, and the importance of a right understanding of it, was in his view so paramount, that the foregoing extracts have been given at the hazard of their being thought to occupy an undue space in this memoir. It is a subject, too, not only important, but according to his opinion greatly neglected, and the space may not lie misspent, which is occupied in recording his sentiments in relation to it. " It is not to be disguised,'' he says at the close of his controversial correspondence, " that many among us have become loose on the subject of baptism. The solemn influential character belonging to it, is nearly lost sight of. The use is declining from day to day, so that from a sacrament it is dwindling down to a mere ceremony for naming a child. Let us endeavour to bring back parents and sponsors to a right understanding of their solemn duty under the baptismal covenant ; and surely no argument can be stronger to produce this serious sense of that duty, than the consideration that they receive from the hands of the Church, a little creature, now in covenant with GOD, prepared to profit by instruction, to repay their anxious love with piety in time, and glory in eternity."

In the year 1823, Mr. Ravenscroft received an invitation to take charge of the large and flourishing congregation at Norfolk. Not conceiving that any call of duty accompanied this invitation, he promptly declined it, " as nothing in the shape of emolument could move him from where he was, and induce him to sacrifice his predilections and attachment to his own little flock." Shortly afterwards, however, he received a call from the vestry of the Monumental Church, in Richmond, to be the assistant to

VOL. I.—5

the venerable Bishop Moore, who had charge of that congregation.   Regarding the services of the Bishop, which were seriously
interrupted and hindered by his large parochial charge, as too
valuable to the diocese to be lost through any impediment
opposed by his private inclinations, Mr. Ravenscroft was preparing to yield to what he considered as an imperative call of
duty, and to accept this invitation—when a call of a yet more
imperative nature reached him from another quarter, which his
conscience, that great master-spring to all his actions, at once
forbade him to reject.

The Church in North Carolina had shared the same fate,
during the Revolutionary war, that had involved all other portions of it in this country in so much gloom and depression.
The violent prejudices—to the injustice of which it is hardly
necessary now to recur—which had brought odium and persecution upon its ministers elsewhere, existed here in their full
vigour.   The effect, indeed, of these prejudices seems to have
been more remarkable in North Carolina than any where else.
The cry of " Down with it, down with it even to the ground,"
accomplished the wishes of the enemies of the Church ; and
long after Zion had arisen from the dust, and put on her beautiful garments, in other portions of her borders, her children here
had still to weep when they remembered her.

It was not until the year 1817, that the three clergymen who
had but recently been called to the towns of Fayetteville, Wilmington, and Newbern, encouraged by some influential laymen
in the two first mentioned towns, proposed a convention for the
purpose of organizing the Church in this state.   A Convention
was accordingly held in Newbern, in the month of June of that
year, attended by three clergymen and six or eight lay delegates ;
when a constitution was adopted, and an address made to the
friends of the Church throughout the state, proposing a second
convention in the ensuing year.   This second Convention was
more numerously attended than the former, and the Church
from that time continued rapidly to increase—or, to speak more
properly, perhaps—to revive from her long and deadly torpor.

Under the patriarchal supervision of the venerable Bishop of
Virginia, who was invited by the Convention to take episcopal

charge of the diocese, this increase assumed a stable and progressive character, and within six years from the time of the first Convention, there were twenty-five congregations attached to the Church. This numerical force, however, exhibits rather an exaggerated view of the real condition of the diocese. Some well-meaning but injudicious missionaries, under the influence of that fervour of feeling usually attendant upon a state of prosperity, had formed nominal congregations where there were in fact very few or no Episcopalians. Bishop Moore's engagements in Virginia, both to the diocese and to his parish, never allowed him time to visit these congregations, and discover their actual condition ; and after remaining some time unfruitful branches of the main stock, and appearing from a distance to add to its strength, they at length withered and fell off, from the want of that vital principle which they had never possessed. And even in the more established and better informed congregations, there were many individuals who had attached themselves to the Church from motives entirely distinct from a discerning and rational preference for her peculiar character. Hereditary predilections, convenience, and accidental circumstances, afforded a sufficient motive with many ; while comparatively few had been led to a candid examination, and a consequent acknowledgement of her distinctive claims.

The number of clergymen was small, in proportion to the extent of country over which the friends of the Church were scattered ; and even of that small number, there were some who, acting under that notion of charity which teaches us to shrink from the search of truth, lest, when found, it should show our neighbour to be in error, avoided the urging of claims which were unpalatable to so many.

These spots of unsoundness in a body otherwise healthy and vigorous, evidently required excision ; and the more intelligent friends of the Church began to look around for some skilful and steady hand to which the operation should be intrusted. The peculiar state of feeling engendered by the existence of these loose opinions, both in the members of the Church themselves and in others, obviously demanded that the agent of reform should possess nerve, as well as skill, and not be deterred from his duty, either by the reproaches of the looker-on, or by the timidity and alarms of the patient. The character of Mr. Ravenscroft, (for he was at this time personally known to but one clergyman in the diocese,) as exemplified by the manner and success of his preaching, appeared to be happily adapted to this emergency. Ardent in his personal piety, zealous in preaching the Gospel in its utmost purity, disinterested in all his aims, and possessing in no ordinary degree talents for pulpit and pastoral usefulness, it was believed that the uncompromising firmness with which he held and preached *the whole* of GOD's revealed will, would at least receive the meed of praise for sincerity and single-heartedness, even from his opponents ; while the sheep of his own fold would be reclaimed from those mazes of error and ignorance into which other shepherds might not have had the hardihood to follow them. This view of Mr. Ravenscroft's fitness for the station operating upon the leading members of the Convention of 1823, and a high respect for his character as a Christian and a minister, influencing others, he was unanimously elected Bishop of the diocese of North Carolina, at a Convention held in Salisbury, and attended by all the clergy and an unusually full delegation of laymen. He did not hesitate in accepting a call which he regarded as being in a peculiar manner a providential one. Personally known to scarcely an individual of the Convention which had unanimously elected him Bishop, it seemed to him " as if the hand of Providence was in it ;" and though the same distrust of himself, that had awakened in him so many doubts respecting his fitness for the ministry at all, yet operated in making him lay aside all self reliance, the same submission to the leadings of his great Master, and the same confiding trust in his sustaining grace, made him determine at once to follow the difficult path now opened to him. His election having preceded the sitting of the General Convention but a few weeks, he was furnished with the requisite testimonial to be laid before that body preparatory to his consecration, and accordingly received his high commission, in the city of Philadelphia, on the 22d day of April, 1823, at the hands of the venerable Bishop White, Bishops Griswold, Kemp, Croes, Bowen, and Brownell, being also present, and assisting.

The pecuniary ability of the Church in North Carolina being but limited, the Convention in offering what they were able to give, allowed to Mr. Ravenscroft the privilege of devoting one half of his time to the service of a parish, so that the conjoined means of the Diocese and the parish might afford a decent and adequate income. The neglect of his private affairs, which has already been hinted at, proceeding from Mr. Ravenscroft's engrossing attention to his ministerial duties, added to some losses sustained by him as surety for others, had now reduced his once ample means so much, that he was obliged to avail himself of this privilege ; and the congregation at Raleigh inviting him to take the pastoral charge of them, he consented to do so, and immediately upon his return from Philadelphia, began his preparations for removal. Knowing, however, how urgent the wants of the Church, were, he did not wait for the completion of his preparations, but set out on his first Episcopal tour in June, within one month after his consecration. It would extend this memoir to an undue length to enter into a minute narration of Bishop Ravenscroft's movements in this, or indeed, in any of his subsequent visitations ; it is designed only to give such occasional extracts from his private journal and correspondence, as are either instructive in point of doctrine, or more than ordinarily interesting in point of fact.

One of Bishop Ravenscroft's earliest endeavours after assuming the care of his Diocese, was to impress upon both his clergy and the people of their charge, a proper estimation of the sacrament of Baptism and its consequent, the apostolic rite of confirmation. These he regarded as the threshold of the Church, and when duly administered and worthily received, would guard the body of the Church from the intrusion of the unprepared. "I consider," says he, in a letter to one of his clergy, "in general terms, Confirmation equivalent to a profession of religion on conviction and experience." And to another he says, "from the nature of things, it is impossible that I can have any knowledge of the qualifications of the persons who offer themselves for Confirmation. I must therefore depend entirely upon your diligence in preparing, and faithfulness in presenting those

only of your charge who have a just view of the rite, and are
properly impressed with the obligations growing out of it, and
the benefits to be derived from it.   Much obloquy has heretofore grown out of the easiness with which candidates for confirmation have been presented and received by the Church, and
occasion has thence been taken against us by our opponents.
This I feel extremely anxious to avoid, and as no lax habits in
this respect have yet obtained in the Diocese, so to commence
and continue by the blessing of GOD, that they may be prevented from creeping in." His views on Baptism have been already
given at large, and need not be here repeated.

During his first visitation, and in the interval occurring between
it and the ensuing Convention, the Bishop discovered in its full
extent the actual condition of the Church, as it has already been
described.   He saw, that as a faithful overseer, it was his duty,
however painful it might be to himself, and however offensive to
others, to correct the mistakes into which so many of his flock
had fallen—to apprise them of the duties resulting from their
connexion with a Church which was founded upon the primitive
model, and to open their eyes to that delusive notion of charity,
which, in its natural consequences, must eventually lead to the
acknowledgement of all error.   He accordingly opened the
deliberations of the first Convention after his consecration with
a sermon containing his views and opinions regarding the Church,
and the most efficient means of promoting its increase and prosperity, and unreservedly communicating the details of the course
which he, as its guardian and Bishop, meant to pursue.   The
stand which he took upon this occasion, and which he maintained during his whole Episcopacy, was perhaps somewhat
higher than would have accorded with his wishes, had he not
been feelingly alive to the solemn responsibility which his peculiar situation imposed upon him.   As the Bishop of a new diocese, which had never enjoyed regular Episcopal ministrations,
and where there consequently existed much looseness of opinions,
and indeed ignorance, respecting the real nature and divine character of the Church, he felt himself called to a more than ordinary circumspection and fidelity.   The future condition of the
diocese was to be determined in a great degree by the character

it was to assume under his forming hand; while her clergy, with a reliance upon him which his eminent piety and great talents demanded, seemed to confide the control of ecclesiastical affairs almost exclusively to him, and to be ready to pursue whatever course his powerful mind and more enlarged opportunities of judging of the wants of the diocese might indicate.   Acting under a sense of obligation resulting from these several causes, after instructing his clergy *in the first place*, to preach "the entire spiritual death and alienation of man from GOD, by the entertainment of sin; the reconciliation of GOD to the world, by the sufferings and death of his only begotten Son; the atonement of his blood; justification by faith; acceptance through the merits of the Saviour; conversion of the heart to GOD; holiness of life, the only evidence of it; and the grace of GOD, in the renewal of the HOLY GHOST, the sole agent from first to last in working out our salvation from sin here, and from hell hereafter"—he proceeds to point out that kind of preaching which was further required of them by the peculiar condition of the diocese.—— " But, with these vital, and heaven-blessed doctrines, other points of edification to those of your charge, and to your general hearers, will require your attention, my reverend brothers; particularly that of the distinctive character of the Church. On this, a most lamentable ignorance prevails, and most unfounded opinions are becoming established, not only among Episcopalians, but at large.   To permit this ignorance to continue undisturbed, is to be false to our ordination vows, to our acknowledged principles, to the interests of our communion, and to the souls committed to our care; and however amiable in appearance the principle on which we act may be, reflection shows it to be a mistaken one, and experience proves it to have been injurious.   If we hold principles that are indefensible, let us abandon them.   But if they are our principles, interwoven into the very frame of our polity, impregnable in their truth, and essential in the great work we have in hand, let us not appear ashamed of them, or weakly afraid of the consequences, and thus become parties to that miserable delusion, which weakens us as a body, strengthens the ranks of our adversaries, and, I will fearlessly say, weakens the cause of true religion, by tacitly owning one division after another, until the great master prin-ciple of the Church of God, its unity, is merged in the mass of Christian names, and swallowed up by the indifference and infidelity thus fostered."

Such was the rule of preaching prescribed by Bishop Ravenscroft in his first official sermon, and it may be considered as descriptive of the course which he ever afterwards pursued himself, and expected of his clergy. While on all occasions he preached with earnestness the doctrine of " salvation by grace, through faith," he deemed it no less his duty to preach the divinely instituted means for the attainment of this end. He rejected as presumptuous the distinction made between the essentials and the non-essentials of the gospel, and felt himself constrained alike to obey and to teach *all* the requirements of God's revealed will. In the view which the bishop took of the character of the Church, and of the course which his vows as a Christian minister would compel him to pursue, he was sustained by the concurrence of a large majority of his diocese, and of all his clergy, with one exception. The difference between that gentleman and the bishop was so fundamental, and the objections to the Church on the part of the former, were so conscientiously entertained, and so deeply rooted, that they eventuated in his voluntary secession, notwithstanding the very great reluctance with which the bishop parted with him.

Much calumny against Bishop Ravenscroft resulted from this circumstance, and as he, from delicate motives, shrunk from a vindication of his conduct during his life, justice to his memory requires that it should here be made. It will be seen that he was wholly passive in the business, and that the clergyman alluded to, withdrew from the Church in consequence of long established opinions, while the official part which the bishop had necessarily to act was characterized by the utmost kindness and courtesy. This can be sufficiently shown by a few extracts from the letters of that gentleman, without making public the whole correspondence. Immediately after the convention of 1824 the bishop received a letter of which the following are extracts.

" My views on many points are so different from yours—the sentiments proclaimed in your convention sermon are so repugnant to my feelings, that I cannot co-operate in the maintenance and propagation of them."—"I look upon all other denominations as branches of CHRIST's Church equally with Episcopalians."—"But as you are so decidedly of an opposite opinion, there seems to be no hope of a cordial concurrence between us in the promotion of the particular interest of the Episcopal Church. I would, therefore, rather withdraw from this station;" meaning his parish. In a subsequent letter the writer says, "You speak of your disposition to render my way easy, and comfortable. I suppose you allude to your assenting to my retirement, if I insist on it. I am still disposed to drop all ministerial functions for a short time." "You ask me whether I am prepared to say that my ordination vows were taken upon me without due consideration? I certainly was ordained more hastily than I should have been, had it been left to my own choice. When I was questioned about my views on the subject of episcopacy, I answered that I knew nothing about it; and if the examination had been as strict as such examinations ought to be, they would have advised me to delay." The following extracts will show the sense of the writer in regard to the manner in which the correspondence was conducted by the Bishop. "I owe you my thanks for the sincere kindness which marks your whole communication, and which would sooner disarm my resolution than any remarks of a different character." "I repeat my sincere thanks for the kind expressions and true friendship which your letter breathes." "Your tone of uniform kindness, and the brotherly tenderness with which you and my other friends are disposed to treat me, deserve my gratitude; and if I were to consult feeling alone, as you seem to imply, my strongest resolutions would be almost ready to melt away before such treatment. Every such letter disposes me to say with St. Paul, *What mean ye to weep and break mine heart.*"

The Bishop was preparing to yield to the wishes of this gentleman in permitting him to leave the church, when another letter from him announced an intention of offering himself to the congregation of which he was pastor, as an independent minister, a step, which, if successful, would of course involve *their* separation from the Church, as well as his own. This only rendered that necessary as an act of discipline, which the Bishop was about to accede to, in compliance with the desire of the interested party ; and the latter was accordingly displaced from the ministry with the usual and necessary forms.

The fatigue and exposure incident to the situation in which the Bishop was now placed, added to the anxiety of mind necessarily attending it, began very soon to make an impression upon his once robust frame and vigorous constitution, and during the whole of the second winter after his removal to North Carolina, he was confined by illness. Besides, "the care of all the Churches," which, to a mind so solicitous as his, respecting every thing that concerned their well being, was a source of constant and corroding anxiety, the mere physical labour of his annual visitations was very great. The farthest western congregation was more than three hundred miles distant from the most eastern one, and yet, long after disease had established its empire in his enfeebled frame, he punctually and resolutely made his yearly visits to both, and it was not until he became utterly incapable of travelling, a short time previously to his death, that he discontinued them. United to these labours were his laborious and zealous services to his congregation at Raleigh as a parish priest, occupying the whole of his time not devoted to his active Episcopal duties.

But even his hours of sickness and confinement were not hours of idleness. Just before his first illness he had been invited to preach before the Bible Society at its annual meeting, in December, at the city of Raleigh, although he had openly expressed his disapprobation of one feature in the constitution of the society. Availing himself of the occasion, he explained his objections, and gave in general his views of the proper principle upon which Bible Societies should be founded to be most efficient in their operations. This sermon having been published, elicited very severe animadversions from various quarters, and eventually attracted the notice of a celebrated professor of theology in Virginia. That gentleman in his strictures upon the sermon, and the publications arising out of it, having assailed the Church of which Bishop Ravenscroft was a member and a minister, the Bishop felt himself imperiously called upon to stand forth to vindicate it from his aspersions. Though worn by a severe and protracted illness, the result of his labours was a masterly and triumphant *vindication of the doctrines of the Church.* This able controversial tract will be found in this volume, and will be alike valuable to the learned churchman and to the unlearned Christian ; to the former, as a clear and comprehensive summary of the learned labours of the fathers, and the brightest luminaries of the Church ; to the latter, as a plain and irrefragable argument, establishing the divine authenticity of those ministrations upon which he relies as means for his spiritual sustenance.

The Bishop's health was never perfectly renovated after this first severe attack, but his constitution, originally hardy and vigorous, frequently rallied and restored him to his usual activity ; the dedication of which intervals to his Episcopal labours would in turn reduce him for a time to sickness and confinement. The last three or four years of his life consisted almost wholly of these alternations of suffering sickness at home and active industry abroad. From the journal of one of his visitations to the western part of the diocese, we make the following interesting extract.

"August 12, 1827—Sunday—I attended the services of the Moravian brethren in this place, (Salem,) which commenced in the chapel of the female school at half past eight in the morning, and was performed in English—by singing accompanied with the organ—extempore prayer standing—and a short discourse from Revelations iii. 11. The school is very numerous, and great order and uniformity is maintained.

"At ten o'clock the services commenced in the church, by singing, accompanied with the organ and other instruments. The line is given out by the minister, and all sing sitting. After the singing, their Bishop, by name Benade, preached sitting, and with great fluency and force—though in the German language, and, therefore, not understood by me and the other visiters. After the discourse, prayer was made, at which the congregation stood, after which they sung and were dismissed. After the services I was asked into the vestry room, and introduced to the Bishop and one of his presbyters, but had no opportunity for conversation, beyond that of civility. It being a festival-day commemorative of some remarkable event in their history, the Bishop's time was very limited.

"At one o'clock their love feast was held, to which I was invited, and attended. At this there were no other services than the singing of a jubilee psalm in parts, by the choir and congregation, accompanied with the instrumental music, during which there was handed to every individual present, a round cake or kind of light bun, and a half pint mug of coffee, which was partaken of by all during the singing, as each was disposed. The parts performed by the choir were executed standing, in opposite galleries; the congregation sang sitting; at the close all stood to sing the hallelujah.

"After the love-feast, I had another interview with Bishop Benade in the vestry room, when he informed me the communion would be administered after an interval of about two hours, say half past three o'clock, at which I could attend, either as a spectator or a communicant. To this I replied, that though curiosity was in part the cause of my visit to Salem, yet it was not the sole cause, it being my real desire, as we were the only two Episcopal Churches in America, which could and would acknowledge each other, (for the Romanists presented an insuperable bar,) to know more of them, and let them know more of us. If, therefore, I was present it would be as a communicant; and I must accordingly request information as to the mode of administering. This was immediately explained to me, and their being nothing in my judgment unscriptural, or inconsistent with the essentials of a sacrament, I concluded to commune with them. At the appointed hour, the Church (meaning thereby the communicants) assembled, amounting to upwards of two hundred persons, and at a signal given by the bell, the vestry room door was opened, the organ began a solemn voluntary, and the Bishop with the priests and deacon walked up to the altar, carrying the bread in two baskets, covered with a white linen cloth, themselves habited in white surplices, bound round the loins with a broad girdle. The wine was previously placed upon the altar in six decanters, with glass mugs to distribute it. The altar was covered with white drapery, ornamented with festoons of artificial flowers.

" On the Bishop's taking the chair, he gave out the line of a hymn, which was sung by the people to the organ, &c. He then delivered a short exhortation, and proceeded to the consecration of the elements, which was exactly similar to our own mode, in the recitation of Scripture, and the laying on his hand on the bread, and on the wine, previously poured into the mugs.

" When the consecration was finished, a priest, attended by a deacon bearing the bread on the right side of the altar, and another priest attended by a deaconess with the bread on the left side thereof, proceeded to administer to the communicants in this wise. The bread was prepared very white and thin, unleavened, and in oblong shapes, sufficient for two portions. On coming to me, to whom it was first presented, the deacon handed one of the pieces to the priest, who brake it, and administered to two at a time, until the whole Church had received, each row of seats rising up to receive, and again sitting down holding the bread in their hands. When the communicants were all served, the baskets were returned to the altar, when the Bishop and clergy having taken the bread likewise, the organ ceased, and all knelt down in silence and ate the bread. A due portion of time was appropriated to private devotion, and towards the close the organ struck a most solemn strain, to which the communicants all responded in a verse of a hymn sung upon their knees.

" When this was finished, all rose up and the cup was then distributed, each drinking and handing to his neighbour—the deacons attending to replenish, and to pass it from one row of seats to another. The ceremony was concluded with a hymn of praise, and dismission of the congregation, I presume with the apostolic benediction : and all I have to regret is, that I was a stranger to their language.

" At half past seven the services again commenced, and were precisely similar to those in the forenoon. One of the priests delivered the sermon, being the same whom I heard in the school chapel in the morning in English—but in a very different style and manner of address and delivery in his native language.

" During this service, Bishop Benade and myself sat together, and at the close we took leave of each other, I trust with mutual Christian regard, and with the desire of a more close acquaintance.

" Many of the original peculiarities of this body of Christian confessors, as respects their civil discipline, are necessarily done away; and the German language is retained only on account of a few Germans among them, whose prejudices for their native tongue are very strong. But as they drop off, and the rising generation become more accustomed to the English language, it will ultimately preponderate. The men and women enter by different doors, and sit on opposite sides of the church. All the females, to the children, wear caps, uniform in their make; and a place is provided opposite to the preacher where the women who have infants sit. Strangers are treated courteously and shown to the seats proper for them, and notified at their lodgings of the hours of divine service."

The increasing infirmities of the Bishop made it necessary for him, in the beginning of the year 1828, to give up the pastoral charge of the congregation at Raleigh, which, under his fostering care had grown into an importance which required more active and uninterrupted service than his declining health and engagements to the diocese permitted him to bestow. The large congregations of Newbern and Wilmington were both desirous of procuring his valuable pastoral services, interrupted and hindered as they were; and accordingly at this time he received from each of those congregations an invitation to become its pastor, but he ultimately selected the village of Williamsborough, to which he had been also invited, as his future residence. The congregation there was small, and having never had the benefit of regular services, he thought it better able to withstand the injurious effects of interrupted ministrations.

It pleased GOD about this time to deprive Bishop Ravenscroft of the whole of his worldly substance, by that means which had become so general in this country. The same benevolent disposition which prompted him to dedicate his life so zealously to the service of his fellow creatures, had induced him at various times to become the security for others in pecuniary transactions, and the issue was his utter ruin. The details of this unfortunate business it is not necessary to relate. Suffice it to say, that he met with kind friends, and in his own bosom found a source of comfort which made him rise superior to his misfortunes, and, like the courser that has shaken off his encumbrances to run his race with renovated speed and vigour.

One earthly tie yet remained to him, besides his connexion with and attachment to the Church, and that also it pleased GOD to sever. Soon after his removal to Williamsborough, the health of his wife, which had been for some time feeble, began rapidly to decline, and in January, 1829, her sickness and sufferings terminated in death. A life spent in the diligent discharge of the various duties belonging to her station, was closed by a death full of the hope of immortality, and it was a source of great comfort to her husband, that during the last stages of her illness, not one cloud of doubt obscured the brightness of her heavenly prospect, and that (to use his own language) "there was not even a distorted feature in the agonies of death, to betray any quailing before the king of terrors." The severance of this last earthly bond was to the Bishop a severe trial. Besides losing an affectionate friend and a faithful counsellor in his wife, the precarious and delicate state of his own health, made him peculiarly sensitive to the loss of a gentle and tender companion and nurse. But even this severe chastisement was not to him without its mitigations. The poverty to which he was reduced in his old age, had only affected him as it rendered it probable that his early death, to which he already began to look forward, would leave Mrs. Ravenscroft in want. The removal of this apprehension by the death of his wife, though it might render the evening of his days lonely and irksome, at once released him from all earthly anxieties; and in speaking of his loss, this thought, next to the consolations of religion, seemed to have been uppermost.

The convention of 1829, sensible of the increasing infirmities of Bishop Ravenscroft, and of the great necessity of relieving

him of a portion of his laborious duties, determined to release
him from all parochial charge.   Notwithstanding his declining
health and strength, his devotion to both his diocese and parish
had continued unremitted.   Often during his visitations he would
spend one day on a sick bed, and the succeeding in preaching
with his usual force and zeal, or in travelling from the place of
one appointment to that of another; and while at home, he
never permitted a Sunday to pass without occupying his pulpit.
This double labour was obviously too much for his reduced
strength and health, and the convention, notwithstanding the
slender means of the diocese, increased his salary so as to make
it adequate to his support independently of any parochial contribution.   But the relief came too late.   The visitation immediately preceding this convention, was the last he was ever
permitted to make to the diocese, which owed so much to his
zealous and faithful labours.   After the adjournment of the convention he visited the newly formed dioceses of Tennessee and
Kentucky, and from thence went to Philadelphia to attend the
sitting of the general convention in that city.   This long journey, which he was induced to take at the urgent solicitations of
the Tennessee clergy, and perhaps by the expectation that it
might benefit his health, he performed in the public stages and
steamboats, travelling more than a thousand miles over a rough
and mountainous country, in the former mode of conveyance.
When the general convention had finished its session he remained for more than a month in Philadelphia, under the care of the
most eminent physicians of that city.   Their skill restored him
to a degree of comfort and health which he had not known for
years, and they gave him reason to hope that, with proper care,
his health might be completely re-established.   But the expectation which they entertained was vain.   Though the Bishop,
previously to this period, was noted for the recklessness with
which he exposed his health and life in the labours of his voca-
tion, he seems to have been impressed by the opinion of these
eminent medical advisers, with the absolute necessity of more
prudence, and thenceforward to have yielded to their injunctions; but a sudden and violent change of weather exposing him
to severe cold on an unavoidable journey to Fayetteville,

(whither he was preparing to remove,) brought back all the worst symptoms of his disease in an aggravated form. Having disposed of his effects in Williamsborough, preparatory to his contemplated removal to Fayetteville, he reached Raleigh in December, where he designed remaining during the session of the legislature. His health was now, once more, evidently and rapidly declining. He was, however, enabled to write a sermon for the consecration of Christ Church, in Raleigh, and to perform that service. After that he daily grew weaker, and his former disease, chronic diarrhœa, returning with renewed violence and being conjoined with the double quartan, soon prostrated him. In a letter written on the last of January, he says, " I am weakening daily, and now can just sit up long enough at a time to scribble a letter occasionally." "But," he adds, " as respects the result, I am, thank GOD, free from apprehension. I am ready, I humbly trust, through the grace of my divine Saviour, to meet the will of GOD, whether that shall be for life or for death ; and I humbly thank CHRIST JESUS, my LORD, who sustains me in patience and cheerfulness through the valley and shadow of death."

For many weeks previous to his dissolution, he was fully persuaded that his sickness was unto death, and spoke of his decease as certain, and at no great distance ; but manifested the utmost calmness in the contemplation of it. " Why should I desire to live ?" said he. " There is nothing to bind me to this world. The last earthly tie has been broken. Nevertheless, I am perfectly resigned to the will of GOD, either to go or stay. I feel no anxiety about the issue." During the whole of his illness, his conduct was such as to satisfy every one, that he felt no apprehensions at the thought of death. He retained the peculiarities of his character to the last ; the same ardent love and zeal for the truth, the same fearless rebuke and condemnation of error, marked his character on a sick and dying bed, which had so eminently distinguished him through life ; and he let slip no opportunity of bearing testimony to the truth as it is in JESUS, and as it is held and taught by the Church of which he was a Bishop. " On one occasion," writes the Rev. Mr. Freeman, (who attended him in his last moments,) " several persons being

present, I turned to the book of Proverbs, and read to those
who were sitting by me, the following passage, (chap. 20. v. 21.)
*An inheritance may be gotten hastily at the beginning, but the end
thereof shall not be blessed,* and proceeded to observe, how little
encouragement was afforded by this passage for a man to make
haste to be rich, &c.   When I ceased speaking, the Bishop,
who I thought was not attending to what passed, exclaimed,
' There is another lesson to be learned from it.   It may be
applied to those who have hastily obtained a religious inheritance—who place their dependence on those sudden and eva-
nescent fervours which they have experienced in some moment
of excitement.'   With respect to his own prospects, he appeared
to entertain no apprehensions.   I asked him, a few days before
his decease, if he had never during his illness been troubled with
doubts and misgivings?   ' Never,' said he.   ' So free have I
been from any suggestions of the enemy, that I have never
doubted for a moment, except that the thought has sometimes
come over me that my tranquillity is possibly an evidence that
Satan thinks himself sure of me, and therefore lets me alone.'
On my answering, that as he had been labouring to pull down
Satan's kingdom—had been constantly engaged in fighting, not
in his ranks, but in opposition to him, it was not reasonable to
suppose that he had any claims upon him.   ' True,' said he,
' but then I have had such a body of sin to struggle against,
and seem now to have been so much engaged in preaching
myself rather than GOD, that I feel humbled to the dust.   My
only ground of consolation is, that as CHRIST suffered in weakness for our redemption, much more may we hope to be saved
by the power of his resurrection.'   Speaking of his enfeebled
state, and what he called the wandering of his thoughts, he
remarked on the folly of delaying repentance to a sick bed, and
expressed, as he had often done before, his desire to warn every
one of the hopelessness of being able to settle on a dying bed so
vast a concern as that of making one's peace with GOD.   ' If I
had my work now all to do, what would become of me?   If I
had put off this matter to this time, it must have been entirely
neglected.'

" He received the Holy Communion once while on his sick

bed, and had appointed to receive it again, a few days before his death. But when the time came, he was so much exhausted by the preparations which he had made, and which he would not omit, in order that he might come, as he expressed himself, 'literally clean to the heavenly feast,' that he was obliged to forego the opportunity. 'I am not in a condition,' said he, 'to partake discerningly, and I have no superstitious notions respecting the Eucharist—I do not regard it as a *viaticum*, necessary to the safety of the departing soul. I believe that in my case the will, will be accepted for the deed; and tell my brethren (who were assembled in the next room to partake with him) that though I am denied the privilege of shouting the praises of redeeming love once more with them, around the table of our common LORD, yet I will commune with them in spirit.'

"The evening before his death, I had left him for a few moments. Soon after, receiving intelligence that he was dying, I hastened to him, and found him nearly speechless, and sinking to all appearance very fast. I asked him if I should pray. 'I cannot follow you,' was his reply, uttered with great difficulty. I then kneeled down by him, and prayed silently. After some moments, he seemed to revive, and motioned to us to retire from his bed-side, and leave him undisturbed. I sat and watched him from that time till he expired, which he did about one o'clock the following morning, (March 5th, 1830,) without having spoken for five or six hours. He appeared, however, to be in the entire possession of his mind to the last, and expired without a struggle."

The remains of Bishop Ravenscroft were deposited within a small vault, which had been prepared under his directions some weeks before his death, beneath the chancel of Christ Church, in the city of Raleigh. The following instructions respecting his burial, were found in his will, and punctually performed. "My will and desire is, that the coffin to contain my mortal remains be of plain pine wood, stained black, and without ornament of any kind—that my body be carried to the grave by my old horse Pleasant, led by my old servant Johnson—that the service for the burial of the dead, as set forth in the Book of

Common Prayer, and none other, be used at my interment, with the 5th, 7th, 9th, 10th, and 11th verses of the 16th Psalm, to be used instead of the hymn commonly sung ; and that the Rev. George W. Freeman, Rector of Christ Church, Raleigh, do perform the said funeral rites."

The following further extract from the Bishop's will exhibits an amiable trait of his character.——" I give to A. M'Harg Hepburn and E. M. Hepburn, whom I have brought up as my children, my servant Johnson, and my favourite old horse Pleasant, believing that they will be kind to Johnson for my sake, keeping him from idleness and vice, but suiting his labour to his infirm condition ; and that they will not suffer Pleasant to be exposed to any hardship or want in his old age, but will allow Johnson to attend to him, as he has been accustomed to do."

His entire collection of books and pamphlets, which were valuable, he bequeathed to the diocese of North Carolina, " to form the commencement of a library for the use and benefit of the clergy and laity of the Protestant Episcopal Church in North Carolina."

To the " Episcopal Bible, Prayer Book, Tract, and Missionary Society," of the diocese, in the formation of which he had taken a very warm interest, he left the copy-right of such publications of his works as his friends might think it expedient to make, which are now collected in the volumes to which this Memoir is prefixed.

To pourtray the character of Bishop Ravenscroft in its true colours, is a task of no ordinary difficulty. Though candid, almost to a fault, he yet shrunk from speaking of himself, except in terms which his deep conviction of sin, and his great abhorrence of self, rendered almost extravagant, and which were calculated to convey, and have conveyed, an impression injurious to himself in a high degree. Glowing with the most devoted gratitude to GOD for having rescued him " from utter ruin of both soul and body in hell," he thought no language of self abasement too forcible to express his own great unworthiness, and to magnify the goodness of GOD's free grace. Such feelings, and the open avowal of them, it is not our purpose to censure; but only to remark, that the same self denouncing language which misled strangers, though it did not deceive those who knew him better, was still calculated to throw a veil over his inward thoughts and feelings which it was difficult to penetrate; and few but those who were admitted to his closet, could see in their full relief, the virtues of his character. How rarely is the veil of humility so impervious! Notwithstanding these difficulties, that mysterious act of Providence which has removed Bishop Ravenscroft from our sight, before a censorious and misjudging world had time to know and appreciate him, renders an effort to make his character better known and understood, an act of justice to his memory; and the writer undertakes the task with the more confidence, as he has, beside his own personal knowledge, the aid and counsel of those who more than any others, knew him long and intimately.

In person, Bishop Ravenscroft was large and commanding, with a countenance, in its general aspect, perhaps austere, but susceptible of the most benevolent expression. His manner corresponded with his person, especially when exercising his ministerial functions; being remarkably dignified, and so solemn and impressive, as to inspire all who witnessed it with reverence. It was impossible not to partake of the consciousness which he ever seemed to feel when at the altar, of being in the presence of the Great JEHOVAH. In his general intercourse with society he was courteous, though when excited in debate, his loud tone of voice and warmth of manner sometimes made him seem dictatorial, and were the pregnant sources of much calumny from his enemies. The infirmity of temper, which in his unfinished memoir of himself he bewails as his chief besetting sin, (but which, it must be remembered, was entirely distinct from that animation and perhaps violence in argument, which, though subjecting him to reproach so often, was purely the result of a naturally ardent temperament, and was unaccompanied by any unchristian feelings,) would occasionally, though rarely, betray him into a momentary forgetfulness of himself. This, however, was witnessed by few; for aware of his infirmity, he struggled and prayed against it, and sought the counsel and prayers of his friends, patiently receiving their rebukes. "I heartily thank you," he writes to one of his presbyters, " for the warning wish with which you notice the infirmity of my ardent temper, and shall always feel obliged by every hint which may keep me on the watch against its injurious influence, and by every prayer which may prevail for grace, to enable me to direct it aright. Of whatever quality my treasure may be, I know that I have it in an earthen vessel, frailer than common in those preservatives which are furnished by nature, which have often failed me ; and therefore the more dependent on the promise, *as thy days so shall thy strength be*."

This concession being made respecting the character of Bishop Ravenscroft, it may be truly said that in all other respects he was *a perfect man, and upright in his ways.*

As a man he was liberal in his views ; independent in his principles ; just, almost to punctiliousness ; honest in his intentions ; warm and kind in his feelings ; bold and fearless in the cause of truth, and remarkably regardless of self in all he said or did.

His moral worth, even before he became a Christian, was such, with the exceptions that he himself has noticed, that an inmate of his family at the time of his conversion, remarks, that except in abandoning the habits alluded to, and in becoming a praying Christian, no outward change was necessary to constitute him the eminent and consistent professor which he became.

As a citizen, he was warmly attached to our free institutions, and was often heard to rejoice that the Church of which he was an overseer, was untrammelled by any alliance with the civil power. As a neighbour, he was kind and charitable. Being considerably skilled in medicine, he was, while resident in Virginia, the chief physician in his neighbourhood, and performed the laborious duties attached to this beneficent species of charity, with cheerfulness and alacrity, promptly and uniformly attending to every call. His hand too, was ever open to follow the leadings of his generous heart, and ministered to the necessities of others with a liberality—we might almost say prodigality—that left him at the last rich only in the affections of his friends and in the approbation of his own conscience. Although his charity was of that expansive kind which embraces within its objects every creature of God——yet his friendships (in the limited sense in which the term is understood,) were few, and founded on a moral and religious estimation of character. He seemed to consider his friends as parts of himself. Though he loved them, he did not express his affection with honied words, or by a wilful blindness to their faults. He knew not how to flatter, and if he had known, he would have met a martyr's fate sooner than have uttered one word more than truth and honesty permitted. Of his "revilers and persecutors," he said but little, but forgot not to pray for them ; while to his friends he was willing to appear at times unsparing, that he might correct in them those weaknesses and sins of which a flattering world might not have told them. His rebukes, though affectionate in manner, were severe, though seldom undeserved, and those who were dearest to him were most likely to smart under his reproofs.

As respects his more remarkable benefactions, this is the testimony borne by one of the objects of his parental love——" In his conduct towards myself and brothers (whom he adopted in infancy and reared to manhood,) he always supported the character of a father, in its truest sense. I was, myself, an infant when thrown upon his bounty, alike unconscious of my loss, and unconscious of my gain——but, though I never knew father or mother, I never knew their want or felt their loss, until I lost those who adopted me for their son." He was, thus, truly and practically, a father to the fatherless.

In the character of a master, Bishop Ravenscroft mingled the care and affection of a parent, with that authority which Providence had placed in his hands, as a means for the good of those who served him. His domestics he regarded as a part of his family, and he was frequent and careful in expounding to them the way of life, and regular in calling them around his domestic altar.

Whether or not the trials of temper to which he makes such frequent reference, in speaking of his early life, had any connexion with the relation in which he stood to his slaves, is not known, but it is certain that in the latter years of his life, if he erred at all in his treatment of them, it was decidedly on the side of indulgence.

As a husband Bishop Ravenscroft was the guide and instructer, the feeling friend, and the affectionate keeper of those to whom he was successively bound in the strongest of earthly ties.

But all the relations of which we have spoken are now dissolved for ever. As a neighbour, a benefactor, a master, and a husband, he will be known no more. But in the enduring character of a follower of CHRIST he continues unaltered and unharmed by death. It remains for us to contemplate him in this character while militant on earth.

When the SPIRIT OF GOD called him like another Saul from the high way of sin, he fell before the power of truth ; he acknowledged himself the chief of sinners ; he renounced all his former dependencies, and gave himself unreservedly to that GOD whom he had opposed. From that day to the one which shone upon his burial, he lived to the glory of GOD and the good of others. In him there was no superficial change : the grace of GOD had done its perfect work, and he, indeed, became a "new creature." His religion had nothing in it austere and repulsive, but was of that cheerful and happy kind which insensibly wins over the thoughtless and disarms the gainsayer. But when in the retirement of his study, he either dwelt upon his own experience in divine things, or listened to the story of some contrite heart, there was a solemnity in his manner which bespoke a heart deeply imbued with the spirit of holiness, and keenly alive to the responsibilities of his sacred calling. In the still more secret recesses of his closet or chamber there was exhibited that earnestness of devotion which added such a lustre to his Christian character. It is truly said by a reverend friend who served with him as a fellow presbyter for years—" He was one of the most devotional men, in private, that I have ever known. After preaching two or three times in a day, and lecturing and praying with a family at night, yet when he retired to his chamber, he would prostrate himself on his knees for a long time, with agonies and internal strugglings almost irrepressible, as though he was wrestling with his GOD for the very life of his soul." These groanings and wrestlings of his heart in prayer have attracted the notice of many, and it is believed were the invariable characteristics of his private devotions.

The most prominent feature of Bishop Ravenscroft's Christian character was love towards GOD, resulting from a feeling sense of the infinite obligations under which the goodness of GOD had laid him. The only subject that ever affected him to tears, was the mercy of GOD in having rescued him from the grasp of Satan. In speaking of this great deliverance, which he seemed to realize in all its force, his heart appeared ready to burst with the fulness of its grateful emotions. It was this ardent love to GOD, which animated his zeal, which quickened his diligence ; which urged him on, even to the sacrifice of life, in the service of his master ; which made him bow, without a murmur, to the various afflictive dispensations of which he was the object ; and which made him, at the last, " lie down in the dust" with the most perfect tranquillity. This principle of action in Bishop Ravenscroft, accounts for much that has been misconstrued in his conduct. Believing all that he preached to be essential to the glory of GOD, it stimulated him to the utmost earnestness and decision ; and thinking especially that the sin of schism was alike destructive to the eternal interests of man, and injurious to the majesty of GOD, like another Curtius he boldly threw himself into the gulf, reckless of what might befall himself, so that he accomplished the salvation of souls and secured the integrity of GOD's law. In the practice of that charity which he revered as one of the plainest injunctions of Scripture, he distinguished between persons and opinions, and while bold in denouncing error, was ever ready to do justice to motives. He esteemed it the highest charity to warn such as he conceived to be in error of their mistake, and earnestly and loudly to call upon them to awake from a delusion which he thought might be fatal. It matters not, in the estimation of the qualities of his heart, whether his opinions were right or wrong ; *he thought* them right, and was, therefore, justified, and even constrained, by his duty as a minister, to preach them. " My dear brother," he writes to the presbyter already mentioned as having withdrawn from the Church, and who had been urging the very charge we have been combating—" is the declaration of the truth, the pressing our principles, upon the authority of Scripture and reason, a hostile and militant attitude ? Is the denunciation of error publicly made, an arrogant assumption of superiority over others? Then were St. Paul and the other apostles the most contentious, arrogant, and contemptuous men in the world—the most hostile to heavenly affections, that ever lived. What harsh censures have I uttered against any denomination of Christians? I beseech you charge me not with any such fault, laying at my door things which I know not of." And again he says, " I respect principle in every man, no matter how much it may conflict with my own ; nor would I take from any man, or set of men, the right, which I hold sacred, of judging and acting for myself." It may be well for those who have attached the charge of *bigotry* to the memory of Bishop Ravenscroft, to inquire whether that so called *liberality* which denounces as bigotry the zealous maintenance of any opinions, be not in itself one of the worst kinds of bigotry? No one who ever heard the Bishop preach, ever doubted that he was sincere ; and if he believed that what he preached was an essential part of the gospel, is it not a species of bigotry to charge this fidelity upon him as a crime? And would he not have been justly deemed a faithless physician of souls if he had kept from the knowledge of his patient, the very existence of a malady which he thought might be fatal unless removed? As has been already said, humility was a distinguishing trait in the Christian character of Bishop Ravenscroft—a humility growing out of a thorough knowledge and distrust of himself. Besides that meekness under rebuke which we have mentioned, it will scarcely be believed, that even in the composition of his most elaborate works, his powerful mind did not scorn the suggestions of his youngest and humblest friends, but would patiently receive, and sometimes adopt them, yielding his own views with entire readiness when convinced that they were erroneous. On the other hand, the spirit of complaisance never tempted him for a moment to withhold what he believed to be the truth, nor to shrink from the detection and exposure of error.

The humility of his character was most eminently displayed in that remarkable loathing of himself to which we have so often referred, and which nothing but an unshaken confidence in the infinite value of CHRIST's sacrifice, could have rendered tolerable to him. But that grace which revealed to him with such awful distinctness, the depravity of his early life, sustained him under the contemplation of it, and enabled him to say on his death-bed, " Though the past is not without its reproaches, the future is without its fears."

As a *minister of the cross,* Bishop Ravenscroft was faithful, diligent, and zealous. He loved to proclaim the goodness of God and the glad tidings of the gospel ; and his appeals to the hearts and the understanding of his audiences were fervid and animated. He preached the gospel in its utmost purity, and though he did not withhold, on proper occasions, the declaration and defence of his peculiar opinions, the themes upon which he most delighted to dwell were, the goodness of God, the depravity of man, the provision made for his restoration by the blood of Christ, and the freeness and fulness of that mercy which offers the inestimable benefits of his death to the whole world.

His success as a preacher no doubt arose in part from the familiarity which his early experience had given him with all the recesses of the unconverted heart, and from the searching fidelity with which he portrayed its most secret workings. Not like the spy who has discovered the outward defences of the enemy's camp, but like one who had been born and bred within its precincts, he knew every assailable point, every defenceless outpost ; and bearing down upon it with impetuous force, it was impossible to withstand his onset.

His solemn and impressive manner, his finely modulated voice, his commanding figure, and evident earnestness in the sacred cause in which he was engaged, never failed to command the attention and to move the hearts of his auditory, while many who had been misled by the misrepresentations of his enemies were constrained to admit his zeal and singleness of purpose.

It may be here observed, that those who most reviled him knew him the least, or were most interested in interrupting the success of his brilliant career ; and many have been the instances, where seemingly inveterate prejudices, have yielded to a personal knowledge, and have been converted into the most ardent admiration and attachment. His defects were superficial, and were discovered at the first glance, and easily made instruments in the hands of his enemies to injure him : but his virtues were sterling, and shed their influence over his whole life and character, and became more and more prominent as the inspection became more close.

As *a scholar and theologian* Bishop Ravenscroft cannot, perhaps, be deemed profoundly learned. He had received an excellent classical education, and had not failed to acquire an extensive acquaintance with general literature ; but the habits and employments of his life before he entered the ministry had not permitted any very enlarged researches in science, or any very great acquisition of learning. When his attention was turned to religious reading, he seems to have confined himself to such authors (and especially the early fathers of the Church) as threw most light upon the Scriptures, and the constitution of the primitive Church ; and his own vigorous mind readily supplied the wants of those lesser aids, which students of more leisure and longer standing have time to use. With the Scriptures themselves he was thoroughly conversant ; and with all such collateral subjects as his station in the Church required him to become minutely acquainted with : but with such subjects as were more speculative than practical, he concerned himself but little. His very retentive memory hoarded up with great accuracy such acquisitions as his limited time allowed him to make, and his rapid and vigorous conceptions enabled him to reach, with far less than ordinary study, the conclusions of truth. These advantages made him appear learned, and, perhaps, gave him all the benefits ordinarily derived from learning ; for his arguments were all of the most masterly kind, and rarely failed to extort admiration, if not conviction. His style was forcible and impressive, occasionally abounding with the most glowing imagery, sometimes a little involved, and more rarely indicated a slight degree of negligence. His reasoning in the pulpit was clear and judicious, while his appeals to the passions were animated and powerful.

As *a Bishop*, he was untiring in his devotion to the duties of his station—more anxious for the promotion of true piety and sound principles, than for the vain extension of the Church over an unfruitful domain, he directed his first attention, when called to preside over the diocese of North Carolina, to the condition of its already established congregations. Many of these, as we have already seen, had been imperfectly instructed in divine things, and needed the fostering and enlightened care of his diligent hand. The establishment and confirmation of these in true and fruitful piety, and in divine knowledge, is the true criterion of the success of his Episcopal labours; while the addition to the Church of several well-informed and zealous congregations, shows that although mainly attentive to the securing the ground already gained, he was not inattentive to its extension. The *substructure* of the Church in his diocese, in some respects weak and defective when placed under his care, he had repaired and thoroughly reformed: the *superstructure* was just beginning to rise when his labours, his self-sacrificing labours were terminated by death.

In his intercourse with his clergy, Bishop Ravenscroft was kind and affectionate. He regarded them as *sons in* God, and they looked up to him with reverence and child-like affection. Although vested with the highest authority of the Church, that authority was never felt except by offenders. In his presence all distinctions vanished, except that which his dignified person, his commanding talents and his superior piety claimed for him.

Such was Bishop Ravenscroft in life, and even more than such did he prove himself in the hours of sickness and death. With humble confession of many offences, both to God and man, he bore his long and wearisome illness with meekness, patience, and even cheerfulness ; and met its solemn termination with that equanimity which the approving grace of God alone can bestow.

The following communication from a reverend gentleman who was an intimate friend of Bishop Ravenscroft, came to hand too late to be embodied in the preceding memoir. As it contains some interesting particulars, the opportunity is embraced of inserting it in this place.

DEAR SIR,
You ask me to give you some of my reminiscences of our late

beloved Diocesan, and I sincerely thank you, in return, for the opportunity thus afforded me of speaking on a subject of which I never can grow weary. And yet I know not where to begin, or how to do justice to a single trait of his marked character. He was indeed a man of peculiar mould. Lavishly endowed by nature, both as to mind and body, he needed only (what he afterward experienced) the transforming power of grace, to make his character as lovely as it was striking. But I will not dwell on his general character, as that is well known to the world. Let me rather call your attention to a few interesting particulars, which, though perhaps unworthy the notice of a more grave biographer, may, notwithstanding, lend their aid in elucidating a character so deservedly dear to us both.

It was my good fortune to be intimately acquainted with Bishop Ravenscroft, and (I think I may say it without being accused of vanity) to enjoy his confidential friendship. Circumstances threw me more frequently in his company, than either of his other clergy, and thus gave me an opportunity, enjoyed by few, of seeing him as he was in his parlour, in his study, and in all those retired relations of life, which, though not often taken into the estimate of character, serve, nevertheless, to show a man in his proper and distinguishing colours. I might further say, that I knew him well in the unreserved moments of private intercourse. But never lived there a man in whom there was less reserve, and who was more perfectly the same in public and in private. "I have no concealments," would he frequently say, "nor do I wish to know the secrets of others." And never did man act more up to his declarations. With a wasteful honesty (if I may so speak) he dealt out the truth to all, regardless of the fear or favour of any. He "kept back" nothing that he thought would tend to the right understanding of the truth. He was "*determined*," to use his own words, "*to call things by their right names.*" In one word, he was far too honest for the age in which he lived. Had his lot been cast in the iron times of the reformation, posterity would have rejoiced in his name, and have ranked him with the Cranmers and Ridleys of those days. But being raised up, as he was, in the midst of an innovating generation, he felt called on, by every consideration of duty, to lift his voice against that strong tide of modern inventions and misnamed charity, which seemed about to drift the Church from the safe moorings of the reformation, and toss it without helm or pilot upon a sea of uncertainty and error. I have often looked with wonder at the man, whilst he has been declaiming with the zeal of an apostle against modern pretences of charity, and have thought that if all heralds of the cross were filled with a like zeal for the truth, and reverence for primitive practice, what another aspect the Church of CHRIST would wear! And it has occurred to me at those times, that his fearless, self-sacrificing character could be summed up in no better language than that emphatic declaration of our Saviour, *Every plant which my heavenly Father hath not planted shall be rooted up.* He might have taken it for his motto; for it was certainly the ruling principle of all he said and did. His *honesty*, I believe, no man doubted—the *policy* of his unreserved declarations was, however, questioned by many, who regarded, more than he did, established forms of speech, and the little courtesies of society which are too often made to conflict with that unbending honesty and sincerity which should ever characterize the Christian.

It fell to my lot to be the bearer of the letter from our Standing Committee, announcing his unanimous election as our first Bishop. And never shall I forget the solemn nature of that interview. I found him happily seated at his fireside, with the friend of his bosom beside him, and his bible open before him. After the usual salutation and inquiries, the documents containing the certificate of his election, &c., were placed in his hands, and as my curiosity was strongly excited to witness the effect produced on him by this unexpected and solemn call, I narrowly watched the workings of his countenance; and there I read a lesson on the awful responsibility of the sacred calling, never to be obliterated. For some moments he seemed to read and read again, as if loath to believe the startling proposition. At length a deep groan relieved the awful heavings of his breast. At this sound his wife looked up from her work, and cast an anxious look upon us both, as if to inquire the cause of such emotion. Not a word, however, was spoken. An impressive silence reigned throughout the chamber, broken only by hard and long drawn breathings, which seemed to say audibly, "LORD I am not worthy! What am I, O LORD GOD, and what is my house, that thou hast brought me hitherto?" At length, after pacing the chamber for a few moments, as if struggling to keep down his emotions, he paused before me, and said in his peculiarly emphatic manner, "Brother, it must be so. The hand of GOD is in this thing, I see it; and with his help I will go where he calls me." Then putting the papers into the hands of her who was literally his "help-meet," he endeavoured to return to his wonted strain of cheerful and edifying conversation. But, although he failed in no iota of attention to his guest, yet there was an evident weight upon him during the remainder of my visit, which made me wonder how "the office of a Bishop" could ever be the aim of worldly ambition. There was something ever to be remembered, in the expression of his countenance, at that time. It seemed to indicate the humility of *David* in the language just quoted, without the apparent reluctance of *Moses* when called into the dangerous service of his Master. All the trials, and labours, and responsibilities of his apostolic office, appeared to array themselves at once before him, as if to intimidate him, and make him doubt the divine call. But like the great apostle of the Gentiles, (whom of all preachers he most resembled,) he took refuge in the gracious promise of our LORD—*My grace shall be sufficient for thee.*

When I next saw him, it was in Philadelphia, standing before the altar of St. Paul's, and receiving from the venerable and truly excellent Bishop White his commission to *rule* as well as *minister* in the Church of CHRIST. And never, while memory retains her seat, shall I forget the startling effect of his responses upon the multitude that looked on. It was as though an earthquake was shaking the deep foundations of those venerable walls. A breathless silence reigned during the whole of the sacred ceremony; and no one, it is believed, left the church that day without feeling as if he could pledge himself for the sincerity and zeal of him who was then invested with the apostolic office.

And yet that this man should have had his enemies, yea, bitter enemies and revilers ! But it need not be wondered at, for he was the unsparing champion of truth—and, *ye hate me*, says our Saviour to his revilers, *because I tell you the truth*. That Bishop Ravenscroft had his faults, must be freely admitted by his greatest admirers. An unfortunate harshness of manner would sometimes repel the timid from approaching him ; and an apparent impatience under contradiction, would deter free conversation in those who knew him imperfectly. But these were blemishes of the *outward man* only, and reached not the "spirit of the mind." Of these weaknesses, however, he was not unconscious ; and oftentimes has he lamented over them before his friends, and prayed against them in secret. But a day or two before his death, the writer of this was conversing with him on the solemn subject of the future, when he said : "My hopes on that score are without an intervening cloud. I know in whom I have believed, and I fear not to trust myself in his hands. But, bear me witness, I look for salvation only as a pardoned sinner. I have much to be forgiven of GOD, and I have many pardons also to ask of my fellow men, for my harshness of manner towards them. But," said he, lifting his eyes to heaven, and striking upon his breast, "there was no harshness here."

I cannot conclude these brief notices of my beloved diocesan without adverting to what I conceive was one of his most distinguishing and lovely characteristics—I mean his devotion in private. On more than one occasion I have been unavoidably placed as an ear-witness of his moments of retired devotion—a devotion to which I am sure that he thought there were no witnesses but himself and his GOD. And it was at such times that I wished a censorious world could have stood in my place. I distinctly remember the first time that I was so situated. Such were the strong wrestlings and deep groanings of that man of GOD in prayer, that my first impulse was to fly to his assistance, fearing lest some sudden and violent pain had seized upon him ; but a moment's reflection convinced me that it was not *bodily* anguish that wrung these complainings from him, but an agony of spirit, which seemed driven for relief to these plaintive moan-

ings.   Oh, how hard would he seem to wrestle with his GOD !
Every groan that burst from his labouring soul seemed to say,
I will not let thee go, except thou bless me.   Nor was his a short-
lived, or transitory devotion.   Three times a day, like the prophet of old, did he kneel upon his knees ; and, unless pressed
by other duties, he continued in prayer for the space of half an
hour.   His usual custom was to go from the reading of GOD's
word to the seeking of his face in prayer.   Indeed I never have
known a more diligent reader of the Bible.   It was ever open
on his desk ; and in the composition of his sermons, he seldom
sought assistance beyond its pages.   Enter his study when you
would, there was his Bible on one side of him, and his Concord-
ance on the other.   And this reminds me of the wide-spread,
but mistaken opinion of thousands as to his views on the subject
of *Commentaries* on the Bible.   So far was Bishop Ravenscroft
from desiring to disseminate with the Scriptures the interpretations of any man, or set of men, that I can truly say I never
have known any one to hold commentaries in such light esteem.
More than once have I heard the young and inexperienced
Christian ask him : " What commentator shall I consult in
reading my Bible ?"   And his reply has invariably been, " No
one.   Read it on your knees, and the SPIRIT of truth will make
all necessary things plain unto you."   Nay, I have heard him
go further, and say, that " seldom, if ever, had he been helped
out of a difficulty by consulting even the most esteemed commentators."   He delighted to drink from the pure fountain of
GOD's word : and his sermons and private discourses showed
plainly that he was neither unlearned nor unskilful in handling
its sacred truths.   In his views of the Christian system, he
seemed to stand on an eminence, with the whole Gospel spread
out before him, in all its length and breadth.   As a practical
expounder of Scripture, I have never known his equal.   He
left to others the applause of critical acumen and deep research,
and sought rather to bring every passage of GOD's word to bear
upon the conscience of the sinner.   And in these practical
applications of Scripture he was peculiarly solemn and interesting.   When in health, I have known him, after preaching
twice or thrice in the day, lecture at family prayers for thirty or

forty minutes, upon perhaps the first chapter that met his eye on opening the Bible. And on these occasions, it has often been thought by his friends that in point of force of manner, and richness of thought, he even exceeded his more deliberate pulpit exercises.

But I must here put an end to these hasty and disjointed sketches. Not that I have nothing more to say of that great and good man, or that I am weary of my subject. But that I fear I have already exceeded the limits which you have fixed for my reply.

One further remark, and I have done. It is reported of Bishop Horne, that such was his admiration of the character of good old Bishop Andrews, that he prayed that he might hereafter be permitted to sit at the feet of that righteous man in glory. For my own part, I have often prayed that I might die as Bishop Ravenscroft died; and now, most heartily do I supplicate our Father in heaven, to permit me to occupy, in the Church triumphant, what I have ever esteemed one of the greatest privileges of my past life—a seat at the feet of Bishop Ravenscroft.

Yours, in Christ, ever and truly.

TO THE

MEMBERS OF THE PROTESTANT EPISCOPAL CHURCH,

IN THE

Parish of St. James', Mecklenburg County, Virginia,

THIS DISCOURSE IS HUMBLY PRESENTED,

AS A TOKEN OF HIS REGARD,

AND

OF HIS EARNEST DESIRE FOR THEIR ESTABLISHMENT IN THE FAITH,

BY THEIR AFFECTIONATE PASTOR,

JOHN S. RAVENSCROFT,

A FAREWELL DISCOURSE.

1 CORINTHIANS xv. 58.

" Therefore, my beloved brethren, be ye steadfast, unmoveable, always abounding
in the work of the LORD, forasmuch as ye know, that your labour is not in vain
in the LORD."

MANY considerations, my brethren and friends, unite in condemning that neglect of revelation, and indifference to the awful
sanctions and encouraging hopes of the gospel, which is so prominent a feature, in the character of the present day ; but none
more directly than that, which forms the subject matter of this
chapter.

That another state of being awaits us, in which we shall live
for ever, no more capable of change or decay, is a doctrine, at
one and the same time grateful and encouraging to our hopes,
and awful and overwhelming to our fears. Because the mind
at once passes forward to the purpose which such an appointment may be made to answer—to the bearing it will have, on
our individual condition, and to those apprehensions, which flow
from our natural knowledge of GOD, and our actual acquaintance with our own nature.

But whatever may be considered the influence of this impression of a future state, on those who either have not, or regard
not, the word of revelation ; it presents to the Christian a subject of the most sublime and encouraging contemplation—of the
most earnest and devoted self-dedication. Realizing not only
eternal life for himself—but the possible re-union of all that was
dear to him in this life—no more liable to change or separation ;
the holy hope re-acts upon the duties of his station, gives to them
a character of eternity, and strengthens him to that firm and
unshaken discharge of them, which shall not be disappointed of
its reward.

What, then, my brethren, must it be to the Christian minister, who knows that he must answer with his own soul, for his faithfulness towards the souls of others, when he comes to realize the awful meeting of the risen dead, and the judgment that awaits him ? Alas ! who can paint the anxious fear and holy hope with which the contemplation is mixed up ? especially, when the connexion between a pastor and his flock, is about to determine—when he looks back on the course of his labours among them—and calls to mind how much is left undone, how much might have been better done—and that ere long they will meet him at the bar of God, and be his crown, or his condemnation ! Oh, it is a feeling which no language can express, under which no human fortitude could bear up, unless strengthened by that grace of God, which is made perfect in weakness, and from which all our sufficiency is derived. Thanks be to God for this his help and mercy !

Under the influence of this feeling I meet you this morning, my brethren, to give you my last exhortation, my last. warning as your immediate pastor—once more to eat of that bread and drink of that cup, by which, when duly partaken of, we are made one body with our blessed Lord—humbly trusting, that however imperfectly—I have not failed to declare unto you that truth by which we are saved ; to counsel you to stand fast in those doctrines, which the holy apostolic Church of which you are members hath set forth, as *the faith once committed to the saints*—and to continue in the use of that *form of sound words* which she hath provided for the public worship of God—that *with the spirit and with the understanding—with one heart and one mouth* ye may glorify his holy name, and with *one hope of your calling* look joyfully forward to that great day when *this mortal shall put on immortality*—and the redeemed of the Lord with crowns of glory on their heads, and harps of triumph in their hands, shall raise the enraptured song, of glory, honour, and salvation, to him that sitteth on the throne and to the Lamb for ever.

Therefore, my beloved brethren, be ye steadfast, unmoveable, always abounding in the work of the Lord—forasmuch as ye know that your labour is not in vain in the Lord.

As the text naturally divides itself into three heads, I shall follow them in their order, and consider,

FIRST, the duty of steadfastness or establishment in religion, with an application of it to some few points of doctrine :—*Be ye steadfast, unmoveable.*

SECONDLY, I shall lay before you the necessity and advantage of diligence and engagement in all your Christian duties :—*Always abounding in the work of the* LORD.

THIRDLY, I shall conclude with a view of the reward which awaits the faithful :—*Forasmuch as ye know that your labour is not in vain in the* LORD.

I. First, I am to consider the duty of steadfastness or establishment in religion, with an application of it, to some few points of doctrine. *Be ye steadfast, unmoveable.*

By steadfastness or establishment in religion, we are to understand that full persuasion of the mind which is the result of knowledge, consideration, and experience ; made effectual by divine grace, to the full assurance of hope unto the end.

Of this persuasion and assurance, the word which GOD *in these last days hath spoken to us by his Son,* as recorded in the holy Scriptures, is the only foundation—as it also is, the only standard, by which to try the truth of our condition, not only as to soundness in doctrine, and holiness of life, but as to our conformity likewise, to those appointments of outward order, in the Church, the ministry, and the sacraments, which our Redeemer has established, as helps to faith, and visible signs and means of that grace, by which he *works in us to will and to do*—and with us—in working out our everlasting salvation.

Of the truth and soundness of this doctrine, it might be supposed there could be no doubt on the mind of any well-informed professor of religion ; because whatever claim we may have on the divine mercy, is by virtue of that covenant made with CHRIST for us, which is revealed in the Scriptures ; and it is just as necessary to comply with the appointments of our Redeemer, in matters of outward order, as in the undisputed attainments of righteousness and true holiness. But further, upon the fundamental principle of the gospel, that *we are saved by grace*, it must follow, that whatever relates to our salvation must be ordered, directed, and determined, by divine wisdom; and so ordered, as not to be subject to any discretion of ours, other than to receive or reject it when proposed. Were it otherwise, there could be no such thing as certainty in this weighty affair: one man's discretion would be as good as another's, and all religion be upturned from the foundation. Neither could there be any kind of ground for *steadfastness* or establishment in the faith, were it left to man's option, what to take in, or what to leave out, in the appointments of GOD for the salvation of sinners.

It hence appears undeniably, my brethren, that the duty of steadfastness is grounded on conformity in our religious state to the *whole counsel of* GOD, revealed in his word. Otherwise it would be the duty of ministers to exhort men to continue steadfast in what was clearly unwarranted by the word of GOD, yea, contrary to it: which is blasphemy even to think of.

This is so clear to the reason of every unprejudiced mind, that it is very wonderful it should be so little attended to; more especially, when the subject is so differently treated in those Scriptures, which all Christians profess to follow as their guide.

In them the exhortations to steadfastness are very frequent; while no latitude or discretion is so much as hinted at, as to what they were to be steadfast in.

St. Paul, in exhorting Timothy to this duty, does it in these words, *But continue thou in the things which thou hast learned, and hast been assured of—knowing of whom thou hast learned them.* Now let us ask ourselves, my brethren, Could Timothy have been as well certified of the truth and certainty of what he was to believe, had he received the doctrines from any other than an apostle of CHRIST? You will answer, No. But why not, if truth is the same by whomsoever spoken? Because the truths of revelation, being articles of faith, must have a divine warrant; and as such, admit of no discretion to interpret or practice them contrary to the standard.

Upon the same principle the apostle presses this duty upon the Colossians, nearly in the words of our text. *As ye have therefore received* CHRIST JESUS *the* LORD, *so walk ye in him, rooted and built up in him, and established in the faith as ye have been taught, abounding therein with thanksgiving.* Adding this most salutary caution, *Beware lest any man spoil you through philosophy and vain deceit, after the tradition of men, after the rudiments of the world, and not after* CHRIST.

It is in his Epistle to the Ephesians, however, that we find this duty of steadfastness in the faith pressed, upon the sole foundation on which it can be required or practised. *There is one body, and one spirit, even as ye are called in one hope of your calling ; one* LORD, *one faith, one baptism—one* GOD *and Father of all, who is above all, and through all, and in you all. And he gave some apostles, and some prophets, and some evangelists, and some pastors and teachers, for the perfecting of the saints, for the work of the ministry, for the edifying of the body of* CHRIST, *that we henceforth be no more children, tossed to and fro, and carried about with every wind of doctrine, by the sleight of men, and cunning craftiness, whereby they lie in wait to deceive.*

Hence it would appear, as well from the nature of the thing, as from the letter and the spirit of Scripture, that steadfastness or establishment in religion, does not refer singly to the spiritual doctrines of the gospel, but to the whole scheme of our redemption—including those appointments of our LORD and his apostles, which are outward and visible ; such as the Church, the ministry, and the sacraments, which are devised and ordered by the wisdom of GOD, as means to an end, for our attainment of those higher and more spiritual qualifications which form the life and power of religion ; or, as it is better expressed in this same Epistle, *till we all come, in the unity of the faith and of the knowledge of the Son of* GOD, *unto a perfect man, unto the measure of the stature of the fulness of* CHRIST.

Hence, my brethren, we are instructed, that the steadfastness to which we are exhorted in the text, does not refer to a part, but to the whole of our duty as redeemed creatures, made wise unto salvation by the revealed word of GOD; and that only as we are thus found submitting ourselves to the righteousness of GOD, can we with any propriety be exhorted to persevere unto the end. If in any thing we be found at variance with this rule, the exhortation must be, to consider and amend our ways, and seek for that good way, which the wisdom of GOD hath marked out for us to walk in, and in which only can we find rest to our souls—*For it is not of him that willeth, or of him that runneth, but of* GOD *that showeth mercy.* To be entitled to that mercy, on the only safe ground, his revealed word, we must be found within the rule which includes it as a covenant stipulation. Of any other state or condition different from this, we can say nothing, because we know nothing. There may be mercy, but it is not revealed : it is no where promised.

Let us cleave then, my brethren, *to the law and to the testimony,* and in imitation of the primitive Christians—*continue steadfast in the apostles' doctrine and fellowship, and in breaking of bread and in prayers.* Thus, and thus only, shall we walk with assurance through our pilgrimage here, finish our course with joy, lie down in peace, awake to glory, and meet at the right hand of GOD— where trial shall be ended, duty be free from hindrance, and love and peace from the presence of FATHER, SON, and HOLY GHOST, grow and increase through the endless ages of eternity.

I come now to apply this duty of steadfastness, to some particular doctrines of our holy religion.

And first to the doctrine of the Church, as that on which the minds of men in the present day, are most unsettled ; and, together with many Episcopalians, farthest led away from the truth of Scripture.

By the doctrine of the Church, I mean that article of our public creed, in which we profess our belief " in the Holy Catholic Church," or as it is more definitely expressed in the Nicene Creed, " in one Catholic and Apostolic Church."

Before I go into the subject, I must explain the meaning of the words *Catholic* and *Apostolic ;* for such is the ignorance which is fast spreading over us, on this and similar subjects, that many, when they hear us express our belief in the Holy Catholic Church, associate us with the Church of Rome, and are thereby the more easily prejudiced against our claims to their notice.

By the word *Catholic,* as used in the Creeds, and applied to the Church of CHRIST, is to be understood Universal ; and Universal in such a sense, as is opposed to national or particular.

By the word Apostolic is to be understood, the derivation of that authority which was committed to the apostles by CHRIST himself, for the founding, extending, establishing and ordering his Church to the end of the world ; and this in such a sense, as is opposed to every other derivation of authority whatever.

That we should have a right understanding of this doctrine, of which we regularly profess our belief, is surely very important, my brethren ! inasmuch as the full persuasion, grounded on the testimony of Scripture, that we are members of that one spouse and body of CHRIST, of which he is the Head—of that Church, which he *bought with his own blood*, and *built on the foundation of the apostles and prophets, himself being the chief corner stone*— that one fold, of which he is the Shepherd—that household, of which he is the Master—that kingdom, of which he is the King— that vineyard, of which he is the Lord—is the first foundation of any hope in the revealed promises of GOD. For, however it may have fallen into disrepute, in these latter days, as a narrow minded and bigotted doctrine, yet certain it is, that there is not a promise from GOD, in the gospel, to fallen man, which is not tied to the condition, that he be a member of CHRIST's visible Church on earth. And we would do well to bear in mind, my brethren, that one " thus saith the LORD," is of more weight, than all the notions, and reasonings, and crooked inventions, and contrivances, of man's wisdom.

On this doctrine of the Church, then, we are instructed from Scripture—

First, that it is but one. *There is one body.* Accordingly, we never find it spoken of, in these same Scriptures, indefinitely, as *a* Church ; but definitely, as *the* Church.

This *oneness*, however, is not to be understood of any particular location ; for in this respect, it hath no limit but the gracious purpose of its divine Founder, *to gather together in one the children of* GOD *scattered abroad.* Hence it is compared to a vine, which, with but one root, has many branches.

Secondly, we learn from the same source, that the unity of this *one Body*, consists in the belief and profession of *the one faith* or system of doctrine, revealed by the one SPIRIT OF GOD, and once committed to the saints, or associated members of the Church of CHRIST, by the preaching of the apostles ; in the service, or obedience to the laws, of *the one* LORD or Head of this body ; in the participation of the same sacraments, as means and pledges of divine grace, and of that brotherly love and Christian fellowship in which we are joined together, in the worship of *the one* GOD *and Father of the spirits of all flesh ;* and in *the one hope of our calling.*

Thirdly, we are instructed from the same word of GOD, that in this one body or Church of CHRIST, there is but one source of authority for administering the word and sacraments ; and, that this authority is of divine appointment. *All power is given unto me, in heaven and in earth ; Go ye, therefore, and teach all nations, baptising them in the name of the Father, and of the Son, and of the* HOLY GHOST—*teaching them to observe all things, whatsoever I have commanded you ; and lo, I am with you always, even unto the end of the world.*

Fourthly, we are taught by the *more sure word of prophecy,* that unto the Church, thus divinely constituted, and *built on the foundation of the apostles and prophets,* the solemn promise is made, that *the gates of hell shall not prevail against it ;* the HOLY SPIRIT given, to abide with it for ever, to enlighten, convince, comfort, and sanctify the children of GOD : and that only as we are members of this one body, fruitful branches of this one vine, are *the promises of* GOD *in* CHRIST, *to us yea, and to us, Amen.*

And now let us ask ourselves seriously, my brethren, What ground of steadfastness and assurance, in the great work of our salvation, can there be to creatures such as we are, other than that of divine authority ? Can that which is merely human, offer any security to our souls ? Or, can any mixture of human wisdom amend the appointments of heaven, and render them more effectual to our good. Alas ! what is there of endurance in the work or wisdom of man ? My brethren, is it not written, that *the wisdom of this world cometh to nought ?* How then can steadfastness be exhorted to, on a ground which is in itself changeable ; which our own observation proves to be so, by the present state of the Christian world, which having once separated from the root of Unity, in the one authority of CHRIST transmitted through his apostles, goes on dividing and subdividing, till every original feature of the Church is lost, and the great and gracious purpose of Christian union and brotherly love, rendered impracticable.

But it may be asked, and very properly, How is a plain man to settle a question on which the learned and the pious are so divided? To which I answer, first—*Search the Scriptures* with a sincere and honest desire to find the truth; remembering, *that the Scripture cannot be broken*, and therefore every conclusion we come to, to be safe and agreeable to *the mind of the* SPIRIT, must be in agreement with its whole purpose, and not merely with partial and insulated passages of the word. And this course I can recommend from my own experience. It was sufficient for me, even against prejudice, prepossession, and profession.

But, secondly, there is a shorter method, my brethren, and that is, on the ground of authority. If the authority by which any denomination of Christians ministers in sacred things, cannot be shown to be derived from the apostles of CHRIST—that is, cannot be verified as a fact; such denomination cannot be a branch of that catholic apostolic Church, in which we profess to believe. And I will venture to say, had this been more attended to, in the controversies on this subject, there would have been less confusion in the minds of men, and less unscriptural hope among professors of religion.

In thus framing my last address to you, my brethren, I know that I am treading on what is considered forbidden ground; yet I am actuated by a deep sense of the responsibility under which I am placed, lest I should be charged with keeping back aught that was profitable for you; and, with something of St. Peter's spirit, I trust, *I would not be negligent to put you always in remembrance of these things which are most surely believed among us—And to endeavour, moreover, that ye may be able, after my departure, to have these things always in remembrance—For we have not followed cunningly devised fables.*

Being aware, also, that mistaken views of Christian charity, and erroneous notions of liberality of sentiment, have shaken many of you from that steadfastness, on this doctrine, which is the only security for consistency and perseverance as churchmen—I am drawn out the more earnestly to lay before you that whole truth in defence of which I am set. And may God pardon me for not having done it sooner, and forgive all his ministers, who from love of peace, and false tenderness to the feelings of others, have kept back these fundamental doctrines from those of their charge.

For let us consider, was this the course pursued by St. Paul and other apostles, towards those who separated themselves from the Church? Did they own such as fellow Christians, and their teachers as ministers of Jesus Christ? Or did they warn them of their danger, endeavour to reclaim them to their duty, and pronounce their schism a deadly sin? Thank God, my brethren, that we have the record of their conduct in this very case to appeal to.

Did St. Paul consider the divisions and separations into parties in the Corinthian Church as venial faults, as points on which private judgment was at liberty to follow its own notions, without guilt and danger? Or does he denounce them as proofs of a carnal mind, and as the actual sin of rending the body of Christ? *Search the Scriptures.* Does he acknowledge the teachers, who had thus disturbed the harmony of the Church, and sown the seeds of strife and contention among them, as fellow labourers with him in the gospel, or does he severely condemn them, and charge them as ministers of Satan? *Search the Scriptures.*

Does he tell the Galatians, that it was a matter of no moment by whom the gospel was preached to them, or what additions or alterations were made in the ordinances of religion, so that they were believers? Or does he put the proof of the fact, that they were believers, on their steadfastness to the doctrine he had preached to them, and the order he had established among them? Again I say, *Search the Scriptures.* Does he speak to them of any other ground of assurance in the faith, than the authority by which he was accredited to them as the minister of Christ! Does he define Christian liberty to be a principle of dissent from established order, at every man's private discretion; a privilege to go where we will, follow whom we like, and believe what suits our particular views, in the Christian revelation? Once more I say, *Search the Scriptures.* No my brethren, No. What then, let me ask, becomes of the specious cant of the present day, the spurious liberality of opinion, so eagerly contended for in this question, that it matters not to what communion of professing Christians a man unites himself; that he is equally safe in one as in another? Is it warranted by either reason or Scripture; or is it not rather one of those deceits, wherewith *Satan, transformed into an angel of light,* is cunningly contriving to defeat the efficacy of the gospel?

With such high authority, then, for our belief and practice, and with even such arguments as I am able to bring forward in confirmation thereof—shall any of you yet halt between two opinions, my brethren; and by continuing to give countenance to separation and division in the Church of CHRIST, contribute to confirm the delusion, under which so many are led away from the only foundation, and deceived into *crying Peace, where there is no peace*—certainly none revealed? GOD forbid! No, let us rather consider afresh the foundation on which such opinions are built, whether on the word of GOD, or the wisdom of man; and separating the precious from the vile, be so grounded and settled in the faith of the gospel order and doctrine, that we may be steadfast, unmoveable, adorning the doctrine we profess, by lives and conversation void of offence.

And you, my dissenting hearers, am I your enemy, because I tell you the truth? GOD knoweth. But whether it is the truth, is the question. Try it, then, by the touchstone of eternal truth, the word of GOD, and as you find it, receive it; for in the words of St. Paul, *We can do nothing against the truth, but for the truth.*

Secondly, to the divinity of our LORD JESUS CHRIST.

On steadfastness, or establishment in the belief of this doctrine, the whole comfort and efficacy of the Christian religion depends. For if JESUS CHRIST of Nazareth is a creature, that is, any thing less than GOD *manifest in the flesh,* no matter how high he may be exalted in the scale of being, no just confidence can be placed in the atonement he hath made for our sins by his death upon the cross, on the virtue of his intercession for sinners, and on his ability *to save to the uttermost all who come unto GOD by him.*

VOL. I.—-11

On the essential divinity of our LORD, also, depends our hope of eternal life; for it is expressly said by St. John, *that GOD hath given to us eternal life; and this life is in his Son.* Our LORD himself also declares the same thing, *My sheep hear my voice, and I give unto them eternal life.* Now without any dispute whatever, if our blessed LORD hath not this life in himself, but by delegation from another in such wise as belongs to the condition of a created being, the security of the believer for the attainment of it, is not only weakened, but shaken to its very foundation. Because faith cannot rationally rely upon any thing less than infinite, for the fulfilment of what is promised; and because all certainty in the revealed word of GOD, as the only ground of faith, is hereby defeated—and the Scriptures rendered of no more value than a novel or a newspaper. And I put the question thus, to show you, my brethren, how much depends upon it; and to warn you against all careless reception of the doctrines of our religion, because no steadfastness can be relied upon, without such conviction as springs from examination and consideration. A man may indeed *adhere* most firmly to a doctrine or opinion, for which he can give no reason, and for which, in fact, none can be given; but such adherence is either *obstinacy,* or *implicit faith;* it is not what the apostle means by *steadfastness.*

This doctrine of the essential divinity of JESUS CHRIST being at once the foundation and the corner stone of Christian hope,— *on this rock will I build my Church,* has from the beginning been a favourite point of attack to the enemy of our souls; because success here, rendered all other temptations needless—it being an actual and fatal denial of CHRIST, to deny his essential divinity; and because also, the entertainment of this heresy is quite compatible with, in fact leads to, that self-righteousness, which apes the morality of the Gospel, and lulls into a fatal security those who, from constitutional temperament or worldly condition, are less exposed to those temptations which lead to gross sin, and out-breaking wickedness.

In the commencement of Christianity, the attack upon this doctrine was supported chiefly by metaphysical arguments, drawn from the nature of GOD; from the expressly revealed, and by all Christians acknowledged, doctrine of the unity of the divine essence ; and from the impossibility, of understanding, so as to believe, the Catholic doctrine of the Trinity of persons, in the unity of the Godhead. In the present day, however, though these weapons are not abandoned, the main reliance seems to be on the resources of learning and critical acuteness, to explain away, or even to expunge, those texts of Scripture which either directly or by consequence assert this vital doctrine.

Against both these modes of attack, therefore, it behoves every Christian, and especially every Christian minister, to be guarded ; and thankful we should be, my brethren and hearers, that unless we believe men rather than GOD—unless we prefer a creature, that is, a created being, to the Most High GOD, as our Saviour—unless we yield to the pride of the carnal mind, choose to be our own Saviour, and risk meeting GOD in judgment, in our own righteousness ; we are amply furnished to withstand the many vain talkers and deceivers, who are now *banded together against the* LORD *and against his anointed,* and are busy to upturn this cardinal point of *the faith once committed to the saints* and with an earnestness that would be commendable in a better cause, are endeavouring to instil the poison of this damnable heresy into the minds of the ignorant, the simple, and the unwary.

Now the means with which we are provided to withstand this master delusion of the devil—are, the word of GOD, and Christian experience.

In the revelation made to us from Heaven by the HOLY GHOST, speaking through the Prophets—by JESUS CHRIST, declaring the will of the Father—and by his Apostles, under the visible and sensible guidance and direction of the SPIRIT of truth ; we find the Redeemer and Saviour of sinful man, represented at once as the Son of GOD, and the Son of man ; and in the personal history of JESUS of Nazareth, and in him only, do we perceive the perfect union of this wonderful designation. For we behold in his birth, in his life, in his death and resurrection, the infinite attributes of JEHOVAH, and the finite condition of our mortal nature, exemplified. Now, why should this be thought a thing impossible with GOD, or incredible with men ?

Is the union of the divine with the human nature, either more incredible or more impossible, than that of an immortal soul with a mortal body ? In no wise, except *in degree*, which operates not at all against omnipotence. All arguments, therefore, framed against the divinity of CHRIST from this source, and from our inability to comprehend the manner of such an existence, are equally good against the being of GOD, and against our own being ; they are therefore good for nothing, but to show the daring impiety of men, who would be *wise above what is written.*

In the purpose which such a mysterious union was to answer, as revealed to us, is there any thing discordant, superfluous, or unnecessary? In no shape or sense whatever, my brethren : for the purpose was to reconcile GOD and man, separated and put at enmity by sin ; therefore none could be competent to this work, but such an one, as was partaker of both natures, and as a mediator, or daysman, as Job styles him, qualified to lay his hand upon both parties in this awful controversy.

It was also in the purpose of this appointment of GOD's rich redeeming love, to procure mercy for man, a sinner, consistently with the dignity of GOD, an offended sovereign. Now this could no otherwise be done, than by the nature which had sinned, suffering the penalty of the law it had broken ; so that full satisfaction might thereby be made to divine justice, and the offender brought within the reach of pardon. But this satisfaction, to be full and complete, must be commensurate with the offence ; which, as against GOD, was infinite. But no finite or created being can perform an infinite condition ; therefore, if we are redeemed at all—if Christianity is not a fable—that being who took our nature upon him, appeared in the world in the person of a man, and according to the predictions of the prophets, suffered and died upon the cross for our salvation, must have been very and eternal GOD. From this argument there is no escape, as the opponents of CHRIST's divinity are well aware—they therefore cut the knot which they cannot untie, and cast away from their system of unbelief, all the distinguishing doctrines of Christianity, denying the fall, and consequent depravity of man's nature, the atonement of the cross, the meritorious righteousness of the Redeemer, as the only ground of our justification and acceptance with GOD, and the gift of the HOLY SPIRIT, as the only root whence all holy desires, all good counsels, and all just works do proceed, in redeemed man. Oh, what a desperate delusion that must be, which thus turns light into darkness, hope into despair, and mercy into condemnation !

From this union of the divine and human nature in the man CHRIST JESUS, results the manner in which he is spoken of in the Scriptures. We read of him as GOD ; as the Son of GOD ; as equal to the Father ; as one with the Father : and we read of him, as man ; as the son of man ; as lower than the Father ; as acting by commission from the Father. Of this necessary manner of speaking of him, the adversaries of his religion would take advantage against his divinity. But what is there in it to stumble any fair mind ? What is there in it inconsistent with either the power or the purpose of GOD in the great work of man's redemption ? Yea, what is there spoken of our Redeemer in the Scriptures, which if unsaid, would not involve the subject in tenfold greater difficulty, and furnish a much more powerful (yea, and reasonable too) ground of opposition and unbelief of this doctrine—the uniform faith of the Catholic Apostolic Church from the day of the Pentecost to the present moment ?

The truth is, my brethren, that there is no difficulty in the question, unless to those who seek occasion against the Gospel. The fact of our LORD's divinity being revealed, is all that we are concerned with. The mystery of the incarnation of GOD the Son, must remain such, while we remain what we are ; but our belief of *the fact* depends in no degree on our being able to solve this mystery. Nor are the benefits to be derived from it, limited upon any such condition. Yea, rather may we observe—and observe to take the warning—that this presumptuous intruding into the secret things of GOD, is most commonly visited with that strong delusion, which leads to believing a lie, or which is the same thing, to unbelief.

On the question of fact, then, it is that this doctrine must ever rest, for its reception or rejection among Christians. This its opponents well know, as also that the fact is against them. To obscure this fact, therefore, and if possible, to disprove it, by invalidating the testimony for it in the *record which* GOD *hath given to us of his Son,* has been their main object. To this end, the learning, the critical skill and ingenuity of the whole body of unbelievers, has been put in requisition. The original text of the Scriptures has been twisted into every contortion of various reading ; the sound and acknowledged canons of criticism have been disregarded and perverted ; the established rules of grammatical construction have been violated : but all in vain, except to *pretenders to science falsely so called,* to superficial sciolists, and proud contemners of the wisdom of GOD, and of the wants of our fallen nature. To the sound scholar, and at the same time fair and candid man, the weakness of their cause, and futility of the arguments with which they would support it, are apparent ; because no otherwise than by a combined violation of the meaning of language, of the rules of grammar, and of the dictates of common sense, can they obtain even a show of success to their cause. To such an one, the word of revelation is strengthened and confirmed by their abortive attempts. It stands amid this war of infidels, like an unshaken rock in the raging ocean, whose proud waves lash themselves to froth against its base, while its summit shines serene and peaceful amid the sunbeams of heaven.

But it is not only to the learned, that it is given to enjoy this satisfactory proof of the divinity of our blessed Redeemer. No, my brethren, thanks be to GOD, every real Christian, whether learned or not, is furnished with it, in his experience of that Gospel in which it is revealed, and which is *the power of* GOD *unto salvation, to every one that believeth.* For there is no one, who has been truly convinced of sin by the SPIRIT of GOD— who has been brought to feel what it is, in its malignity, as an offence against GOD, how infinite in its guilt, and damnable in its very nature ; and has been enabled by the same HOLY SPIRIT to believe in the LORD JESUS CHRIST, as the great sin-offering, through whom only pardon and grace can be obtained—who can entertain any doubt of the infinite virtue of that atonement (and, of course, of the infinite nature of him who made it,) whereby GOD *can be just, and yet the justifier of him that believeth in* JESUS.

Being thus furnished, my brethren, in the express revelation which God hath made to us concerning his son JESUS CHRIST our LORD, and (if we are Christians indeed) in our experience of the efficacy of his word and grace upon our hearts and lives, with the most irrefragable testimony for the divinity of our LORD and Saviour, let us cleave to this true and faithful witness ; and building ourselves up in our most holy faith, *continue steadfast and unmoveable*, in the belief of this article of the catholic faith, as the only doctrine which makes Christianity consistent with itself—with its author—with its object ; as the only foundation on which faith can be fixed with assurance, hope entertained with reason, and eternal life realized by the sinners who descend from Adam. If there are any in this world descended from another stock, they may sport with this doctrine : but to us, my brethren, there is hope only in *the* LORD *our righteousness ;* and in him no otherwise than as he is GOD *over all, blessed for ever,* and therefore *able to save to the uttermost all who come unto* GOD *by him.*

I did intend, my brethren, to have applied this duty to the belief of the doctrine of the Trinity, as the faith of the one Catholic Apostolic Church : but the time will not permit. This, however, is the less to be regretted, as whatever tends to establish the divinity of the Saviour, is conclusive, so far, for the Trinity of persons in the unity of the Godhead. Let me say this much, however ; that it is a doctrine, like that of the incarnation, or the being of GOD himself, revealed to our *faith* only ; that is, dependent for its reception and obligation, solely on the authority of the revealer, and not on any capacity in us to understand and unravel its mysteries.

I come now to the

Second head of my text, which is, to lay before you the necessity and advantage of diligence and engagement, in all your Christian duties.

It is a humbling reflection, my brethren, but one which may be very profitably applied, that the constant tendency of our fallen natures is, rather to become remiss, to faint and grow weary in the Christian race, than to *press towards the mark, for the prize of our high calling of* GOD *in* CHRIST JESUS. To this various causes contribute ; the corruption of our nature, the weakness of our faith, the temptations of the world, the care of our necessary business, and the use made of all these by the enemy of our souls, ever on the watch to ensnare us. There is, however, one more, not often thought of; and that is, the measuring ourselves by others, the taking a standard of Christian attainment from those around us, and not from the word of GOD.

In exhorting you, then, to diligence and earnestness in all your Christian duties, let me warn you against the insidious influence of this false estimate; let me beseech you to guard against it with care, for it is the commencement of that slothfulness, which begets indifference, and ends in *a form of godliness without the power.*

My brethren, it is not sufficient that our lives be orderly and decent, free from the crying enormities of the openly profane and ungodly. This will not fulfil the injunction of *abounding always in the work of the* LORD. A higher example is called for, from the Christian, both in his own private deportment, and in his connexion with others. He is to *let his light shine before men;* which certainly implies such a marked and decided preference of his eternal interests, and such a constant and habitual pursuit of them, as shows that he is *seeking* FIRST *the kingdom of* GOD, *and his righteousness.*

Yes, my brethren, the religion of the Gospel is a living, practical principle, of love to GOD, of obedience to his holy laws, of faith in his revealed word, and hope in his precious promises, through JESUS CHRIST, wrought in the heart by the power of the HOLY GHOST, pervading our whole condition, operating on all our concerns, and manifesting its sanctified influence by fruits of righteousness in the life and conversation of the man. Yet while it is thus heavenly and spiritual in its origin and nature, it is a principle wisely adapted to our condition as moral beings, requiring our hearty concurrence and co-operation—our faithful, and diligent improvement of grace given. It is GOD indeed *that worketh in us both to will and to do of his good pleasure,* or, rather, as the word should be translated, of his *goodness;* but it is for this very reason that he requires us *to work out our own salvation with fear and trembling,* that is, with care and diligence; and enforces this practical principle of all godliness with the solemn and equitable declaration, *unto every one that hath, shall be given, and he shall have abundance, but from him that hath not, shall be taken away even that which he hath.*

Hence the necessity of diligence and earnestness in religion, is just the necessity of being saved at all : without these, there can be no progress, no advancement, no growth in grace, no improvement, and, as we learn from the parable of the talents, no salvation. *Cast ye the unprofitable servant into outer darkness,* because he slothfully hid his talent in the earth, and gave not my money to the exchangers.

And the advantage of thus *abounding in the work of the* LORD, is precisely the advantage of greater inclination to, and enlarged ability for, the performance of our various duties ; with increased enjoyment of that inward peace and satisfaction of spirit, which flows from conformity to the will of GOD. And herein, my brethren, the appointments of divine wisdom in the kingdom of grace, are directed upon the same principle with those in the kingdom of nature. As knowledge, industry, care and diligence, yea and self-denial too, are essential to success in worldly under-takings ; so are they indispensable to the same end, in those which are heavenly ; and we may just as reasonably expect to reap where we have not sowed, as to hope for the reward of glory, without earnest and persevering endeavour.

Shall, then, the children of this world still be wiser in their generation than the children of light? Shall they bring every thought into obedience, every passion into subjection, and every effort to bear upon the master-wish of their souls? and Christians remain cold and languid, and indifferent to the holy hope which they profess to entertain? Shall the servants of the god of this world, by their zeal and earnestness, put to shame the servants of the GOD of heaven? Shall they who strive for an earthly crown, leave behind them in the race, those who strive for one heavenly and eternal? GOD forbid !

Yet how is it with us, my brethren, in this respect? Where are our affections laid up ; in heaven, or upon earth, or mixed of both? O, purge out the dross, *that ye may grow up an holy temple unto the* LORD. O, keep near your hearts the solemn thought of that awful morning, when the voice of the archangel

and the trump of GOD shall call up our sleeping dust, to meet
the judgment of CHRIST ; and let it re-act to stir you up to that
diligence, without which there is no crown of glory—to diligence
in personal religion—to diligence in those duties which you
have solemnly engaged, before GOD, to perform towards your
children—to diligence in watchfulness—against the deluding
and dangerous pleasures of that world, which you have openly
renounced for them and for yourselves—to diligence in the performance of all the charities of life, which spread peace and
good-will around you, and mark you as the disciple of that master *who went about doing good.* Seek no release from the full
measure of your duties ; yield to no compromise with the world
and the flesh ; fear no reproach for the name of CHRIST ; but
*continue steadfast, unmoveable, always abounding in the work of
the* LORD, *forasmuch as ye know that your labour is not in vain in
the* LORD.

Which brings me to the last head of my discourse, to wit :

III. The reward which awaits the faithful.

To what this is in itself, my feeble tongue can add nothing,
my brethren ; for even inspiration shrinks from the attempt, as
beyond the reach both of utterance and imagination : but the
reward is not, therefore, either the less sure, or the less glorious.

Suffice it, then, to say, that it will be happiness ; unmixed
felicity, flowing from the unclouded presence and favour of GOD,
upon creatures sublimated and prepared for its reception and
enjoyment. It will be unalloyed bliss, increased by the presence
of that merciful Saviour, who *loved us, and washed us from
our sins in his own blood,* and drawing forth from every heart
those rapturous ascriptions of glory and praise to GOD and the
Lamb, of which immortal natures alone are capable ; adding
even to the blessedness of our Redeemer, when he thus *sees
of the travail of his soul,* and reaps the full fruit of his mighty
conflict with sin and death, in the millions for ever rescued from
their power.

It will moreover be eternal ; liable to no diminution, subject
to no change, free from all interruptions, and knowing no end,
for ever blessed, and for ever increasing in blessedness : and
what can I say more, my brethren, but this ? Who then shall

separate us from the love of CHRIST, which hath purchased so lively a hope for us ? Shall unbelief freeze up our hearts against the love of GOD in CHRIST JESUS ? Shall indolence and carelessness beget indifference to so unspeakable a reward, shall the cares of this life shut out the care of our immortal souls, shall the pleasures or the profits of the world ensnare us to barter eternity for time ? In a word, shall CHRIST die in vain for any of us, to whom he is offered as a Saviour ? GOD forbid ! Keep, then, ever present to you, my brethren, that special doctrine, upon which the exhortation of my text is founded, *resurrection of the body.* This gives to that eternal life which we hope for, a peculiar character, and to the religion of the gospel, a singular influence. We shall meet again, dear brethren, and with a personal knowledge of each other. We shall meet again with a clear recollection of all that we have enjoyed or suffered together here. We shall meet again under the influence of all those sweet charities, which constitute the happiness of the present life, refined and spiritualized to the nature of immortals, yet forming a part of the blessedness of heaven. Upon these, therefore, it is, that the practical duties of religion are made to bear. Our love to GOD must be manifested by love to each other, and our fitness for heaven determined by its influence on our lives here. Let, then, this solemn and encouraging doctrine be realized in all its extent ; for by this, we look forward with hope and joy, to a re-union with those who have already fallen asleep in CHRIST before us : by this, we are enabled to surrender to GOD, without murmuring, those he sees fit to take from us, however dear : by this, the duties we are prompted to by natural affection, towards our families, friends, and neighbours, are sanctified to a holier purpose : by this, the narrow boundary of time is overstepped, and what we now are, is united with what we shall be, when time shall be no longer, and GOD *shall be all in all.*

And now, dear brethren, what remains, but that I *commend you to* GOD *and the word of his grace*—which I do most heartily. The near relation in which we have stood to each other for the last seven years, is about to determine. But nothing, I think, can determine the affection I bear towards you, but that stroke, which shall determine all earthly things. *Ye are in our heart to live and die with you;* but the providence of GOD hath ordered otherwise : for I sought neither the change nor the promotion. In many things, doubtless, I have come short in the duty I owed you, but not with intention : for all which I humbly crave pardon of GOD, and of you : but in nothing have you failed that you owed to me, save, only, in carrying your respect for me too far ; and would you make me more your debtor, continue your regard to my successor, in whom I feel a confidence which lessens my anxiety in leaving you.

Under the pain of separating from you, it is pleasant, however, to reflect, that during the whole time I have been in charge of this parish, I have had no necessity to resort to public censure upon any of the members of the Church : private admonition having been sufficient : and even to that, but in a few instances. Continue thus, then, my brethren, that your own comfort and peace may be increased, and that the GOD of love and peace may be with you.

Now, unto him who is able to keep you from falling, and to present you faultless before the presence of his glory, with exceeding joy ; to the only wise GOD *our Saviour, be glory and majesty, dominion and power, both now and for ever.* AMEN.

A SERMON ON THE CHURCH;

Delivered before the Annual Convention of the

PROTESTANT EPISCOPAL CHURCH OF NORTH-CAROLINA;

BY THE

RIGHT REVEREND JOHN S. RAVENSCROFT, D. D.

A SERMON ON THE CHURCH.

Amos viii. 5, *latter clause.*

"By whom shall Jacob arise? for he is small."

THE providences and dealings of Almighty GOD, for and with his Church, form a very conspicuous and instructive portion of the inspired writings. Indeed we might be justified in observing that the whole scheme of revelation and prophecy is predicated on the existence of a body or society of men, distinct from and called out of the world, as *the peculiar people of* GOD; and that the dealings of GOD, whether in acts of mercy, or in the infliction of judgments, refer primarily to this his inheritance; through that, to the rest of mankind, and ultimately, as we are warranted in believing and saying, to the higher intelligences of the unseen world. *To the intent,* (says the apostle to the Ephesians, iii. 10,) *that now, unto the principalities and powers in heavenly places, might be known by the Church, the manifold wisdom of* GOD.

Thus divine in its origin, influential in its character, and single in its designation, it presents a subject of the most impressive consideration to all mankind; inasmuch, as it is only in connexion with this body or society, that the revealed promises and hopes given in and by JESUS CHRIST, are assured to men, and the appointed means of grace and salvation brought within their reach.

Under this view, a brief notice of the distinctive character of the Church, as presented in the Scriptures, will prepare the way for an appropriate improvement of the text.

That this point has been greatly neglected, and held back from the public edification of Christians, even by those who were nevertheless entrusted with its defence and support, is unhappily too evident, and the consequences are such, as to warn both ministers and people, that it is time to retrace their steps ; and by considering this vital doctrine in its application to the hope of man as a sinner, to learn its influential bearing on the advancement of pure and undefiled religion in the world.

I feel, my reverend brethren, as I doubt not you also do——the full difficulty with which long neglect, and the consequent prevalence, and almost establishment, of erroneous opinion, invests the subject. But I trust that I feel, and that you feel, the awful responsibility of our respective stewardships, and are prepared to meet whatever may be required by a conscientious discharge of duty. And I trust also, that you, my brethren of the laity, feel that lively interest in the cause we have in hand, which shall ensure your hearty co-operation in such plans for the revival of the Church in her pure and primitive character, as its present condition, and the means in our control, shall render advisable ; while I cannot permit myself to suppose, that amid the variety of opinions on this subject now before me, there can one be found, by whom it will be considered an unnecessary or unprofitable discussion. Error, my dear hearers, however sanctioned by time and numbers, still retains its character : truth, however obscured by ignorance or prejudice, or rejected by men, is yet eternal and unchangeable as its author. And when eternity, with all its glories, or with all its horrors, is suspended upon truth or error, here received and followed ; the astounded exclamation of Pilate, before our blessed LORD, *What is truth ?* should burst from all our lips, and engage our inquiries.

To every class of my hearers, then, I must believe that a candid and scriptural, though necessarily brief, inquiry into the origin and purpose of the Church, and of the appointments of Heaven in it, for the salvation of man, must be both desirable and profitable. While to us, my clerical and lay brethren of this convention, it is essential to the right performance of the duties devolved on us, that we view the subject in this light, as well as in the causes which contributed to its decline ; otherwise, with the best intentions, our efforts may prove abortive, because erroneously devised and improperly directed. If *Jacob* is ever *to arise*, it must be as Jacob, and not as Esau.

First, as to the origin of the Church.

That the Church is divine in its origin, and in the appointments connected with it, is so generally admitted a doctrine, that the less may suffice on this point ; yet it ought ever to be borne in mind, that this divine institution of the wisdom and goodness of GOD, is not an abstract idea to be entertained in the mind ; but an actual, visible, accessible body or society, for practical use ; deriving its constitution, laws and authority, directly from GOD. As such, it is placed beyond the reach of any human appointment, addition, or alteration ; and this so strictly, that all the wisdom, piety, and authority in the world, congregated together, is just as incompetent to originate a Church, as to call another universe into existence. This, however, will be more evident, when we come, in the *next place*, to consider the purpose of such an institution. And as this is the key which unlocks all the difficulties that surround this subject, from the divided state of the Christian world, it will be necessary to consider what led to the appointment of the Church as a distinct body, with a visible and verifiable character.

The dispensations of Heaven's mercy and wisdom for the salvation of fallen man, are presented to us under various aspects ; all of which are closely connected with each other ; yet with marks of distinct discrimination, manifesting, nevertheless, that it is the same plan, modified and fitted by the Almighty himself, to the condition of that poor, perverse, and opposing being, for whose benefit it was all provided, and who has never ceased to corrupt and depart from it, in every age of the world.

Under the *first*, or Patriarchal dispensation, as it is called, of religion, as the benefits of the covenant of redemption were to be continued in their knowledge and operation, by the influence of parental instruction, and a family priesthood, no particular designation as a Church, or visible society, with privileges and obligations, promises and helps, of a special description, was marked out. Each family composed a Church for the worship of GOD, and was furnished with the necessary means of grace within itself, in the offering of that sacrifice which prefigured *the Lamb slain from the foundation of the world*, and was appointed and intended, to keep alive in the minds of men the knowledge of their fallen condition, and of the only method of recovery from it.

When, however, an experience of one thousand and five hundred years had proved that the corruption of human nature was too powerful to be withstood and counteracted by this method of continuing the influence of religion in the world ; and when a farther trial of the same means, for the space of five hundred years more, under the fresh remembrance too, of the recent destruction of the ungodly by the general deluge, and the still more recent visitation of the dispersion at Babel, had demonstrated, that they *did not like to retain* God *in their knowledge ;* but had *corrupted their way before him,* and departed from both the letter and spirit of his institutions——then it pleased the merciful Saviour of poor sinners, again to interpose ; and by selecting from this mass of corruption, another family, through that to restore, and continue in the world, the true knowledge of God, of the worship acceptable to him, of the expectation of a Deliverer, in the promised seed of the woman, and of the means of that grace by which only can fallen man be *renewed in the spirit of his mind,* delivered from the guilt and power of sin, and from that eternal death which is its only wages.

In this, the *second* dispensation of true religion provided for mankind, the distinction from that which preceded it, to be most carefully marked and considered by us, is, its covenanted and peculiar character ; in other words, the limited and pre-scribed conditions, on which only, its privileges and advantages can be obtained. If we overlook this, we overlook its most distinguishing feature, lose that deeply impressive lesson, which it was intended to teach us, and pass over the most interesting, because most influential part of the whole transaction ; that of a new relation to God, conferred upon men by outward and visible marks, and henceforth confined and limited within this institution. For it is this, and this only, my brethren and friends, which marks its separation from the rest of the world, as the Church, the peculium, the elect of God. Because of this its distinctive character it was made the visible and only depository of his revealed will and precious promises. For certainty and assurance, to this Church were committed those lively oracles of divine truth, which were corrupted and lost under the custody of tradition. And in it was prepared and established that body of testimony to the person and offices of JESUS CHRIST, as the promised seed of the woman, which shines so bright, so enlivening, comfortable, and irrefragable to us, under the gospel. Through this channel only, was to flow hereafter, that chain of revelation, prophecy, and providence, which constitutes and confirms the hope of man. And to mark its dignity and preeminence, and to fulfil the wise purposes of its founder, the condition of the rest of the world, in the rise and fall of its kingdoms, and in the operation of its various events, is overruled, and made subservient to the advancement, enlargement, and final establishment of this kingdom of GOD upon the earth, against all the opposition of men and devils combined.

For the order and uniformity of the public, prescribed, and, therefore, only acceptable service of GOD, in this his sanctuary, a divinely constituted priesthood was appointed, through which alone, were the people permitted to present their united worship, to offer up the proper sacrifice for personal as well as general sin, and to draw assurance of forgiveness, through the efficacy of that great sin-offering, atonement, and expiation, which all their sacrifices represented.

Hence, my brethren, the singular and personal character under which it is spoken of, throughout the Scriptures; that sacred unity with which it is invested : hence that zeal for its purity and interest, so constantly manifested, and that care with which its constitution and government were fenced against all intrusion.

Hence also, the strong language in which its endurance or everlasting continuance is spoken of in the Scriptures ; which proves that it was not a temporary appointment; but inseparably connected with the wonderful plan of man's redemption, and to run parallel with it, and efficient in it, *until the earth shall be filled with the knowledge of the* LORD, *as the waters cover the great deep—and the kingdoms of this world become the kingdoms of our* LORD *and of his* CHRIST.

Here, then, my brethren and friends, let us pause a moment, and look back and reflect, what would have been the state of the world, what would have been our individual condition, had this wise and merciful provision of the love of GOD never been appointed ; had men been left, as justly they might have been, to the influence of traditional knowledge, as the ground and the means of salvation for sinners—and let the awful religious blank which the thought reflects back upon the mind, awaken us to consider more carefully the foundation on which we are building for eternity ; whether on this certified and verifiable basis of GOD's appointment, or on some presumptuous imitation of its lineaments, by the weak and incompetent intrusion of human wisdom.—*I speak as unto wise men, judge ye what I say.*

But to proceed. Thus divine in its origin, constitution, and appointments, definite in its purpose, and singular in its character, the Old Testament Church stands alone in the world, like the ark on the waters of the deluge, the sole depository of the truth and of the people of GOD ; nor is their access to it, nor admission within its saving enclosure, otherwise than according to the institution of its founder. It was competent to no man— not even to Lot, or to Melchisidek—to obtain its privileges, without its seal. Whatever of mercy might be in store for them and the rest of mankind observing *the law written in the heart*, it was not the pledged and promised mercy made over to the Church. Whatever the truth or reasonableness of any religious duty might be; however well founded the hope of GOD's favour, from conformity to the dictates of natural conscience ; it was not the truth confirmed by express revelation : it was not the hope which springs from the promise of GOD, certified by outward, visible, and appointed ordinances, as helps to faith, means of grace, and assurances of a relationship to GOD in which none other stood, transacted through an authorised and accredited agent.

This, my brethren and hearers, is that deeply impressive and influential character in which *the Church of the living* GOD is presented to our notice and use, in working out our eternal salvation. This is that commanding feature, by which it is to be distinguished by us from all imitations of it by either the piety or the presumption of fallible men ; and it is by tracing it, according to this its specific character, through all the dealings and providences of its founder, that we, at this day, are enabled to discover and distinguish this ark of safety, this special deposit of the promises of GOD to a fallen world, this authorized source of agency between heaven and earth. For the Church of CHRIST, under the New Testament dispensation, is not a *new* or *fresh* appointment of GOD, in the sense and meaning too commonly entertained ; but a *continuation* of the old, in all its essential provisions. The same, and not a new divine origination ; the same, and not a fresh devised constitution of government, administration, and authority ; with the same and not another holy purpose of separation, certainty and assurance to men, in things spiritual and invisible ; and this, upon the sure ground, that JESUS CHRIST *is the same, yesterday, to-day, and forever.*

From not attending to this essential point to the very being of a Church, room has been given for the intrusion of man's presumption into this sacred appointment, and to deal with it as the creature of his contrivance, as a thing subject to his alteration and amendment. By losing sight of the intimate relation and analogy between the Old and New Testament dispensations ; by failing to consider the one as perfective of the other, confusion and obscurity on this subject has spread over the Christian world ; and division and distraction, instead of union and peace, has been the bitter fruit ; while the event has fulfilled the prediction of our LORD, in impeding the progress of the gospel, and encouraging that infidel spirit which turns away from the truth because those who call themselves the disciples of CHRIST, bite and devour one another. Above all, by neglecting to apply the test which GOD himself has provided, whereby to determine the certainty with which we are transacting our spiritual affairs, in the very natural inquiry—*By what authority doest thou these things ?* and substituting, in lieu thereof, the reputed piety and holiness of particular men, has the darkness become thicker and blacker, and the powerful prejudices of pride and profession, been enlisted against the truth ; so that men—reasonable beings, with the light of GOD's word in their hands—contentedly trust their souls to a security, on which they would not risk their estates.

Yet the truth remaineth, my brethren and friends, unaffected in its heavenly and unchangeable nature, by any perverseness and opposition of men. And to us it is given, by the distinguishing mercy of GOD, to know and ascertain the truth, to the comfort and health of our souls. The Church also—*the pillar and ground of the truth,* the peculium of GOD—by the same distinguishing mercy, yet remaineth, lingering as it were, with us, and verifiable, by the same heavenly original, divine authority, and saving purpose, which constitute its sacred character. As such, it is presented to your consideration this day, my hearers, in a point of view in which you may never have regarded it; briefly, it is true; yet sufficiently plain to enable every man, with his bible in his hand, to determine the question for himself. And sure I am, that this is the only representation of the subject which can correct erroneous notions, or confirm those which are true; the only ground on which there is any foundation for faith to rest upon, any assurance of hope in the revealed mercy of GOD. For I am yet to learn, where a promise of GOD to fallen man is to be found, that is not limited on the previous condition, that he be a member of CHRIST's visible Church upon earth.

Having thus given a faint outline of the origin, purpose, and importance of the Church, as an appointment of Almighty GOD in the gracious plan of our redemption, I will make a few remarks on that branch of the true vine which has been planted in this portion of the LORD's vineyard.

Of the early state of the Church in this diocese, the notices are so scanty, and my information so limited, that there is no safe ground on which to form an estimate of the state of religion within our communion, previous to the recent effort to revive the cause in the year 1817.

The journals of the General Convention, and the lists of the clergy in each state therein published, give no notice that the Episcopal Church was even known by name in North Carolina. It is nevertheless certain, that the Church was coeval with the establishment of a regular government, and had spread the knowledge of her doctrines and liturgy, and formed regular congregations for the worship of GOD, as far west as the middle counties of the state.

We must, therefore, refer the decline, and almost extinguishment of the Church here, to the same causes which operated throughout this vast continent, to wit : the just judgment of Almighty GOD, on the sins and iniquities of his people. To ascribe the depression of the Church to political causes *solely*, is to reverse the order of His providence who over-rules and directs the affairs of the world, to the final triumph of his spiritual kingdom.

The long period, however, during which the people were deprived of the services of the sanctuary, could not fail to operate injuriously. We gradually forget our dearest friends, my brethren, when removed from all intercourse with them. We soon seek to form new connexions, and we cleave to them the closer, perhaps, because of previous privation. And thus it fared with the Church. Multitudes, who would never have deserted the fold, were forced by want and privation into strange pastures. Still greater numbers have grown up in ignorance of her claims, and even of her existence ; while the pride of opinion, reluctance to acknowledge an error, and the modern fallacies of liberality in religious opinion, and equal safety in all religious denominations, keep back many who once enjoyed the benefit of her sound and safe ministrations, and bid fair to establish the notion, that no religious profession is necessary—thus demonstrating by experience, that in proportion as you weaken the vital doctrine of the visible unity of the Church of CHRIST, by acknowledging communions erected by human authority, you encourage the growth of infidelity and impiety. And it requires but a fair consideration of the effects which have followed the divisions among Christians, and the consequent adoption of liberal opinions, to demonstrate the alarming fact, that if the Church of GOD may be found every where, it will soon be sought no where. Indifference to religion is the inevitable result of such pestilent notions ; and this is the sum total of gain from this so much boasted system of liberal opinions.

Yet the arm stretched out upon his inheritance was, and is, an arm of mercy. A remnant was left. *Jacob*, indeed, *was made thin, and the fatness of his flesh became lean ; yet gleaning grapes were left in the vineyard, as the shaking of an olive tree ; two or three berries in the top of the uppermost bough.* It was a praying remnant, and it pleased GOD to open his ear to hearken.

For that remnant, then, it is, and for those whom GOD hath added to them, and for the deluded multitudes who are living *without* GOD *in the world,* we are met, in the fear of GOD, I trust, and in the hope of his guidance and direction in our counsels, to consult and devise things profitable, prosperous, and happy ; the things which accompany salvation. Let us then inquire

Thirdly, by whom shall Jacob arise ?

And by whom, my brethren and friends, can Zion *arise and shake herself from the dust, and put on her beautiful garments, and become the praise of the whole earth,* but by that Almighty arm which upholds the universe ; by that ever living Head, who hath pledged his promise, that *the gates of hell shall not prevail against her ?*

On that promise I am built : on that providence I am staid : and when I consider the marked interposition of his hand in the commencement and progress of this work ; when I reflect, that by him who inspireth the counsels and ordereth the doings of the children of men, I meet you here this day, in the station which I fill in his Church, I bend in humble adoration before his wonder working power ; I rely, with unshaken confidence, in his abiding faithfulness ; and give myself to the work, in the firm belief that the set time to favour Zion is come. Well may we say, dear brethren, *What hath* GOD *wrought ?* and in contemplation of what he hath already done, be strengthened and encouraged to be workers together with him, in *building up the waste places of Jerusalem.* I have been among them, my brethren——among the earliest records of the piety of our forefathers ; and my heart yearned over the ancient, and decaying, and now too often silent temples. I have been among the ancient Simeons and Annas, servants of the LORD, who *take pleasure in the stones, and favour even the dust of Zion ;* who have prayed and fainted not, through a long night of darkness and bereavement ; and I have seen the smile of transport, and the flush of hope, and the fervour of devout and grateful praise, light up their patriarchal countenances as the promise of a brighter day dawned upon their children ; and I felt that it would not be disappointed.

In this holy hope, then, let us continually look-up to our great covenant Head, and ever merciful Redeemer ; beseeching him to inspire our prayers, direct our counsels, and prosper our endeavours " to the advancement of his glory, the good of his Church, the safety, honour, and welfare of his people."

But while it is by the LORD only, that *Jacob can arise,* it is by the use of means within our reach—by joining our earnest endeavours to our united prayers, that this most desirable work is to be carried on and effected.

First, then, because of the highest concernment, let us, my brethren, ever bear in mind, from what causes the depression and downfall of the Church originally proceeded, and guard carefully against a return of the same evil. Throughout the whole history of GOD's dealings with his Church, we may see, that the light of his countenance upon his people, or the hidings of his face from them ; the communication of his favour to them, or the infliction of his judgments on them ; have ever been regulated, according as piety or ungodliness prevailed among them. Now, all these things, we are instructed, *happened unto them for* ENSAMPLES, *and are written for our admonition, upon whom the ends of the world are come.* Happy, then, will it be for us, my brethren and hearers, if we take warning by this more recent example and proof, that the same order of his providence yet subsists ; and keep ourselves from the evil way of profession without practice, religion without holiness. Many suppose, that in the Episcopal Church, a greater laxity is allowed, than in other denominations. But this manifests a total ignorance of all our institutions. No countenance is given or allowed to what is sinful ; nor can any denomination pretend to greater strictness, than is required by the Canons and Rubricks of the Church. We cannot help it, my brethren, if persons whose conduct is a scandal to all Christian profession, will call themselves Episcopalians : the discipline of the Church can be applied only to those who are known and received as communicants ; and by those compared with any other denomination, we fear not to be tested ; yet with us, whatever may be the

case with other professions, we know and confess, that much
of the old leaven has to be purged out; and this will we do, if
God permit.

To this point, then, my brethren, let us bend our united
attention; taking away occasion from those who seek it, and
wiping out the reproach against us; firmly setting our faces
against all conformity with the world in its ungodliness; and
withholding our fellowship from all who walk disorderly.   This
we owe to our own souls, to the honour of God, to the credit
and advancement of the Church, and to the souls of others : we
owe it to that forbearing goodness which has once more revived
us, and in agreement with which only, we can hope to prosper.

As holiness is the mark of God's children, we are called to
holiness, to severance from the world, its idolatrous pursuits, its
vain and vicious pleasures, in ourselves and in our families.
*Wherefore come out from among them, and be separate, and touch
not the unclean thing, and I will receive you, and be a father unto
you, and ye shall be my sons and daughters, saith the* LORD *Almighty.—Having, therefore, these promises, dearly beloved, let us
cleanse ourselves from all filthiness of the flesh and spirit, perfecting
holiness in the fear of* God.

This is the doctrine of the Episcopal Church; this is the
practice in the life, which all her precepts inculcate upon her
members; which her discipline is constructed to enforce, and
which no endeavours of mine shall be wanting, God being my
helper, to bring to full effect.   And here I am truly thankful
that so many circumstances concur to favour us in this essential
work.   No wide spread, inveterate habit of ungodliness, has yet
had time to take root among us, and cause alarm at the extent
of the excision required. *Jacob,* indeed, *is small,* but he is young
also, and comparatively free from the great transgression.   Be
it our care, then, one and all, dear brethren, that as he increases
in stature, he may *grow in grace,* and *increase* also *in favour both
with* God *and man.*

Whatever reproach of this nature is brought against our communion as yet, is brought from a distance, and there let us re-
solve that it shall remain ; whatever is now to perform of the
painful duty of reproof and correction, is comparatively light ;

and (blessed be GOD for it) there is no diversity of opinion among those who have the care of the flock. United in this, as in all other points which concern the peace and prosperity of our Zion, we may humbly trust to build up those committed to our charge, *an holy temple unto the* LORD.

Secondly, that *Jacob may arise* as Jacob, it is essential that the doctrines and worship prescribed in the articles and liturgy of the Church, be faithfully preached and adhered to by all of her communion.

On you, my brethren of the clergy, depend the hopes of the Church in this diocese, for this means of resuscitation. This precious deposit she has committed to your fidelity, and at your hands does she require that it be exercised for the increase of the body.

And here again I have to bless GOD, that *the lines are fallen to me in pleasant places*—that however small the number, it is a little phalanx of men sound in faith, and united with me in one mind, and in one doctrine ; that on no point is there such a division of sentiment as leads to a diversity of practice ; but all can go hand in hand to the object before us ; that however feeble in the eyes of the world, it is a band of brothers, who have themselves experienced the power and efficacy of the truths they preach—who know and feel that they are *the power of* GOD *unto salvation*, and are therefore able to teach others also—who admire and love the scriptural simplicity, devotional sublimity, and doctrinal security, of that form of sound words, in which they lead the public worship of the sanctuary—who know that the liturgy of the Church is the great bulwark of *the faith once committed to the saints*, the tried safeguard against the heresies of the day, of all who use it with the understanding and the affections.

Thus favoured of GOD, my burden, dear brethren, is comparatively light—while my hope is animated, that with such workmen, the edifice will arise, beautiful in its proportions, resplendent in holiness, and *the praise of the whole earth*.

The foundation on which it rests, is *the rock* CHRIST, confessed, and believed on, as GOD *over all, blessed for ever*—" who for us men, and for our salvation, came down from heaven, and was incarnate by the HOLY GHOST of the Virgin Mary, and was made man, and was crucified also for us, under Pontius Pilate." The beauty of its proportions, consists in the harmony of that unsearchable wisdom—whereby *mercy and truth are met together, righteousness and peace have kissed each other*—in the unspeakable mystery of GOD *made sin, that* man might *be made the righteousness of GOD in him.* And the splendour of its embellishment, in the union of all its members, in the *faith which worketh by love,* the *hope which maketh not ashamed,* and the *charity which never faileth.*

This is the blessed fruit of the doctrine of the Gospel, and of the Church, " truly preached, truly received, and truly followed." The mystery of godliness, that GOD *was manifest in the flesh, justified in the spirit, seen of angels, preached unto the Gentiles, believed on in the world, received up into glory,* is the *new sharp threshing instrument* predicted by the prophet, wherewith to break down the kingdom of sin, Satan, and death. *Fear not, thou worm Jacob, and ye men of Israel, I will keep thee, saith the* LORD, *and thy Redeemer, the Holy One of Israel. Behold I will make thee a new sharp threshing instrument, having teeth. Thou shalt thresh the mountains, and beat them small, and shalt make the hills as chaff. Thou shalt fan them, and the wind shall carry them away, and the whirlwind shall scatter them ; and thou shalt rejoice in the* LORD, *and shalt glory in the Holy One of Israel.*

On the doctrines of the cross, then, as you have taken, maintain your stand, my reverend brethren. Preach them in the simplicity and sincerity of hearts that feel them, with the earnestness of men who wish to save their own souls, and the souls of others. The entire spiritual death, and alienation of man from GOD, by the entertainment of sin ; the reconciliation of GOD to the world, by the sufferings and death of his only begotten Son ; the atonement of his blood ; justification by faith ; acceptance through the merits of the Saviour ; conversion of the heart to GOD ; holiness of life, the only evidence of it ; and the grace of GOD, in the renewal of the HOLY GHOST, the sole agent from first to last, in working out our salvation from sin here, and from hell hereafter. In fewer words, SALVATION *by grace, through faith, not of works, lest any man should boast.*

But with these vital and heaven-blessed doctrines, other points of edification to those of your charge, and to your general hearers, will require your attention, my reverend brothers; particularly that of the distinctive character of the Church. On this, a most lamentable ignorance prevails, and most unfounded opinions are becoming established, not only among Episcopalians, but at large. To permit this ignorance to continue undisturbed, is to be false to our ordination vows, to our acknowledged principles, to the interests of our communion, and to the souls committed to our care; and however amiable in appearance the principle on which we act may be, reflection shows it to be a mistaken one, and experience proves it to have been injurious. If we hold principles that are indefensible, let us abandon them. But if they are our principles, interwoven into the very frame of our polity—impregnable in their truth, and essential in the great work we have in hand; let us not appear ashamed of them, or weakly afraid of the consequences, and thus become parties to that miserable delusion, which weakens us as a body, strengthens the ranks of our adversaries, and, I will fearlessly say, weakens the cause of true religion, by tacitly owning one division after another, until the great master principle of the Church of God, its unity, is merged in the mass of Christian names, and swallowed up by the indifference and infidelity thus fostered.

If, then, we would be found faithful to ourselves, to the Church whose commission we bear, and to the souls committed to our trust; this doctrine of the distinctive character of the Church, must be fully unfolded, and laid before our people. Their attention must be called to it, on the grounds of scriptural reason. The purpose of this wise and merciful appointment of Almighty God, in the salvation of sinners, must be dwelt upon and enforced, by all those weighty arguments and authorities which the word of God so richly supplies. The importance and efficacy of authorized ministrations—of valid sacraments, must be elucidated and confirmed, by the analogies which govern men in temporary things, and by the method so demonstrably resorted to by God himself, both under the law and under the gospel; to give certainty and assurance to men in things so unspeakably important. These are the points to be presented to our people, to be pressed upon the understandings and the feelings of our hearers, in connexion with the other doctrines of the gospel—that they may learn to estimate aright their privileges ; and valuing, to cleave to them.

Thirdly, that *Jacob may arise* in his true character, a steadfast and uniform adherence to the liturgy and offices of the Church, as set forth in the book of Common Prayer and Administration of the Sacraments, must be observed.

In this duty it is my happiness to believe that you, my reverend brethren, are found faithful. As honest men, independent of your Christian character, I could expect no less. But in this liberal and latitudinarian age, this duty is sometimes rendered painful, by the wish to yield in some degree to the prejudices of a mixed congregation ; and by the hope that conforming in this respect, they may be won over. In aid of this dereliction of duty, the points objected are artfully represented as things indifferent in themselves, and therefore, to be yielded in favour of Christian fellowship. All this, however, is mere pretence ; for, if they are points really indifferent, the fault must ever be with those who on such grounds separate themselves from what never can be viewed with indifference by any serious person. And whatever pretences may be urged, they are all fallacious, and proved to be so by experience. For whatever the principle of accommodation may be capable of in other things, it has ever failed in points of religious dissent ; and I am yet to learn, in what instances the surrender of principles, or even of distinctive points, has profited those who have tried the dangerous experiment. My brethren, the attempt has ever been in vain, and has issued in weakening and degrading those who have resorted to it ; and the reason is obvious : principles, religious principles especially, are presumed to be well considered—adopted as the best, and on the highest authority. To hold them, then, as things that may be dispensed with, may be accommodated, may be yielded, is viewed as the mark of a weak or an insincere mind.

To act upon this expectation, then, is to court defeat, while it is at the same time to expose ourselves to contempt, as men of lax principles, and designing conduct ;—a stigma of all others the most severe upon a minister of religion ; who, in common with all Christians, but in a higher degree, ought to *have his conversation in the world, in simplicity, and godly sincerity.* And what has been the effect of such a course, in the trials that have unhappily been made by Episcopal clergymen ? Has our communion gained or lost by it ? Where is the addition obtained by this surrender of private and public principle ? It has lost, my reverend and lay brethren, by this Judas-like method of betraying it into the hands of its enemies, with a kiss.

And what have the individuals, who have thus acted, gained by it ? They have gained the name, perhaps, of liberal and charitable ; and have lost the esteem of all sound churchmen ; while they have not gained the confidence of those, who, nevertheless, flattered their enlarged views of Christian liberty, and evangelical piety ; because, in the midst of this flattery, they are obliged to view them as false to the most solemn pledges that can be given of sincerity of opinion, and integrity of practice.

In all such cases, the question with an Episcopal clergyman, is not, whether our general principles, or our method of conducting public worship by a fixed form, be scriptural, profitable, or even evangelical ; this ought to have been settled on the most serious investigation, before he assumes the orders of the Church. Whatever discretion he had as to this and other points of required conformity, is then given up ; nor can he continue to wear the livery of the Church, and thus act, without the guilt of the most sublimated perjury.

Alas ! that it should be necessary to warn against the influence of such an example elsewhere. But as the evil exists, and this view of the subject includes every plea for nonconformity to the doctrines and worship of the Protestant Episcopal Church, in the United States, I think it due to you, and to the sincerity with which I am bound to act, to show distinctly, at the commencement of my administration, the principles by which I am guided.

Fourthly, for the increase and advancement of true godliness, let me recommend the observance and cultivation of family religion.

Without this root and spring, under GOD, of "all holy desires, all good counsels, and all just works," hope is vain for the Church and the state; we shall sink into a nation of infidels.

That the practice has declined in the families of professing Christians; that it is abandoned in all others, is known by all who hear me at this moment. And that the consequences are the bitter fruit of increasing crime and profaneness, is recorded in every court, and witnessed by every Sabbath.

But, my brethren and hearers, could this be so, were the principles of our holy religion early and carefully instilled into the minds of the rising hope of this great and growing Christian nation? Were the fear of GOD, and the reverence of his most holy name, and the observance of his worship, and the knowledge of his life-giving precepts, inculcated and manifested in our families, would so little of it be seen in the world? Awake, then, from this torpor, ye Christian fathers and mothers—from this deadly delusion of adulterated religion, which is so fast swallowing up the dearest hope you can entertain of a happy eternity, with those who are dearest to you here. Trample under your feet, those pestilent doctrines which inevitably lead to this criminal neglect, by confiding the hope, and by necessary consequence, the duties of the gospel, to a chosen few. Arise to the blessed assurance of GOD's public message by his only begotten Son—*that he hath not appointed you or them to wrath, but to obtain salvation by our* LORD JESUS CHRIST *;—who, by the grace of* GOD, *tasted death for every man.* Believe this, his true and faithful word, against all the sophistry of men; diligently use and apply the means provided by the wisdom and goodness of GOD, for your advancement in knowledge, and growth in grace; and no longer suffer your children to grow up like the wild asses colt, alike ignorant of GOD and of themselves, of the word of his grace, of his Sabbaths, his ordinances, his mercies, his judgments, and that eternity, in which all these end, and where you and they must meet, to enjoy or to suffer forever, according to the improvement or abuse here, of the talents committed to your trust.

Oh! it is an awakening thought to contemplate a family, godless, under the gospel, assembled before the judgment seat of CHRIST, and to carry out the consequence to the misery that awaits them; and that misery doubled by the near and dear ties which connect them; hell made hotter by the endless reproach —we neglected our children's souls—my father and mother hardened me against GOD—they trained me to perdition.

Oh! it is a heart-cheering, soul-enlivening vision, to go in the mind's meditation, with the faithful father and mother, to the same awful tribunal, and see the holy confidence with which they stand and say—"Behold us LORD, and the children thou hast given us." We have taught them thy fear; and by thy grace kept them in the way; we surrender them to thy mercy, through thy dear Son. *Well done, good and faithful servants, ye have been faithful in a few things, enter ye into the joy of your* LORD. But who can speak that joy, when all the dear ties of nature in this life shall be refined, purified, and perpetuated in glory; when conjugal, parental, and filial love, shall be swallowed up, but not lost, in the love and enjoyment of GOD forever?

And is this, dear brethren, a result in the one case to be shunned as destruction; in the other to be desired as life? O, if it be! (and what Christian parent does not feel that it is all this?)—let the plain and certain road to the attainment of this blessedness, be pursued by all. Discard for ever, my brethren and hearers, this murderous neglect of the souls of your children and servants; and as you are able, call them round the family altar, and invoke the blessing, the promised blessing of GOD, upon your holy purpose: restrain them from all violations of the Lord's day; cultivate his fear in their hearts; and show, by the example of your lives, that you fear his name, and hope in his mercy.

Especially upon you, my Episcopal brethren, is this primary duty enforced, by every principle you profess, by every obligation that can be undertaken, and by every sanction known to time and to eternity. Your baptismal sponsion for your children involves it, by the solemn stipulations then entered into; and the promises of GOD therein sealed to them is your full and sufficient warrant to engage in this fruitful work, with assurance of success. Let, then, the inscriptions on your dwellings be,

As for me and my house, we will serve the LORD. To this source of supply the Church looks, for the enlargement of her border, the extension of her communion—for the spread of the gospel, and its triumph over all its enemies.

And to what other source can we reasonably look, my brethren, not only for the advancement, but for the continuance of religion among us? Let us ask ourselves, and reflect seriously upon it—what proportion do the conversions, which we occasionally hear of, bear to the numbers annually coming into and going out of life? In this State, do they amount to five hundred in the year—to one for every hundred thousand of its population? I know not; but I doubt it. But say they amount to five times this number, and are all sound conversions of the heart to GOD—what is this to the annual drain by death, of souls dead to GOD, unprepared for eternity? What to the multitudes *who know not* GOD, *and obey not the gospel of our* LORD JESUS CHRIST; who have grown up without him, and must in all probability die without him? What is this to the thousands coming forward into life, the hope of days to come, equally unfurnished?——O let the alarming calculation startle us from this delusion of double death, and convert us from dependence on the extraordinary, to the serious use of the ordinary means which GOD has provided, commanded, and promised to bless, in *training up our children in the nurture and admonition of the* LORD; that his converting grace may change their hearts, transform their lives, and enrich the Church and the world with sound and instructed believers, serious and experienced Christians, and firm professors of the hope of the gospel. Thus, and thus only, shall the objections of the infidel be done away; the vain reasonings of the disputer of this world be answered and refuted; and the means corresponding with the end, and the fruit crowning the work, make all men see, that GOD *is with us of a truth.* Thus *adorning the doctrine of* GOD *our Saviour,* by the union of profession and practice, *Jacob shall arise,* and his light shine. Thus shall *his seed possess the gate of his enemies,* and *the* LORD *whom we seek shall suddenly come to his temple,* and *the glory of this latter house shall be greater than the former, saith the* LORD *of Hosts.*

Lastly.—Our pecuniary means must be reserved for the wants of our own communion.

This is so plain and obvious a duty, that at first sight, it would appear superfluous to mention it; yet certain it is, that in this respect, Episcopalians have manifested an easiness in yielding to the solicitations of other denominations, which can be justified on no sound principle of regard for the Church, or feeling sense of the wants and privations of their immediate brethren; and the time I think is come, when it is absolutely necessary to act differently. *Jacob is small,* and he must continue so, if his patrimony is squandered upon strangers. It is the dictate of inspired wisdom, my brethren, *that if any provide not for his own, especially those of his own house—he hath denied the faith, and is worse than an infidel.* This rule, both of reason and religion, will apply in the closest manner to the present condition of the Church in this diocese, and to the present duty of all the members and friends of our communion, and should regulate and restrain the indiscriminate expenditure of her means, for purposes, which if not hostile, are certainly unprofitable.

If I could paint to you, as vividly as I have witnessed and now feel, the destitute condition of our brethren—men agreeing in faith, doctrine, and worship with ourselves—and the general call there is, *come over and help us;* the necessity as well as propriety, in the truest religious sense, of adopting and acting henceforth upon this principle, would need no enforcement from me. Your hearts would feel for congregations destitute of ministers and ordinances; Jacob's feeble hands would not be lifted up in vain; the Church of your fathers, and of your affections would no longer be dry nursed, to succour her opponents; but all would be united for one object, and your bounty flow in one enriching stream of nourishment, growth, and strength to our Zion. Oh! if I had but the thousands, which have heretofore been drawn away from her exigencies, how easily would all our wants of this kind be supplied. It is gone, however, and regret will not bring it back. But if it shall teach us to adopt and adhere to a different course for the time to come, it will so far be a gain, and there is yet enough left in the piety, and affection, and affluence of the Episcopal body in this diocese, to meet all our reasonable demands. All that is required, is to act upon principle, by system.

Much will be said against this my advice to you, my brethren, and I doubt not it will be called illiberal, uncharitable, perhaps unchristian. But by whom will such truly unchristian terms be applied to it? By those only, whose interest it is that you should not discriminate. By those, who act themselves, as a body, and rigidly too, upon this very principle—who have drawn largely on the easiness, or indifference of your liberality; but have never returned a cent for the dollar, to our wants, and never will; or by those who cloak real disregard to all religion, under the motley mask of equal regard for all denominations. Regard them not, therefore, my brethren; but strong in the soundness of the principle, and the obligation of the duty, as Christians and Churchmen, reserve what you have to spare in the service of religion, for the wants of your own communion. That certainly has the first and highest claim upon your ability, upon your bounty; a claim which no sophistry can invalidate— which no mistaken views of liberality and charity towards the opinions or the practices of others, should either weaken or defeat.

According, then, as the distinctive character of the Church is understood in its principles, applied in the use, and regarded in the hearts of its members,' will it be cherished and will flourish. According as the walk and conversation in the world of those who call themselves Episcopalians, shall be *as becometh the gospel of* CHRIST, will its high, because heaven-descended claims, be owned, acknowledged, and acted upon, in the regeneration of a fallen world; and according as we show, that it is all this in our estimation, my clerical and lay brethren, by the zeal and earnestness with which we unite and persevere in the work we have in hand, *will Jacob arise—will a little one become a thousand, and a small one a strong nation.*

To this work you have called me; to this work the LORD through you hath devoted me; and to your service, such as I am, I give myself without reserve. Accept, then, the first fruits of the deep concern I feel for your advancement; of the observation and experience I have had opportunity for, and of that sacred regard for your present and eternal welfare, which occupies my thoughts, my prayers, my labours. And may He that *holdeth the seven stars in his right hand,* who *walketh in the midst of the seven golden candlesticks,* be with us in all our undertakings, to bless and prosper us in building up the old waste places; in raising up the foundations of many generations; that we may indeed be called the repairer of the breach, the restorer of paths to dwell in.

Now unto Him, &c.

A SERMON ON THE CHRISTIAN MINISTRY;

DELIVERED BY THE

RT. REV. JOHN S. RAVENSCROFT, D. D.,

IN

ST. PETER'S CHURCH, WASHINGTON, ON SUNDAY, APRIL 24th, 1825;

AT THE ORDINATION OF THE

REV. JOSEPH PIERSON AS PRIEST, AND OF THE REV. C. C. BRAINERD AS DEACON.

A SERMON ON THE CHRISTIAN MINISTRY.

JOHN xx. 21.

"As my Father hath sent me, even so send I you."

The baptism of John, whence was it? From heaven, or of men? was the answer made by our blessed LORD to the Jews, who inquired into the authority of his ministry.   And in the effect it produced upon them, we learn, my brethren and hearers, to estimate the power of prejudice upon the human mind, by seeing it able to resist at once the evidence of sense and the conviction of reason.   We learn, also, from this example, that the excuses we are apt to make for error, from the influence of established habits of thought and action, are not always—perhaps we may safely say, are rarely—of that justifiable character we would willingly persuade ourselves ; there being something in the very sound of truth, especially divine truth, to alarm the prejudice that is opposed to it—to set it instantly at work to provide a defence, and, by this very effort, (would we permit it thus to react,) to convince us of the fallacy and folly of such a sacrifice to pride.   In the case before us, we have a pregnant instance, how readily truth, even when indirectly proposed, will flash upon its object—how equally quick its bearing will be seen, and, when there is no other escape, how prejudice will resist it, even at the extra expense of a falsehood.   Hence we learn, my friends, of what great importance a fair mind is to the attainment of truth generally ; and, also, how this qualification is enhanced by the unspeakable value of religious truth.   But in this, alas ! it is, that our prejudices are both most numerous and most powerful.

Yet is there no necessity that it should be so, my hearers. Prejudice, in a great degree at least, is voluntary, and, after all

VOL. I.—16

the allowances which can be asked for the influence of education, and other circumstances of a like nature, there is provision made to counteract its sway over the mind, did we faithfully and humbly seek the truth in its great Author, and not in the systems and inventions of men.   In our religious concerns especially—the care of our souls, is this a paramount duty ; and, as we are fully provided for it, by the wisdom and goodness of Almighty GOD, and furnished with the law of faith and life in his holy word, there can be no excuse, either for the neglect or perversion of the Scriptures, which, as men, we can apply with confidence, either to ourselves or others.   What may be in reserve for such cases, in the equity and mercy of our omniscient Judge, as he has not seen fit to reveal, so we can say nothing, unless to warn against speculations into the secret things of GOD, or against remaining satisfied with a dependance which rests for its foundation, rather on our own vain reasonings, than on the declared counsel of his revealed will.

It is not, however, to evidence the power of prejudice over the mind, that I have noticed this awakening answer of our LORD, to the chief priests and elders of the Jews.   By transposing the question contained in the answer and applying it to the gospel, we obtain the governing principle which pervades every advance in religion, and is alone competent to arrest the power of prejudice, and give solid comfort to the soul, in the awful interests of eternity.

The gospel of CHRIST, whence is it ?   From heaven, or of men ?   Now, while there will be but one answer to this question, from this assembly of Christian people, to many, it is to be feared, were it pressed home, it would be equally embarrassing as the original question to the Jews.   If we shall say, from heaven, may be the musing of some minds present—we are met by the unanswerable inquiry, Why, then, do you not believe and profess it ?   But, if we shall say, it is of men, a mere human production, we rank at once with infidels.   And why not, my hearers ?   Where else can you, or would you, rank, seeing there is no middle ground on which you can take your stand ?   In the sight of GOD, and in the judgment of right reason, there is no medium between receiving unqualifiedly, and rejecting absolutely, his public message to the world, by his only begotten Son. No man can be, at the same time, both a believer and an unbeliever. *He that believeth not, is condemned already.—He that is not for me, is against me.* This is an awakening thought, and I pray GOD it may be sanctified to those whose condition it meets.

But it is not only to the gospel as a whole, that this inquiry is applicable. Every particular doctrine, every prescribed ordinance, every point of instituted order, with every personal duty as Christians—all rest, for their sacredness to us, on the governing principle, Is it from heaven, or of men? No conceivable fitness, or reasonableness, or expediency, or accommodation to external circumstances, can be allowed to supersede the fixed, unchangeable nature of what GOD hath appointed. And the reason is obvious—as it proceeded from GOD, no human power or wisdom can intermeddle without impiety. As faith can rest only on the authority of GOD, and that authority capable of being verified; as faith constitutes the essence of every religious act; the foundation on which it is built must be fixed and unchangeable as GOD himself.

These positions, which, it appears to me, my brethren and hearers, cannot be controverted with any show of reason or Scripture authority, prepare the way for that improvement of the words of my text, which I propose to make of them; and, as they directly refer to the Ministerial Commission under the gospel, furnish a subject of general as well as particular edification, not so frequently presented to the consideration of professing Christians, as, from its great importance, it deserves to be; and on which there is as much erroneous and unsettled opinion as upon any other doctrines of the Christian revelation. And my apology, if apology can be needed, is to be sought and found in this fact, and in the particular duty now before me.

And here, my friends, I must take leave to enter my public protest, in behalf of the Church, against the unjust and ungenerous denial to us of what is so fully conceded to other denominations, and very freely exercised—the privilege of presenting, and pressing upon their members, the distinctive tenets of their several creeds. In this respect, we claim to stand upon that ground which is equally the privilege of all in this free and happy land ; nor do we wish to stand upon any other or higher ground than is due to the soundness of our doctrine and principles ; to their agreement with Scriptural truth and order ; and to their tendency to promote and ensure the three great blessings of civil liberty, social happiness, and pure and undefiled religion.   If any represent us otherwise, we only say, that we sincerely pity their ignorance or malevolence, and heartily beg of GOD to give them repentance, and better minds.

I now proceed to the consideration of the words of my text, *As my Father hath sent me, even so send I you.*

That these words refer to the ministerial commission, is clear, from the context, and from the parallel passages of Scripture. According to the testimony of St. John, they were uttered by our LORD after his resurrection, and on the evening of that day, at his first appearance to the eleven.   And what farther took place at that time, puts beyond dispute our LORD's intention : *And when he had said this,* [the words of my text,] *he breathed on them, and saith unto them, Receive ye the* HOLY GHOST. *Whosesoever sins ye remit, they are remitted unto them ; and whosesoever sins ye retain, they are retained.*

This application of the words of the text is further confirmed by the parallel passages in the other gospels.   In St. Luke's gospel the same commission is conferred in these words : *And I appoint unto you a kingdom, as my Father hath appointed unto me.* In St. Matthew's gospel, the ground of the authority to send, or appoint, and the commission itself, are thus expressed : *And* JESUS *came and spake unto them, saying, All power is given unto me, in heaven and in earth.   Go ye, therefore, and teach all nations, baptizing them in the name of the* FATHER, *and of the* SON, *and of the* HOLY GHOST ; *teaching them to observe all things, whatsoever I have commanded you.*   And according to St. Mark, the commission is the same as in St. Matthew, with a slight variation of the phraseology : *And he said unto them, Go ye into all the world, and preach the gospel to every creature.   He that believeth, and is baptized, shall be saved ; but he that believeth not, shall be damned.*

In addition to this, it may be helpful to state, that this commission was addressed exclusively to the eleven.   Neither the hundred and twenty disciples, mentioned in the first chapter of the Acts of the Apostles, who followed our LORD during the latter part of his personal ministry, nor the five hundred brethren, who saw him alive after his passion, as St. Paul assures us, are included in it, as is abundantly evident from the historical part of the New Testament.

To form a just estimate, therefore, of this very important subject, it will be necessary to consider,

FIRST, The nature and extent of our LORD's own commission, as the Messenger, the Apostle, of GOD the Father, to a sin-ruined, but redeemed world.

SECONDLY, The connexion, or parallel, between this and the commission conferred on the Apostles, as the messengers of CHRIST to the same world.

THIRDLY, The continuance of this commission in the world.

FOURTHLY, The object or purpose of a divinely authorized ministry, in the Church, or Kingdom of CHRIST.

And then conclude with such practical inferences from the whole, as shall be suitable to the solemn duty we have this day to perform.

As my Father hath sent me, even so send I you.

I.   First, to consider the nature and extent of our LORD's own commission, as the Messenger, the Apostle, of GOD the Father, to a sin-ruined, but redeemed world.

To avoid confusion of mind, and, of course, error of judgment, by blending distinct and separate things in one view, it is necessary to confine our consideration to that part of our Saviour's office which could be transferred.

In what pertains to the inherent divinity of his nature, as he received no commission, so there was none to be continued. In his merciful undertaking to suffer the penalty of sin, by tasting *death for every man*, there could be no transfer.   It is therefore to the administration of that kingdom which the Father hath appointed unto him, as the Son of Man, that we are to direct our attention, on the point under consideration ; indeed, to bear constantly in mind, my brethren, that, as it was by the assuming of the human nature into union with the divine, by the Son of GOD, that the purposes of Heaven's mercy to man were to be accomplished—so the whole economy and management of the gospel dispensation is committed to the LORD JESUS CHRIST, in this his assumed character ; in which, for an appointed period, he stands in equal relation to GOD and man, and thus competent to meet the claims of the one, and the necessities of the other. And were this duly attended to, my hearers, there would be less difficulty in detecting the vain reasonings of those who, from the mystery of his incarnation, and the necessary reference to both natures, in the language of Scripture, dispute and deny his essential divinity.

To obtain this kingdom, however—this intermediate dispensation, rendered necessary by the entrance of sin into the world, conditions were to be performed. The oblation of himself, therefore, to the justice of GOD, by our Redeemer, was to precede his assumption of the kingly office, and was, in fact, the price paid for his exaltation to that kingdom, *in which,* says St. Paul, *he rules as a son in his own house.* Hence he is said to have *purchased a Church with his own blood ;* to have *bought us* (the subjects of this his kingdom) *with a price.* It was, therefore, subsequent to his resurrection, that his exaltation as the Son of Man commenced ; it was then that he received the kingdom appointed unto him of his Father ; and it was then that he commenced the exercise of his authority, by commissioning his apostles for its establishment and government in the world.

In this view of the subject, my brethren, we shall find the question simplified, freed from many difficulties which otherwise attend it, consistent with all that is said in Scripture concerning it, and profitable to correct some prominent errors which prevail on the subject of the Christian ministry.

Our LORD'S own commission, then, as the messenger (the apostle) of GOD the Father, of a sin-ruined, but redeemed world, is derivative in its nature. Hence St. Paul, discoursing of our LORD'S priestly office, in the Epistle to the Hebrews, speaks in this wise : *And no man taketh this honour unto himself, but he that is called of* GOD, *as was Aaron.* So, also, CHRIST *glorified not himself to be made an High Priest ; but he that said unto him, Thou art my Son, to-day have I begotten thee. As he saith also in another place, Thou art a Priest forever, after the order of Melchisidek.* And again it is repeated, with the same reference to the Old Testament priesthood, *For the law maketh men High Priests, which have infirmity, but the word of the oath, which was since the law, maketh the Son, who is consecrated forevermore.* That it is derivative in its nature, we learn further from the circumstance of its being limited in duration of time. This St. Paul also informs us of, in his first Epistle to the Corinthians, *Then cometh the end, when he shall have delivered up the kingdom to GOD, even the Father; and when all things shall be subdued unto him, then shall the Son also be subject unto him that did put all things under him, that GOD may be all in all.*

The extent of our LORD's commission embraces whatever is needful to the fulfilment of the purpose he has undertaken. Within this it is unlimited and omnipotent ; beyond this it does not reach.

Thus, we read in the Epistle to the Ephesians, that GOD *hath set him at his own right hand, in the heavenly places, far above all principality, and power, and might, and dominion; and every name that is named, not only in this world, but also in that which is to come, and hath put all things under his feet, and gave him to be head over all things to the Church.* And St. Peter tells us, that *angels, and authorities, and powers, are made subject unto him.* And St. Paul again, in his Epistle to the Philippians, lays down the same doctrine : *Wherefore,* says he, that is, because CHRIST became obedient to the death of the cross, *wherefore, GOD also hath highly exalted him, and given him a name which is above every name ; that at the name of JESUS every knee should bow, of things in heaven, and things in earth, and things under the earth, and that every tongue should confess, that JESUS CHRIST is LORD, to the glory of GOD the Father.*

These Scriptures, with many others to the same amount, which might be produced out of both the Testaments, declare sufficiently, though in general terms, the extent and importance of that office which the LORD JESUS CHRIST sustains, in the economy of man's redemption and salvation. It is by the particulars, however, that we shall best discern its practical use to ourselves. And these consist in his Prophetic, Priestly, and Regal offices.

As the Prophet or Teacher of his Church, he was commissioned to make a full disclosure of the will of GOD to the world. And this he has done, partly by his own preaching, but more fully by the revelation made through the prophets and apostles, in the Old and New Testaments, which contain all things necessary to be known, believed, and done, by men, in order to secure their eternal salvation.

As the great High Priest of our profession, *He has passed into the heavens, there to appear in the presence of* GOD *for us :* to present the prayers and praises of his people, whether public or private, purified from their imperfection by the merit of his name, and rendered acceptable to GOD the Father, by the prevailing intercession of GOD the Son.

In his regal office, he exercises all power in heaven and in earth, with reference to his Church. He rules it by his laws, and appoints his servants to their several stations ; he defends it by his power ; sustains it by his providence ; directs it by his wisdom ; extends it by his word ; sanctifies it by his SPIRIT ; and, when the number of his elect shall be accomplished, will judge it in righteousness, according to the word spoken unto it in the gospel, and reward or punish everlastingly, according as every man's work shall be. And for this great and awful purpose, his commission extends to raising the dead. *Verily, verily, I say unto you, the hour is coming, and now is, when the dead shall hear the voice of the Son of* GOD, *and they that hear shall live. For, as the Father hath life in himself, so hath he given to the Son to have life in himself, and hath given him authority to execute judgment also, because he is the Son of man. Marvel not at this, for the hour is coming, in the which all that are in the graves shall hear his voice, and shall come forth ; they that have done good, unto the resurrection of life, and they that have done evil, unto the resurrection of damnation.*

In the extent of its operation, our LORD's commission includes the Church triumphant, as well as the Church militant—the Church in heaven, as well as the Church on earth. Being the same body, of which he is the living Head, they are both under his jurisdiction ; and, as the purpose of the Church upon earth is to prepare members for the Church in heaven, to this end all

its laws, and orders, and worship, and appointments, are directed. All have a close connexion with the moral and spiritual
condition of his people, and are calculated to sustain faith, and
defeat sin, and increase holiness. And as our LORD's undertaking for mankind embraced the whole human family, so does
his commission include the boundary of this world in this operation. *Ask of me*, says the ALMIGHTY, through his prophet,
in the 2d Psalm. *Ask of me, and I shall give thee the Heathen
for thine inheritance, and the uttermost parts of the earth for thy
possession.*

From all which we learn, my brethren and hearers, that the
LORD JESUS CHRIST, by the appointment of GOD the Father,
is, to his Church, the source of all wisdom, in the knowledge of
divine things; the ground of all hope, in the intercession of his
priestly character; and the root or foundation of all authority
for administering the affairs of this his kingdom, by virtue of the
supreme dominion of his regal office. And if to these we add,
my brethren, all that he is to us, in the full splendour of his
mediatorial character, well may we exclain, *What hath* GOD
wrought! and learn to realize the depth and importance of his
affectionate admonition, *without me ye can do nothing.*

II. Secondly, I am to consider the connexion, or parallel,
between this and the commission conferred on the apostles, as
the messengers of CHRIST JESUS to the same world of sinners.

And here, my brethren, the more we examine into this subject, according to the limitation already laid down, the more
satisfied we shall be of the exactness of the parallel, and of the
importance of a right view of it, to the full comfort of our religious condition, as redeemed by the blood of CHRIST, and call-
to this state of salvation by the gospel.

First, then, as our LORD JESUS CHRIST derived his commission and authority immediately from GOD the Father, so did the
apostles derive theirs immediately from the LORD JESUS CHRIST:
This is my beloved Son, hear ye him, said the voice from heaven.
*And I appoint unto you a kingdom, as my Father hath appointed
unto me.*

Next, as the man CHRIST JESUS was visibly anointed with
the HOLY GHOST, and with power from on high, previous to

VOL. I.—17

commencing his ministerial office, so were his apostles baptized with the HOLY GHOST on the day of Pentecost, from their ascended and glorified Master, according to his promise, *Ye shall be baptized with the* HOLY GHOST *not many days hence ;* and according to St. Peter's argument with the Jews, on that day, *This* JESUS *hath* GOD *raised up, whereof we all are witnesses ; therefore, being by the right hand of* GOD *exalted, and having received of the Father the promise of the* HOLY GHOST, *he hath shed forth this, which ye now see and hear.*

Thirdly, as the LORD JESUS CHRIST evinced the divine authority of his commission by the miracles which he wrought, in like manner were his apostles provided with this testimony to their commission, as the Ambassadors of CHRIST.

If I bear witness of myself, my witness is not true, said our LORD. *Ye sent unto John, and he bare witness of the truth; but I have greater witness than that of John ; for the works which the Father hath given me to finish, the same works that I do, bear witness of me, that the Father hath sent me.*

Verily, verily, I say unto you, he that believeth on me, the works that I do shall he do ; and greater works than these shall he do ; because I go unto my Father.——And with great power, gave the apostles witness of the resurrection of the LORD JESUS. *And by the hands of the apostles were many signs and wonders wrought among the people, and believers were the more added to the* LORD.

Fourthly, as the commission of our LORD and Saviour JESUS CHRIST, (as the revealer of the will of GOD,) included the race he came to redeem and save, so, also, is the commission to his apostles alike comprehensive in the extent of its jurisdiction. *As by the offence of one, judgment came upon all men to condemnation ; even so, by the righteousness of one, the free gift came upon all men, unto justification of life.——Go ye, therefore, and teach all nations.——Go ye into all the world and preach the gospel to every creature.*

Fifthly, as our LORD is ordained and commissioned as the Judge of quick and dead, by the GOD *and Father of the spirits of all flesh,* so, also, has the great Head of the Church clothed his apostles with a similar distinction. *When the Son of man shall come in his glory, and all the holy angels with him, then shall he sit upon the throne of his glory; and before him shall be gathered all nations, and he shall separate them one from another, as a shepherd divideth his sheep from the goats. And JESUS said unto them, Verily I say unto you, that ye which have followed me, in the regeneration, when the Son of man shall sit in the throne of his glory, ye also shall sit upon twelve thrones, judging the twelve tribes of Israel.*

From the connexion and parallel thus shown, my brethren, (and doubtless it might be more minutely traced,) what can we infer, but that the Christian ministry is of that important and influencial character to revealed religion—so connected with its divine original, and so bound up with the hope of man, in the administration of its saving ordinances—as to claim, from every rational believer, that verification which alone can give to any agency the stamp of assurance. And we have but to suppose the apostles of CHRIST, at the first promulgation of Christianity, unable to prove their divine commission by its then proper testimony; to learn how impossible it would have been for the gospel to have prevailed against established superstition, and the vices thereby generated, and even consecrated among the heathen nations of the world; and thence to derive those conclusive arguments which demonstrate the continual necessity of a like verifiable authority to every generation of men, in transacting what GOD requires at their hands in order to their becoming and continuing parties to this great salvation, as a system of reciprocal covenants, between GOD and man.

Indeed, my brethren and hearers, it is only as a scheme of covenanted mercy, on declared conditions, that any outward order and appointment, any Church ministry and sacraments, are requisite to religion. Abstracted from this, every man might be his own administrator in religious things, and all hope and assurance be vacated, until the judgment of the great day. Disjoined from this, also every thing like union and fellowship in the Saviour's religion would be an impossible requirement, inasmuch as there would be nothing outward and visible, to test internal agreement in faith and charity; and man would be left to travel through his pilgrimage here, solitary, unconnected, unaided, and unencouraged, towards eternity. It is a cold and comfortless thought, my hearers, yet is it inseparable from the denial of a verifiable divine commission to the Christian ministry.   It is a cheerless, gloomy condition, my brethren, to which a merciful God has not consigned us, notwithstanding such numbers adopt it; to which the Scriptures of our faith give no countenance, and to which the searching question—*By what authority doest thou these things?* if seriously applied, would unmask the disguises, and tear away the sophistry, wherewith the right and the efficiency of a ministry not apostolically derived, is covered up and defended.

III. Thirdly, I am to consider the continuation of this commission in the world.

That it was to accompany the gospel in its progress, as an integral part of the dispensation, may be shown from a variety of considerations, but chiefly from this : That to every generation of men, as it comes forward to accountable life, the gospel is in fact a revelation ; has to be considered, in its evidences, its authority, its obligations, its benefits, as the personal concern of each individual ; has to be met or rejected, in is faith, its duties, its grace, its ordinances, as the prescribed conditions of salvation.   Nor do the advantages of early initiation into its hope, or nurture and admonition in its precepts, at all alter the case, except as these are advantages—additional talents increasing responsibility for their improvement. Christianity is for ever a substantive consideration, my brethren, and religion a personal attainment, to all who are called by the gospel to the knowledge of this grace.   It does, indeed, derive confirmation from the accumulating testimony of centuries and numbers, in behalf of its truth and divine original. But it is, nevertheless, independent of this aid, resting on its own evidences for the wisdom or the folly of receiving or rejecting it.   For it was just as true and divine, at its first promulgation, as at any subsequent time.

Had, then, the gospel commission been confined to a few persons, a few generations only could have reaped the advantage of their ministry. Unless, therefore, the lives of such persons were miraculously continued, all who came after them must be deprived of the benefit of authorized religious ministrations. Hence, if there is any connexion between Christianity and its author; if there be any dependence, for religious benefit, on religious instruction, on religious ordinances duly administered—in short, on keeping alive in the world *the knowledge of the only true* GOD, *and of* JESUS CHRIST *whom he hath sent ;* it can only be done (miracle always excepted) by a continued succession in the ministry, from the one original root of all authority to minister in the affairs of CHRIST's kingdom.

And such, in fact, is the method infinite wisdom hath adopted. *Lo, I am with you always, even unto the end of the world,* are the words of encouragement and perpetuity, which our LORD addressed to the apostles for their personal comfort, and to the Church for its lasting assurance that *the gates of hell should not prevail against it ;* and no other or reasonable interpretation can be given of them, than as applicable to their successors in the ministry. The apostles, individually, soon finished their laborious and painful, but heaven-blessed and glorious race. They had this treasure in earthen vessels, materials which could not last. But before they finished their course, respectively, they committed unto faithful men, by divine direction, that commission and authority for the rule and government of the Church, for the guardianship of the faith, and fulfilment of the gospel dispensation, which they received from CHRIST, and CHRIST from the Father. In which transfer, they gave instructions for the due and faithful performance of the duties peculiar to their office ; with directions that they also should, in like manner, *commit the same to faithful men, who should be able to teach others,* and thus continue the line of apostolical succession, unbroken, to the end.

Paul, an apostle of JESUS CHRIST, *by the commandment of* GOD *our Saviour, and the* LORD JESUS CHRIST, *according to the gospel of the ever blessed* GOD, *which was committed to my trust, whereunto I am ordained a preacher, and an apostle. This charge I commit unto thee, son Timothy ; and the things that thou hast heard of me among many witnesses, the same commit thou to faithful men, who shall be able to teach others also.*

This is the language of St. Paul to Timothy, when transferring to him the authority to rule, censure, restrain, and ordain in the Church; which manifests in what sense he understood the continuance of the apostolic commission ; and, in connexion with the uniform, undeniable practice of the Church of CHRIST for fifteen hundred years, might put at rest, forever, all dispute upon this subject, as a matter of fact, as a point to be tried by its proper evidence.

But, independent of this, from the words of my text, and the parallel passages of Scripture, it would appear that a contrary conclusion does violence to the only possible purpose and design in the appointment of a visible Church with an authorized ministry. These, if they mean and effect any thing in the salvation of men, must be considered as provisions in aid of union and assurance of faith among Christians. And in what way this purpose can be answered, other than by a fixed and unchangeable standard of unity, in faith, doctrine, and worship, referable to a derived, transmitted, and thereby verifiable, authority, to act as *ambassadors of* CHRIST, and *stewards of the mysteries of* GOD, is difficult to conceive, and still harder to make appear. *As my Father hath sent me, even so send I you. I appoint unto you a kingdom, as my Father hath appointed unto me.* Hence it is clear,

First, That whatever the authority of CHRIST in the gospel dispensation was, with reference to the Church, of the same extent was that of his apostles. As he alone could purchase, so they only could plant and govern his Church. All others were interdicted from any interference.

Secondly, As the Church and ministry, in this dispensation, were intended for perpetuity, *even till the earth be filled with the knowledge of the* LORD; therefore, this authority must also continue, and run parallel with it, through all generations. As CHRIST's commission and authority, derived from the Father, admitted a transfer of it to his apostles, in like manner the commission and authority of the apostles, derived from CHRIST, admitted, and in fact included, a like transmission to others, and equally verifiable with theirs. Each were invested with powers and qualifications suited to the exigencies of the Church——to its condition at the time ; and as there were many things in which the apostles were inferior to their Master, as the head, but were yet truly his successors in things necessary to the Church, so are there many things in which the subsequent governors of the Church were inferior to the apostles; yet were they truly, and to all necessary purposes, their successors. And this may serve as an answer to the childish cavil so much relied upon, that the apostles, as inspired men, endowed with miraculous power, and eye witnesses of the resurrection and ascended glory of JESUS CHRIST, could have no successors. In *these things*, indeed, they could have no successors; neither was the continuance of such qualifications needed by the Church. The apostles lived to establish the Church, and complete the canon of Scripture, as the standard of faith. Their extraordinary powers were given for this end, which being answered, they were withdrawn. But in the necessary powers and qualifications for its government, preservation in unity, and extension in the world; as these were continually needed, essential to the very being of the Church, as a visible society; so, in them the apostles both could have, and did have, successors; which have continued in an unbroken line of transmitted authority to this day, through the order of Bishops, as the only lawful and verifiable source of spiritual rule, in the kingdom of CHRIST.

IV. Fourthly, I am to consider the object, or purpose, of a divinely constituted ministry in the Church, or kingdom, of CHRIST.

That every regular society, whether civil or religious, to be either permanent or profitable, must be administered by its proper officers, duly authorized, is too obvious to require either proof or illustration. The Church of CHRIST, therefore, differs in no respect from all other societies, as to this necessity. Order, and not confusion, is the signature of the Almighty on all his works, and equally conspicuous in the constitution of his holy Church, which he has put under the regular subordination of a government suited to the objects of such an institution.

Neither does the Church differ from other societies in the application of the rule, inseparable from every regular government, *no man taketh this honour unto himself;* a self constituted or irregularly appointed magistrate being, in every sense, an intruder, whether in the Church or in the state. The Church differs, however, in the source from which the honour or authority is derived.   As civil societies derive altogether from common consent of the parties associated ; the Church on the contrary, as a spiritual society, derives directly from its divine Head : *My kingdom is not of this world,* saith the Saviour.

Another design of a divinely constituted ministry in the Church, with a verifiable authority, is, for assurance in the administration of the ordinances of religion.   Without this, there can be no more certainty and assurance, no more validity and effect, in the sacraments of religion, than there can be in civil affairs, from transacting the requisitions of government with self appointed officers ; and as, in the latter case, though the men may be very competent, and the person transacting perfectly sincere in his intentions, yet, for want of due authority, the whole is a nullity, and cannot be recognised ; so, in the former case, if we would act with assurance, we must act according to the rule and order laid down for the government of the Church, as a divinely constituted society, under its proper officers.   And did men allow this plain analogy its proper weight, there would be less danger of being seduced into the pernicious paths of division and discord.

It is, therefore, for the benefit of third persons, for those who desire the aids and the hopes which CHRIST's religion presents to mortals, that a fixed and authorized ministry is an integral part of the gospel.   As it is a communication from heaven to man, through men of like passions with others, some mark of discrimination, some distinctive character, of a higher order than man can supply, is necessary to designate those to whom is committed the ministry of reconciliation, and dispensing the mysteries of GOD's grace in the sacraments of the gospel.   But where would be the benefit, had we no means of determining the true from the surreptitious authority ? The very reason of the thing, therefore, points to transmitted succession from the apostles.   This the divine wisdom has seen fit to provide and appoint, and this we are bound to follow, if we would have our religion what it is intended to be, to wit, a reasonable service, and a source of comfort and assurance during our journey through life, and of revealed hope for eternity.

The apostles of our LORD gave to the world the incontestible evidence of miraculous power, that they were messengers of heaven, commissioned servants of the Saviour, *to show unto men the way of salvation.* And though, from the very nature of things, this mode of proof could not continue, inasmuch as a perpetual miracle would cease to be such, from constant recurrence ; yet we are not deprived of sufficiently satisfactory evidence on this leading point of revealed religion. The authority of the Church planted and ordered by these very apostles, regularly transmitted from them, and attested by the public ordination of her ministry, being the true and only substitute for miraculous attestation to ministerial commission. Since the cessation of miraculous gifts in the Church, no man can prove *a priori* that he is called of God——moved by the HOLY GHOST to take upon him this ministry. But an *a priori* proof of this as a fact, must precede the very first ministerial act, if we would avoid uncertainty and confusion. Therefore, the authority of the Church, regularly deduced from the apostles who founded it, as it is the only verifiable, so it is the only valid proof of ministerial commission.

The sum is this : The Christian ministry is either at large, that is, the right and privilege of every private Christian, to assume at his pleasure ; or it is limited, that is, confined to a particular order of men, acting under apostolical authority.

But, according to the Scriptures, CHRIST limited his authority to preach and baptize——to found and govern his Church——to the apostles. Therefore, if there is a Christian ministry upon this earth, if the promise, *Lo, I am with you always, even unto the end of the world,* has not failed, that ministry must be sought in apostolical succession. From this position there is no escape, but a determined adherence to the opposite notion, in defiance of Scripture and reason.

Where, and with whom it is to be found, is the deep and previous question, which every man, as serious for his soul as for his estate, has to settle at his entrance on a religious course of life. One thing, however, is beyond dispute ; no apostle has appeared in the interval which has elapsed since those first appointed finished their course. No subsequent origination of names and orders in the Christian community, therefore, can claim the sanction of apostolic origin.

V. I come now to conclude, with such practical inferences from the whole, as are naturally suggested by the solemn duty we have this day to perform.

And, first—If the view I have taken of this subject be at all founded on Scripture and reason, it is not of that unimportant, indifferent nature, which some endeavour to represent it, but so intimately connected with the certainty or uncertainty, the safety or insecurity of our eternal condition, according to the public stipulation of the gospel, as to give that colour to our religious condition in this world which is entitled to assurance, or divested of revealed hope.

Secondly, if *the order* of the gospel is as much a part of God's revealed will as *the faith* of the gospel, it is equally entitled to our reverence and observance ; and no reasonings should be listened to, which go, in any way, to separate what God in his wisdom hath seen fit to connect together, for the comfort and edification of his creatures. It is ever at our personal peril, my friends, if we venture to stretch our measure beyond its proper limit, and create a standard for the gospel, instead of making the gospel the safe standard to our thoughts and actions.

Thirdly, if the means of determining the lawfulness of the authority, by which our spiritual guides act, be thus furnished to all, under the gospel dispensation, there can be no excuse for negligence or remissness on such a commanding interest ; for the very first religious ordinance, by which we obtain a title to the covenanted mercies of the redemption that is in CHRIST JESUS for ourselves and our children, prompts the inquiry, as to the administrator, *By what authority doest thou these things ?* And, while no worldly-wise man will purchase, for himself or his children, an earthly inheritance, without careful scrutiny into *his* right and title who conveys it to him ; no serious Christian can be justified, even in the eye of reason, who accepts a title to a heavenly inheritance, either for himself or his children, without an equally careful examination of his right to convey who proffers to transfer it.

Thus, my brethren and hearers, do we find the maxims and the prudence of common life our schoolmasters, to teach us our duty in this infinite interest, of our claim to, and rightful Scriptural expectation of GOD's revealed mercies in CHRIST JESUS. And, in laying them before you on this occasion, I fulfil an imperious duty, for which I feel and know that I am responsible to GOD ; but on which there is a guarded silence preserved by those whose very existence depends on keeping this inquiry from general attention, and who stigmatize every attempt to give information, as an uncharitable effort, to disturb the peace and harmony of the professing world.

But, my brethren, such railing accusations have no weight with me. The truth—*the truth as it is in* JESUS, is all I live for ; is what, by the grace of GOD, I would die for ; and nothing else, how specious soever in its structure, will avail either you or me, in the great day of eternity. I am not calling your attention to the title to your estates, but to that title on which your souls rest for their hope of a heavenly inheritance. And could I but rouse you to feel the same interest for the one, which you manifest for the other, GOD would be glorified in the triumphs of divine truth, and an evangelized world resound his praise, who, *when he ascended up on high, led captivity captive, and gave gifts unto men ; and he gave some apostles, and some prophets, and some evangelists, and some pastors and teachers, for the perfecting of the saints, for the edifying of the body of* CHRIST, *till we all come, in the unity of the faith, and of the knowledge of the Son of* GOD, *unto a perfect man, unto the measure of the stature of the fulness of* CHRIST.

To you, my brethren, whose purpose it is, by the good motions of the HOLY GHOST, to devote yourselves to this ministry, and, in the presence of GOD and of this congregation, to pledge yourselves this day, to the advancement of the Redeemer's kingdom, I now turn, and, from the consideration of the high authority under which you will be commissioned to act, would call your attention to the proportionally high and solemn obligations under which you are about to come.

Separated to the gospel of GOD, henceforth all profane and secular occupations, beyond those indispensible to the common duties of life, in every calling, are put beneath your notice.

Your ambition must now be directed to the attainment of *the honour that cometh of* GOD. Your labour and diligence must henceforth be applied to approve yourselves faithful to him who hath called you into the spiritual vineyard. Your riches must now consist in accountable souls won over from darkness and death of sin, to glory, honour, and immortality, by the power and grace of CHRIST, through the word preached unto them.

All conformity to the world is henceforth peculiarly interdicted to you. To the Ministers of CHRIST, and Messengers of salvation to a sin ruined world, its vain and vicious pleasures, its ensnaring temptations and unhallowed pursuits, must be guarded against, with that care and watchfulness, which the deepest conviction of their danger and fallacy alone can supply. *Ye are not of the world,* said our LORD, to his first disciples ; and it is yet true, in the just application of the words of all who are moved by the HOLY GHOST to take upon them this office and ministration. Let your deportment, then, show, that you can so use the world as not abusing it ; that your treasure is elsewhere laid up, and your affections settled on another and a better country, even an heavenly.

Ambassadors of CHRIST ! A station more dignified and exalted, more influential and extensive, than the kingdoms of this world can match ; but withal, my brothers, more highly responsible, by all the difference between time and eternity. As envoys of the LORD JESUS CHRIST, the ministry of reconciliation is committed to you. You have to negotiate terms of peace between earthly rebels and their heavenly Sovereign ; between dying sinners and their living Saviour ; and diligence and faithfulness alone can offer you the hope of success, and enable you to deliver your own souls.

In this labour of love, bear ever in mind, my brothers, the instructions from your embassy, contained in the word of GOD ; and, within that gracious limit, draw out every affection of nature and grace, to win immortal souls to eternal life. Contemplate your merciful Master, loving them, even unto the death of the cross, and cultivate the mind that was in him. Use the *terrors of the* LORD *to persuade men;* the promises of GOD, to engage them ; the love of CHRIST to constrain them ; and the example of your own lives to encourage them to lay down the weapons of a mad rebellion, and embrace the mercy that spares and saves. Assure them, with all the earnestness of personal experience, that none were ever rejected who sincerely and penitently sought unto GOD, through his only begotten Son; and that, through faith in his blood, pardon, grace, and everlasting life, are the rich exchange you are authorized to offer them for guilt, and sin, and eternal death, the only fruit of their rebellion, if persisted in. Address their hopes, their fears, their reason, their self-love, if by any means you may save some, making full proof of your ministry.

Stewards of the mysteries of GOD! Intrusted with the rich deposit of his grace, in the word and sacraments of the gospel! That grace, without which fallen creatures can do nothing in the great work of spiritual renewal, and in working out their everlasting salvation. That grace, which is the purchase of CHRIST's death, the root of all holy desires, all good counsels, and all just works, in redeemed man, which is given to every man to profit withal, and shines bright and cheering in those very offers of mercy you are commissioned to bear forth among your fellow sinners. This you have to deal out in measure and season to the household of faith, watching that all be duly supplied according to their several wants, and that none be deprived, by your negligence, of that spiritual nourishment which is the food of the soul. Remember then, my brothers, that it is *required of stewards, that a man be found faithful;* and keep full before you *the prize of your high calling,* that, giving yourselves wholly to this work, your crown may be bright with jewels, in the day of the LORD JESUS. To whose holy keeping and all-sufficient grace, I commit and commend you; and to whose holy name, with the Father and the HOLY GHOST, one only and ever-living GOD, be glory and praise from redeemed man, world without end. AMEN.

REVELATION THE FOUNDATION OF FAITH;

A SERMON,

PREACHED BY

THE RIGHT REVEREND JOHN S. RAVENSCROFT, D. D.,

IN ST. LUKE'S CHURCH, SALISBURY, NORTH-CAROLINA,

AT THE ORDINATION OF THE REV. PHILIP B. WILEY, SUNDAY, MAY 24, 1829;

AND

Published by request of the Convention.

REVELATION THE FOUNDATION OF FAITH.

ROMANS x. 14, *and part of* 15.

" How, then, shall they call on him, in whom they have not believed ? and how shall they believe in him, of whom they have not heard ? and how shall they hear, without a Preacher ? and how shall they preach, except they be sent ?"

IN this series of questions, it appears to be the apostle's object to show, that revelation is the only foundation on which religion can be either required of, or practised by, fallen creatures ; and as it is of the highest importance to the interests of our souls, my hearers, that men should be fully convinced of this primary truth, I shall endeavour to explain and confirm it, by showing,

FIRST, that discoveries are made in the gospel of CHRIST, which were otherwise impossible to men.

SECONDLY, that these discoveries are adapted to a state or condition of the world, from which it was desirable to be delivered.

THIRDLY, that the preaching of the word is the regular appointed means for making known to the world the methods of GOD's grace, in the salvation of sinners.—*How, then, shall they call on him, in whom they have not believed ? and how shall they believe in him, of whom they have not heard ? and how shall they hear, without a preacher ?*

FOURTHLY, that as the discoveries of the gospel are of divine revelation—so is the preaching of the word and the administration of the gospel, by a divine commission—*And how shall they preach, except they be sent ?*

I. First, I am to show that discoveries are made in the gospel of CHRIST, which were otherwise impossible to men.

To those who are acquainted with that gospel, this proposition would seem to require no proof.   But on a little more consideration, we shall find that the actual condition of the religious world renders it both necessary and proper, to vindicate the claims of *revealed* religion, against religion in the general or abstract notion of the unbelieving indifference of too many, in this latter-day state of the gospel.   It is a part of our weakness, my brethren, against which we should be steadily on our guard, that admitted truths, however high their importance, lose by length of time, that relish and impression, which the freshness of discovery imparts to them.   Hence, though the acknowledgement is general, in all Christian lands, of those truths, which by revelation are made our own—and though the awful consequences which depend upon them, are just the same now, as at the beginning—yet it is past all contradiction true, that they are not listened to with that reverence and attention, they do not occupy and fill the minds of men with that deep and serious interest, which so tremendous an alternative, as salvation or damnation, must present to every reflecting mind. Having been so long in possession, we are apt to overlook the source from whence we derive them—to consider them as antiquated, and far distant, in their application ; when, nevertheless, in their vital influence upon the heart, they are to this day, and will be to the end of days, as new and as fresh as when first promulgated.

To this cause it is owing, that experimental religion is so little sought after—that so many are satisfied with the knowledge of the truth, and are careless about the effect—that numbers rest contented with the form, while they are strangers to the power of godliness ; forgetting *that the letter killeth*—that mere acquaintance with religious truth possesses no saving power, being equally in reach of the worst, and of the best of men ; and not bearing in mind, *that the* SPIRIT *giveth life*, in the saving application of truth to the heart, and from thence to the conversation, of every believer.

To this cause, also, I am disposed to refer that trait in the freethinking philosophy of the present day, which boldly assumes as its own the deep things of GOD, deals with them as with mere natural verities, and putting in the back ground the only source of truth and wisdom, presumptuously speculates on the condition of man, and on the purposes of GOD respecting him, as if the *counsels* of him who is perfect in knowledge were within the grasp of a finite and fallen creature. Hence much of that indifference, not to say deadness, to the religion of the gospel, which marks men of literary pretensions in the present, as well as in primitive times. Full of the *wisdom of the world*, but empty of that *wisdom which cometh down from above*, they overlook the never to be shaken truth, that, but for the page of revelation, the boasted powers of human reason could never have advanced a single step in the science of salvation. *The world by wisdom, knew not* GOD. To this, also, I doubt not, it is owing, that *not many wise, not many noble, are now called—because that, though they profess to know* GOD, *they glorify him not as* GOD, *neither are thankful, but become vain in their imaginations, and their foolish heart is darkened*, so that GOD permits strong delusion to lay hold of them—even to believing the impossible lie, that they can be their own Saviours. And were this evil confined to this description of persons, though deeply to be deplored, it might be submitted to ; but unhappily the example is spreading among the rising hope of future days—in the young men of this generation, who are caught by the glitter of false learning, and seduced by the *great swelling words of vanity*, according to the description of the apostle, *wherewith they promise them liberty* from what they are pleased to call the trammels of superstition, and whereby they are seduced to doubt, and to deny, the truth *which is according to godliness.*

But were the revelation of the gospel fairly considered—what it is that it brings to our knowledge, with what it proposes to our attainment—it could not fail, I think, to interest and engage, even the commanding and commendable acquirements of literature ; unreservedly in its behalf. For it meets us, with its soul cheering discoveries, exactly where the powers of human reason come to a full stop. When observations and experience introduce us fully to that confusion and disorder which pervade equally the natural and the moral world, they can go no farther ; and just at this point, the discoveries of revelation step in to save us from the gloomy conclusions of fate and necessity—of chance, creation, and Atheism.

One single example out of many, may serve, my hearers, to confirm this remark. How are we to account for the origin and existence of evil, either natural or moral, in the creation of a perfectly good, wise, and omnipotent Being ? Can reason and philosophy account for this ? Alas, it is powerless. We may conjecture and speculate, and build up theory upon theory, till we lose ourselves in thought——but still we have only the miserable certainty, that evil is present with us. To revelation alone, therefore, are we indebted for this discovery.

But admitting for the moment, that it is possible to be satisfied on this point, without the aid of revelation——let me ask, what are we the better for it ? Can this knowledge, however attained, furnish a remedy for, or arrest, the mortal malady under which the world labours ? No, not at all. *Man knoweth not the price thereof, neither is it found in the land of the living——the depth saith it is not in me, and the sea saith it is not with me. But* GOD *understandeth the way thereof,* and hath showed unto us in the gospel of his Son, *the place where wisdom may be found*——that wisdom, compared with which, all the wisdom of the world is foolishness :——that truth, in the light of which the wisest systems of human contrivance vanish into their original darkness :——that truth, which shall endure, and shine brighter and brighter, when this world, with all its wisdom and philosophy, *shall pass away with a great noise,* and be no more seen for ever.

To the gospel, then, my brethren and hearers, and to the gospel alone, must we look for the solution of every difficulty, and of every doubt, which attends our present condition. To that also must we come——and, thanks be to GOD for the blessed privilege, to that may we freely come——for help and deliverance, for comfort and consolation, for grace and truth, through JESUS CHRIST our LORD. Man, the favoured creature of Almighty GOD, made in the image of his Creator, and amply provided with all that was needful for his happiness, by wilful disobedience drew down upon himself, and upon creation, the curse of GOD. Hence the origin of that sin and misery, which prevails in this world. But mercy, in the person of JESUS CHRIST, the eternal and only begotten Son of GOD, interposed in behalf of the condemned criminal, arrested the uplifted stroke of infinite justice by the substitution of himself ; and thereby converted the present life, with all its load of guilt and suffering, of sorrow and disappointment, into a state of renewed trial and probation for the attainment of eternal life, on the condition of faith and renewed obedience.

To satisfy the demands of infinite justice, purity, and holiness, invaded by the presence of sin—to bear the punishment, which the broken law inexorably demanded, and without which no propitiation could be effected ; for *without shedding of blood there is no remission*—to teach us authoritatively the will of GOD, and to set before us an example of all holiness, humility, and patience, in the very nature which had sinned—the Son of GOD took our nature upon him, became the representative of the human race, paid with his own spotless life the ransom of their forfeited lives, and ratified in the blood of his cross a new covenant of grace and mercy between GOD and man ; in which repentance is accepted, and made available to the pardon of sin, through faith in the atoning virtue of his blood poured out upon the cross for the sins of the whole world. And the sincere though imperfect obedience of sinful creatures, is accepted before GOD, through his mediation and intercession. This, my brethren, is the *gospel of the ever blessed* GOD—*the glad tidings of great joy, which shall be to all people*—to the blessings and benefits of which state of salvation, it hath pleased GOD to call you, my friends. This is the *wisdom of* GOD *in a mystery*—the revelation of *the hidden mystery, which was kept secret since the world began ; but now is made manifest, and by the Scriptures of the prophets, according to the commandment of the everlasting* GOD, *is made to all nations for the obedience of faith.* These are the high discoveries which the gospel makes to our faith, and which nothing but infinite love and wisdom could have so adapted to our wants and wishes, that in the fulness and freeness of gospel grace, their is a sufficiency, even for the chief of sinners. *O, the depth of the riches both of the wisdom and knowledge of* GOD.— Sin condemned and atoned for, by the same act—the law satisfied, its rigour relaxed, and *the righteousness which is of faith,* established—*life and immortality brought to light,* by the clear and full discovery of another life after this—a judgment day declared, and the very manner of that judgment represented, wherein all who have ever lived shall *give account of themselves to* God, and be rewarded or punished everlastingly, *according to the deeds done in the body.*

Now let me ask, in what wilderness of thought could the wisdom of the world have stumbled on such discoveries as these, and so put them together as to harmonize with the perfections of God, and the imperfections of his fallen, sinful creature, as is manifested in the glorious plan of our redemption by JESUS CHRIST? O ye disputers of this world, who vainly strive to bolster up the misgivings of your own hearts, by an affectation of doubt on the revelation of the gospel—but in the hour of danger give the lie to your own vain talkings, and flee to the consolations and hopes which that alone can give—why do you thus sin against your own souls? Is there any thing disgraceful in accepting mercy or receiving favour at the hand of Almighty God? Is there any thing low or unbecoming in humbling yourselves to submit to the righteousness of God, that he may save you by a way you know not of? Come on now, bring your boasted reason to the trial, and let us see what you can substitute for *that grace of* God *which bringeth salvation.* Suit yourselves every way, so that no earthly objection shall be found against your method of salvation—and what then! Alas, yourselves dare not trust it. It is of man, the production of a perishing creature, and must go, with its author, to a tribunal that is eternal. For it is written, *As I live, saith the* LORD, *every knee shall bow to me, and every tongue shall confess to* God.

II. Secondly, I am to show that these discoveries are adapted to a state or condition of the world, from which it was desirable to be delivered.

The condition of man as a sinner, and consequently liable to wrath and punishment, and conscious that he is thus liable, is demonstrated by all that has hitherto been discovered concerning him. Wherever he is found, whether civilized or savage, a sense of guilt cleaving to him is manifested; and religion, in some shape or other, is the refuge to which he flees for relief and comfort. Conscious that he is under the control and within the power of an invisible and omnipotent Being, with whom he is at variance, and whom it is both his duty and his interest to propitiate, every device which ignorance and fear can prompt superstition to invent, has been resorted to, to appease the wrath and avert the indignation of that Supreme Being who is thus ignorantly worshipped. In this universal worship there is one circumstance, my brethren, which is common to all the shapes and forms with which it has been invested : which is this—the vicarious substitution of man or animal, as a sacrifice, to avert wrath from the worshipper himself. Wherever man is found, even in the most degraded and brutal state in which recent discovery has represented him to our notice, where no other trace of religion is to be seen, the victim bleeds, and life is offered up to appease and propitiate. An experience thus general, my hearers, is with me a most conclusive argument for the truth of revelation; for it is not to be accounted for, that such should be the universal impression and practice, but from the identity of the human race, the community of guilt, and the tradition of that sacrifice which was instituted upon the entrance of sin, as a type of that great sin-offering presented on calvary, *which taketh away the sins of the world.*

The great volume of nature, my brethren, unquestionably points the creature to the Creator, and as GOD, it is his first duty to honour and to worship *Him*, who *giveth to all his creatures life and breath and all things.* But alas, the power of sin hath so weakened and corrupted his faculties, that this grand and universally legible record of GOD is a sealed book to him, as to himself. Amid the beauties and bounties of nature, man sees and feels the effects of the curse, and shrinks in terror and dismay from that awful being, who rides in the whirlwind and directs the storm. If he reflects at all, he perceives that himself is nothing, even here, where he is lord of all below. And if an anxious thought should burst the barrier of sensible things, and inquire beyond the grave, nature has no sweet discovery wherewith to relieve the anxious soul, which pants for immortality. If he has advanced to the supreme and eternal Cause of all being by the study of his works, he beholds GOD in all the plenitude of his incommunicable attributes, he beholds himself without any claim to his notice and regard, but what he has in common with every other creature to whom life is given. Nature's volume contains no record of sympathy and compassion for deceived and ruined mortals.   Yet something within him would claim a nearer relationship——the immortal aspiring principle, which God breathed into him with the breath of life, would soar to its original kindred in the heavens.   But guilt, the guilt of sin, hath put a bar between them, which nature cannot remove.   No, dear brethren, without the gospel, there is neither help nor hope for sinners.

Thus surrounded by a power which he cannot escape ; conscious of a guilt, which he cannot remove ; desirous to propitiate, but ignorant of what will be acceptable ; exposed to the evil which sin hath entailed upon the present life ; death, sooner or later, certain and inevitable ; another state of being, after this, shrouded from his view in all the uncertainty of unrevealed conjecture, yet nevertheless what gives shape and substance to all his fears :——what is there in such a condition desirable ? or, rather, my friends, what is there in it, from which it is not above all things desirable to be delivered? And, thanks be to God, by the revelation of JESUS CHRIST in the gospel, we are delivered from this dark and dismal state of doubt and dismay.   It is our unspeakable blessing, my dear hearers, to know the gracious purpose of Almighty God, in permitting that mixed state of moral and natural evil which this present world presents to our notice.   It is ours to know, that his power and providence stand engaged to make it work together for his glory and our good. It is ours to look up to him with reverence and love, as our reconciled father in CHRIST JESUS.   It is ours to know the propitiation which is always acceptable in his sight, even the blood of his only begotten Son, *which cleanseth from all sin.* It is ours to know his will, and to have power to do it, through the grace given us in CHRIST JESUS. It is ours to look beyond the grave, to a never-ending existence, in which the awful sanctions of religion shall be applied to the deeds done in this body, by the righteous judgment of God, in the rewards and punishments of eternity. And it is our high privilege, my brethren in the LORD, by virtue of the victory given us over death, hell, and the grave, through the resurrection of CHRIST, to look forward with humble yet joyful hope—with lively and assured faith, *to an inherit-ance incorruptible, undefiled, and which fadeth not away,* reserved in heaven for us.

These are the discoveries of the gospel, and of the gospel alone.   These are the otherwise impossible discoveries, made to mankind by revelation, adapted to that destitute and helpless condition in which sin had sunk the world ; from which it was surely most desirable to be delivered : and which GOD hath *commanded to be preached among all nations for the obedience of faith.*   Which brings me to what was proposed as the third head of this discourse.

III. Thirdly, I am to show, that the preaching of the word is the regular, appointed means for making known to the world the methods of GOD's grace in the salvation of sinners.

To our habits of thought and action, my hearers, the propo-sition stands in need of no proof: *Go ye into all the world, and preach the gospel to every creature,* is the commission of the author of our religion to his ministers : But to impress upon you more deeply, the great importance of the appointment, and to point out the benefits which in every age of the world man-kind have derived, and will yet derive, from a preached gospel, it will be necessary to consider more at large, the fitness of the means to the end.

It is certainly not for us to say, by what various methods the wisdom and the power of Almighty GOD might have provided for the spread of the gospel in the world.   But this we may say —that unless by resorting once more to the already abortive channel of tradition, or by the intervention of a perpetual miracle ; the appointment he hath been pleased to make of public preaching of the gospel, is the wisest and best, because best adapted to the nature and condition of those for whom it is designed.

For, had it pleased GOD, that this revelation of his will should have been made to all men, in every place and in every age of the world—to every generation of men, and to every individual in each generation—we cannot comprehend how this could be done, without involving a standing miracle : which circumstance, independent of the infringement it would be of that freedom which alone constitutes us moral agents, must soon cease, from the very nature of things, to be miraculous to us; for to apprehensions such as ours, a perpetual miracle involves a contradiction. Besides, on the plan of a perpetually renewed revelation, *must CHRIST often have suffered since the foundation of the world.*

On the other hand, had tradition again been resorted to for the spread, and continuance in the world, of the revelation made by the Son of GOD, all experience went to prove, that however high and holy the deposite—however express the command, to transmit it down from generation to generation—it would speedily have been corrupted, and become as impure as the channel through which it flowed, as uncertain and inefficient as any other legend.

But now, my brethren, by a fixed revelation of his will, attested and verified with a precision which renders criminal the obstinacy that will not receive it as the truth of GOD; and by the appointment of public preaching of the word, by persons having his commission therefor; GOD hath graciously removed every difficulty, and wisely provided, that every generation as it comes forward on the great theatre of life shall, in this respect, be equal—and that to *every nation, and kindred, and tongue, and people that dwell on the face of the whole earth,* the word of this salvation shall thus be sent, and all mankind be furnished with the high discoveries and holy hope of the gospel of CHRIST—that high and low, rich and poor, bond and free, as they all stand in the same relation to GOD, may alike be partakers of the riches of his grace, and of the means, and of the hope of eternal life, through JESUS CHRIST our LORD.

But not only to make known the terms and conditions of the gospel for salvation to sinners, is the preaching of the word appointed; but to keep alive, also, the impressions of divine grace, to convey and confer that grace in the sacraments of salvation, and to further and help—to instruct and build up—the disciples of CHRIST, in the most holy faith, is the office and duty of those *who are put in trust with the gospel.* As it also is, to call sinners to repentance, to warn the unruly, to reprove the disobedient, to rebuke the rebellious, to encourage the timid, to strengthen the feeble minded, and to comfort the mourner, *warning every man,* (says the apostle,) *and teaching every man, that we may present every man perfect,* in CHRIST JESUS.

With so high and holy a purpose, dependent on this provision of the wisdom of GOD for our salvation, the interest we all have that it should be encouraged and promoted, is exactly equal to the consequences which are connected with it. And as these are infinite and eternal, most presumptuously do those offend against GOD, and sin against their own souls, who needlessly absent themselves from the public appointments of religion, or attend upon them without reverence. When we consider, moreover, my friends, that *faith* itself *cometh by hearing,* and that GOD hath specially promised the light and comfort of his HOLY SPIRIT to the devout and reverent hearing of his word preached, it might serve to convince many, who are negligent in this respect, what a risk they run, of never *coming to the knowledge of the truth, that they may be saved ;* and how foolish, and even impious, it is, to expect GOD's blessing, while they neglect the very means he has appointed for obtaining it.

But let me not be misunderstood, as if I confined our duty, under the blessing of GOD's word, to the mere hearing of it preached. No, my brethren; what is preached according to *the mind of the* SPIRIT, must be retained and acted upon.——Nor yet, that I confine the influences of the HOLY SPIRIT to the word preached. No, my hearers ; reading the Scriptures, with meditation and prayer, is an excellent and fruitful means of grace. Neither our private, nor our public religious duties, are substitutes the one for the other. When they go hand in hand together——when, like the Bereans of primitive times, we search the Scriptures to see whether what we hear preached is the truth of GOD, and as such receive it ; then it is, that the full benefit of the gospel is most surely to be expected, and is most generally found.

IV. Fourthly, as the discoveries of the gospel are of divine revelation, so is the preaching of the word and the administration of the gospel by a divine commission——*And how shall they preach, except they be sent ?*

On this point but little would be required to be said, were it not for the operation of those dissensions and divisions in Christianity, which by length of time, and the established habit of thought, and the power of prejudice, and the pertinacity of party feeling, and, I may add, the apathy and indifference of an unbelieving age, have fulfilled the predictions of the Author and Finisher of our faith, defaced the beauty and simplicity of the gospel, and cut the nerves of revealed religion.

Yet, my hearers, in this, as in all other the appointments of heaven for our good, God hath not left himself without witness, or placed his creatures under any necessity of erring from his way, or of defeating the comfort and assurance derived from the gospel, by reason of uncertainty in the administration of the word of his truth, and the means of his grace. By an undeniable appointment of the first preachers of the gospel, certainty and assurance was given to the first converts to Christianity, that their faith was not built on a cunningly devised fable, the contrivance of human wisdom, but on the power of God, certified to their senses by the mighty power of the HOLY GHOST. On this foundation the Church of CHRIST was planted and built up ; and on this foundation it must continue to the end of the world, or cease to be the Church of the living God. For, while faith shall continue to be the essence of religion, it must be derived from the same source ; while revelation shall continue to be the only ground of faith, it must be derived from the word of God ; while the word of God shall continue supreme for the direction of man in his spiritual concerns, it must be certified to his senses, as the standard of all duty and of all hope ; and, while it shall continue to be preached to all nations for the obedience of faith, it must be accompanied with the same divine commission and authority by which it was verified at the beginning, as the truth of God, for man's salvation. Now as faith, considered as a religious principle, is inseparable from divine operation and divine warrant for what is believed, not only is the revelation itself, but all other ministrations connected with the religion thus established, dependent for certainty and effect on the same principle. As it is competent to no man to declare the will of God without revelation, so neither is it competent for any to administer the affairs of CHRIST's kingdom, *except he be sent*—that is, as the apostle evidently means, except he be duly authorized thereto : a conclusion so clear and so reasonable, and at the same time so wise, and so profitable to creatures dependent on the use of means for spiritual attainment, as to create wonder that it should ever have been, or yet continue to be, overlooked and disregarded by Christian people.

Hence is derived the importance of all the services here to be performed this day—the worship of GOD—his law proclaimed—his word preached—his sacraments administered—and his commission transferred to an approved servant, professing to be moved by the HOLY GHOST to take upon him this office and ministry, but outwardly commissioned for the assurance of those to whom he shall minister. What, my brethren and hearers, would they all be worth, separate from the divine authority, whereby they are certified as the appointments of GOD for your salvation ? *How shall they preach except they be sent ?*

Such, my brethren and friends, being *the gospel of the ever blessed* GOD, which hath reached so far as even unto us, bringing with it the grand and profitable discovery of our wants, and of GOD's mercies—and such the appointment of his wisdom for continuing the knowledge of his will and the help of his grace among men, by the ministry of the word—what becomes us, who are so highly favoured, and so richly provided for in our greatest interest ? Shall it be a dead letter to us through neglect, or life and power unto salvation, through attention ? This question it is your part to answer ; and *I beseech you, by the mercies of* GOD, to lay it near your heart. Every thing will depend on the temper and spirit with which you consider it. For the apostle tells us, that in the preaching of the gospel the ministers of CHRIST *are a savour of life, or a savour of death,* according as *the word preached, is mixed' with faith in them that hear it.* I have met you to-day, my brethren and hearers, in the simplicity of that gospel in which you stand, and have laid it before you, in its first lines, as it were. Shall I then be the savour of life, or of death, to you, or any of you ? This also will depend greatly on yourselves ; and I pray to GOD, to help you to a right understanding of what may turn, perhaps, on the choice of this hour—even your future and eternal condition.

The gospel is your salvation or condemnation, as you receive or reject it ; you cannot escape from that fixed rule by which you must be judged and sentenced everlastingly. But a little while, my friends, and *he that shall come, will come, and will not tarry.* He comes to take account of his servants, according to what he hath committed unto each man's trust. At your hands he will demand an improvement of gospel light, gospel privileges, and gospel grace—and nothing short of improvement will answer. The unprofitable servant, remember, returned his lord's talent safe and uninjured ; but was consigned to outer darkness because he had not made an increase of it. What then must be the portion of those, who not only have not improved, but have abused, wasted and dissipated, profaned and despised, this richest gift of GOD's love? And think me not your enemy, my friends, because I thus speak—No : GOD knoweth, that for your souls I would spend and be spent—and O that I had a tongue of fire, that I might consume every opposing thought, and bring every soul now before me, to know the gospel of CHRIST to be *the power of* GOD *unto salvation!* You are here, my brethren, this day, in the house of GOD, and as the people of GOD. The everlasting gospel is proposed to you ; and what hindereth, that you should not close in with its most gracious offers. *All things are now ready, come to the marriage.* O begin not *with one consent to make excuse, and go away, one to his farm, another to his merchandize, and another* to his profession ! For there is an awful threat in this very gospel, that those who make such excuses, shall not taste of the marriage supper of the Lamb.

Oh ! it is a fearful thought, my brethren and hearers, to reflect on the heedlessness and inadvertence of redeemed sinners, under this rich provision of the love of GOD in CHRIST JESUS for their salvation ! It is a heart-sinking prospect to behold the thousands of accountable immortals, who, Gallio like, *care for none of these things,* but follow the carnal mind in its rejection of GOD, and preference of the world. Yet if we have hearts awakened for ourselves, they must feel for the sin deceived multitudes, who madly put away from them the words of eternal life. And what they thus feel, they must manifest ; for there is no middle ground on which we can contemplate man in any moment of his existence, other than as in the favour, or under the curse of his Maker.

This, my brethren of the clergy, is the anxious, oppressive thought, which weighs down the spirit of the ministers of CHRIST, under the apathy and indifference wherewith the gospel is received. But *whether they will hear, or whether they will forbear—necessity is laid upon us; yea, woe be to us if we preach not the gospel.* Arm yourself, therefore, my brother, who will this day be invested with CHRIST's commission to preach the gospel and administer the sacraments of the grace of GOD. Arm yourself with a steadfast mind, fully and faithfully to administer the trust committed you. You have to go forth among this heedless and unconcerned race of fallen creatures. You have to rouse them from the lethargy of unbelief—to awaken them from the dream of mortality, and point their thoughts, their anxieties, their exertions, to the realities of another being—and to apply the sanctions of eternity to the pursuits and occupations of time. You profess to be called of GOD to this great work. Believing this, we this day clothe you with CHRIST's commission, derived from his holy apostles, to *call sinners to repentance.* Commending you to the grace of GOD, and exhorting you to *make full proof of the ministry,* and to bear in mind that you have to account for immortal souls; we bid you GOD speed. And may he who hath the remainder of the SPIRIT, and who alone giveth the increase, be with you in your work, to the advancement of his glory, the good of his Church, the safety, honour, and welfare of his people.

Now unto GOD the FATHER, GOD the SON, and GOD the HOLY GHOST—the only living and true GOD, be all honour and glory—now and forever.

A SERMON,

PREACHED BEFORE THE BIBLE SOCIETY OF NORTH-CAROLINA,

On Sunday, December 12, 1824;

BY THE

RIGHT REVEREND JOHN S. RAVENSCROFT, D. D.,

BISHOP OF THE DIOCESE OF NORTH-CAROLINA.

PREFACE.

IN presenting the following discourse to the public, no other view is entertained, than that of enabling every person who chooses to pass upon the question, to have the question itself, and not the misrepresentations of either editors or enemies to found his judgment upon.

That the view taken of the subject is novel, is, in one sense of the word, true—in the more general meaning of that word, it is not true. It is novel or new, in that sense only, in which it is in opposition to the current in which the public mind has long been directed by the tenor of the public or pulpit instruction given to it. But it is not novel or new, as respects the fundamental and irrefragable principles of that religion, on which the hope of man for hereafter is founded; nor yet is it novel or new, in the sense of being first presented by the author. Hundreds, whose names will never perish, have stood forth to stay the plague, and have in substance, though not perhaps in manner, advocated the same cause. If these publications have not reached this length, the greater the pity, and the greater the necessity that the thousands of immortal souls who live in trust of the integrity of their spiritual guides, should be informed and induced to examine for themselves. But this they will not do, so long as those to whom they naturally look up, are themselves the advocates of a specious but dangerous error. And when an erroneous principle has received the sanction of great names, and numerous associations, it is next to impossible to stem the tide of popular prejudice. Yet the obligation is not thereby lessened on the part of those, whose exclusive duty it is to deal with divine truth—who in the emphatic language of scripture *are put in trust with the gospel.*

On this ground the author rests, for the defence of the course he has taken in the following discourse. He has long lamented the injurious tendency of the favourite principle of the Bible Societies in question. He thinks he has witnessed its dangerous, because irreligious, effect; and he took the opportunity afforded by the Anniversary Sermon, to lay before this Bible Society, and all who should be present, what he believes to be a just view of the subject, without once reflecting on any collateral propriety.

It has been attempted on former occasions, as well as on the present, to deny the interpretation given to the words "without note or comment." But that it is the only true interpretation—the only practical meaning of the phrase—is evident, from the unanimity, with which all descriptions of Religionists adopt it; and even the enemies of Christianity subscribe to it. It leaves the field free for their respective emissaries to give their separate and opposite constructions to the *one* faith of the gospel. Yet certain it is—Emperors and Kings and Princes and nobles, and opposing religious denominations, amalgamated into Bible Societies, to the contrary notwithstanding—certain it is, there is but one saving interpretation of divine truth, one prescribed channel of hope, and means of grace, revealed to fallen man.

That the interpretation of the words "without note or comment," adhered to by the author of the Sermon, is in deed and truth, that of the Societies themselves, he offers to submit to the following test:

Let any Bible Society, not an auxiliary—let the great mother of all, the British and Foreign Bible Society—be convened, to decide on which of the various denominations of Christians shall be authorized by them, as a body, to interpret the faith, and administer the sacraments of the gospel—yea, to present some single commentator as a safe guide to the ignorant and unlearned—and then see whether they can agree. If they can, or, if in the mind of any reasonable man, there is the remotest probability of it—on the contrary, if it does not split them into shivers, then is the author wrong in the view he has taken of it. Otherwise, he must retain the meaning he has annexed to the talismanick words "without note or comment." Let the North Carolina Bible Society try it at their next general meeting, and thus prove or disprove what this enemy to Bible Societies has had the temerity to call in question. This will refute the Sermon better than all the railings of men who vainly think that the truth of GOD is the creature of human opinion, and to take its character from the fluctuations of such a standard. If theirs is the truth of this controversy, let them meet this ordeal.

Of the injurious effect of this principle upon religion at large, in lowering the importance of the Bible, lessening the reverence due to the sacraments of the gospel, and encouraging the infidel notions exposed in the body of the Sermon, the author, unhappily, can desire no more striking proof, than the sentiments expressed in the first of that series of newspaper publications, which followed the delivery of the sermon.*

As it seems to be the determination of many, who write and speak on this subject, to denounce the author as an enemy to the distribution of the Scriptures, notwithstanding his express declarations to the contrary, he thinks proper to repeat, most solemnly, that the charge is wholly unfounded. He is opposed only to the erroneous and injurious principle, on which the greater number and most efficient, but *not all*, Bible Societies act: there being, both in Europe and America, Bible Societies, who are operating with zeal and effect, in disseminating the word of GOD to all who are in want, both Heathen and Christian, accompanied with the authority of GOD, and with the sacraments of consolation and assurance. And nothing but the poverty and depression of the Episcopal Church in this Diocese has prevented the attempt to unite her exertions with them, in so sacred a cause.

Nor yet is the author opposed to the reading of the Scrip-

---

* The following are the sentiments referred to. "Nor do we consider the diversity of opinion among men on the subject of religion, as an evil to be lamented. All that is necessary to produce happiness under such circumstances is, that men should think charitably of each other, and agree to differ, believing that every one who professes himself to be guided by the principles of the gospel, leads a good life, is sincere in his profession, and will hereafter be approved by his Maker."

tures without a commentator, as is falsely charged against him. On the contrary, he has many witnesses, how earnestly and repeatedly he presses the study of the word of God upon his hearers; and it is his invariable rule, when consulted what commentator to begin the reading of the Scriptures with, to answer, none; recommending to all, to be first well grounded in the Scriptures themselves, by reading, meditation, and prayer, when a sound and judicious commentator may be helpful; but previous to which, he will only lead the beginner into his own particular views, whatever these may be, so that, if he happens to be right, it is not understandingly—he may easily be shaken; if he happens to be wrong, he is fortified in error, and cannot readily be set right.

It is due to the subject, and to the public also, to state, that the short compass of a sermon is inadequate to the full developement of the principle and its consequences. The author, therefore, confined himself to those objections which lie most level to every apprehension, and can be most readily understood and felt by every serious Christian.

JOHN S. RAVENSCROFT.

Raleigh, Dec. 24, 1821.

A SERMON,

BEFORE THE BIBLE SOCIETY OF NORTH CAROLINA.

ACTS viii. 31.

"And Philip ran thither to him, and heard him read the Prophet Esaias; and said,
Understandest thou what thou readest? And he said, How can I, except some man
should guide me?"

THE circumstances which precede and follow the relation of
this fact, in the history of our religion, for the details of which I
refer you to the chapter itself, point out the connexion of my
text with the more special purpose of this day.

Favoured as we are, my brethren and hearers, with the word
of life, with those *Scriptures which are able to make us wise unto
salvation, through faith which is in* CHRIST JESUS, it would be a
libel on our Christian name, were neither wish or effort manifested, to supply the manna of souls to the needy and the destitute. From this reproach, however, the Christian community
has long been released; and, as if to atone for former remissness, seems now to be absorbed, as it were, in the one object of
disseminating the Scriptures *to every nation, and kindred, and
tongue, and people under heaven.* And what heart that circulates
Christian blood, but must prompt both to approve and to aid a
purpose so divine? What Christian, who has himself *tasted of
the good word of* GOD, *and the powers of the world to come*, but
must wish and pray, and, if consistent, strive to promote that
blessed and promised period, *when the knowledge of the* LORD
shall cover the earth as the waters cover the great deep.

That a purpose so glorious—a plan so beneficent—should
have captivated the public mind, and rushed forward to its ac-
complishment, with an impetus which left far behind those more
sober considerations, which alone can give effect and perma-
nence to the good intended, is not to be wondered at my hear-

ers; for it is the very nature of high wrought public feeling to outstrip reflection—it is of the essence of general as well as personal enthusiasm, that it cannot be trammelled with details. Of the Bible cause, therefore, it may be said, as was happily said of a similar excitement, (that which produced the crusades for the recovery of the holy land,) "a nerve was touched of exquisite feeling, and it vibrated to the heart of Christendom." Nor yet is it to be wondered at, that the same cause should have produced a like oversight of those precautions, which are indispensable to the success of every moral effort.

But it is not to excitement alone, that we are to ascribe the adoption of what is here considered an error, in the original principle of the most extensive Bible Society in the world, and recognized by the one I am now addressing, in the second article of its Constitution. To the unhappy divisions in the Christian world must we, in great part, attribute the currency—I had almost said, the consecration, of the dogma—"that the distribution of the Bible, without note or comment, is the only just principle on which to disseminate the Scriptures of our faith."

This specious position, while it seemed to give to the word of God that pre-eminence which it challenges, as exclusively saving truth, and to leave, also, exclusively to the SPIRIT OF GOD, which inspired them, the effect to be produced on the hearts and lives of those to whom it was sent, presented to Christians of every denomination, one point, where they could all meet. And as it recognized, what is considered, the leading Protestant principle, "that the Bible is the religion of Protestants," less consideration than it deserved was given to the principle itself. Great and good men of every persuasion, sick of the dissensions which deform the fair face of Christianity, were glad to find one object, in the forwarding of which all could cordially unite—which promised the extension of. blessings beyond all price—and in the magnificent issue of an evangelized world, held out the fulfilment of their daily prayer, *thy kingdom come.*

Under the influence of such feelings, the Bible itself was overlooked, in the clear directions which may be drawn from it, as to the only safe and effectual manner of disseminating its saving knowledge: and a mark of reproach was fastened upon all who ventured to call in question the soundness of the favourite notion. Their sentiments are held in contempt, as narrow and bigoted. Their authorities and arguments are met, not by reason and Scripture, but by splendid details of Bible society extensions—by gorgeous declamation of Heathen nations furnished with the bread of life—and by overwhelming catalogues of the names enlisted, and the millions disbursed, for this despotic favourite.

Yet, my brethren and hearers, the march of truth, though slow, is sure, and her victory certain. Examination of the subject has given a juster direction to the minds of many; and, though they cannot equal the numbers of those who follow the direction of the first impetus, they are sensible of a progressive accession of strength, and look forward with confidence to that period, when principles, equally impregnable with revelation itself, will be owned and acted upon; and to this they look with the greater confidence, because, though inconsiderately and injudiciously charged with being opposed to the spread of the Scriptures, they yield to none in the sincere desire and earnest endeavour to place in every hand, and instil into every heart in this sin-struck world, *the saving knowledge of* GOD, *and of* JESUS CHRIST, *whom he hath sent.*

In these prefatory remarks—very different, perhaps, from what you have heretofore been accustomed to on such an occasion—my object is, to present the subject to your thoughts in a connexion in which you have not been taught to view it. My wish and intention is, to lead you to the serious consideration of the purpose for which you are associated, for which your affections are enlisted, and your contributions expected; to compare the declared principle of your operations, with the instrument you have undertaken to wield; to estimate the means used, in connexion with the end proposed; and by the result of such an examination, to place your feelings under the control of your understandings, as the only safe principle of moral conduct.

I might, indeed, my hearers, have taken the beaten track, with more ease to myself, and perhaps with greater satisfaction to many of you. It presents a wide field for affecting declama-

tion, a plenteous magazine of facts and figures to work upon
the feelings——yea, a well furnished store house, from which to
draw materials to confirm the prejudices of an erroneous judgment.   But such is not my office—-such is not the purpose
wherefore I am *separated unto the gospel of* God.   A higher tribunal will pass upon the faithfulness of this day, both to you and
to me.   Under a present sense, then, of the awful account we
have mutually to give in, let us now speak and hear.

*And Philip ran thither to him, and heard him read the prophet
Esaias, and said, Understandest thou what thou readest? And
he said, How can I, except some man should guide me.*

From these words I propose to show, that the principle recognized and acted upon, by this and other Bible Societies, "that
the Scriptures are exclusively sufficient for their own interpretation," is unfounded and dangerous, and, ultimately, subversive
of all revealed religion.

I. First, from the structure of the Scriptures themselves.

The purpose of revelation being to bring to our knowledge
things divine and spiritual, and which otherwise are entirely out
of our reach, the language made use of must be appropriate to
the subject matter of the communication, and to our capacity
of apprehension.   And since there is an infinite disproportion
between the things themselves and the capacity of men, the use
of figure or metaphor is resorted to, to convey this knowledge.
Under the letter of Scripture, therefore, is couched that spiritual
meaning and application, which constitutes their value and importance to us as saving truth.   Hence we find, that while the
preceptive parts of revelation are plain and perspicuous, so as to
be immediately apprehended, those which are doctrinal partake
of different degrees of clearness, according to the nature of the
doctrine inculcated ; and those which are mysterious, are clothed
in an obscurity which even *the angels desire to look into.*   Yet
they are all made the subject matter of our faith and obedience,
my hearers, and operative, according to our diligence, in preparing us for still higher and brighter spiritual attainments.

Unless, therefore, it can be made out, that the mysterious and
obscure parts of revelation can be safely and truly interpreted
by those which are clear, (for that is the amount of the prin-

ciple acted upon as fundamental, by the Bible Societies in question,) the very structure of the Scriptures shows the fallacy of the proposition.

On this point, which is of great importance to a just view of the subject, and, I presume, new to many of you, the observations of a prelate of high character for ability and piety, are so clear and convincing, that I shall lay them before you in his own words :

"The principle (says this writer) of explaining those parts of holy Scripture which appear more obscure, by those which are manifest and clear, involves a very serious inconvenience. It is obvious that, in the sacred word, different degrees of clearness and obscurity can have arisen only from the various nature of the subject matter. In promulgating a design so vast, comprehensive and profound, as the design of Christianity, what St. Paul terms *the deep things of* GOD must frequently come into view. In every enunciation of these great mysteries, an awful obscurity must unquestionably overhang the subject ; still, however, all the instances may not be equally inaccessible : some may reward research, though others may baffle investigation. But if passages of obvious plainness are to limit the import of profounder passages, it is manifest, that all profounder passages must be at least comparatively, and in many cases totally, neglected. On the assumption that the profounder and the plainer language refer to the same subject, and express the same, or nearly the same idea, it would be difficult, perhaps, to defend the wisdom, and sometimes even the humanity of the HOLY SPIRIT, who indited the Scriptures ; for why employ dark and doubtful sayings where obvious and familiar sayings would have answered every reasonable purpose ? But the fact is far otherwise. Simple truths are simply expressed, majestic truths are clothed in appropriate majesty of language, and mysterious truths are invested with that sacred veil which they alone may venture to penetrate who are at once illuminated by Christian grace, animated by christian love, and regulated by Christian humility. Such spirits are invited, and expected, to search out the wonders of GOD's word, no less than the works of his creation. But what an obstacle will be opposed to their researches,

what a bar to their spiritual improvement, if the highest truths
are to be measured by the lowest standard ! If the depths are
to be sounded with a plummet, which can scarcely reach the
bottom of the shallows !"   "But a still more serious consequence may be dreaded.   The clearer passages of Scripture,
will, in general, be those which recognize principles deducible
from nature and providence; and, by parity of reason, the
obscurer passages will commonly be those in which pure matter
of revelation is promulgated.   If, therefore, it be adopted as
the leading principle of interpretation, that the sense of this
latter class of passages should be limited or settled by the sense
of the former class, it may be reckoned upon, that through the
continual application of this rule the appropriate and peculiar
truths of revelation will gradually be absorbed in mere natural
varieties."   "The question may now be asked, have not these
consequences been actually realized? Is it not but too certain,
that a diminishing scale of interpretation detracts from the
fulness of Christian belief; and that where the less appropriate
and peculiar parts of revelation are made the limits of all the
rest, the system commonly terminates in Socinianism; perhaps
in something, if possible, more removed from the semblance of
Christianity ?"

Thus writes the present Bishop of Limerick, not on the subject of Bible Societies, but upon the principle which distinguishes
the British from the reformed continental Churches; and it is
for the observation and experience of those who now hear me,
to apply the reasoning, and to consider whether similar effects
are not following to us, and whether, upon the whole, the reverence due to the Bible as the word of God, is not declining,
under the operation of this unwise and unwarranted assumption ?

But it may be said, since the canon of Scripture is complete,
and admitted by all to be in itself sufficient for every Christian
purpose, what more can be needed?   To this it is replied by a
Christian father of the fifth century, "That, from the very depth
of holy Scripture, all men cannot receive it in one and the same
sense.   One person interprets the divine oracles in one manner; another person in a manner totally different; insomuch,

that from the same source, almost as many opinions may be elicited as there are men. Therefore, amidst so great perplexity of such various error, it is extremely necessary that the line of prophetic and apostolic interpretation be regulated by the standard of ecclesiastical and catholic judgment."

To close this head of my discourse, I would observe, that if the foregoing arguments needed any confirmation, it is to be found in the order pursued by the Divine Wisdom in making known his will to his creatures. Under each dispensation of his grace, the revelation made has been accompanied by authorized and accredited interpreters and administrators of spiritual things. In no case is the word of GOD disjoined from the Church of GOD—the grace of GOD from the sacraments of the Church—and the end proposed and promised, separated from the means provided and commanded. All of which the present system keeps entirely out of view; and is, therefore, so far, at variance with the wisdom of GOD.

II. Secondly, the fallacy of the principle will be further evidenced by the condition of man as a fallen creature.

As such, his tendency has uniformly been to corrupt revelation—to bring it down to his own unholy standard. *The natural man receiveth not the things of the* SPIRIT OF GOD. With difficulty does he retain them even when received, and slowly do they grow and increase, under the most diligent instruction. What, then, are we reasonably to expect when he is deprived of these advantages, and thrown back upon himself, to search out the mystery of godliness from the unaided word? What must be the result, but either total neglect, or as many and various systems of belief, as there are varieties of mental capacity?

Unless, therefore, it can be shown that it is a matter of perfect indifference what system of religious opinions we draw from the Scriptures; and that we are equally safe, as regards another life, under an erroneous, as under a true interpretation of the word of life; the condition of man as a fallen creature, in connexion with the structure of the Scriptures is yet further in opposition to the principle in question. For, as the apostle tells us, there is but *one faith*, or system of saving truth, to all Christians; and when we further consider, that to man religion is a forced state, that is, not his natural state, the calculation is very wild, that he will seek and find it in the naked knowledge of the facts and doctrines of the Scriptures.   But,

III. Thirdly, from the agency of the HOLY SPIRIT in giving effect to the word of GOD, the principle under consideration is shown to be erroneous, dangerous, and eventually destructive of all revealed religion.

No doctrine of Christianity is more firmly established, than that of the exclusive necessity of spiritual illumination to a right understanding and application of the Scriptures ; and it is equally sure that the HOLY SPIRIT is given to lead us into all needful truth.   Is it thence to be assumed, however, that the simple volume is necessarily accompanied by the SPIRIT OF GOD, and that every impression made on the mind of the reader of that volume, is *the witness of the* SPIRIT to the truth and certainty of the interpretation he comes to ? Have we any warrant, from what is revealed to us of the connexion of spiritual influence with the written word of GOD, to believe that such is the agency of the HOLY GHOST upon inspired men ? Yet such is unavoidably the extent, to which the favourite principle of this and other Bible Societies carries the essential doctrine of Spiritual influence.

According to the principle, the Bible is to be exclusively interpreted from itself : according to the doctrine of the Scriptures, no saving knowledge and application of divine truth can be had, but by the operation of the HOLY GHOST. It, therefore, follows, if the principle be true, that the effect produced through the word of GOD read, must be received as the immediate dictate of the SPIRIT by the person under its influence, and, indeed, by all others.

This, it appears to me, is the unavoidable conclusion, assuming the principle to be well founded. Whether it is intended to be carried this far, may reasonably be doubted ; but whether intended or not, an awful responsibility is incurred, by sanctioning so dangerous a position, on a subject of such vital interest, by such an imposing weight of character as Europe and America have leagued in its favour.

With whatever intention, however, a more erroneous notion could not be suggested ; for it goes the whole length of making every man's private imagination the test to him of saving truth, and sanctions the destructive, but prevailing, notion, that the discordant and opposite views of Christian faith and practice which deform the gospel, have all alike the witness of the SPIRIT OF GOD that they are the truths of GOD, and equally to be relied upon for salvation. But is such the doctrine of the religion we profess? Is the hope given to man, by the revelation of JESUS CHRIST, built upon so sandy a foundation? Are its fundamental doctrines, wise directions, and bright examples, of so vague and indeterminate a character as to give countenance to so broad a delusion? I ask Christian men—I ask men who stand forward as Christian teachers—I ask men who say they reverence the Bible, and wish to present it as the best of all gifts to their fellow-men; and I beseech them to meet the question, not under the influence of assaulted feeling—not under the calculation of party interests—but under the solemn influence of that account which we must all give in to GOD: in particular, I intreat those who are capable of embracing the argument in its extent—who are competent to try its truth and soundness—to reflect, that they owe to others, not so gifted, the benefit of their counsel and example; and that, however popular an error may be, it is not, therefore, the less, but the more, injurious, and demands the united efforts of the wise and good to counteract its effects. In the case before us, it appears to your preacher, that the best interests of pure and undefiled religion are at stake—that they are compromised on grounds most difficult to meet, because ostensibly fortified with zeal for the interests of the Redeemer's kingdom. Yet there is a zeal without knowledge, which is to be guarded against, and the surest guard must forever be a close adherence to that system of divine truth, and prescribed ministrations, which GOD hath indissolubly joined together, for the assurance of faith to man in the hope of the gospel.

Under the influence of this principle, I have taken the view of the subject now submitted, conscious that I throw myself in the face of high authority, of strong prejudice, and inconsiderate feeling. But what then? If this is never to be done, where is the stopping place for error to be found? And if the ministers of the sanctuary shrink from this duty, who else shall stand in

the gap ?   On this, and on all other points, I hold and act upon
the principle, that the temperate arraignment of what we believe
to be error at the bar of public opinion, is the truest friendship
to those who entertain the error, and the only lawful means of
defeating its influence. I speak not a word this day, my hearers,
against the free and full distribution of the word of GOD.   No,
GOD forbid !   I speak only against an unfounded and dangerous
principle, which Bible Societies have adopted and consecrated,
and declared unalterable, in the articles of their constitution.   I
speak not a word to repress your zeal and liberality in the cause
of religion but, according to my poor ability, to give to that
zeal a right direction, and to make that liberality fruitful and
lasting in its effects ; to preserve it from evaporating in hypothe-
tical good ; and to return it back into your own bosoms tenfold,
in the happy fruits of sound knowledge and pure religion, instilled
and established in your own hearts, in the hearts of your children, your neighbours, your countrymen, and the world.   This
must all be done from the Bible.   It is our only warrant—it is
our only weapon.   The Bible is alone sufficient to heal the divisions among Christians ; but this surely never can come to pass,
under the operation of a principle which sanctions division without limit, and consequently ends in the subversion of all revealed
religion.   Nor can it be brought to pass, by carelessly casting
out a dollar, or an hundred or a thousand of dollars, to aid in
printing and circulating the Scriptures.   No : to obtain this
blessed end, the Bible must be imprinted upon our own hearts,
and reprinted in our lives—its types must be set in the hearts
of our children, and the same impression struck off, in each
succeeding generation.   There is no new version, no new edition,
of the spirit of religion—*it is the same, yesterday, to-day, and for
ever ;* and thus must its triumphs extend, from families to kindred,
to country, to the universe.   It is the order which GOD, *the only
wise* GOD, hath appointed ; which he hath promised to bless : it
is the order of all other events, under the control of his providence : and only by conforming thereto, can we entertain a
reasonable hope of success.   Let us not, then, depart from it,
in the great concern of our own souls, and the souls of others,
however specious the theory may seem.   Let our liberality in

the things of God be regulated by the terms of that trust-deed, whereby they are committed to our stewardship; and our sense of its true meaning and interpretation be guided and directed by the universal consent of that body of holy men, who heard with their own ears the exposition of those to whom were committed the words of eternal life, by the Great Head of the Church. Then shall the Bible, indeed, speak *the mind of the* Spirit and the gospel be found *the power of* God *unto salvation to every one that believeth.*

In conclusion, I recur to my text. It has been kept out of view——but not, I trust, out of remembrance——by the course of the argument. Its application, however, cannot be mistaken.

Understandest thou what thou readest? This is a question, my friends, which enters into the very essence of spiritual attainment from the Scriptures. Religion is, throughout, a reasonable service. Nothing connected with its hope, and its comfort, its assurance and its reward, is divested of this distinguishing feature. Nor can these rightly be claimed or entertained, without rendering a reason for them.

Suppose the Scriptures in the hands of one, of whom, to our shame as a Christian nation be it spoken, we have multitudes. He can read, perhaps; yet with such incoherence, that attention is absorbed in mastering letters and syllables. What to him is the word of life? It is a task book——a work of labour—— which, after a few efforts, he abandons. Suppose this done away——that he reads fluently, yet without intellectual cultivation: what can he gather, beyond the law written in his own and every other heart by the finger of God, except a mass of vague and undigested notions, equally at war with reason and religion? *Understandest thou what thou readest?* must ever bring from him, if he is an honest inquirer after truth, the answer of the Ethiopian——*How can I, except some man should guide me?* My Christian hearers, I think I have but to appeal to your own experience on this subject. With all your advantages, understand you what you read, in your daily application to the Scriptures? Are there no depths which you cannot fathom——no mysteries which you cannot penetrate——no connexions which you cannot make out? How, then, are those into whose hands they fall, in fact, as a revelation ; and who are refused all guidance, but from the word itself—how are they to compass what is attainable *of the length, and breadth, and depth, and height, of* GOD's *rich redeeming love ;* and trace the connexion and dependence of prophecy, promise, and fulfilment, as bound up with the hope of man ; and in this boundless field of heaven's mercy, find *the strait and narrow way which leadeth unto life ?* Does heaven warn us needlessly *that few there be which find it ?* Are there no parallel paths marked out by the invention of men, which an uninstructed traveller may mistake for the King's high-way—the royal road, trodden by the King of kings himself, in faith and obedience, and marked with the assurance of a verifiable signature ? Are there no cross roads and intricate divergencies, all professing to point to the City of Refuge, which are, nevertheless, unmarked and unverifiable, unless by a counterfeit signature ; and, though much trodden, are yet, comparatively, but newly opened ? Is there no need of a pilot—an instructer, a guide, through this labyrinth ? Are we to turn loose the ignorant in Christian lands, and the Heathen in Pagan lands, to wander unguided through the mysteries of revelation—oppressed by its discoveries—uncomforted by its ministrations—and deprived of those authorized guides and interpreters of his word, whom GOD hath bound to faithfulness at the peril of their own souls ? No, my Christian brethren, let us hear them calling unto us in the words of the Ethiopian in my text—*How can I, except some man should guide me ?* and, with the word of GOD, send them the Church, and the ministers, and the sacraments of GOD. Then shall the end and the means correspond, and the ravishing spectacle be presented to an admiring and adoring universe, of a redeemed world, furnished with the light of life, and made wise unto salvation, with one heart and one mouth ascribing *glory, honour, and dominion, unto Him that sitteth upon the throne, and to the Lamb for ever.*

A SERMON,

ON

THE STUDY AND INTERPRETATION OF THE SCRIPTURES,

DELIVERED IN

THE EPISCOPAL CHAPEL, RALEIGH, ON THE 20th OF MARCH, 1825;

BY

THE RIGHT REVEREND JOHN S. RAVENSCROFT, D. D.,

BISHOP OF THE DIOCESE OF NORTH-CAROLINA :

And published by the Vestry.

A SERMON

ON THE STUDY AND INTERPRETATION OF THE SCRIPTURES.

JOHN v. 39.

"Search the Scriptures."

MUCH, my brethren, depends upon the importance we attach to the Bible, and the unqualified dependence we place in it, as the infallible word of GOD. Much also depends upon the disposition with which, and the manner in which, we consult the divine oracles, to draw from them that *knowledge which is able to make us wise unto salvation*. That they are the well spring of life and hope to fallen man, and the infallible rule of his faith and practice to every Christian, is assented to by all. Yet that the Scriptures are so framed, that we may pervert them to support and defend almost any preconceived system of doctrine, is equally evident, from the actual condition of the Christian world. Hence the great importance of sound and correct views of divine truth, and of such information as shall render the duty enjoined in my text both pleasant and profitable, and guard you against the awful ruin of building your hope for hereafter upon perverted Scripture. And hence my duty, rendered more imperious by recent circumstances, to take up this subject for your edification, and, as I humbly trust, for the edification of many, on a subject of vital interest to all, embarrassed by many specious, but fatal errors.

I shall therefore, in the

FIRST place, lay before you some observations calculated to direct you to a safe and satisfactory compliance with the Christian duty of searching the Scriptures.

SECONDLY, I shall endeavour to obviate some prevailing and popular errors on this fundamental subject. And then

CONCLUDE with some plain and practical inferences from the

whole.   And may the SPIRIT of truth preside over my meditations ; and your attention.

Search the Scriptures.

I. First, I am to lay before you some observations, calculated to direct you to a safe and satisfactory compliance with the Christian duty of searching the Scriptures.

1. As the Scriptures to which our blessed LORD referred, in giving this direction to those to whom the words were spoken, were the Scriptures of the Old Testament—that testimony of JESUS, which GOD was pleased to commit to the keeping of the Old Testament Church ; we are fully warranted in asserting the identity of the two dispensations, and in considering the New Testament as perfective of the old.   This is a point of great importance, my brethren, to any rational fulfilment of the duty enjoined in the text ; inasmuch as by separating the two dispensations, we neutralize both, and expose ourselves to every variety of deception which interested ingenuity can draw from a partial view of divine truth.   To search the Scriptures, therefore, to any profitable purpose, we must begin with the foundation, and regularly go on to the finishing of the superstructure ; and *comparing spiritual things with spiritual*—that is, a recorded purpose with its exact fulfilment—obtain that full conviction of the infallible truth and divine authority of revelation, which is indispensable to any thing worthy the name of rational assurance, in working out our everlasting salvation.   For, as nothing can induce us to commence this work but the full persuasion, drawn from GOD's public message to the world by his only begotten Son, that GOD invites and commands us to it ; so nothing can encourage to perseverance, amid the trials and disappointments of our condition, but an equally fixed reliance on the promised guidance and help of the HOLY SPIRIT.   From first to last, my brethren, *we walk by faith and not by sight.*   And faith, to deserve the name, and become a foundation for eternity, must, in its commencement, and throughout its whole progress, rest upon a divine and verifiable warrant—*Thus saith the* LORD.

2. To search the Scriptures, however, does not mean simply *to read* them, and acquaint ourselves with the facts and doctrines therein contained.   Hundreds have done, and yet are doing

this, without profit. The duty enjoined and under consideration, involves the careful examination and comparison, not only of the several parts with each other, but of each part with the whole. This is evident, not only from the reason of the thing, and the general purpose of revelation, but also from the particular circumstances under which the words were spoken. The unbelieving Jews, having rejected the evidence of John the Baptist to the person and office of JESUS as the promised Messiah, and resisted the testimony of our LORD's own miraculous power in attestation of the same fact, are by him referred to their Scriptures. *Search the Scriptures,* said he ; *for in them ye think ye have eternal life, and they are they which testify of me.* In which reference to the Scriptures, it must be clear that our LORD meant such a careful consideration and comparison of what was foretold by the prophets concerning the Messiah, with the events then fulfilling before their eyes, as must be sufficient for correcting their erroneous prejudices, and for producing a rational conviction of the truth. In like manner, my hearers, must we lay aside our prejudices, and with sincere and ready minds desire the whole truth, if we would search the Scriptures to advantage, and draw from them the bread of life.

3. Another consideration, my brethren and hearers, of the last importance to a safe and profitable fulfilment of this duty, is a just view of *the unity* of Scripture—that is, of the connexion and dependence of all the parts with and upon each other, and of the end and design of the communication, as a whole. Of this unity, I have no hesitation in asserting, that it is as complete as that of its glorious Author. *The Scripture cannot be broken,* says our blessed LORD. It cannot be taken to pieces, and made to subserve systems of conflicting doctrine and practice in the religious world. This must be evident to the slightest reflection, from its acknowledged purpose, as a standard—an infallible measure, of saving truth ; which it never could be, were it allowable and safe to take a part here and a part there, in order to patch up the semblance of a support for those many inventions which presumptuous men have sought out.

As this is a cardinal point, my brethren, standing upon such undeniable grounds of authority and reason, that none can excusably be ignorant of it, or neglect it, I feel bound to press it upon your most serious attention and observance ; and this the rather, because it is beyond contradiction, that a broken Scripture is the root of those divisions which deface and defeat Christianity, and the prevailing snare in which the ignorant and unwary are taken captive *by the cunning craftiness of men who lie in wait to deceive them ;* and because it is equally beyond dispute, that the carelessness or easiness of public opinion is yielding to the assertion of a contrary doctrine by those whose foundation can only be found in a partial or mutilated view of divine truth.

In searching the Scriptures, therefore, their unity is never to be lost sight of ; for it is this alone which can preserve us from being led away by false doctrine, and seduced into the specious, but dangerous delusion of marking out a plan of salvation for ourselves, at variance, in some of its features, with that which heaven has revealed and prescribed.

From this sacred unity also, duly estimated and applied, we learn, that no conflicting or opposite doctrines can equally claim the warrant of GOD's holy word. If, therefore, we are at any time inclined to construe any part of the Scriptures in such wise as to conflict with any other part, or with its general import, we may be sure beforehand that such construction is, to say the least, doubtful, and not to be relied upon as an article of the faith. Deep and mature examination is necessary before we commit our souls on the truth and certainty of a doctrine which has any thing opposed to it, in *the letter* of Scripture even—to say nothing of the *general tenor* and *design* of that blessed communication to sinners. All reasonings, however specious, must go for nought, if in their result the Scripture shall be broken, and the unity of its purpose and meaning be severed or perverted.

Bearing in mind then, my brethren, these three essential rules, to wit : the identity of the Old and New Testament dispensations ; the careful comparison of the more obscure delineations of the gospel contained in the Law and the Prophets, with their fulfilment and completion in the person and doctrine of JESUS CHRIST, and the teaching of his apostles, and the unity of Scripture in the connexion and dependence of all its parts as a whole ; you will be furnished to fulfil the duties enjoined in my text with advantage : while at the same time, you will be guarded against the ruinous influence of a partial and unconnected view of divine truth, that fruitful source of all the divisions which deform Christianity, and which encourage and increase the infidelity of a *world that lieth in wickedness.*

Profitable, however, as these rules unquestionably are, and essential to any just and saving view of the word of life, there is yet one more of the deepest interest, and without attention to which, those before mentioned are neutralized if not defeated. And that is *the rule of interpretation* of Scripture, as the one standard of the *one faith* of the gospel. Now, my brethren and hearers, while it is indubitably certain, that "holy Scripture containeth all things necessary to salvation, so that whatsoever is not read therein, nor may be proved thereby, is not to be required of any man, that it should be believed as an article of the faith, or be thought requisite or necessary to salvation," as it is expressed in the sixth article of the Church ; it is neverthe-less equally certain, that uniformity of belief and practice among men—in other words, Christian unity, must depend upon the interpretation given to the Scriptures—upon the sense and ap-plication made of the doctrines and precepts therein revealed. It is, therefore, of the last importance to the very being of the Scriptures as the only standard of saving faith, as well as to the comfort of your own souls, that your minds should be grounded and settled on this point. To this end I shall give the rule, and then explain and enforce it by some plain and obvious examples.

The rule then is, "That interpretation of Scripture is to be followed and relied upon as the true sense and meaning which has invariably been held and acted upon by the one Catholic and Apostolic Church of CHRIST."

In explanation of this rule, it is to be borne in mind, my brethren, that while GOD hath fully and clearly revealed his will to us, yet he hath so done it as to form a part of our trial. While all things necessary to salvation are set forth in his word for our learning, Scripture is nevertheless so constructed, that *the unlearned and the unstable can wrest it to their own destruction* ; and the word of the gospel is either *a savour of life or a savour of death,* as we receive and apply it.   Now if this was the case in the apostolic age, as St. Peter and St. Paul both declare that it was ;   much more is it possible, and to be expected, in these days of multiplied divisions and latitudinarian departure from the faith : and, therefore, the more earnestly to be contended against by those who are *set for the defence of the gospel.*

If the inquiry then be, which of two or more conflicting doctrines or systems of religion be the right one, and to be received and relied upon as the truth of GOD?   I answer, first, *How readest thou ?   What saith the Scripture ?*   Is one of the the doctrines or systems clearly revealed therein ; or reasonably without force and refinement, to be deduced from what is thus revealed ?   Is it free from opposition to the other doctrines and general design of revelation ?   If so, there need be no difficulty. The doctrine or system thus supported is to be received as true.

But suppose the ingenuity of man's wisdom, in support of some favourite system, shall have thrown over the subject such a gloss of perverted Scripture and specious reasoning, as to render it difficult for a plain mind to disentangle the sophistry of the argument, and for a humble mind to resist the authority of great and learned names and numerous bodies of professing christians built upon this system : what then is the only standard to which we can have recourse?   To this, I answer : the word of GOD, as received, believed, and acted upon universally, by the primitive church—that body of holy confessors and martyrs, who received the true interpretation of every doctrine from the lips of inspired and infallible men—who themselves kept the faith and order of the gospel, and committed it, pure and unadulterated, to faithful men—their successors in this mighty trust —who watched against every innovation, fearlessly denounced every heresy, and kept the Church, what it was constituted by its Almighty Head, and what it is called in the inspired volume, *the pillar and ground of the truth.*

And I hazard nothing, my friends, by asserting in the most unqualified terms, that this method of determining disputed doctrine must be admitted and acted upon as the only safe rule, or the Scriptures be abandoned as containing any practical standard of faith. There is no medium, my brethren, between this standard and none. For, however desirable, however necessary it may be to the comfort of those numerous bodies of professing christians, whose systems of doctrine are opposed to each other though drawn from the same Bible, that the standard of faith should not be determined by this rule; yet certain it is—nor can the principle be controverted—that of opposite views of divine truth, one only can be the true one. From the nature of things, both cannot be right; and which of them is so, can no otherwise be determined, than by comparing them with the standard, as above explained.

As this is a point of great importance to you, my brethren, and indeed to all who hear me, I shall endeavour to illustrate it, by some examples of opposing doctrine.

Whether the doctrine of a trinity of persons in the unity of the GODHEAD, or the opponent doctrine of a unity not thus constituted, be the true interpretation of what is revealed to us concerning this point of the faith; evident must it be, from the very opposition of the terms, that both doctrines cannot be true, and equally safe to those who entertain them.

Whether the essential divinity of the man CHRIST JESUS, or his mere humanity, be the true doctrine of the Scriptures; certain it is, that one must be false, and false in such wise, as to be fatal to those who hold it.

Whether the redemption wrought out for sinners by the sufferings and death of the Son of GOD; be general, that is, for all mankind; or particular, that is, embracing only certain persons styled the elect; is a question of the true or false interpretation of Scripture, involving the very possibility of religion, as the highest duty of rational redeemed creatures. Yet one of those doctrines, with all that is built upon it, must be false and unfounded.

Whether the punishment of the impenitent and ungodly, in a future state, shall be eternal; or only for a limited duration, issuing in universal salvation; is a question of Scripture well or ill interpreted, which involves the very essence of moral obligation from man to his Maker, and from man to man.

Yet, my brethren and hearers, it is within your own observation, that these opposing doctrines, with many others which I have not time to notice, are all held by different bodies of professing Christians, as the infallible truth of revelation——who declare the most unqualified belief of their truth and certainty, and claim, without a blush, the witness of the HOLY GHOST in their favour, from their success in making proselytes.

In like manner of those doctrines of revelation which relate to the Church of GOD, as a means of grace and assurance to man, in working out his eternal salvation.

Whether the Church of CHRIST, which he *purchased with his own blood* is a divinely instituted, visible society, built on the same foundation, professing the same faith, and united in the same doctrine, discipline and worship; or a loose, unconnected medley of separate assemblies, the creatures of human presumption or convenience, holding opposite doctrines, and inculcating opposite practices; is a vital question to the hope of man for hereafter, which depends on the interpretation of Scripture, and can be true only of one.

Whether the ministry of the Church of CHRIST is by divine appointment, and of three orders; or of human convenience, and of one grade; is a question which meets the Christian at the very entrance of his course, and can only be settled by the word of GOD rightly understood, and cannot be true of both.

Whether a divine and verifiable commission and authority is requisite, to give effect to the sacraments of the gospel, as instituted means of grace; or whether they are equally valid and efficacious, by whomsoever administered; is an inquiry which enters into the continually recurring duties of the Christian, and involves his title to the covenanted mercies of GOD: one of which must be false.

Yet these doctrines, you also know, my brethren, are variously held, and even considered as secondary and unimportant points, by numerous bodies in the Christian world. Yet surely they are a part of that revelation which GOD hath given us, and dependant for their truth or falsehood on the interpretation of his word!

Now, let us suppose, for a moment, a plain, sincere person, truly desirous of the truth of GOD, but perplexed with these conflicting doctrines, of all of which he finds something said in the Bible, yet sees them differently held by the various religious denominations around him: how is he to find, among them, *the rule of faith*—that standard of belief and practice, which all, nevertheless, admit is to be found in the word of GOD? Is he to expect a miraculous direction of the HOLY GHOST, as some most ignorantly and dangerously teach? Even under this discussion, he is no nearer his object, for all claim the witness of the SPIRIT of GOD for their respective systems: but it is utterly impossible that all should have it, without admitting the horrid blasphemy, that the HOLY GHOST gives equal testimony to the truth of doctrines so opposite, that both cannot be true. Is he, in this case, to have recourse to the judgment of men? The difficulty still continues. The men themselves are at variance, and one will deny what another affirms. Is he then to consider it a matter of such entire indifference what system of belief he embraces, that personal preference and convenience may determine his choice? This would be to reverse all certainty, in a matter of such moment: inasmuch, as it exalts human opinion in religion into a standard of the Scriptures, instead of bringing down human opinion to the word of GOD, as the only standard in matters of saving faith.

What then, my hearers, is the only resort? To what quarter can he turn his perplexed mind, but to that cloud of Christian witnesses who *continued steadfastly in the apostles' doctrine and fellowship, and in breaking of bread, and in prayers*—that is, to the primitive Church—as the best expositor of the obscure parts of Scripture—the sure and safest guide to the truth of conflicting doctrines and practices. But it may be said, this, after all, is an appeal to the judgment of men. In one sense, it is so. But to what sort of men? To men, who saw with their eyes the miracles which established the gospel; who heard with their ears, the instructions of infallible guides; who spent their lives in the faith and order established in the Church by the apostles, and sealed the truth of that faith and order with their blood.   Whether they are competent to decide, judge ye.

Thus have I shown you, my hearers, the importance and the application of the rule given for determining the true sense of Scripture, as the one only standard of faith and obedience; and though the view taken has necessarily been brief, I think I can appeal to the understandings of all present, whether it is not both reasonable and effectual ; and competent, moreover, if duly observed, not only to preserve every sincere person from departing from *the faith once committed to the saints*, but to arrest the spreading mischief, and to awaken and bring back the multitudes who blindly and inconsiderately, but not excusably, have committed their souls to a security on which they would not risk their worldly interest.

II.   I come now, as was proposed in the *second* place, to obviate some prevailing and popular errors, on this fundamental subject.

1. And first (because most extensive and injurious in its operation,) the principle acknowledged and acted upon by all anti-episcopal denominations, that "the scriptures are exclusively sufficient for their own interpretation."   Now, my brethren and hearers, if these words have any practical meaning, it must be this; not that men *may* draw from the Bible those directions which shall be sufficient to secure their salvation, if faithfully followed, but that they *will* do so.   As this, however, must depend on the true or erroneous interpretation given to the Scriptures by each individual person, the principle itself is hereby shown to be, both theoretically and practically, unfounded. Of this, I conceive, there needs no other proof than the actual condition of the Christian world, with its hundreds of discordant and conflicting professions of faith and practice—all drawn from the same word of GOD—when contrasted with the spirit of Christianity, and with the affecting prayer of the great head of the Church, at the close of his ministry upon earth—*that they all may be one, as thou Father art in me, and I in thee, that they also may be one, in us.*   But were other proof required, it is easily found in those summaries of doctrine which many of those

bodies who assert the principle have nevertheless provided, to instruct their respective members in what they conceive to be the true meaning of scripture; thus manifesting, either the insufficiency of the principle, or its dangerous tendency : and, beyond dispute, nothing but disunion and division, without limit, can grow from such a root.

2. In support of this principle, and as a kind of corrollary from it, it has come to be considered as the dictate and the duty of an enlightened charity to look upon all varieties of religious profession as right—that is, right in such a sense, as to be safe for salvation.   And it is beyond denial, that whoever attempts to expose the fallacy of this notion, lays himself liable to the charge of bigotry and intolerance—not only from Christian denominations, but from infidel contenders for some share of the Christian name.   Now, my brethren and hearers, as this is one of the most specious deceptions with which revealed religion has to contend—as it is fortified in its operation by an erroneous and modern view of the doctrine of Christian charity—as it is rendered captivating, to the young and thoughtless, by being tricked off with the epithet of *liberality*, and meets in the secret chambers of the heart something like the wish, that it could be so—I feel it my bounden duty, to arm you against its seducing influence, and to furnish you, and all who choose to profit by it, with such a short and convincing refutation, as can be met by no fair argument of reason, or authority of revealed religion.

If all varieties of Christian profession are right, in the sense of being safe for salvation, then none are right—there is no such thing as revealed religion in the world—there is no assurance of faith—there is no comfort of hope, to man, for hereafter : and this I say upon the sure ground, that no power, not even omnipotence (with reverence be it spoken) can make *contradictions* to be *the same thing*.   If all are right in the above sense, the Scriptures cannot be an infallible standard of faith and duty. They only serve to give us information, which every man is at liberty to use as he pleases ; and from this the transition is easy, to the entire neglect of them.

3. But it is said—and it is relied upon by those who have a miserable interest in the prevalence, and establishment, of a

misdirected judgment—that all the conflicting denominations of Christian profession, nevertheless, hold the great fundamental doctrines of the Christian revelation, and differ only in *non-essentials*—as they venture to call them.

But, my hearers, this is not the fact, as respects the fundamental doctrines of the gospel; unless, indeed, actual, known, and published, opposition of professed belief, on some, if not all, of those doctrines, be to hold them as a common stock. Is the extent of the redemption that is in CHRIST JESUS—that is, whether it extends to all, or only a part of mankind—a fundamental doctrine of the Christian revelation? And can those who are opposed to each other on this point, be said, with any show of common sense, to hold the doctrine in common? Is the essential divinity, or the mere humanity, of our Redeemer, (considered as conclusive of the doctrine of the Trinity,) a fundamental doctrine of Christianity, or a non-essential? And can the opposite opinions upon this article of the faith, be said to hold it in common? Why, where is the resentment of the public understanding, at such a barefaced insult to its power of discrimination.

But it may be said, that the Unitarians stand alone, and incur the censure of all other denominations of professing Christians. But why so? Upon the principle, that Scripture is exclusively sufficient for its own interpretation, and that all varieties of belief are equally right, that is, safe for salvation; I ask, and I wait the answer—What privilege has the Calvinist or Arminian, in the interpretation of Scripture, which is not equally due to the Unitarian or the Universalist? And thus, perhaps, may be seen and felt, how unfounded and fallacious—how dangerous, and destructive of all revealed religion, such an erroneous principle must be.

With respect to those points called non-essential, to which their differences are affirmed to be confined, there is a complete deception, either of themselves or of others; for it betrays an unpardonable ignorance of the nature and design of religion, to assert that the only wise GOD, who doeth nothing in vain, hath revealed any thing to the faith and obedience of his creatures, which they are at liberty to treat as *non-essential*—that is, of no practical importance. But it is denounced as uncharitable and illiberal, to deny the soundness of such opinions ; and many who doubt them, are deterred from following out their doubts, by reason of this popular notion. Yet sure I am, my brethren and hearers, that it is not Christian charity that is hereby wounded ; for the charity of the gospel, properly understood, has no application to *opinions*. It can have no fellowship with error in faith, or corruption of doctrine. In fact, it is bound to oppose them. It is to *persons* only, especially to those labouring under the fatal consequences of religious error, that the beauty and efficacy of this divine grace can be manifested ; whereas, the modern notion of this doctrine is the reverse of this, instilling the persuasion that its right exercise regards opinions chiefly. But were this so, who does not see, that religious truth and error would be of no importance ? It is, therefore, a perversion of the doctrine of Christian charity, and fatal to its very existence, as a Christian duty : its certain and only fruit being indifference, and not love.

With respect to the *illiberality* of denouncing error, either in doctrine or practice—as the Scriptures know nothing of this word in such a connexion, nor yet of what is meant by it—so neither do I : I will, therefore, only say, that those are commonly most earnest in requiring it, who, whether they know it or not, stand most in need of its exercise towards their own opinions on religious subjects.

III. I might pursue this investigation, my brethren, to many other delusions of the same kind ; but as time fails me, and they are all to be detected by the application of the principles laid down for your guidance in searching the Scriptures, I shall conclude with a few plain and practical inferences from what has been said.

1. If such be the effectual nature of the provision made for our religious comfort and edification in the word of God, it must be our bounden duty to cleave to it with earnestness, affection, and diligence. To remain wilfully ignorant of, or unaffected by, the mighty discoveries of revelation, betrays such a disregard of God, and our own souls—such a contempt of his promises and threatenings, and so great a preference of the world—as

deserves to be given over to a reprobate mind; and, as this is threatened—has been inflicted—and is yet in operation, it should awaken and alarm all, who are conscious of this neglect, to escape from the snare, *before the things which make for their peace, are for ever hid from their eyes.*

2. As the Scriptures are so constructed as to form a part of our trial; and offer and supply the treasures of divine wisdom, in preference, to the humble, teachable, and desirous soul; it should be our constant care to acquire and retain this temper and habit of the mind—carefully guarding against all prejudices, whether of natural disposition, or acquired inclination—ever ready to receive instruction from those who are qualified, or authorized, to impart it; yet not blindly and implicitly, but with concurrence of the understanding, certified by obvious agreement with *the law and the testimony* of Scripture; that so, *the word being received into an honest and good heart,* and nourished with prayer for divine grace and direction, may *bring forth fruit with patience.* For mysteries are yet revealed unto the meek, while, in the order of the divine wisdom, they are *hid* from those whom our Saviour styles *the wise and prudent.*

Lastly. As the holy Scriptures contain the standard, or only infallible rule, of faith and practice; our chief care should be, to be in all things conformed to this pattern: not, as the manner of some is, considering some parts more important than others; but wisely judging all to be of such vital consequence, that only as we are found in agreement therewith, can we take to ourselves the comfort and assurance of those *promises,* which are then, and not otherwise, *yea and amen to us, in* CHRIST JESUS.

Wherefore, my beloved brethren, as ye are *built upon the foundation of the apostles and prophets,* JESUS CHRIST *himself being the chief corner stone,* and are *made wise unto salvation,* through the word of life furnished in the Scriptures; *therefore, be ye steadfast, unmoveable—not carried about by every wind of doctrine—always abounding in the work of the* LORD; *for as much as ye know, that your labour is not in vain in the* LORD.

To whose holy name be glory and praise, now and ever—world without end. AMEN.

A SERMON,

PREACHED

AT THE CONSECRATION OF CHRIST CHURCH,

𝕽𝖆𝖑𝖊𝖎𝖌𝖍, 𝕹𝖔𝖗𝖙𝖍=𝕮𝖆𝖗𝖔𝖑𝖎𝖓𝖆,

ON SUNDAY, DEC. 20, 1829,

BY

THE RT. REV. JOHN S. RAVENSCROFT, D. D.,

LATE BISHOP

OF THE PROTESTANT EPISCOPAL CHURCH IN THE DIOCESE OF NORTH-CAROLINA.

PUBLISHED BY THE VESTRY.

A SERMON,

PREACHED AT THE CONSECRATION OF CHRIST CHURCH,
RALEIGH, N. C.

I KINGS vi. 11, 12, 13.

"And the word of the LORD came to Solomon, saying, 'Concerning this house
which thou art in building, if thou wilt walk in my statutes, and execute my
judgments, and keep all my commandments, to walk in them ; then will I perform
my word with thee, which I spake unto David thy father. And I will dwell
among the children of Israel, and will not forsake my people Israel.' "

The connexion of the text with the purpose which we have
met to accomplish, and the services in which we have been
engaged, must be sufficiently obvious, I presume, to all present ;
and the train of thought necessarily thereby suggested to every
serious and well ordered mind, must lead to the solemn considerations which are connected with our religious condition, as the
provision and appointment of the most wise and merciful GOD,
for the present and eternal good of his rational creation. The
range is indeed a wide one, my brethren and hearers ; too wide
and extended to be fully followed out in the reasonable compass
of a single discourse : yet, in the leading particulars which it
suggests to our meditations, there will be found abundant matter
for edification to all present ; while there will not be wanting
sufficient grounds of encouragement and satisfaction to those
who have devoted their time and their substance to provide this
appropriate accommodation for the public worship of Almighty
GOD. *And the word of the LORD came to Solomon, saying,
' Concerning this house which thou art in building, if thou wilt walk
in my statutes, and execute my judgments, and keep all my commandments to walk in them ; then will I perform my word with thee,
which I spake unto David thy father. And I will dwell among
the children of Israel, and will not forsake my people Israel.'*

The reflections suggested by this passage of Scripture, and by the context, in connexion with the present occasion, point to three subjects of general edification, which I shall present in their order; and then conclude with an application of the whole.

I. First, the subject of religion in general is necessarily presented to our consideration, by the particular circumstance to which the text refers.

On this subject, it is all important, my brethren and hearers, that we entertain just views; a mistake, either as to its nature, its derivation, or its application to moral condition, must be attended with danger, and can only lead to some false and spurious exhibition of an unfounded hope. Yet on no other subject, perhaps, with which men engage, is there less previous thought bestowed, even by serious persons; and, as a natural consequence, upon no other is there so great a variety, both of opinion and practice.

If, then, it be inquired, "What is religion?" the answer is ready, That it is the cultivation of the divine nature and image, impressed upon moral beings at their creation. It is the rendering to the glorious and underived Author of all being the homage of the affections, the conformity of the will, and the obedience of the conduct, singly and unceasingly. This is religion as exhibited before the throne of GOD, by those pure and holy beings who have never swerved from the love of their Creator. This is religion, as enjoyed and practised by our first parents, before their apostacy from GOD, and will be that of their posterity, when, purified from the corruption of their nature, and recovered to holiness by the grace of the gospel, they shall be restored to the bright inheritance forfeited by sin. But such is not, cannot be, the religion of sinners. A religion calculated for fallen, depraved, and corrupt creatures, alienated from GOD, must be suitable to their condition, commensurate with their powers of moral improvement, and calculated to try and to prove the sincerity and strength of their faith. Faith, as a moral virtue, as a religious duty, is unknown to the religion of heaven. But on earth, it is the foundation on which the entire superstructure is built up, and without which the whole aim, purpose, and design of religion is defeated, and its attainments rendered impossible.   The religion of heaven is neither derived from revelation, nor enforced by command, nor produced with effort, nor assisted by sacraments as means of grace, nor encumbered with ministers and places, and times and seasons for the performance of its holy duties.   No, my brethren ; the love of GOD is the unmixed element of their being, and its exhibition in adoration and praise, the spontaneous offering, the overflowing of the ravished spirit, the unceasing and happy employment of those pure and uncontaminated spirits who dwell for ever in the presence of GOD, and derive from the unveiled brightness of the heavenly glory, continual increase of love, and joy, and peace, and blessedness unspeakable ; whereas the religion of redeemed sinners is a prescribed and limited institution, with ritual observances, and outward and visible ordinances, in the hands of an appointed ministry ; all derived from express revelation—authorized by divine appointment—enforced by positive command—attainable only through the painful efforts of watchfulness, self-denial, and mortification of the natural inclinations —and after all, prompted and wrought out in the desire, and enlightened and assisted in the endeavour, of the fallen creature, by the divine grace of a divine Saviour, as the source and spring of "all holy desires, all good counsels, and all just works."

In our estimate of religion, therefore, to confound what is peculiar to our condition as a state of trial and moral improvement, with what belongs to the same thing, under opposite circumstances ; and thence to decry, undervalue, and cast away ritual observances and positive institutions as weak and beggarly elements, unworthy of our care and observance ; is to make shipwreck of the faith, and, in the unbridled license of a heated imagination, to surrender the soul to the deceits of an inexplicable mysticism, or to the equally dangerous delusions of an enthusiastic and unbalanced mind.   While, on the other hand, to be wise above what is written, in departing from the revealed appointments and commanded duties of the wisdom of GOD for the attainment of eternal salvation, is to vacate revelation as the foundation of faith, and to incur the awful risk of being surrendered to that strong delusion which GOD threatens to send upon those *who receive not the love of the truth that they might be saved.*

Yet all wish to be saved—yea, we may say with truth, that all *hope* to be saved—that there is not one in this congregation—no, not one, even in the wide range where the Christian revelation is known, or in the still wider range, where "darkness covers the earth and gross darkness the people"—who does not hope, on some principle, true or false, that another state of being will place him in unchangeable enjoyment. For, my hearers, in the very elements of his nature, man is a religious being ; and though fallen, degraded, and blinded, and, over the greater part of this poor world, alike ignorant of GOD and of himself, yet claims relationship with eternity, and intuitively seeks to propitiate and appease the unknown GOD, whom he fears, but cannot love. And it is well worthy of your serious notice, my friends, that man never has been found in the circumference of this world, so devoid of intellect, and degraded in condition, as to be divested of all religious impression. Yea, more than this—he hath no where been found collected into a community, without exhibiting the shadow of that substance contained in the revelation we are favoured with. The temple, the priest, the altar, and the victim, of the grossest and most disgusting superstition, set the seal of universal humanity to the fundamental truth that sinners can approach GOD acceptably only through a representative, and be cleansed from guilt no otherwise than by an atonement of blood, washing away the defilement of sin.

To a testimony thus universal, in favour of religion, we refer, on the present occasion, as calculated, in the judgment of your preacher, to arrest the prevailing disposition of the present day to strip the religion of the gospel of its peculiar distinctions and external rites, to divest them of the sacred character of divine appointments, equally bound upon our observance with the body of revealed doctrine, and to reduce the Christian system to the nakedness of an abstraction which may safely be modified according to the convenience or the caprice of individual inclination. That the influence of some such mistaken principle is at work in the world is rendered certain, not only by the existence of those divisions which deform the beauty, and destroy the unity of the gospel, but still more by the indifference and disregard manifested by the great majority of our population to any mode or form, under which it has been attempted to render Christianity more palatable to the pride and prejudice of a depraved nature. That this exists to an alarming degree, in all Christian lands, cannot justly be questioned; and to account for it, we must resort either to absolute infidelity, or to indifference, on the grounds just mentioned. And the consciences of all present, who are, unhappily for themselves and for their country, unconnected with the gospel, can best witness to which of these two causes their disregard of God's gracious and only provision for the salvation of sinners is to be referred. For it is not my province to judge, my hearers; but it is strictly so to give you grounds on which to examine and judge yourselves.

Of absolute infidelity—that is, of actual rejection of revelation—none present, I trust, stand convicted to themselves. On the contrary, I am almost sure, that belief of the Scriptures, as a revelation from God for the good of mankind, would be the serious confession of all who hear me. To the delusion, then, that the great purpose of the gospel, in their eternal salvation, can be answered without the external profession, the practice, the fellowship, and the sacraments of religion, must this neglect be referred. Otherwise, rational beings must be convicted of the desperate folly of deliberately choosing and following out their own perdition.

Yet, my dear friends and fellow sinners, what but perdition of soul and body in hell, must be the consequence to those who, under the *grace and truth which came by* JESUS CHRIST, pass their short and uncertain period of probation and improvement for eternity unconnected with the requirements of the gospel, and regardless of the conditions on which alone the mercy of God is tendered to a world of sinners? Remember, I beseech you, in the first place, *that* God *hath no need of the sinful man;* therefore, salvation is wholly of grace. *Of his mercy he saved us by the washing of regeneration, and renewing of the* HOLY GHOST. In the second place, remember that God *now commandeth all men, every where, to repent* and *believe the gospel;* because *he hath appointed a day in the which he will judge the world in righteousness.* And in the third place, bear in mind, that *except a man be born again*, except he be *born of water and of the* SPIRIT, and do *eat the flesh and drink the blood* of the divine Saviour, in the sacraments of his death and resurrection, this salvation is unattainable. And most earnestly and affectionately are we cautioned by the HOLY SPIRIT, in the word of GOD, not to be wise in our own conceits—not to listen to the self-righteous pride of our corrupt hearts, tempting us to hew out cisterns of salvation for ourselves, and by departing from prescribed conditions, to cast away from our hope the precious promises of GOD, ratified in the blood of CHRIST.

II. Secondly, from this passage of Scripture, in connexion with the building of the temple at Jerusalem, we are led to inquire into the design and obligation of ritual and ceremonial appointments in religion.

I think it must be admitted, my brethren and friends, that in the degree in which the circumstantials of any positive institutions are respected, will the institution itself be esteemed, or lightly regarded. The inquiry, therefore, I trust, will not be without its use, as a subject of general edification on the great concern which I wish to impress upon your consciences this day.

It is very true, that though religion is in itself prior to, and independent of, all ritual appointments, and external accommodations—yet, never in this world has it been presented to mankind, abstracted from outward and visible observances, as a part and an essential part too, of every dispensation revealed to the faith and obedience of redeemed man. The patriarchal, the Jewish, and the Christian dispensations of *grace given us, in* CHRIST JESUS, *before the world began*, had, and have, each of them, peculiar rites and positive institutions, which, under some variety of modification, have continued integral parts of each succeeding dispensation of revealed religion; and as their origin was the same, so was the purpose they were intended to answer, in the economy of divine grace.

In their origin they come from GOD; they are of his appointment, and only as such can they be the objects of faith to ra-

'tional beings, or be required of them as religious duties. Their obligation, therefore, is supreme, and binds every soul under the particular dispensation to a faithful observance of what is thus appointed. Of this, we have a very instructive example given us in the earliest record of the worship of his Creator enjoined upon fallen man. The rite of sacrifice, being the chief external observance of the patriarchal religion, and the animal and the manner of the offering being expressly designated, a departure on the part of Cain, the first-born from Adam, from what the ALMIGHTY had prescribed for his observance, was visited by rejection of his unbidden offering. Presenting an awful warning to will worshippers of every age, and a most pointed condemnation of those many inventions of men, wherewith the gospel is both disfigured and impeded.

The positive institutions, common to every dispensation of revealed religion, are five in number—viz: The day of rest, or Sabbath, or Lord's day; as it has successively been called, in commemoration of the finishing of the works of creation; marriage, or the union of one man and one woman in holy matrimony; the rite of sacrifice; the priestly office, to minister in holy things; and the temple, or place set apart for the public offices of religion. And by considering the design or purpose of Almighty GOD in the appointment of the three last mentioned, as more directly connected with the subject, we shall more clearly understand their obligation for our observance.

1. And first, of the rite of sacrifice as a divine institution.

Now this was evidently, in the first place, to show to the sinner the utter hopelessness of his condition, from any thing in himself. That he had become unworthy to approach GOD, even as a worshipper. And that, as his own life was forfeited to the divine justice, by his disobedience, he could never hence forward be heard or accepted, but through a divine Mediator.

In the second place, the appointment of an animal slain by the shedding of its blood, was intended to keep alive among mankind the knowledge and effect of the first and most gracious promise made to fallen man: that in the fulness of time the seed of the woman should overcome the enemy of the human race, deliver mankind from the power and dominion of sin, and by offering an adequate atonement to the offended justice of GOD, restore them to his favour, and recover for them the bright inheritance which was forfeited by sin.

And, in the third place, to furnish a visible channel or means of divine grace, through which only can fallen, spiritually dead creatures, be regenerated; that is, restored to moral competency, and rendered capable of religious attainments.

This is a design, my brethren and hearers, which, while the world shall continue to be peopled with successive generations of sinners, must needs be continued in operation ; and only as it is truly realized, and heartily embraced and followed out, can those successive generations escape from the curse and condemnation which rest upon unbelief, with the superadded guilt of rejected salvation.

2. Secondly—Of the priestly office.

To minister in holy things, and especially to serve at the altar, offering gifts and sacrifices to GOD for man, is the natural right of no sinful mortal. It must be conferred by the Almighty, and be certified to be so conferred, not only to avoid presumptuous sin on the part of the offerer, but to give certainty and effect to those outward and visible religious ordinances, which by the appointment of GOD, have an inward and spiritual grace annexed to their due administration and reception. From the beginning, therefore, it has been so ordered, that *no man taketh this honour unto himself.* Under the patriarchal period, the priestly office was the privilege of the first-born son. Under the Jewish economy, a particular tribe, that of Levi, was set apart by divine direction for the service of religion generally ; and in that tribe a particular family, that of Aaron, was specially selected for the succession to the highest grade of the priesthood, as then modified. And under the Christian dispensation, the Author and finisher of our faith selected the twelve apostles, who were eye witnesses of his resurrection and ascension into heaven, as the visible and verifiable root from which the succession of the Christian priesthood should be derived, to the end of the world. When, therefore, we consider the inseparable connexion betwixt a sacrifice or a sacrament, as divine institutions, and a priest or divinely authorized person, to offer them to GOD on the part of others—when we reflect on the signal manner in which the contempt of this high distinction—as in the case of Esau—or the invasion of its sacred rights—as in the case of Corah and his company in the wilderness, and of king Uzziah, who was smitten with leprosy because he attempted to burn incense upon the altar—was vindicated ; the obligation to reverence the office, and to profit by this provision of the wisdom of God for the regular and effectual administration and participation of the sacraments of the gospel, must be understood and felt by every serious person.

It has indeed been contended, that the priestly office ceased with the Jewish dispensation ; and that, as there are no longer proper sacrifices to be offered up to God, the ministerial office under the gospel is not a proper priesthood; not to be estimated according to what was particular to it under the law.

Into this question I enter not on the present occasion, further than to observe, that the assertion itself, and the argument constructed for its support, are derived from the necessity of those who, in comparatively modern times, have assumed the ministerial office without due warrant and authority : and that the whole is founded on the erroneous notion that the priestly character is confined to the acts of sacrificing and offering the victim ; whereas, in truth, the priestly character is derived altogether from its being a representative office, instituted to administer the things of God to and with men ; dependent wholly on the mediatorial scheme of religion, to continue until that scheme shall be completed, and of the same sacredness and obligation, whether the sacrifice offered be proper, as of a slain animal, or symbolical, as in the eucharist. Every priest, lawfully called and set apart to his holy office, from the first born under the patriarchal dispensation, to the apostolic succession of the present day, has been, and was intended to be, a representative of our great High Priest, the man Christ Jesus. The material sacrifices of slain beasts, and purification by the sprinkling of actual blood, have indeed been abrogated by the offering up of the body of Christ, once for all.   But the representative sacrifice of his death, and of the purification of his atoning blood, still continue to be administered in the sacraments of the

Church; and derive their whole benefit to us as instituted means of grace—receive their true character as sacraments from the authority to consecrate and administer them as divine appointments.

GOD hath indeed most wonderfully provided Himself and us with a Lamb for a burnt offering. This *Lamb of God, which taketh away the sins of the world,* the worthy Christian communicant discerns by faith, as slain for him, in the sacrifice of the cross. By faith he offers this to GOD, through the appointed channel of the Christian priesthood, as the substitute for his own forfeited life, a spiritual sacrifice, acceptable to GOD; and partaking of the bread of life, by eating the flesh and drinking the blood of the great sin offering, under the appointed symbols of consecrated bread and wine, he derives therefrom the strength and consolation which faith imparts to the soul, and that measure of divine grace which enables him to hold fast his profession without wavering, and to *press towards the mark for the prize of the high calling of* GOD *in* CHRIST JESUS.

3. Thirdly—Of the temple, or place solemnly set apart for the public offices of religion.

That proper accommodations for the performance of the public duties of religion are indispensable to a visible society of professing believers, we are taught, my brethren, not only by the precepts and example of former dispensations, but by the reason of the thing. As we are commanded *not to forsake the assembling of ourselves together,* there must be a suitable place to assemble at. And as the Christian sacrifice of the Eucharist is continually to be offered, *until our* LORD *shall come again,* there must be an altar and a priesthood for the sacred purpose. In the infancy of the world, indeed, and before it became expedient to institute the Church as a visible society, every family, every particular household, possessed an altar, and a priesthood thereat to serve, in the person of the head of the family or of the first born son. But when the corruption of religion, the increase of idolatry and wickedness, and the approach of the appointed time for the fulfilment of the original promise, rendered it necessary to select a particular family from which the Messiah should spring; the Church in its distinctive and particular character, was called into being, and constituted the sole depository of the revealed will, prescribed worship, precious promises, and enlivening presence of their GOD and Saviour. And when, in process of time, the increase of their number and their deliverance from Egyptian bondage, rendered a place of public assembly for the performance of their religious services necessary, GOD was pleased to command the erection of the tabernacle in the wilderness, and afterwards, of the temple at Jerusalem, as habitations for his holy name ; as places to receive the offerings of his worshipper, and to dispense his blessings to his people, through the divinely appointed office of the priesthood : as he also was pleased to manifest his acceptance of the buildings, by a visible display of his glory at their respective dedications.

In like manner, when our blessed LORD had purchased to himself a kingdom, by finishing the work which his Father had given him to do, he founded his Church, his mystical body, and sent forth his servants, the apostles, to teach all nations—to proclaim the glad tidings of a reconciled GOD, of the pardon of sin, and of eternal life through faith in his name ; and to receive into his Church by baptism all who should embrace their doctrine. These, his faithful servants, accordingly went forth and preached every where ; GOD, *also, bearing them witness, both in signs and wonders, and with divers miracles and gifts of the* HOLY GHOST, *according to his own will ;—so that believers were the more added to the Church.* And as *their* numbers increased, and the circumstances of the times permitted, *they,* too, erected places of worship, and solemnly dedicated them to the service of Almighty GOD. It is true, we read of no miracles indicating the acceptance of their houses of prayer, on the part of Almighty GOD ; neither have we any certain information of fixed places for the performance of Christian worship, during the period that miracles were wrought in confirmation of the gospel. While exposed to the persecuting Heathen power, Christians were obliged to meet *secretly* and as they *could,* for the performance of their sacred solemnities. Yet, whether in private houses, in the recesses of some forest, or in the concealment of some cavern of the earth, they were still the Church, the peculium of GOD ; and whether in Rome or Jerusalem, in Greece or in

Egypt, in Asia or in Africa, they collectively formed that one visible body, of which CHRIST is the Supreme Head and Almighty Saviour ; of which every national Church, derived from the apostles of CHRIST, is a branch, and every particular congregation a member ; against which no weapon formed shall prosper ; against which the gates of hell shall not prevail ; and with which CHRIST hath promised to be *present*, by his SPIRIT, *to the end of the world.*

Such, my brethren and hearers, is the gracious and merciful provision which the wisdom of GOD hath made in the external and positive institutions of religion, for the furtherance and help of our faith.   A Church, a ministry, and sacraments, are indispensable to the religious condition of fallen, sinful beings, reprieved from condemnation, and placed in the hand of a Divine Mediator for recovery and salvation. The whole economy of grace, therefore, is so constructed as to keep before their eyes, in the boldest relief, this master-principle of encouragement, exertion, and success ; and with a design so gracious, a provision so excellent, and an obligation so commanding, it is deeply to be lamented that so few, comparatively, are drawn by these cords of love to the Father of Mercies, for that eternal life which is in his only begotten Son—that under the *light* of the gospel multitudes of accountable immortals pass through their day of trial and grace without opening their eyes to the light—and, that under the *preaching* of the gospel, still greater numbers resist the convictions of divine truth, and say to their consciences, *Go thy way for this time ; when I have a convenient season, I will call for thee.*

III. In the third and last place—From this passage of Scripture we have confirmed in a very striking manner the reasonable and unchangeable conditions on which alone the promises of GOD can be attained by us.   The conditions are, a full, unreserved, and sincere obedience to the revealed will of GOD—a thankful reception of his offered mercy, through our LORD JESUS CHRIST ; and a diligent cultivation of the means of grace, for the attainment of that *holiness, without which no man shall see the* LORD.

And the word of the LORD *came to Solomon, saying, Con-*

cerning this house which thou art in building, if thou wilt walk in my statutes, and execute my judgments, and keep all my commandments, to walk in them; then will I perform my word with thee, which I spake unto David thy father: and I will dwell among the children of Israel, and will not forsake my people, Israel.

These are the conditions on which, to you also, my friends and hearers, as to Israel of old, the promises of GOD are suspended; and you must fulfil the conditions, on your part, otherwise you forfeit the glorious reward held out to your hopes. Revealed religion, remember, is a matter of strict covenant engagement, and to every baptized person is strictly a personal contract. In this contract you have solemnly engaged, on your part, to "renounce the devil, the world, and the flesh"; and "diligently to keep GOD's holy commandments": and on his part, your Heavenly Father hath engaged to give you the assistance of his Holy Spirit, to enable you to perform your engagement; and to reward your faith and obedience with eternal life. To expect it, therefore, on any other conditions, is the grievous folly of expecting to reap where you have not sowed, and to be transferred to a situation for which you have made no preparation.

That the promises of GOD are conditioned on our faithfulness to the baptismal engagement, is an awakening thought at all times; and particularly so on the present occasion, my brethren of the Church, when the cloud which has so long hovered over your prospects appears to be withdrawn, and the promise of a brighter day to be dawning around you. Almost against hope, and through various disappointments, the zeal and liberality of a few praiseworthy individuals have succeeded in erecting a commodious and respectable building, in which to worship the GOD of your fathers and to participate in those sacred ordinances which are the divinely appointed channels of grace to your souls. This building you have surrendered to GOD, and called upon me, in virtue of mine office, to consecrate and set it apart, exclusively, to the worship and service of his holy name. This duty I have performed this day, before many witnesses, and before GOD the Judge of all. I have laid before you the nature of your religion —the design and obligation of the positive institutions connected with it—and the conditions on which alone can this or any other religious advantage be truly profitable to you.   Before these witnesses, then, and before that heart-searching Eye, which now looks down upon us, I charge you to bear in mind and faithfully to fulfil the conditions on which only will his promised blessings continue with you.   Bear in mind, my brethren, that this house is now separated from all unhallowed and common uses.   Be diligent therefore, to discharge from your hearts the unhallowed love of the world, and from your lives the too, too frequent conformity with its vain and vicious practices ; lest by your irreverent coming into his presence, you profane that which is now *holiness unto the* LORD.   *Keep thy foot when thou goest to the house of* GOD, says the wise preacher and king of Israel to his people.   That is, prepare for the solemn service of GOD, by searching your hearts, and trying your spirits, and examining your lives, in the retirement of your private devotions. This will preserve you from *offering the sacrifice of fools* in a mere unmeaning lip service—will enable and prepare you to pray with the understanding for the relief of particular wants, and with the fervency of spirit for general blessings.   *Come out from among them, and be ye separate, saith the* LORD, *and touch not the unclean thing, and I will receive you; and I will be a father unto you, and ye shall be my sons and daughters, saith the* LORD ALMIGHTY.   And thus preached the inspired apostle St. Paul, to the fashionable Christians of the dissolute city of Corinth.   From his Epistles to them, it would appear that they were fond of the shows and feasts made in the idolatrous temples; of the exhibitions and games presented in the amphitheatre and circus ; and of the other vanities in which wealth, idleness, and irreligion, sport away the burden of their superfluity. But such, St. Paul well knew, *was not the spot of* GOD's *children;* and to reclaim them from this vicious and ruinous conformity with the world, he showed them, by arguments of reason; how every way inconsistent such conduct was with their holy profession.   *What communion hath light with darkness ? and what concord hath* CHRIST *with Belial ? and what agreement hath the temple of* GOD *with idols ?*   And to stir them up to higher and better things, he sets before them the promises of

GOD, and reminds them of the high privileges they were entitled to as his adopted children. And the same precious promises, and the same exalted privileges are yours, my brethren; but on the same conditions of distinct separation from the vanity and ungodliness of the times. Therefore, my beloved brethren, *touch not, taste not, handle not;* but *come out* from among the votaries of the world, *and be separate ;* as in profession, so likewise in practice. Study to *adorn the doctrine of* GOD *our Saviour in all things*, keeping ever before you *the hope of your high calling*, and the unchangeable conditions on which only *the promises of* GOD *are Yea and Amen to us, in* CHRIST JESUS.

I come now to apply what has been said.

If I have not failed altogether in my object, I cannot but hope that the attention with which I have been favoured, must already have suggested this reflection to many, who are yet strangers to the power and influence of religion :—" Why have I been so long negligent of that which is of such infinite importance and immeasurable obligation ?" And have you been able, my brother, to answer the question otherwise than by confessing it to be by your own proper fault ? And if not, what is the improvement which both reason and interest will tell you should be made of the discovery ? Surely it must be the part of every ingenuous mind, which has been betrayed into carelessness and indifference, hitherto, on the great interests of eternity, or into an erroneous view of revealed religion, to rouse from the delusion, and to search and look into those things which are presented to its consideration, with such a show of reason, and on such high authority. Surely it may be expected, that those for whom a gracious GOD hath done so much, will at least inquire what their part and duty is as redeemed to GOD, called to the knowledge of his grace, and furnished for the attainment of eternal life, through faith in the LORD JESUS CHRIST. Otherwise, eternal life and endless felicity in the presence of GOD can have no attractions, and everlasting misery and despair no terrors, to rational beings.

Yet, reasonable as this expectation surely is—and GOD grant it may be realized even in one instance this day—I fear it will be in vain. Practical unbelief is so common—disregard and indifference to religion so general—and the love of the world, and exclusive engagement with its pursuits so prevalent, as to stifle and silence the occasional awakenings of the conscience. But let me entreat you, my dear hearers, to reflect where this disregard of GOD, and of your immortal souls, must end—to consider how conscience will be quieted when it awakes upon a death bed, under the agonies of an unprovided-for eternity—under the remorse of abused mercies, disregarded warnings, and a rejected Saviour.   O, that I could raise up a spirit of consideration and inquiry on this unspeakable interest.   Surely there is yet left to us so much of Christian knowledge, of enlightened reason, and of moral worth, as might form a wall of defence for what remains of Christian principle and Christian practice, could it but be prevailed upon to step out and avow itself as on the LORD's side.   But alas! my brethren, we must take up the lamentation of the prophet, over Israel of old—*The whole* HEAD *is sick*—the learned, the noble, and the wealthy of the land—the *heads* of society, with a few shining exceptions—for which GOD be praised—are *ashamed of the gospel of* CHRIST. *The whole* HEART *is faint*—the middle class of society, the *heart* and strength of our country are doubting and divided, scattered and peeled by every wind of doctrine which can blow from misguided zeal, misplaced ignorance, honest error, and dishonest deceit; while all *below*, the poor and the ignorant of our population, is *full of the wounds and bruises and putrifying sores* of blasphemy, drunkenness, and sensuality. Oh! what an account has this every way favoured land to give in to GOD the judge of all!   But it must be given, remember, my dear hearers, by its *individual* population; for *nations*, as such, cannot answer at the judgment seat; and in the dread account which awaits this generation, the influence of example will not be overlooked.

And may GOD in mercy, impress his truth upon every heart present.

Now to GOD the Father, GOD the Son, &c.

THE

DOCTRINES OF THE CHURCH VINDICATED

FROM

𝕿𝖍𝖊 𝕸𝖎𝖘𝖗𝖊𝖕𝖗𝖊𝖘𝖊𝖓𝖙𝖆𝖙𝖎𝖔𝖓𝖘 𝖔𝖋 𝕯𝖗. 𝕵𝖔𝖍𝖓 𝕽𝖎𝖈𝖊;

AND

THE INTEGRITY OF REVEALED RELIGION DEFENDED

AGAINST THE

"NO COMMENT PRINCIPLE" OF PROMISCUOUS BIBLE SOCIETIES;

BY

THE RIGHT REVEREND JOHN S. RAVENSCROFT, D. D.,

BISHOP OF THE DIOCESE OF NORTH-CAROLINA.

PREFACE.

In presenting the following pages to the public, the author conceives it due to a reasonable expectation, to account for the delay which has intervened between the appearance of the Reviews of his printed Sermons in the Literary and Evangelical Magazine, and the reply now published. This delay was occasioned by the constant demand, upon his time and thoughts, and upon his personal labour, in the duties required by the care of an extensive Diocese, in travelling for six months of every year —in the correspondence consequent on his station—and in the preparation necessary to the discharge of the weekly and other duties, arising from the charge of a particular congregation. These, as of the first obligation, have occasioned repeated and extended interruptions in preparing the work for press; and they are mentioned, as forming a reasonable ground of excuse for the delay—and of allowance for any want of connexion, either in the train of thought, or in the arrangement of the argument. Much is felt to have been lost from this cause. Yet it is hoped, that nothing of material consequence to any of the leading points in the controversy, has been overlooked.

To have entered minutely into every question, which the ingenuity, the necessity, or the hardihood of assertion of his adversary, presented, would have been endless. The main points only, therefore, have been taken up; yet these have swelled into a small volume, in spite of every care to curtail unnecessary discussion. This the Author knows, is against him. Numbers will read a paragraph, or a pamphlet, who shrink from undertaking to read a book.

In this respect, the command of a periodical publication is of great importance. And Episcopalians have grievously to lament their own backwardness and supineness in this behalf—and to suffer from the superior discernment manifested by dissenters, in furnishing this means of disseminating their respective tenets, and providing for their defence. It is not however a recent discovery, that men are more alive and alert in the cause of error, than in the cause of truth. It has been so from the beginning, and will continue, while our fallen nature predominates. Yet the lesson is an impressive one; and the more minutely the inquiry is carried forward in this direction, *viz.* that of literature and the press, the more evident will it appear, that the steady, progressive aim of the most learned and respectable body of the dissenters in this country, perhaps in any country, is to obtain possession of the schools, academies, and presses of the land. They are able men, calculating men, united men, and well know the moral power of these two mighty engines.

Let Episcopalians then take a lesson from them. *Fas est ab hoste doceri.* It is not yet too late. A quarter of the union and exertion on our part, which they put forth in this behalf, would be sufficient to counteract all their efforts; would prove like the worm at the root of Jonah's gourd, withering the lofty and spreading expectations wherewith they are filled.

Let Episcopalians also take a nearer view of their distinctive character, that they may learn to respect it. They will then put forth their abundant ability to support and defend it. It will become venerable in their eyes. It will become dear to their hearts. It will be considered a desirable legacy, to bequeath, pure and unmixed, to their children.

The work now offered to their patronage, will give them some insight into the high and heavenly nature of their foundation, as *the Church of the living* GOD. It will point out to them the only safe and scriptural ground for assurance of the exceeding great and precious promises of GOD our Saviour, made over to his Church through JESUS CHRIST our LORD. It will show them, with what fear and alarm the preaching of these irrefragable truths strikes their adversaries; to what desperate shifts they are driven to evade or avoid their effects; and how impregnable is the faith and order once delivered to the saints, to all the force of assertion, and to all the artifices of false reasoning.

That the distinctive character of the Church of CHRIST has

long been lost sight of in this southern country generally, and was almost merged and sunk into nothing more than the name of a particular sect among Christians, is beyond the need of proof. That advantage was made of this circumstance, and high and towering hopes built upon it, by one dissenting denomination at least, is demonstrated by the hostility manifested by that denomination in chief, on the announcement of this distinctive character by the Bishop of this Diocese. Yet it must be revived, and, at whatever risk, restored to its place in the estimation of Episcopalians, or the Church will dwindle into insignificance. To that end, it must be preached, and explained, and enforced by all those commanding motives which give life and power to the obligations of revealed truth.

And as the Bishop would have proved a traitor to the trust reposed in him, had he failed to rouse the members of the Church put under his care, from the torpor induced by the opiate of a spurious modern charity ; so would he prove an unfaithful watchman, did he suffer the arraignment of her pure and primitive doctrines to pass unnoticed, and unrepelled. These have been arraigned as Popish and even as Anti-christian, by a writer in a periodical work published in Virginia ; and much exertion has been put forth, to give a false impression of their influence on the civil and religious liberties of this country.

Against this unfounded, and most ungenerous appeal to prejudices, which were gradually wearing out, the author has endeavoured to defend the Church, her doctrines, her ministry, and her members ; and now commits to the consideration and support of the Episcopal body in particular, and to the public at large, this sincere, though very inadequate, endeavour, to rescue the cause of truth from the misrepresentations of an adversary less scrupulous, as to the means made use of to gain his point, than is consistent, either with Christian candour or literary fairness.

DOCTRINES OF THE CHURCH VINDICATED.

SIR,

It having suited your sense of duty, your inclination, or your interest, to pass your judgment, as a theologian and a Christian, on several of my published sermons ; and having stated to the world your deep regret, at being obliged to oppose the doctrines advanced by me—not only as unsound, and unwarranted by Scripture, but as calculated to stir up a spirit of contention and uncharitableness, detrimental to the progress of true religion·: it becomes my bounden duty, not only to examine carefully my own foundation, but also to weigh and consider impartially the facts and arguments adduced by you, in opposition to the principles laid down and supported by me, in the sermons in question, as the *truth of* GOD as contained in his *revealed word.*

To be instrumental in impeding the progress of CHRIST's religion, even unintentionally, would be cause of the deepest sorrow to my soul. To be the means of producing, or of increasing, contention among Christians, would cover me with shame and confusion of face. But to be justly chargeable with withholding from them any part or portion of GOD's *revealed will*— to have upon my conscience the overwhelming load, that for the fear or for the praise of men, I had refrained from declaring *the whole counsel of* GOD—would expose me to a condemnation so deep and desperate, that I dare not encounter it ; though the alternative shall be the loss of your favour, and the denunciation of the whole dissenting interest of this wide extended country.

The question between us, Sir, is of the fundamentals of religion —of those things which enter into the very essence of the hope given to man, in the gospel of our salvation. It ought not, therefore, to be trifled with, or discussed with a view to obtain a victory in a literary contest, but as bearing upon the everlasting welfare of our fellow creatures, and upon the account you and I have to give in to God. As such, I am pleased that I have the opportunity given me by your opposition, to bring the doctrines I have advanced to a fresh scrutiny, and to a strict examination of their spiritual soundness, under the objections of so able an adversary as Dr. Rice. And still better satisfied I should have been, had the subject been so treated by you, as to spare me the unpleasant task of exposing the perversions of my words and meaning, to which you have permitted yourself to descend.

In meeting the course you have pursued in your Review of my Sermons, therefore, I shall first notice these perversions to such an extent, as to require from you an explanation of the cause of such unfair and such unjustifiable conduct, as being equally due to the public and to me : and as every number of your Review is justly liable to this charge, in order to avoid repetition, where either my language or my meaning is perverted in one number and repeated in any of the others, I shall include both under the same statement, noting the page where it is to be found. Your objections to the doctrines inculcated in my Farewell and Convention Sermons, will next be met in full, and answered in their whole extent. The Bible Society Sermon, and that *on the Study and Interpretation of Scripture,* will be re-considered in the next place, under the full weight of the objections raised against the principles maintained in them. And I shall close with such notice as I think it deserves, of your attempt to fasten the charge of foreign influence upon the Protestant Episcopal Church in this country, and to excite popular prejudice against me, individually.

The public will thus be fairly in possession of our respective principles, and of the grounds on which they rest for the deepest consideration of every accountable being.

As introductory to this examination, I must observe that the general complexion of these reviews is not tinctured with that candour and fairness, which might be expected from a lover of truth in general ; and still more from one who professes so much personal respect for the individual he differs with, and such earnest desire for the promotion of brotherly love among Christians.   This, however, is not to be wondered at.   The best intentioned men are unconsciously swayed by their particular prejudices ; and in nothing is this influence more visible, or more powerful, than in the case of religion.   A sincere man feels keenly, when any part of his dependance for hereafter, is, or appears to be questioned.   If on a particular point he is not fully persuaded, yet is pledged to it by a particular profession of faith ; on that he is still more sensitive : and if, from better and subsequent information, he knows certain points to be so exposed to attack, as renders them justly untenable, which are, nevertheless, distinctive of, and fundamental as to his particular profession ; on these he is still more tremblingly alive to any thing like question or opposition.   Just as a person in possession of property by what lawyers call *a pretence title*, feels anxious, alarmed, and even angry, at any reference to his deed ; and thinks it struck at by the most remote allusion.   And thus has it fared with the Sermons in question.   In three of them, I have not uttered a sentiment, which any Christian minister, believing the Bible, and fully impressed (as every sincere minister of religion must be) that he is acting by divine warrant and in accordance with its precepts, could not as freely advance—nay, I will go further, and say, which he ought not to advance—if he would maintain the dignity of his office, if he would not admit a flaw in his title.   And yet, all whom I call *Dissenters*, as the best understood and least offensive designation—and particularly the Presbyterians—conceive themselves struck at, and lay aside their particular animosities, and take sweet counsel together, and join their forces to withstand this disturber of the common peace, as you are pleased to denominate me.   But surely, if what I advance be the truth as contained in the Oracles of GOD, ought any to be offended who are with the truth ?   If what I advance be *contrary* to the truth, may not the falsehood be shown, without identifying it with any particular denomination of Christians ?   And if it be thus identified, does it not betray a consciousness of defect—the very anxiety and petulence of *a pretence title*, in such as thus act ?   To your skill in casuistry, Sir, this can be no' difficult question, and to that I leave it.

The first perversion of my words and meaning which I will notice, is contained in the December number of your Magazine, p. 638.   After quoting an extract from my Sermon on the Church, you go on to say—

" We would acknowledge as a brother, and heartily join in communion with any one, on this confession of his faith, but Bishop R. will not—and why ?"—" we receive the same Bible, believe in the same Saviour, profess substantially the same doctrines, partake of the same sacraments ; why then do we not belong to the Church ?   Plainly on account of some matters of *outward form and order—because we have not diocesan bishops, and the Book of Common Prayer, and administration of the sacraments.   And precisely because we want these, the preacher thinks that we have departed from that Church, with which* GOD *has made his covenant stipulation, and which* ' is beyond the reach of any *human appointment, addition, or alteration.*' "

Now, Sir, in what part of either of the sermons under your consideration when you penned this paragraph, do you find the remotest warrant for the assertion that '*plainly on account of some matters of outward form and order,*' and '*precisely because we want these,*' you do not, in my judgment, belong to the true Church ? On the contrary, is it not *explicitly* stated in both the sermons, that my refusal to acknowledge the Presbyterians and other dissenters as branches of the catholic and apostolic Church of CHRIST, rests solely on the ground, that their *authority* to administer the affairs of CHRIST'S kingdom, is *not apostolically derived,* and, therefore, *is not of divine right ?*

In my *Farewell Sermon,* then before your eyes, my words are these, page 8th :

" If the *authority* by which any denomination of Christians minister in sacred things cannot be shown to be derived *from the apostles of* JESUS CHRIST, that is, *cannot be verified as a fact ;* such denomination cannot be a branch of that Catholic Apostolic Church in which we profess to believe."

In my *Convention Sermon*, equally under your notice, the same principle is maintained throughout, though not as definitely expressed.   After stating its divine origin——the divine authority of the priesthood, its peculiar covenanted character as the sole depository of the truth, of the people, and of the revealed mercy of GOD, p. 6 and 7 ; I go on to say, p. 8th :

"This is that commanding feature, by which it is to be distinguished by us from all *imitations* of it, by either the piety or the presumption of fallible men ; and it is by tracing it according to this *its specific character*, through all the dealing and providences of its Founder, that we at this day are enabled to discover and distinguish this ark of safety, this special deposit of the promises of GOD to a fallen world, this authorized source of agency between heaven and earth." "For the Church of CHRIST under the New Testament dispensation, is not a new or fresh appointment of GOD, in the sense and meaning commonly entertained, but a continuation of the old in all its essential provisions."

Again, Sir, is there here a word about outward form and order, about Diocesan Bishops and Book of Common Prayer ? Is there in either of the sermons a single passage that can be rightly applied in the artful direction you would give to my open, undisguised, and published declarations on this point ?   No Sir, and you knew it, and your own words shall prove that you did. For, in the fifth, sixth, and seventh of the deductions you have drawn from the two sermons then under review, and which form the heads of the subsequent application of the review, you represent me, *so far truly*, as holding and saying,

"That no ministry ought to be regarded as *authoritative and rightful*, which cannot trace back its descent, and the derivation of its power, to the apostles : but this the Episcopal Church can do."——*Fifth head.*

"Of course, all who do not belong to this Church, are out of the Church of CHRIST ; strangers to the covenant of promise ; without Scriptural title to the hopes of the gospel ; and with no reliance on any but the uncovenanted mercies of GOD. That their ministers are intruders into the sacred office, that they have no valid ordination or sacraments, and do in fact belong to the world, and not to the body of CHRIST."—*Sixth head.*

"Of course, he cannot acknowledge them as brethren, nor hold communion with them, or, indeed, exhort them to do any thing but to amend their ways and seek for the good way."— *Seventh head.* p. 637.

These, Sir, are your own considered and recorded opinions of the principles supported in my two sermons under review ; and after such a statement from yourself, what can be said of so barefaced a perversion as that I have just noticed ? Is it honest as a man ? Is it fair as a scholar ? Is it charitable as a Christian ? Am I to ascribe it to inattention, or to want of knowledge on the subject ? In a man of your standing this cannot be admitted. Am I to charge it then to accidental or wilful misrepresentation ? If I attempt the former, the whole structure of your subsequent argument to the close of the piece, contradicts me. If I resort to the latter, I encounter the whole stream of your denunciation against my uncharitable judgment. Of necessity I must offend either your head, or your heart, perhaps both; or yield the point to this modern craft of controversy. But, Sir, you have mistaken your man. You have tried your hand upon one who does not start at shadows, who is not deceived by the most flowing professions of fraternal love or solemnity of purpose ; who does not fear to tell the theological professor of the Presbyterian synod of Virginia, that he has evaded the question, and escaped into a gross perversion of the plain language and meaning of his opponent: and who confidently throws himself on the public intelligence to sustain him in this charge. He regrets deeply that it is necessary to speak in such terms ; but he has reflected maturely upon it, and is convinced that the time is fully come, when this cunning claim to a liberal construction of the most illiberal and uncharitable conduct must be resisted and exposed ; or it will sweep into the vortex of indifference, disregard, and abandonment, all that is peculiar to or distinctive of revealed truth.

A similar perversion of my words and meaning you have been guilty of, in the review of my *Sermon before the Bible*

Society of North-Carolina—and that in two instances.   They are found in page 204 of the Magazine, and are continued throughout the argument got up as an application or improvement of the review in the succeeding number, more particularly in p. 250, 252, 253.   Page 204—you say,

"If any ask then, in what does his error consist—we answer, that the following appears to be the true state of the case. Bishop R. has, together with his love of the Bible, so high an admiration of the Book of Common Prayer, and such an unqualified devotion to its forms, that he verily thinks that the Bible ought not to be distributed without it.   These strong feelings, and, we are obliged to add, prejudices, have *perverted* his better judgment, and hurried him to the adoption of such opinions as are contained in his Sermon, and to the strange course of conduct which we have seen him pursue.   *We act advisedly when we give this form to our statement.*"

Now a more *false* and *unfounded* statement, never was ventured, even by a writer intending to mislead his readers.   In what part of my *Bible Society Sermon* do you find the Book of Common Prayer mentioned, or even hinted at?   Lay your hand upon it—present it to the public.   But this you cannot do.   It is therefore a wilful perversion.   Nor yet can you show that, in the *manner* and *connexion* in which I have there or elsewhere used the words "Church," "Ministry," and "Sacraments," it necessarily and fairly follows that I meant the *Book of Common Prayer and Administration of the Sacraments.* It is, moreover, a forced and cunning perversion—and proved to be such by the use made of it in the May number of the Magazine, by the construction of the argument there raised upon this unfair foundation.   For it is not to be supposed that a scholar and a divine of your pretensions, and a veteran controvertist, would have resorted to so poor a trick, but on the calculation that he would gain more by the unscholarlike use made of it than he would lose by the subsequent exposure. Especially as the influence and effect of the perversion would have some months the start of its detection and exposure, and would be read and repeated to numbers who would never see any notice of this jesuitical dealing.   In page 251, you further say—

"Now we happen to know what the Right Reverend Preacher means, by *Church* and *Sacraments*."

Will you be kind enough, Sir, to say how you have obtained this knowledge ?   Is it from any thing written by me, in which I have put the Book of Common Prayer on an equality with either the Bible or the sacraments ?   If so, you will be pleased to show it.   Is it from personal intercourse, and exchange of sentiments in conversation ?   You will hardly venture to say so ; for you well know, there never passed more in the shape of language between us than the mere civilities of introduction ; there never passed an exchange of words betwixt us of ten minutes duration ; and never a syllable on any religious topick. Is it from the information of others, that you have ventured this unfounded assertion?   If so, let us know who they are ; that the blame may rest upon the right person.   For you have been misinformed on this and some other things respecting me, which I have to notice.

It is however true, that I wish to be considered second to none, in the reverence and regard I entertain for the sublime, scriptural, and spirit-stirring Liturgy of the Church.   But it is equally true, that it has never entered into my head to place it on a par with things of divine appointment and authority, such as the word of GOD—the Church of GOD—the Ministry of GOD, and the Sacraments of GOD.   And in my *Bible Society Sermon*, I was guardedly careful to avoid the remotest allusion to it.   It suited your purpose, however, it seems, to find it there —and you have not been at any loss for the means.

After the same manner have you perverted my meaning in the use of the words, " without note or comment," in the same Sermon—though not against such plain and express statements, as in the cases mentioned.   If I have any thing to regret on the score of the *Sermon before the Bible Society of North Carolina*, it is, that I did not more explicitly define the sense which I applied to the talismanick words, (for such in truth they. are,) " without note or comment."   Yet I did suppose, and I still think, that, when the whole context showed in what sense I used them—when I contrasted the *practical use* of these words by the Society with the method pursued by the divine wisdom, in the revelation of his will to mankind—and asserted, p. 14, that, "in no case is the word of GOD disjoined from the Church of GOD—the grace of GOD from the sacraments of the Church —and the ends proposed and promised separated from the means provided and commanded. All of which the present system keeps entirely out of view, and is, therefore, so far, at variance with the wisdom of GOD,"—my meaning could hardly be mistaken. Nor do I believe it was, unless by those whose ignorance, prejudices, or interest, rendered them incapable or unwilling to take my fair and true meaning. Still less could I have anticipated, that a man of your calibre, and in the teeth of those specious professions which usher in the Review, p. 193, 194, would have fastened upon this oversight—applied it contrary to the plain and obvious meaning of the context—and used it to construct an argument overstrained in every position, evidently thrown out *ad captandum*, and as far from the truth and soberness due to the substantial difficulties of the subject, as the framer of it is from the candour of his very prominent professions. (See the argument *passim*, in the May number of the Magazine, which is framed exclusively on the gratuitous assumption, that by the words "the Church," "the Ministry," and "the Sacraments," I mean nothing more than the Book of Common Prayer.) But, Sir, when you are assured that in the use of these words "the Church," "the Ministry," and "the Sacraments," I meant only what they express and convey to every plain but sound mind, I trust you will see the necessity, (not only as claiming the character of a Christian divine, but as an honest man, and a fair writer,) of disabusing your readers, and doing justice to me. As you have by this unjustifiable course given strong ground to believe, that this main objection to the principles on which promiscuous Bible Societies act, cannot be fairly met; and as the resort to such a perversion, amounts to a tacit acknowledgment on your part, that the talismanick words, "without note or comment," do virtually amount to a severance of the Word of GOD from the Church of GOD; you surely owe it to the cause of which you are so warm an advocate, to meet the arguments of my *Bible Society Sermon* fairly, and without any perversion.   By the course you have pursued, you give me room to say, (*and I do say it,*) that it is a cause that cannot be defended on any ground of Scripture and reason —that it depends for its whole magic influence on sectarian artifice and delusion—and that every advantage which the Bible is fraught with, and intended to confer on the world, is neutralized if not defeated, by being thus separated from *the pillar and ground of the truth,* and from the sacraments, as the seals of that truth, and from the ministry, as alone authorized to apply them.   While, therefore, I decline any notice of the puerile and hackneyed argument which you have constructed on this gratuitous perversion of my language and sentiments, I stand prepared to meet you, or any other champion of this cause of disorder, confusion, and irreligion, upon the *actual ground* taken in my *Bible Society Sermon;* and though that is confessedly not the strength of the opposition—for it was prepared in a hurry, and under the depressing influence of a diseased body— I nevertheless know that the general principle cannot be shaken, and am willing to meet the utmost that the ingenuity of its adversaries can bring forward, of Scripture authority, and fair argument. The malignant aspersions of the British and American Episcopal Churches however, with which you have spiced and seasoned this piece of popular delusion, will not be passed over, when I come to notice your strictures on this particular Sermon; at present I am only noticing your plain and palpable perversions of my plain words and meaning.

I have next to notice a minor species of perversion, in the gloss you have attempted to throw over my use of the words *identity, interpretation,* and *authority*—words, I did suppose, either in themselves, or in the connexion in which they are used by me, as little liable to be mistaken, and as easy to be understood, as any in the language.   Yet so keen are your fears of the Church and her sound and scriptural doctrines, or so ravenous your appetite to find some occasion against her, that your ingenuity must be put upon the stretch, to find either a foolish or an injuriou sconsequence in all that I have said in behalf of her distinctive character, and of its importance to the assurance of that hope which Heaven in its mercy has given to man through the LORD JESUS CHRIST, and *limited* within the sacred enclosure of that Church which he *purchased with his own blood*, and which is *built on the foundation of the apostles and prophets*, JESUS CHRIST *himself being the chief corner stone.*

On the *identity* of the Old and New Testament dispensations, and in the connexion in which the expression is used by me—I would ask, is it fair that you should confine the word to its most restricted meaning, on purpose to lead your readers into an error, by ascribing a design to me in the use of the phrase, not necessarily flowing from it, or at all connected with my argument, as you have done, page 304 ?   Is the word *identity* never used in the sense of *sameness*, or *agreement—not diverse*—or implying diversity in the sense of opposition ? and in this most common use of the word, is there not *an identity* of origin, of design and of end in the two dispensations ?   Do you design to insinuate into the minds of your readers, that either the parties, the purpose, or the means have been so changed, that the *opposite of identity* can justly be affirmed of either to the other ?   If so—and I see not what else you can have in view—it would be a more manly part to speak it out, and let the public see at once how much of the unity of revealed truth, as well as of the visible Church, must be surrendered, to sustain the great Diana of parity ?   This, Sir, is no trifling point, though it is so little thought of and applied by Christians and Christian teachers of the present day. I, therefore, ask you again—is not the New Testament dispensation of the grace of GOD to the world in such wise connected with, and perfective of, the Old Testament dispensation of the same grace, as could with no truth be affirmed of them, were they not *identical*, in the sense of *implying the same thing ?* And if this shall be the judgment of all sound, impartial, and informed Christians ; what must be thought of the vicious reasoning resorted to by you on this subject, in order to fasten upon the absurdity of asserting that ' the shadow and the substance are the same identically ;' which is no where affirmed ?   " It does seem strange," you say, p. 304, " that it should be necessary to show that two different things are not one and the same thing ! But so it is."   But with all due deference to Dr. Rice—it is not so. No part or purpose of my argument from the identity of the two dispensations warrants the course he has taken. It is a *perversion*, and a perversion springing from that wakeful anxiety on the subject of the ministerial commission (the petulance of a *pretence title*) so prominent in these reviews. His fears, also, expressed in the next paragraph, were premature as to the consequences Bishop R. 'derives from his strange assertion, that the old dispensation and the new are identical.' And, however willing Dr. Rice may be, to answer for what was in the Bishop's mind at the time, it is only another proof how little he knows, either of the Bishop, or of the controversy betwixt them. And really, if the science of *Hermeneutics* has enabled Dr. Rice to draw the just meaning of St. Paul's argument on the two dispensations, in the Epistle to the Hebrews, no better than in the present instance, he had better not trust to it any more, but take to himself the advice he so affectionately bestows on the Bishop, p. 320, ' and learn a better system of Hermeneutics, and take a totally different ground in the interpretation of Scripture.'

Equally evasive and deceptive is the representation you give your readers, of the sense, in which I make use of the words ' interpretation of Scripture.' No man, Sir, knows better than you do, in what sense I used the word : no man, Sir, knows better than you do, the overwhelming power of the rule given in my Sermon *on the Study and Interpretation of Scripture*, and quoted by you, p. 308 : and nothing shows more distinctly your fear of its just application, than the artful manner in which you have led your readers away, from the sense in which the word ' interpretation' is used and applied by me in the Sermon in question, and the *desperate* and *unfounded* assertions of opposition on the part of our standard writers to the rule therein given.

As the rule itself, however, with your strictures upon it, will necessarily call for a full examination, I shall, in this place, confine myself to the perversions of the word ' interpretation' with which you have filled several pages. Page 308, you say,

" Our first remark here is on the unusual language employed by the right reverend author : ' that interpretation, (says he,) is the true sense and meaning, &c.' " " Writers on Hermeneutics are accustomed to say that interpretation is—not ' the true meaning'—but the *act* or *art* of giving the true meaning. But this is a mere bagatelle."

Why then meddle with it, where there was so much more weighty matter ? Was it done that you might again introduce your favourite word *hermeneutics*, and make your plain country readers stare at the vast extent of your learning ; or to gratify that pedantic itch for verbal criticism, which pervades your pages ? But, your authority to the contrary notwithstanding, if the word *'interpretation'* is properly used to express the *sense* given by an interpreter—in other words, the *exposition* or *clearing up the meaning* of a passage—I must maintain that the language made use of by me, in giving the rule, is not *unusual*— " That interpretation of Scripture is to be followed and relied upon *as the true sense and meaning*, which has invariably been held and acted upon—by the one Catholic and Apostolic Church of CHRIST."* This is the rule as given in my Sermon. Now suppose we read it thus—" That *exposition* of Scripture is to be followed and relied upon as the true sense and meaning"— where would be the difference, as to any precision of idea, in understanding or applying the rule? The interpreter or expounder —or the act or art of interpreting or expounding—gives the interpretation or exposition. But this when given, is certainly a substantive thing, and may with propriety be used as I have done it, in the rule in question.

It was not sufficient, however, to make it appear that I knew so little of what I was about as neither to see the consequences of my critical cannon, or to use language proper to convey my meaning to others ; but you must fasten upon the word *'interpretation,'* the artful perversion which graces or disgraces pages 313 and 314 of your Magazine. Page 313, thus you write.

---

* ADDISON, as quoted by JOHNSON, makes this very use of the word—". The primitive Christians knew how the Jews, who preceded our Saviour, *interpreted* these predictions—and the marks by which the Messiah would be discovered—and how the Jewish Doctors, who succeeded him, deviated from the *interpretations* of their forefathers."

"But it may be said that we are referred to the primitive Church as the best expositors of the obscure parts of Scripture; the surest and safest guide to the truth of *conflicting doctrines and practices*. Be it so. Let us then put the rule thus limited, to a plain and simple trial. The pages of our work shall be open to Bishop R. to any extent, if he will only be so kind as to let us know—how the primitive Church, how the martyrs and confessors, understood the Book of Apocalypse, as interpreted by infallible men. We should be most exceedingly glad, too of an inspired interpretation of the Epistle to the Hebrews. Or if the bishop is too much occupied to afford so large an exposition, we should be happy in receiving an explanation of a single chapter (for instance the 9th of Romans) as expounded by inspired men. And if this is asking too much, we will moderate our desires, and try to be satisfied with a solution of the difficulties in Col. ii. 8 and 23; or even if he will tell us how Peter or Paul, or whoever it was that performed the service, understood 1 Cor. xv. 29. Easily contented, however, as we are, we must say, that it has not been kind in those who know how 'inspired and infallible men' expounded 'the obscure parts of Scripture,' to keep back their knowledge all this time from the world."

To this sneering escape from what could not be fairly met, Bishop R. would certainly feel himself fully justified in making no reply, had all the readers of this review the sermon before them. But as this is not the case, he must call their attention to the fact, that in the sermon, the rule itself, and the word "interpretation" used in the rule, is applied *exclusively* to determine the truth or error of *conflicting doctrines and practices in religion,* for which the parties holding them equally rely upon the Scriptures. Of this, its just and profitable application, all the examples of opposing doctrines and practices in the profession of religion, given in the sermon in illustration of the rule, and of the meaning given to the word interpretation, are irrefragable evidence, but totally disregarded by this candid reviewer. Had it been in the purpose of Dr. Rice to meet this point fairly, and to give his readers a just view of the subject, it is not conceived possible that he could have made so wild and unreasonable a perversion, as undeniably he has done. In what way he will account for it, and excuse himself, is hereafter to be seen; as it also has to be reconciled with literary honesty, and the candour of his professions.

It is very true, that Bishop R. has no inspired exposition of the Apocalypse, or of the other passages referred to by Dr. Rice, as it is equally true, that he never professed to be thus furnished. He, therefore, feels himself quite clear of the charge of unkindness, in withholding from the world such valuable information. He is, however, able and willing to show the application of the rule and the use of the word 'interpretation' to the difficulties proposed by Dr. Rice. If, for instance, it shall be disputed whether the 'angels of the seven churches' mentioned in the Apocalypse were diocesan Bishops, or Presbyterian moderators, Bishop R. is able to show that the primitive Church interpreted and understood the word *angels*, of diocesan Bishops, —that is, of a distinct order in the Christian ministry, having the rule and oversight of Presbyters, Deacons, and Churches, and possessing powers never exercised by either of the other two orders. In like manner, should it be asserted that the ninth chapter of the Epistle to the Romans sanctions the doctrines of particular redemption, and unconditional decrees, Bishop R. is able to show, that no such interpretation of that chapter, or of any other part of the Scriptures, was given by the primitive Church; nor were such doctrines known to, or held by, the Church in the three first centuries. And if Dr. Rice will point out any heresy, or other ground of dispute on doctrine or practice, growing out of the other two passages of Scripture referred to— whether it shall be of some *invention of men, intruding into things not seen, vainly puffed up by a fleshly mind*, or of *will-worship*, in separating from the primitive faith and order of the gospel—or even of Romish traditions, the Bishop will do his best to make a faithful application of the rule, to ascertain the sense of the primitive Church on the particular point, and thus exemplify its indispensable use to determine the truth or error of opposing doctrines or practices in the religion of the gospel.

On the use I have made of the word 'authority' in the sermons reviewed by you, a still greater obliquity of understanding in you, or of wilful perversion of my language and meaning, is

VOL. I.—30

to be observed. In the review of my *Farewell Sermon*, p. 595, 596, you thus express yourself:

"The preacher, in the next paragraph, turns to a *truth* before stated, and zealously urges what nobody disputes—that firm faith can only rest on *divine* authority—that nothing merely *human*, can afford any security to our souls. This repetition is made apparently for the purpose of introducing the following sentence. 'How then can steadfastness be exhorted to on a ground which is itself changeable, which our own observation proves to be so by the present state of the Christian world; and having once separated from the root of unity, in the one authority of CHRIST, transmitted through his apostles, goes on dividing and subdividing, till every original feature of the Church is lost, and the great and gracious purpose of Christian union and brotherly love rendered impracticable,' *Farewell Sermon*, p. 8. To the very pertinent question, which this exhibition and dispute would call forth, how is a plain man to come to the truth? The preacher gives two answers: one, the genuine Protestant answer, *Search the Scriptures*. The other, an answer which we are truly grieved to hear from any one, but much more from so respectable a man and minister as Bishop Ravenscroft—*By authority*. 'The Bible, the Bible, is the religion of Protestants.' This quotation from the accomplished but changeful Chillingworth, contains the only remark we shall now offer on this unfortunate position."

And pray, Sir, what difficulty is there in the passage which you hope to be pardoned for not being able to understand? When taken in connexion with the rest of the discourse, does it not plainly refer to the absolute nullity of the Apostle's exhortation in the text; if (as is claimed for them) all the existing and opposite divisions and subdivisions of religious profession are really branches of the one apostolic Church of CHRIST? Can you inform us, how any one is to be exhorted to be stedfast to some hundreds of disagreeing denominations? Or, can you show, how the visible Church of CHRIST is to be ascertained, amid this mass of conflicting pretensions, unless by the possession of apostolic succession? If you can do this, you might have spared yourself a great deal of useless writing, and put these Sermons down at once. But as this is a point of which you are very shy, it was easier to brand the passage which included it, as a piece of nonsense.

And why could you not have met it at the outset? Wherefore was it, that at the very spot where the sense in which I use the word authority is most evident, there, you choose to assert an improper and injurious meaning? Was it to pre-occupy the minds of your readers to prepare the way for an escape from the just use of the word as applied to the existing divisions among Christian denominations? But more than this: if this is such an 'unfortunate position,' why did you not give it to your readers as it stands in the Sermon? Why did you garble the quotation? My words are these, (the question being on *steadfastness*, as reconcileable with existing divisions:)

"But it may be asked, and very properly, How is a plain man to settle a question on which the learned and the pious are so divided? To which I answer, first, *Search the Scriptures* with a sincere and honest desire to find the truth, remembering that *the Scripture cannot be broken;* and therefore every conclusion we come to, to be safe, and agreeable to the *mind of the* SPIRIT must be in agreement with its whole purpose, and not merely with partial and insulated passages of the word." "But, secondly, there is a shorter period, my brethren, and that is, *on the ground of authority*. If the authority by which any denomination of Christians ministers in sacred things, cannot be shown to be derived from the Apostles of CHRIST, that is, cannot be verified as a fact, such denomination cannot be a branch of that Catholic Apostolic Church, in which we profess to believe."

Now, Sir, is it as thus speaking that you represent me to the readers of your review? Or have you, contrary to my plain and obvious meaning, led them to believe that I use the word *authority* in an ill and improper sense? Were you aware, that the divided state of the Christian world is by *no means* reconcileable with the unity of the Church of CHRIST, as set forth in the Scriptures, and commanded to be held and followed by all his disciples, as a practical doctrine, and a personal duty? Did you perceive what a sweeping erasure of the claim to divine authority is contained in this 'unfortunate position,' and that you were bound, at every risk, to keep it from the *notice* of your readers? Really, Sir, you give strong ground to infer that you are at least dubious as to your own foundation, by escaping from so fair a method of ascertaining the fact of divine commission to the ministry, into a perversion of the use made of the word 'authority.'   For I think I can appeal to every reasonable and competent person, whether the use I have made of the word 'authority,' as actually found in the Sermon, is justly liable to the construction you have here given it, resumed at p. 639, 640, continued p. 651, 653, and again resorted to, in the review of my *Bible Society Sermon*, p. 248, and elsewhere.

What connection is there, Sir, between the *ground or source of authority*, as respects the ministerial commission, and the quibbling you have resorted to, on the *authority of the church to decree rites and ceremonies*, and in controversies of faith ?   Were these the points pressed in my sermon ?   No, Sir : but it suited your purpose best to shift the question, that you might bring in the following startling positions, as fairly deducible from my use of the word 'authority,' p. 640.

"Are we to understand, then, that on pain of being cast out of the range of God's covenant mercies, we are to submit to *any decrees,* made by the rulers of the Church, which are not contrary to the word of God."——" In a question, then, as to what ought to be believed, the rulers of the Church have a right to decide, and I am bound to obey ! my conscience must submit to their decisions, otherwise I have no right to hope in God's promised mercy."   "If this is not making man, for the rulers of the Church are but men, the lord of conscience—what is ? It is lamentable, that a Protestant Bishop—a pious, zealous, evangelical preacher, should allow himself to be hurried into such indiscretions, and to use such rash expressions."

Lamentable indeed, Sir, were this a *true* exposition either of his words, or of his meaning as conveyed by his words—But as this is *not* the case, it is equally, if not more, to be lamented, that such should be the hood-winked ignorance of his readers, that the conductor of a periodical publication dare venture to palm upon them so violent a perversion of plain language and plain meaning—and this too, in a case which concerns their souls.   You continue, however, to press it upon them, and at page 651, you thus speak—

"And does a Christian minister think himself authorized to employ the terrible words of an apostle, used on such an occasion as this, towards men whose only sin is, that they *will not lay stress enough* on outward things ; that they will not place the authority of the Church on a level with the authority of CHRIST —that they had rather trust in the promises of GOD made in the gospel, than to the declarations of a Bishop or a priest."

Indeed ! and is it the considered and recorded opinion of Dr. Rice, the Theological Professor of the Synod of Virginia, that the authority by which men administer the sacraments of salvation, and thereby bind and loose upon earth, *is a mere outward thing, on which no stress is to be laid?* For of this, and of this only, was I speaking in the passage in question. Is it indeed of no importance as to the assurance of faith, whether the ministers of religion be self-commissioned—authorized merely by men, or clothed with the authority of CHRIST, as the supreme Head of the Church, and sole Source and Fountain of all spiritual power ? For such is the fair inference from the passage just quoted. Have the Seceding Presbyterians of America abandoned the claim to the power of the keys, which has heretofore been so stoutly insisted on against the Independents, and Congregationalists, by the old Presbyterians ? Or is it only your present necessity that forces this abandonment from you ? And where can you find a promise from GOD, which is independent of the one apostolic Church of CHRIST ? The declarations of all the bishops and priests upon earth, are certainly nothing worth, divested of the authority of the Church to make them : (and I heartily wish that those who call themselves both bishops, priests, and deacons, would well consider this :) but with the authority of the Church to make them, and the warrant of Scripture for them, I have certainly a spurious Bible if they are not the words of CHRIST himself—and their sacerdotal acts such as will be recognized in Heaven. I am indeed glad that those men, who so pertinaciously deny and resist the authority of CHRIST in his Church, have but this one sin to answer for, and I humbly hope, that in so far as it is a sin of ignorance it will be forgiven them. But there is none the less occasion to remind them, that schism is a Scripture-denounced sin, and that (Professor Campbell to the contrary notwithstanding) its essence consists in separating from the one

authority of CHRIST, committed to his apostles, for the extension of the Church among all nations in unity of faith and
order; and in setting up another authority in his name, in opposition to it.   Not satisfied however, you resume the perversion
at p. 653, as follows :

" As to that shorter method of verifying the true Church 'by
authority' of which the Bishop speaks—it can amount to nothing
but this, *that the people are to receive implicitly the tradition of
their priests on this subject.*"   Again at the same page—"A
shorter way indeed ! most obviously then, the Bishop would
have *the people exercise implicit confidence in ecclesiastical tradition.*
Here, therefore, is a priesthood to be regarded as the accredited
agents of Heaven, in whom we must place our faith as to things
essential to our authorized hope of salvation.   Now if this is the
preacher's meaning, we are unable to express our sorrow and
astonishment, to hear such sentiments from an evangelical
minister in a Protestant country, and that country America."

But, Sir, ought not common honesty (to say nothing of Christian charity) to have suggested to you, to be sure, that such
' was the preacher's meaning,' before you indulged yourself,
and misled your readers, by attributing to him such conclusions
as your jealousy and fear of the distinctive doctrines of the
Church as exhibited in these Sermons, have forced you to
resort to ? Yes, Sir : and the preacher tells you, that you have
violated every rule of just construction, to draw from his words
a meaning every way foreign to his thoughts and to his intentions.
The preacher does not indeed parade his protestantism as much
as some others, because he is quite certain there is no ground
on which it can be questioned.   He is, however, a Protestant
on the true ground of the reformation—who, while he abhors
the very idea of implicit faith, implicit obedience, and implicit
submission, except in and to the word of GOD as revealed in the
Scriptures ; yet does not therefore consider either himself or
others warranted in departing from the faith and order of the
gospel, as understood and acted upon in pure and primitive
times.   He is Protestant enough to believe and to teach, that
the genuine principle of the reformation was, *renunciation and
abandonment of the corruptions engendered in the Church, not*

of the Church itself, or of the authority of its Founder, as transmitted through his apostles in the line of Bishops, as distinguished from Presbyters. And he is perfectly sure that this authority by succession, is the only verifiable root of unity—the sole test of catholicism in the visible Church of CHRIST. But so far is he from claiming or asserting implicit submission to the authority of man, that he is Protestant enough to know, that this very claim to infallible direction of the conscience by the clergy, was the entering wedge to all the corruptions that followed. It is, therefore, a *base and flagitious* insinuation, that such sentiments are either held or taught by himself personally, or by that Church which is the bulwark of the reformation, or by that branch of it of which he is (however unworthy) a governor. And his whole course, he conceives, demonstrates the injustice of such a charge. His great object is to give, not to withhold, information. He calls upon all around him to exercise their privilege as Protestants, as Christians, as men, to search and examine for themselves on what foundation the claims of the various denominations calling themselves Churches of CHRIST, rest for this distinction. He offers them the aids which he himself has derived from *Scripture, reason, and authority,* (in the just and proper use of the word,) to enable them to determine understandingly in this chief of all inquiries. Nor can he be justly charged with a single attempt to mislead his hearers or his readers, or to evade an objection to his positions ; and he humbly trusts, that though this is done in Protestant America, it is not, therefore, the less allowable ; and he submits it to the public judgment, whose course betrays the strongest tendency to stifle inquiry and withhold information— that of the reviewer, or that of the preacher.

I forbear to notice here the continuation of your perversions of this ' unfortunate position,' (certainly very unfortunate to *one* of us,) at p. 248, 254, 312, and 327—because they would necessarily be taken up again, in examining your strictures on my Bible Society Sermon, and also on that *on the Study and Interpretation of Scripture.* I likewise leave, for the present, your attempt to enlist political prejudice in favour of your cause ; as this will require to be noticed in repelling the charge of foreign influence, brought forward by you against the Church.

And this I do, because I am really tired of the painful work; and also, because I believe that sufficient proof is adduced to make good the charge of perversion, and to determine whether your management of the controversy, so far, is consistent with your declaration at the outset—with a supreme regard for truth —or with those flowing professions of charity and personal regard which are so prominent in the language of these reviews.

I come now, Sir, to consider your objections to certain points of doctrine laid down in my *Farewell Sermon* to my former parishioners, and that delivered *before the Convention of North-Carolina.* The subject matter of each was well considered, was uttered under a deep sense of the responsibility of my ministerial character, and if in any point I have erred from the truth of revealed doctrine, I owe it to myself, as well as to others, to correct it. If these two Sermons are, indeed, ' firebrands of discord,' and calculated to ' do greater injury to the cause of Christianity in the Southern country, than twenty of the ablest preachers can do of good in their whole ministerial life,' (page 590,) I cannot be too prompt, or too earnest, in a full and public recantation of such unworthy and dangerous sentiments. But as Presbyterianism and Christianity are not synonymous, at least in my judgment ; and what may be considered injurious to the former, may, nevertheless, be innocuous, if not helpful, to the latter ; I trust to stand excused for venturing to dispute so strong an assertion, and for exposing the fallacies with which it is endeavoured to be supported. In your June Number, p. 301, you observe—

" In our Southern country, subjects of this kind have been so little discussed, that the great body of the people have no ideas of their true bearing, or of the manner in which they affect their vital interests."

Most true, Sir, and as you doubtless know in whose hands the religious instruction of the southern people has, almost exclusively, been for the last forty or fifty years, perhaps you can tell the reason why subjects of this kind have been withheld from public discussion.   But for this very reason, and because he deems them *vital subjects* and affecting *vital interests*, did Bishop Ravenscroft feel it his bounden duty to present them to those more particularly under his charge, and eventually to the public.   And most unquestionably, if they are of this important description, and the people have *no ideas* of their true bearing, it is high time that their attention should be called to them ; and every way reasonable, that Bishop R. should stand justified for discarding that false tenderness to the feelings of others, which had been instrumental in keeping back these fundamental doctrines from the edification of the pulpit.

These doctrines are—the Church and the ministry, as divine and authoritative appointments of revealed religion.   And the objections taken by you, are rather to the conclusions I draw from them—to the views I give of them as practical truths, bearing vitally upon the hope given to redeemed man—than to the doctrines themselves.   For, at p. 637—

" We most fully maintain," say you, " the divine origin, unity, and perpetuity of the Church ; we believe that the ministry is of divine institution, and that none ought to take upon themselves that sacred office, but such as are rightly called to it."

Your opposition, therefore, must be to the use or purpose of the Church, as a visible body or society—to the nature and kind of the unity, which is an inseparable characteristic of it, as divine and true—and to the divine right of the ministry in the Church, as explained and enforced in these two Sermons. And here I cannot help expressing the wish, that your objections had been more definite—that you had come more directly to the issue between us ; because it would have saved much time and trouble, and put the question more immediately in reach of the reader.   No doubt, however, you have your reasons for this diffuse method of treating the subject : whether they will appear in the sequel, remains to be seen.

And, first ; of the purpose or design of the Church, as a divine appointment in the salvation of sinners.

VOL. I.—31

In my *Convention Sermon,* p. 5, I lay down this position: That the Church, as a divine institution, 'is not an abstract idea to be entertained in the mind; but an actual, visible *body* or *society,* for practical use, deriving its constitution, laws, and authority, directly from GOD. As such, it is placed beyond the reach of any human appointment, addition or alteration; and this so strictly, that all the wisdom, piety, and authority in the world, congregated together, is just as incompetent to originate a Church as to call another universe into existence.' In the next page I proceed to show that the purpose of this divine appointment was—to give a covenanted character to the religious condition of man—to confer upon men, by outward and visible marks, a new relation to GOD, henceforth confined and limited within this institution;—that this, and this only, marks its separation from the world, as the Church, the peculium, the elect of GOD:—and that because of this its distinctive character, it was made the visible and only depositary of his revealed will, and precious promises. Hence I draw the conclusion, as well of the New, as of the Old Testament Church, (p. 8 and 9,) 'That it was competent to no man, not even to Lot or to Melchisedek, to obtain its privileges without its seal. Whatever of mercy might be in store for them, and the rest of mankind observing the law written in the heart, it was not the *pledged* and *promised* mercy made over to the Church. Whatever the truth or reasonableness of any religious duty might be—however well founded the hope of GOD's favour, from conformity to the dictates of natural conscience; it was not the truth confirmed by express revelation—it was not the hope which springs from the promise of GOD certified by outward, visible, and appointed ordinances, as helps to faith, means of grace, and assurances of a relationship to GOD, in which none other stood, transacted through an authorized and accredited agent.'

Such, Sir, are the views of the purpose of the Church, to which you oppose yourself, and which you denounce as uncharitable, and fire-brands of discord. Yet when it suits your purpose, you can speak as nearly the same language, even, as you here denounce, on the *peculiar covenanted character* of the Church of GOD—of its *origin and object.* In your *Essay on*

Baptism, p. 14, you thus express your views *at that time* on this subject.

"The question then recurs, when was the visible Church—that is, a Church admitting members by external rites, and adopting some principle common to every association that is to be held together—when was this Church organized? It was not by John the Baptizer. He pretended to no such authority; and in truth was a Jew, conforming, during the course of his ministry, to the Jewish ritual, and embodying no distinct society. It is not imagined that any of the Prophets organized the Church of God. In a word, we first find the institution in the days of Abraham. God entered into covenant with him; constituted him the father of the faithful, and he received *circumcision as a seal of the righteousness of faith*. From the beginning there was only one way of salvation, that is through the LORD JESUS CHRIST. But there was no *visible Church* until God had appointed a visible sign and seal of that righteousness by which he would pronounce a sinner just; and glorify himself in his salvation."

You then assume the views of a writer in the *Christian Magazine*, and show that circumcision as the visible seal of the covenant—

"Certified to the seed of Abraham, by a token in the flesh of their males, that the covenant with their great progenitor was in force; that they were under its full operation; and entitled to all the benefits immediately derived from it," p. 15—And, that it also was "to all who walked in the faith of Abraham, a seal of their *personal interest* in that same righteousness by which Abraham was justified." Hence you conclude, that the covenant made with Abraham and certified by the seal of circumcision," was a covenant ecclesiastical, by which JEHOVAH organized the visible Church, as one distinct, spiritual, society, and according to which, all his after-dealings with her were to be regulated." p. 16, "With this Church, as with the *whole*, composed in the first instance of Abraham's family, and to be increased afterwards by the addition of all such as should own his faith, was the covenant made. This covenant has never been annulled—the proof of the affirmative lies upon the affirmer." p. 17.—"If the Abrahamic covenant is no longer in force, the Church of God, as a visible public society, is not in any sense connected with him by covenant relation. This may weigh light with those who discard the doctrine of a visible Catholic Church; but it draws much deeper than they suspect. *The whole administration of the covenant of grace proceeds upon the principle, that there is such a Church. All the ordinances are given to it, all the promises are made to it.* To the elect as such they are not, cannot be given—the application of them would be impossible without a special revelation: and the whole administration of the covenant of grace, by visible means, would be at an end. *Nor is a single instance to be found, excepting in virtue of immediate revelation, in which the* LORD *ever gave an ordinance or a promise to particular Churches. They always receive their privileges in virtue of their being parts of the Church universal. Now this Church universal, which is the body of* CHRIST, *the temple of his* SPIRIT, *the depository of his grace, stands in no covenant relation to* GOD, *in her public character, if the covenant with Abraham is annulled.*" p. 18.

On these recorded sentiments of Dr. Rice in 1819, I must first request whoever shall read this, to be assured that I did not copy from him in laying down the doctrines contained in my sermons; next, that my whole fault consists in being *explicit* in my views, and carrying out these very doctrines to their *legitimate consequences.* And to Dr. Rice himself I will say, that the controvertist whose principles can shift with his interest, ought to have a good memory; of which further proof will be given before I finish. I must, however, return to the tangled bank, which the *necessities* of the reviewer have given me to unravel. I am well aware, indeed, that to the intelligent and reflecting this *argumentum ad hominem* would be sufficient to shed a very different light on the subject: but, alas, these are the few, and the reviewer evidently writes for the many. The subject also is of the highest interest, and I owe it to the first of duties to guard the charge committed to me, from the attacks of its enemies, however friendly their professions; and to give to all within my reach the best helps I am possessed of, to detect sophistry, escape from error, and find the truth.

Against the unchangeable nature of the Church of GOD, as expressed in my sermon (p. 5.) and which you desire the reader to mark, (p. 609 of the Review,) the objections you bring forward, p. 638, 639, 640, 641, &c. are of a description as completely irrelevant to the subject as can well be conceived. What have all the changes you ring throughout five or six pages, "on forms of prayer, sponsors, and the sign of the cross in baptism—immersion, or pouring the water in that sacrament, confirmation, kneeling at the LORD's table, consecration of churches, and modes of dress" as decreed and practised by the Protestant Episcopal Church—what have these to do with the unchangeable nature of the Church as a divine institution? Do you mean to assert, or even to insinuate, that the Protestant Episcopal Church, either in England or America, considers and uses these rites and ceremonies (confirmation always excepted, which is as ancient and scriptural as baptism, and a term of communion) as laws and statutes of CHRIST's kingdom—as things necessary to be believed and practised in order to salvation? If you do, I must ask you, is it not asserted against your better knowledge? Do you not know that these stumbling blocks to the pride of Presbytery, these bugbears to the spiritual pride of ignorant and deluded fanatics, are decreed and practised only as primitive, orderly, and edifying ceremonials, and changeable according to circumstances? Where have you ever heard or read that they are held as the essence of religion, and grounds for rejecting from communion and Christian fellowship any denomination of Christians episcopally constituted? How often have you yourself, who certainly do not hold or use them, received the holy communion from episcopal hands? How often have you been told, that the reason why they cannot in return receive at your hands is—not that you do not use forms of prayer, and sponsors in baptisms, &c. &c. but because they believe in their consciences, that you have no authority to administer? Why then commit yourself against such plain truth, and give such just cause to say that you write to mislead? And as the subject I am upon suggests it, let me ask you further—if you can receive the communion once from episcopal hands with a good conscience, why not always? What possible justification can there be for separation from a communion, which you can partake of with a good conscience? Are the rites and ceremonies of the Church which you decry so bitterly, in such sort sinful as to warrant breach of communion? Are they in any respect contrary to the love of GOD, or to the love of man? If not, how can they touch the conscience ?   They may, indeed, offend the pride, prejudice, and caprice, of unreasonable or contentious men, but they cannot touch the conscience in any just sense of that much abused word ; or furnish an excuse for rending the body of CHRIST.

Your remarks on the Nineteenth Article, p. 639, are perfectly gratuitous, as to the limitations of the article : they are unknown to Burnet, who was to the full as well acquainted with the history of the article—that is, with the particular views of the framers of it—as you can possibly be ; and from his known character, would not have withheld the notion you assert, had there been any foundation for it. Neither is it 'undeniably true,' that the fathers and reformers of the British Church, as a body, acknowledge the Protestant Churches in Scotland, France, Holland, &c. as true branches of the Church of CHRIST. They were very cautious and prudent not to excite any prejudice against the reformation that could be avoided without a surrender of principle—perhaps too much so for the subsequent peace and welfare of the Church.   And the most that could be got from them on the subject of the foreign Churches that reformed on the Presbyterian model was, to admit that where necessity compelled them to reform in this manner or not at all, such necessity was a justification.   Nor did Calvin himself, at the first, resort to any other plea or ground of defence ; but even deplored the necessity he was under as a great misfortune. After the English reformers, indeed, refused his assistance in re-organizing the Church, his tone was changed, and if he ever really entertained any episcopal principles, they were abandoned.   Your assertion, therefore, is wholly unsupported, and can be considered no otherwise than as mere make-weight in your general scheme.

Your remarks on my view of the purpose of the Church as a divine institution, are next directed against the position at p. 9 of the sermon, that it is ' the authorized source of agency between heaven and earth.'   That there is something exceedingly alarming to you in this position, is evident from the more than common pains taken to distort it into an attack upon every thing deservedly dear to men and Christians. For, at p. 641, you endeavour to rouse your readers to the stoutest resistance of so dangerous a claim for the Church, as that of an agency in the salvation of men, in the following words :

" Here then, in this one Church, to which, according to the preacher, none may add, and in which none may change, it is authoritatively decreed that rites and ceremonies—such, we presume, as kneeling at communion, the cross in baptism, sponsor's saint's days, &c. &c. may be changed or abolished ; yet such is the authority of the Church, as the authorized source of agency between heaven and earth, that while she retains any of these things we are bound to retain them under the awful forfeiture already stated ; and when she changes any rite or ceremony not prescribed in the word of God, we are bound to change our observance or be cut off from the covenanted mercies of God ! Where then is the liberty wherewith CHRIST has made us free, and what yoke of bondage is heavier than this ? What has become of the principles of Protestantism ? And where are the blessings of the reformation ?"

And let me ask, where is common sense, where is self-respect, where is the respect due to a discerning public, to say nothing of love of truth, when a writer ventures upon so barefaced an evasion of the point before him ? What has the admitted authority of any particular Church to decree and change rites and ceremonies, to do with the origin and constitution of the Church, as a divine appointment ? Still more, what has this to do with the question of its agency in the purpose of its institution ? Where is the connexion between them, and the object of the reviewer in putting forth his might against a shadow ? Connexion certainly there is none, and it is easier as well as safer, to contend with a shadow than with substance. But to show the utter futility of the argument—to establish the position, and bring this Proteus to his answer—let me ask, What is the gospel but a message of grace to rebels and enemies to Almighty God, offering them pardon and reconciliation on certain prescribed conditions ? What is the Church, but the heaven appointed, visible, and accessible depositary and dispenser of this grace through her commissioned officers ? Now, where must these rebels one and all, come to fulfil on their part the prescribed conditions, to make their submission and receive the seal of reconciliation and adoption into a new and covenanted relation to GOD? There can be but one answer, and that is, To the visible Church through her authorized ministry. And what are the officers of the Church called in Scripture? *Ministers—Stewards of mysteries—Ambassadors.* Are not these then agents for a specified purpose, and their work an agency? Stand they not in the gap, as it were, between Heaven and Hell, on this sin-ruined, death-stricken world, sent of GOD to win souls to CHRIST, and pluck sinners from everlasting burnings? Stand they not commissioned to *feed the flock of* CHRIST—to prepare, and give to each, his portion from the spiritual treasury of the divine word, and to administer the sacraments of salvation? Have they no stores of admonition, reproof, and censure—no provision of encouragement, comfort, and consolation—to deal out, according to the several conditions of their charge, amid the sundry and manifold changes and chances of this mortal life? And in all this, are they not the agents of a higher power—even of Him, who hath promised to *be with them* in this arduous work, *to the end of the world?*

Dr. Rice—is this any thing like the work *you say you are commissioned by Heaven to perform?* When you baptize, do you not profess to bring an alien into covenant with GOD, and to seal him to the day of redemption? When you preach, do you not declare the conditions of salvation, denounce the punishment of sin, exhort to repentance, and instruct and build up unto faith and holiness? When you administer the LORD's supper, do you not negociate afresh the pardon of the penitent, and replenish and confirm the grace of worthy partakers? When you visit the sick and dying, are not the consolations of religion at your disposal according to the circumstances of the case? And in all this are you not an agent—feel you not that you are an agent—deriving your warrant and authority for all you do from the great Head of the Church, through the visible Church on earth? Where, then, is the wrong, or the error on my part, in this view of the purpose of the Church? Wherefore did you resort to so unconnected and irrelevant a set of objections as

you have heated yourself into ?   Was it because you foresaw
the bearing of this position, and of some others, too, on the
principle of dissent from the Church, and felt your ministerial
character struck at ?   Why, even in that view, my good Sir,
you have hereby helped yourself nothing, and me much; for
undeniably, an agent without a verifiable commission from his
principal, cannot be safe to transact business with : and it must
be a doubtful cause indeed, which betrays such alarm at every
allusion to it.   Yet it appears to me, that this master mischief in
these sermons, has haunted you throughout, and tinged every
page you have penned in this review with the complexion of
your own jealous apprehension.

A third objection taken by you, to my view of the purpose of
the Church, as a divine institution, is grounded on a declaration
found in both sermons, and is a conclusion drawn by me from
the position, p.' 9, of the *Convention Sermon*, that the Church is
the ' special deposit of the promises of GOD to a fallen world.'

In the *Farewell Sermon*, p. 6, it is expressed in the following
words :

" To be entitled to that mercy on the only safe ground, his
revealed word, we must be found within the rule which includes
it as a covenant stipulation.   Of any other state or condition
different from this we can say nothing, because we know
nothing.   There may be mercy, but it is not revealed—it is no
where promised."

In the *Convention Sermon*, the same sentiment is thus expressed, p. 10 :

" For I am yet to learn, where a promise of GOD to fallen
man is to be found, that is not limited on the previous condition,
that he be a member of CHRIST's visible Church upon earth."

On this you remark, p. 595, ' If this declaration had been
made with greater caution, we should have admitted it, but it
makes too wide a sweep for us.'   But why so ? Are either the
premises assumed by me, or the conclusion thence deduced in
either of the Sermons, false or unscriptural ? If so, you ought

to have shown it, and directed your readers to the promise independent of the Church, This would have been conclusive. But this you could not do; and as this 'wide sweep' included a certain foundation, on which you are very sensitive, and not a little apprehensive, it suited you better to sweep away into the South Sea, and fetch thence the inhabitants of Pitcairn's Island, to give it their support.

"What would the preacher say of the inhabitants of Pitcairn's Island—who have the Bible, but have no preacher, no sacraments, no holy Catholic Apostolic Church? When they read such words as these—*believe on the* LORD JESUS CHRIST, *and thou shalt be saved,* and are conscious of faith, and love, and hope, and rejoice in prospect of eternal life; are they relying without a promise? Are they presumptuously relying on the uncovenanted mercies of GOD? Who will affirm it? We dare not."

To try the worth of this delusive sort of reasoning, let us reverse the question: Are they, especially their unbaptized descendants—are they relying *with a promise?* Are they, unpresumingly, relying on *covenanted mercies?* Dare you affirm it? But further; (for it is a captivating and wide spread delusion, to exalt internal consciousness above commanded duty;) when, in addition to the words you have quoted, they read in their Bible, that the person to whom they were addressed, *was forthwith baptized;* when they read, *except a man be born of water and of* SPIRIT, *he cannot enter into the kingdom of* GOD; when they read, *he that believeth and is baptized, shall be saved,* can their assurance be equal to what it would be, were the conditions prescribed fully complied with, and the promises certified by the appropriate seal? But—to meet your question fairly, and answer it satisfactorily—it being not of their choice, but of the providence of Almighty GOD, that they are deprived of the Church Ministry and the Sacraments; the *necessity* of the case is their only dependence. GOD requires no impossibilities of his creatures. Therefore, if from the Bible alone these mutineers have been brought to repentance and faith, the promises of GOD may be relied upon for comfort and hope, even without the seal of the covenant.   Nor is it either necessary or proper, to affirm either way, of the kind or character of the mercy which is in store for them.   It is what St. Paul calls an *unlearned question*.

But the case is *an exception* to the general rule, as laid down in my Sermon : it therefore strengthens it.   It is also an *extreme case*, and therefore ought not to have been, and would not have been, put by a fair reasoner.   Moreover, the impression made by it, whether intended or not, is calculated to do unspeakable injury among the careless and thoughtless part of the community, by lowering the importance of the ordinances of religion, already too low in their estimation.   I must, therefore, enter a caveat against this danger, by warning them that the case is irrelevant to the point between the Reviewer and myself.   Cases of plain necessity stand upon very different ground from that of those who may read either these Reviews, or this reply to them.   In Christian lands, he that would secure the comfort and benefit of the promises and provisions of God to and for a fallen world, must previously, on his part, comply with the conditions on which they are plainly and expressly limited in his revealed word ; otherwise, his hope is not founded—it cannot bear the scrutiny to which it ought to be brought, as a reliance for so infinite an interest as salvation.   Nor is the modern doctrine of *internal consciousness, and assumed assurance*, (that sectarian opiate of deluded souls,) any substitute for those *external ordinances* which designate the covenant of mercy to redeemed man.   It is the union of these two—of internal effect, by the blessing of God, with external obedience—that *the hope which maketh not ashamed* is to be obtained ; and *what God hath joined let no man put asunder.*   Your objections, therefore, to the doctrine as laid down in both the Sermons, that ' there is not a promise of God to fallen man, that is not limited on the *previous condition* that he be a member of CHRIST's visible Church upon earth,' are a mere escape from the question, of which, as I think, no sincere man could avail himself—an appeal to the ignorance and prejudice of his readers, on a point of vital importance, which I am at a loss to conceive how a divine can justify to his own conscience—and every way inconsistent with those high professions of exclusive regard to truth, which you record at the outset of these Reviews, as the duty of all, and as your governing principle as a clergyman.   If there is a promise to fallen man, independent of his connexion with the *visible Church of Christ*, you can surely find it—and when you do, you will then have met this point fairly, and as a champion for the truth ought to do.   But until `you do this, I must consider all that you have raked together as argument, as a mere quibble; and, what is painful in the extreme to express, a quibble on the eternal interests of the immortal souls who hang upon your *dicta*, as upon divine oracles.

Against this doctrine—that the Church is an integral part in the salvation of the gospel—and the conclusions thence drawn in the Sermons, you repeatedly resort to the use of the term 'uncovenanted mercies' in such a way as to leave on the mind of the reader, more especially dissenting readers, that the Protestant Episcopal Church holds and teaches, that all the other denominations of religious profession are, in consequence, cut off from salvation.   Now, Sir, as you must know these two things—first, that such is the hasty conclusion, which uninformed and unreflecting minds come to from this doctrine—secondly, that it is not a just conclusion, or even such an one as those called high churchmen draw from it; did you not owe it to candour and fair argument, to meet this point otherwise than you have done in these Reviews?   Did you not owe it to those who look up to you for direction?   Did you not owe it to your own character?   Whatever you may think of these questions, Sir, or however you may be pleased to answer or to pass them by, I feel that it is due to myself, and to the cause of truth and order, to state explicitly—that Episcopalians hold no such views of these doctrines as are unjustly and illogically drawn from them, and abundantly insinuated throughout these Reviews; they do not hold that the multitudes who dissent from them on the faith and order of the gospel, are, therefore, consigned to perdition.   No, God forbid!—They say, simply, as it is expressed in my *Farewell Sermon.*   For such there may be mercy, but it is not revealed, it is no where promised.   And they say this to rouse them to search the Scriptures, to reflect, to compare their condition with the revealed word ; whether it agrees with it in the directions and limitations therein set forth.   They only wish them to act with the same discretion in the case of their souls as they manifest in the case of their estates ; and inquire, whether those persons who profess to confer a title to the covenanted privileges of the gospel, by administering its sacraments, have authority for what they do.

What Presbyterian, or other dissenter, will risk the purchase of property from a distant owner by power of attorney, upon the mere assertion of the agent that he is empowered to convey the title ?   Know you of any, who would not require to see the power of attorney—that it was in due form of law, and such as would bind the principal, before he paid the price, or even became bound for it ?   And know you not of thousands, who bargain for the rich inheritance of the gospel, for themselves and their families, without the slightest security, beyond the mere ' say so,' of the agent ?   Alas, how very true are our Saviour's words that *the children of this world are in their generation wiser than the children of light.*   Episcopalians present these doctrines to their hearers, in the full persuasion that the Church, the ministry, and the sacraments, are as distinctly and truly appointments of GOD in order to the salvation of sinners, as the faith of the gospel : and that only as these are united in the profession of religion, can the hope thereby given to man, be worthy of the name of assurance.   Episcopalians consider the grace and mercy of the gospel, as matters *of strict covenant stipulation ;* as bound up with the authority to dispense them ; as inseparable from that authority ; and only by virtue of that authority (with reverence be it spoken) pledging the glorious source of all mercy and grace to His creatures.   But they presume not to pass beyond their written warrant, either to extend or to circumscribe the mercy of GOD : they know what is promised, and on what conditions ; and of that only do they venture to speak.   Those persons who profess to be acquainted with the secret decrees of Almighty GOD, may also be acquainted with the extent and the rule of his uncovenanted mercy, and prefer it to that which is promised ; but Episcopalians dare not thus speculate on eternity. And they feel themselves well supported in presenting and pressing this distinction upon their hearers, by the whole analogy of Scripture.   Consider the case of Abraham and Lot, or of Abraham and Melchisidek.   What constituted the difference between Abraham and either of these ?   Was it not the seal of that peculiar covenant, in and by virtue of which he stood in a relation to God, altogether different from that in which they stood ? And is not this a clear illustration of covenanted and uncovenanted mercy ?   Does it not show that God's mercy is not exhausted by a peculiar covenant, while at the same time the advantages annexed to it are such as nothing but ignorance, or presumption, or the power of prejudice, will venture to sport with !

But to make this plainer still, and meet your sneers at the distinction taken in the Sermons between covenanted and uncovenanted mercy, with an answer in point—Suppose Lot had been desirous to partake of the privileges, blessings, and promises, made over to his kinsman, and, in consequence of this desire, had applied to Melchisidek to affix the appropriate seal, and he had done so.   Would this have availed Lot, and conferred a title to the blessings of that covenant ?   Could any persuasion of his own mind, or any reasonings of others, or any holiness in the administrator, have supplied the defect of divine warrant to perform the act ?   Surely there can be but one answer to these questions.

Is an Episcopal minister, then, to be denounced as a disturber of Christian peace, for applying this analogy to the seal of the Christian covenant in the sacrament of baptism, and warning the thousands who receive baptism at any hand almost that offers it, to consider on what they are building ?   Are the privileges annexed to baptism in the gospel, less strictly limited as to their covenant character, than those annexed to circumcision under the law ?   Is there any *revealed means* of obtaining an interest in the covenant ratified in the blood of Christ, other than by the application of its seal in the sacrament of baptism !   Can we become members of Christ's visible Church, otherwise than by being baptized into his death and resurrection ?   When you have answered these questions directly, and as a lover of truth must do, you will then be prepared for two more, which

shall close my answer to the first objection, and at the same
time refute the sophistry you have resorted to on the subject of
the sacraments, p. 641.

Is an unbaptized person in covenant with GOD ? Can a
third person be pledged or bound by the acts of one, to whom
he has given no commission or authority ?

SECONDLY, of the unity of the Church.   On this point you
say, p. 637—'We most fully maintain the divine unity of the
Church.' Your objection therefore, must be to the *nature* and
kind of that unity, as set forth in the Sermons.   This I infer,
rather from the general tenor of your remarks, than from any
thing so explicit as to enable me to meet it with precision ; but
particularly from the address you have in the outline given of
what is said on this subject in the *Farewell Sermon*, as will be
more evident by comparing p. 595 of the Review, with the
Sermon itself.   Your outline is thus given—

" Of this doctrine of the Church (see p. 7) [the preacher
doubtless means the Church itself] he says, that it is one ; that
this unity consists in the profession of one faith or system of
doctrine, and in participation of the sacraments; that there is
but one source of authority for administering the word and
sacraments ;   that to this Church is the promise made that *the
gates of Hell shall never prevail against it ;* and that (*ecce iterum*)
only as we are members of this one body have we a right to rely
on the promises of GOD."

In the Sermon itself, what is above given to your readers as
a fair outline of my sentiments, is thus expressed :

" On this doctrine of the Church then, we are instructed
from Scripture—first, that it is but one—*there is one body.*
Accordingly we never find it spoken of in these same Scriptures
indefinitely, as A *Church*, but definitely, as THE *Church*.   This
oneness, however, is not to be understood of any particular
location, for in this respect, it hath no limit, but the gracious
purpose of its divine founder to *gather together in one, the children of* GOD *scattered abroad.*   Hence it is compared to a vine,
which, with but one root, hath many branches."
" Secondly, we learn from the same source, that the unity of

this one body consists, in the belief and profession of the *one faith* or system of doctrine, revealed by the *one* Spirit of God, and once committed to the saints, or associated members of the Church of Christ, by the preaching of the Apostles ; in the service or obedience to the laws of the *one* Lord, or head of the body ; in the participation of the same sacraments, as means and pledges of divine grace, and of that brotherly love, and Christian fellowship, in which we are joined together in the worship of *one* God and Father of the spirits of all flesh, and in the *one hope* of our calling."

" Thirdly, we are instructed from the same word of God that in this one body or Church of Christ—there is but one source of authority for ministering the word and sacraments, and that this authority is of divine appointment :—*all power is given unto me in Heaven and Earth : go ye, therefore, and teach all nations, baptizing them in the name of the* Father, *and of the* Son, *and of the* Holy Ghost, *teaching them to observe all things whatsoever I have commanded you*—*and lo, I am with you always, even unto the end of the world.*

" Fourthly, we are taught by the *more sure word of prophecy* —that unto the Church, thus divinely constituted and *built on the foundation of the Apostles and Prophets,* the solemn promise is made that *the gates of Hell shall not prevail against it ;* the Holy Spirit given, to abide with it forever, to enlighten, convince, comfort, and sanctify, the children of God ; and that only as we are members of this one body, fruitful branches of this one vine, are *the promises of* God *in* Christ *to us, yea and to us, amen.*

" And now let us ask ourselves seriously, my brethren, What ground of steadfastness and assurance in the great work of our salvation can there be, to creatures such as we are, other than that of divine authority ? Can that which is merely human offer any security to our souls ? Or can any mixture of human wisdom amend the appointments of Heaven, and render them more effectual to our good ? Alas, what is there of endurance in the work or wisdom of man ? My brethren, is it not written that *the wisdom of this world cometh to naught ?* How then can steadfastness be exhorted to, on a ground which is itself changeable—which our own observation proves to be so, by the present state of the Christian world—and having once separated from the root of unity, in the one authority of Christ transmitted through his Apostles, goes on dividing and subdividing, till every original feature of the Church is lost, and the great and gracious purpose of Christian union and brotherly love rendered impracticable."

Now, Sir, it is submitted to your readers, whether you have given a just outline of the above extract from my sermon ; and whether there is a single sentiment in it which is at variance with Scripture, or which any plain Christian can object to.   To you, however, it presents a different aspect, as it is evident from the contemptuous *ecce iterum* with which you greet the inseparable conclusion, that only as we are found in the unity of the Church are the promises of GOD sure to us.   This doctrine seems to have a peculiar effect upon your nerves, and whatever even points to it, is, therefore, sure of your opposition, either direct or indirect.   To bring this vital subject, however, into some definite shape, and you to your answer—I ask, On what possible principle is the divine unity of the Church of CHRIST reconcileable with the existing state of the Christian world ? Are all the varieties of religious profession throughout Christendom true branches of the true Church—the one spouse and body of CHRIST—or, only some of them ?   Will you answer this plainly and directly, and give us the grounds and reasons of your determination, whatever it may be ; that we may know the extent of that fraternity, which modern Presbyterians manifest for Congregationalists, Independents, Methodists, Baptists, &c. &c.— and may also learn, if it can be communicated, how separation and exclusion are transformed into union and fellowship ?   In what does the unity of the visible Church consist according to your view of it ? Is it in agreement in *faith and order*, or of *faith* singly, or *order* singly ?   If the unity of the Church is not to be referred ultimately to the authority of CHRIST, originally lodged with his apostles as the root, to what is it to be referred ?   Is there another principle or root of unity, as a divine character or mark of the Church of CHRIST, which is equally verifiable and conclusive in all ages and by all capacities of men ?   If there be, let us have it, plain and direct.

"Here, Sir, is the dividing line between us: it is the point which involves all the rest, as you well know, and decides the momentous question of Church, or no Church, in a divided Christian world.   And I have put it thus directly, that by the answer given, my ignorance of the subject may be edified, or the delusion spread over the dissenting community of Christians may be removed.

Sir, in these Reviews you frequently beg the patience, the charity, and forbearance, of your readers for me, on the ground that I see not the consequences of my positions.   Let me not have to request the same favour for you, because you *do see* those consequences, and, therefore, either decline or evade the issue offered you on your objections to this, and to the doctrines generally which I maintain.   Sir, *my* principles are open and avowed, I have no purpose of concealment or deceit to answer. If *your* principles are of the same character, you will meet these questions with the frank and fearless spirit of the man who is sincere in what he holds, and who knows that he must be a gainer by the establishment of truth.   If we are what we profess, and what we ought to be, no pitiful consideration like that of a victory by Dr. Rice over Bishop Ravenscroft, or by Bishop Ravenscroft over Dr. Rice, will be allowed to overrule the commanding claims of GOD's truth upon men, who say they are *set for the defence of the gospel*—who watch for souls, and for souls must give account.

THIRDLY, the divine right of the Ministry in the Church.   In this case also your objections are directed against the view given of this doctrine, and the conclusions drawn from it in the sermons, rather than against the doctrine itself ; for you say, p. 637, 'We believe that the ministry is of divine institution, and that none ought to take upon themselves that sacred office but such as are rightly called to it.'   The point then between us is this, How shall this rightful call be certified to third persons ? What is the just and satisfactory evidence of this divine right, as committed to and exercised by them ?

In my *Farewell Sermon,* p. 8, I lay down the following as the just and only certain method of determining this question.

"If the authority by which any denomination of Christians minister in sacred things cannot be shown to be derived from the apostles of CHRIST, that it cannot be verified as a fact, such denomination cannot be a true branch of that catholic apostolic Church in which we profess to believe."

In your Review, p. 647, you give your view of the subject in these words :

"If an association calling itself a Church, administers baptism in the name of the FATHER, SON, and HOLY SPIRIT, celebrates the LORD's Supper—giving bread and wine to the communicants as memorials of the broken body and shed blood of the LORD JESUS—puts the pure word of GOD into the hands of the people —teaches the doctrines of CHRIST, such as 'the entire spiritual death and and alienation of man from GOD—the reconciliation of GOD to the world by the sufferings and death of his only begotten Son—the atonement of his blood—justification by faith—acceptance through the merits of the Saviour—conversion of the heart to GOD—holiness of life, the only evidence of it—and the grace of GOD, in the renewal of the HOLY GHOST, the sole agent from first to last in working out our salvation from sin here and from hell hereafter ; and finally, has a ministry trained for the work, and qualified to impart spiritual instruction—we have no doubt but there is a true Church of CHRIST, whether their ministers are set apart to their work *by the laying on the hands of the presbytery* as in the days of Paul, or by the ordination of a Bishop, as is the practice of some modern Churches."

Without stopping to notice the abundant matter for animadversion which this very guardedly equivocal expression of your views on the divine right of the Christian ministry presents ; I accept it as an acknowledgment that you consider ordination *essential* to that office. But as you do not say in what sense you consider it *essential*, I must, therefore, ask, Whether it is as a mere designation to office for notoriety of the person, or as imparting a character, that you think it essential? On the answer to this much depends, through whatever channel the ordaining power is transmitted, whether through Presbyters or Bishops. As you admit, however, that the ministerial office is a divine institution, I must suppose you also to admit that ordination confers or imparts a character ; and as the ministerial character is a divine right to transact the affairs of CHRIST's kingdom, ordination must consequently be the only evidence (miracles excepted) of divine right—the substitute to us for miraculous attestation to the ministerial commission. If this reasoning be correct, it also follows necessarily, that as this evidence of divine right is for the benefit of third persons, it must be verifiable, it must be capable of proof, as a fact.

According to your view as above expressed, it is a matter of perfect indifference whether this evidence of divine right is transmitted through either or both of two channels of conveyance ; but as this is evidently impossible to be reconciled with the unity of the Church of CHRIST it cannot be sustained. A divided unity is a contradiction ; and could such a thing possibly be, its only effect would be self-destruction. A divided root will have divided branches, as we so wofully experience in the actual operation of this unfounded notion. While, therefore, I admit that it would be a matter of perfect indifference as to evidence of divine right, in *which of the two* channels the root of unity was originally planted, I cannot, for the above reasons, agree with you that it is to be found in *both*—notwithstanding all the ingenuity that has been exerted to convert a community of *names* into proof of a community of *office* in the Church. The question then is, in which of the two channels contended for is it found ? In the order of Presbyters, or in the order of Bishops ? This is a question of fact, to be determined by its proper evidence ; and a question of fact exclusively. It is one however that is fiercely contested in the Christian world, and not likely to be settled ; yet it is fundamental, and vital to the hope of man for hereafter ; and in my humble judgment, when divested of the prejudices, passions, and interests connected with it, as capable of ready and satisfactory determination as any other question of fact.

The question then resolves itself into this inquiry—Is *parity* or *imparity* of order in the ministry the original constitution of church government as settled by the apostles of the LORD JESUS CHRIST ? And the evidence by which this is to be determined is, first, the Scriptures ; and next, the practice of the purest and primitive ages of the Church.

If *parity* in the ministry, by which is meant a single order, is tried by the evidence of Scripture, it goes down at once, and that by a double proof. First, it is clear beyond reasonable denial, that there was an order of men in the Church, styled Deacons, who were ordained to the ministry by the usual form of prayer and imposition of hands, and who, in consequence, preached and baptized.   This order of Deacons was instituted shortly after the day of Pentecost ; so that thus early in the commencement of the Church, there is, undeniably, by Scripture testimony, Acts, vi. 6, Deacons and Apostles as church officers : from which it is evident, that parity did not continue in the Church a single month.   Secondly, it is equally clear from Scripture, that there was another order of men in the ministry, styled indifferently (perhaps interchangeably) Elders, Presbyters and Bishops—distinct from the order styled Deacons, Acts xiv. 23.   Here then is another undeniable proof from Scripture, against parity of order in the Church of CHRIST.   That these were distinct and established offices in the Church is past contradiction from the Epistles to particular Churches written many years afterwards : as in that to the Philippians—*Paul and Timotheus the servants of* JESUS CHRIST, *to all the saints in* CHRIST JESUS, *which are at Philippi*, WITH THE BISHOPS AND DEACONS. And in 1st Tim. iii. 1, where they are described as distinct offices—*This is a true saying, if any man desire the* OFFICE OF A BISHOP *he desireth a good work*.   The qualifications for this office are then set down for Timothy's direction in ordaining them. In like manner concerning deacons, ver. 10—*Let these also first be proved ; then let them use* THE OFFICE OF A DEACON, *being found blameless*, with similar directions as to their qualifications.

For parity then, as the constitution of the Christian ministry, there is no foundation in Scripture : the evidence is directly against it ; even if the apostles, as a distinct order of ministers, are allowed to be discontinued. If to this we add the elucidation and confirmation given to these proofs from Scripture, by the practice and usage of the Church in the first and purest ages, and uninterrupted for fifteen hundred years ; there is such a body of testimony against this claim to parity of order in the ministry, as gives a very frightful cast to the prejudice which can resist it.   Here, strictly speaking, the question of fact is closed ; for, if you take your stand upon parity, as the divine constitution of the Church, and fail to establish it by proper and sufficient testimony, your cause is gone, and imparity proved to be the will of the founder of the Church.

No fact can be established by reasoning solely; whatever then hath been reasoned by the ingenuity and research of men contending for parity is of no moment until the fact be previously established by proper evidence. And so sure am I of the fact being the very reverse of parity that if in Scripture, or in ecclesiastical history, you can point to any branch of the Church of CHRIST in the apostle's days—or from thence to the fifteenth century inclusive—modelled and governed upon this principle, and acknowledged in communion with the catholic or universal Church, I will publicly recant every word I have written or spoken on the subject.

The establishment of imparity, however, does not necessarily establish any particular number of orders in the ministry—*two* orders being as good as *two hundred* to defeat the pretensions of parity. The question as to the number of orders in the Church is still open, and is as much a question of fact as that of one order only; and on this fact I maintain, that the testimony of Scripture is direct for three orders in the ministry of that Church which CHRIST purchased with his own blood, and planted and established in this world by his apostles.

That the apostles were ministers is clear from their own acknowledgment—*Who then is Paul, and who is Apollos—but* MINISTERS *by whom ye believed?* 1 Cor. iii. 5. *Let a man so account of us, as of the* MINISTERS *of* CHRIST, 1 Cor. iv. 1. *Who also hath made us able* MINISTERS *of the New Testament,* 2 Cor. iii. 6. From the testimony of Scripture then, we have these three orders existing and acting in the Church from the beginning.

First—*Deacons,* who were ordained by *the laying on the hands of the apostles,* Acts vi. 6; who were authorized to preach and baptize, Acts viii. 12, 38; Secondly—*Presbyters,* styled indifferently *Elders* and *Bishops*—why so called is of no consequence as to the fact—they were a distinct order from the Deacons; Thirdly—*the Apostles* themselves, as that order from which both the others derived their commission and authority. The fact then that there were three orders in the Church of CHRIST, during the life-time of the apostles, is established by the irrefragable testimony of Scripture; and as *the fact* is all that we are at present concerned with, you must show that I have quoted the Scriptures wrong, or lose your cause. Again, therefore, I say, if you can produce any branch of the Church of CHRIST, either national or particular, from the time of the apostles to the fifteenth century inclusive, and in communion with the church founded by the apostles—which was not constituted on the principle of *imparity*, and which was not governed by three distinct orders of ministers—I will surrender Episcopal pre-eminence to Presbyterian parity.

The question however has yet to be settled, to which of the three orders was the ordaining power committed? That the Apostles possessed this power in right of their office, you will not dispute. That it was not conferred upon the order of Deacons, you will readily admit. It must therefore have been committed either to that order styled indifferently Elders, Presbyters, and Bishops, in Scripture, or to another order, distinguished by possessing this as well as the other *ordinary* apostolical powers. On this question you assert, that the ordaining power was transferred to the order of Presbyters. This assertion I deny as a fact, and I support my denial in the following manner from the Scriptures.

The ordination of Timothy, not to say his consecration, is marked by St. Paul with such a peculiar character, as is, in my view, utterly incompatible with the parity you contend for. Authority is given him over the doctrine, the ministers, and the members of the Church at Ephesus—*I besought thee to abide still at Ephesus, that thou mightest charge some, that they teach no other doctrine.* 1 Tim. i. 3. From the 11th to the 18th verse, the apostle refers to his own commission, as intrusted with the gospel, and at the 18th verse transfers it to Timothy, *This charge I commit unto thee, son Timothy.* In the second chapter he gives him directions as to the qualification of Bishops and Deacons, and at the 14th verse, states the object of his writing to him, in such wise as clearly designates his supreme authority in that Church. *These things write I unto thee, hoping to come unto thee shortly ; but if I tarry too long, that thou mayest know* HOW THOU OUGHTEST TO BEHAVE THYSELF IN THE CHURCH OF GOD :—an expression which cannot be construed of personal deportment when engaged in the public duties of religion, and must therefore refer to the exercise of his episcopal authority over the Church. In the fifth chapter, accordingly, Timothy is directed, *Rebuke not an Elder, but entreat him as a father,* verse 1 : *Against an Elder receive not an accusation, but before two or three witnesses,* verse 19. His authority over the members generally is evidenced by the whole chapter, particularly by verse 20—*Them that sin, rebuke before all ; that others also may fear.* And that the power to ordain was committed to him singly is clear from both the Epistles, particularly 1 Tim. v. 22, and 2 Tim. ii. 2. *Lay hands suddenly on no man——The things thou hast heard of* ME *among many witnesses, the same commit thou to faithful men, who shall be able to teach others also.* If to this we add the affecting circumstances under which the second Epistle was written, there can hardly remain a doubt, that it was the apostle's object in committing this charge to Timothy, to transfer to him the oversight, government, and rule, of the Ephesian Church—*For I am now ready to be offered, and the time of my departure is at hand,* says the apostle, chap. iv. 6. Under the impression, and with the assurance he was filled with, that a crown of righteousness awaited him, what could occupy his care and thoughts more, than to provide for the security and establishment of this favoured people in the faith and order of the gospel, by placing them under the care and oversight of one who had *fully known his doctrine, manner of life, purpose, faith, long-suffering, charity, patience ;* and whose tried affection for St. Paul gave assurance that he would continue in the things which he had learned, which had been assured to him both by miraculous testimony and his own experience, which he had learned from this apostle, and were confirmed by the gift of GOD which was in him, by the laying on of St. Paul's hands ?

This view of the subject, as the plain scriptural view of it, is confirmed by the Epistle of this same Apostle to Titus :—*For this cause left I thee in Crete that thou shouldest* SET IN ORDER *the things that are wanting, and* ORDAIN ELDERS *in every city, as* I HAD APPOINTED THEE, Chap. i. 5. Directions are then given him as to the qualifications of those to be ordained, and as to his general duty as a governor of the Church, of the same character as those given to Timothy, with this particular charge, *a man that is an heretic, after the first and second admonition, reject.*

From the letter and obvious unforced meaning of Scripture, therefore, I consider it *established as a fact,* by express testimony of Scripture, that, even in the life time of the Apostles, the episcopal office was instituted in the Church by the Apostles themselves as a distinct order of ministers—that to this order was committed the apostolical power of ordaining, restraining, judging, and governing, in the Church—and that *through this order only* does the ministerial commission, as a divine right, descend from the Apostles. Here I conclude, that, in order to verify the divine right of any particular ministry, it must be derived from the Apostles through the succession in the line of Bishops, and not in the line of Presbyters. If, however, you can show that I have quoted Scripture either falsely as to the letter, or unfairly, or unusually, as to the plain and connected meaning of the passage; or can produce from the records of ecclesiastical history, for fifteen centuries, *a single instance of Presbyterian, as contradistinguished from Episcopal ordination, in any acknowledged branch of the Catholic Church;* I surrender the cause I maintain, and with it every claim or title to covenanted mercy.

Do not however suppose, Sir, that I am unaware of the ground you take, to obviate this plain testimony from Scripture on these points, as matters of fact. No, Sir, the Presbyterian hypothesis, that the order of Deacons was not a distinct clerical office, in the Christian ministry, but provided exclusively for the care of the poor, is unsupported by any thing but assertion. * I have proved from scripture, that the Deacons in the primitive Church were solemnly set apart to that office by prayer and imposition of the Apostles' hands—that they preached and baptized—that thirty years after the first mention of them, and in a

---

* Some persons may feel surprise perhaps, at the Presbyterian hypothesis respecting the order of Deacons, considering what is so plainly said in the 7th chap. of the Acts and elsewhere, of their proper ministerial character. Yet Dr. Rice does not scruple to assert, that they were not preachers of the gospel. See his *Irenicum,* page 140.

distant Church, they are recognized and addressed by St. Paul as
an established order in the ministry. I have given you Scripture and fifteen centuries of ecclesiastical history, to contest this
as a fact, or to produce the slightest ground to believe that they
were chiefly, and as their proper official duty, appointed to the
care of the poor—or that this order is in any sense analagous
to that class of men styled Deacons in the Presbyterian system
of government. And unless you can do this, the 6th chapter of
the Form of Government of the Presbyterian Church in these
United States, is bottomed on a perversion of the texts of Scripture, brought to support the assertion there made, as to the
order of Deacons, and is also in direct opposition to the judgement and practise of the Church of CHRIST, from the Apostles'
days to the reformation. Was Stephen, I pray you, serving
tables and waiting upon the poor like a Prebyterian Deacon,
when, *full faith and power, he did great wonders and miracles
among the people ?* Was such the occupation of Philip, when
he preached CHRIST to the Samaritans ?—converted and baptized them—was he thus employed when he baptized the
Ethiopian Eunuch, and preached unto him JESUS ?

Equally unwarranted by Scripture and ecclesiastical history,
is the usual subterfuge resorted to by contenders for parity in
the Christian ministry, against the episcopal character of Timothy and Titus. They were *Evangelists,* it is said, and not
Bishops ; and as Evangelists only, were clothed with a special
power to ordain and govern in the Church.

This, Sir, also, is mere assertion ; and you are required to
show, either from Scripture or the records of antiquity, that
there was a distinct order of ministers in the Church styled
Evangelists, and as such possessed of authority distinct from,
and superior to, the order either of Deacons or Presbyters.
Unless you can do this, you must be aware, Sir, that the reasoning founded on this assertion, and the conclusions drawn from
it, are equally gratuitous with the assertion itself ; and very
wonderful indeed it would be, that an office, which from the
very nature of things must run parallel with the gospel, so long
as there was a heathen land into which to carry its joyful sound,
should have been discontinued in the Church ! But as the

work of an Evangelist cannot cease, so long as the glad tidings of the gospel of CHRIST are *unheard* by any nation, kindred, tongue, or people, so neither can the office. Every Deacon, Presbyter, or Bishop, proclaiming these glad tidings to such, is—thereby, and not in virtue of any official designation—an *Evangelist,* in the proper Scriptural and only just meaning of that word. Nor was any other notion ever annexed to the word, until it was found convenient, by the contenders for parity, to consider an Evangelist as a distinct office in the Church, in order to evade the clear and direct precedent for parity given in the case of Timothy and Titus. You well know, Sir, that Philip, one of the seven Deacons, is called an Evangelist. Acts xxi. 3. Are you, therefore, prepared to assert, that he was clothed with the same powers, as a minister of the Church, wherewith Timothy and Titus were invested? But this you must do, or yield whatever support is given to parity, by this modern notion of the word *Evangelist.* But further, and to show the opposition of parity, both in principle and practice, to the order of the gospel—I ask you, would the preaching and baptizing of Presbyterian deacons, or even of ruling elders, be allowed and acknowledged by that Church? If not—where is your conformity with the order of the gospel? For indubitably, the primitive Deacons and Elders, ruling or not ruling, both preached and baptized; and where is your warrant for depriving these Scriptural orders in the Church of their ministerial privileges? What authority had Calvin, or the Assembly of Divines, to depart from the primitive apostolical order of Church ministers, and discontinue an order (as in the case of Deacons,) which, when *used well, purchased to them a good degree,* (that is, entitled them to advancement in the ministry,) *and great boldness in the faith which is in* CHRIST JESUS. 1 Tim. iii. 13. By what right did they split up the sacred order of a Scriptural Elder, or preaching Presbyter of the Church of CHRIST, into a mere secular office? Surely this parity must be a most despotic thing—suffering neither an inferior or superior in office, to come near it! If, then, no authority can be produced, either from Scripture, or elsewhere equivalent to Scripture—the mildest thing that can be said of the Presbyterian platform is, that it is a mistaken view of primitive truth and order. I again repeat, Sir, that *it is as a question of fact only* that any serious man can consider the disputed subject of orders in the Christian ministry. As such, it is accessible to every capacity : as such, if you will meet it, I shall most gladly profit by what your superior attainments in sacred Hermeneutics, Theological Science, and Ecclesiastical History shall bring forward. On any other ground it can only occasion collision of opposite views, productive of heat without light, upon which I shall not waste my time.

Assuming, then, till better informed, that the fact is against you, I now return to the course of reasoning you have adopted in support of parity, or rather, in opposition to Episcopacy. Page 643, you ask, ' Does Episcopal, in contradistinction to Presbyterial ordination, enter into the essence of the Church of CHRIST ?' To this I answer, without the slightest hesitation, that it does, and for this plain reason—because I believe the one to have a divine and verifiable commission to ordain, which the other does not possess. And if, according to your own acknowledgment, p. 637, divine right is essential to the validity of ministerial acts ; the authority to ordain must be of the essence of the Church of CHRIST, and in such sort essential, that with it there is a Church, authorized for the high and holy purposes of this Heaven-appointed institution, without it there is no Church. If this is not so, I cannot see what possible purpose a divinely instituted ministry, or a Church, or sacraments, are to answer. All reliance upon them, as revealed means of grace in the salvation of sinners, and as grounds of assurance to the hope of believers, *must forever rest on* THE FACT, *not on* THE IMAGINATION *that they are divine.* The sacraments of the Church are the seals of GOD's covenanted mercies : these sacraments must be administered by men ; and by what men, can no otherwise be determined than by the verifiable authority of the Head of the Church, transmitted through his apostles. To the case you put in the same page, then, in the following words—

"If we suppose two men ; one, with barely as much religion as to afford evidence that he is a Christian, who receives the sacrament from an ungodly, fox-hunting parish priest, and another of the highest piety and spirituality, who receives the sacrament from such a man as Philip Doddridge or Samuel Davies—are we to believe that the former has a divine warrant to hope for salvation, and that the other is cast off without any Scriptural hope of mercy?"

I answer, in the words of the 26th article, "Although, in the visible Church, the evil be ever mingled with the good, and sometime the evil hath chief authority in the ministration of the word and sacraments, yet, forasmuch as they do not the same in their own name, but in CHRIST's, *and do minister by his commission and authority*, we may use their ministry, both in hearing the word of GOD, and in receiving the sacraments.   Neither is the effect of CHRIST's ordinance taken away by their wickedness, nor the grace of GOD's gifts diminished from such, as by faith and rightly do receive the sacraments ministered unto them, which be effectual, because of CHRIST's institution and promise, although they be ministered by evil men."

To this answer you do in effect subscribe, by the declaration which immediately follows the case you put.   'Certainly (say you) *we do not limit the validity of a Christian ordinance to the worthiness of him who administers it.*'   Yet you certainly have put a case, which favours strongly the conclusion that the piety of the administrator is a substitute, and a safe one, too, for authority to administer; and as such it will be taken by nine-tenths of your readers, notwithstanding your feeble declaration by way of off-set.   But to show the fallacy of this conclusion, and strip the case of its power to mislead the ignorant and unreflecting, I ask you, To what is the recipient of a sacrament to refer for assurance that the application of water in the name of the Trinity, or the reception of bread and wine as memorials of CHRIST's death, are sacraments—are means of grace—are valid and effectual transactions with GOD in the infinite interests of salvation?   What is the Presbyterian ground of assurance that the sacraments are sacraments?   Step from under your veil, and let us know on what ground your people rely for confidence, that in the ministrations of religion, the sanction of the Almighty is with the actings and doings of those who call themselves his servants and ministers? We shall then be able to form a just opinion of the effect intended to be produced by this insidiously constructed case. But to sift it thoroughly, and counteract its injurious tendency—I ask you, what constituted the difference between your pious communicant, and either Doddridge or Davies? Whence had either of these a right to administer to him which he had not to administer to them? Was it their piety or their learning, or the choice of their respective congregations, which made the difference? Was it a compound of all these, with the ordination they had received? Was it their ordination itself? Was it any confidence or persuasion of mind in the recipient, that they were really lawful ministers of CHRIST, acting by divine authority? What was it, in your opinion, which gave to the bread and wine, administered as memorials of CHRIST's death, by Doddridge and Davies, a sacramental character? If you say, as you must do to keep clear of a greater difficulty, that the divine right conferred by their ordination constituted the difference between them, and the equally pious recipient, I agree with you, provided it was an authorized and Scriptural ordination—otherwise, their ministerial acts were worse than mere nullities. Thus your overwhelming case brings us to where we must for ever resort to ascertain the validity of ministerial acts, *viz :* the authority by which they are performed. Nor is there, in the compass of possibility, any other way to determine between a sacrament and the profanation of a holy mystery ordained by CHRIST himself, and instituted in his Church as a means of grace, a seal and pledge of covenanted mercies.

If, then, the ungodly, fox-hunting parish priest, was truly and Scripturally ordained, his ministrations are valid, and the recipient has to answer for his own qualifications, according to which will the effect of the sacrament be. Whereas, if Doddridge and Davies were not truly and Scripturally ordained, their piety can avail nothing as to conferring a sacramental character upon their acts—it gives them no authority to bind and loose, to receive or reject, to and from the communion of saints, in the sacraments of the Church. Their sacramental acts, however decently, orderly, and solemnly celebrated, (p. 642,) possess no character whereby the relation of the recipient to the covenant engagements of GOD is validly and efficaciously marked.

And I must be permitted to say, Sir, that you might have presented the contrast between an ungodly parish priest, and a godly dissenting minister, so as to test the influence of piety without authority, and of authority without piety, on the efficacy of the sacraments, without giving such just ground to accuse you of unfairness and uncharitableness, as this particular passage, and the whole structure of your argument exposes you to. If the validity of dissenting orders requires in its defence a resort to such miserable artifice, to keep alive the prejudices of the ignorant in its favour, it is a sign, either that its foundation is shaken, or that its present advocate is unacquainted with its real strength. As, however, you have chosen this course, I must follow you, at least so far as to expose the fallacy of your statements and reasonings, and check their deleterious influence in weakening, and eventually effacing from the minds of Christians, *the importance of the revealed order of the gospel, to the revealed hope of the gospel;* GOD hath seen good to bind them inseparably together, and together they must go to his tribunal. If the liberty wherewith CHRIST hath made us free, is in your estimation such, that *you are justified* in treating one half of his message as the creature of human convenience, and subject to human alteration or amendment—I confess, *I am thus not free;* I am in bondage to, *thus saith the* LORD, whether that be read in his holy word, or may be proved thereby, or be plainly certified by the faith and practice of the primitive Church, as the surest and safest guide to the truth of contested or corrupted Scripture.

At the same page, 643, you go on to ask,

" Is it necessary, in order to establish the validity of any ordination, to have recourse to authority? to be able to trace an ecclesiastical pedigree through each successive age to the apostles? We doubt whether the best ecclesiastical historian on the earth can do this. Besides, if it could be done, is there no breach in the line? Does not every body know, that the whole reformed Church, Bishops, Presbyters, and all, were excommunicated by the Church of Rome, from which they received ordination? Would Bishop Ravenscroft admit the ordaining power of an excommunicated and deposed Bishop? And now we ask, do the hopes of men for Heaven depend on such a foundation as this? If we cannot show that something was transmitted through the whole line of Popes and Bishops, to the man who ordained our humble and pious Pastor, are we shut out from GOD's promises, and cut off from his covenant mercies, and left in all the uncertainties of the benighted heathen? How does the man who has the courage to make the assertions prove them? Where is his *thus saith the* LORD for this? Surely Christian charity ought not to let him rest a moment, until by plain declarations of Scripture, he has put this thing beyond all possible doubt!"

Such, Sir, is the direction you choose to give to the principles laid down in these two Sermons; and though, for reasons obvious enough, you have made an *extreme case* of it, yet I flinch not from your ordeal. Religious principles, which cannot bear being extended to their *fair conclusions*, are not safe—they cannot be cherished—they savour not of the truth, or of the *wisdom which cometh down from above*—nor are they compatible with that sincerity and singleness of heart, which identifies them with our being. And be you from henceforth sure, Sir, that the man who has the courage to avow principles, thus *bone of his bone, and flesh of his flesh*, will always have the magnanimity to meet *fairly and openly*, every objection to them; will resort to no subterfuge, nor appeal to any prejudice. His charity, indeed, may not be of the modern liberal stamp, or blazoned in multiplied professions, as if it was liable to dispute; yet such as it is —and he strives that it may be what it ought to be—the man who makes these assertions, leaves it to Him who sees through every pretence, and discerns every motive, and meets your queries, as follows:

To your first inquiry—'Is authority, and succession from the apostles, necessary to establish the validity of any ordination?' I answer unqualifiedly in the affirmative—They are not only necessary, but essential and inseparable. The authority of CHRIST is the *only warrant* to act in his name; and succession from his apostles the only *satisfactory evidence* that any man, or body of men, are possessed of this warrant. And from the very nature of things, ministerial commission and authority can no otherwise be so verified, as to be consistent with assurance as to the validity and efficacy of religious ministrations in the name of CHRIST. The ministry in the Church *is a substitution for the* LORD JESUS CHRIST *in person*—"*As though* GOD *did beseech you by us, we pray you in* CHRIST's *stead*," says the apostle—nor can the ingenuity of all the dissenters upon earth propose or provide, (miracles excepted,) another method equally conclusive and satisfactory. If, however, they think they can do this, let us look at it, and try its worth.

But as this cannot be done—as three hundred years of the most persevering ingenuity and unwearied research, has advanced no farther than to reiterate objections, and renew assertions, which have again and again been answered, refuted, and disproved, and you continue to harp upon the same string —I must buckle on my armour, and go forth against this Goliah of dissent.

'We doubt (say you) whether the best ecclesiastical historian upon earth, can trace an ecclesiastical pedigree back through each successive age to the apostles.' Indeed ! then is there no such thing as a Christian minister of any order, or a Christian Church of any name, or Christian sacraments, or Christian religion, in Europe or America, certainly—perhaps not in the world. For such is the inevitable result of your doubt, if you can make it good. Alas, what a Japanese temper must this parity possess, that will even kill itself to slay its adversary ! But this is only a doubt of yours—in order to clear it up, as far as is in my power, I shall request your attention to the following facts and arguments, the substance of which I have extracted from Mr. Leslie's *Discourse on the Qualifications requisite to administer the Sacraments ;* an author with whom, as a theologian and a controversialist, you are doubtless acquainted.

That the succession from the apostles of the LORD JESUS CHRIST in the Protestant Episcopal Church of Great Britain, and consequently of America, has been traced ; and the individuals through whom it runs, named, both through the British Bishops, from the first planting of Christianity in that Island before the close of the first century, and also through the Bishops of the western or Latin Church, down to the present day ; is a matter

VOL. I.—35

of notoriety to every student of Ecclesiastical History——and however the lists therein given may be doubted or disputed, there is such weight of testimony in their favour as can only be overcome by contrary evidence. From the ancient British historians two things are clear——First, the line of succession in that Church is traced through the Bishops, and not through the Presbyters. Secondly, this succession is traced by these historians through the Archiepiscopal See of London, until the arrival of Augustine the Monk in Britain, in the seventh century—— after which, the See was removed to Canterbury, through which it is subsequently traced. And not only the ancient historians of Britain, but those also of all other countries where Christianity was planted, do show, *without exception*, that the government of the Church of CHRIST was episcopal and not presbyterian. *There not being a record extant, nor even an intimation in any historian, of a single Church, in any country, founded and governed on the presbyterian principle, previous to the sixteenth century.*

That Bishops were found in all branches of the Church of CHRIST, without exception, before the reformation, is *prima facia* evidence that such were the chief officers of the Church from the beginning ; nor can this testimony be overthrown, otherwise than by sufficient proof of the fact, that at some particular time, the Church was constituted on some other principle than that of episcopal rule and superintendence. Suppose then it be admitted, that some of the smaller branches of the Church are unable to show the succession of their particular Bishops and apostles——yet if the majority, especially the larger and more noted ones——such as Rome, Antioch, Alexandria, and other once famous Churches——are able to do this, it is a sufficient proof for all the rest ; because they all stand upon the same authority, and are all derived in the same manner——and it rests with those who deny the succession, to assign the breach, and prove it by sufficient testimony : it being the dictate of reason and common sense, as well as a maxim of law, that if I am in possession, my title is held to be good, until by proper evidence, it is shown to be unfounded. In such a case, asserting a defect in title is nothing to the purpose, nor will the most specious assumptions, or ingenious reasonings, avail any thing, in the absence of facts sufficiently proven. It were an easy matter for me to present you with the succession, under which the episcopate in this country claims and holds apostolic authority. I could extract it from Mosheim, from the Gospel Messenger, printed in South Carolina, or from a little work (which perhaps you have seen) called the *Trial of Episcopacy:* but as you have no doubt access to some of these, and it would needlessly swell this pamphlet, I decline it, at any rate in the body of the work. Well persuaded I am, that you stand in no need of information to this point ; and could you have succeeded in assigning and supporting a breach in the chain of episcopal succession, it is hardly to be supposed you would have let this opportunity slip, and contented yourself, as all your predecessors have done, with bold but unsupported assertion, erroneous quotation, and mere declamation. How comes it to pass, pray, that in three hundred years of controversy on this subject, not one of you have been able to bring forward any thing worthy the name of *proof*, either *for parity* as a matter of fact, or *against imparity* as a fact. Surely, on so momentous a subject —if this has not been done hitherto, we may safely conclude that it cannot be done at all. But suppose you could succeed in scattering episcopal succession to the winds, what would you gain by it ? Would the divine right of presbytery be thereby established ? No, by no means. That would still remain a substantive proposition to be established by its proper proofs, against Congregationalists, Independents, and names without end. And if doubt and difficulty and even failure, as you insinuate, attends the succession in the line of Bishops, how much more intricate and unsearchable must it be to hunt it through the line of Presbyters ? Your whole gain then would be demolition of such a thing as a Christian ministry in Europe, Asia, and America ; and unless we could recover it again in the wilds of Hindostan, (where I should certainly go to find it*) faith must fail, and certainty and assurance perish, from the hope of man.

---

* The reader is directed to a work republished in this country under the title of *Christian Researches in Asia, by the Rev.* CLAUDIUS BUCHANAN, D. D., for a very interesting account of a numerous body of Christians, episcopally constituted in the

Of the same *felo de se* description, is your poor resort to papal excommunication, as an argument against episcopacy. 'Does not every body know,' say you, 'that the whole reformed Church, Bishops, Presbyters, and all, were excommunicated by the Church of Rome, from which they received ordination?' And what then? Do Presbyterians regard it? If not, why should Episcopalians? The objection might have some weight if brought forward by a Papist; but by a Protestant of the purest breed, I confess I do not see its bearing on the present question, unless to cast us all back into the arms of the Pope.

As, however, you labour hard to instill into the minds of your readers, that Episcopal are but little removed from Popish doctrines, and thereby continue and increase prejudice, I will endeavour to put you and them in the way to obtain a better informed mind on this point. In order to which, I must take the liberty to contradict your assertion, that all the world knows that the British Church received her orders from the Bishop or Pope of Rome; for that is the notion invariably attached to the words "Church of Rome" by ninety-nine in the hundred, who either hear or read them. Whether it is the meaning you meant to convey, you best know; but in this, the most common acceptation of the words, *it is not the fact*, and therefore, neither you, nor all the world, can know any such thing.

It is not the fact, that the succession of any Protestant hierarchical Church is derived *through the person of the Bishop or Pope of Rome*. Perhaps not a single Bishop who reformed from popery in the sixteenth century received his consecration by imposition of the Pope's hands—perhaps not one in a hundred of the existing bishops in the Latin or Western church during any Pontificate from the rise of the Papacy were thus consecrated. And it is not an unreasonable or unfounded assumption, that in the wide and extended boundary of the Western Church, the ordaining power was canonically transmitted in the regular

interior of India. But as the support thereby given to the cause of episcopacy was supposed by some one to be too strong for the interests of parity—an edition was published some where to the north, with the same title, in which all that related to the episcopal character of the Syrian Christians is suppressed. A full edition was published in New-York, in 1812, by Richard Scott.

succession from Bishop to Bishop, without contracting any *fancied contamination* from the person of the pope. With respect to the succession of the British Church in particular, and so far as that flows through the Western Church, we know that the Bishop of Rome had, personally, little or nothing to do with it up to the seventh century. It was an independent apostolical Church under its own Bishops—its connexion with the Church of Rome commenced with Augustine the monk, who was consecrated the first Archbishop of Canterbury, not by the Bishop of Rome, but by the Archbishop of Arles, in France, early in the seventh century. And I notice this, not because there is any real force in the objection derived from the succession passing through even the person of the Bishop or Pope of Rome—but in order to remove the prejudices so studiously instilled into the minds of the ignorant on this subject. For, admitting the utmost that the bitterest enemy of the Church can ask for, that the British Bishops were all, in succession, consecrated by some of the Popes of Rome, what can you gain by it? If the Bishop of Rome had a true succession from the apostles of CHRIST, was the transfer of that succession to other Bishops nullified by his usurpations, or even by his personal ungodliness? Among the many and grievous corruptions of that Church, is the succession of its Bishops to be so considered? I suspect if this is properly searched into, the most grievous corruption the succession of the Christian ministry from CHRIST's apostles, as the root of the ordaining power in the visible Church is capable of, will be found to originate with those men who, in the sixteenth century, usurped the power of commiting to others what never was committed to themselves—what they never possessed in any previous age of the Church ; and for whose right to exercise the ordaining power, not the shadow of a proof has ever been produced either from Scripture rightly interpreted, or from antiquity ; and whose author cannot be shown ever to have had orders of any kind, Popish or Protestant. If such an uncertainty (not to say breach) could be asserted of the ministerial succession through the line of Bishops, as can be asserted, and assigned too, in the line of Presbyters, so far as Calvin is concerned, no sincere man could contend for it. He would have to look elsewhere than in the succession of the Western Church, for that appointment of heaven which alone gives certainty to the Church, as the one undivided spouse and body of CHRIST—to that *truth*, of which it is *the pillar and ground*—to *the faith once delivered to the saints* —to the sacraments as seals and pledges of covenanted engagements and means of grace—to the hope of man as founded on revealed mercy, and built on the firm and unsevered foundation of the faith and order of the gospel mutually confirming each other.

Since, therefore, the reformed churches, especially the British Church, did not derive their orders from the Bishop of Rome personally, there is the less force in the objection raised from his withdrawing them by excommunication. But again, supposing that every single reformed Bishop was such by the laying on of the Pope's hands, does it follow that the exercise of an usurped and unlawful power destroys the effect of his acts performed in virtue of a power of which he was rightly and lawfully possessed? Certainly, Sir, you know that it is a maxim of the soundest reason, though I doubt whether you will acknowledge it, that usurped power cannot pass into lawful authority. That the supremacy claimed by the Bishop of Rome was an usurpation, and no part of his original and rightful episcopal authority can require no proof to a Protestant; nor yet is it needful to show that such of his equals, in spiritual office, as had submitted to this usurpation in the darkness of the middle ages, were not thereby precluded from shaking off this lawless authority usurped over them, and from resuming the independence of their character, and the exercise of their just and equal rights, as the spread of knowledge and the investigations of inquiry laid open and exposed the corruptions on which this anti-christian domination was built up.

While, therefore, Bishop Ravenscroft would not admit the ordaining or any other power of an excommunicated and deposed Bishop, he would yet take the liberty to examine and determine whether such excommunication and deposition were lawfully and regularly pronounced, and thereupon decide for himself. Nothing like a superiority of spiritual power or authority is known or owned among Christian Bishops. The Episcopate is one, of which each Bishop holds a part.   This part is equal in each, *and includes all powers originally annexed to the office by its founder*—'*the Shepherd and Bishop of our souls.* These original powers do not include the tremendous power of excommunicating each other.   No single Bishop can exercise it towards another Bishop.   Where it becomes necessary to resort to it, it must be the act of that particular body or Church to which the offending Bishop belongs; and if regularly and canonically pronounced, will be respected by the Church catholic.   But if founded upon usurped power, or uncanonically and irregularly pronounced, it cannot rescind and annul the power conferred on a Bishop or Bishops by their regular and canonical consecration.   And this is a necessary consequence from the very nature and fundamentals of society, or associated individuals, whether the purpose of their association be civil or religious.   If, for example, the Bishop and Clergy of the diocese of North Carolina should undertake to fulminate a Bull of excommunication against a particular Bishop, or against all the American Bishops, would it any way, or in the judgment of any sound mind, be entitled to respect, or considered as at all affecting their lawful power and authority?   And precisely of the same worth is the excommunication of the reforming Bishops, clergy, and people, by the Bishop of Rome, and his consistory of cardinals.   It was a mere nullity, sanctioned by no principle of reason or religion, and is of no avail even to a contender for parity, in assigning it as a breach in the apostolical succession of the Protestant Episcopal Church.

Not satisfied, however, with these startling inquiries, so well calculated to feed the prejudices of the ignorant and ill informed, you rise in all the majesty of Presbyterian climax, and ask, 'If we cannot show that something was transmitted from St. Peter or St. Paul, through the whole line of Popes and Bishops, to the man who ordained our humble and pious pastor: Are we shut out from GOD's promises, and cut off from his covenant mercies, and left in all the uncertainties of the benighted heathen?'   In reply to which, I would just ask you who hold the divine right of the ministry in the Church, how the divine right 'in our humble and pious pastor' is to be ascertained without something transmitted from the apostles of CHRIST, which is capable of proof as a fact? I would also ask you *how those persons who cut themselves off from the line in which these promises and mercies are revealed and limited, can claim the benefit of them?* And I might here leave you to all the ingenuity you are master of, without the slightest fear of your being able to escape from the difficulty of a divine right in the ministry asserted, and the only possible proof of it rejected. But as your question is an appeal to the feelings and passions of your dissenting readers, and an argument addressed to the ignorant and prejudiced of every class, I must meet it and refute it. And this I am happily able to do in the most decisive manner. Whether the ground work of your question is taken from Bishop Hoadly you best know—it is, however, so similar in its character to his views on the subject of uninterrupted succession in the Christian ministry, that I shall meet it with the arguments of Mr. Law.

The position laid down by the Bishop of Bangor is, in substance, that the claims to regular and uninterrupted succession in the ministry of the Church of CHRIST are vain words, mere niceties, trifles, and dreams. To which Mr. Law replies in the following manner, "Thus much surely is implied in these words; that no kind of ordination or mission of the clergy is of any consequence or moment to us. For if the ordination need not be regular, or derived from those who had authority from CHRIST to ordain, it is plain that no particular kind of ordination can be of any more value than another. For no ordination whatever can have any worse defects than being irregular and not derived by a succession from CHRIST"—"for if there be not a succession of persons authorized from CHRIST to send others to act in his name, then both Episcopal and Presbyterian teachers are equally usurpers, and as mere laymen as any at all; for there cannot be any other difference between the clergy and laity, but as the one hath authority from CHRIST to perform offices which the other hath not. But this authority can be no otherwise had than by an uninterrupted succession of men from CHRIST, empowered to qualify others. For if the succession be once broke, people must either go into the ministry of their own accord, or be sent by such as have no more power to send others than to go themselves.   And, my LORD, can these be called ministers of CHRIST, or be received as his ambassadors? Can they be thought to act in his name, who have no authority from him?   If so, your lordship's servant might ordain and baptize to as much purpose as your lordship; for it could only be objected to such actions, that they had no authority from CHRIST.   And if there be no succession of ordainers from him, every one is equally qualified to ordain.   My Lord, I should think it might be granted me, that the administering of a sacrament is an action we have no right to perform, considered either as men, gentlemen, or scholars, or members of a civil society. Who then can have any authority to interpose but he that has it from CHRIST?   And how can that be had from him, without a succession of men from him, is not easily conceived.   Should a private person choose a Lord Chancellor, and declare his good authority, would there be any thing but absurdity, impudence, and presumption in it?   But why he cannot commission a person to act, sign, and seal, in the king's name, as well as in the name of CHRIST, is unaccountable."

"My Lord, it is a plain and obvious truth, that no man, or number of men, considered as such, can any more make a Priest, or commission a person to officiate in CHRIST's name as such, than he can enlarge the means of grace, or add a new sacrament for the conveyance of spiritual advantages.   The ministers of CHRIST are as much positive ordinances as the sacraments, and we might as well think that sacraments not instituted by him, might be means of grace, as those pass for his ministers who have no authority from him.   Once more—all things are either in common in the Church of CHRIST or they are not; if they are, then every one may preach, baptize, ordain, &c.   If all things are not thus common, but the administering the sacraments and ordination, &c. are offices appropriated to particular persons, then I desire to know how in this present age, or any other since the apostles, Christians can know their respective duties, or what they may or may not do with the several acts of Church communion, if there be no uninterrupted succession of authorised persons from CHRIST?   For until authority from CHRIST appears, to make a difference between them, we are all alike, and any one may officiate as well as another. If there be no uninterrupted succession, then there are no authorized ministers from CHRIST ; if no such ministers, then no Christian sacraments; if no Christian sacraments, then no Christian covenant, whereof the sacraments are the stated and visible seals." *First Letter*.

From this unanswerable and most convincing reasoning, which applies as strictly to the principles you support, and to the whole scope of your argument and assertions in these Reviews, as to the principles of Bishop Hoadly ; I think it clear, even to demonstration, that the ground you take on the subject of the Christian ministry is both dangerous and untenable. That you know it to be such, is not to be presumed : yet you must know how readily, and even gladly, the world catches at the slightest objection to the truth and certainty of revealed religion ; and you must be aware, that, whatever tends to throw obscurity and uncertainty over the appointments of the divine wisdom for assurance to man of those invisible things of which faith is the evidence, does in an equal degree at least, foster and cherish the daring infidelity of this latter day. To your cooler reflection then, I must leave it to determine, how far the structure of your argument throughout, and particularly what you present and support as the just and scriptural view of the Church and ministry of JESUS CHRIST, is calculated to mislead the ignorant and unwary, to cast down the defences of the gospel, and turn men adrift on the ocean of life, without chart or compass to guide them *to the rest that remaineth for the people of* GOD.

But while I trust that you will seriously reconsider your ground, I must yet pursue the track you have taken, and for the sake of myself as well as others, detect and expose every error I think you have committed, either in assertion, quotation, or reasoning. Page 644, you go on to say—

"We know that the founders of the Church of England did not hold these sentiments : (on the succession of the ministry in connexion with the gospel covenant :) we are sure too, that it is not in the Bible as we read it, and we feel prepared to make our assertion good."

Presuming, that by the word *founders*, you mean the *reformers* of the Church of England, (its foundation being in the first century and apostolical,)—you must be able then to show that the men who gave their bodies to the flames in behalf of the truth, were double minded men ;—that the men who declared in the Preface to the Ordinal that "it is evident unto all men, diligently reading Holy Scripture and ancient authors, that from the apostles' times there have been these orders of ministers in CHRIST's Church, Bishops, Priests, and Deacons"—"and therefore to the intent that these orders may be continued and reverently used and esteemed in the Church, no man shall be accounted or taken to be a lawful Bishop, Priest, or Deacon in this Church; or be suffered to execute any of the said functions, except he be called, tried, examined and admitted thereunto, according to the form hereafter following, or hath had Episcopal consecration or ordination :" did, nevertheless, consider uninterrupted succession from CHRIST's apostles, in the line of Bishops, as incapable of proof and unimportant to the validity of the ministerial commission ; and did confess and allow, that persons otherwise than episcopally ordained had, equally with themselves, a divine right to administer the affairs of CHRIST's kingdom in the world.   For this you must do, to redeem your pledge and escape the censure justly due to so unfounded an assertion.   I think I know what you can bring forward on this point ; and doubt not that it will be fully met ; in the mean time, I am sure that the reformers no where contradict those well considered principles, which they have set forth as fundamental, in the Articles, Rubrics, Liturgy and Ordinal.   They were, it is true, men of great moderation and forbearance, and did not heedlessly commit themselves, or weaken the general cause of reform by obtruding their views, uncalled for, upon the continental Churches: but they were firm men, and never flinched from their principles in the hour of trial.   When you make good your assertion, then, by producing from the reformers, as such, a declaration contrary to that given you from the Ordinal, I will credit it.

In what manner you read the Bible, I have no means of knowing ; this I know, however, that it may be so read as to give countenance and fancied support to the most opposite as well as the most unfounded notions—witness the present state of the Christian world. From the specimen given in these Reviews, however, it would appear that it is searched rather with a view to find out what is in favour of a particular previous profession, than to ascertain the real connexion of the faith and order of the gospel, with the revealed hope of man. To this must be attributed the insidious nature of the assertion, that there is no direct or express declaration in the Scriptures, concerning the importance of an uninterrupted succession of the ministry. Hence (as you well know) the hasty conclusion of most of your readers, ' If it is not in the Bible, it need not be believed' ; and thus the whole subject is dismissed from the attention, and the mind pre-occupied against just information. Yet I would humbly suggest, that the wonder-working system of Hermeneutics which can draw from the Bible the doctrines of particular redemption ; of predestination to eternal life of a part, and to eternal death of the rest of mankind by the most merciful GOD, without respect or foresight of any good or evil by them done ; might find in that same Bible at least equal support for an uninterrupted succession from CHRIST, through apostles, to give validity, and effect too, to sacraments, as seals of the grace of the gospel. This you say is not to be found in the Bible, *as you read it*, and that *you are prepared to make your assertion good*. And here, Sir—though I might safely leave the point on this issue, and put you upon proving your negative, which you can never do—yet for the sake of those who might be still further misled by the boldness of the assertion, I will present such proofs for the affirmative as cannot be denied by any reasonable man, however they may be unreasonably resisted ; and here again I shall avail myself of Mr. Law's reasoning against the Bishop of Bangor.

" It appears from Scripture, that all the sacerdotal power is derived from the HOLY GHOST. Our SAVIOUR himself took not the ministry upon him, till he had his consecration ; and during the time of his ministry, he was under the guidance and direction of the HOLY GHOST. Through the HOLY GHOST, he gave commandment to the Apostles whom he had chosen. When he ordained them to the ministry, it was with these words,

Receive the HOLY GHOST. Those whom the Apostles ordainèd to the same function, it was by the same authority; they laid their hands upon the Elders, exhorting them to *take care of the flock of* CHRIST, *over which the* HOLY GHOST *had made them overseers.* Hereby they plainly declared, that however this office was to descend from man to man, through human hands, it was the HOLY GHOST which consecrated them to that employment, and gave them authority to execute it."

" From this it is manifest, that the priesthood is a grace of the HOLY GHOST; that it is not a function founded in the natural or civil rights of mankind, but is derived from the special authority of the HOLY GHOST, and is as truly a positive institution as the sacraments. So that they who have no authority to alter the old sacraments, and substitute new ones, have no power to alter the old order of the Clergy, or introduce any other order of them. For why can we not change the sacraments? Is it not because they are only sacraments, and operate as they are instituted by the HOLY GHOST? Because they are useless inefficient rites without this authority? And does not the same reason hold as well for the order of the Clergy? Does not the same Scripture tell us they are equally instituted by the HOLY GHOST, and oblige only by virtue of his authority?

" How comes it, my Lord, that we cannot alter the Scriptures? Is it not because they are divinely inspired and declared by the HOLY GHOST? And since it is express Scripture, that the priesthood is instituted and authorised by the same HOLY SPIRIT, why is not the HOLY GHOST as much to be regarded in one institution as another? Why may we not as well make a gospel, and say it was writ by the HOLY GHOST, as make a new order of clergy, and call them His, or esteem them as having any relation to Him?

" From this it likewise appears, that there is an absolute necessity of a strict succession of authorized ordainers, from the apostolic times, in order to constitute a Christian Priest. For since a commission from the HOLY GHOST is necessary for the exercise of the office, no one can now receive it, but from those who have derived their authority in a true succession from the Apostles.   We could not, my Lord, call our present Bibles the word of God, unless we knew the copies from which they are taken, were taken from other true ones, till we came to the originals themselves.   No more could we call any true ministers, or authorized by the Holy Ghost, who have not received their commission by an uninterrupted succession of lawful ordainers."——"And as to its not being mentioned in the Scriptures——the doctrine on which it is founded, plainly made it unnecessary to mention it.   Is it needful for the Scriptures to tell us, that if we take our Bible from any false copy, that is not the word of God?   Why then need they tell us, that if we are ordained by usurping false pretenders to ordination, not deriving their authority to that end from the Apostles, we are no priests?   Does not the thing itself speak as plain in one case as the other?"   " I shall therefore, my Lord, take leave to lay it down as a plain undeniable Christian truth, that the order of the clergy is an order of as necessary obligation as the sacraments, and as unalterable as the Holy Scriptures ; the same Holy Ghost being as truly the author and founder of the priesthood, as the institutor of the sacraments, or the inspirer of the divine oracles.

"What your Lordship charges upon your adversaries as an absurd doctrine, in pretending the necessity of one regular, successive, and particular order of the clergy, is a true Christian doctrine ; and as certain from Scripture, as that we are to keep to the institution of particular sacraments ; or not to alter those particular Scriptures which now compose the canon of the Old and New Testament."   *Second Letter.*

Nevertheless you ' are sure, it is not in the Bible as you read it.'   And how many things by you considered more sacred than uninterrupted succession, have no express—*thus saith the Lord*—in the letter of Scripture ?   Are they therefore unscriptural, and to be cast away from the observance of Christians ?   But whatever you may think, or say, the truth of the matter is undeniably this, ' If nothing is to be esteemed of any moment among Christians, which is not expressly required in the Scriptures, then it is of no moment whether we believe the Scripture to be a standing rule of faith in all ages—whether we have any clergy at all—whether we observe the Lord's day—whether we baptize our children—or whether we go to public worship; for none of these things are expressly required in so many words in Scripture. But if you, and those who follow your faith will take these things to be of moment, and well proved, because they are *founded in Scripture,* though not in express terms, or under plain commands—if you and they will acknowledge these matters to be well asserted, because they may be *gathered from Scripture,* and are confirmed by the universal practice of the Church in all ages, (which is all the proof they are capable of) I do not doubt but it will appear, that this successive order of the Clergy is founded on the same evidence, and supported by as great authority; so that it must be thought of the same moment with these by all unprejudiced persons. For though it be not expressly said, that there shall always be a succession of Episcopal clergy yet it is a truth founded in Scripture itself, and asserted by the universal voice of tradition, in the first and succeeding ages of the Church."

Your objection, then, to episcopal succession in the ministry, from the want of express words of Scripture for its institution, by proving too much, proves nothing but the weakness of the cause which is reduced to so poor a shift. For, to be consistent, you must abandon every Christian doctrine and practice not thus supported. In truth, you must surrender the Bible as the word of God : for its claim to that high distinction rests on the same foundation, and is established by the same testimony with the uninterrupted line of episcopal succession in the Church of CHRIST.

As, however, this objection is the strong hold of the dissenters, and widely spread in its operation, not only upon the illiterate and ignorant, but upon those, also, who might be presumed, from their advantages of education, and the supreme importance of the subject, better informed respecting it ; I must carry out the argument from Scripture, for uninterrupted succession from the apostles in the Christian ministry, to the different orders in that succession.

To proceed with the argument, then. "The order of the clergy, is not only a positive order instituted by God, but the different degrees in this order are of the same nature. For we find in Scripture that some persons could perform some offices in the priesthood, which neither Deacons nor Priests could do, though those Deacons and Priests were inspired persons and workers of miracles. Thus Timothy was sent to ordain Elders, because none below his order, who was a Bishop, could perform that office. Peter and John laid their hands upon baptized persons, because neither Priests nor Deacons, though workers of miracles, could execute that part of the sacerdotal office.

" Now can we imagine that the apostles and bishops thus distinguished themselves for nothing ? That there was the same power in Deacons and Priests to execute those offices, though they took them to themselves ? No, my Lord, if three degrees in the ministry are instituted in Scripture, we are obliged to think them as truly distinct in their powers as we are to think that the Priesthood itself contains powers that are distinct from those of the laity. It is no more consistent with Scripture, to say that Deacons or Priests may ordain, than that the laity are Priests and Deacons. The same divine institution making as truly a difference betwixt the clergy, as it does betwixt clergy and laity. Now if the order of the clergy be a divine positive institution, in which there are different degrees of power, where some alone can ordain, &c. whilst others can only perform other parts of the sacred office ; if this (as it plainly appears) be a doctrine of Scripture, then it is a doctrine of Scripture that there is a necessity of such a succession of men as have power to ordain. For, do the Scriptures make it necessary that Timothy (or some Bishop) should be sent to Ephesus to ordain Priests, because the Priests who were there could not ordain ? And do not the same Scriptures make it as necessary that Timothy's successor be the only ordainer, as well as he was in his time ? Will not Priests in the next age, be as destitute of the power of ordaining as when Timothy was alive ? So that, since the Scriptures teach that Timothy, or persons of his order, could alone ordain in that age, they as plainly teach, that the successors of that order can alone ordain in any age : and, consequently, the Scriptures plainly teach a necessity of an episcopal succession.

" The Scriptures declare there is a necessity of a divine commission to execute the office of a Priest.   They also teach that this commission can only be had from particular persons; therefore, the Scriptures plainly teach, there is a necessity of a succession of such particular persons, in order to keep up a truly commissioned clergy.   Suppose, when Timothy was sent to Ephesus to ordain Elders, the Church had told him 'We have chosen Elders already, and laid our hands upon them.' Would such a practice have been allowed of in the Ephesians, or would ministers so ordained, have been received as the ministers of CHRIST?   If not, why must such ministers be allowed of in any after ages?   Would not the same proceeding against any of Timothy's successors have deserved the same censure, as being equally unlawful?   If, therefore, the Scripture condemns all ordination but what is episcopal, the Scriptures make a succession of episcopal ordainers necessary.   So that I hope, my Lord, we shall be no more told that this is a doctrine not mentioned in Scripture, or without any foundation in it."   *Ibid.*

Thus, Sir, have I met your objections to the claim of uninterrupted episcopal succession from the apostles of CHRIST from the want of express warrant of Scripture for it, in the words, and with the arguments, of Mr. Law, in the controversy with Bishop Hoadly.   As the objection on your part, is identically the same with that of the Right Rev. Prelate, the complete refutation of it, as advanced by him, contained in Mr. Law's *Second Letter*, is equally solid and satisfactory when used against it as revived by you.

You next inquire, p. 644,

"Are the great body of the laity, by the constitution of the Church of CHRIST, brought to this point, that they must either trace back an ecclesiastical pedigree to the apostles, a thing plainly impossible, or believe the declarations of Priests and Bishops, that they themselves are the accredited agents for transacting business between GOD and man, or be cut off from the scriptural hope of salvation?   Where do we find any thing like this in our Bible, that charter of our Christian liberty?"

To which I reply, that I have already showed to you, and to
VOL. I.—37

all who may read this, what the Bible says, and warrants us to say, on this point. To any rational Christian assurance, the authority by which we are admitted into the Christian covenant, and continued in it through the sacraments, must be verified as a fact; otherwise our persuasion is a blind credulity. But as the church of CHRIST, like every other form of social government, when once established, needs not to be the subject of continual doubt and investigation; no greater difficulty is presented to the laity, from the nature of the thing, in ascertaining the Church of CHRIST, than in ascertaining the government under which they live. They find them both in existence, acting by their proper and constitutional officers; and this is, and ought to be perfectly satisfactory. In times of rebellion and usurpation in the State, and of separation and division of the Church, there may indeed be difficulty; but no greater *impossibility* exists in the one case than in the other, to determine the true from the false and usurping rulers, or the right or the wrong of opposite claims to the lawful authority, when tried as matters of fact, and not as things of shifting opinion and private liking. It is only when bold assertions, and plausible but unfounded reasonings, are substituted for facts—when habit and the prejudices of education have perverted the judgment, and when the lapse of time has shed something of sacredness over existing institutions, whether civil or religious, that the difficulty is really felt. But in the case of the Church, it never can amount to *impossibility;* for GOD requires nothing such from his creatures: and yet he certainly requires of them to conform to the conditions on which his mercy is promised, if they would obtain a title to it. And one of those conditions being, *membership in his visible Church on earth*, it is rather a rash assertion on your part to say, ' *it is plainly impossible*' to discern the only mark by which the true Church can be verified, in the divine right of its ministry derived by succession from the Apostles of CHRIST. And I would be really glad to know, if 'the declarations of the Priests and Bishops that they themselves are the accredited agents for transacting business between GOD and man' present no sufficient ground of rational confidence, what better security the declarations of Presbyterians and other dissenters, that they are the agents of Heaven's grace, afford to the laity? Does this charitable Reviewer mean to insinuate, that Priests and Bishops are *ex-officio* liars and deceivers; and Dissenters, by virtue of their schism, true and lawful men? I hope not; yet from the structure of this sentence, and the gall visible in every allusion to Episcopal claims throughout his work, I think he is bound to show on what grounds the declarations of Priests and Bishops are less worthy of credit than the declarations of Presbyterian' and other dissenting ministers, to the same agency. Assuredly, I contend for no implicit reception by the people, of assertions and declarations of Bishops and Priests, or pretenders to priestly authority. On the contrary (and that is my offence) my sole aim is, to rouse the deluded portion of this Christian land to demand of their respective spiritual guides evidence of their commission from CHRIST, as a fact. If they have it, let them produce it, and put to silence all opposition. If they have it not, let them manifest their sincerity by the surrender of their pretensions.

Again, Sir, we are come to the very point betwixt you and myself. And though an ignorant layman may not be able to trace an ecclesiastical pedigree back to the apostles, yet a learned divine, and deeply read Theological Professor, can be under no great difficulty on such a requirement. Give us, then the list of your ordainers, or those of any other Presbyterian clergyman on earth, *through the line of Presbyters*, back to the apostles. Show us, by good and sufficient evidence, that in the apostle's days, there was a branch of the Church of CHRIST founded by them on Presbyterian principles, with one order of ministers only, from which you are derived; and you will do more for the peace and union of Christendom, and for the advancement of the Redeemer's kingdom, than if you were to fill the world with *Irenicums*, and other meek and lowly question-begging publications, or with such gratuitous assertions and unfounded and fallacious reasonings as these Reviews are filled with. Do this, Sir, and all bar to acknowledgment and communion on my part, is done away. It is, to be sure, a small offer, and is felt to be of little worth, but it is all I have.

The point to which the attention of your readers is next called, is set forth in the following words, at the same page :

"What portion of the New Testament affords the slightest foundation for the opinion, that the Christian Ministry ought to be modelled according to the pattern of the Jewish Priesthood?"

" None, that I know of, in the restricted sense in which it is evident you mean the question to be taken by your readers. Yet surely there is to the full as much warrant for the similarity between the legal and evangelical priesthoods, in appointment, order, and use, as there is for the respective dispensations to which they belong—as there is for the respective sabbaths—for the corresponding festivals of the Church, with the paschal and pentecostal feasts—and for the respective sacraments of the Law and the Gospel. There may not be a *thus saith the* LORD, for this opinion, to which you would restrict it ; and yet there may be sufficient foundation for it from Scripture : for certainly there is such a thing as analogy of positive institutions, as well as of faith. If then, St. Paul, when speaking of the Christian priesthood to converted Jews, says, that *no man taketh this honour unto himself, but he that is called of* GOD *as was Aaron ;* is there in this no allusion to the model of that priesthood with which they were familiar ? And if the same apostle states in his Epistle to the Corinthians, chap. x. that the Jewish sacraments were types of those sacred institutions under the gospel, through which, as channels, the same spiritual blessings were and are derived to his people ; might not a Christian divine have expressed himself more guardedly ? Especially, when he cannot but know what a cloud of Christian witnesses, in the preceding ages of the Church, have found sufficient foundation in the New Testament, as they understood it, to warrant the direct assertion, that thus the Christian priesthood was constructed. And might not a Presbyterian divine have recollected, that he whom, of all the Christian fathers, they most admire, and oftenest quote as with them, even St. Jerome himself, asserts expressly in his Epistle to Evagrius, that " what Aaron and his sons and the Levites were in the Temple, *that same* are Bishops, Presbyters and Deacons in the Church ? "

But it seems this argument ' Is not Protestant enough for our country,' p. 645.   But if it is supported by Scripture soundly interpreted by the unanimous voice of Christian antiquity, and by the reason of the thing, I trust it will be considered so truly Protestant as not to be shaken in its just application by the bare assertion of an interested declaimer for parity, who has given full proof, as in his Essay on Baptism, that when it suits his purpose he can contend for doctrine on the analogy and construction of Scripture, and can find the primitive fathers (in other words, recorded tradition) good and sufficient witnesses and safe expositors of holy writ.   But further,

" The soundest reasoners among Episcopalians have long ago given up this argument, because, if it proves any thing, it proves too much."

Who these ' soundest reasoners' are, I have no means of knowing ; and certainly I have not resorted to it.   But this I know, that no sound and well informed Episcopalian, who knew, and understood, and felt the unshaken security of his foundation, ever used this argument otherwise than by analogy and correspondence, to illustrate and support what was, by other testimony, proved and established.   And this I also know, that the consequence you draw from it, ' that there ought to be but one Bishop as the visible head of the Christian Church,' no more follows from the right use of the argument, than it follows from any mode of using it, that there ought to be but one order of ministers in the Church of CHRIST.

Every well instructed Episcopalian will tell you, that this great High Priest (of whom the Jewish High Priest was a visible type, and therefore but one) *is passed into the heavens, now to appear in the presence of* GOD *for us,* and that he is the only Head of his body—the Church.   But he will also tell you, and make good the fact by the clearest testimony which any matter of fact is capable of, that *when he ascended up on high, he gave* —various orders of ministers to his Church—*for the perfecting of the saints, for the work of the ministry, for the edifying of the body of* CHRIST ; and that because in various orders of the same office, there must necessarily be degrees of authority—therefore, that order in the Christian ministry, to which the chief authority is committed, and from which the other orders derive their commission, is aptly illustrated by a corresponding order to the Jewish Hierarchy. And did Presbyterians only reflect, that Christianity was first preached to Jews, who were already familiar with different degrees of order in the ministerial office; they would surely think it more reasonable to explain what is obscure in the New Testament writers, as to the delineation of the order of the Gospel, by what was established and familiar in the Church under the Law, than obstinately to insist upon this obscurity, in order to support a recent invention of men, for which, as a matter of fact, they cannot bring forward any thing deserving the name of testimony, either from Scripture, or usage in the Church, before or since the coming of CHRIST.

Your next objection to the claim of uninterrupted succession from the apostles of CHRIST, through the order of Bishops, is founded on the assertion, that the apostles, as extraordinary officers, endowed with peculiar gifts, and eye witnesses of CHRIST's resurrection, could have no successors ; p. 645. And it is granted in the fullest extent, as to these *peculiar distinctions* of the apostolic office. Episcopalians lay no claim to apostolic endowments for their Bishops. They claim only the transfer of the apostolic powers of ordaining and governing in the Church, which the Apostles certainly possessed, which are indispensable to the existence and progress of the Church, which can be exercised without miraculous power, and which they indubitably committed to faithful men for perpetuity of the Church, for order and discipline in the management of its affairs, and for certainty and assurance in the faith. In this sense only are Christian Bishops ever considered, or spoken of, as successors of the apostles, by Episcopalians.

As I have had occasion, however, to notice this point in a Sermon, delivered at the first Ordination I ever held, which the Convention of this diocese thought good to publish, and which has not fallen under your observation, I will present you with an extract from it.   The text is from St. John's Gospel, Chap. xx. 21.   *As my Father hath sent me, even so send I you.*   From these words, at the 11th page, I draw the following conclusions:

" First. That whatever the authority of CHRIST in the gospel dispensation was, with reference to the Church, of the same extent was that of his apostles. As he alone could purchase, so they only could plant and govern, his Church; all others were interdicted from any interference.

" Secondly.   As the Church and ministry in this dispensation, were intended for perpetuity *even till the earth be filled with the knowledge of the* LORD—therefore this authority must also continue, and run parallel with it, through all generations.   As CHRIST's commission and authority derived from the Father, admitted a transfer of it to his apostles; in like manner, the commission and authority of the apostles derived from CHRIST, admitted, and in fact included, a like transmission to others, and equally verifiable with theirs.   Each was invested with powers and qualifications suited to the exigencies of the Church—to its condition at the time; and as there were many things in which the apostles were inferior to their Master as the head, but were yet truly his successors in things necessary in the Church; so are there many things, in which the subsequent Governors of the Church were inferior to the apostles, yet were they truly, and to all necessary purposes, their successors.   And this may serve as an answer to the childish cavil, so much relied upon, that the Apostles, as inspired men, endowed with miraculous powers, and eye-witnesses of the resurrection and ascended glory of JESUS CHRIST, could have no successors.

" In these things, indeed, they could have no successors, neither was the continuance of such qualifications needed by the Church.   The apostles lived to found and establish the Church throughout the bounds of the Roman Empire, and to complete the canon of Scripture as the standard of the faith.   Their extraordinary powers were given for this end, which being answered, they were withdrawn.   But in the necessary powers and qualifications for its government, preservation in unity, and extension in the world; as these were continually needed—essential to the very being of the Church, as a visible society; so, in them, the apostles both could have, and did have successors, which have continued, in an unbroken line of transmitted authority, to this day, through the order of Bishops, as the only lawful and verifiable source of spiritual rule in the Kingdom of CHRIST."

On a point so very obvious, I confess it is very extraordinary, that men who possess high character for intellectual ability—who certainly have read much, and profess the utmost sincerity in their objections, should not be able to see how very futile they are—how impossible to reconcile with either Scripture, reason, or matter of fact, as attested by the whole Christian world for fifteen hundred years.   And the wonder is increased, when I come to consider your next objection, and the manner in which you support it.   You inquire, p. 645,

" Who were appointed by the apostles as *standing* officers in the Church, to do after their decease, all things necessary to be done for the promotion of the Christian religion ?"

To this you boldly reply, in substance, that these standing officers were the single order of Church ministers, called indifferently by the sacred writers, Elders or Bishops ; and you assert, p. 646, that,

" The whole language of the New Testament is such, as to have extorted from many learned Episcopalians the confession—that Bishops and Presbyters were the same."

Sir, I am sorry that any man having a character to lose, whether for Christian candour or literary fairness, should so commit himself.   For what is this but the threadbare, exploded argument, from the *community of names*, which no Episcopalian pretends to dispute.   But you cannot bring forward a solitary learned Episcopalian, by whom the confession ever was made, that Bishop and Presbyter were the same order in the ministry. Far less can you establish your assertion, either from Scripture or antiquity.

Were you conversant with the writings of Mr. Charles Leslie, I think that even the necessity of your case could hardly have driven you to so weak a defence of your cause, as you have here resorted to.   And as the objection is old, and unadorned with any thing new or even ingenious in its support, I shall reply to it in his words, as I find them in the discourse before mentioned.

"If the Presbyterians will say (because they have nothing else left to say) that all London (for example) was but one Parish—and that the Presbyter of every other Parish, was as much a Bishop as the Bishop of London, because the words Bishop and Presbyter are sometimes used in the same sense ; they may as well prove that CHRIST was but a Deacon, because he is so called. Rom. xv. 8.   And Bishop signifies an *overseer*, and Presbyter an *ancient man* or *elder man*—whence our term of Alderman.   And this is as good a foundation to prove that the Apostles were Aldermen, in the city acceptation of the word ; or that our Aldermen are all Bishops and Apostles, as to prove that Presbyters and Bishops are all one, from the childish jingle of the words.

"It would be the same thing if one should undertake to confront all antiquity, and prove, against all the histories, that the Emperors of Rome were no more than the Generals of Armies, and that every Roman General was Emperor of Rome, because he could find the word *Imperator* sometimes applied to the general of an army.

"Or, as if a commonwealth's man should get up and say, that our former Kings were no more than our Dukes are now, because the stile of Grace, which is now given to Dukes, was then given to Kings.

"And suppose that any one was put under the penance of answering such ridiculous arguments ;   what method would be taken, but to show that the Emperors of Rome, and former Kings of England had Generals of armies, and Dukes under them, and exercised authority over them ?

"Therefore, when we find it given in charge to Timothy, the first Bishop of Ephesus, how he was to proceed against the Presbyters when they transgressed—to sit in judgment upon them—examine witnesses against them—and to pass censures upon them, it is a most impertinent logomachy to argue from the etymology of the words, that, notwithstanding all this, a Bishop and a Presbyter are the same thing.   Therefore that one text 1 Tim. v. 19, is sufficient to silence the pitiful clamour of the Presbyterians.   Our English translation reads it *against an Elder* (which is the literal translation of the word *Presbyter*,)

VOL. I.—38

against a Presbyter receive not an accusation, but before two or three witnesses; and them that sin rebuke before all, that others also may fear.   Now upon the Presbyterian hypothesis we must say that Timothy had no authority or jurisdiction over that Presbyter, against whom he had power to receive accusations, examine witnesses and pass censures upon him; and that such a Presbyter had the same authority over Timothy; which is so extravagant, and against common sense, that I will not stay longer to confute it: and this is enough to have said concerning the Presbyterian argument from the etymology of the word Presbyter and Bishop."

Thus far Mr. Leslie; and though I perfectly coincide with him, that it is a sufficient answer to all that has or can be said, from the community of names; yet as you refer your readers to the 20th chapter of the Acts of the Apostles for proof of your assertion, it is necessary to meet you on your own ground, lest it should be said, that I could not do it.

The part to which you refer, is the affecting circumstance of St. Paul's farewell charge to the Elders of the Church of Ephesus, under the solemn foresight that they should meet no more in this world.   Here then it is fairly to be presumed, that the man who could appeal to his hearers—*that for the space of three years he had kept nothing back that was profitable to them, but had taught them publicly, and from house to house,* would be full and particular in his instructions and directions.   I therefore ask the reader to look if there is a single word of instruction or direction to these Presbyters or Bishops on the exercise of the ordaining power, or if a single word on this very important part of their office, is addressed to persons of this order in the ministry, in any of the Epistles, by any of the Apostles?   If then, as is asserted by you, Episcopal power and authority, in the proper acceptation, belonged to these Presbyters of the Ephesian Church, in virtue of their office as such it is most unaccountable, that not the remotest allusion is made to it by St. Paul, at this particular and very proper time: and still more unaccountable how, if they possessed it, they could have exercised it upon each other.   If all had equal right to rule—to judge of doctrine and conduct—to censure and absolve—who were to obey and submit themselves ?   The very idea of such a state of things, is so absurd as to refute this argument in favour of parity.   But to put the matter out of all reasonable dispute, and to satisfy every fair and candid mind—let the instructions and directions given by St. Paul to these Ephesian Bishops, or Presbyters, or Elders, (for the name is nothing) be contrasted with those given to Timothy and Titus by the same Apostle—and then say whether Bishop and Presbyter are the same in order and office, as ministers of the Church—whether the Elders assembled at Miletus, possessed, either individually or collectively, the powers and prerogatives conferred on Timothy and Titus ?

That the Elders who attended St. Paul's summons were *Bishops*, in the then use of the words, that is, *overseers*, in charge of particular congregations, there is no dispute ; therefore the Apostle's exhortation is confined to this their proper duty—*Take heed therefore unto yourselves, and to all the flock over the which the* HOLY GHOST *hath made you overseers, to feed the Church of* GOD, *which he hath purchased with his own blood.*

That Timothy and Titus were Bishops, that is, *overseers*, in the sense of judging, restraining and governing, as well as ordaining the Bishops, or Overseers, or Pastors of particular congregations, can be disputed or denied by none, unless under the influence of the most pitiable prejudice ; and therefore the exhortations and directions of this same Apostle to them, are suited to this their special office.   Nor can the difference, either in the matter or manner of the address, be otherwise, accounted for.   I therefore most cordially second your request 'that the reader carefully peruse the Letters of Paul the Apostle to Timothy and Titus,' and then judge, whether the Apostle 'uses phraseology exactly conformed to your position.' He will indeed find the words *Elder* and *Presbyter* and *Bishop*, applied indifferently to denote the office of a Pastor of a single congregation ; but searching for the whole truth, he will also find an office of oversight and authority *over these very Bishops*, and all of their order, conferred upon Timothy and Titus, with directions how to discharge it, and with injunctions to Timothy to continue the office after him.   *This charge commit I to thee,*

*son Timothy. The same commit thou to faithful men, who shall
be able to teach others also.*

We are now, Sir, prepared to meet, as they ought to be met,
the following desperate assertions, p. 646, 647.

"The indisputable fact is, that at the death of the apostles
there was no episcopacy in the whole Christian Church, but a
Parochial episcopacy. There was no superiority of one clergyman over another. But each Bishop in his parish had the oversight of the flock committed to his care."

Now Sir, so far is this from being the 'indisputable fact,' that
it is contradicted by the direct testimony of Scriptures, and by
every record of ecclesiastical history, up to the commencement
of the Presbyterian schism in the sixteenth century. And here,
Sir, I might most securely rest my cause—my denial being to
the full as good as your affirmation—until you prove your
'indisputable fact' by proper testimony. But, for the sacred
cause of truth and order, as set forth in the New Testament;
and for the sake of the many who surrender themselves implicitly to such sweeping assertions; I must support my denial of
your 'indisputable fact,' both from Scripture and antiquity.

You take your stand on the fact, as at the death of the apostles; thereby insinuating, if not asserting that diocesan episcopacy, as contradistinguished from the episcopacy of parity, was
unknown in the Church during the life time of any of the apostles. Against this, I bring forward from Scripture the episcopal
character of Timothy and Titus; who certainly were diocesan
Bishops, if by the word *diocesan* we are to understand one who
has the oversight and authority over a city, district, or country,
containing a number of particular congregations, with their
respective Pastors or Bishops. In this sense, Timothy 'in-
disputably' had charge over the whole Church of Ephesus,
consisting of several particular churches, with their respective
Pastors. We are not indeed informed of the exact number of
Elders convened by St. Paul at Miletus, but they are spoken of
in the plural number.

In like manner, Titus had similar jurisdiction over the whole island of Crete, which is represented as very populous, and famous in history for its hundred cities.   In every one of these, where a church was or could be gathered, Titus was authorized by St. Paul to ' ordain Elders, and set in order the things that are wanting.'   Here then, are two instances, in the life time of St. Paul, of men, not in any sense apostles, advanced to the apostolical rule and government of the Church, peculiar to the order of Bishops as such ; which are in the very teeth of your ' indisputable fact,' and must be disproved by something of more weight as testimony than bare assertion, or presumptive reasonings.   And when to this testimony of Scripture we add the confimation thereof by ecclesiastical antiquity, and bring forward the succession of such diocesan Bishops derived from the apostles, ruling over many particular Churches with their respective Bishops, (if you must have the name) for a long series of years ; what sort of a reasoner must he be who will stand it out against such decisive testimony, upon the miserable evasion of a community of names in the ministerial office at a particular period of the Church ?   But to return to Scripture.

In the life time of John, the beloved disciple, we have further proof of diocesan episcopacy in the seven Churches of Asia, to whose respective Angels or chief Governors, were addressed through St. John, the admonitions of the great Head of the Church.   I enter not into the unprofitable and childish jangle raised on the word *Angel*, in order to support the Presbyterian hypothesis.   Sufficient it is for me that the Church of Ephesus is in the number of the seven thus admonished ; in which, we have already seen from Scripture, that a diocesan Bishop was appointed ; and have good reason to believe, that the succession from Timothy was acted upon before the Apocalyptic vision ; because upwards of thirty years elapsed between the appointment of Timothy to the government of the Ephesian Church, and the giving the revelation to St. John ; and we well know, that the primitive Bishops, or Angels of the Churches, had but a short space given them by the persecuting powers.

If then, the Bishop or chief governor of the Ephesian Church is addressed in a revelation from heaven, as *the angel* of that Church, and is commended for the just exercise of his episcopal authority, in *trying them which said they were apostles, but were not*, (Rev. ii. 3.) the same official character and station must be assigned to the Angels of the other six Churches : we have, therefore, at once, and from Scripture too, six additional testimonies against your 'indisputable fact.'

If to this we add the testimony which Ecclesiastical antiquity gives in support of the diocesan character of these Angels, it is not easy to understand upon what principle it can be resisted. For we have extant the Epistles of Ignatius, Bishop of Antioch, ordained by the apostles, to three of these Apocalyptic Churches —the Ephesian, the Philadelphian and the Smyrnean—in all of which he recognizes the three orders of the Bishop, the Presbytery, and the Deacons : particularly in that to the Ephesians, he speaks of Onesimus, their Bishop, who of course must have been such subsequent to Timothy ; and in that to the Smyrneans, of Polycarp, their Bishop, who was also apostolically ordained to this office of Angel or Bishop.　To this we can add the testimony of many witnesses, particularly of St. Augustine and Epiphanius, that by the *Angels* of the Apocalyptic Churches, the *chief rulers* or *Bishops* of those Churches were always understood.

Another testimony to this point, less objectionable perhaps in your eyes than the early historians of the Church, is found in the more modern ecclesiastical historian Mosheim. In his Commentaries on the Three first Centuries (Vidal's Translation, p. 227, 228, note) he thus expresses himself: " In support of this opinion, (that episcopacy was established during the life-time of the apostles and with their approbation) we are supplied with an argument of such strength, in those 'angels' to whom St. John addressed the Epistles, which by the command of our Saviour himself, he sent to the seven churches of Asia—as the Presbyterians, as they are termed, let them labour and strive what they may, will never be able to overcome.　It must be evident to every one, even on a cursory perusal of the epistles to which we refer, that those who are therein termed ' Angels,' were persons possessing such a degree of authority in their respective Churches, as enabled them to mark with merited disgrace, whatever might appear to be deserving of reprehension :

and also to give due countenance and encouragement to every thing that was virtuous and commendable."

Another, and decisive proof from Scripture in favour of diocesan episcopacy, is furnished in the constitution and government of the first Christian Church that ever was gathered in the world, the Church in Jerusalem. The converts to the faith in that city, are counted by thousands in the New Testament, so that it was impossible they could all assemble in one place, and must, for convenience, if not for safety, have had different places of worship. Over these separate congregations, with their respective Presbyters and Deacons, a near kinsman of our blessed LORD presided, as is evident from the manner he is spoken of in the Acts of the apostles.

That James, the LORD's *brother*, as he is called in Scripture, was truly the Bishop or Chief Governor of the Church in Jerusalem, and ordained thereto by the apostles themselves, is attested by all antiquity——by Hegesippus and Clemens Alexandrinus, in the second, and by Chrysostom, and your favorite Jerome, in the fourth century. To this I will add the testimony of the same Mosheim before mentioned, extracted from the same work, p. 229, 230, note——" As the early Churches are well known to have taken all their institutions and regulations from the model exhibited to them in the Church of Jerusalem, it appears to me, that scarcely a doubt can be entertained of their having been also indebted to this last mentioned venerable assembly, for the example of appointing some one man to preside over the Presbyters, and general interest of each individual Church, and that the first instance of any one's being invested with the episcopal office, occurred in that city."

However, therefore, you may be disposed to receive the testimony of the ancient fathers, or the opinions of more modern ecclesiastical historians——yet the ten instances I have produced from the New Testament, of distinct and distant provincial Churches, consisting of many separate congregations under their particular Presbyters or Bishops, all episcopally constituted and governed, must be sufficient to prove to your readers, if not to yourself, that what you assert as an 'indisputable fact,' is as far from fact as the east is from the west. It therefore does not 'appear from the New Testament, that at the death of the apostles, there were no Bishops in the world but parochial Bishops,' though you boldly re-assert it, p. 647.

Neither are the subscriptions to the Epistles to Timothy and Titus, any more 'forgeries,' as you venture to pronounce them, than the headings of the chapters in the Bible, or than the division of the Bible into chapters and verses.   They are not Scripture, nor considered as such, but as declarations of matters of fact, sufficiently attested by other evidence to render it both safe and useful, to give the information to the readers of Scripture. Eusebius, Chrysostom, Epiphanius, Jerome, and Hilary, the Deacon, as quoted by Bingham, (Eccles. Antiq. Vol. I. Book 2d, chap. 1st, page 20, folio edition,) all declare, that Timothy was ordained Bishop of Ephesus by St. Paul.   Most of the same authors agree in the same declaration as to Titus, that he was ordained Bishop of Crete by St. Paul also.   Therefore, another assertion of yours, that ' at least three hundred years passed off before any thing was heard of the episcopate of Timothy and Titus,' is not the truth, these writers being witnesses with the Scriptures ; nor yet is it true that 'there is nothing but uncertain tradition to support this notion'—both which rash and unfounded assertions you make at p. 647.   The tradition for ' this notion,' as you call it, being evidence just as certain as that on which all Christians rely for the authenticity of the canon of Scripture, and for the fact that it is a revelation from God.

Whether, then, 'the New Testament itself affords decisive evidence (as you also assert) that these companions and aids of the apostles, *were not Bishops*,' must now be left to the judgment of your readers.   'Search the Scriptures is our motto,' say you, ' nay, we insist on a decision of the question by the Scriptures ; we are not willing to appeal to any other authority.   The Bible is the religion of Protestants.'   Yes, when it suits your purpose.   When the modern notion of ministerial parity is to be supported against episcopacy, then nothing but the *strict letter* of Scripture is to be heeded ; the recorded testimony of the primitive Christians is worthless ; mere ' uncertain tradition,' and proves nothing. But when infant baptism is to be supported, against those who impugn it as a modern innovation and a corruption of Christianity ; then the case is altered, and the self-same testimony which is rejected in the one case, becomes safe and substantial evidence in the other, as will be shown more at large in its proper place.

But you ask exultingly, p. 646,

" Where was the Bishop of Rome when St. Paul wrote his Epistle to that Church ?"

To which I might answer, by a question fully as pertinent, but of more consequence to your cause, than your question is to mine—Who was the ordainer of John Calvin ?

It can do the cause I support no injury to acknowledge, that at the time St. Paul's Epistle was written, there was no Bishop in the Church of Rome—because it is the truth.   Had there been such an officer in that Church, it might have been cause of regret to the Christian world at large, and particularly to that part of it of the same doctrinal persuasion with yourself ; because the occasion for it being prevented by the care and oversight of their own Bishop, the Epistle to the Romans might never have been written.—You next inquire,

" Where was the Bishop of Corinth, of Galatia, of Ephesus, of Colosse, of Thessalonica ?"

I presume you mean, when the respective Epistles to those Churches were written.   To which I answer, that St. Paul himself was their Bishop at the times when he wrote to them—they were all his own converts—Churches of his own planting, and were retained under his own superintendance.   This is abundantly evident, not only from the tenor of the Epistles, but from the circumstance of an Epistle being addressed to them as Churches.   St. Paul knew too well what belonged to clerical propriety, to have addressed an Epistle to any Church collectively, that was under the care of its own Bishop.   Had his apostolic duty required such an interference, there can be no doubt that, as an inspired man, he would have acted upon the principle adopted by his Divine Master towards the seven

VOL. I.—39

Churches of Asia, and addressed his admonition to the Angel or Bishop of the particular Church. From the difference of the style also, so easily observable in these Epistles, from that of the Epistle to the Romans ; it is evident, that in them, he writes as one having a special and personal authority over them, while in the other he uses such a style as belonged rather to his general apostolical relation to the Church Universal, than to his episcopal rule over particular Churches. Yet, in due time, these very Churches all had their particular Bishops, and were constituted and governed upon the one universal principle of all true Churches of the LORD JESUS CHRIST—unity in derivation, in faith, and in order.

Upon the whole, I trust it will appear, that whatever advantage you supposed you possessed, from the letter or the meaning of Scripture, has not been denied you, or avoided or evaded by me. The Scripture is my supreme rule, in all that concerns religion. " What is not read therein, or may not be proved thereby," I neither hold myself, nor require of others, as necessary to salvation. But I do not consider myself at liberty, either from its silence, or from its obscurity, to construe one part so as to conflict with any other part, or with the plain, obvious intent and meaning of the whole. I do not feel myself at liberty, for instance, because of some fancied obscurity in the meaning and use of the words *Bishop* and *Presbyter* in the New Testament, to separate *the order* of the gospel from the *faith* of the gospel. The Bible tells me, that the one is just as much a revelation from GOD for my observance as the other. Where any real obscurity, therefore, exists, on either of these subjects, I gladly resort to the light and assurance afforded me in the belief and practice of the primitive Church—that cloud of Christian witnesses, upon whose testimony alone you and I must receive the Bible as of divine and infallible authority, or be left *without* GOD *in the world.*

As the Bible thus received, warns me expressly of two deadly sins—heresy and schism—the one against the faith, the other against the order of the gospel, *as once delivered to the saints,* by the apostles of the LORD JESUS CHRIST : to the faith and order observed in the primitive Church, therefore, I bring myself, and endeavour to bring others; that we may escape the condemnation denounced equally against these two distinct and too common sins.   As neither the faith nor the order of the gospel oblige men, otherwise than as founded on divine right, to declare the one and institute the other; and as divine right is a nullity until verified as a fact; and moreover as the Bible expressly declares, that the religious condition of redeemed man, is one of explicit covenant relation to GOD, through outward and visible sacraments as its seals, administered by divine right certified to mankind at first by miracles, and subsequently by derived succession: therefore, I count that doctrine *heretical*, which is contrary to the plain language or general tenor of the Bible, as understood and professed by the primitive Church; and that order *schismatical*, which is separated and divided from the root of unity, in the authority of CHRIST transmitted through his apostles as the only verifiable warrant for the administration of the sacraments of salvation.

For example—The denial of the inherent divinity of the man CHRIST JESUS, I consider to be a damnable heresy; because contradicted by the express words of Scripture; which, though disputed by some, are yet confirmed by the unanimous belief of the primitive Church, which *held and taught* the inherent divinity of the Saviour.

Wilful separation from the communion of the visible Church in the word and sacraments, instituted by CHRIST through his apostles, evidenced by the setting up another authority, and administering and partaking of sacraments in the name of CHRIST, by virtue of such assumed and underived authority, I consider to be the sin of *schism*, or rending the body of CHRIST, denounced in Scripture.   And this from the express language and meaning of Scripture, confirmed also by the unvarying testimony of the primitive Church, which thus describes it.

For example—If any layman, by reason of his piety and learning, or by any other means, should obtain followers, organize them into a Church state, as it is called, and proceed to ordain ministers, and administer sacraments in the name of CHRIST; such person and his followers would be guilty of the sin of schism.

So also—If any clergyman under the degree of a Bishop, should in like manner obtain followers, and proceed to confer orders in the name of CHRIST, setting up a separate altar, or communion, administering sacraments; such clergyman and his followers would be schismatics, in the true, genuine, Scriptural, and primitive meaning and usage of the word. Nor can any piety, or soundness of faith, cure or even palliate the enormity of this sin; which is an actual rending the body of CHRIST, the destroying that unity, in which it is constituted and commanded to abide, and which is the mark by which it may be distinguished from any counterfeit of its divine character and saving efficacy.

On the doctrine of divine right in the ministry, I hold and teach, that it can be derived only from the apostles of our LORD JESUS CHRIST by succession in the Church, through the line of Bishops, as distinct from Presbyters; that it is essential to the validity of the sacraments, and from its very nature incapable of any graduation. It is either divine right or no right at all: I therefore know nothing of any barometrical measurement into high and low Church; higher than its source I attempt not to carry it—lower than its origin I will not degrade it, and only by its proper proofs will I acknowledge it.

These, Sir, are the principles on which the doctrines enforced in these two sermons are founded; which you have felt yourself bound as a Christian to oppose. From your misrepresentations I have endeavoured to rescue them, and to free myself from the imputation of preaching false doctrine. In performing this duty I have also endeavoured to give the public such further information on the points to which you oppose yourself, and which have been systematically withheld from their consideration, as will enable it to form a safe judgment of the scriptural soundness of our respective professions. From this also it will be able to determine whether you have met the points betwixt us fairly, and as the friend of truth, or as the advocate of a party. And what is more, I trust it will be drawn to consider deeply the effect of those religious principles, under which, the order of the gospel, one half of GOD's express appointment in the salvation of sinners, is rejected as a non-essential, and abandoned to the profane encroachments of those daring intruders, who sport with the unity of the Church, and scatter the assurance of faith to the four winds of heaven.

What remains unnoticed of your review of these two sermons is not therefore avoided or escaped from ; but being of a political and personal cast, is reserved until I come to matter of the same kind, in your review of my *Bible Society Sermon,* and of that *On the Study and Interpretation of Scripture ;* to which I now proceed.

And first of the *Bible Society Sermon.* Having already exposed the unworthy perversions of my language and meaning to which you have descended, I will not again revert to them, but come at once

"To the great principle which our prelate opposes with so misplaced and illtimed vehemence. The principle is, that the copies of the Scripture circulated by the Bible Society, shall be without note or comment. This is transformed by the preacher into the principle, that ' the Scriptures are exclusively sufficient for their own interpretation.' Now we directly deny that this is a just interpretation of the Bible Society principle." p. 241.

This is the point between us—and as I have seen no cause to change my views, after much and very serious consideration of the subject, but am rather confirmed in the injurious tendency of the principle to the interests of revealed religion ; I am constrained by the highest motives, to re-assert the ground taken in the sermon—to press it upon the most serious consideration of all concerned—and to defend it against all that you have as yet brought forward in favour of the principle.

Notes and comments on any book, are always intended to explain and render more intelligible, and of course more practically useful, the subject matter contained in the book. This is the declared object of those who compile them ; and the benefit is acknowledged by those who read them. The exclusion of notes and comments, then, is in effect to say that the book requires no explanation—that it is sufficiently intelligible in itself. This being true of books in general, it must also be true of the Bible as a particular book, unless it be shewn that it is an exception to the rule.   But the common sense and common usage of the Christian world prove that it is not an exception, there being no book in the world, upon the explanation and illustration of which so much labour and research have been bestowed.   The adoption of a principle, therefore, which excludes notes and comments from the Bible, does in fact assert that the Bible requires no extraneous help to understand it aright, and, (as it is assumed in the Sermon) that it is *exclusively* sufficient for its own interpretation.   I have therefore done no violence or injustice to the Bible Society principle, in holding it responsible for this most just and direct conclusion from it.   But further, as I have done no violence or injustice to the principle adopted and acted upon by these Bible Societies, so neither have I drawn from it a single consequence, that it is not equally direct and unavoidable.   For, if the Bible is in itself so clear and plain as to require neither notes or comments to render it more intelligible, it follows inseparably, in the judgment of the Bible Society, as a body, that there is no danger to any man of mistaking its meaning, or misapplying its truths.   But the Bible Society, as a body, are aware of the fact, (and the very materials of which it is composed confirm the fact to their senses,) that the Christian world is split up and divided into hundreds of opposite systems of doctrine and practice, all professedly drawn from the Bible, as its exclusive truth.   Hence, it is the opinion of that body, witnessed by the adoption of the principle as their fundamental rule, that all these various and opposing systems of religious profession, are equally consistent with the truth of God's word, and equally safe for salvation.   Nor is there an escape from this consequence, that will not show that the favorite principle is wrong, and ought to be abandoned. For, of necessity, the Society must either believe that all varieties of religious profession drawn from the Bible are equally right, in the sense of being equally safe ; or they must believe that some of them are unscriptural and unsafe.   If the former of the alternatives is adopted, the principle is demonstrated to be productive of divisions in religion without limit.   If the latter shall be resorted to, it shows the principle to be justly liable to the charge of withholding from the Bible what is essential to a right understanding of its contents, and to a just application of its life-giving truths.

That such conclusions and consequences are not seen by the individual members, I am well aware; that they are hid and concealed from them, by the intrinsic merit of the work, and the enthusiasm it so powerfully kindles, I can readily conceive; yet that they are unavoidable from the principle, is beyond all reasonable denial: and it is for this reason, and this alone, that I have raised my voice against it; and not without taking into consideration how much more probable it was, that I was mistaken, than that thousands of great, and learned, and pious men should be guilty of such an oversight, as to adopt for the foundation of the most extended religious co-operation, a principle demonstrably subversive of all revealed Religion.

But the Bible Society principle operates yet more extensively, and more certainly, against the interests of revealed Religion, than in the exclusion of all helps to understand and apply the Scriptures according to their true meaning, and to their saving purpose; for it authorizes the conclusion, that the sacraments are not necessary to give effect to the word of GOD. All comments are excluded. Preaching and sacraments are, in the truest sense of the word, comments on the Scripture—comments which GOD has commanded to accompany them: yet, by this principle, these are separated from the Bible; not only by fair and necessary inference from the principle as adopted, but practically and in fact. This consequence from the Bible Society principle was stated in the Sermon, and pressed as an argument against it. But of this you have taken no notice, beyond giving the paragraph in which it is found, and resorting to your ready scape-goat, the Book of Common Prayer, as what I mean by the Church, the Ministry and the Sacraments. But, Sir, you knew better. You knew well what my real meaning was in this objection, and you felt that it was fatal; and yet the principle which goes this length must be supported.

Against this objection I have heard many, and read some answers; but not one that to my mind was even plausible. It is admitted on all hands, that a proposition to send the sacraments with the word, would be the signal to dissolve the society. It is confessed, that no such thing is contemplated by the society. By some it is replied, that the sacraments are already furnished. But even admitting this, as it respects Christian lands——(though the Society are not entitled to it) yet it is *not true*, as respects the heathen, who are embraced in the operations of the Society. The principle, as to them, is an actual separation of the Sacraments from the word of GOD.   And its operation in Christian lands, is to weaken the impression of their indispensable necessity to give the word its saving effect.   It is in vain to contend, the Society is associated for a specific purpose, which does not embrace the sending of the sacraments with the word ; because no necessity can be conceived for their separation ; because no Christian can comprehend any saving benefit from the mere letter of Scripture, without the sacraments ; because no necessity existed for the adoption of a principle thus pregnant with mischief.   If it was felt to be a Christian duty to disseminate as widely as possible the word of life, the duty was equally Christian, and equally imperious, not to deprive the word of those accompaniments which the wisdom of GOD had joined inseparably with it, as essential to its saving effect.   I cannot perceive any just ground for the exercise of discretion even in this case, particularly as respects the heathen——and far less of justification for the adoption of this principle as their bond of union, and the best method which their collective wisdom and piety could devise for presenting to all nations, *the whole counsel of* GOD *for their salvation.*

If the sentiments entertained by myself and many others on this subject, were mere speculations from the nature of the principle, it appears to me there is such a show of reason in them, as to entitle them to dispassionate consideration.   But when these reasonings are confirmed by the experience and observation of missionaries on the spot, I think it calls loudly upon the Society to reconsider the principle of its association.

This experience and observation, is furnished in a communication to the American Churches and Christians, from Gordon Hall, and Samuel Newhall, American missionaries at Bombay; *Andover,* 1818.   "Preachers are wanted, in the first place, to call the attention of the ignorant and careless heathen to the word of God.   Secondly, to direct his mind to such parts of the sacred volume as are best adapted to his capacity and circumstances.   Thirdly, to make explanations, where the sense is not obvious; and finally, to enforce the truths of Scripture by argument and persuasion.   Without Christian teachers, an indiscriminate distribution of the Bible in Heathen and Mahometan countries, would be but little better than throwing it away. Some solitary instances of conversion there have been in Heathen and Mahometan lands, which were occasioned by reading the Bible only : but there is no instance on record, of a nation being evangelized by the Bible, without the preaching of the gospel.   Bibles should by all means be circulated extensively among the heathen ; but ministers of the gospel should be sent along with them.   Thousands of Bibles may be sent with every preacher of the gospel ; but they should not be sent alone. Sending teachers without the Bible, was the error of the Church of Rome.   Let it not be the error of Protestants to send the Bible without preachers."   p. 8.   Again.   "Is the distribution of the Bible in this new era, to supercede the sending of preachers? *Is there not some great and alarming error, which makes the Church so zealous in providing for the heathen to read the gospel, and so remiss in providing for them to hear the gospel ?* Is not the latter, rather than the former, the great means which CHRIST has ordained for evangelizing the world? *Why then should the order which he has prescribed be reversed?* Especially when it is considered, that in heathen nations all have ears to hear the gospel, while comparatively but few of them, through their great ignorance, could read the Bible, if given to them in their own language.   Besides, as to those who might be able to read, their degraded minds are so deplorably darkened, and so completely absorbed in every thing that is hostile to the purity of the gospel, that while perusing the mysteries of godliness, were any one of them interrogated, as Philip asked the Eunuch, *Understandest thou what thou readest ?*—would he not answer as the Eunuch did, *How can I, except some man should guide me ?*" p. 75, 76.

What bearing these extracts have upon the Bible Society

principle, you can be at no loss to judge; nor yet apply the facts and reasonings therein contained, to the condition of much of our population, both white and black. Perhaps also, you may be able to say wherefore it is, that with much similar information, their ears are yet closed against reason and experience, and this false, injurious, and yet consecrated principle, still rules the divisions of religious profession, in Christian Europe and America.

Lest, however, you should feel reluctant to betray the secret of its ascendancy—I will state to the public, what my very limited means of information and observation lead me to refer it to; and that is, the sanction and support which this 'no comment' principle gives to the two very prevalent delusions of this latter day—the one, that every man may *safely* form his own system of faith and order in religion—the other, that all who profess and call themselves Christians, no matter how separated and divided in faith, origin, and order, are nevertheless members of the one spouse and body of CHRIST, and ought to be acknowledged as such. This, I verily believe, is the real cause of the popularity of this Bible Society principle; and I am much mistaken if a careful and informed reader of these Reviews does not discover in them its operation throughout. Only acknowledge us as branches of CHRIST's Church, upon every thing else let us "agree to differ." But, Sir, the religion of the gospel is a *positive institution*, which Bible Societies, and sectarian professions of faith, cannot control, and model to suit their particular views, but by which they ought to and must be regulated. And a principle in religion, or connected with religion as revealed, which cannot bear being carried out to its 'legitimate consequences and results, is not of GOD. The wisdom of GOD sends us nothing in his word, or connected with his religion, of this abstract unmanageable character—beautiful in theory, impossible or injurious in practice. And the very fact, that in favour of this very principle, every shade of sectarian belief, every grade of speculative and actual unbelief, can, and does unite, is conclusive proof that the principle is unsound, vicious, and ultimately subversive of all revealed religion. Each sees in it something favourable to its particular views; none perceives in it any thing inimical to its distinctive tenets; all find in it something which may be turned to account in the rivalry for accession to particular denominations in a divided Christian world; while in their aggregated capacity of a 'no comment' Bible Society, they flatter and greet each other with the name of Christians. *Deistical* Christians, *Unitarian* Christians, *Universalist* Christians, *Quaker* Christians, *Independent* Christians, *Congregational* Christians, *Presbyterian* Christians, *Methodist* Christians, *Baptist* Christians, *Lutheran* Christians— names without number Christians, *Nothingarian* Christians, and alas, alas! some *Episcopalian* Christians, all meet here upon the same level, all unite to send the naked Scriptures into the world; all being aware, that in the confusion of mind as to its real and single truth, consequent on existing divisions as to what is truth, each may give that gloss to the discoveries and doctrines of the Bible which shall suit its own views.

But is this at all akin, either with the declared purpose of GOD, or with the nature of revealed truth? Did our LORD JESUS CHRIST come *to gather in one*—or into one hundred, or one thousand, *the children of* GOD *scattered abroad?* Is the presiding principle of the gospel of CHRIST *unity* or division? Is divine truth multiform, or like its author, one? These are the tests by which to try the soundness of the 'no comment' principle of these Bible Societies. *To the law and to the testimony, if they speak not according to this word, it is because there is no light in them.*

If on this subject I am in an error, it is one which the defenders of this principle, and you, Sir, in particular, labour to confirm. I meet with nothing which serves to remove the substantial difficulties of the case; nothing that meets them fairly; but much that evades the truth of the question, and strives to gain its purpose by false reasoning, by appeals to prejudice, and by vituperative declamation. And in these I have now to follow you through; for thus you proceed to support your *direct denial* that my interpretation of the Bible Society principle is a just one, p. 241, 242.

" **All Protestants agree that the Bible is the only rule of faith,** that no other Book in the world has authority to bind the conscience ; that from the sacred records alone, can we derive authentic information of what we must do to be saved ; and that its universal dissemination is a consummation devoutly to be wished."

True, Sir, but not the whole truth—The value of the Bible to mankind for ever depending on its being rightly understood, believed and followed ; and also, that it be *the whole counsel* of GOD—the Bible accompanied by those sacred ministrations commanded in it, sent with it by its Author, and without which, ordinarily speaking, it is but a book, and not *the book of life.*

"Now, while these things are so, there are six hundred millions of human beings without the Bible—Heathens, Mahomedans, and nominal Christians, perishing in ignorance and sin."

As respects nominal Christians, that is, persons under the light of the gospel ; the assertion is true, and would to GOD that this overflowing benevolence, of which so much is said, could be directed, in this country at least, to *their* really destitute and dangerous condition, instead of evaporating in this great emulation of misguided zeal which, literally, takes the children's portion, and squanders it unprofitably upon strangers. As respects the Heathen, properly so called, the assertion is not true, either in its terms, or in the sense in which it is taken by the general class of readers. *The Heathen are not perishing because they have not the Bible.* The want of it will not be charged to their account, nor its conditions required of them, neither will they be judged by its law. It is not of their procuring, that they have not the Bible, but of the providence of Almighty GOD. He has not seen fit in his wisdom, to call them as yet into covenant with him ; but the time is coming ; and assuredly when the work is of GOD his word and his sacraments, the seals of his covenanted mercies, will not be separated. In the mean time, his uncovenanted mercies are towards and over them, and I doubt not that many a Heathen will rejoice before GOD for ever, when Christians with the Bible, will be howling in everlasting darkness.   Yet this is one of the stalking horses, behind which to take aim at contributions for ‘no comment’ Bible Societies.   Nevertheless, it is most heartily to be wished, and most devoutly to be prayed, and earnestly laboured for, that the Heathen may be furnished with the Bible—not naked and shorn of its strength, but as GOD was pleased to send it at the first, with his Church, his ministers, and his sacraments, as his seals of its precious promises to all who receive them, and as means of his heavenly grace to a fallen world.

“ Roman Catholics are known to prohibit althogether, or greatly to discourage the circulation of the Scripture.”

On this I will only say, for the present, may they speedily learn a better mind !   But the inuendo contained in it will not be overlooked in another place.

“ Protestants are divided, chiefly owing to matters of external observance, into a number of different denominations.”

This is true, as respects the sectarians themselves.   It is not true, as respects the separation of the sectarians from the Episcopalians.   It is totally false as respects myself.   I am divided from no Protestant denomination, nor yet is the Church to which I belong so divided, on a matter of mere external observance, on a point that is not of *positive institution, and fundamental importance to religion as revealed*.   Yet this is also one of the deceits practised on the ignorant.   We differ only on non-essentials, on matters of outward order ; such, say you, as forms of prayer, the cross in baptism, saints’ days, &c.

“ All, however, derive their religion from the Scriptures.   The pious among them of *every name*, have felt the power of Divine Truth, and know the preciousness of the Bible.   Here is ground on which all can meet.   One calm and peaceful place in the agitated and stormy scene—one association, where all may feel a common bond of brotherhood, and indulge the emotions of unbounded benevolence, and unmingled confidence”

True it is, that all profess to derive their religion from the

Scriptures; and I verily believe they think they do so: I hold it as a debt due to real charity, to consider all denominations as acting with integrity in this matter—that they do verily believe, not only that they have the warrant of Scripture, but that they have it in such wise as to be safer, as concerns their souls, under this construction of Scripture, than they could be under any other construction of it; and your charity may go further if it can. But this affects not in the least, the right or the wrong—the truth or the error of their respective professions: that must ever be tried by a different standard. The darkest and most preposterous fanatic that ever lived, equally with the more dangerous heresiarch, and orthodox Christian—John Bockholt, and George Fox—John Calvin, and John Wesley—Anna Lee, and Joanna Southcote—Archbishop Cranmer, and Bishop Ridley, all professed to derive their religion from the Bible, all claimed the Scriptures as with them. Yet forever and forever, must it not hold good—that whether right or wrong, true or false, religion or no religion must depend on Scripture, well or ill interpreted, understood and applied? These all could not be right, some must be radically wrong. Yet, according to your argument, upon the principle of a 'no comment' Bible society, the very delusion which abandons the Scriptures to any and every sort of interpretation, 'is ground where all can meet;' yes, and be acknowledged, too, as faithful Christians. For, if this were not a consequence, practically, of the principle, your numbers would be wofully thinned. But so it is. In these societies the Deist and the Trinitarian, the Calvinist and the Arminian, the deniers of the divinity of CHRIST and its defenders, the asserters of universal salvation and the teachers of eternal punishment, the Quaker and the Churchman, the Presbyterian and the Episcopalian, the Baptist and the Pædo-Baptist, the true believer and the infidel of every shade, can find 'one calm and peaceful place' wherein 'to indulge the delightful emotions of *unbounded benevolence, and unmingled confidence.*' And is such wild and visionary declamation tricked out in the tinsel of a spurious charity, ventured upon the public intelligence by a Divine and a Theologian of the nineteenth century? Are we from this to understand that there is unmingled confidence betwixt the

Presbyterians and the Unitarians? Or is there some talismanic charm in this Bible Society principle, which fosters 'unbounded benevolence,' while it interdicts the orderly prelude of joint prayer to GOD for his blessing on their joint work of enlightened charity? Or is the jesuitical maxim, that the end justifies the means, once more in operation?

Would you lend your aid in any way to circulate the Unitarian version of the New Testament? You will answer No. Upon what other ground, then, than upon some calculation (whether right or wrong is immaterial) that the 'no comment' principle is favourable to his views, do you expect the Unitarian, or the Universalist, or any other name or description of religionists, to aid in the circulation of the commonly received Scriptures? The Unitarian, in particular, can have no possible motive, but the perfect freedom (which the 'no comment' principle so broadly recognizes) of interpreting the Scriptures as he pleases, wherewith he is allowed to take part in this disgraceful scramble for deluded souls. 'But the pious among them, of *every name*, have felt the power of divine truth, and know the preciousness of the Bible!' Indeed! Then it follows of course, that it is a matter of perfect indifference what system of doctrine and practice we extract from the Bible. If piety is found in all denominations, from John Calvin to Joanna Southcote—and piety, be it remembered, can only flow from the SPIRIT OF GOD—no conclusion can be more direct from these premises, than that the *witness of the* SPIRIT is equally given to the most discordant and opposite systems of faith and practice. Now Sir, I know you did not mean to say this; but you must either say it or renounce your argument, and with it the defence of the 'no comment' principle. If it be undeniable that some, in every denomination of Christian profession, have had the *witness of the* SPIRIT OF GOD to their piety, that is, to their faith and holiness, the most opposite doctrines and practices, founded on Scripture, are equally the truth of GOD; and consequently, the Bible is exclusively sufficient for its own interpretation, and ought to be circulated 'without note or comment.'

But if this assertion involves a contradiction, then it is equally undeniable that some systems of faith and practice have not this witness, and also, consequently, that the Scriptures are not exclusively sufficient for their own interpretation, and ought not to be circulated without 'note or comment.'

In reviewing this point as very briefly presented in the Sermon, you indulge yourself, (p. 252,) in the exposure of what you are pleased to call my 'intellectual chivalry,' and request your readers patiently and candidly to hear me.' I hope they will do so, and that they will not be blinded, and shifted away from the true point in the case, by your customary, but unknightly conduct of turning aside in the career, to avoid your adversary's weapon.

The point in the Sermon is, the witness of the SPIRIT to the different and opposite systems of religious profession, drawn from the Scriptures. Are they all equally entitled to it, from what is revealed in Scripture concerning the office and agency of the HOLY GHOST?

As an objection to the 'no comment' principle of these Bible Societies, I undertake to show that 'such is unavoidably the extent, to which the favorite principle of this and other Bible Societies carries the essential doctrine of spiritual influence'— To which you reply,

"Unavoidable! So far from it, that there i probably not a single individual on the face of the earth, who ever thought of this thing, before it was suggested by the Bishop of North-Carolina. Who, of all that believe in the HOLY SPIRIT, believe that he necessarily accompanies any means of Grace? Does he necessarily accompany the use of the Book of Common Prayer? Or the administration of the Sacraments? Or the preaching of legitimate Ministers?"

Now, Sir, whether this is a new thought of the Bishop of North-Carolina, or not, he feels perfectly confident of its correctness. The present point, however, is not whether the HOLY SPIRIT *necessarily* accompanies the means of grace, but whether the 'no comment' Bible Society principle 'unavoidably' involves the doctrine, that he so accompanies the reading of the naked word. This, the Bishop of North-Carolina conceives, must be an unavoidable conclusion from the principle; or the humanity as well as the wisdom of the Society must be deeply implicated, in depriving mankind, so far as it is concerned, of all other helps to understand and apply it aright. But the Bishop conceives, that such is the unavoidable conclusion from the principle itself, and your defence of it, by the strictest reasoning. The Bible Society principle asserts the sufficiency of the Scriptures for salvation, without the Church, the Ministry, and the Sacraments.

Many *opposite systems* of religious profession are derived from the Bible, in which 'the pious of every name have felt the *power* of divine truth, and know the preciousness of the Bible,' and are saved:

But no saving knowledge can be drawn from the Scriptures, but by the HOLY GHOST :

Therefore, the witness of the SPIRIT OF GOD is equally given to opposite interpretations of Scripture.

And this, I hope, will satisfy your desire for a regular syllogism, (p. 253) will teach you to look to the consistency and agreement of the principles you advocate, with the reasonings you resort to—will lead you to be sorry for your so frequent and needless attacks on that which, if you have either piety or taste, you must love—the Book of Common Prayer.

" It is seen to be of unspeakable importance, that Latins and Greeks, Mahomedans and Pagans, should feel the united influence—the whole moral power of Protestantism. It is better that the Bible should be given, no matter what interpreter may be selected by the recipient—or even that he should have had none at all—than that the nations should be destitute of the word of life. It is understood, that each separate denomination, in its collective capacity, may promote Christianity according to its own creeds and confessions, without let or hindrance. Where they cannot agree, they will agree to differ ; but on this one point, they will unite and co-operate as brethren."

I hope not. What! the whole moral power of Protestantism assent to such monstrous doctrine—that it is of no consequence whether the Bible be truly or falsely interpreted ! Is it so perfectly a matter of indifference, what doctrines men draw from the Scriptures? Then, indeed, is it high time, that this 'no comment' principle, this crusade against revealed religion, should be met by abler pens than mine.   But, after all, it is even so.   Every evil charged against it in the Sermon, is conceded by its defender.   The Scriptures are in such wise exclusively sufficient to their own interpretation as to require no interpreter—and even to bid defiance to a false interpreter, to corrupt the saving faith contained in them, to the injury of the recipient.   I wonder of what advantage the Scriptures would be to a Pagan, or a nation of Pagans, interpreted by an Unitarian?   B.t, 'with no interpreter, it is better that the nations should have the word of life, than remain deprived of it.'   And what is this but the acknowledgement that preachers and sacraments are not necessary to give effect to the Scriptures; and consequently, decisive proof, so far as your authority goes, that the 'no comment' principle involves the separation of the Church of God from the word of God?

It is understood—that is, it is tacitly agreed upon—that each separate denomination is to find no let or hindrance in promoting Christianity according to its own views.   Then it is the true meaning of the 'no comment' principle, that all the various and opposite professions of religion, drawn from the Bible, are equally true, and equally safe for salvation; for, otherwise, how can they promote Christianity, or how can the Bible Societies be justified in the adoption of a principle which places them all upon a level, provided they receive the naked Scriptures, and lend their aid to disseminate them?   And is this the secret of the burning wrath poured out against me?   Is my poor Sermon looked upon as infringing this agreement—and, therefore, denounced as a 'let and hindrance,' to this license to proselyte?

How the Heathen are to be benefited by this concession, does not so readily appear.   They have no denominations to help them out.   This is a disadvantage, however, under which they will not long labour.   Denominations will rise up in plenty, under the operation of this principle.   Whether they will be *Christian*, indeed, is another question.   Unity, a visible and verified unity, in origin, faith, order, and worship, is the Christian mark.   Not merely *holding the head*—but so holding it, as that *from which all the body, by joints and bands, having nourishment ministered, and knit together, increaseth with the increase of God*;

and I confess that I am not skilful enough to reconcile this Christian unity with a principle which so unqualifiedly sanctions, and even encourages, division without limit.

Equally unable do I find myself to reconcile the sentiments I have been considering, with these which follow, p. 244 :

" But let it not be said, that we nullify the ministry of the gospel, and the sacraments of the Church. A thing may be done by one set of means, which will be done more readily, frequently, and effectually, by the use of additional means. This is a matter of common experience. So it is in the efficient communication of Scriptural instruction. God can communicate saving knowledge to every individual by immediate revelation; but he does not choose to do this. He can accomplish the work by means of the Bible. This is sometimes done, where other opportunities are wanting. But that man may be made a blessing to his fellow, and that society may be bound together by new bonds of love, he sees fit chiefly to carry on this work by human instrumentality, by the preaching of the gospel, and the administration of the sacraments. We are, therefore, perfectly consistent in maintaining the sufficiency of the Scriptures, and at the same time the necessity of a gospel ministry and the ordinances of the Church."

Much do I wish to know, which set of sentiments I am to consider as those you will stand to. Your declaration that it is better the nations should have the Bible, even without an interpreter, or with the risk of an erroneous one ; and your maintaining the necessity of a gospel ministry and the ordinances of the Church ; present a species of consistency which is new to me. It is, however, not very material to the present question— this very statement serving to support my objection to the ' no comment' principle, as being at variance with the wisdom of God, in that method pursued by him in making known his will to his creatures.   *Sermon*, p. 14.

' For the *efficient* communication of spiritual instruction to mankind, God sees fit,' say you, ' among several ways in which it might be done, to select human instrumentality, in the preaching of the word, and the administration of the sacraments.' Now, Sir, does the Bible Society principle, or the Bible Society as a *body*, pay the least regard to this example? On the contrary, by expressly excluding them—'no notes or comments,' 'the Bible alone'—does it not practically reject them as necessary, and so far 'nullify' them? And am I not justified for the opinion expressed in the *Sermon*, p. 8, that 'the Bible itself was overlooked, in the clear directions which may be drawn from it as to the only safe and effectual manner of disseminating its saving knowledge.' And is such a palpable departure as this, both from divine precept and example, to be sustained and defended as one of the buttresses of religion? And all this, because it presents 'one calm and peaceful place,' where Christian divisions may rest themselves, and take sweet counsel together, and send forth the fruitful seeds of more division, in the Bible stripped of all help to understand it—of all means to profit by the personal application of its hope, in the sacraments of salvation? But 'we maintain the sufficiency of the Scriptures.' Unquestionably : and even their *exclusive* sufficiency, which is the error charged to the 'no comment' principle, and you are drawn out to defend. But their sufficiency *to what?* To the '*efficient* communication of spiritual instruction without the ordinances of the Church? If this is your meaning, as it certainly is of the 'no comment principle, I consider it subversive of all revealed religion, being plainly contrary to the word of GOD. If it is not your meaning, as I believe it is not, you ought to have been more explicit. Neither yourself nor any other, maintains more absolutely than I do, the sufficiency of Scripture ; but it is their sufficiency to make men *wise unto salvation*—not to save them. It is their sufficiency to direct men what they must do to be saved. It is their sufficiency as an infallible rule of faith and manners, when truly interpreted and followed. It is their sufficiency to direct and bring sinners to CHRIST for life and salvation, in the external appointments of the Church, the ministry, and the sacraments—and not their sufficiency as a *substitute* for these integral parts in the plan of salvation.

But while I maintain their full sufficiency for all these purposes, I also maintain that they are not in such wise sufficient, that men cannot be mistaken or misled, in drawing from them their true meaning—I therefore assert, against the 'no comment' principle, the *utility* and the *necessity* of explanations, illustrations, expositions, enforcements of their sense by notes and comments ; not only in the literal meaning of these words, but in the higher, equally just, and more profitable application of them to the ordinances of the gospel, as alone giving life, and power, and assurance to the word. This is the sense, and the only sense, in which the Scriptures are considered insufficient to their own interpretation, by either the Bishop of Limerick or the Bishop of North Carolina. In support of this insufficiency, they present the actual condition of Christendom, with its hundreds of opposite constructions of the vital doctrines of the Scriptures. Against the difficulty and the danger hence arising, they offer the best advice their ability enables, and their station requires them to give ; leaving it to the discretion of their hearers and readers, whether, on so momentous a subject as the truth or falsehood of opposing systems of religion, they will resort to the Saints and Confessors of the primitive Church as safe interpreters of Divine Truth, or to the naked Scriptures.

"Now, while the hearts of millions are rejoicing in this ' era of good feelings,' and thanking GOD that sectarian coldness is warmed and melted by this new display of fraternal love ; we hear this Bishop and the other interposing, and saying, No, we cannot unite with you, unless you will join the Book of Common Prayer with the Bible ! Unless you all become Episcopalians, and join with us, we cannot have any connexion with such societies."

And pray, Sir, is this the objection taken in my sermon to the Bible Society principle ? Is the separation of the Book of Common Prayer from the Bible in its distribution, given as the reason why I cannot warm myself at this genial source of sectarian fervour ? Or is this one of Dr. Rice's charitable fabrications, to catch his readers ? Certainly, Sir, I am free to acknowledge, for myself, that CHRIST's religion forbids me to have fellowship with, or to countenance in any way, either men or measures, which I conscientiously believe to be injurious to the interests of revealed religion ; even if that injury shall proceed from well meant, but mistaken intention to serve it. But I cannot allow you or any other person to attribute motives to my conduct, without contradiction, which are notoriously false ; as is the case in the present instance.

That any 'other Bishop' has given you reason to assign this as the cause of his refusing to unite with 'no comment' Bible Societies, I do not know ; but I do not believe it, because so many stronger and juster reasons can be given for this refusal, that such as you have chosen to put into our mouths, would hardly be thought of.

The objection of every consistent Episcopalian to promiscuous 'no comment' Bible Societies is to the *principle* of their association in its practical results—to the inevitable consequences of that principle, on the unity of faith, order, and fellowship in the gospel ; to the separation of the word of GOD from the Church of GOD as an efficient means of grace—and to the countenance given to the monstrous delusion, that whatever a man, or body of men, draws from the naked Scriptures, as a system of faith and practice, is good to him or them, as the religion GOD hath enjoined to be believed and practised in order to obtain eternal life. All of which, (unintended, I admit ; surely unperceived,) do necessarily follow from, and are the practical results of the 'no comment' principle, adopted and acted upon by these Bible Societies.

And the 'one and the other Bishop' presumed to be intended by you, do verily believe, and think themselves competent to show, that cause and effect are not more certain, than the subversion of all revealed religion by the necessary operation of this 'no comment' principle, so far as corruption of the faith, and separation from the order of the gospel as instituted by the LORD JESUS CHRIST is subversion.

For admitting, even, that the principle is not abused in Christian lands to the formation of new systems, and sects of religion by the readers of the naked Scriptures ; and that men are stirred up by the Bible *alone*, to seek the salvation of their souls : they must of necessity, unite themselves with some one of the various religious denominations around them, or adopt the notion of an invisible Church, and rely on inward assurance, &c. becoming *liberal* Christians, that is, Christians indifferent alike to the faith and order of the gospel, on the plea that all are right in so far as salvation is concerned. Now what is this but plainly and palpably sanctioning the prevailing notion, that contradictory creeds and confessions of faith, and oppositions of external order, are equally safe for the attainment of the salvation offered by the gospel? In what does it come short of giving the whole weight of these Bible Societies to the infidel notion, that the Scripture-denounced sins of heresy and schism are no longer within the range of our commissions? For one of these two things is infallibly certain. Either all the various denominations of Christian profession within the range of Bible Society circulation of the Scriptures are equally true and orthodox branches of the Church of CHRIST, and equally safe for the attainment of salvation; or some of them are in heresy or schism, or both heretical and schismatical, and not thus safe. But the Bible Society principle, that the Scriptures alone are sufficient to determine the truth or error, the heresy or schism, of opposite denominations, all alike claiming the Scriptures to be with them; does give the sanction of that body to the monstrous proposition, that it is a matter of entire indifference and equal safety, whichever denomination a man unites himself with as a church member; and by a similar consequence, that the sins of heresy and schism are either abrogated, or yet future.

You do, indeed, (p. 249, 250,) beg to be excused from admitting either that the tendency of the Bible Society principle to produce an endless variety of systems of belief, is a valid objection to the principle; or from maintaining 'that it is a matter of perfect indifference what system of religious opinions we draw from the Scriptures.' The latter, you say, 'we hold in utter abhorrence;' and ask, if 'I do not know that you do?' I know nothing about your private sentiments further than your choice of one dissenting denomination out of many, declares them. Neither have I any thing to do with the private sentiments of Dr. Rice, who is so clear sighted to his own weak side, that he refuses fundamentals, and attacks ceremonies. Bishop R. has never charged Dr. Rice with 'indifference to truth.' He has arraigned a public principle, supported and defended by Dr. Rice, as sanctioning, and encouraging, and necessarily leading to this indifference to the unity, and consequent efficacy of revealed truth.   To this Dr. Rice replies, 'No, this is not our sin ; it (the sin) consists in believing that the word of GOD is sufficient without the book of Common Prayer'—thus artfully substituting the book of Common Prayer for the Church, the Ministry, and the sacraments of GOD, as inseparable from the right knowledge, and saving virtue, of the word of GOD.   Yet Dr. Rice cannot but know, that in resorting to this trick—indeed, in his entire defence of the Bible Society principle—he is liable to be confronted with the highest authority of his own denomination (the General Assembly) in favor of the Westminster Confession of faith, as indispensable to a right understanding of the Bible ; and also with the recorded opinion of a brother divine and Theological Professor, in favour of creeds and confessions—in other words, expositions and comments, as *essential* to the unity and purity of faith in the Church.   How these solemnly considered and authoritative sentiments of his own Church are reconcileable with the support of the ' no comment' principle is for Dr. Rice to make out ; and to assist him in this difficult job, Bishop R. refers him to the recantation by the General Assembly of 1825, of the sentiments published in 1824 ; and to Dr. Miller's Letter on the Bible Societies, subsequent to his published Lecture on the utility of Creeds and Confessions.

" We ask—But, dear brethren ! why can you not co-operate with us in this work of love? It is haughtily replied, 'because in the constitution of your society you maintain that the Scriptures are exclusively sufficient for their own interpretation.' We answer, whatever may be our sentiments, we maintain no such thing in our association ; we only agree that, as a Bible Society, we will not undertake to interpret Scripture. You, as individuals, or united in another society, may distribute as many Commentators, Prayer Books, and Homilies, as you please.   We have nothing to say to this ; we pretend to no power to prevent it.   We only ask you to join with us, in presenting the whole Protestant world, as united in one work of Christian benevolence."

What a pitiful quibble ! What miserable sophistry ! 'We are not associated to interpret Scripture.'   And yet the very principle of your union is capable of no other practical meaning, than that the Scriptures need no interpretation—no comment, no exposition, no illustration! What name, pray, would the Bible Society, as a body, deserve for adopting this principle, could it be shown that it really did believe that the Scriptures required explanation, for men to understand them aright, and the Sacraments, to make them effectual to their declared purpose? Does not every one joining this society, then, declare his assent to the public principle of its foundation? Or is there a public mind for it as a body, at variance with the private mind of the individuals composing it? If this be so, it is certainly, in more respects than one, a novel institution. 'We are not associated to interpret Scripture.' No, your principle tells me that; and it tells me, moreover, that, as a body, you are associated to declare your belief that every man, without regard to his capacity, and without danger of error, may derive from the naked Bible the saving faith and commanded duty of redeemed creatures. And I am considered 'haughty,' for giving this as a reason for refusing to unite in support of such a principle—and the reasons are met by the reply 'we are not associated to interpret Scripture.'

'One work of Christian benevolence.' Certainly—though it ought to be shown that it is such a work, before those who refuse to co-operate in it, are branded either as haughty or malignant. But what in its genuine results is this work? What language does the circulation of the Scriptures, on the Bible Society principle speak? Says it not to every shade of error in religion, Be satisfied, you are founded on the Bible; you hold the head; you have felt the power of Divine truth; you know the preciousness of the Bible; the Church, the Ministry, and the Sacraments—the unity and fellowship of believers in *one body, one spirit, one faith, one* LORD, *one baptism, one* GOD, *and Father of all*, are matters of mere form and order?

Sir, I trust I would not knowingly force the principles or the arguments, even of an adversary, beyond their fair and evident consequences; and if these are not the practical conclusions from this principle, and confirmed to be such both by the matter and the manner of your defence of it, I have yet to learn the meaning of language, and the connexion of reasoning.   Sir, the best intentions, the most affectionate expressions, the most earnest professions, alter not the nature of things.   The most dangerous thing in the world, is an unguarded abstract generality—such as the ' no comment' principle of the Bible Societies.   When it is once thrown out, you cannot controul, you cannot limit its effects ; men rush to its obvious—most commonly to its most remote and unconsidered—conclusion, at once ; and what was meant for good, produces the most irremediable evil. Of this ill-considered, unguarded, abstract description, is this Bible Society ' no comment' principle ; and such have already been, and such in greater degree, will yet be, its effects.   The knowledge of divine truth may, indeed, be extended, but it must and will be, divine truth severed from divine institution, from those positive appointments of heaven which illustrate, apply, and confirm divine truth, to the faith of mortals.

' One work of Christian Benevolence.'—Sir, Christian benevolence, like Christian charity, is a grave and considerate virtue. It is not an impulse of mere feeling.   It calculates its means, it weighs consequences, it looks to the end.   It is not taken with the glitter of the action, but with its fruits.   Of what character, then, is that benevolence, which says in effect to the Christian world, prone to and warned against divisions in religion,—Never mind, go on, circulate the Scriptures without any help to understand them, and deprived of the means to realize them, and then exert yourselves, according to your several contradictory views of divine truth, to obtain proselytes to your different systems of faith and order.   Distribute as many Commentators, Prayer Books, Homilies, Westminster Confessions of Faith, Saybrook Flatforms, Methodist Books of Discipline, Bible Society Speeches, Tracts, Irenicums, Magazines and Reviews, as you please—true or false—orthodox or heretical—orderly or schismatical.   We have nothing to do with this, we pretend to no power to prevent it.   We are not associated to guard the ignorant from error, or to enforce what we severally or singly believe to be divine truth and order, but simply to disseminate the Scriptures ' without note or comment.'   And it is a haughty, and of course a reprehensible reply, to refuse to take a part in, or to give countenance to a principle, which, if it has a meaning, means all that I have attributed to it.   Where have we a more unqualified acknowledgment, and even enforcement, of entire safety, in a religious sense, in whatever system of faith and obedience a man may frame for himself, from the Scriptures? For this, (unintended, I admit, but not, therefore, the less certain or the less dangerous,) is the only practical meaning of the far-famed 'no comment' principle of these Bible Societies.

If, therefore, I am considered guilty of *hauteur*, in proposing the test of the principle, mentioned in the preface to the Sermon —my haughtiness must be still more reprehensible, when I confirm the application of the test, by referring to the fact that these promiscuous, 'no comment' Bible Societies, from the parent down to the remotest descendant, do not generally open or close their meetings with prayer.   Their very composition forbids it; the materials are too heterogeneous even for supplication, as a body, to the Father of Mercies to bless and prosper their work.   They feel and know, that to propose it even, would "split them to shivers," and by common consent, the religious character of the association is left to be inferred only, from the name of the Book they distribute.   In their composition, and in their principle of action, Bible Societies of this stamp are representatives, and in fact encouragers, of the foulest blot upon Christianity—its divisions.   And the more I reflect upon it, and the more I see of the growing consequences of this fatal principle, the more confirmed I am, that the secret of its popularity is that mentioned in the preface to the Sermon. 'It leaves the field free for their respective emissaries, to give their separate and opposite constructions of the *one faith* of the gospel.'   And when we add to this that the Society itself, as a body, is a virtual acknowledgment of every separate denomination as a lawful and Scriptural branch of the Catholic Church, we need not resort to supernatural influence, of a heavenly character at least, to account for the torrent-like nature of its success in a divided Christian world.

You may, therefore, shrug your shoulders yet more significantly, and say,

"Dear Sirs, what would you have? We have associated on a certain principle, and you wish us to try whether the Society will hold together when we abolish the principle of association. We tell you again, that we did not unite for the *interpretation*, but the *distribution* of the Bible."

No, Sir; the proposition alluded to in the preface to the Sermon, was offered to try the soundness of the conclusions drawn in the Sermon, from your boasted 'no comment' principle—to demonstrate that its obvious necessary consequence is, division without limit, and the ultimate subversion of all revealed religion. For what other conclusion can be drawn from the principle on which the Society is formed, and acts, but this, that the Scriptures are *safe and profitable*, however interpreted— that it is not only unnecessary, but *unsafe*, to give the ignorant and unlearned any help to understand and apply them beyond what the letter of Scripture affords? And, what, I pray you, Sir, is the fair and required presumption, but that the one adopted is the best and most consistent principle, in the judgment of the Society, on which to disseminate divine truth? Nay, that in their opinion as a body, no other principle ought to be acted upon, in the distribution of the Bible among men? Surely, candour, Christian charity, requires it to be presumed that so respectable, and learned, and pious an association, chose the best, the very best, of many ways in which this work might have been performed. Undoubtedly it is the best plan, that has yet been devised, to increase and multiply copies of the Bible, and with them to confirm existing divisions, and generate fresh ones. But whether this is consistent either with the purpose of GOD, or with the methods of his wisdom in every communication of his will to this world, you, as a divine and a theologian, may be able to show.

'How is it then, that *you* do not perceive that there is not an atom's force' in the quibble you have resorted to, as to the purpose of the association; and that your whole defence of the principle of the society is made to turn on the individual views and privileges of its members, and not on the obvious and necessary tendency of the principle in its practical operation? Sir,

I know well, that the principle of these Bible Societies restrains no one, from even the wildest and most discordant interpretation of Scripture. On the contrary, it gives the sanction of the various and opposite denominations of religious profession, who have adopted this principle as the constitutional rule of their operations as a body, to the very root of division, in such unwarranted and opposite interpretations of Scripture countenanced as divine and saving faith. 'And how is it that you do not perceive' that the objections taken in the Sermon are strictly confined to the *principle*—the 'no comment' principle of these Bible Societies; that they have no reference to the *individuals* composing it, and that your whole defence of it tends only to expose more broadly its deleterious consequences?

"But it is of no use, we cannot prevail with them. And we who love the Gospel, and the Universal Church, more than the peculiarities of a particular denomination, must content ourselves with sharing our labours, our pleasures and our honours, with these brethren."

Certainly, Sir, these brethren cannot unite in such labours; and for the reasons above given : nor do they claim any share in either the pleasures or the honours which spring from them. But they would humbly put in their claim to be considered among the number of those who love the Gospel and the Universal Church; who love them so well, that they feel bound to guard them from whatever would corrupt the faith of the one, or the unity of the other. *Set for the defence of the gospel,* and appointed to *watch for souls,* they cannot give their countenance and support to a principle so pregnant with danger as they verily believe, and think they have demonstrated, the 'no comment' principle of these Bible Societies to be. The purity of *the faith once delivered to the saints ;* the unity of the Church which the SON OF GOD *purchased with his own blood,* and constituted a visible society in the world ; the validity of the sacraments therein administered by his authority, as seals of the the promises, and means of the grace of GOD given in CHRIST JESUS : *these* are the peculiarities of these denounced brethren, as a Christian denomination. As you therefore 'love the Gospel and the Universal Church' more than *these*, it must be a Gospel and a Church, of which they are as yet ignorant. Give them then to know and understand whence cometh the one, and by what marks the other is verified as the Church of GOD. The Gospel which 'these brethren' have received, and *wherein they stand*, came from GOD by JESUS CHRIST, through his Apostles. The Universal Church, of which they are members, is *the Church of the living* GOD—*the pillar and ground of the truth*, planted by the Apostles, and verified by succession from them. Of any other Gospel, or Universal Church, they have no knowledge, and ought not to be accused, even by implication, of any want of affection towards them.

In this whole matter, all they wish is, to be fairly represented. They have no hostility to the Bible—no wish to impede its *widest* circulation. They have no peculiarities, as a Christian denomination, which are bars to communion in the rightly informed conscience of any believer. Nor do they hold a single tenet, or require a single observance, *which is not warranted by Scripture, by antiquity, and by universality of consent in the Catholic Apostolic Church of* CHRIST.

Having thus disposed of the main point in the controversy on the Bible Society Sermon ; and the rest of your strictures upon it, being, in substance, the same as those you have made use of in the Review of the *Sermon on the Study and Interpretation of Scripture*, I shall pursue them no further in this place. There are, however, three other points growing out of the Bible Society Sermon, yet unnoticed, which ought not to be passed over.

The first is, the repeated insinuation, and occasionally the direct assertion, that the doctrines laid down in my Sermons of the subjects of the Church and Ministry, and in the two last particularly, are of a character too 'nearly akin to Popery, to suit the meridian of Protestant America.'

What purpose this insinuation is intended to answer, beyond that of profiting by the prejudice it may serve to excite and continue against the Episcopal Church, you best know. But that there is the slightest foundation for it in fact, is just as false, as it is true that you have made it. And I wonder it did not occur to your sagacity, how easily it might be retorted on you, that if the general interests of dissent, or the particular interests of 'no comment' Bible Societies, required their patrons and defenders to resort to such shifts, the cause must be a bad one. Truth, Sir, disdains trick or chicane. Honesty, even honest error, stands in need of no subterfuge. Candour is a stranger to duplicity; and the temper of a Christian is *simplicity and godly sincerity*.

The first insinuation of this stamp, in the review of the Bible Society Sermon, is found p. 197, 198. In the sermon, p. 9. I have expressed myself thus: 'I might, indeed, my hearers, have taken the *beaten track*, with more ease to myself, and perhaps with greater satisfaction to you;' but however plain and direct, in signification and reference, the words 'beaten track' are, to the usual course pursued by the preachers of Anniversary Bible Society Sermons, neither this, nor the solemn professions which usher in your review, were sufficient to restrain you from the following sacrifice of Christian candour and literary fairness on the altar of prejudice:

"But yet he does not walk in a new way. According to his own showing, he goes in a track marked out and trodden by others. In the *Raleigh Register* of the 28th of January, the Bishop gives us to understand that a number of the rulers of the United Church of England, that all the Scotch Bishops and more than two of the American Bishops, are decidedly opposed to the present organization of the Bible Society. He might easily have swelled the list of oppugnation to a much more formidable length. The Bishop of Rome, with almost all the Romish Bishops in the world, are zealous opponents. And we can now add, it was not known when the sermon was preached, that the Grand Seignor is *almost* as much opposed to the distribution of the Bible in his dominions, as *any Catholic or Protestant Bishop* can be. We say *almost*, in a spirit of candour and justice; for it appears, by the last accounts from the missionaries in Palestine, that the Grand Turk was instigated to this measure by the Latins (that is, the Roman Catholics.)"

Now, Sir, will you be pleased to come forward, and point out any Protestant Bishop, either in Europe or America, who is opposed to the distribution of the Bible. For this you must do, or stand convicted of fostering prejudice at the expense of truth. And I speak thus plain, because the case is of that sort which precludes mistake as to the fact. You have said, ' that the Grand Seignor is almost as much opposed to the distribution of the Bible in his dominions as any Catholic or Protestant Bishop can be.' Unless, therefore, you can show some Protestant Bishop who is opposed to the distribution of the Bible, as Roman Catholics are opposed to it, you are justly chargeable as a *false accuser of the brethren.*

The character of your candour and justice also, is hereby strikingly exemplified. It is carefully manifested towards the Grand Turk—it is withheld from a Protestant Bishop. And wherefore is it thus? Is it indeed the case, that the ' no comment' Bible Society principle is to be supported at every hazard? Are the interests of parity so bound up with those of his foster-parent of religious division, that the whole body of Protestant Bishops are to be falsely denounced as opposed to the distribution of the Bible? Or does this reviewer write at random, under the impression that no one will venture to contradict him? I should be glad to know. For I would not willingly suppose any man, much more a man calling himself a minister of religion, capable of such a cool, calculating surrender of candour and justice, and I might add, of truth, to keep alive the prejudices of a misguided judgment, in the very persons who look up to him with confidence for instruction and direction. With Dr. Rice, therefore, it rests, to support or to abandon this charge, as it is made. Again. at p. 248 :

" We lament," say you, " that the indiscretion of his zeal hurries him unawares into errors so near akin to popery."

Now, it might reasonably be supposed, that either in the *Bible Society Sermon,* or some where else, I had laid down some doctrine, or expressed some sentiment, hostile to the fundamental principles of the reformation ; which the Protestant zeal of the reviewer was constrained to animadvert upon. Whereas, and in very good truth, the ' error so near akin to popery,' is one of the reviewer's own forced, and even false constructions of a principle which was the very light of the reformation, and is to this day the only safe-guard against heresy aud schism. The point in the sermon is, the rule of interpreting the mysterious and obscure parts of Scripture, which I conclude in the words of a Christian Father of the fifth century, as follows :

" From the very depths of Holy Scripture, all men cannot receive it in one and the same sense. One person interprets the divine oracles in one manner, another person in a manner totally different ; insomuch that from the same source almost as many opinions may be elicited as there are men. Therefore, amid so great perplexity of such various error, it is extremely necessary, that the line of prophetic and apostolic interpretation be regulated by the standard of ecclesiastical and catholic judgment."

This only safe rule in questions of disputed doctrine from Scripture, and which was adopted and relied upon before popery was even thought of, the reviewer transforms into the assertion on my part, that men must ' surrender understanding and conscience to diocesan bishops, and the men on whom they have laid their hands ;' and upon this gratuitous perversion of the rule, he not only insinuates a charge of popery, but constructs the greater part of the reasoning, followed out through the remaining pages of the Review. Now while I freely admit that if I had ever thought, spoken, preached, or published a word or sentence that could fairly be construed into the assertion of such a claim over the understandings and consciences of men, popery, and any other wicked kind of conspiracy against religion, might justly be charged to me ; I must insist, as I have not done this, not to be delivered over to the unjust and injurious prejudices, growing out of so barefaced a perversion of the sound Protestant principle contained in the rule above given.

The Reviewer does indeed express a doubt, ' whether the Right Reverend preacher has considered the extent to which his principles carry him,' and this he does, to plead my excuse with his readers for the Popish errors he ascribes to me. In several other places, also, he repeats his conviction that I do not see the consequences of my position ; but I cannot accept the excuse because it would be to admit that I engaged in the serious duties of the pulpit, without carefully considering and preparing my discourses. As however I pretend to no extraordinary share of acumen, I may not see entirely through the application of this rule; and if so, the Reviewer has the advantage of me, for it is very evident that he does see, and too clearly for his quiet, the just, safe, and unavoidable consequences, not only of the rule given in this Sermon, but of some other also, of my 'unfortunate positions.' This, however, is but the distant rumbling of the thunder—the storm will burst anon, in all its fury, upon the devoted rule and its supporter. Once more, p. 241.

"Roman Catholics are known to prohibit altogether, or greatly to discourage, the circulation of the Scriptures."

On this I have already remarked, that I hope they will speedily learn a better mind. And it is not to defend them in this antichristian denial of the light of life to benighted souls, that I again notice it; but to show that the reproach comes with a very ill grace from a staunch defender of the 'no comment' Bible Society principle. This I shall do, in the words of one of the Vestry of the Episcopal Chapel, Raleigh; to whose judgment, as a body, you refer the quality of the logic used by you, p. 309. And I am exceeding happy to inform Dr. Rice—for I feel great comfort in it, that there are gentlemen and Christians in that Vestry, to whose competent judgment he might safely commit deeper things than his logic, and from whom even *he* might derive an accession of knowledge, both on religious and other subjects.——But to the argument:

" The Romanists contend, that the *Scriptures* are confided exclusively to the clergy; that the laity are to receive implicitly, without inquiry or examination, what is by them declared to be the truth of these Scriptures. To the people they give the *Church* and the *Ministry*, but retain for themselves the *Scriptures*. They thereby *separate* the former from the latter, and deny the people at large, one of the most efficient means of grace.

" The doctrine of the Bible Society, involved in the rejection of comments—that ' the Scriptures are exclusively sufficient'— produces a like separation with that of the Romanists; the difference being, that the former give to the people the *Scriptures without the Church*, while the latter give to them the *Church, and refuse the Scriptures*.   In opposition to the latter error the reformers and standard writers of the Church contended, because it was the prominent error of their day.   In opposition to the former, Bishop R. and those who think with him, contend, because it is the prominent error of our own time.   The Bishop, and those who think with him, are perfectly consistent in refusing to countenance these Bible Societies ; because they maintain, that *all the institutions of* GOD, designed as means of conveying and giving assurance of his favour to fallen man, should be communicated to the people——that those things which He has *united*, should never be *separated* by a vain confidence, which rushes into the counsels of the Most High, and acting as GOD, profanely elevates one of his institutions by the depression of another.   The Bishop, and other opponents of the principle and practice of these Bible Societies, unite in condemning all separation of the means of grace, one from the other ; whether devised by the craft of Romanists, or suggested by the mistaken liberality of the Bible Societies ; and in affirming that the gospel, as *one* in its doctrines, order, and ministrations, should be afforded *entire* to the people.

 " They hold, that a true Church, in which the pure word of GOD is preached by those having authority thereto, valid administrations of the sacraments, and the Scriptures to be examined and read by all who can read them, *are* TOGETHER *the sure means*, prepared by divine wisdom for our salvation.   That in their *union* there is *safety ;* in their *separation* there is *danger.*   That *separation* of the one from the other is *erroneous*, whether it be made by Protestants or Romanists——whether it be the result of designing policy or uninformed benevolence——whether it be a corruption of the dark ages, which benighted Christianity and learning ; or a meteoric error, kindled into blaze in our own day, by the collision of different elements in religious belief, chafing themselves into an attempt at unnatural union."

Secondly——The opportunity afforded you by an expression of mine in the Note in the *Raleigh Register*, before noticed, which you eagerly catch at, in order to cast reproach on, and excite prejudice against the American Bishops.

The Note was occasioned by an anonymous publication in the previous *Register*, altogether erroneous in the statement made to the public, of the support given to ' no comment' Bible

Societies by the British and American Bishops; and the passage alluded to is as follows :

"I have no hesitation in asserting, that more than two, perhaps a majority, of the American Bishops, are not in favour of Bible Societies, on the principle adopted by the British and Foreign Bible Society, and copied by a majority of those in this country. While of those who are known to have given them countenance, reasons and motives very different from those of sanctioning such principles, have operated in inducing them to have any connexion with such societies."

On this you remark, with your usual candour, p. 205, 206 :

"What is the meaning of these words, as it forces itself upon our attention? Plainly this. American Bishops, who have taken an active part, and borne offices in Bible Societies, are opposed to the fundamental principles of the institution ; but yet have their reasons and motives for appearing to favour them —or, to use the significant and striking words of the Prelate of North-Carolina, for having 'any connexion with such societies'!!! If we were enemies, what an occasion for triumph is here! What an opportunity for assaulting the whole corps of American Bishops is afforded by this confession of one of the fraternity, who might be supposed to know the secrets of his order ! But no——we are unwilling to admit the justice of this reproach."

Generous, candid, charitable man ! But as I am altogether unwilling to bear the reproach transferred to me, as the writer of the Note, I will just say, that so far is it from being the *plain meaning* of the passage, that no one would have made this use of it who was not himself capable of all the perfidy which it implies. And so far from refraining from an assault, it is actually made, and in that way too, which is well understood to be most effectual with the uninformed and the prejudiced, by insinuation of more than appears; while the cunning disclaimer is put in, as the loop-hole of retreat. But, Sir, it shall not answer your purpose——for I am happily able to free both the Bishops and myself, from the injurious imputation of your implied charge.

It does not follow, either plainly or necessarily, from 'the striking and significant words of the Prelate of North-Carolina,' that the reasons and motives for 'having any connexion with such societies,' were either bad in themselves, or coupled with any insincerity or duplicity, in acting upon them. To infer bad motives, therefore, unnecessarily, is at once unjust and uncharitable. In the mind of the writer of the Note, the most distant idea of any thing culpable in the reasons and motives of the American Bishops, connected with ' no comment' Bible Societies, or even capable of being twisted into wrong, was not entertained. To assume it gratuitously, therefore—to clutch it even with avidity, in order to circulate an injurious imputation on the writer, and on the body to which he belongs, betrays a disposition not easily reconcileable with either candour or justice.

But further. Reasons and motives perfectly innocent, and even praiseworthy, and yet 'very different from those of sanctioning such principles,' present themselves readily to every ingenuous mind. What does Dr. Rice think of the desire to conciliate—to soften the asperities of religious dissent, by such concessions to prejudice as can be made with a good conscience? Are these, and such as these, reasons and motives of a character so unknown among the American Bishops, that he could not even suppose them to be meant by the writer of the Note, or acted upon by the Bishops connected with the Bible Societies? And when to this is added, what I firmly believe, but have no authority to assert it as a fact, that in one such case at least, Dr. Rice had the best means of being satisfied that the reasons and motives for taking an active part, and bearing office, in a 'no comment' Bible Society, were entirely of a conciliatory nature, it could have been no great stretch of his abundant charity, to have inferred the same of the few other instances of connexion with these Bible Societies which have occurred among the American Bishops. Dr. Rice's ' alas !,' therefore, is sadly misplaced. ' The good man' (as he is pleased to call me) has not permitted himself, either ' in the warmth of his zeal against an object which appears *very good*, to bring into question the sincerity of his brethren,' or in ' his ardour to support episcopacy, to impeach the character of his brother Bishops, and cast a slur on the whole sacred office.' This has been the work of another man, whose reasons and motives for forcing this incident into his service, and in this way, are best known to himself.

Thirdly. The use made by yourself, and others equally uninformed, but equally willing to fasten a charge of inconsistency on me, of the part I took in the formation of the Mecklenburg Auxiliary Bible Society. On this subject, you thus express yourself, p. 302 :

" But, notwithstanding this pertinacious consistency, we have satisfactory evidence that the Bishop is capable of changing his opinions. It has been stated to us, as undeniably true, that a few years ago a Bible Society was organized in Mecklenburg county, auxiliary to the Bible Society of Virginia ; and that its Constitution was written by the then rector of St. James' Parish ; and that an article in it corresponds with the famous article in the Constitution of the Society in North-Carolina, which has given so great offence to the Bishop of that diocese. How is it that the Bishop's views differ so widely from the Rector's ? We do not pretend to explain this matter : nor do we blame a man for changing his opinions, when he assigns adequate reasons for the change. This we are sure the Bishop thinks that he has done : but it is our misfortune to differ, and we never bow to human authority."

" It is ' undeniably true,' Sir, and never has been gainsaid by me, that an Auxiliary Bible Society was formed in the county of Mecklenburg, and that the constitution thereof, and perhaps some other papers belonging to its formation, are in my hand-writing ; nevertheless, the current opinion on the subject, is not the correct one. The facts are briefly these. The Rev. Mr. Treadway, recently ordained a deacon in the Protestant Epis-copal Church, was appointed an Agent of the Virginia Bible Society, at the instance of Bishop Moore, for the formation of Auxiliary Societies. In this capacity, he visited my then parish, and was received by me with all the attention due to his clerical character, and was assisted in his particular object, so far as introducing him to the people, and making appointments for him to preach, and explain the views of the Society, from the respect due to my diocesan. Mr. Treadway having succeeded in obtain-ing a sufficient number to form a society, and a day being appointed for them to meet at the court house, and being himself obliged to visit some other places in the interval, he requested me to draw up a constitution and rules for the regulation of the society.   This I assented to, as an accommodation to him, and performed it by copying a printed form, which I found among some loose pamphlets in my study.   I believe also, that I gave a dollar, or some small contribution to the society—preached an extempore sermon to a small congregation convened on an appointment made for Mr. Treadway, which he did not attend, and at a meeting of the Society to elect their officers, when only three or four attended, I advised, as the only probable means of becoming organized; that the few who were present should name the officers, and notify them of their election.   The plan was agreed to, and at the request of those present the nomination was made by myself, embracing all classes of religious profession in the county, except Episcopalians, not one of whom was nominated to any office in the Society; having previously refused to have any thing to do with its transactions myself. This is the whole extent of my intromissions with the formation of this Auxiliary, or any other Bible Society.   Less I could not well do consistently with my respect for Bishop Moore—more I could not do, consistently with respect for myself.   And though you wish to make it appear that I have changed my views on some inadequate ground, you happen to be mistaken in this, as in many other instances, respecting me.   The Bishop and the Rector have never been of contrary sentiments on this subject. And even suppose an alteration of opinion had taken place ; a man of your acuteness and experience—to say nothing of the very friendly feeling professed toward me—might have considered, that as the Bishop's sphere of observation is necessarily far more extensive than that of the Rector, and his means of ascertaining the effects produced by such bodies much more ample, he had doubtless good reasons for an actual change, both of opinion and conduct—were such the fact.   The Bishop can, therefore, give Dr. Rice no hope that he will return to the ground supposed to be occupied by him, ' when under his auspices the Bible Society of Mecklenburg was instituted.' p. 317.

I come now, Sir, to your review of my *Sermon on the Study and Interpretation of Scripture.*

In this, the main point is, the rule known among Theologians as that laid down by Vincentius Lirinensis, a Christian father of the fifth century. From the purpose and the structure of the sermon, this rule is necessarily the governing principle, and pervades the whole discourse in some example of its very practical and profitable application. As it occupies, consequently, an equally conspicuous place in your review of the sermon, and is moreover the very *jugulum causæ*, you know, Sir, it is entitled to the chief notice: I shall, therefore, proceed at once to the examination of your objections to the rule, and to the means by which you endeavour to sustain them. At p. 308, you thus introduce the subject:

"Our readers see, that after having given three 'essential rules,' Bishop R. proceeds to lay down another, which he calls 'the rule of interpreting Scripture, as the standard of the one faith of the gospel.' On this rule he lays very great stress, and presents it as the very sum and substance of the Biblical Interpreter's Manual. The rule then is, 'That Interpretation of Scripture is to be followed and relied upon, as the true sense and meaning, which has invariably been held and acted upon, by the one CATHOLIC AND APOSTOLIC CHURCH OF CHRIST.' From the beginning, we suspected that some such notion as that contained in this pretended rule, was *wildering* through the preacher's mind. But really, notwithstanding all our previous suspicions, we were astonished to find this worn out, obsolete principle patched up by a Virginian Protestant, and brought out in these broad, unequivocal terms. Expressions of surprise and regret are however useless. The principle must be brought to a severe test. If it stands the trial, we pledge ourselves to adopt it. It will certainly remove us entirely from the ground we now occupy—but it will carry us directly to the [Roman] Catholic Church."

But if it is a 'pretended rule,' 'a worn out, obsolete' principle, why this deep anxiety and alarm? Is the ground you occupy so insecure as to be shaken even to its centre, by a piece of 'patchwork?' Does the very sight, the first blush as it were, of the bewildered imagination of 'a Virginian Protestant,' flush conviction on the mind of a learned divine and theologian, that his foundation is on the sand? Really, Sir, there is something strangely inconsistent between the cause and the effect, as stated by yourself. A 'worn out, obsolete' principle, revived, no matter by whom, can present no great difficulty to one well enough acquainted with the subject, to assert this : such an one can at once give its history, and show wherefore it is abandoned. And a 'pretended rule' being, in fact, *no* rule—I cannot see why or how it must or can be brought to a severe test; neither can I understand upon what principle you pledge yourself to adopt it, if it be what you affirm it is—especially with so dreadful a consequence staring you in the face as that of converting a Presbyterian Theological Professor into a Papist. The meaning of this, however, is plain enough. As either the rule, or the Reviewer and his cause, must fall ; it is so much gained for a weak argument, that the case should be prejudged. But in the same broad and unequivocal terms in which the rule is brought out, (and I trust you would not have me speak equivocally in the pulpit) I promise, that if you will stand to your pledge—I will land you in the Roman Catholic Church.

To your argument then.

" Our next remark is, (p. 308) that the rule contains that sort of bad logic, which is usually distinguished by the phrase, *reasoning in a circle.* For, we ask, how shall we ascertain the one *Catholic and Apostolic Church,* whose interpretation of Scripture is to be received and relied upon ? The Roman Catholic tells us, that his is the *true Church,* out of which there is *no salvation.* Bishop R. has given us to understand that the Protestant Episcopal Church, has the 'verifiable' characters of *Catholic* and *Apostolic,* and that separated from it, we are left to 'the uncovenanted mercies of God.' The stern and sturdy covenanter gives his *notes of a true Church,* as loudly and confidently as any—so of others. But the Church is *one.* Now amidst these conflicting claims, we repeat the important question, how are we to ascertain, that 'sense and meaning' of Scripture, on which reliance may be placed for salvation ? It is in vain for Bishop R. to tell us he means the *primitive Church.* Because he will admit, nay, insist upon it, that we must now go to that one Catholic and Apostolic Church, which is the depository of the faith of the primitive Church. And what Church is that ? There is but one way to answer our question —'search the Scriptures.' This then is the duty of *all ;* for all are under obligation to be members of the true Church of

CHRIST. They must search and *judge for themselves*. Because we have as good a right to tell the inquirer, that the Church of which we are unworthy members is the true Church, and that our parochial Bishops are true ministers, as Bishop R. has to affirm the same thing of the Protestant Episcopal Church and her Bishops. And some of our number would make the assertion with equal confidence. The inquirer then must search the Scriptures, and find the characters of the true Church; that is, he must *learn the meaning of the Scriptures*, that he may ascertain to what body of men calling themselves Christians he must apply, that he *may learn the meaning of the Scriptures!* We are willing that the Vestry of the Episcopal Chapel in Raleigh, who published this Sermon, should say whether this is good logic."

This is your state of the case for the application of the rule laid down in my Sermon, with an example of the illogical circle, in which you make it tread; and though characteristically unfair, inasmuch as it assumes for me what I have no where claimed, *viz.* an exemption of the Protestant Episcopal Church from the operation of the rule as to the faith and order therein held, upon the ground that *that* Church now occupies the place of the primitive Church, as the only resort in controversies of disputed Scripture; whereas, (nor can my intention be fairly misunderstood) I place the rule as paramount, and submit the claims of the Protestant Episcopal Church to the sacred verity of that character, equally with those of all other Churches, to the determination of the rule as the only possible resort : it is nevertheless sufficient to test the rule, to free it from the halo of absurdity wherewith you invest it, and put the circular wreath on your own brows.

On opposite views of the faith or order of the Gospel, the Reviewer says, Search the Scriptures—and the Bishop says, Search the Scriptures, for he holds them supreme. Well, this has been done ; but each remains stiff in his own particular opinion of the sense or meaning derived from the Scriptures, believing that his everlasting interests are at stake.

The doctrines respectively held are fundamental—that is, of the essence of religion ; and so opposite, that one must necessarily be false—that is, contrary to the true sense and meaning of Scripture, to *the truth once delivered to the saints.*

In this difficulty, and in order to preserve unity, the Bishop proposes to submit this difference of judgment to the determination of the best testimony, and the safest decision, which the nature of the case admits—that is, to the judgment of the primitive Church, ' as the best expositors of the obscure parts of Scripture ; the surest and safest guide to the truth of conflicting doctrines and practices.'

No, says the Reviewer, I appeal to the Scriptures, "the Bible is the religion of the Protestants."

We have already appealed to the Bible without effect, says the Bishop, and as the determination of the truth or error of our respective views on this subject is of infinite consequence to our own souls, and to the souls of others, we ought to resort to such means as are in our reach, and present a reasonable prospect of bringing us to agreement. You will surely admit, that the truth of doctrine and order in the religion of JESUS CHRIST was committed to the primitive Church, and to all its branches, planted by the Apostles. And as the Scriptures are owned by both of us as the standard—though we differ as to the true meaning, can there be any other or better judgment to refer to ? Is there no period subsequent to the Apostles, in which what was universally held by the Church as the true sense of Scripture, may be safely relied upon by us as the truth of GOD, and justify our full assent to it as an article of the faith ?

No, answers the Reviewer, the Bible says nothing of any such tribunal to settle these disputes.

"Undeniably that is the true Church, which preaches the true doctrine of CHRIST, and duly administers the sacraments by men who hold a divine and verifiable commission and authority to give them effect as instituted means of grace. It is clear then, that the man who wishes to learn what society teaches the true doctrine, must first ascertain from the Scriptures, what doctrines are true, and what are false. Must not he who wishes to learn who are authorized ministers, and who intruders, first verify from the Scriptures the commission of the one, and detect, so to speak, the counterfeit of the other ?" p. 311.

By no means, says the Bishop, is it clear, either in the one case or the other, but the contrary. The question is of disputed doctrine from Scripture, and the Scriptures are claimed alike by each; if therefore, neither will yield, or submit to the decision of a competent judge, the question never can be settled. But the mischief stops not here. If such reasoning be correct, the purpose of GOD in the revelation of his will is reversed, and private judgment, competent or incompetent; (for you cannot limit,) made the standard of the word of GOD. Thus, faith is uptorn from its foundation, and religion scattered to the winds. In like manner of a question of disputed order, or authority to minister in religion. The Scriptures can only show, that a prescribed order for the administration of divine things in the Church was originally settled by the apostles, who were infallibly directed. But in a dispute as to what the Scriptures do, or do not say, as to any particular man or body of men being regularly authorized to act in this behalf, these Scriptures cannot determine, for they are claimed by each side—what the Scriptures say, being the very point in dispute. The verification of ministerial authority, therefore, in a particular case disputed, must of necessity be *dehors* the Scripture—must be by a proof derived from some other quarter. And if this is rejected, and the Scriptures pertinaciously insisted upon, for a purpose they are incompetent to, and never were intended to answer from the very commencement of revelation; all the evils which spring from divisions and uncertainty, must continue and increase *ad infinitum*.

It won't do, says the Reviewer.

"Is it not as clear as day-light, that we must search the Scriptures, until we ascertain the truth and falsehood of these several opinions, before we can know where to find the true interpreter of Scripture? That is, *we must not settle these questions* before we can find the one Catholic Apostolic Church to *settle them for us?*" * p. 311, 412.

"The Bible, the Bible is the religion of Protestants"—I

---

* The absurdity involved in this argument led for a moment to the suspicion, that the Reviewer is speaking ironically. But it is so perfectly of a piece with the general strain of his reasoning on this troublesome rule, that this idea was abandoned, and the argument met, as perfectly consistent with the circular logic of Dr. Rice.

appeal to the Scriptures ; thus we end where we began, and the circle is complete.

In this statement of your argument, Sir, I trust I have put no force on your language, or on the conclusions from it ; my wish is to avoid every strained meaning. It therefore appears that the vicious circular quality belongs to your own logic ; and not to the rule of Vincentius, as given in the Bible Society Sermon, or to the abstract of it, now under consideration.

Your argument being thus vicious and illogical in its structure, as well as unfounded in the ground assumed ; I will now examine of what worth your other objections to the rule are.

"Its application as a practical rule, is absolutely impossible. Bishop R. may assume any Church he pleases, as the one Catholic and Apostolic Church, the depositary of the true sense and meaning of Scripture, as delivered by inspired men ; and he cannot, with all his brethren to aid him, tell us, what that Church has invariably held." p. 312.

And does this Reviewer think to make his escape, and evade the operation of the rule, by a perversion of this sort ? Assuredly he must be hard driven. Bishop R. confidently asserts his ability to show what the primitive Church invariably held, as the true sense and meaning of Scripture, on any point of disputed doctrine or order which the Reviewer may please to select—to which points only does the rule apply, either in itself, or as set forth in the sermons. Bishop R. confidently asserts his ability to show what the Protestant Episcopal Church has invariably held, as the true sense and meaning of the Scriptures, in the like case. Nay more—he confidently asserts, that he can show what the particular denomination of Christians calling itself the Presbyterian Church has invariably held as the true sense and meaning of Scripture, on contested doctrine, and in exclusion too, to any other meaning. And to do this, he has only to refer to the Fathers, Councils, and Creeds of the three first centuries, for the faith and order of the primitive Church ; to the Articles, Liturgy, and Homilies of the Church of England, for the public faith and order of the Protestant Episcopal Church ; and to the Westminster Confession of Faith, as the Presbyterian platform of the faith and order once delivered to the saints.   These speak the true sense and meaning of the Scriptures, according to the mind of the framers and holders of each particular interpretation of the Bible, and more especially on disputed points. These are the public and declared sentiments of each Church as a body.   These are, respectively, the standards by which they are regulated, and by which their soundness as to the faith and order of the gospel is to be tested.   These are, to each particular body, what the rule in question ought to be to all in general ; and not the varying opinions of the individuals belonging to the particular body.   In proof of this, we have only to take a disputed point of faith or order, and apply the fixed standard of the particular body to it, to determine what that body has invariably held, as the true sense and meaning of Scripture, as to that point.   And one step further carries us to all the certainty we either need or can obtain, on disputed doctrine or practice from Scripture ; and that is, to take all these varying Creeds, Confessions, and views of modern Christianity, and test their soundness by their agreement with the faith and order of pure and primitive times, according to the rule under consideration. And I have no hesitation in recording my considered opinion, that the theologian who refuses to submit the tenets of the denomination to which he belongs to so impartial an umpirage, betrays his consciousness that the foundation on which he relies, is in something at variance with *antiquity, universality, and consent* as to the true sense and meaning of Scripture.

Your questions, therefore, in the same page, present no difficulty ; nor is the stability of the standard at all shaken, by the various views taken of it by individuals.   And had you meant to put the question fairly, you would have asked—not ‘ What was the true interpretation of Scripture held by the Protestant Episcopal Church in this country, when the Prayer Book was published without the thirty-nine Articles ?’—but, What means had the members of the Church of readily determining the sense of that Church on the leading doctrines of revelation, during this short period ?   To which I answer—It is convenient and expedient, certainly, that the whole should go together ; but it is not indispensable, that they should be in the same volume.   The

Articles, though not published with the book of Common Prayer, were, nevertheless, accessible, and could be appealed to when wanted; just as the ordinal, or Book of Offices, though now, for convenience, and because of the improvements in the art of printing, bound up with the Liturgy and Articles, is not at all essential to the daily and weekly uses of the congregation, for their joint or common prayer. But further, had you been a fair opponent, you would have looked deeper into the case, and perhaps have informed your readers, that the Thirty-nine Articles were never separated from the book of Common Prayer under any intention of rescinding them, as obligatory upon all the members of the Church; and that whatever might have been contemplated, or even proposed by some individuals, in the various consultations which led to the re-organization of the Church in these United States—no act of the Church as organized, has authorized the separation, or the consequence you would insinuate from it.

Your next question is,

" Nay, what does it (the Protestant Episcopal Church) hold now, as the true sense and meaning of the seventeenth Article?"

On this subject, Sir, I am happy to tell you, that the Church has in nothing altered her views in the adoption of the Article; nor is there the least difficulty in it, but with determined Calvinists, whether in or out of the Church. The Articles themselves being the best expositors of each other, and the Liturgy of the whole; the Church refers every inquirer to these, to ascertain what she holds as the true sense and meaning of the seventeenth. Taken altogether, then, it is utterly impossible to make the seventeenth article speak the sentiments of Calvin, or of the Westminster Confession of Faith, on the doctrine of Predestination. The thirty-first article is an impregnable barrier against this most favourite desire of Calvinists. And I speak without fear of any reasonable contradiction, when I say, that the Articles, Liturgy, and Catechism of the Church, are *decidedly and unequivocally* opposed to the corner-stone of Calvinism, the *doctrine of particular redemption.* The true sense and meaning of the seventeenth article, as *now* held by the Church, is what it always was, nor can it be forced, by any fair construction to give support to the doctrine taught by Calvin, and adopted by the Assembly of Divines—that Confession of Faith, which you have solemnly pledged yourself to, as the *exclusive* truth of God's revealed word, but which (I speak advisedly, and stand prepared to support the assertion) not one in a hundred of you dares to preach, *in the terms* in which you have subscribed it ; and which, if I am rightly informed, Dr. Rice himself, on his late visit to the Presbytery in Guilford county in this state, abandoned entirely in his public preaching. On the other question,

" What does the Church believe concerning the efficacy of Baptism ? When administered by a ' divinely commissioned clergyman' does it effectuate regeneration, or not ?"

To this the Church answers directly and distinctly in the affirmative, as is plain from the Baptismal Office. But this she affirms, in the original Scriptural meaning of the word *regeneration*,[*] as understood by the primitive Church, and of qualified subjects. The Church knows nothing of the use of this word, in the novel, improper, and unscriptural meaning, which Calvinists cling to. Nor is there a stronger proof of the anti-Calvinistic structure of her Articles, than the Baptismal Office, as it stands in the Liturgy. As in her thirty-first article she asserts, with the plain language, primitive interpretation, and general tenour of Scripture, "that JESUS CHRIST, by the grace of GOD,

---

[*] By the modern meaning attached to the word *Regeneration*, which is entirely unscriptural, great injury is done to the cause of religion. By making it synonymous with *conversion*, much confusion of mind is occasioned, and it becomes difficult to speak understandingly on either subject. The chief mischief is in the case of infant baptism. It sounds strange to speak of the conversion of an infant, a few weeks old ; with many it is an objection to the baptismal office in the Liturgy of the Church, and with some to the sacrament itself; all of which would be avoided, were the proper distinction between the two words restored and observed. *Regeneration* is a special grace, certified to us in the sacrament of baptism ; *Conversion* is a subsequent operation of the HOLY SPIRIT upon the practical sinner, and is inconceivable even without previous regeneration.

tasted death for every man"—that "it is not the will of our Heavenly Father that one of these little ones should perish;" so in this initiating sacrament of grace, she asserts of infants *absolutely*, and adults *conditionally*, that they are *regenerate*. She "thanks the most merciful Father, that it hath pleased him to regenerate this infant with his HOLY SPIRIT, to receive him for his own child by adoption, and to incorporate him into his Holy Church." And the difference observable in the thanksgiving prayer and exhortation to baptized *adults*, is referable solely to the difference of condition between the parties; the benefit to the adult being limited on the qualification of the person for this ordinance—while to the infant, it is absolute and unrestricted.

And, Sir, I make bold to say, that the wit of man cannot invent a scriptural and reasonable objection to this view of the subject, which is not derived from the Calvinistic views of the nature and effect of divine grace. This is the root from which has sprung the whole difficulty, and out of which has grown the change in the meaning and use of the word *regeneration*, with all the confusion of mind consequent on the adoption of strange doctrine. Doctrine, I will take leave to say, is as much at war with the word of GOD, and the attributes of Jehovah, as it is abhorrent to the common sense and rewardable condition of moral beings. Doctrine, which never has been, and never can be demonstrated from Scripture, which cannot even find a colour of support, but at the expense of a broken Scripture—which rests upon the assumption, the naked assumption, that the grace of GOD, in other words, the assistance provided for and given to fallen creatures by the SPIRIT OF GOD, to enable them to work out their eternal salvation is, in its nature and effects, *indefectible and necessitating*—cannot be *resisted*, cannot be *abused, grieved, quenched, driven away*, and *extinguished*. But until this be demonstrated—until this be proved *a priori*, from *express and agreeing* Scripture; Calvinism proper—the Calvinism of Geneva, and of the third chapter of the Westminster Confession of Faith (for I speak not of the diluted, inconsistent, nondescript thing, wherewith the lurid horrors of its parent is endeavoured to be disguised and rendered bearable in the present day) is a naked, unsupported assumption, a mere *invention*

VOL. I.—45

of men, who would be wise above what is written, intruding into things not seen, vainly puffed up by a fleshly mind. Yet in favour of this unproved dogma, the true, and fundamental, and comfortable doctrine of CHRIST is to be put in jeopardy, the hope given to parents in the baptism of their children neutralized, and the encouragement thence to be drawn for the performance of solemnly undertaken duty defeated. And all this, as you well know, Sir, in the very teeth of the express declarations of your far-famed and honoured founder, of your own fundamentals, and of every reputable platform of Christian faith. For, however strange it may appear, all these assert in the plainest terms, the inseparable union of the grace of regeneration with the Christian sacrament of baptism.

Thus CALVIN expresses himself. *Institut.* Lib. iii. ch. 6, and Lib. iv. ch. 15, 16. "I consider it (baptism) as a figure—but at the same time it has the substance connected with it. For GOD, in promising his gifts *does not deceive us.** Therefore, as forgiveness of sins and newness of life are offered to us in baptism, *so it is certain they are received by us.*" Again he says, "CHRIST hath purified us in the laver of his blood, and hath communicated this purification by baptism." Again, "those who have imagined that baptism is nothing more than a mark or sign by which we profess our religion before men, have not considered that which was the principal thing in baptism ; which is, that we ought to receive it with this promise, *He that believeth and is baptized, shall be saved.*" "We are baptized into the mortification of the flesh, which commences in us at baptism, which we pursue from day to day, and which will be perfected when we shall pass out of this life unto the LORD."

In the Westminster Confession of Faith, Ch. 28, Art. 1. baptism is declared to be "a sacrament of the New Testament, ordained by JESUS CHRIST, not only for the solemn admission of the party baptized into the visible Church ; but also to be to him a sign and seal of the covenant of grace, of his ingrafting into CHRIST of *regeneration*." And Art. 6, "The efficacy of baptism

---

* *Quere.* Did Calvin mean to say, he does not "keep the word of promise to the ear and break it to the hope ?"—*Shakspeare.*

is not tied to that moment of time wherein it is administered; yet notwithstanding, by the right use of this ordinance *the grace promised is not only offered, but really exhibited and conferred by the* HOLY GHOST, to such (whether of age or infants) as that grace belongeth unto, according to the counsel of GOD's own will, in his appointed time." In the larger catechism, in the answer to the 165th Question, this definition is in substance repeated, and baptism is declared to be " a sign and seal of—*regeneration* by His SPIRIT."

Not having access to the particular modifications of the one faith of the gospel, which are indulged in by the different denominations of professing Christians, I cannot quote their words; but I run no risk in asserting, that the Dutch Church of the Netherlands, the Dutch Presbyterian Church, the Congregationalists, the Lutherans, the Methodists, all assert, unequivocally, the connexion of spiritual regeneration with the sacrament of baptism. And I will here take leave to ask this learned reviewer, to what purpose he would press the doctrines and duties of the gospel on, or in what method he would proceed to produce, the conversion of a fallen being—*absolutely unregenerate?*

In continuation you say, " We could easily urge many such questions as these.' And what then? They could certainly be as easily answered. Nor do I give you the smallest credit for forbearance; believing as I do, that could you put a question of any difficulty—could you find a point of attack against the Church, which has not already been attempted, and defeated too, in the judgment of every informed and unprejudiced person—you would glory in it, and every Presbyterian Periodical be struck off in double impressions. But 'matter of this might' is not found in the meridian of Hampden Sidney, otherwise we should not have seen you reduced to the shifts and evasions you have resorted to. We should not have had such totally irrelevant questions, as are found immediately following:—As to what was held as the true sense and meaning of Scripture by the Church of England, from the time of Archbishop Cranmer forward? As to the respective merit of her controversial writers?—with a long list of names, calculated

to make your subscribers stare at the vast extent of your reading, and to give colour to the insinuation that her standard is
unsettled, and nothing but laxity of doctrine and discipline to
be found within her pale.   But to bring this insinuation to a
point, I ask you, Sir, have her Articles, Liturgy, and Homilies,
been changed or altered in substance since the days of Cranmer?
Has the foundation then laid, been departed from at all, by
any public authoritative act of the Church, as a body?   And
are not the Articles, Liturgy, and Homilies the authentic declaration of the sense and meaning in which she receives and holds
the Scriptures of our faith?   To what purpose, then, the catalogue of authors differing in opinion on particular points of this
fixed summary of Christian doctrine?   Do these authors
compose the Church?   Or to what purpose the catalogue of
opposite doctrinal opinion, which you assert is contained in her
bosom?   Is it recognized by the Church as a body?   Admitting it to be true, which yet I have the best reason to discredit
on your *single assertion,* (viz. the perversions and misrepresentations you have made of my own words and meaning, and
the erroneous view you give of the words and meaning of her
standard writers, as I shall show distinctly before I close,) what
purpose is it to answer, unless to escape from this mischievous,
troublesome, yet 'pretended rule,' this 'worn out, obsolete
principle, patched up by a Virginia Protestant.' Well may you
assert the rule to be impossible in its application, when you
create the impossibility to fit the assertion.   The man, with the
pretensions and admitted character for learning and information, of Dr. Rice, should have paused, before he asserted that it
is 'impossible to say how the Church of England has invariably
interpreted Scripture,' and 'that the Church of England is no
older than the days of Elizabeth.' p. 313.

Another objection, made by you to this rule is :

"It is contrary to the fundamental principle of the reformation." p. 315.

And if this, or any thing in the likeness of this, can be made
to appear, or can be supported by any sufficient authorities, or
colour of reason, the rule shall find no support from me.   But

so far is this from being the case, that I affirm, and shall make it good, that this rule, either expressly in its terms, or virtually in its principle, was the actual basis of the reformation ; inasmuch as *antiquity, universality,* and *consent* were the tests by which the reformers, every where, were determined, both as to *corruptions* and *reform.* You commence your proof of this objection to the rule, by saying :

" The claim of the Romish Church, which was most strenuously resisted by the reformers, was that of interpreting Scripture."

You further state as from Bishop Hurd.

" That when the Reformers had renounced allegiance to the Papal chair, and were for regulating the faith of Christians by the sacred Scriptures, it still remained a question, on what ground those Scriptures should be interpreted ? [The very question at issue between us, and the Bishop of North-Carolina.] The voice of the *modern Church*, was without ceremony rejected. But the fathers of the primitive Church were still in great repute among the Protestants themselves—they dreaded more than any thing else, the charge of novelty. The Papists took advantage of their fears, and appealed to the ancient fathers. The Protestants, who were proud of their superior skill in the old literature, accepted the challenge, ' and thus shifting their ground, they maintained henceforth, not that the Scriptures were the sole rule of faith, but the Scriptures as interpreted by the primitive fathers.' [This is precisely the error of Bishop R.]" p. 319.

It may be so, admitting Dr. Rice to state the subject in dispute, to suit himself. But as Bishop R. does not admit the claim of infallibility in a Presbyterian, any more than in a Roman, Doctor ; he must state ' the question at issue' more clearly, as well as more fairly.

The rule is not set up as an interpreter of Scripture, in the sense in which you present it to your readers ; but as the best, because the only possible, and most reasonable method of determining controversies from Scripture. But the claim of the Romish Church was, to an infallible interpretation of divine

truth, whether clear or obscure, whether controverted or agreed
—lodged by divine authority in the Church, as the mother and
mistress of all Churches; together with the claim of an oral
tradition from the apostles, of equal authority with the Scriptures
themselves; so as to bind the conscience, even in the most
palpable contradictions and impious perversions of the letter and
spirit of the written word. This claim the reformers most nobly
and effectually resisted on the never to be shaken, and never by
me to be questioned ground, that the Bible, containing all things
necessary to be known, believed, and practised by men in order
to salvation, was itself the only infallible interpreter of the will
of God; and hence the abbreviate maxim, that *the Bible is the
religion of Protestants.*

Now, wherein does the rule conflict with this maxim? On
the contrary; is it not the only conceivable principle which can
make this fundamental maxim of any practical use? For,
beyond all dispute, the true value of the maxim, ‘the Bible is
the religion of Protestants,’ must for ever depend on the circumstance, that the Bible be *well* or *ill* interpreted. Here, then,
the wisdom and importance of the rule is at once exemplified.
For, from the Deist who rejects revelation, to the wildest fanatic
who ever ventured to corrupt its pure and perfect truth I defy
you, or any other man, to produce a heresy or a schism, which
may not be determined by, and which ought not to submit its
pretensions to, the reasonableness, truth, and certainty of the
rule, *under Scripture, as supreme.* Strange indeed it would be,
if that testimony on which the Bible itself depends (particularly
the New Testament) for its value and obligation to us as the
word of God, should be derided and rejected, as incompetent to
determine the truth or error of doctrine drawn from the Bible,
as the whole counsel of God. The rule, therefore, does not
occupy the place of Romish infallibility, as you very laboriously,
artfully, and unjustifiably, too, endeavour to make out. On the
contrary, it is the surest and most effectual support which the
fundamental principle that ‘the Bible is the religion of Protestants’ can ask for or obtain. What else, let me ask, can guard this
maxim from these errors and corruptions of true religion, which
the ignorance or the artifice of fanatics and heresiarchs have

already, and will yet engender? What else, for instance, can counteract the fertile and fatal source of division and departure from the one faith of the gospel, demonstrably contained in the 'no comment' principle of promiscuous Bible Societies? Sir, I fear that its bearing in this, and some other directions, was seen; and, therefore, it behoved you to represent it in any way that promised to withstand its effect: because, as a theologian, you could not excusably be ignorant of the place which the rule holds in controversial science; and if really ignorant, you would not have ventured to speak of it as you have done. But to support my assertion, ' that this rule, either expressly in its terms or virtually in its principle, was the actual basis of the reformation,' I bring forward for your consideration and the information of your readers, the following facts.

Presuming that you will not dispute, (what nevertheless can be proved,) that all the hierarchical (that is Episcopal) Churches recognize this rule as the governing principle on which they are constituted, I shall content myself with but one proof out of many.

That the reformed Church of England is constituted on the very terms, as well as on the principle of this rule, you admit, p, 321. But as this admission might be qualified in a variety of ways, and I am under no need of it, I shall put all denial or qualification out of your reach, by the testimony of the following reformers, martyrs and standard writers of that Church.

First, Bishop RIDLEY; than whom none stands higher, if indeed any stand so high among the reformers and martyrs of the British Church: of him it is affirmed, that so convinced was he, "that to surrender Catholicity in the whole or in part, would be to sign the death warrant of the English reformation, no efforts of his opponents could dislodge him from the bulwarks of the ancient Church. Nothing could be more laborious, nothing more trying to every power of the mind, than to maintain defensive warfare on so vast and debateable a ground. Nothing, on the other hand, more easy, than to have intrenched himself at once within the fastnesses of Scripture. Latimer, his companion in suffering but not his copartner in wisdom, had strongly advised him to this latter course: that he rejected this counsel, and maintained his arduous post, can be ascribed only to the most immoveable conviction, and the deepest sense of duty."—JEBB's *Appendix*, p. 387,

Next Bishop JEWEL; "We are come as neere as we possibly could to the Church of *the Apostles, and of the old Catholic Bishops and Fathers*, and have directed *according to their customs and ordinances, not only our doctrine, but also the sacraments and the forme of common praier.*"—*Apology, Works*, p. 614.

Bishop OVERALL; "I believe there are few things in your book, which will not be approved of by the Bishop of Ely, (Launcelot Andrews) and the rest of our more learned divines; unless, perhaps, they may hesitate respecting those passages which seem to give to lay powers a definitive judgment in matters of faith; to deny the true power and jurisdiction of Pastors of the Church; and to rank episcopacy among unnecessary things. For our divines hold, that the right of definitive judgment in matters of faith is to be given to Synods of Bishops, and other learned ministers of the Church, chosen and convened for this purpose, according to the usage of the ancient Church: *who shall determine from the Holy Scriptures, explained by the consent of the ancient Church—not by the private spirit of Neoterics.*"—*Letter to Grotius*, translated from *Epistolæ præstantium et eruditorum Virorum.* p. 486.

Bishop HALL; "He that hath willingly subscribed to the word of GOD, attested in the everlasting Scriptures—to all the primitive Creeds—to the four General Councils—to the common judgment of the fathers, for six hundred years after CHRIST (*which we of our reformation, religiously profess to do,*) this man may possibly err in trifles, but he cannot be an heretic."— Translated from *Concio ad Clerum*, 1623.

Bishop BEVERIDGE; "Since the *consent of the Universal Church*, wherever it can be had, *is the surest interpretation of Holy Scripture*, it hence most clearly follows of what, and of how great use, the ancient fathers, and other ecclesiastical writers of all ages, must be; and how necessary to be consulted in matters of controversy, by those who lay to heart either their own salvation, or the peace and order of the Church."—Translated from

BEVERIDGE's *Præm. ad Cod. Can.* p. 1—3, apud *Coll. Patr. Apost.*

Bishop BULL; "All persons, not absolutely strangers to our history, are aware, that so far as it was practicable and the age allowed, *our Reformation was, in all respects, conformed to the example of the ancient Catholic Church.* Hence was the order of Bishops retained in England, and that new form of Ecclesiastical government rejected, which, by the advice of Calvin, was adopted in other Churches. Hence *were certain ancient doctrines, though most abhorrent from the sentiments of Calvin, established and confirmed by our Church.* Hence, almost at the commencement of our Reformation, in the year 1571, was that remarkable canon respecting preachers sanctioned by the consent of a full Provincial Synod, and further confirmed by the royal authority of Elizabeth. '*Let preachers, above all things, be careful that they never teach aught in a sermon, to be religiously held and believed by the people, except that which is agreeable to the doctrine of the Old or New Testament, and which the Catholic Fathers and ancient bishops have collected from that very doctrine.—Coll. Can. Lond.* 1691, p. 238.

Doctor HAMMOND; "Our most beloved mother, the Church of England, is certainly solicitous to avoid, with all cautious diligence, this rock of innovators. It is her ambition to be distinguished, through the whole Christian world, and judged by an equitable posterity, under this character, that *in deciding controversies of faith or practice,* it has ever been her fixed and firm resolution—*and on this basis she has rested the British Reformation—that in the first place, respect be had to the Scriptures; and then, in the second place to the bishops, martyrs, and ecclesiastical writers of the first ages.* Therefore, whatsoever hath been affirmed by the Scriptures in matters of faith; whatsoever concerning ecclesiastical government, she hath discovered to be the appointment of the Universal Church throughout the world after the apostles; these things she hath taken care to place, as fixed and established among the Articles of religion; determined never to permit her sons to alter or abolish, what hath been thus decided." "*It is her principle,* that, as whatsoever is clearly proposed from the Scriptures is to be embraced with the whole mind ; so, whatsoever is obscurely set forth in Scripture, but explained by consent of the first ages, and definitely settled on one side, *that* she determines her sons must either believe as of faith, or place among pious credibilities, not to be re-modified by any of us, after the lapse of so many ages."—*Works*, Vol. IV. p. 270.

JOSEPH MEDE ; "Our Church, you know, goes upon differing principles from the rest of the reformed ; and so steers her course by another rule than they do. *We look after the form, rites, and discipline of antiquity, and endeavour to bring our own as near as we can to that pattern.* We suppose the reformed Churches have departed further therefrom than needed, and so we are not very solicitous to comply with them. Yea we are jealous of such of our own, as we see over zealously addicted to them ; lest it be a sign they prefer them before their mother."—MEDE's *Works*, Vol. II. p. 1061.

Sir Dudley Carleton, in his speech to the States General, 1618, thus expresses himself ; "When the King thinks it fitting and necessary to cause any matter of religion to be examined and decided in the Church of England, his Majesty causes a Synod to be called, consisting of bishops and other ecclesiastical persons ; appoints them a time and a place for their meeting, and communicates to them the affairs in general about which they are to treat ; giving them, by his letters patent, a power to debate upon, and decide the same. They, conforming themselves to such orders, set about the work, and confer upon the points which are in dispute, in order to regulate them, *according to the word of* GOD, *the canons of ancient Councils, and the doctrines of the fathers.*"—G. BRANDT's *History of the Reformation*, Vol. II. p. 447.

MR. CHARLES LESLIE : "But though we think no Church to be infallible, yet we have an infallible assurance of the faith, in its being delivered down to us by such an universal consent of all ages and Churches as that it was not in their power, though they should be considered so wicked as to design it, at such vast distance, even when all correspondence was stopped, to have combined together, and all agree in the self-same doctrine, if it had not been the same which was taught from the beginning.   And the rise of heresies does rather confirm the truth of this ; because such were found to be novelties, and to go against the universal tradition ; *which, whatever has* (according to the rule of VINCENTIUS LIRINENSIS—'quod semper, ubique, ab omnibus') *we willingly receive ; and what has not this evidence, we cannot admit as of faith.*"   *Answer to Bossuet. Theol. Works,* Vol 1, p. 581.

These, Sir, though but a small part of the testimony which can be produced in favour of the adoption and practical application of this rule by the reformers of the British Church, I conceive quite sufficient to confirm my position respecting the rule, so far as the British and all other reformed hierarchical Churches are concerned.

That this rule virtually, in its principle, formed the basis of the reformation in the continental non-episcopal Churches, is proved by the following extracts from their public confessions, so far as I have access to them.

Saxon Confession.   "We distinctly affirm, before GOD and the universal Church in heaven and in earth, that we embrace with sincere faith, all the writings of the prophets and the apostles ; and according to that *genuine interpretation of them, which is set forth in the Apostles', the Nicene, and the Athanasian Creeds.*"   "This is the sum of the doctrine which, by the blessing of GOD, we proclaim with one voice in our churches.   Nor have we the smallest doubt that it is an incorrupt transcript of the doctrine, divinely delivered in the prophetic and apostolic writings, and in the creeds ; *and from the more genuine ancient writers, it may be perceived to accord with the faith of the old and purer Church.*"

Wirtemberg Confession.   "We believe and confess the Trinity, according as is taught in the prophetic and apostolic Scriptures, and *explained by the three Creeds—the Apostles' the Nicene, and the Athanasian.*"   *Art. de* DEO.

"We believe and confess JESUS CHRIST to be GOD," "according to the doctrine *which the holy fathers in the Nicene, the first Ephesian, and the Chalcedonian Councils,* set forth by testimonies drawn from holy Scripture."—*Art. de filio* DEI.

"We believe and confess that the HOLY SPIRIT from all eternity proceeds from GOD the Father, and GOD the Son, and that he is truly and eternally God, of the same essence, majesty, and glory with the Father and the Son," "*according as the holy fathers in the Council of Constantinople,* on the authority of the sacred Scripture, rightly explained the doctrine, in opposition to Macedonius."—DE SPIRITU SANCTO.

"We directed our preachers to draw up a summary of their doctrine, as a public testimony that nothing but the true apostolic, catholic, and orthodox doctrine has any admittance into our churches."

"We have, therefore, thought proper to make public this written exposition; and we trust the universal Church of the pious will thus be satisfied by actual proof, that nothing can be more foreign from our Churches than the adoption, either of any doctrine to be preached, or of any rite to be administered, which is at variance with the prophetic and apostolic Scriptures, *and with the consent of the true Catholic Church.*"

Helvetic Confessions. "Concerning the mystery of the incarnation of our LORD JESUS CHRIST, whatever things are laid down out of the sacred Scriptures *and comprised in the creeds and decisions of the four first and chief councils so highly celebrated;* namely, those of Nice, Constantinople, Ephesus, and Chalcedon, *together with the Creed of the blessed Athanasius, and all the similar Creeds;* we believe with a sincere heart, and profess ingenuously with pure lips, condemning all doctrines contrary to these.   And in this manner *we retain inviolate and entire, the orthodox and Catholic Christian faith,* being satisfied that the above-mentioned creeds contain nothing which is not agreeable to the word of God, *and altogether conducive to the right understanding of the faith.*"

Helvetic Confession of 1536—"Art. 2.   The interpretation of Scripture is to be sought only from Scripture itself, that thus Scripture may be its own interpreter; under the directing rule, however, of charity and faith."

"Art. 3.   So far as the holy fathers have adhered to this species of interpretation, *we not only accept them as interpreters of Scripture, but venerate them as beloved instruments of God.*"

Bohemian Confession. "These things irrefragably prove, that we, as well as our predecessors, belong to the holy Catholic

Church ; and that we do not in the smallest degree dissent from her with respect either to rites, or to the teaching of the word, or to religious worship, or to the function of the keys, or to the administration of the sacrament."—*Præfat.*

"*The writings of learned men of the Church, particularly of the ancient ones, we hold to be true, and worthy of belief, and useful for the instruction of the People, yet always in those points in which they do not differ from the Scriptures.* For they themselves thus prescribe the measure of respect due to them, that they are to be believed, and allowed so far as they agree with the divine Scriptures."

Augsburg Confession. "This is the sum of the doctrine which is delivered in our Churches. And we judge it to be in consonance with the prophetic and apostolic Scriptures, *and with the Catholic Church ; and lastly, even with the Church of Rome, so far as that Church is to be known from writers of approved authority. For we do not reject the consent of the Catholic Church ; nor are disposed to introduce into the Church any Dogma new and unknown to the Catholic Church.*"

"*We have made no alteration, except according to the example of the ancient Church.*"—Chap. 21.

Polish Confession. "Lest, however, any doubt or controversy should arise with regard to the genuine interpretation of these leading documents of the Christian faith (the Scriptures) we further profess that we embrace, as undoubtedly exhibiting the true meaning of Scripture, the Nicene and Constantinopolitan Creed." "With this creed we acknowledge to agree the creed which is commonly called the Athanasian ; likewise the confessions of the first Ephesian and Chalcedonian Councils." "And, indeed, whatever the primitive Church, from the times of the apostles downwards, believed and taught, with unanimous and notorious consent, as an essential article of the faith, we also profess to believe and teach out of the Scriptures." Ann. 1645.

To these I will add the testimony of your founder JOHN CALVIN : "So those ancient councils, the Nicene, the Constantinopolitan, the first Ephesian, the Chalcedonian, and others similar to these, which were held for the confutation of errors, *we embrace cordially ; we revere them as sacrosanct, so far as respects points of faith ; for they contain nothing but the pure and genuine interpretation of Scripture, applied by the spiritual wisdom of the Holy fathers, to beat down the enemies of religion."——Instit. Lib. iv. c. 9. sec. 8.*

From these authorities, which I have copied from an article in the *Christian Observer* of August 1816, a correct judgment may be formed, how far this rule presided over the conduct of those who conducted the reformation in Continental Europe, and how far you are justified in saying that 'it is contrary to the fundamental principle of the reformation.' Wherefore they have abandoned it, in its just application to the order as well as the faith of the gospel, is for some champion of parity to show ; my business, at present, is to sustain the rule, as a principle of the reformation, as a sound and safe principle to determine the truth or error of disputed Scripture, against all who dread its application, and therefore decry it.

Your last objection to the rule is, that 'in effect it denies the right of private judgment.' As, however, you do not condescend to support your assertion with either authority or argument, I can only answer in the general, that when you can show that what aids and assists private judgment in coming to a just and safe conclusion on matters of dispute and difficulty, is a denial of the right of private judgment, your objection will lie, and not till then. For this is all that is claimed for the rule by myself or others. We do believe with Stillingfleet, and common sense, that, "he who questions a clear, full, universal tradition of the Church from CHRIST's time to this, will, by the same reason, doubt of all matters of faith, conveyed by this testimony to us." —"Because the ground or rule of faith, the Scriptures is conveyed to us, only through this universal tradition."—*Grounds of the Protestant Religion*, fol. p. 84.

I am sorry, that instead of referring the reader to a particular part of the Sermon, to gather thence the proof that the rule was in effect a denial of the right of private judgment, it had not suited your purpose to show by some example, or induction of reasoning, in what way it thus operated ; as I could then have learnt my own error, or corrected yours. I have examined the extracts from the Sermon to which you point the reader, with great attention, and do most sincerely declare, that my imagination cannot conceive of another equally safe, satisfactory, and certain mode, of coming to the Scriptural truth of the disputed doctrines and practices there mentioned : nay, more than this, I cannot conceive any alternative between adopting this rule, and surrendering the word of GOD to the caprice of man.

That you have either not understood the rule, or have misrepresented it to your readers, is most evident, and I would gladly adopt the former supposition, did not both the manner and the matter of your objections to it, forbid this resort.   You present it to your readers as that to which Scripture, and conscience, and the right of private judgment, are all to yield at discretion, and under this view of it, you heat yourself, and endeavour to rouse them, to a holy fury against it ; whereas you well know, that the rule is held by all who receive it, and is laid down and applied by me in the Sermon as subordinate to the Scriptures, looking to them as supreme, and applicable only to disputed questions from the Scriptures.   As clearly then as can well be expressed, the rule is given and is presented by me, as a help to private judgment—as a safe guide to disputed truth, on a subject of the highest interest.   " It is not, therefore, implicit subjection to any existing authority, but an admission of concurrent evidence, intelligently examined, and soberly estimated ; which Vincentius inculcates.   The habit of mind which he was desirous to form, instead of superseding reason and judgment, involved their unfettered and enlightened exertion.   It was a habit, not of mental contraction, but of mental enlargement : a rejection of all confined views, all party prejudices, all temporary misconceptions ;   and a recurrence to the widest range of inquiry, the purest fountain of information, and the most ennobling sphere of generous and manly feeling.   In a word, Vincentius was a Catholic Christian ; and as a Catholic Christian he would fix our view on the Christian *cloud of witnesses,* in like manner as the view of St. Paul in the eleventh chapter of the Hebrews was fixed on the Jewish *cloud of witnesses ;* he is solicitous that from the luminaries of our brighter hemisphere, we should derive the confirmation and encouragement, the instruction and religious elevation, which an Apostle did not blush to receive from the weaker radiance of Old Testament faith and piety."——JEBB's *Appendix*, p. 377.

Having thus answered your objections to the rule, and showed, I trust, how every way unfounded and unreasonable they are, I have now to follow you through what, I presume, you consider the severe test to which the principle must be brought.

This test consists in an attempt on your part, to invalidate the authority of the primitive fathers—in an appeal to the standard writers of the Church, as having yielded and abandoned what you choose to call the *Patristical authority*—and in the worthlessness of the rule to produce uniformity of faith, exemplified by the present condition of the Church of England, where you acknowledge the rule is adopted.

First, then, your attempt to invalidate the authority of the primitive Christian fathers. Did it never once occur to you, Sir, that in the manner in which you have represented them to your readers, at p. 245, 246, 314, 315, and in many other parts of these Reviews, you were aiming a blow at the very foundation of all religion? Pray, Sir, on what (in your considerate judgment) does the Bible depend, for its binding obligation as the word of GOD? On what testimony do we receive this as a fact—and a fact too, previous to all reasoning from internal testimony, and independent of it? As there can be but one answer, I leave you to make it, and as your conscience shall bind you, to make amends to your readers, to the Christian public, and to those calumniated fathers, for the unfounded, dangerous, and degraded character in which you have chosen to represent them, in order to get clear of this troublesome rule.

Again. Did it never once enter your recollection, that by thus casting off the authority of the primitive Christian fathers, you were contradicting yourself? For, most certainly, you have resorted to their testimony, in support of your particular interpretation of Scripture—for the baptism of infants—and against the claims of Episcopacy. For proof of which, I refer to your *Essay on Baptism*, p. 68, and to your *Irenicum* p. 217, et seq. It will therefore be necessary for you to show, that the rule contemplates a different use of these fathers than you have actually made of them—than you actually rely upon, against the antipedo-Baptists on the one hand, and Episcopalians on the other.   But this you cannot do, either from the rule itself, as given in my Sermons, or from the examples there set forth to exemplify its use.   You and myself think alike in the interpretation of Scripture, as warranting and requiring the administration of the sacrament of baptism to infants.   Antipedo-Baptists interpret the same Scriptures differently, and denounce our view of it, as a corruption of Christianity : and what do we do, but appeal to the Christian fathers from the earliest period, as witnesses that from the beginning, the Scriptures were thus interpreted and acted upon.   And I put it to your candour as a man, to your credit as a theologian, and to your conscience as a Christian, either to show (without any subterfuge from the word *interpretation*) wherein the rule differs from your own recorded practice, or to undo the mischief of your attack on the credibility of the primitive Christian fathers, as witnesses of the sense and meaning of Scripture, on points now disputed among Christians.

The direction, however, which you have given to this part of the subject, necessarily involves a more detailed consideration of what you have advanced.   With some minds, the general principle is sufficient of itself—with others details are necessary to comprehend and apply the general principle ; and with others, such is the power of prejudice, neither general principle or details, have any efficiency—the unreasonable *sic volo* of determined dissent, being sufficient to defeat the power of fact and argument, combined against it.

It was not actually necessary, Sir, to inform us who was your master, in the objections taken to the rule, as avouching the Christian fathers.   The pupil of DAILLE declares his teacher ; but it required even Corinthian assurance to assert, that his work, *on the right use of the fathers*, was *useful* to the men you name. p. 315, in the only sense in which the word can be taken by your readers—that is, useful in the sense of destroying or defeating some previous view entertained by them, of the authority of the Christian fathers in determining controverted points of faith or order in revealed Religion.   Useful I admit, it might be to them or to others, in the sense in which a buoy or a beacon warns the mariner of shallows and sunken rocks, which may mar his voyage and make shipwreck of his hopes. But no otherwise, unless perhaps, it may be thence apparent how the power of a preconceived notion can master and overcome both facts and arguments, which are opposed to the particular prejudice.

DAILLE, you tell us, 'was a French Presbyterian.' He was therefore pledged to parity, and like some modern contenders for the same doctrine, overlooked the fatal blow inflicted on revealed religion, by impugning the credibility of the primitive Christian fathers. I say not, that it is thus *meant*, in either case; but I say, such is the inevitable consequence. If they are not credible witnesses, as to the truth of any particular fact—be it infant baptism or the Christian sabbath—episcopacy or parity—general or particular redemption—secret decrees, or a fully declared will of GOD—or any other modern dispute— they are not credible witnesses for the fact of a revelation, and for the canon of Scripture. The hope of man is built upon the sand—*we are without God in the world.* But if these primitive Christian fathers are allowed on all hands as credible witnesses for the greater, wherefore are they to be discredited as to the less ?

It is not a little remarkable (though it is not the only point of coincidence between them) that Presbyterians and Unitarians occupy exactly the same ground, as to the right use of the Christian fathers. Can it be, because they are both aware that the application of this rule is fatal to their distinctive doctrine ? Be this, however, as it may, the fact is certain ; and I see not, for my part, how either can consistently throw a stone at the other. For I am not casuist enough to determine what part of GOD's revelation we may abandon and gainsay with impunity ; or which is *more a sin*—to reject the Church of CHRIST, or to deny the divinity of CHRIST ; or how a mistake as to the one, should be considered fatal—and as to the other, trivial. For in my Bible, it is as clearly revealed, that we must be members of CHRIST's visible body on earth, as that we must believe in him as GOD *over all, blessed forever.*

In SPARKS' *Letters on the Episcopal Church*, p. 28, that writer thus expresses himself: "Daillé, in his celebrated work on the right use of the fathers, has stated *seventeen reasons* why these writers are not to be implicitly relied upon, *each of which is enough* to invalidate their authority in a question of so much importance as the divine origin, and divinely protected succession of a religious institution." In this Review, Dr. Rice thus speaks, p. 315.

"Should the Bishop include in the meaning of the primitive Church the Antenicene fathers, all we have to say is, that no man living can say how they invariably interpreted Scripture, nor can any one draw out of their writings a complete system of Christian theology. If we descend below the Council of Nice, the difficulty is immeasurably increased. May we recommend to all who have any doubt on the subject, the perusal of a work written by the learned DAILLE, *on the right use of the Fathers?* He perhaps pushes his conclusions too far, yet his work is masterly."

We thus see, that a writer, whose work strikes at all assurance that the Scriptures are the word of GOD——an authentic revelation from Heaven to mankind, is yet recommended as celebrated and masterly, by the Unitarian and Presbyterian; and by both on the same principle, *viz.* that it is favourable to their particular views on the subject of religion. While, therefore, I am fully persuaded that Dr. Rice would not admit, even for a moment, the thought that was derogatory to the verity and divine authority of the Bible, I must nevertheless hold him answerable for the dangerous tendency, in this infidel age, of the contemptuous manner in which he treats the Christian fathers and their testimony, generally throughout these Reviews, and particularly at p. 245, 246. And I can foretel, without the gift of prophecy, that if the Unitarians can succeed in casting public opinion loose from the witness and authority of antiquity in behalf of revelation as a fact, and of universal consent in the interpretation of its doctrines, as conclusive of truth or error in religion; no system of Hermeneutics 'will be of an atom's force to withstand the desolation of their damnable heresy.'

Again.   Mr. SPARKS thus writes, p. 29, of the same work :
" No one has attempted lately to defend the genuineness of all
the Epistles, which were formerly ascribed to Ignatius.   Five at
least have been given up ; and the seven which remain, are
universally allowed, even by those who are most zealous in
proving them genuine, to be disfigured by interpolations."

In this Review, Dr. Rice asserts as follows, p. 246 :

" And as for Ignatius, it is, in the judgment of many able
critics, uncertain whether the Epistles which go under his name
are genuine or not.   If they are, *it is well known*, that they have
been sadly interpolated."   And at p. 314, " to Ignatius, whose
seven Epistles are *even now believed* to have been sadly interpolated."

Yet both these writers cannot but know, that the genuineness of these Epistles has been unanswerably vindicated by
PEARSON and HAMMOND, against this very DAILLE and others
—by HORSLEY, in his answer to Priestly ; and that they are
received as genuine by the great majority of the learned, generally.   To call them in question, then, in this unqualified manner, is indefensible on any plea.   But when not only particular
doctrines, but the Scriptures themselves are at stake, as a revelation from GOD, it is a most flagitious act to invalidate one of
the witnesses, by a most flagrant untruth.   Mr. Sparks and Dr.
Rice are at perfect liberty to form their own estimate of the
facts and arguments brought forward on both sides, and make
up their respective opinions accordingly, and to publish them if
they please ; but they are not at liberty, morally speaking, to
lead the uninformed reader astray by such unqualified assertions
as those in which they have indulged themselves, as to these
Epistles.   Necessity however has no law ; and these Epistles,
together with the testimony of the other Christian fathers, must
be put down, or their respective distinguishing tenets be proved
heretical and schismatical ; and what that necessity is, shall be
explained by DR. MILLER, another Presbyterian divine and
Theological Professor.

This learned divine, in his first *Letters on the Christian
Ministry*, says, that " the Epistles which go under the name of

this venerable Christian Bishop, have been the subject of much controversy," and that, "in the opinion of the ablest and best judges in the Protestant world, they are unworthy of confidence." Nevertheless, in his answer to Sparks, this same learned gentleman quotes them as authority. Hence it would appear, that the genuineness of the Epistles depends upon the use to be made of them. When *parity* is to be supported against episcopacy, they are ' interpolated' and ' unworthy of confidence ;' but when the divinity of the Saviour is to be defended against the Unitarians, they are genuine, and of conclusive authority. And thus it has fared with the rule in question. When the testimony of the fathers is wanted to support Dr. Rice's interpretation of Scripture against the Antipedo-Baptists, they are good and sufficient authority ; but when the same fathers are brought forward to testify on the interpretation of Scripture in favour of episcopacy, as of divine appointment in the Church, they are altogether unworthy of confidence.

Happily, however, we stand in no need either of French or American Presbyterians, or yet of Unitarians, to instruct us in the right use of the primitive Christian fathers. As we have occasion for them only as witnesses, " it is as witnesses only that we plead for them ; and as witnesses they are entitled to the fullest credit. Their reasonings are often weak, and their criticisms puerile ; but it is impossible to question the *integrity* of men, who laid down their lives for the truth. What they affirm they witnessed, they *undoubtedly* witnessed. Even the *opinions* in which they were unanimous, '*quod semper, quod ubique, quod ab omnibus,*' are not to be hastily rejected, merely because they tally not with the dogmas of this or that modern school."—*Review of Haweis' Church History.*

Secondly—Your appeal to the standard writers of the Church, as having abandoned what you choose to call patristical authority.

Though I consider what I have already brought forward from the reformers, martyrs, and standard writers of the Church of England, as to the adoption of this rule as the basis of their reformation, amply sufficient to refute this assertion of yours ;

yet as you have referred me to particular persons in support of your position, it is incumbent on me to meet you.

And first, you refer me to ' CHILLINGWORTH's most masterly work on the Popish Controversy,' and conclude your quotation in these words, ' Plainly then, Chillingworth, the great Protestant champion, is against the rule of the Bishop of North-Carolina.' Not having the work from which you quote, or not knowing it by the title you have given it, I can say nothing as to the correctness of the quotation, or of the connexion in which the words, as given by you, are used by him. But I have good reason to believe that there is some error. For in his *Religion of Protestants a safe Way of Salvation*, folio edit. p. 109, Chillingworth thus expresses himself on the very point between us. "This assertion, that Scripture alone is judge of all controversies in faith, if it be taken properly, is neither a fundamental nor unfundamental point of faith, nor no point of faith at all, but a plain falsehood. *It is not a judge of controversies, but a rule to judge them by ;* and that not an absolutely perfect rule, but as perfect as a written rule can be, which must always need something else which is either evidently true, or evidently credible, to give attestation to it ; and that in this case, is universal tradition. *So that universal tradition is the rule to judge all controversies by.*" It does not, therefore, 'plainly' appear, that the 'incomparable Chillingworth' 'is against the rule of the Bishop of North-Carolina.' A more unqualified acknowledgment of the rule and of its application as given in the Sermon, the Bishop of North-Carolina could not ask for. But it does plainly appear, either that you have quoted his words disjoined from the context, so as not to express his real meaning, (a very easy, and a very common thing too, when a controversial writer is hard driven,) or, that he has contradicted himself ; but as you bring him forward again, we shall then see more into this, and into his real sentiments as to this rule, and as to some other notions which you would father upon him.

You next refer me to HOOKER, ' the judicious Hooker, whose authority stands as high as that of any man in the Church of England.' Certainly it does, and your quotation from him is correct as to the words, but is entirely irrelevant to the question between us. The sentiments contained in them I hold without reserve, in common with every Protestant. But the conclusion you furnish your readers with, that of course, he held the 'exclusive sufficiency' of the Scriptures to determine controversies in religion, is not correct, but alien both to the occasion and object of his great and unanswerable work.

In the preface to his work *on Ecclesiastical Polity,* having noticed the challenge of the advocates for the new discipline (that is, the Presbyterian form of Church government) to a trial by public disputation, he remarks, " what success GOD may give unto such kind of conference or disputation we cannot tell, but of this we are right sure, that nature, Scripture, and experience itself, have all taught the world to seek for the ending of contentions, by submitting itself unto some judicial and definitive sentence, whereunto neither part that contendeth, may under any pretence or colour refuse to stand. This must needs be effectual and strong ; as for other means without this, they seldom prevail. I would therefore know whether, for the ending of these irksome strifes, wherein you and your followers do stand thus formally divided against the authorized guides of this Church, and the rest of the people subject unto their charge ; whether, I say, ye be content to refer your cause to any other higher judgment than your own, or else intend to persist, and proceed as ye have begun, till yourselves be persuaded to condemn yourselves ? If your determination be this, we can be but sorry that ye should deserve to be reckoned with such, of whom GOD himself pronounceth—*the way of peace they have not known.* Ways of peaceful conclusion, there are but these two certain ; the one, a sentence of judicial decision, given by authority thereto appointed within ourselves ; the other, the like kind of sentence, given by a more universal authority. The former of which two ways, GOD himself prescribeth ; and his SPIRIT it was which directed the very first Christian Churches to use the latter."—Octavo edit. p. 163.

And yet ' the judicious Hooker' must be passed upon your readers, as favouring the absurd notion, that the Scripture alone is sufficient to determine controversies of faith, between parties who each claim the true sense of Scripture to be with them ; which is as much as to say, that the laws of the land can declare their true meaning, and maintain the peace and order of the state, without judges and other officers.   The rule itself is not indeed here mentioned by Hooker in so many words, but the principle on which the rule is founded is recognized throughout, and enforced by the authority both of revelation and reason.   I therefore proceed to ask you in the words of Hooker to your progenitors, " Are ye able to allege any just and sufficient cause wherefore, absolutely ye should not condescend in this controversy to have your judgments overruled by some such definitive sentence ; whether it fall out to be given with or against you, that so these tedious contentions may cease ?   Ye will perhaps make answer, that being persuaded already, as touching the truth of your cause, ye are not to hearken unto any sentence, no not though angels should define otherwise, as the blessed apostle's own example teacheth.   Again, that men, yea councils may err ; and that unless the judgment given do satisfy your minds— unless it be such as ye can by no further argument oppugn—in a word, unless you perceive and acknowledge it yourselves consonant with God's word ; to stand unto it, not allowing it were to sin against your own consciences.   But consider, I beseech you, first as touching the apostle, how that wherein he was so resolute and peremptory, our LORD JESUS CHRIST made manifest unto him, even by intuitive revelation, wherein there was no possibility of error : That which you are persuaded of, ye have it no otherwise than by your own probable collection ; and therefore, such bold asseverations as were in him admirable, should in your mouths argue rashness."   " For if GOD be not the author of confusion, but of peace, then can he not be the author of our refusal but of our contentment, to stand unto some definitive sentence ; without which almost impossible it is, that either we should avoid confusion or ever hope to obtain peace.   To small purpose had the Council of Jerusalem been assembled, if once their determination being set down, men might afterwards have defended their former opinions.   When, therefore, they had given their definitive sentence, all controversy was at an end.   Things were disputed before they came to be determined. Men afterwards were not to dispute any longer, but to obey. The sentence of judgment finished their strife, which their disputes before judgment could not do. This was ground sufficient for any reasonable man's conscience to build the duty of obedience upon, whatsoever his own opinion were, as touching the matter before in question."—*Preface*, p. 165, 166.

And not only on the general principle on which the rule is founded, does the judicious Hooker thus reason unanswerably, in favour of its just and Scriptural authority as the safe and conscientious resort in controversies of faith or order—but also to the same kind of objections of that day to the authority of the fathers and of councils to determine controversies, as are by you again relied upon against this rule, he argues at length, in the body of the work, in this manner. Speaking of the authority and use of councils in the Church, he thus expresses himself: " A thing whereof God's own blessed Spirit was the author; a thing practised by the Holy Apostles themselves ; a thing always afterwards kept and observed throughout the world ; a thing never otherwise than most highly esteemed of, till pride, ambition, and tyranny began by factious and vile endeavours to abuse that divine intention, unto the furtherance of wicked purposes."—" To speak of this matter as the cause requireth, would require very long discourse. All we will presently say is this, whether it be for the finding out any thing whereunto divine law bindeth us, but yet in such sort, that men are not thereof on all sides resolved ; or for the setting down some uniform judgment to stand, touching such things as being neither way matters of necessity, are notwithstanding offensive and scandalous, when there is open opposition about them ; be it for the ending of strifes, touching matters of Christian belief, wherein the one part may seem to have probable cause of dissenting from the other ; or be it concerning matters of polity, order, and regiment in the Church, I nothing doubt but that Christian men should much better frame themselves to those heavenly precepts which our Lord and Saviour with so great instancy gave, as concerning peace and unity, if we all did concur in desire to have the use of ancient councils again renewed, rather than these proceedings continued, which either make all contentions useless, or bring them to one only determination, and that of all other the worst, which is by sword."——*Ecclesiastical Polity*, Book I, p. 225. 8vo.

On the objection to the authority of the fathers, in matters of disputed doctrine from Scripture, then taken and now renewed ; having showed that the " strength of man's authority is affirmatively such, that the weightiest affairs in the world depend thereon," he thus argues against the objection taken to it from human authority.   " If the question be of the authority of a man's testimony, we cannot simply avouch, either that affirmatively it doth not any way hold, or that it hath only force to induce the simple sort, and not to constrain men of understanding and ripe judgment to yield assent ; or that negatively it hath in it no strength at all.   For unto every of these the contrary is most plain."

" Neither doth that which is alleged concerning the infirmity of men, overthrow or disprove this.   Men are blinded with ignorance and error ; many things escape them, and in many things they may be deceived—yea, those things which they do know, they may either forget, or upon sundry indirect considerations let pass ; and although themselves do not err, yet may they, through malice or vanity, even of purpose, deceive others.   Howbeit, infinite cases there are wherein all these impediments and lets are so manifestly excluded, that there is no show or colour whereby any such exceptions may be taken, but that the testimony of man will stand as a ground of infallible assurance.   That there is a city of Rome ; that Pius Quintus, and Gregory the thirteenth, and others, have been Popes of Rome, I suppose we are certainly enough persuaded.   The ground of our persuasion, who never saw the place nor persons before named, can be nothing but man's testimony.   Will any man here notwithstanding, allege those mentioned human infirmities, as reasons why these things should be mistrusted or doubted of?   Yea, that which is more, utterly to infringe the force and strength of man's testimony, were to shake the very fortress of GOD's truth.   For whatsoever we believe concerning salvation by CHRIST, although the Scripture be therein the ground of our belief, yet the authority of man is, if we mark it, the key which openeth the door of entrance into the knowledge of the Scripture. The Scripture doth not teach us the things that are of GOD, unless we did credit men who have taught us that the words of Scripture do signify those things. Some way, therefore, notwithstanding man's infirmity, yet his authority may enforce assent. Upon better advice and deliberation so much is perceived and at length confessed, that arguments taken from the authority of men, may not only so far forth as is declared, but further also, be of some force in human sciences; which force, be it never so small, doth show that they are not utterly naught. But in matters divine, it is still maintained stiffly, that they have no manner of force at all. Howbeit, the very self same reason, which causeth to yield that they are of some force in the one, will at length constrain also to acknowledge that they are not in the other altogether unforcible." —" For the controversy is of the weight of such men's judgment. Let it therefore be suspected; let it be taken as gross, corrupt, repugnant unto the truth, whatsoever concerning things divine above nature shall at any time be spoken out of the mouths of mere natural men, which have not the eyes wherewith heavenly things are discerned; for this we contend not. But whom GOD hath endued with principal gifts to aspire unto knowledge by; whose exercise, labours, and divine studies he hath so blessed, that the world for their great and rare skill that way, hath them in singular admiration; may we reject even their judgment likewise, as being utterly of no moment? For mine own part, I dare not so lightly esteem of the Church, and of the principal pillars therein." But further, having showed the futility of objections taken to human authority in things divine, from some observations of Irenæus, Jerome and Augustine, he goes on to say, " Yea, but we doubt what the will of GOD is. Are we in this case forbidden to hear what men of judgment think it to be? If not, then this allegation might very well have been spared. In that ancient strife which was between the Catholic fathers and Arians, Donatists, and others of the like perverse and froward disposition, as long as to fathers and Councils alleged on the other side, the like by the contrary side were opposed, impossible it was that ever the question should by this means grow to any issue or end.   The Scripture they both believed ; the Scripture they knew could not give sentence on both sides ; by Scripture, the controversy between them was such as might be determined. In this case what madness was it with such kind of proofs to nourish their contention, when there were such effectual means to end all controversy that was between them ?   Hereby, therefore, it does not as yet appear that an argument of authority of men affirmatively, is in matters divine nothing worth.   Which opinion, being once inserted in the minds of the vulgar sort, what it may grow unto, God knoweth.   Thus much we see, it hath made thousands so headstrong in gross and palpable errors, that a man whose capacity will scarce serve him to utter five words in sensible manner, blusheth not in any doubt concerning matter of Scripture, to think his own bare *yea*, as good as the *nay* of all the wise, grave and learned judgments, that are in the whole world ; which insolency must be repressed or it will be the very bane of Christian religion.—*Ecclesiastical Polity*, Book II. p. 327 to 336.

Thus, Sir, speaks ' the judicious Hooker,' in connexion with his whole subject, and with his actual purpose ; and not as you have represented him, or as any other author may be made to speak, by taking a detached passage of his writings.   And it is confidently submitted to the public intelligence, whether this great and good man, this learned and able, and just, and moderate man, is opposed to the principle of the rule of the Bishop of North-Carolina, as you call it ; or of one mind with the Bishop on this subject ?   Whether he gives any countenance to the ' no comment' principle of promiscuous Bible Societies ?   And whether this Reviewer is really acquainted with his writings, and honest in the representation of his sentiments to his readers ?

In the close you refer me to the learned Bishop HORSLEY, and the ingenious Bishop HURD.   But as I have not access to their works, I can form no judgment as to the fairness, and connexion, in which you refer to them.   I entertain not the least doubt, however, that on the *true point* betwixt you and myself, *viz :* the rule to determine the true meaning of the Scriptures, on disputed questions of the faith or order of the gospel, they will be found firm in the ranks of that impenetrable phalanx of piety and learning, whose judgment you reject, on these very subjects.

To this opinion I am the more inclined, because, through Bishop Hurd you make Chillingworth speak a language which he expressly denies, and considers as a scandalous charge, brought against him by the Papists. The quotation from Bishop Hurd is given, p, 319 of the Review, in the following words :

"This discovery [namely, that the fathers had no authority] had great effects. It opened the eyes of the more candid, and intelligent inquirers. And our incomparable Chillingworth," (who by the way had been a Papist on the very ground here opposed) "with some others, took advantage of it to set the controversy with the Church of Rome once more on its proper foot, *and establish for ever the* OLD PRINCIPLE *that the Bible, and that only,* INTERPRETED BY OUR BEST REASON, *is the religion of Protestants.*"

On the contrary, Chillingworth thus expresses his own sentiments, in his own words, "Your injuries then to me, (no way deserved by me,) but by differing in opinion from you, (wherein yet you surely differ from me, as much as I from you,) are especially three. For, first, upon heresy, and refusing to give me opportunity of begetting in you a better understanding of me, you charge me with a great number of false and impious doctrines, which I will not name in particular, because I will not assist you so far in the spreading of my own undeserved defamation : but whosoever teaches or holds them, *let him be anathema !* The sum of them all cast up by yourself, in your first chapter, is this, *Nothing ought or can be certainly believed, further than it may be proved by evidence of natural reason ;* (where I conceive natural reason is opposed to supernatural revelation :) and whosoever holds so, *let him be anathema !* And moreover to clear myself once for all, from all imputations of this nature, which charge me injuriously with denial of supernatural verities, I profess sincerely, that I believe all those books of Scripture, which the Church of England accounts canonical, to be the infallible word of God : I believe all things evidently contained in them ; all things evidently or probably deducible from them : I acknowledge all that to be heresie, which by the act of Parliament, *primo* of Queen Elizabeth, is declared to be so, and only to be so.   And though in such points which may be held diversely of divers men, *salva fidei compage*, I would not take any man's liberty from him, and humbly beseech all men, that they would not take mine from me !   Yet thus much I can say, (which I hope will satisfy any man of reason,) that whatsoever hath been held necessary to salvation, *either by the Catholique Church of all ages, or by the consent of fathers, measured by Vincentius Lyrinensis his rule;* or is held necessary by the Catholique Church of this age ; or by the consent of Protestants, or even by the Church of England ; that, against the Socinians, and all others whatsoever, I doe verily believe and embrace."— *Preface to the Religion of Protestants a safe Way of Salvation.* Sec. 28.*

---

* It may be useful here to show how Chillingworth actually argued with the *jure divino* Presbyterians of his own times, upon the chief point of dispute between Bishop Ravenscroft and Dr. Rice.   To give more force to his argument he takes the lowest ground, *viz :* "That episcopacy is *not repugnant* to the government settled in the Church for perpetuity."   "Whereof I conceive," says he, "this which follows is as clear a demonstration (as) any thing of this nature is capable of.

" That this government was universally received in the Church, either in the Apostles' time, or presently after, is so evident and unquestionable, that the most learned adversaries of this government do themselves confess it."

Petrus Molinæus, in his book, *De Manere Pastorali,* purposely written in defence of Presbyterian government, acknowledgeth, ' That presently after the apostles, or even in their time (as ecclesiastical story witnesseth) it was ordained, that in every city one of the Presbytery should be called a Bishop, who should have pre-eminence over his colleagues, to avoid confusion, which often times ariseth out of equality. And truly this form of government all Churches every where received.'

Theodorus Beza, in his tract, *De triplici Episcopatus Generi,* confesseth in effect the same thing.   For having distinguished episcopacy into three kinds, divine, human, and satanical, and attributing to the second (which he calls *human,* but we maintain and conceive to be *apostolical*) not only a priority of order, but a superiority of power over other Presbyters, bounded yet by laws and canons provided against tyranny ; he clearly professeth, that of this kind of episcopacy is to be understood whatsoever we read concerning the authority of Bishops (or presidents, as Justin Martyr calls them) in Ignatius and other most ancient writers.

Certainly from* these two great defenders of Presbytery, we should never have

---

* To whom two others also from Geneva may be added : *Daniel Chamierus* (in *Panstratia,* Tom. II. Lib. x. cap. 6. sec. 24.) and *Nicol. Vedelius,* (*Exercitat.* III. *in Epist. Ignatii*

Whether therefore, the mistake is yours or Bishop Hurd's, two things are perfectly evident; first, that the 'incomparable Chillingworth' *is not* 'against the rule of the Bishop of North-Carolina,' but on the contrary, that he is not only

---

had this fair acknowledgment, (so prejudicial to their own practices, and so advantageous to their adversaries' purpose,) had not the evidence of clear and undeniable truth enforced them to it.   It will not, therefore, be necessary to spend any time in confuting that uningenuous assertion of the anonymous author of the *Catalogue of Testimonies for the Equality of Bishops and Presbyters*, who affirms, that their disparity began long after the apostles' time.   But we may safely take for granted that which these two learned adversaries have confessed, and see whether upon this foundation, laid by them, we may not by unanswerable reason raise this superstructure :—

That seeing Episcopal government is confessedly so ancient, and so Catholic, it cannot, with reason, be denied to be apostolic.

For so great a change as between presbyterian government and episcopal could not possibly have prevailed all the world over in a little time.   Had episcopal government been an aberration from, or a corruption of the government left in the Churches by the apostles, it had been very strange that it should have been received in any *one* Church so suddenly, or that it should have prevailed in *all* for many ages after. ' *Variasse debuerat error ecclesiarum : quod autem apud omnes unum est, non est erratum, sed traditum.*' '*Had the Churches erred, they would have varied : what therefore is one and the same amongst all, came not sure by error, but tradition.*' Thus *Tertullian* argues, very probably, from the consent of the Churches of his time, not long after the apostles, and that in a matter of opinion much more subject to unobserved alteration.   But that in the form and substance of the necessary government of the Church, a thing always in use and practice, there should be so sudden a change as presently after the apostles' time, and so universal as received in all the Churches ; this is clearly impossible.

For, what universal cause can be assigned or feigned of this *universal* Apostacy ? You will not imagine, that the Apostles, all or any of them, made any decree for this change when they were living ? or left order for it in any will, when they were dying ? This were to grant the questions, to wit : That the Apostles, being to leave the government of the churches themselves, and either seeing by experience, or foreseeing by the Spirit of God, the distractions and disorders which would arise from a multitude of equals, substituted episcopal government instead of their own. General Councils, to make a law for a general change, for many ages there was none. There was no Christian Emperor, no coercive power over the Church, to enforce it. Or if there had been any, we know no force was equal to the courage of the Christians of those times.   Their lives were then at command, for they had not *then* learnt to *fight* for Christ ; but their obedience to any *against* his law was not to be com-

---

ed *Philadelph.* cap. 14. and *Exercit.* VIII. *in Epist. ad Mariam*, cap. 3.) which is fully, also, demonstrated in Dr. Hammond's *Dissertations against Blondel*, (which never were answered and *never will be*,) by the testimonies of those who wrote in the very next ages after the apostles.

'plainly' but expressly *totidem verbis,* in favour of it.   Secondly, that in truth the Reviewer is not acquainted with the writings of those men, with whose names, nevertheless, he shows his

---

manded: for they had perfectly learnt to *die* for him.   Therefore there was no power then to command this change, or if there had been any, it had been in vain.

What device then, shall we study; or to what fountain shall we reduce this strange pretended alteration ?   Can it enter into our hearts to think, that all the presbyters and other Christians then, being the Apostles' scholars, could be generally ignorant of the will of CHRIST, teaching the necessity of a presbyterial government ? Or, dare we adventure to think them so strangely wicked all the world over, as against knowledge and conscience to conspire against it ?   Imagine the spirit of Diotrephes had entered into some, or a great many, of the presbyters, and possessed them with an ambitious desire of a forbidden superiority ; was it possible they should attempt and achieve it once without any opposition or contradiction ?   And besides that the contagion of this ambition should spread itself, and prevail without stop or constraint ; nay without any noise or notice taken of it, through all the churches in the world ; all the watchmen in the mean time being so fast asleep, and all the dogs so dumb that not so much as one should open his mouth against it ?

But let us suppose (though it be a horrible untruth) that the presbyters and people then were not so good Christians as the presbyterians are now ; that they were generally so negligent to retain the government of CHRIST's Church commanded by CHRIST, which we are so zealous to restore ; yet certainly we must not forget nor deny, that they were *men* as we are.   And if we look upon them as mere natural men, yet knowing by experience how hard a thing it is, even for policy armed with power, by many attempts and contrivances, and in a long time, to gain upon the liberty of any one people ; undoubtedly we shall never entertain so wild an imagination as that, among all the Christian presbyters in the world, neither conscience of duty, nor love of liberty, nor averseness from pride and usurpation of others over them, should prevail so much with any one, as to oppose this pretended universal invasion of the kingdom of JESUS CHRIST, and the liberty of Christians.

When I shall see, therefore, all the fables of the metamorphosis acted, and prove true stories ; when I shall see all the democracies and aristocracies in the world lie down and sleep, and awake into monarchies ; then will I begin to believe, that presbyterial government, having continued in the Church during the Apostles' times, should presently after, against the Apostles' doctrine and the will of CHRIST, be whirled about like a scene in a masque, and transformed into episcopacy.   In the mean time, while these things remain thus incredible, and in human reason impossible, I hope I shall have leave to conclude thus :—

Episcopal government is acknowledged to have been universally received in the Church, presently after the Apostles' times :

Between the Apostles' times and this *presently after,* there was not time enough for, nor possibility of so great an alteration :

And therefore, there was no such alteration as is pretended.   And therefore, Episcopacy, being confessed to be so ancient and Catholic, must be granted also to be Apostolic : *quod erat demonstrandum.* CHILLINGWORTH's *Works,* p. 388 and seq.   See also FABER's *Difficulties of Romanism,* in which the author shows by

readers he is so familiar.   The man who had sounded the depths of Hooker and Chillingworth, in their published labours for the support of true religion, could not maintain the sentiments which this Reviewer does attempt to maintain, and father upon them.   *The Bible, and the Bible only, interpreted by our best reason, the religion of Protestants*, may suit the meridian of a defender of the 'no comment' Bible Society principle of modern times; may suit the man, who sees in this element of discord and division nothing hostile to the unity of CHRIST's body; but it is unknown to such men as Hooker and Chillingworth; it is unknown to the Church of which they were members, and equally unknown to every sound theologian; and I may go further, it is unknown to, and indefensible upon, any principle of right reason.

Equally unjustifiable, in the judgment of such men, is the charge attempted to be fastened on this rule, and on the application made of it in my Sermons, by this Reviewer, that it is Popish and anti-protestant.   This I trust has been fully refuted already, by the proof of its universal adoption as the

---

his practice, as well as by his declared judgment, the importance of the evidence of the early Christian writers " on all the great leading points of divinity."   He thinks "those who lived nearest to the times of the Apostles must have best known the mind of the Apostles."   *Preface to Difficulties of Romanism.*

Dr. VAN MILDERT in his fourth *Bampton Lecture*, after stating some objections against the authority of the primitive fathers, adds, "In answer, therefore, to such objections, it may suffice to observe, that supposing the primitive fathers to have been men of only common discernment and integrity; their testimony respecting the doctrines then actually received by the Church and maintained against the heresies then prevailing, must have peculiar weight.   Those among them who had been personally conversant with the Apostles, and who derived their knowledge of the Christian faith from what they continually heard of their preaching and discourse, as well as from their writings, seem to have claims to a regard only short of that which is due to their inspired preceptors.   To place such men as *Clement, Ignatius,* and *Polycarp* no higher in the scale of authority, with respect to the value of their testimony on these points, than bishops and pastors in later times, betrays an error of judgment, which on any other subject of investigation analogous to this, would be deemed preposterous."   pp. 114, 115.

See SIMPSON's *Plea for the Deity of Jesus*— page 457 and seq.

These references are made to show that the authority of the primitive fathers in matters of controversy continues to be regarded, notwithstanding the assertions of Dr. Rice and others to the contrary.

VOL. I.—49

basis of the reformation; but as Chillingworth is relied upon, as 'plainly against the rule of the Bishop of North-Carolina,' let us hear his own sentiments, in his own words. It being objected to the Protestants, "that if the true Church may err, in defining what Scriptures be canonical, or in delivering the sense thereof, then we must follow either the private spirit, or *else natural wit and judgment*, and by them examine what Scriptures contain true or false doctrine, and in that respect ought to be received or rejected." Chillingworth replies as follows :- "All which is apparently untrue, neither can any proof of it be pretended. For though the present Church may err in her judgment touching this matter, yet have we other directions in it, besides the private spirit, and the examination of the contents, and that is, *the testimony of the primitive Christians.*"—Same *Preface* Sect. 13. And again, Sect. 25— "What if Protestants be now put in mind, that for the exposition of Scripture, they are bound by a canon *to follow the ancient fathers;* which whosoever doth with sincerity, *it is utterly impossible he should be a Papist?* Is there in all this, or any part of it, any kind of proof of this scandalous calumny?" (For the calumny referred to, see Sect. 20 of the *Preface.*) And I trust that the Bishop of North-Carolina may ask, and with the same confidence, Is there, in all the assertions of Dr. Rice against this rule, and the application made of it in the Sermons, any kind of proof, either of Popery, or of opposition to the fundamental principle of the reformation?

We are now prepared, Sir, I think, to answer the question you put so triumphantly, at p. 320 :

"We would now ask, is the united authority of the *incomparable* Chillingworth, the *judicious* Hooker, the *learned* Horsley, and the *ingenious* Hurd, *good* enough, and *high* enough to satisfy Bishop Ravenscroft ?"

Perfectly sufficient, Sir, when they speak their own sentiments. Bishop Ravenscroft would examine with great care, any opinion entertained by him, which was opposed by the judgment of such highly gifted, learned, and faithful men. He would greatly doubt any conclusion, however reasonable it might appear, which was not sanctioned by their opinion, and by their practice. Dare this Reviewer say as much? No—for he knows, intimately knows, that they spent their talents and their lives, in direct opposition to his public and most cherished sentiments. He knows, that tried by their judgment, and that of their fellows, his whole system crumbles into dust. Yet he would make his readers believe, that they are his friends and allies, engaged in the same cause—and he quotes them—I suppose I shall be called uncharitable, but the proof is before the public— he quotes them to mislead.

But as this deification of human reason is a most captivating fallacy, and daily gaining ground under the patronage of promiscuous 'no comment' Bible Societies—as it is moreover, another of those curious coincidences of sentiment betwixt Presbyterians and Unitarians, which have already been hinted at —it demands further notice, and fuller exposure; and as you have given it your unqualified sanction, you can have no objection to its being tried by an example.

Suppose, then, you have to meet an Unitarian on this ground; (and I select the Unitarian, because you have asserted him impregnable to the authority of the Church, and told us, 'he laughs to scorn the spiritual meaning hid under the letter of Scripture,' p. 249) from Scripture, interpreted by his best reason, he declares that he can see no ground for the distinguishing doctrines of Christianity; that he does not believe in the inherent divinity of the Saviour—the fall of man—the atonement of the cross—the necessity of renewing grace—the being and inspiration of the HOLY GHOST, &c. Now what have you to oppose to *his* best reason, but *your* best reason? Spiritual influence is out of the question on both sides; on that of the Unitarian by his professed belief; on your side by the wording of the rule. You are deprived also, of all benefit of consentient testimony in favour of the doctrines of Christianity: nothing will touch him, say you, 'but the meaning of Scripture, elicited by the best rules of Hermeneutics.' Suppose then, your natural abilities and acquired knowledge are superior to his—you refute his arguments, you answer his objections, you overthrow all his defences. And what then? Is he thereby

convinced; or is he even put in the wrong, morally speaking?
You will answer, that he ought to be convinced—that he is
obstinate and unreasonable, if he does not yield the point.   Be
it so ;   but let us give just measure.   Suppose the Unitarian
proves superior to you in natural and acquired endowments,
and on the ground of human reason, shuts you up in silence.
What follows? Are not you equally obstinate and unreasonable,
if you refuse to surrender your faith to him, and renounce your
Saviour?   If you say No ;   you abandon your own principle.
If you say Yes ;   you surrender the faith and certainty of
revelation.   For be it well remembered, that in this case, the
points disputed are chiefly mysteries—things above reason,
which reason touches at her peril, beyond the terms in which
God hath spoken of them.   The doctrine of the Trinity—the
incarnation of the Son of God—the operation of the divine
grace, &c. as facts revealed, and attested by sufficient evidence,
reason is competent to inquire into, and to decide ; but beyond
this, a higher principle than reason is required, even *faith*—
which, though not independent of the understanding, is yet
chiefly an act of the will.   When reason, then, can rectify and
rule the will in fallen man, the principle may be a sound one ;
till then, it is an infidel and ruinous position.

But further.   If this fundamental principle of the reformation, as you assert it, is consecrated as the true principle of
interpreting the Scriptures ; then, Sir, I desire to know what is
to prevent as many forms of faith, as there are men who can
obtain followers? According to you, our best reason, whether
informed or not (and recollect, I pray you, there is no qualification mentioned, nor can you limit a broad abstract generality
of this kind,) is to be the *sole guide ;* and in a world like this,
what does all experience prove will be the consequence, but
divisions multiplied into each other, until religion moulders away
into the dust of individuality, and infidelity treads in triumph
upon the hope of redeemed man? And is this a result to be
desired—to be aided and assisted in its progress? Was it in the
mind of Chillingworth, or Hooker, or Horsley, or Hurd, to
sanction a principle leading to such consequences? Assuredly,
neither their writings nor their lives give any countenance to

such an assertion.   But are not such indeed the consequences of the principle asserted by you to be maintained by them ? And is it not demonstrated, by the existing state of the Christian world, with its multiplied and increasing religious divisions ?— These have chiefly sprung from the pride of human reason undertaking to sit in judgment on the *mystery of godliness*, and to measure *the deep things of* GOD, with the shallow line of this world's wisdom.   And they will continue, and increase too, until men are brought to understand that in things divine, reason is given them, that they may learn the will of GOD ; not that they may make and declare it according to any such imperfect and variable standard.   For what material light is to the bodily eye, that in like manner, is revelation to reason, the eye of the mind.   And as the best formed eye would be perfectly useless without material light—so is our best reason totally useless in things spiritual, without the light of divine revelation.   How a Christian divine, then, has been betrayed into the acknowledgment and assertion of this infidel principle, of revelation subservient to human reason, is to me unaccountable ; unless indeed the subtle Unitarian poison is at work where we do not (as yet) suspect it, silently undermining the religion of JESUS, that it may build upon its ruins, the religion of reason.   That this is the grand principle of the Socinians and Unitarians, in all their various ramifications, requires no proof.

Again. On this principle, as contended for by you, with what propriety do you make use of the phrase *Orthodox Churches* ?* or how can you consistently refuse communion with Anna Lee, or Joanna Southcote, or the Swedenborgians, or the Universalists, or even the Unitarians, or any other description of reli-

---

* It is not a little amusing to observe the use now made of the word *Orthodox* by the Dissenters.   For a specimen of it, the reader is referred to DR. MILLER's *Letters to Professor Stuart, of Andover*, on the subject of the eternal generation of the SON OF GOD, where the word *Orthodox* is nearly exclusively confined to the acknowledgment of the Divinity of the Saviour ; and where the Andover Professor is most plentifully *orthodoxed* by his brother of Princeton, even while the latter is striving to show, and from the Primitive Fathers too, the *heterodoxy* of the former on this subject.   I wonder if there is any system arranged among them, on a calculation of advantage from a change in the meaning of leading words, gradually introduced ? Such as *Regeneration, Evangelical, Orthodox, &c.*

gionists? By one so filled with charity as you represent yourself, it must be presumed, that on an affair of such importance, they have interpreted Scripture by their *best reason;* you interpret it differently, to be sure, in the use of the same means; but this should make no difference; because, by the appointment of Almighty GOD the faculty of reason in man varies so much in degree originally, and by cultivation and improvement subsequently, that no blame can attach to different, and even opposite interpretations of his revealed will.   Upon this principle, the greatest difficulty reason would have to surmount, would be the giving of a revelation at all.   For beyond all doubt, if our best reason is supreme in the interpretation of divine truth, Holy Scripture is nullified as the rule of faith, and the *Bible* is no longer the *religion of Protestants.*   For the celebrated words of Chillingworth, "the Bible, I say, the Bible only, is the religion of Protestants," is a very different maxim from that which you would father upon him, from Bishop Hurd—"that the Bible, and the Bible only, *interpreted by our best reason,* is the religion of Protestants."*   The one becomes so incomparable a man and pious Christian.   It gives honour, where honour is indeed due; and asserts the supremacy of the word of GOD, as the standard of revealed truth to man—the fixed and unchangeable rule of his faith and practice.   The other becomes no well informed, pious and humble Christian; inasmuch as in its obvious and fair construction, no less than in its terms, it exalts

---

* Since these pages went to press, I have had opportunity to see Bishop Hurd's Work, from which Dr. Rice makes the quotation, and, as I expected, I find it unfair in fact, and actually false in the use made of it.   But that the public may judge for themselves, the original and the quotation are given, exactly as they stand in the respective publications.

BISHOP HURD.	DR. RICE.
"And to establish forever the old principle, that the Bible, and that only, (interpreted by our best reason) is the religion of Protestants."	"And to establish forever the old principle, that the *Bible, and that only,* INTERPRETED BY OUR BEST REASON, *is the religion of Protestants.*"

The words are indeed the same—the manner of presenting them to the reader, constitutes the difference.   What Bishop Hurd puts in a parenthesis, as not material to the sentence, and certainly not the words of Chillingworth, Dr. Rice puts in *capitals,* and presents as the considered sentiments of that great and good and learned man.

the wisdom of the world above the wisdom of GOD, and surrenders and subjects his holy word to the control and determination of the most variable, uncertain, and unmanageable of the perverted faculties of human nature.

The first, as laid down by Chillingworth, is assented to and held in full by every Protestant. On this ground they can meet without reserve; though, unhappily, they differ widely on the true interpretation of its sense and meaning; and some of them betray the most pointed hostility against the most reasonable means of coming to agreement, by submitting their differences in doctrine and practice to the Bible, as understood, believed, and acted upon by consentient antiquity—by the pure and primitive Church.

The other is asserted and maintained only by those, who find in the latitude of the principle, the best defence of their particular practice; and who cling to it as the specious but flimsy excuse for their departure from the faith and order *once delivered to the saints.* But to show beyond dispute, not only the fallacy, but the dangerous tendency of this popular delusion, as asserted by you, "that the Bible, and that only, interpreted by our best reason, is the religion of Protestants;" let us suppose, for a moment, that it is acted upon throughout the Christian world, and then ask, what *possible,* (for I will not say *reasonable,*) expectation could be entertained, that the unity of faith and fellowship enjoined upon Christians by the gospel, and enforced by such awful sanctions, would or could be kept? Let us ask our best reason, and require it to answer, under the revealed sanctions of eternity. Wherefore, in the wisdom of GOD, a visible Church, Ministry, and Sacraments, were connected inseparably with his word under every dispensation of his grace to mankind, to preserve uncorrupted, and render effectual to salvation, the revealed mysteries of his holy will; if this purpose was within the province of the broken and perverted reason of fallen creatures? Suppose Christianity had commenced its progress under the control of this modern delusion: what do common sense and experience tell us our best reason would have made of it? Sir, the calculation is easy. As the *preaching of* CHRIST, *crucified, was to the Greeks foolishness* to the same class of persons it would have still remained a *hidden gospel.* The pretenders to *science, falsely so called,* would have continued to measure *the wisdom of* GOD *in a mystery* by their best reason—they would have scorned to *become fools that they might be wise :* and. from what has taken place in the Christian world, notwithstanding the counteracting effect of a visible Church, ministry, and sacraments, and the adoption and influence of a safer rule for the interpretation of doubtful or obscure passages of Scripture, we may anticipate the havoc this proud parent of all heresy and schism would have made of the one faith of the gospel ; and thereby be warned against the mischief it may yet perpetrate.

To this principle, therefore, as asserted and contended for by you, I will apply the words of the judicious Hooker, on an analogous case—" which opinion being once inserted into the minds of the vulgar sort, what it may grow unto, GOD knoweth. Thus much we see ; it hath already made thousands so head-strong, even in gross and palpable errors, that a man whose capacity will scarce serve him to utter five words in sensible manner, blusheth not in any doubt concerning matter of Scrip-ture, to think his own bare Yea, as good as the Nay, of all the wise, grave, and learned judgments that are in the whole world ; which insolency must be repressed, or it will be the bane of Christian religion."—Book II. 8vo. edit. p. 336.

The third test to which you would bring the rule of the Bishop of North Carolina, as you are pleased to call it, is its worthlessness to produce uniformity of faith ; exemplified by the present condition of the Church of England, where you acknow-ledge the rule is adopted.

Whatever the actual condition of the British Church may be at present, as to uniformity of faith in her clergy and members, it is evident, that it formed no part of your plan to extenuate it ; and as you thought you found in it a weapon of some force against this alarming and troublesome rule, it was laid hold of and wielded without due consideration. Whatever its intrinsic worth may be, no claim has been put in for it by me, to stand even upon equal ground with the Scriptures, as to this effect of uniformity of faith. Yet that the Scriptures were intended to produce uniformity of faith among men, you will hardly venture to deny.   That they have not done it, you will also admit.   Are they therefore worthless, and to be thrown aside as incompetent to the gracious purpose of their Author?   In like manner is this rule, which, next to the Scriptures, is the grand instrument to bring men to one mind on the doctrines of revelation, to be branded as worthless, because it is overlooked by some, and denied and resisted by others?   Are you prepared to assert that the abuse or neglect of a remedy renders the remedy itself worthless?   Yet this you must do, or abandon the ground you have taken at p. 251, 313, and elsewhere in these reviews.

The differences in doctrine and opinion, stated by you as now existing in the British Church, do not arise from the *use* of the rule, but from the *neglect* of it.   The rule is, therefore, in no shape answerable for the various sentiments entertained among the clergy of the Church of England, on points of religious belief; any more than the Bible itself is answerable for the various systems of faith and practice into which Christianity is split up.   However tempting, then, the opportunity to assail at once this troublesome rule, and the Church which regards it as the only safe resort in controversies from Scripture, you have missed your aim, as respects the rule.   It was found effectual by the British reformers, to detect and expose the corruptions and errors of the Church of Rome; and to enable them to restore the ancient and apostolic Church of Britain, to the soundness and purity of primitive times.   And it is yet competent to detect and expose the corruptions and errors of all classes of dissenters in the present day, and to bring them back to the same happy condition.   But they will not resort to its safe and certain counsel, proudly preferring their own ' best reason' to the clear and unbroken testimony of the saints, confessors, and martyrs of antiquity, and to the collected judgment of the most pious and learned of modern times.   Were it indeed the worthless thing you represent it to your readers, and at the same time so dangerous and destructive to the cause of true religion; we might reasonably expect from one who betrays an instinctive dread of its operation, something of more weight, and worthy of deeper consideration, than the miserable sophistry you have raked together to assail it.   For it is not a new point in religious controversy, but one which has been repeatedly canvassed, and has never been answered otherwise than by the determined *sic volo*, of *resolved* dissent.

Whether you have not likewise missed your aim in the wanton attack you have made on the integrity of the British and American clergy of the Protestant Episcopal Church, remains to be examined.

"In the Church of England," say you, p. 251, "there are high churchmen and low churchmen, Deists, Arians, Socinians, Calvinists, Arminians, and Swedenborgians."

And in a note on this passage you go on further to say:

"For the Evangelical clergy of England, we entertain the highest respect and the sincerest affection. We mention the facts above stated with great pain. Our object is to show, that Bishop R's plan won't do; and by the way, to prove that a great injury is done to a Church when government encourages bad men to seek a living in it. We take great pleasure in stating that the number of Evangelical clergy is increasing."

That in so numerous a body of men as the clergy of the united British and Irish Church, there should some be found unsound and unfaithful, notwithstanding every care and diligence used to prevent it, we are prepared to expect from experience observation of much smaller bodies. That the evils inseparable from an endowed establishment of religion by the state, particularly one with such tempting prizes in its range, as that of the British Church, should occasionally allure ambition, cupidity, and infidelity, to the commission of perjury, the depravity of our common nature, alas! renders too probable. But that it should predominate in such a body; that it should infect to such an extent, as to warrant the charge here made; ought to be substantiated by better proof than the mere assertion of an interested reviewer.

Not content, however, with this wide range of denunciation, which includes the British Bishops as unfaithful, and their clergy as unsound and unprincipled, you make another sweep, and bring in the majority of the Episcopal clergy of this country, as insincere and double-minded men, at their very entrance upon the sacred trust committed to them.   For at p. 312, you ask :

"Are we to look to the *minority* in that Church, who subscribe *ex amino ;* or to the *majority* who regard the Articles as articles of peace ; for the interpretation of the one sense of Scripture, and for the proper meaning of their standard of doctrine ?"

Now, Sir, will you be pleased to make known the grounds on which you venture to charge the *majority* of the Episcopal clergy as subscribing the articles of the Church, *not ex animo,* that is with the sincerity of men who call GOD to witness, but with a duplicity which construes the articles against the sense of the Church which imposes them ?   Will you also be pleased to inform us, upon what scriptural or reasonable ground the Calvinistic clergy are exclusively entitled to the name of *Evangelical,* and represented as the *only ex animo* subscribers of the Articles, the *only men* who present themselves for ordination according to the principles of that Church, whose orders they receive ?   These questions, Sir, I feel that I have a right to ask, and that you are bound to answer, as to a charge of moral wrong; for I have embraced these articles *ex animo ;* in common with every other Episcopal clergyman in this country, though not actually, yet I have virtually, subscribed them in my ordination vow ; I am not an *Evangelical,* in the modern, artful, and false acceptation of the word ; as one of the falsely accused majority, therefore, I must be allowed to repel this slander, by whoever made, and to warn the clergy at large against the cloven-footed cunning of the old maxim, "divide and overcome."   I must also take leave to caution them against the influence of a word artfully and systematically changed from its original, scriptural meaning.   There is no necessary connexion between the words *Calvinistical* and *Evangelical :* on the contrary, they are radically opposite.   Evangelical doctrines are tidings of great joy, good news, to *all mankind,* through the redemption that is in CHRIST JESUS.   Calvinistical doctrines are good news only to *a part of the world,* filling with despair, (could they be believed) the non elect.   Yet gradually, but very generally, the word *Calvinistical* is retiring from general use, and the word *Evangelical* is taking its place ; and if not resisted will, ere long, cause as much confusion of mind, and become the occasion of as much disturbance, as the equally unscriptural and unwarranted change which has taken place in the use and meaning of the word *Regeneration.*

That for the *Evangelical* clergy of England (and I doubt not for those of America likewise) in this novel acceptation of the word, Dr. Rice ‘ entertains the highest respect and the sincerest affection’ needs not to be disputed ;   nor yet, that he rejoices at their increase.   Strange indeed it would be, when men must think alike, and act as near as possible by the same rule, that the bonds of fellowship should not be strengthened !   In this case, there is but the mere trifle of episcopacy betwixt them ; and as observation has taught me, so doubtless it has not escaped Dr. Rice, that where the principles of Calvin are entertained the revealed *order* of the Gospel is proportionably, lightly regarded.   Hence the flattery which this description of persons receives from the Presbyterians, and the high gratification all classes of Dissenters manifest, at receiving countenance from any portion of the Episcopal Church.

But in what way do these facts, (if facts they are, and which you say you mention with great pain,) in what way do they show ‘ that Bishop R’s plan won’t do ?   Has the rule pro- posed by him from Vincentius, for settling the disputed meaning of Scripture, been resorted to by any class of dissenters? Have the Deists, or the Arians, Socinians, Swedenborgians, whom you reckon up, or even the Calvinists, ever consented to submit the truth and soundness of their respective doctrines, to this umpirage ?   No, they refuse it——they dread it, they know it would be fatal to their pretensions.   How is it then, that you undertake to say, ‘ Bishop R’s plan wont do ?’   Are the Presby- terians——or is Dr. Rice for himself——willing to submit the pretensions of parity to divine appointment, to the determi- nation of Scripture, as understood, believed, and acted upon by the primitive Church ? Bishop R. is perfectly willing to submit the claim of episcopacy to this high and essential distinction, to the judgment of such a competent and impartial tribunal.   Why is it then, that 'his plan won't do?'   Certainly it never can do, if one of the parties refuse to be bound by it. But does this prove that the plan is inefficient?   Or does it prove, incontestibly, that the party refusing is conscious of defect in his foundation?   And what better proof can be required that such is your case, Sir, than the manner in which you have met this point in these Reviews?

If indeed, the efforts made by the contenders for parity to destroy the credibility of the Christian fathers of the three first centuries, as witnesses of facts and opinions within their immediate observation, could be sustained; with what good reason might you say, 'Bishop R's plan won't do?'   But when the canon of Scripture is received solely on this testimony—when it is resorted to, and relied upon by you, in support of your interpretation of Scripture in the case of infant baptism—by Dr. Miller against the Unitarians, and against Professor Stuart's heterodox notions on the eternal generation of the SON OF GOD; wherefore is it, I would be glad to know, that they are not equally good and sufficient witnesses as to the true interpretation of Scripture, on the subjects of particular redemption and parity of order in the Ministry? Yet 'Bishop R's plan won't do.'   Why?   Because the testimony is so clear and unanimous against you, that you dare not meet it.

But these facts are mentioned 'to prove by the way, that a great injury is done to the Church, when Government encourages bad men to seek a living in it.'   A point certainly requiring not even a way-side proof, because self-evident.   But did it never once occur to Dr. Rice, whence he was to draw his proofs that the British, or any other Government thus circumstanced, either had originally, or now have in view, by an Ecclesiastical Establishment, the encouragement of bad men to enter the Church?   With what propriety does such an insinuation—not to say direct accusation—come from the man professing such unbounded charity, and so tremblingly alive (see p. 345) to impugning motives.'   Can Dr. Rice produce the most distant ground to believe that such a motive was entertained by any government adopting an Ecclesiastical Establishment, from the days of Constantine to the present moment? Can he bring forward the remotest resemblance of proof that such a motive was in the intendment of Queen Elizabeth and the Parliament of England, when the ancient and apostolical British Church, reformed and purified from the corruptions of Popery, and resorted to, and re-established upon, the primitive model of faith and order, was taken into union by the State? Can this, or any other Reviewer, produce proof that such is the motive which sways the present government of Great-Britain, with respect to the Ecclesiastical Establishment of that Kingdom? For unless this can be done, the charge must be rejected, as equally rash and unfounded.

That this ' way-side' assertion (for there is no *proof* offered, nor in the nature of things is it *capable* of proof) is meant as a side blow at religious establishments, is pretty evident; and coupled as it is, with the unqualified denunciation of Bishop R's plan (this troublesome rule of Vincentius) may be understood by your readers (whether so intended or not by you,) as if it was the purpose of Bishop Ravenscroft, or the policy of Episcopalians in this country, to prepare the way for an establishment here. I think it my duty, therefore, to express plainly and distinctly, for myself—and as I firmly believe, for the whole Church—the utter *rejection of any such plan, purpose, or even wish.*

Experience has proved, beyond reasonable denial, that the taking one denomination of religious profession into union with the state, and endowing it to the exclusion of others, though coupled with the broadest toleration, is yet productive of great injury to religion itself, and to the peace, union, and stability of civil government. Tests, and richly endowed benefices—things inseparable from an effective church establishments, are, in their very nature inimical to vital piety; while the jealousies and heartburnings of the excluded sects—the most intense and bitter of all the bad feelings known to our fallen nature—not only mar the private concord of families and neighbourhoods, but threaten continually the public repose, and gradually compel a transfer of power to the government, verging upon despotism.

While, therefore, I should feel bound to oppose every attempt of the kind, I am yet fully aware of the high and binding obligation all Christian governments are under (inasmuch as their stability is based upon revealed religion) to provide effectually for the religious instruction of the people ; and so to provide for it, that every Christian denomination shall be able to obtain for its respective families the benefits of education, without compromising their religious principles.   That this can be done, without the establishment and endowment of a particular denomination, I have no hesitation in expressing my full conviction ; and if such a measure should be taken into consideration in my fast waning day, will most gladly contribute my mite to the general stock of friendly and patriotic exertion in this behalf.

Yet, while opposed, upon principle, to any union of Church and State, I am not therefore obliged to see nothing but unmixed evil in the religious establishment of another country—far less am I warranted to make that the theme of denunciation and abuse, from which the whole Christian World has derived incalculable benefit.   I would wish and endeavour to show myself grateful, while I proved that I was independent.   In working this most difficult and most momentous problem, I would strive to hold the balance with an even and a steady hand, and to draw from the experience of others those aids and guards, which may give to the people of this favoured land the full benefit of religious instruction ; while at the same time, it preserves the State from appearing under the weakening and dissolving character of a step-mother to any portion of her children.

On the particular subject, therefore, which has led to these remarks, I cannot help thinking that if Dr. Rice would institute a fair inquiry, and cast up a fair account of the evil and of the good, which the cause of true religion has derived from the English establishment, he might perhaps find occasion both to think and to speak of it, with more candour ; and instead of ascribing to that government the anti-christian purpose of alluring bad men into the Church, by the remuneration provided for the servants of the altar, he might learn that the true motive, the real purpose, was to stimulate and reward piety and learning, in devoting themselves exclusively to the elucidation, support, and defence of revealed truth. And, methinks, while this learned theologian was sitting in his study, meditating his weekly discourses, preparing his *prelections* for his divinity students, or even dissecting Bishop Ravenscroft's Sermons, the company of the mighty dead surrounding him, might have suggested a better motive than the one he has pitched upon, for that liberal endowment, to which we are altogether indebted for their learned labours. Alas! what a meagre, vapid collection would this theological Professor's Library contain, were it stripped of all those works which ecclesiastical endowment has enabled their authors to produce! what a starved and stunted aspect would his divinity class present, were it excluded from the rich pastures of the fathers and standard writers of the Church! Other men have laboured, and we have entered into their labours: surely then, the smallest return we can make, is to manifest a grateful sense of the mighty benefits we thence derive!

Thus might a little calm reflection have saved you from being betrayed into this rash and unfounded denunciation, and led you to understand that the evils growing out of the Church establishment of Great Britain, or of any other country, are no part of the intention of the government, but inseparable from every institution merely human. The corruption of our fallen nature will sooner or later taint every thing connected with it. It will elude the wisest laws, trample on the most sacred obligations, and even defy the wrath of God. Yet laws, and oaths, and the sanctions of eternity are not therefore to be accused as causing this corruption, or as intending to encourage it.

Having thus followed you through the main objections taken to the rule of Vincentius in your review; and having showed satisfactorily, I trust, that they are utterly unsupported either by authority or just reasoning, I might safely, as I think, here conclude my remarks. There are, however, one or two observations of yours connected with your opposition to the rule, which call for a short answer. At p. 320, you take occasion thus to speak:

"Every observer has noticed what a movement is now being made by the Papists through the whole world. The Holy Alliance has infused new courage into the adherents of the Pope. 'His chosen instruments the Jesuits have been re-established in the fulness of their power. Those extraordinary and most dangerous men are again exerting their skill, and trying all their arts. They know that the universal diffusion of the Bible, on the true Protestant principle, is the great obstacle to their success.'* The great battle with the Beast is yet to be fought in this land of ours. Let Bishop R. be upon his guard. Should his life be prolonged, (may GOD preserve it many years,) he will in all probability be called upon to guard his diocese against the inroads and his flock against the artifices of the Jesuits. And we do now solemnly and affectionately forewarn him, if he does not learn a better system of hermeneutics, and take a totally different ground in the interpretation of Scriptures, he will be worsted in the conflict. An ingenious adversary from St. Omers would desire no better assurance of victory than that given by the Bishop in his great canon of interpretation. But let him take his stand on the Bible alone, and he is safe. He may rely upon it he is safe no where else."

Thanking Dr. Rice for the affectionate advice which *his experience* of Jesuitical arts enables him to offer, and assuring him that I will endeavour to profit by it when the dreaded emergency arrives——I trust he will not be offended at my endeavouring once

---

* It is worthy to be noted, how perfectly indifferent such interested declaimers as Dr. Rice, are, either to the consistency or accuracy of their assertions. Whatever may be the truth or the falsehood of what is here said of the courage infused into the Pope by the Holy Alliance, or of the fears of the Jesuits from the dissemination of the Bible, certain it is, that by no individual in the world has so much been done for the distribution of the Bible, and upon the no comment principle, too, as by the late head of the Holy Alliance, the deceased emperor Alexander of Russia. To give encouragement to the Pope and the Jesuits, is certainly no part of the purpose of the Holy Alliance: yet the Pope and the Jesuits too may think they see herein wherewithal to co-operate successfully for their never forgotten interests, and after all be mistaken; just as Dr. Rice may calculate on giving an increased impetus to the prejudices against the Church, by squinting at some connection between that branch of it in this country and the politics of Europe, and thereby manifest to every reflecting mind, that the Church of Rome is not the only Christian denomination which finds it necessary or profitable to employ 'these extraordinary and most dangerous men,' called Jesuits. *Query*—Is the attention of the religious world directed so constantly to the march of popery, in order to call off its observation from the strides of Presbytery to a similar domination ?

more to put him right, as to the place which the rule in question occupies in my system of sacred hermeneutics. Be pleased then to understand distinctly, that in all that relates to salvation, *my stand is on the Bible as supreme.* It is already taken; and I trust, through the grace of GOD, never to be dislodged from it, either by the artifices or the arguments of Romish or Protestant Jesuits. My 'great cannon of interpretation,' as you term it, is only resorted to in cases of disputed doctrine from Scripture; and it is thus resorted to as the most rational, safe, and certain means within the reach of uninspired men, of attaining the truth as it is in JESUS; as is repeatedly stated and exemplified in my *Sermon on the Study and Interpretation of Scripture.* Nor can Dr. Rice, with the collected ingenuity and learning of all the dissenters in the Christian world to help him, present a substitute equally safe and satisfactory to every sincere inquirer after revealed truth. Neither is there a middle ground betwixt the adoption of this rule and the abandonment of unity and agreement in the *faith once delivered to the saints.* If, however, Dr. Rice thinks he can do this, he owes it to the peace of the Christian world, and to his own credit as an honest and sincere man, to bring it forward to public consideration. Especially in the foresight of such a tremendous contest as he predicts, ought this to be the object and endeavour of every true Christian. Divided and split up into fragments as the Christian world at present is, it is in no situation to resist, with the efficacy it might otherwise do, the attacks of an 'ingenious adversary,' whether that adversary shall come from Rome or from Geneva—from Poland or from New England. And in Bishop R's opinion (which he has no desire to conceal) it is not a matter of much though it is certainly of some importance, whether the victory be gained against the *faith* or against the *order* of the gospel. Those are *equally* the revelation of Almighty GOD to the world, and *alike* fundamental to the hope limited on the observance of them as divine appointments. Nor can the Bishop conceive upon what principle of justice or fair reasoning, a corrupt and erroneous view as to the *order* of the gospel, is less an offence against GOD than a corrupt and erroneous view as to the *faith* of the gospel. In other words, why an *honest Unitarian* is less excusable before

GOD than an *honest Presbyterian, Congregationalist*, or *Indepen- dent.* When Dr. Rice can solve this spiritual problem, and show by warrant of Scripture, that a *schismatic* is in a less dangerous condition than a *heretic*, as respects the righteous judgment of GOD, there may be some excuse for the dogmatism of this reviewer *against Unitarians as to the faith of the gospel*, and *in favour of Unitarians as to the order of the gospel.* And though it may be considered presumptuous, Bishop R. hesitates not a moment to express his individual opinion, that the public at large, and the Presbyterian body in particular, have a right to demand at the hands of Dr. Rice, or any other more capable man belonging to it, something better than mere assertion, and delusive *ad captandum* reasoning, on a point so clearly funda- mental as the *order* (in other words, the *authority*) by which the gospel is administered to them, by those men to whom they look up as their spiritual guides.   Yet, to avoid giving room for mis- representation, Bishop R. would caution against any declaration as made by him on the relative magnitude of *heresy* and *schism*, as sins against GOD.   Sufficient it is for him, and as he thinks, for all other men, to know that there are such sins : and that it is both the wiser and the safer part, to avoid the commission of them, than to speculate on their comparative malignity, however ingeniously the theory of essentials and non-essentials may be constructed.   The gospel knows nothing of any such distinction as to the things therein revealed, to the faith and obedience of redeemed man; and, therefore, Bishop R. cannot intrude beyond his warrant, in forming a scale of *comparative* guilt in the observ- ance or neglect of those things which are equally divine in their appointment, and consequently in their obligation.   This may suit a pupil of St. Omers or of Geneva, and may give him an opportunity to show the versatility of his talents ; but is every way unworthy of a Christian bishop, and the cause committed to his guardianship.

Should, therefore, the great battle with the Beast come 'to be fought in this land of ours,' within the limit allotted to Dr. Rice and the Bishop for continuance in this world, Dr. Rice shall see, that Bishop R. will intrench himself within the impregnable bulwark of Scripture, and that he will fight with the sword of the Spirit ; but Bishop R. will not be persuaded to cast away any part of that armour of proof, bequeathed to their successors by the renowned champions of the Protestant faith—Ridley, Jewel, Overall, Andrews, Hall, Beveridge, Bull, and a host of other noble and never-dying names.   Nor yet will he consent to exchange it for any modern system of Hermeneutics ; he has no wish to be led away after *opposition of science, falsely so called,* preferring words to things.   With the Bible in one hand, and the testimony of consentient antiquity as to its true meaning, in the other, he feels *strong in the* LORD *and in the power of his might,* to meet the beast—whether it shall be the many-horned monster of Popish blasphemy, or the anti-christian unicorn of Socinian heresy.   What was so profitable in the contest with the Church of Rome at the time of the Reformation, must again be equally serviceable, should the battle be renewed ; and what occasions Unitarians, whether as to the *order* or the *faith* of the gospel, to writhe and twist so fearfully under its bare announcement, must prove fatal to their cause under the just application of its unerring blows.   And whatever the event may be, of which he certainly feels no depressing apprehensions, if Bishop R. is doomed to fall in the contest, whether by Dissenters, or by Romanists, or by Unitarians, his resolution is immoveably taken, that it shall be under the banner of the cross, and in the armour of the primitive Church.

At page 324, you further remark :

" We are very sorry to find Bishop R. treading in the steps of high churchmen in England, who persist, with deplorable ignorance, or inexcusable perverseness, in confounding *Separatists* from the Established Church, with such as they call *Heretics.*"

Do they, indeed ?   Really I should have supposed, that high churchmen understood better the meaning of words, and would rather have denominated such persons *Schismatics.*   But the ' ignorance' and ' perverseness,' I presume, consists in applying either name to them.   Will Dr. Rice, then, be pleased to tell us, by what name to distinguish those persons who, in the first place, hold doctrine *unknown* to the primitive Church, and con-

trary to *the faith once delivered to the saints ;* and in the next place, have actually rent the body of CHRIST, and originated orders, and set up a communion (indeed communions) for themselves? For high churchman although I am, I do very sincerely declare, that I have no wish to give offence. Yet I cannot consent to betray that cause, for defence of which I am set, because unreasonable men choose to be offended at the use of Scripture language.

The Scriptures certainly tell us of *damnable heresies,* in the plural number; so that the denial of the Saviour's Divinity is not the only one, though very artfully insinuated, by some writers and many talkers of the present day. The same Scriptures likewise, warn most earnestly against the sin of *schism,* as a breach of external order in the Church of CHRIST, and not as a breach of the royal law of Christian love. Now, beyond all controversy, there must be some plain and certain method whereby to determine what constitutes a *heresy,* and what amounts to the deadly sin of *schism ;* and this so readily, as to condemn every man who refuses to submit his case to the test. And here again this troublesome rule comes in, which, with unerring precision, determines the question as a matter of fact. And when thus determined, assuredly there can be neither perverseness nor uncharitableness in calling things by their right names.

But there may be great perverseness, in refusing so competent and so impartial an umpire as the universal judgment of primitive antiquity. And there may be great address manifested, in so stating the case, as to mislead the mere general reader; which has unhappily been resorted to in the present instance.

For it is not because they have separated themselves from the Church as by law established, that those ignorant and perverse high churchmen consider these *Separatists,* either heretics or schismatics; but because, together with new and erroneous doctrine, they have divided themselves from that branch of the catholic and apostolic Church of CHRIST, which is established by law as the national Church of that kingdom. Its being the established Church is a mere accident, nowise constituting the offence, as against GOD. Heresy and schism, as Scripture-denounced sins against the *one faith and order* of the gospel, are altogether independent of Acts of Parliament and religious establishments.   As human laws cannot create either of those offences, so neither can they rescind them.   As we have the most undeniable proof that they were committed before such a thing as an alliance between Church and State was thought of; so is it equally certain that we may be guilty of them, where no religious establishment is known.   On the other hand, where the Church by law established is not apostolically derived, the separating ourselves from the communion is not the sin of schism, denounced and warned against in the Scriptures of our faith— the essence of that sin consisting wholly in its opposition to, and separation from, the *external order of the Church of* CHRIST, *as instituted by divine authority.*   And if Dr. Rice's system of sacred Hermeneutics has not enabled him to draw this view of the subject from the word of GOD, it forms an additional reason why Bishop R. cannot accept of it as a substitute for that which he has already adopted.

But if Dr. Rice will take the trouble to imagine a heresy, or a schism, which cannot be clearly detected to be such by the application of this rule to the passage or passages of Scripture on which it is founded, Bishop R. will not only be thankful for the new light thus shed upon the meaning of Scripture, but he will cast away the rule as worthless.   Yea more; if Dr. Rice will condescend to show by authority from Scripture, or from the judgment of consentient antiquity, or even from the reason of the thing, that opposite and contradictory *doctrine*, and separated and divided *order*, in religion, may exist among Christians, without involving the sins of *heresy* and *schism* on one side or the other, Bishop R. will certainly cease to be what is called a high churchman ; indeed he will, in such case, cease to be a churchman of any grade ; for when this shall be done, *the law shall perish from the priest, and counsel from the ancients*—all trust and confidence in revelation, as the unchangeable word of the Most High GOD, will be scattered to the four winds of heaven.

But why not come at once to the point ? Of necessity Bishop Ravenscroft, and those who think and act with him, must be *heretics in doctrine*, and *schismatics in order* to Dr. Rice ; OR, Dr. Rice, and those who think and act with him, must be *heretics in doctrine*, and *schismatics in order* to Bishop Ravenscroft : because they profess doctrines as opposite to each other, as the east is to the west ; and are as far separated, in derivation of order, as heaven is from earth.   Now as it is equally the duty and the interest of both parties, to avoid the guilt of those sins ; and as their bare assertions are of no worth to decide the point, Bishop Ravenscroft offers to submit to the judgment of the primitive Church, as to the true interpretation of the passages of Scripture respectively relied upon, but which each charges the other with understanding and applying erroneously.   This judgment, however, Dr. Rice refuses to stand to, for reasons best known to himself.   But for the sake of faith and charity—for healing divisions, and promoting the cause of true religion—will Dr. Rice be entreated to devise some plan, equally scriptural, comprehensive, and certain, to which the several pretensions of the various Christian denominations may be submitted ?   If he will do this, Bishop R. promises faithfully to submit to its determination.   And surely the man who decides so confidently, that ' Bishop R's plan won't do,' must be able to point out its defects, and to supply what shall better promote so every way desirable an event, as real Christian unity !

But if this shall not seem good in his eyes, let him at least understand better what the principles of high churchmen really are, before he undertakes to brand them with the epithets of ignorant and perverse.   That they are ignorant of this modern delusion of a spurious charity, which claims for opposite and divided classes of religious profession, the right to be considered and treated as true branches of the one catholic and apostolic Church of CHRIST, they most freely admit.   They are ignorant of it, because such a right is no where conceded to inventions of men, by any just construction of Scripture as the standard to all.   And in things of this nature, high churchmen acknowledge no other ground of certainty, than the word of GOD rightly interpreted.   That they are perverse men, they humbly venture to consider as a mere railing accusation, unsupported by any thing better than the Reviewer's bare assertion ;—unless indeed it shall be considered a mark of perverseness, to hold the word of GOD as interpreted by the first and purest ages, in preference to all modern systems of Hermeneutics. To perverseness, in this sense, they most cheerfully plead guilty, and hope by the help of GOD to continue steadfast in this mind, though every form, shape, and shade of heresy and schism, shall unite in denouncing it. Other than in this course they cannot keep a good conscience; and they are willing even to suffer for it, should it please GOD to require this of them.

Yet, though High Churchmen, they are not indiscriminate in their views. While they declare error in doctrine publicly maintained, and made a term of communion, to be heresy; and separation from the apostolic order of the Church of CHRIST, to be schism; they are, nevertheless well aware of the difference in the degree of guilt, which is consequent on the circumstance of the case. To those who are nurtured and brought up in error—who drink in with their mother's milk, as it were, the seeds of heresy and schism, yet manifest the good effects of that portion of divine truth which is therewith mixed up; High Churchmen gladly hope, that His mercy, *who knows how to have compassion on the ignorant, and* ON THEM THAT ARE OUT OF THE WAY, will be extended—that as GOD is pleased to permit such things to be, and to continue, for the trial of the faith of his elect, so in the plenitude of his *infinite and unpledged mercy* there will be found a place of refuge for their souls, through the *unlimited* atonement of the blood of CHRIST. But as they find no warrant in the word of GOD for this latitude of condition among Christians, but rather the reverse; they dare not resort to their own reasonings, *as a ground of revealed hope* to such persons. High Churchmen *Preach not themselves, but* CHRIST JESUS *the* LORD. They therefore denounce these sins of heresy and schism, and warn against them, and by every means sanctioned by the word of GOD strive to bring back those who are in error to a better mind. Amongst which means they consider none better calculated to awaken reflection, than the *true* and *Scriptural* doctrines; *That* GOD's *promises are limited to the visible Church. That the Church can be verified no otherwise than by apostolical succession, through the line of Bishops, as distinct from Presbyters ; and that consequently, every religious condition, not thus verifiable, is destitute of revealed hope, and can have no Scriptural ground of assurance.* And they confidently call upon Low Churchmen, and Dissenters of every name, from Theological Professors and D. Ds, downwards, to lay aside invective and assertion, and show wherein in this, or any other particular of their real principles, High Churchmen are unscriptural. But as a mere assertion amounts to nothing but impudence, when unsupported by sufficient proof ; as it is as competent to one man as to another, to lay claim to the ministerial character, and to every denomination of Christians, to call themselves Churches of CHRIST ; and as all mankind are in the highest degree interested in the subject, inasmuch as the whole virtue and validity of the sacraments as means of grace, and visible pledges of purchased and promised blessings, depend on the divine right by which they are consecrated and administered ; High Churchmen most willingly submit their claim to the high distinction of *stewards of the mysteries of* GOD, to the most rigid scrutiny, as a matter of fact. They reject, as unscriptural and fanatical, any internal persuasion of a man's own mind, or any pretences to a call of the SPIRIT, as a sufficient ground to assume the ministerial office, and *supercede a lawful external, scriptural, ordination.* They earnestly exhort all serious persons to examine carefully the authority by which their spiritual guides undertake to assume that office ; and if in this there is any thing unscriptural, uncharitable or disrespectful to any one bearing the Christian name, be pleased to point it out, and it shall be amended.

The last point growing out of your objections to the rule, which I shall notice, is found at p. 325, 326.

To show the fallacy of the very common and favourite notion of the Dissenters, that the various divisions of Christian profession differ only in *non-essentials ;* in the *Sermon on the Study and Interpretation of Scripture,* I put the following questions :

" Is the extent of the redemption that is in CHRIST JESUS—that is, whether it extends to all, or only a part of mankind—

a fundamental doctrine of the Christian revelation? And can those who are opposed to each other on this point, be said, with any show of common sense, to hold the doctrine in common? Is the essential divinity, or the mere humanity, of our Redeemer, (considered as conclusive of the doctrine of the Trinity,) a fundamental doctrine of Christianity, or a non-essential? And can the opposite opinions upon this article of the faith, be said to hold it in common?"

On these questions you remark, p. 325.

"We know not how to express our astonishment that a distinguished prelate in the Protestant Episcopal Church should manifest such very imperfect knowledge of the history of theology, as is here indicated. The *fundamental* doctrine of the divinity of CHRIST (including the doctrine of the Trinity) is joined with the question concerning the *extent of the atonement,* for the purpose of showing that *Christian denominations* do not agree in fundamentals!"

By your leave, Sir, your astonishment might have been better bestowed; for whether from ignorance or artifice, you have misstated the point. The divinity of CHRIST is *not* joined with the question concerning the extent of the atonement. The questions, as put in the Sermon, are distinct, and perfectly disjointed. But as the first question was rather too direct for a precise answer from a Calvinist; the second must be shuffled into it, to open the way for an escape: and what follows, at p. 326, furnishes as complete a specimen of evasive management, as if it had come from St. Omers itself.

"We would ask of the bishop (say you) will all men be finally saved? He answers in the negative—Well: one class of men holds that *redemption* is unlimited in its *nature,* but confined in its application. To this class we suppose Bishop R. belongs. Another class holds that the atonement is sufficient in its nature for the whole world, but designed by him who made it only for those who will finally be saved. Does not Bishop R. see, that much here is held in common? And that there is the widest imaginable difference, between these brethren, and the unhappy men who deny the atonement altogether?"

Whatever Bishop R. may see, or may not see, to be held in common by the two classes who profess to believe the doctrine of atonement to some *extent*, is wholly unimportant at present. The question is, does the atonement made upon the cross by the SON OF GOD, *extend to all, or only a part of mankind ?*   To this Dr. Rice replies with all the guardedness of indefinite language, and in changed terms ; that some 'hold a *redemption* unlimited in its *nature*, but confined in its application ;' that others 'hold an *atonement* sufficient in its *nature* for the whole world, but *designed* by him who made it only for those who will be saved;' and very adroitly shifts the attention of his reader to the wide difference between the two classes who hold the doctrine of atonement at all, and those who reject it entirely.

But as the question was put—first, to refute the unfounded, but extensively relied upon, and industriously circulated notion, that Christian denominations differ only in *non essentials ;* and secondly, to show the use and application of the rule given in the Sermon, to the Calvinistical doctrine, as to the *extent* of the atonement ; I must call Dr. Rice back to it, and in the very terms in which it is worded : I cannot accept the word *redemption*, for the word *atonement ;* or the word *nature* for the word *extent ;* or the word *sufficient*, for the word *unlimited ;* or even the word *designed*, for the word *limited ;* in the discussion of this point. For I do mean to affirm, even at the risk of betraying my ignorance 'of the history of theological doctrine,' *that the extent of the atonement is fundamental to the Christian revelation :* and in such wise fundamental to any rational preaching of the gospel, that no ingenuity can show the reasonableness of requiring the conditions of the gospel from those, who have neither part or lot in that atonement, upon which *alone* the gospel is founded, and without which, it never could have been revealed, and *commanded to be preached* AMONG ALL NATIONS *for the obedience of faith.*

And I earnestly desire to know, and in such language as a plain man can understand, how it is possible for a Minister of CHRIST who holds a *Calvinistically limited atonement*, to press the duties and obligations—the hopes and the fears—the grace and the assurance of the Gospel, upon all mankind without exception.   Show us, if you please, upon what principle of reason or religion it can be said to a fallen creature, debarred all benefit from the atonement of the cross of CHRIST, *Believe in the* LORD JESUS CHRIST, *and thou shalt be saved !*

But to expose the sophistry in which you have endeavoured to wrap up this vital, and therefore fundamental subject, I observe further, that I do belong to that class of men who hold, that the atonement made upon the cross for human sin by the SON OF GOD, *our* LORD JESUS CHRIST, is not only *sufficient* in its *nature* for the whole world ; but was *designed* by him who made it, and does actually embrace and include in its *extent,* every fallen sinner, from Adam to the end of time—as well those who *perish,* as those who are *saved.*   I also hold that this atonement, thus unlimited in the *design* of him who made it, and in the *extent* of its comprehension, is yet *limited in its application.*   On the other hand, you belong to that class of men, who hold an atonement *sufficient in its nature* for the whole world ; but *designed by him who made it, only for those who will finally be saved.*   Now while this representation of the subject is so worded, that readers in general would suppose that much is held in common by you and myself, and the respective classes to which we adhere, on the doctrine of the atonement: it is nevertheless as complete a deception as can be played off upon the mind, by the use of indefinite language.   For, in truth, there is nothing in common but the word *atonement.*   As a practical doctrine—as the foundation of the Gospel—as the groundwork of hope to a fallen, sin-ruined world, there exists such a direct opposition of professed belief, as places one of us in the wrong, beyond the reach of palliation : because it is not an opposition of argumentative conclusion from admitted premises, but an opposition as to the premises themselves—as to the actual declarations of GOD, in the word spoken unto us by his Son.

I believe and profess, in agreement with the Scriptures and the standard set forth by the Church in her Articles of Faith, that the atonement of the cross of CHRIST *is limited in the application of its benefits to mankind no otherwise, than by their own perverseness, impenitence, and ungodliness ;* whereas you believe and profess, in agreement with the Westminster Confession of

THE DOCTRINES OF THE CHURCH VINDICATED.

Faith, which is the standard of Presbyterian doctrine, that the atonement of CHRIST's death *is limited in its application to men, by the act and decree of* GOD *himself.*   This is plainly and precisely the difference between us on this point.   I believe and teach *that* JESUS CHRIST, *by the grace of* GOD, *tasted death for every man :—that* GOD *is not willing that any should perish, but that all should come to repentance.*   On the contrary, you believe and teach (if, as I am bound to presume, you are an *ex animo* subscriber of the Westminster Confession of Faith) that JESUS CHRIST, by the grace of GOD, tasted death for *a part only of mankind*—that GOD *is willing that a part of his creatures should perish*—*having doomed them to perdition from all eternity.*   Now what is there held in common between us, on this fundamental doctrine, beyond the word ' atonement' ?   As ministers of *the manifold grace of* GOD, can we meet our fellow-sinners on the same ground ?   Can we propose to them the same gospel, the same means of grace, the same Saviour, the same GOD ? Surely not.   For if a part of mankind are precluded from all benefit of the atonement of CHRIST's blood, by a decree of Almighty GOD, how can the man who really believes that such is the case, press the gospel duties of faith and holiness, and the end everlasting life, upon every soul of man ?   Hence it is evident, as I think, not only that the *extent* of the atonement is a fundamental doctrine of the Christian revelation, *but that such a difference of opinion as to the extent of it,* as exists betwixt you and myself, is also *fundamental ;* inasmuch as the error, on whichever side that shall be found, amounts to blasphemy.   And to determine which is in error, I propose in the *Sermon,* to submit it to the determination of the Christian Church of the three first centuries, as the best qualified, and most impartial tribunal before which this controversy can be brought.   This, however, you refuse ; and wisely, in one sense of the word ; nothing being more certain, than that to have held and taught, as an article of the Christian faith, that a part of mankind were precluded from all possible benefit of the atonement of CHRIST's death, *by a decree of Almighty* GOD, would have been considered and treated *as a blasphemous heresy* by the primitive Church.

I trust, therefore, that we shall hear no more of the Calvinism of the seventeenth, or of any other of the thirty-nine Articles of the Protestant Episcopal Church, however desirable it may be to bolster up that hideous doctrine with so sound and Scriptural a standard of the faith.   Nor has Bishop R. any fears, that his views on this subject are calculated to 'cut off from the one catholic and apostolic Church, many who have long been regarded as its brightest ornaments.' For beyond all reasonable dispute the *predestination* which is held, subscribed, and preached from the seventeenth Article, in full connexion with the *general redemption*, grounded on an *atonement unlimited in its extent by any act or decree of Almighty* GOD, which is set forth in the thirty-first Article ; is something *very distinct* from that *predestination* which is held, subscribed, and preached, in *ex animo* connexion with that *particular redemption*, grounded on an *atonement limited in its extent by the decree of Almighty*, set forth in the 3d chap. of the Westminster Confession of Faith.   And let this be forever borne in mind, as the complete refutation of every attempt to fasten the *predestination* of Calvin upon the standards of the Church, in her Articles, Liturgy, and Homilies. These know nothing of the *horribile decretum* of Geneva, and for this plain and sufficient reason—neither the Scriptures, nor the primitive Church in its purer days, knew any thing of any such decree.

But not only have you misstated the point, by blending the two questions put in the Sermons to show that Christian denominations are not divided upon non-essentials only ; but by choosing to confine the denial of our LORD's divinity to the modern Unitarians, the full design of the second question, as connected with the rule, is defeated.   'Does not Bishop R. know,' say you, 'that no Church has ever acknowledged Unitarians as a part of the body of CHRIST ?'   Bishop R. certainly knows, that *the Church* has never acknowledged them as such ; but he cannot undertake to say what some of the many varieties of Christian Dissent may have done in this respect.   So far as his own immediate observation goes, persons of this way of thinking prefer the service of the Dissenters, particularly the Presbyterians, to those of the Church.   There is something too direct, and too constantly recurring, against their views, in the Liturgy of the Church, for them to feel easy under it ; and they consequently resort where they are less harrowed in their feelings. But the Bishop also knows, and to this point the second question is directed, that the doctrine of the atonement is held by those, who yet deny the *essential divinity* of the Redeemer of sinners. The Bishop's 'very imperfect knowledge of the history of theology,' has taught him, that the acknowledgment of the atonement made by the Saviour, is not decisive, either of his *essential divinity*, or of the *doctrine of the Trinity, as fundamental to the faith of a Christian*. The Arians held the doctrine of the atonement. The second edition of that heresy in the older Socinians, allowed "not only that the death of CHRIST and the pouring out of his blood for us, was an offering and sacrifice to GOD ; but that this sacrifice may be said to have been offered up for our sins, in order to their being forgiven." Some anti-trinitarians, as Mr. Tomkins and Dr. Watts, nevertheless, hold the doctrine of the atonement in some sense. It is by the modern Socinians, self-named Unitarian Christians, that both the divinity and the atonement of the LORD JESUS CHRIST are denied and rejected. And surely, Dr. Rice ought to be aware, that in such an unlimited latitude of non-belief as is permitted by this class of religionists, too much care cannot be taken to guard against their intrusion into the Christian name. They already claim it ; and that indifference to the *distinctive, limited character of the Church of* CHRIST, which the principles advocated by Dr. Rice throughout these Reviews tend so palpably to encourage, defend, and establish, will ere long yield it to them, as a duty of that *liberal charity*, which is now so fashionable. Nor can Bishop R. possibly see upon what ground it can be denied to them, whilst it is yielded to the rest of the numerous divisions and subdivisions into which Christianity is split up. Upon Dr. Rice's great principle, *the Bible interpreted by our best reason*, they cannot consistently be denied this concession ; and may justly complain, that what Dr. Rice claims so absolutely for himself, and other Dissenters, he yet refuses to them.

But Bishop R. cannot yield this point. He cannot surrender GOD's true and faithful word to the goddess of reason. And he trusts that he has showed sufficiently that such was not the fundamental principle of the reformation. He would, therefore, bind down himself and Dr. Rice, and all dissenters, both Trinitarian and Unitarian, to the Scriptures of truth, as understood, believed, and acted upon by the Church catholic of the three first centuries. In his judgment, no other method of settling disputed doctrine, of ending divisions, and producing that unity which is so desirable, and which is so essential to the triumph of the gospel, can be proposed equally competent and impartial, and alike reconcileable with the just claims of reason and conscience. And he would gladly hope, that when generally known in the extent of its application, when considered and digested into practical form by some abler head than his own, there will be found so much of real Christianity amid the shapeless mass of its modern profession, as to resort to it with a sincere desire that Christians may all *speak the same thing,* and *with one heart and one mouth glorify* GOD.

. This would indeed be a result worthy the sacrifice of all prejudice and party distinctions ; a result to be desired and prayed and laboured for by every true Christian. But it is to be feared that the set time is not yet come. Nevertheless, until, in the providence of Almighty GOD, it shall be brought round, there is an intermediate duty equally imperious, and never to be lost sight of by Christians, which is, *to contend* EARNESTLY *for the faith once delivered to the saints ;* to which apostolic injunction, Bishop R. will take leave to add—and *as it was delivered.* This was his governing principle in preparing the sermons which have so greatly alarmed Dr. Rice not only for his own particular form of faith and order, but for the general interests of religion. This is his governing principle in the notice he has found himself bound to take of the perversions, mis-statements of authorities, unfounded assertions, and erroneous reasonings, contained in these reviews. This was his single aim in proposing originally that rule of interpretation of Scripture, as to points of disputed doctrine or order, against which such an effort has been put forth. It is his sole purpose in the extended examination he has given to the objections brought against it. And it is for the public to determine, whether the rule has stood the severe test to which it has been subjected ; and Dr. Rice whether consequently bound, by his voluntary pledge, to adopt it, even under the foreseen alternative of enriching the Church of Rome, at the expense of the Church Presbyterian.

In drawing his remarks to a close, Bishop Ravenscroft would have been truly glad, had it suited Dr. Rice to confine himself to what appeared to him objectionable in the sermons themselves. The interests of his party, however, or, as he may choose to term it, the interests of the community, have led him to mingle political considerations with questions purely religious; and to bring forward the serious charge of the surrender of the Episcopal Church in America to the views of a foreign influence, alike hostile to our civil and religious institutions. His words are these :

"Here, therefore, is a priesthood to be regarded as the accredited agents of heaven ; in whom we must place our faith as to things essential to our authorized hopes of salvation ! Now if this is the preacher's meaning, we are unable to express our sorrow and astonishment to hear such sentiments from an evangelical minister, in a Protestant country, and that country *America.* Our astonishment arises from this, that with these opinions Bishop R. professes to derive every thing from the Bible : our sorrow, from the fact that many of our countrymen are greatly prejudiced against Christianity, from its supposed hostility to civil and political liberty; and we greatly fear that the avowal of such sentiments by a distinguished and justly admired preacher, will serve to strengthen these prejudices : *especially at this time when strenuous efforts are made to bring the influences of religion, as it is modified by European establishments, to bear on the moral feeling and opinion of this country.* In the United States we have happily thrown off the yoke of ecclesiastical bondage ; *and religion, as it prevails among us, is admirably suited to support our political institutions, and give security to our liberty.* And we have no doubt but that *all* Christians rejoice in their privileges. But while this is so ; what would one of our jealous politicians say, on scanning the sentiments of these sermons ; and particularly the parts under consideration ? Would he not ask, and with great earnestness too, What will be the result if these opinions should become general ? Where would be the limits of ecclesiastical influence and power ?"—December No. p. 653, 654.

Again. "*Many of the sentiments here advanced are, as we verily believe, at war with the best interests of religion, and with the true genius of our institutions ;* and we regard it as a solemn duty to oppose them in every way consistent with the character of Christians."—April No. p. 203.

Once more. "We clearly see to what all these things tend. A vigorous effort is being made in this country, privately by some, openly by others, to persuade the people that there is no true Church of CHRIST, but the Episcopal Church ; no true ministers but her ministers ; no scriptural hope of salvation, but such as is warranted by her administrations ; no ecclesiastical authority, but that vested in her Bishops ; and that the only way by which the people at large can verify the true Church, and learn what they must believe and do for salvation, is to hear the Bishops and Priests, and commit themselves exclusively to their spiritual direction. *There are many more influences at work to accomplish this object, in this country than the people are aware of. It is high time for the public attention to be awakened to this thing. We do conscientiously believe that success in this project will deeply injure the Episcopal Church in her true interests ; will be destructive to the cause of piety ; will operate against those principles which are most dear to us as Americans."*—May No. p. 254.

"*There is an American principle in regard to these matters,* which exerts itself with mighty efficiency. And on the fullest examination, we believe that it is *the very principle which prevailed in the primitive Church.*—p. 255.

Lastly.—"Bishop Ravenscroft, in two Sermons, with which our readers are somewhat acquainted, set up the highest pretensions of High Church, and denounced all preachers who have not received episcopal ordination, as intruders into the sacred office, and as ministers of Satan, &c. &c. He also, begs pardon for having in times past, yielded to the pretensions of a *spurious modern charity,* and promises hereafter to discard all 'false tenderness' from his bosom. True to his purpose, on being requested to preach the annual Sermon of the Bible Society of North Carolina, he delivered a discourse directly against that institution, and all others of a similar organization in the world. The great object of the preacher was *to prove the insufficiency of the Scripture as a guide to heaven.* This is followed by a fourth Sermon, in which he fills up his system, and tries to persuade us, that we must acknowledge the Church as the authorised interpreter of the Bible. We have been made to understand, that the episcopal clergy of North-Carolina follow their Diocesan. *We know that sentiments of a similar character are boldly advanced in New-York, by a man of learning and talents ; and that the wealth of the richest church in the United*

States is pledged for their support. We have satisfactory evidence, too, that influence from abroad is made to bear on the religious character of our population. In a word, exertions are made to extend opinions among us which we do conscientiously believe to be injurious both to the Church and to society."—June No. p. 330, 331.

Such are the terms in which Dr. Rice is pleased to express himself, on the subject of the Protestant Episcopal Church, of her Bishops, Clergy, and Laity, in these United States, and of the plain and evident tendency of the principles laid down and supported by Bishop Ravenscroft in his published Sermons. Here is no allowance made or provided for, that either the fears or the fancy, or the prejudices, or even the ignorance of Dr. Rice, may have led him astray, and caused him to form an erroneous estimate, either of the circumstances on which his charge against the Church is constructed, or of the fair and reasonable conclusions from the authorities and argument of his opponent. Bishop R. is certainly surprized at the turn thus given to the controversy, but he is at the same time pleased and even thankful; a direct and open adversary, or a plain and direct accusation, he knows how to meet; the subtle ingenious management of the St. Omer's school, is less congenial to his mind.

To the charge then as brought against the Church, Bishop Ravenscroft can here oppose nothing but his most fixed belief that it is totally void of all colour, even, of support; and those which refer to himself personally, are gratuitously false and slanderous. He cannot, to be sure, know what may be going on in every diocese, of this extended country; but as he feels that *he* would spurn the very thought of subserviency to any foreign influence, he judges by the same rule, of *the rest* of his brethren.

As the charge however is made, and with a name to it, he desires that it may be sifted to the bottom, and a full and fair investigation had, whether there is any just and reasonable ground for it; or whether it is one of those desperate appeals to existing prejudice, of which an honourable man would disdain to avail himself. Bishop Ravenscroft, therefore, demands at the hands of Dr. John Rice, the Theological Professor of the Presbyterian Synod of the State of Virginia, as an act of justice to the Episcopal Church, and to the community at large, to give form and substance to this treasonable charge—to produce ' the *satisfactory evidence*' he says he is possessed of, ' *that foreign influence is made to bear on the religious character of our population*'—to name the guilty persons engaged in this conspiracy against the civil and religious liberties of this Country ; that public odium may fall where it is merited, and the innocent be shielded from so wanton and unwarranted a denunciation.

For himself personally, as implicated in this charge, Bishop R. demands, that Dr. Rice shall specify and point out those sentiments in his published Sermons, or even in his private discourse, which ' *are at war with the best interests of religion, and with the true genius of our institutions.*' This he demands, as a right, which Dr. R. is *morally* bound to render, not only to Bishop R. but to the public. If the Bishop is this *wolf in sheep's clothing*, prostituting the sacred station which he fills by the providence of Almighty GOD, to undermine the civil and religious liberties of his country, in the name of justice let him, or his accuser, be dragged forth to merited disgrace and punishment. In the mean time, and until Dr. Rice shall come forward to sustain his charges, Bishop R. will take leave to say, that the whole of these kind and charitable insinuations are as totally void of any foundation in fact, as it is utterly devoid of truth that the great object of the Sermon before the Bible Society of North Carolina was, ' *to prove the insufficiency of the Scriptures as a guide to heaven.*'

With these proofs of a disposition on the part of Dr. Rice to impute a high degree of moral turpitude to some part of the Episcopal Church not yet designated, and personally to Bishop R. both as a man and as a minister of religion, he cannot consent to accept the artful salvo with which these charges are qualified.

" We do not insinuate," (says Dr. Rice) " that Bishop R. or any of his brethren, are less zealous friends of civil and political liberty than other Christians. We protest utterly against an inference of this kind." " We think it necessary again to declare, that we do not make Bishop R. and his associates responsible for the consequences of these opinions. We believe these gentlemen to be sincere in their devotion to Christianity and in their attachment to the institutions of our common country."

What, then, does Dr. Rice mean to insinuate? For what, then, are Bishop R. and his associates made responsible; if not for the consequences of their considered and published opinions? And wherefore did Dr. Rice take the pains to hunt out this moral treason, in some part at least, if not in the whole of the Episcopal Church, and obtain satisfactory evidence of the fact, and denounce Bishop R. as a religious aristocrat, (p. 255) hostile alike to the civil and religious liberties of his country, if it is to be neutralized by an artifice of this kind? But the trick is too stale, to pass upon any man who regards his character. In the present instance, it is adding insult to injury; for Dr. Rice is old enough, and sufficiently experienced in human nature, to be well aware that the *charge* will be taken by his readers in full, and without any abatement, while the *qualification* will remain unheeded. Bishop R. therefore holds Dr. Rice responsible for a wanton attack upon the character of the Church, and upon himself, personally; and appeals to the public, that the charge may be substantiated, and the guilty exposed.*

[* The remainder of the tract, as originally published, containing the refutation of a personal charge, is omitted, in conformity with Bishop Ravenscroft's erasure.]

AN EPISCOPAL CHARGE.

DELIVERED TO THE

CONVENTION OF THE PROTESTANT EPISCOPAL CHURCH,

ASSEMBLED IN WASHINGTON, N. C., IN APRIL, 1825.

AN EPISCOPAL CHARGE.

THE period has arrived, my brethren, when personal observation of the state of this diocese enables me to fulfil a duty of my station, in an Address, by way of Charge, to the clergy and laity of the Protestant Episcopal Church in North Carolina; and I very gladly embrace the opportunity of this annual assemblage of the representatives of the Church in Convention, to present to their consideration those particulars which are of greatest importance, at present, to the progress and success of the cause we have in hand.

From the information given to this Convention in my Episcopal Journal, and the subsequent Parochial Reports, the gradual improvement in the external circumstances of the Church is very evident; and it is no more than a reasonable expectation, that a continuance of the same course of labour and diligence in the clergy, and attention on the part of the laity, will be followed by a like favourable result.

There are some causes, however, more remote from general observation, which operate injuriously to the advancement of the Church, but which are in the reach of a remedy, and which it is our joint duty to endeavour to remove.

The first I shall mention is WANT OF INFORMATION in the people at large, and in too great a degree among those of our own communion, ON THE DISTINCTIVE CHARACTER OF THE CHURCH OF CHRIST, and the obligations which thence follow to man, thus furnished with this means of grace.

That it exists in a very extensive and injurious degree, is a point which needs no proof; it being the daily experience of most of those who hear me. And while it can be accounted for very satisfactorily, in my opinion, it is from the causes producing it that we shall best learn what is most proper to counteract it.

We have, then, but to direct our attention to the state of things produced by the downfall of the Church at the period of our revolution, and to what has followed progressively since, until within a very few years, to find ample means of accounting for this state of the public mind. The Episcopal Church, never very strong in this State, was reduced by that great event to a condition of actual silence. Political feelings were associated with its very name, which operated as a complete bar to any useful or comfortable exercise of duty, by the very few clergymen, perhaps not more than three or four, who were left.

The public instruction of the people in religion, therefore, fell exclusively into other hands, and into hands disposed, both by principle and interest, to complete the ruin of the Church; and, by their particular systems of doctrine, precluded from treating, with any precision, that branch of Christian edification which refers to the unity of the Church of CHRIST, its distinctive character and religious purpose, and to the authority of the Christian ministry, as an integral part of that system of of faith and order revealed in the Gospel. On such points of doctrine, those who have separated from the Church are necessarily silent; or, if they are occasionally hinted at, it is in such vague and indefinite terms as tend rather to obscure than to elucidate the subject. It is not to be wondered at, then, my brethren, that these doctrines, as held by the Episcopal Church, should gradually lose their impression on those who entertained them, be lost sight of by the people at large, and at length be forgotten; and that a prescription of forty years should possess an influence difficult to dislodge from the minds of those who have been taught to view every thing relating to the external order of the Church as unimportant and non-essential. That this is the more general state of the public mind, I have all the certainty which observation and declared opinion can give; and the very painful knowledge, that many who call themselves Episcopalians cherish such every way inconsistent notions, and are further led into this error by the modern but erroneous views of charity and liberal opinions. While this state of things continues, we shall deceive ourselves egregiously if we expect any real or extensive increase of the Church; our numbers may indeed be added to, but the *numerical* is not always the *real* strength either of the Church or of an army.

On you, then, my brethren of the clergy, will devolve the imperious duty of so framing and directing your public ministrations, as well as your private instructions among your respective charges, as to embrace these long neglected but vital doctrines, and to explain and enforce them, from the word of GOD and the reason of the thing, as parts of that system of revealed truth, which forms but one whole, and cannot be broken up to suit the particular notions of any man or body of men. In coming to this duty, however, my reverend brethren, it is my part to warn you to set your faces, like a flint, against the misrepresentations and reproaches of pretended friends and real enemies, who will be sure to combine against you, and to throw every obstacle in the way. But, for your encouragement, let me remind you that it is a work of necessity, mercy, and charity : of necessity, as to the edification of your own flock ; of mercy, as to those multitudes who are perishing for lack of knowledge; of charity, as to those who have embraced the error, in presenting them with the means of detecting and escaping from it. But, further, as you are to *declare the whole counsel of* GOD, and to *keep back nothing that is profitable* to your hearers, so are you bound by your ordination vow, " to be ready, with all faithful diligence, to banish and drive away from the Church all erroneous and strange doctrines, contrary to GOD's word."

Against this, my admonition to you, and against your attention to it, you must be prepared to meet and to disregard the odium attached to a controversial spirit ; because it can in no sense be made to apply to the duty every pastor owes to his flock, in warning them against error, however that error may be sanctioned by others ; and it is high time that this cunning method, of giving religious error time to establish itself and eventually interdicting the only possible method of refusing and overturning it, be resisted. Those, and those only, who have a miserable interest in the prevalence of error, will resort to such an untenable argument against the discussion of those points on which the professing world is so divided; and when it is evident that the operation of this and similar deceptive principles is gradually producing an indifference, coldness, and deadness, to revealed religion, which indicate the temper predicted of the latter day, it surely becomes the duty of the ministers of CHRIST to *contend earnestly for the faith*—to remember that they are watchmen in Zion, and that if they give no warning, the price of blood will be required at their hands. But it does not follow, my reverend brothers, that in exposing error an angry and acrimonious temper or style is necessary. No : on the contrary it is to be avoided, both for our own sakes and the sake of others ; and the only just objection to religious controversy is the intemperance into which it is too apt to degenerate. This, then, is to be guarded against, while we equally bear in mind, that the time is come when great plainness of speech is required, if we hope to rouse men to the serious consideration of those things which make for their peace ; if we would, indeed, draw that line between divine truth and human error, whereby all may profit who are disposed to come to the light.

A second point, on which a cloud has been thrown over the public mind, injurious to, and, in the end, destructive of, revealed religion, is THE LOWERING OF THE SCRIPTURES OF OUR FAITH IN GENERAL ESTIMATION, BY HOLDING THEM OUT AS EQUALLY CONCLUSIVE IN FAVOUR OF OPPOSITE SYSTEMS OF DOCTRINES. This, by men of any reflection, especially by men desirous of some escape from the obligation all feel they are under to bear the word of GOD, and to keep it, is seized upon as an argument against the Scriptures themselves, as the only rule of faith and duty ; and not, as in justice it ought, as an argument of the strongest kind against all such perversion of their use and neglect of their warning. Hence the deplorable ignorance of the Bible itself, which is so visible among the better informed and more active part of society, and the consequent indifference to the claims of revealed religion. Hence the approximations to infidelity, in the various shades of unbelief which the different systems of morality, as a substitute for revealed religion, exhibit.

And hence the prevalence of that liberality of opinion in which they tolerate every thing as true, but *the truth as it is in* JESUS.

Upon men of less information of mind, and of little leisure for reading and reflection from the pressure of laborious occupation, the injury is doubled ; they not only become remiss in procuring and acquainting themselves with the Bible, but, from the example of those above them, to whom they more or less look up, are encouraged in that neglect of religion—that surrender of themselves to the world and its pursuits, and to the indulgence of the flesh, which, like the worm at the root of Jonah's gourd, separates the hope of man from its foundation, cuts asunder the ligaments of society, and blasts and withers the overshadowing love of GOD revealed in the gospel of his Son.

Here, again, my reverend brethren, you are called upon to interpose, and, with all the earnestness and diligence which the love of souls, and a deep sense of accountable duty can beget, to meet this wide-spread delusion with every argument which revelation and reason can supply ; to call back your flocks to the only foundation, in the word of GOD ; to exhort them to the diligent perusal and study of its inspired wisdom ; and, with the Bible in your hand, and the love of GOD in your heart, explain and point out to them the connexion and dependence of its parts, the harmony of its doctrines, the efficacy of its sacraments, the beauty and fitness of its order, and its sufficiency to answer the great purpose of its divine Author, in giving light—the light of life, to a benighted world, in order to *make them wise unto salvation.* In fulfilling this imperious duty, fear not to expose those fallacious inventions of men which have observed the simplicity and efficacy of the doctrine of CHRIST—which have led men's minds into the devious mazes of error and unsettled opinion, and call loudly for the united efforts of all who value religious and civil liberty, to engage heartily in this work. Take St. Paul's rule, as expressed in the first Epistle to the Thessalonians, to govern and encourage you in this part of your duty in particular : —*But, as we were allowed of* GOD *to be put in trust with the gospel, even so we speak ; not as pleasing men, but* GOD, *which trieth our hearts.* And thus shall you be fortified against that *fear of man,* which *bringeth a snare.*

We are but a small body, my reverend brethren ; but, by the good blessing of our GOD upon us, we are increasing.   Help hath come forth for us from his right hand, during the past Conventional year ; and, if we continue faithful, we may confidently look for its continuance.   Let this hope, then, animate us all to renewed diligence in those duties, in the faithful discharge of which only can we expect to *save our own souls and the souls of those who hear us.*

To you, my brethren of the laity, it is also my duty to present such admonition, on those interests of the Church which depend on your co-operation, and can be promoted by the countenance and support you give to her ministrations.

Now, this is confined chiefly to three things :

First, YOUR OWN DEPORTMENT, whether as members and friends, or members and communicants of the Church.

The most efficient support which the members of the Church can give to her advancement, is by their own personal religion. This is literally *manifesting the tree by its fruit,* and is *an epistle of* CHRIST, *to be read of all men.*   If therefore you really and truly desire the prosperity of the Church, from whatever cause this desire may proceed, labour, and strive, and pray, that you may imbibe the spirit of her doctrines ; that you may manifest the purity of her discipline ; that you may experience the efficacy of her means of grace ; and, by thus promoting the cause of the Church, which is one and the same with the cause of true religion, promote and secure, at the same time, the salvation of your own soul.

Another very effectual means of promoting the interests and advancement of the Church, is, EXACT CONFORMITY TO THE COURSE AND ORDER SHE HATH PRESCRIBED FOR HER PUBLIC SERVICES.   And in this there will be no difficulty, where her distinctive character is understood and felt ; because this gives a point and impression to her ministrations, which belongs not to those who have separated themselves from her communion.   Occasional conformity, therefore, by which is meant, a mixed attendance upon the Church and upon those who dissent from her—sometimes with the one, sometimes with the other——is so far in opposition to her advancement, as it is sure to keep the person thus acting unfixed and wavering. Where there is no settled principle there can be no consistent conduct ; and experience teaches us, that it is only what we love that we lay ourselves out for.

The peculiar situation of the Church at present, and for many years back, whereby the congregations can only be occasionally supplied, has had a tendency to lessen the danger of this practice, in the opinions of Christians, and to induce many who nevertheless have a true regard for the Church, to attend the services of others, when they had none of their own. Now, while it may be said, that hereby a good example was given of reverence for the Sabbath, and good instruction was received from the Sermon delivered, it is not considered, on the other hand, that countenance has also been given to ministrations which the Church considers irregular and invalid——not to say schismatical ; and that, by this kind of conduct, we actually encourage the dangerous delusion, that one system of doctrine is as true as another, and one Church just as safe as another ; and thus, without meaning it, perhaps, pull down with one hand the fabric we are rearing with another. For, according to St. Paul's reasoning, in a parallel case, *If any man see thee, which hast knowledge, sit at meat in the idol's temple, shall not the conscience of him which is weak be emboldened to eat those things which are offered to idols !——and, through thy knowledge, shall the weak brother perish, for whom* CHRIST *died ?* But, though it is to be lamented that the different congregations cannot be supplied with regular services on every Sunday, yet is every family provided with the means of spending the vacant day profitably and to edification at home, in the Liturgy, Scriptures, and standard writers of the Church ; so that every member of the family may have this advantage, which some must be deprived of if they have any distance to travel to the place of meeting.

As this want of conformity, therefore, to principle and order as Churchmen, is not defended by any necessity, is well provided against in the use of the Liturgy, Scriptures, and standard writers, and has an evident tendency to retard, rather than to promote the advancement of the Church, I trust that you, my lay brethren, will take in good part the admonition now given, and, by future steadfastness, shew that you are members of the Church rather from principle than from mere choice and convenience; and that, as your affection, understanding, and interests, are all on the side of the Church, so will your conduct declare it, by *continuing steadfast in the Apostles' doctrine and fellowship, and in breaking of bread and in prayers.*

A third and most important means for the advancement of the Church, exclusively in the power of the laity, is found in THE EDUCATION OF THE RISING GENERATION.

But a little while, my clerical and lay brethren, and the place that now knows us will know us no more. Who, then, is to succeed to that blessed hope, through the power of which we contemplate this awful change without dismay, if not with with desire? Surely it is bound upon every father, upon every mother, upon every Christian who himself rejoices *in hope of the glory of* GOD, to do what in him lies to perpetuate that foundation on which this hope is built.

To education, then, we must look, not only for the future advancement, but for the very being of the Church. If religion is not instilled in early life, if it begin not in our *families*, and continue not to be carefully cultivated throughout the whole period of juvenile instruction, we shall in vain look for its prevalence in the world. Not to detain you on what is so evident—what you are so solemnly pledged to in the baptismal covenant—I will mention what I consider as injurious and inconsistent, in the performance of this duty.

First—The neglect of early catechetical instruction; that is, preparing your children for public examination on the Catechism, in the Church, by the clergyman. This, my own experience tells me, is sadly neglected in many places; and thus is lost the most favourable time to lay a good foundation, and to implant those sound and saving principles, which grow with their growth, and strengthen with their strength.

Secondly—An alarming carelessness as to the religious tenets of those to whom that part of the education of our children is committed, which has to be completed at a distance from the parents and guardians of youth. That this also is a negligence which calls loudly for a remedy, must be most evident. That it betrays an indifference, a deadness to religion, a want of serious heartfelt impression of its awful realities, is to me the most distressing symptom. And it is my duty, my brethren, to direct my attention rather to those things which mark the *general* than the *particular* indications of religious impression among the members of the Church.

When, therefore, we see Christians, so called, sending their children to Jews, to educate; when we see Protestants trusting their offspring to Roman Catholics to train up; when we see believers in the divinity of the LORD JESUS CHRIST surrendering their sons and their daughters to professed Unitarian teachers; and Episcopalians committing the hope of the Church to Dissenters; what can be the conclusion, but that such an indifference on the subject of religion generally, and such carelessness on its particular distinctions, prevails, as is sufficient to alarm every serious mind? And as no necessity, nor yet commanding convenience, can be pleaded for this inconsistency, (for it is the wealthy who thus risk their children, and by a little concert with each other might remove the reproach,) it calls the more loudly for this notice from me to the lay members of the Church. I pretend not to insinuate that the general advantages of education may not thus be obtained; nor yet do I say that any system of proselyting is in these schools carried on. But this I say, without the slightest fear of contradiction, that either there is no attention paid to religious instruction at all, or it partakes of the character of that which is professed by the teachers. Upon you in particular, my Episcopal brethren, I am bound to press this subject, as of the last importance to the well-being of the Church; and to warn you, that however careful you may be in laying the foundation in infancy, if you afterwards commit your children to those who are the enemies of your faith, the most you can hope for is, that it will not be pulled down. You cannot reasonably expect that it will be built up, as you would have it to be, if sincere in your own profession.

To your serious consideration, then, my brethren of the clergy and laity, I commit these remarks, trusting that their deep importance to our general and particular well-being, as a religious body, will gain them that attention which they deserve. And, wishing you a safe return to your respective places of abode, I beg you to take with you the assurance of the deep interest I feel in your prosperity and happiness individually, and of the prosperity and increase of the Church over which I am called to watch.

AN EPISCOPAL CHARGE,

DELIVERED TÓ THE

CONVENTION OF THE PROTESTANT EPISCOPAL CHURCH,

ASSEMBLED IN HILLSBOROUGH, N. C., IN MAY, 1826.

AN EPISCOPAL CHARGE.

My BRETHREN OF THE CLERGY AND LAITY—The important interests to which your attention has been directed during the session of this Convention, are calculated to engage the most earnest endeavours that the counsels agreed upon for the advancement of the Church, and the kingdom of the Redeemer, should be successful. But to this end it is not only necessary that the measures directed by this body should be correct in principle, and required by the interests of the Church, but practically attainable, also, by the reasonable ability of the members. That such is the character of the resolutions you have now come to, must be evident to all who consider the magnitude of the objects to be attained, with the means which are at the reasonable disposal of the representatives of the Church.

Past experience, however, teaches us, that neither the necessity nor the advantage of a particular measure, nor yet the ability to carry it into effect, are in themselves sufficient to insure general co-operation. The Convention of the Church, though the proper representative of the particular congregations comprising it, and in fact a legislative body ; yet, as it is clothed with no coercive power, is liable to find its best devised and best intended measures, paralyzed, if not altogether defeated, by the negligence or indifference of its constituents.

That this every way indefensible, and, if much longer continued, most ruinous state of insubordination to the fundamental principle of all regularly associated bodies, is, in our particular case, my brethren, the consequence of inconsideration in some, and want of proper information in others, I am well persuaded ; and am, therefore, induced to give my annual Charge to the diocese such a direction as may tend to obviate this evil, by laying before the members of the Church such a plain, yet

concise view of the popular nature of our frame of ecclesiastical government, as shall tend to engage and secure the ready
concurrence and co-operation of all our members in favour of
the measures agreed upon, either for particular or general good,
by the regularly elected representatives of the particular congregations of the diocese at large.

The first delegation of power and authority by the members
individually, is that committed to the Vestries of each particular
congregation. These are bodies of men, varying in number
according to the constitution of particular dioceses, but most
commonly limited to twelve, annually chosen by a majority of
the votes of each particular congregation; and form, as it were,
the legislative council of the parish or congregation by which
they are elected. To the Vestries it appertains to direct and
transact the secular concerns of the congregation; to assess
and collect the pecuniary contributions required of the members;
to appoint the delegates to the diocesan Conventions; to elect
the church-wardens out of their own body; and to act as counsellors and assessors with their clergyman, if required, in cases
of discipline, and other matters of common concern. They
are also required to keep a regular record of the members of
the congregation, of the marriages, baptisms, and burials, in the
parish or congregation, and to enter a statement of their proceedings at every meeting.

To the Church-wardens it more especially belongs, to take
care of the church buildings; of the communion plate, books
and vestments; to provide the elements for the holy communion, at the common expense; to maintain order and
decorum during public worship; and to regulate the necessary
provision for the poor of the parish. It is their duty also, in
the absence, or at the desire of the minister, to preside according to seniority of appointment, at all meetings of the vestry;
to direct the entries to be made by the secretary according to
the determination of the majority; to sign the proceedings of
each meeting; and to certify all extracts from the records,
particularly all certificates of delegation to the diocesan Conventions.

From this brief view of the appointment and purpose of

vestries it must be evident, I think, that provision is made for the administration of parochial affairs upon the most popular model compatible with order and effect. The vestry-men being themselves members of the congregation, must be intimately acquainted with the condition and circumstances of their constituents ; and as they must themselves be affected, in a proportional degree, by the resolves of the vestry, every security is obtained that nothing like oppression or injustice towards the rest of the members will be attempted. But even if such a case should occur, the congregation retains the remedy in their own hands, in the annual elections.

The next delegation of power and authority from the members of the Church, is that which is exercised mediately, through the vestries, in the appointment of lay delegates to the diocesan Conventions.

These bodies are to the dioceses at large, what the particular vestries are to the several congregations composing them : the only difference between them being that which arises from the charge and management of general and particular interests, and the consequently superior importance of their determinations.

To the diocesan Conventions, and of course to this body as such, it appertains to consult and provide for the general interests of the diocese ; to enact, amend, or repeal canons, or laws ecclesiastical, for the regulation of the members at large ; to elect the Bishop, to appoint the standing committee, or council of advice for the Bishop, to choose the clerical and lay delegates to represent the diocese in the triennial Conventions of the General Church in these United States ; and to assess and regulate the pecuniary contributions which are required for the general interests. And as the particular vestries are the organs through which the enactments of the diocesan Conventions are carried into effect, so are the diocesan conventions also the organs whereby the General Convention fulfils its still higher and more comprehensive duties. Through these, as links in the chain, the frame of our ecclesiastical government is compacted together by joints and bands which are essentially popular. It is based upon the will of the majority of the members, personally exercised in the immediate election of the vestries, and it returns to them again in the annual controul which they retain over those elections ; and that they may act with judgment on their affairs, provision is made for their full information by the public manner in which the conventions hold their sessions, and by the general dissemination of the annual journals of their proceedings.

With a frame of ecclesiastical government as directly assimilated to, and equally as congenial with, the civil institutions of our country as that of any other known religious denomination in it, Episcopalians may surely be permitted to express their sorrow that so persevering an effort should have been made to impress upon the public mind the false and unfounded persuasion, that the principles of their government and the tenets of their religious belief, are alike hostile to the free and happy institutions of this favoured land ; and to indulge the hope, that both those who circulate and those who receive so injurious and uncharitable a misrepresentation, will at least take the pains to be more truly informed.   As, however, the remainder of a most unhappy prejudice has been widely spread, and long entertained, I feel it due to the interests committed to me to show further, that in the administration of the frame of government adopted by the Protestant Episcopal Church in these United States, nothing contrary to the will of the individual members of the Church, expressed by a majority of their representatives, can be forced upon them.   Every Bishop is elected by the votes of the Clergy and laity of the diocese, assembled in Convention ; every pastor of a particular parish or congregation, is called to the charge by the vestry of the parish ; and the vestry being elected by the members themselves, every precaution is taken, that as the whole is instituted for the common benefit, common consent shall be the basis from which all necessary power and authority to administer the system with advantage and effect, shall spring. Nothing despotic, nothing unregulated by laws passed by the representatives of the members of the Church, is admitted in the constitution of the Protestant Episcopal Church.   Even the Bishop is only an executive officer, restrained and directed by express canons in the exercise of the authority committed to him ; the only absolute power possessed by him being that of a negative nature, and this confined to matters purely conscientious—such as the refusal to admit a candidate for ordination, although recommended by the examiners as in their judgment qualified to receive orders, and cases of a like nature. A bishop can neither suspend, displace, nor degrade a clergyman, otherwise than as the canons direct. Nor can a clergyman exercise the discipline of the Church upon a communicant, except according to the rubrics and canons, and ultimately liable to the decision of the bishop, to whom, in every such case an appeal lies.

Every security being thus taken against the oppressive exercise of the authority confided to the different officers who are appointed to administer its affairs, and no authority being conferred but what is absolutely necessary for the edification of the body; it should surely be a prevailing argument with Episcopalians to respect and support their ecclesiastical constitution, by the observance of all the duties it imposes upon them.

And first, they owe to their own interest, to the credit and welfare of the Church, and to the advancement of true religion, a CONSCIENTIOUS PERFORMANCE OF THEIR RIGHT AND DUTY IN THE ELECTION OF THE MEMBERS OF THE VESTRY. On this every thing may be said to depend, because to the vestries all subsequent measures for the year are referred. And not only is it a conscientious duty that every member of the Church should *personally attend* on the annual election day, but that he should vote also for those persons who, for their piety, their standing in public estimation, and other qualifications combined, give the best assurance of a faithful and profitable performance of the trust committed to them. In electing these men, respect should be had, in the first place, to their standing as Christians; a Christian body should surely be represented by Christians. In truth, it is desirable, that in every case the representatives of the Church should be communicants. But as this unhappily is not in all cases possible, it is therefore not insisted upon; nor is any particular congregation, or the Church at large debarred by any regulation from the services of those friendly laymen, whose orderly lives, and respect for religion, encourage the happy hope that they are *not far from the kingdom of* GOD.

Secondly, they owe it to conscience and to consistency, to OBEY THE REGULATIONS, TO CARRY INTO EFFECT THE LAWFUL RESOLUTIONS AND ENACTMENTS OF THEIR REPRESENTATIVES. As the members of a particular Church are morally bound by the acts of their vestry; so are all the congregations in a diocese, equally bound by the acts of their Convention; and all the Conventions of this country by the acts of the General Conventions of this Church. And the ground of this obligation is plain and obvious. As the individual members are bound by every principle of right reason to perform the duties and fulfil the engagements growing out of the lawful acts of their immediate representatives; so are these also, in the same manner, equally bound by the lawful acts of their immediate representatives, up to the highest judicatory known to the Church.

From this very brief but just statement of the popular principle upon which the frame of our ecclesiastical government is founded, the members of the Church in this diocese, I trust, will be induced to pay more attention to the election of their immediate representatives, and feel that the carelessness and indifference, too frequently manifested as to this duty, is, in fact, a surrender at once of private and public obligation, and a mark of great laxity of principle, both as churchmen and Christians.

As an additional and very powerful reason to give the whole of this subject the serious consideration its real importance demands, I would remark, that as the whole power possessed by the administrative bodies of the Church is of a moral nature, and dependant for its effect on the influence of this principle over the members, all unnecessary neglect of the personal duties consequent on the right of election by them, of the relative duty of representatives, with all refusal to carry into effect the decisions of the vestries and Conventions, is, so far, very conclusive proof of the weakness of the moral principle—of indifference to the interests of religion—and of disregard for the only just and safe ground on which either civil or religious liberty can be maintained, viz. submission to the will of the majority, constitutionally declared.

Let not, then, the Church of which we are happily members, have to take up the reproach of her great Founder and Head, as expressed by the prophet Isaiah, *I have nourished and brought up children, and they have rebelled against me.* Our nursing mother appeals to us for support ; let us not prove ourselves unnatural children by devouring the breasts which we have sucked, and refusing the support and defence which our spiritual parent requires in the day of her need. She has given all to her children ; she has reserved nothing for herself, but the comfort and consolation which springs from unfeigned love and devoted attachment in them, grounded on the irrefragable testimony of heaven and earth united in favour of her divine origin and saving purpose, as held and maintained by the Protestant Episcopal Church in these United States.

AN EPISCOPAL CHARGE,

DELIVERED TO THE

CONVENTION OF THE PROTESTANT EPISCOPAL CHURCH,

ASSEMBLED IN FAYETTEVILLE, N. C., IN MAY, 1828.

AN EPISCOPAL CHARGE.

My Brethren of this Convention.——Among the various subjects of general interest to the Church in this Diocese which your own observation, the Episcopal Journal, and the Parochial Reports, present for particular consideration, none seems more worthy of special notice, or more called for by existing circumstances, than the relation in which the ministry and the members of the Church stand to each other, and the obligations thence mutually arising.

From various causes, the difficulty of obtaining and retaining a supply of clergymen for our fixed congregations, seems to be increasing. This necessarily adds heavily to the many other anxieties which press upon me ; and more especially when I look forward to the more than probable removal of more of our very limited number. Under so serious an obstacle to the progress and prosperity of the Church in this diocese, my thoughts have necessarily been much occupied in searching out the cause, and in providing to counteract it ; and I feel constrained by a sense of duty, deepened by my increasing bodily infirmities, to present the result in this way, to the attention of this body——in the hope that it may prove beneficial, not only by conveying information, but by bringing this vital, but certainly much neglected subject, closer, both to the understanding and to the feelings of those interested, than it can possibly be, while viewed with the indifference and want of interest which our population manifests.

Religion in the abstract, and revealed religion with instituted means of grace, are things totally different from each other, my brethren. Natural religion, as it has been called, is a mere creature of the imagination, which never did, and which never could, exist in a fallen world, labouring under the palsy of spiritual death. In whatever degree, therefore, we assume the gratuitous reasonings derived from either abstract or natural religion as the ground of duty and hope towards GOD, we depart from the only foundation, and prepare the way for infidelity and indifference to triumph under the guise of external morality. Nor are there wanting in the judgment of him who addresses you, strong indications, from the actual condition of society in Christian lands in regard to revealed religion, that some such deleterious principle is in operation, indisposing the minds of men to give that close and earnest attention to the subject, which it most surely merits, as a special institution and appointment of the wisdom of GOD; and seducing them to rest satisfied with the hasty conclusions of indolent or ill-directed research, and to receive unquestioned, the comparatively modern inventions of men, as *the faith once delivered to the saints*. To correct this dangerous delusion, therefore—or rather to avert its pestiferous influence from the charge committed to my accountability —and to prepare the way for the particular subject of this address, the following preliminary remarks are submitted.

To derive advantage from any institution of a moral and spiritual nature, it is evident that the institution must be understood and applied in the extent and integrity of its appointments. Hence, as religion is the most commanding interest which moral beings can either reflect or act upon, it claims the most serious investigation, and the most diligent and unreserved application of its directions and precepts. To expect to reap the benefits which it is intended to confer, without resorting to the means appointed to that end, is to vacate religion as a reasonable service, and to reduce the first duty and the highest attainment of accountable man to such an uncertainty as paralizes the one, and renders the other altogether fortuitous; a state of things, when considered in connexion with moral condition, productive only of heartless disregard, or of wild enthusiasm. Like its Almighty Author, religion must be sought unto; for the happiness of a future state is proposed to mankind, not as the fate of their nature, but as the reward of their duty, faithfully and religiously performed.

The same obvious and rational principle pervades whatever is connected with religion as a practical duty. Hence, in the provision which the wisdom of GOD hath made, that the ordinances of his grace for the salvation of sinners shall be ministered to their fellows by men of like passions with themselves, the same foundation for confidence and assurance is given, with that on which the religion itself rests for its obligation upon men, *viz :* the authority and appointment of heaven—that authority and designation to office, which was originally certified to the world *by signs and wonders and mighty works,* by *the power of the* HOLY GHOST, and is to be verified to the end of time no otherwise than by derivation from this root.

As, therefore, no well informed and serious man will take his religion on a lower authority than from GOD, the reason is equally strong, that he should require from those who undertake to administer its ordinances to him that their authority for so doing shall be derived from the same source. And as, in the one case, the ground of his belief that his religion is divine and true, rests on the proper testimony that it came forth from GOD ; so likewise in the other case, the authority to act for GOD, in the external appointments of religion, should first be ascertained by its proper testimony, before any rational confidence can be derived from participation of its ordinances, as means of grace.

These appear to be principles which carry their truth and certainty, and consequently their obligation to moral beings, so undeniably in the very terms in which they are expressed ; and are, moreover, so intimately connected with the comfort and assurance of religious condition ; that it may be conceived superfluous to present them to such a body as that now before me. Yet when it is considered, that many equally undeniable truths are assented to in terms, and forthwith laid aside—that many most concerning truths are rendered null and void, by the influence of ignorance, prejudice, and prepossession—that the effect of popular opinion, moulded into a particular form, can clothe error, and particularly religious error, with the properties of truth—and that the as yet loose and ill-considered views of many who call themselves episcopalians, are all interested to escape from this close scrutiny into religion as a revealed

VOL. I.—57

appointment of GOD, I trust, that neither my intention in presenting them, nor their own intrinsic importance, will be mistaken or overlooked by those to whom I address myself; and with whose comfort here, and hope hereafter, they are so closely allied. Moreover, when it is taken into consideration that loose, indefinite, and mere general notions on so momentous a subject as salvation, operate to produce indifference and disregard, as to the external appointments of religion; and to induce a supine acquiescence in whatever bears a resemblance to the gospel, and is professed with a claim to superior sanctity; and that this is in truth, the prevalent state of the public mind, in the present day; it is hoped that what has been said, with the views about to be submitted on the subject of the Christian Ministry, will neither be deemed superfluous nor out of season, in the present circumstances of the Church in this diocese.

The Christian ministry being an appointment of Almighty GOD for the benefit of redeemed man, the connexion between the pastor and his flock is spiritual in its nature—refers exclusively to the care of their souls, and has no concern with their temporal affairs, only as these affect their religious condition. Its object and purpose is accordingly expressed in Scripture by the word *edification*, which comprises instruction, exhortation, warning, reproof, correction, and example—and, as necessary, indeed indispensable preliminaries, knowledge, experience, piety, and authority. So very obvious is this, as justly to excite surprise that the qualifications derived from education should come to be so lightly esteemed, and the importance of a lawful commission disregarded by any who call themselves Christians. Yet it is the unhappy condition of much of Christendom, as well as of our own country, to labour under the delusion, that piety, however ignorant, with pretensions to the ministerial office destitute of all proof, indeed utterly incapable of any other proof than the mere assertion of the party—are safe and allowable substitutes for such plain and necessary pre-requisites, in whoever undertakes to act between GOD and man in high concerns of salvation.

This office being spiritual in its nature, and concerned exclusively with spiritual things, must be derived from GOD, there being no other source of spiritual communication and authority to mankind, but GOD the HOLY GHOST. Being derived from GOD it must be the object of faith, that is, of firm and considered confidence, that it is thence derived; and being the object of faith, it must be grounded on, and be in conformity with the revealed word of GOD; that being to men the only ground and rule of faith, as to all spiritual things, GOD himself excepted, who is necessarily prior to and independent of any communication of himself to created beings.

Considered in this light, which is submitted as the just and scriptural view of the nature and object of the Christian ministry, the high responsibility of the pastoral office is evidenced by its origin, by its purpose, and by the sanctions wherewith it is enforced. And as the *responsibility* of the office refers chiefly to you my brethren, of the clergy, and its *importance* and *use* refers in like manner to you, my brethren of the laity, I shall be guided by this distinction in what I propose to say on this subject.

First, ITS ORIGIN. This being divine, and the office to be no otherwise undertaken than by the direct influence of GOD the HOLY GHOST, imagination can ascend no higher, as respects either the responsibility or the dignity of the Christian priesthood. As ambassadors from CHRIST, and acting in his stead in the awful controversy between heaven and earth, occasioned by sin; as entrusted with the ministry of reconciliation, and authorized to declare the conditions, and to administer the divinely instituted pledges of pardon and acceptance, to a world that lieth in rebellion and wickedness; your office my reverend brothers, is eminently one of unceasing labour, of constant watchfulness, of deep anxiety, and of unshaken fidelity; requiring that entire surrender of yourselves to this great work, and that abiding sense of the responsibility you are under, without which the expectation is vain that it will be so exercised as to be profitable either to yourselves or to others. But it is likewise an office in which the most powerful motives to exertion are presented, and supported by the brightest hopes, the most unfailing assurances ; and energy and activity in the performance of duty are prompted and encouraged by the highest considerations which an accountable being can contemplate.   The balance, therefore, is held with an even hand by the wisdom of God in this appointment.   As your responsibility is great, so is your help mighty : as your labour is unceasing, so is your wages beyond all price : as your privations are many, so are your consolations firm and steadfast as His word, who hath promised to *be with you always, even unto the end of the world.*

Of the same divine character is the evidence by which the designation of particular persons to this office and ministry by the Holy Ghost is certified to men.   The ministerial office being for the benefit of third persons in things pertaining to God, must, from the very nature of the office, be the subject matter of proper proof that it is derived from him ; otherwise, that faith, *without which it is impossible to please* God, and according to which the effect of the ordinances of religion, as divinely instituted means of grace, is expressly limited, must be wanting, and its place be supplied either by the formality of customary assent, or by the confused workings of an unbalanced mind rushing without discernment to assumed assurance of spiritual benefit.   Hence, at the commencement of Christianity, miraculous gifts pointed out to an astonished world the particular persons to whom Christ had previously committed the charge of establishing and governing his Church.   These were incontestible proofs of a divine commission—and it was to these that the apostle referred the obligation of Jew and Gentile to believe and embrace the gospel.   The first ministers of Christ went not forth claiming to be sent of God without credentials suitable to their high and holy office.   The world was not required to believe them on their naked assertion that they were called of God, and sent to preach the gospel.   Nor is it now required to receive any as ministers of Christ upon so uncertain a security as an unsupported and unproveable assertion.   For as Christ's commission to teach and baptize the nations was originally certified to the world by miraculous attestation to his apostles personally ; it is only as derived from them, by a verifiable succession, that a true and lawful ministry is to be ascertained since miracles have ceased. And as the fact is equally certain to third persons by the one testimony as by the other, the ground of Christian assurance is neither changed or lessened, nor the obligation or the efficacy of religious ordinances impaired. And let it never be forgotten, my reverend and lay brethren, that the revealed religion of the LORD JESUS CHRIST, from its commencement to its close, in all its appointments, in all its requirements, in all its attainments, and in all its hopes, is a *reasonable service*, resting upon divine faith pervading its whole structure. Its ministry, and sacraments, then, as integral parts of the religion, and without which it cannot be savingly administered, must forever derive their authority and efficacy from divine institution ; and the assurance of faith prove a delusion, or a reality, according as it is built upon the foundation CHRIST hath laid, as exhibited to the world by his holy apostles, received and acted upon by the primitive Church, and recorded in the inspired Scriptures of our faith ; or as it is assumed upon some invention of man, utterly devoid of that testimony to divine origin and authority, upon which alone a rational being is presumed to rest the unspeakable interests of eternal condition.

To place the ministerial office, then, upon any other, or upon lower ground, than as derived from GOD, is at once to vacate the responsibility of the office to him who holds it, and to defeat its use and efficacy to those for whose benefit it is instituted. For if less than divine in its origin, it is not perceived how any man can with truth and understanding say, that he is moved by the HOLY GHOST to undertake it ; or where the only proper testimony to this its divine origin is wanting, how any thing deserving the name of Christian assurance can be derived to those whose spiritual condition is inseparably connected with the visible sacraments of the visible Church of CHRIST. Nor need we be in the smallest degree afraid to assign the low and erroneous views as to the origin and proof of the Christian ministry, which the divisions and separations among Christians have forced into currency, as one of the chief causes of the disregard of religious ordinances, and indifference to and disuse of the instituted means of grace, and of the consequent decline of vital godliness, which casts so awful a shade over the otherwise happy condition of this favoured country.

But, my reverend brothers, it is a part of the responsibility of your sacred office, to magnify that office—not only by adorning your divine commission as ambassadors of CHRIST, and stewards of the mysteries of GOD, by a holy life, and by unwearied and faithful exertions for the advancement of his kingdom, but by asserting its high derivation, and by demonstrating its inseparable connexion with the revealed hope of the gospel. To be silent on this fundamental subject to those of your charge, is to be unfaithful to them, and unjust to yourselves ; while it serves to cherish the delusion in others, that because pretensions to ministerial character unsupported by verifiable succession from the apostles of CHRIST as the only root of unity in his visible Church, are unquestioned, that therefore they may be relied on. We can look back, my reverend brothers, on a wide and wasteful desolation of the fold of CHRIST, through remissness on this primary and fundamental subject. Let past experience, then, teach us to pursue a wise course for the time to come. We can look forward to a most powerful host of prejudice and party arrayed against us; but let us not therefore be cast down. Truth must at last prevail over error—and by turning the public mind to a sounder judgment on the concerning subject of religion, prepare the way for its final triumph over all opposition, and for that union among Christians, which forms the beauty and the strength of the gospel.

If we consider, in the second place, THE PURPOSE of the Christian ministry, the view here taken of its origin, and of the proof by which it is verified, will it is humbly conceived, be confirmed. Now this purpose is threefold. The first is, the communication of the discoveries of the gospel to mankind, in order to recover them from the ruin and misery of sin, and from eternal death as its wages. The second is, to transact the conditions of this recovery, receiving the submission of penitent sinners, and by administering to such the divinely instituted pledges of pardon and adoption into the family of God. The third is, to watch over the household of faith, thus gathered into one body ; to provide for their instruction in righteousness, and to exercise the discipline of CHRIST, for the peace and edification of the Church.   Now, to either of these purposes singly—and much more to all of them collectively, as the sum of ministerial duty—a divine commission and authority to act is indispensable, too, prior to any performance of the duty.   For, *How shall they preach except they be sent ?*   Or, Who has any natural right to administer the sacraments of the gospel ?   Or, who are bound to submit themselves to discipline, where no lawful authority to inflict censure is possessed ? Above all, who will be found to regard the discipline of CHRIST, unless upon the firm persuasion, amounting to fixed faith, that to be justly cut off from the peace and privileges of his visible Church upon earth, is a virtual excision of such person from the *Church of the first-born, which are written in heaven?*

Evident as this must be to every reasonable mind, and confirmed as it is by the analogies of all social bodies, the subject presents itself with the highest interest to the consideration of believers, when viewed as the express appointment of the wisdom of GOD, in the structure of that religion which he hath revealed to fallen man for his salvation.   In that religion as established by its divine Author, the unity of the Church, and the assurance of faith, are inseparably connected with CHRIST's commission to preach and baptize the nations.   But this commission was not given to the whole body of believers who embraced the gospel during his personal ministry ; nor yet to his Church, properly so called : for the Church of CHRIST was not organized and set up in this world until the day of Pentecost. CHRIST's commission was given exclusively to the eleven, who continued with him in his temptations, and with whom he continued for forty days after his resurrection, *speaking to them of the things pertaining to the kingdom of* GOD.   It was to them, and to them only, that he said, *As my Father hath sent me, even so send I you.*   His passion being accomplished, the purchase of redemption completed, and a kingdom conquered from sin and death, then it was, that he conferred on the eleven, and on their successors to the end of the world, authority to plant and govern his Church. *I appoint unto you a kingdom, as my Father hath appointed unto me——All power is given unto me in heaven and upon earth,* said the Saviour. *Go ye therefore into all the world and preach the gospel to every creature. He that believeth and is baptized shall be saved; he that believeth not shall be damned.* It was when his resurrection had demonstrated his triumph over death and hell, that he transferred his divine commission to his eleven apostles; that he *breathed on them, and said unto them, Receive ye the* HOLY GHOST. *Whosesoever sins ye remit, they are remitted unto them; and whosesoever sins ye retain, they are retained.* And it was when his glorious ascension into heaven had established his supreme dominion over a redeemed world, that he poured out upon them the HOLY GHOST, to qualify them for their great work, and to certify to the world that they were messengers of heaven, and the depositaries of all lawful authority in *the kingdom of* GOD'S *dear Son.*

In like manner, the sanctions by which ministerial duty is enforced, furnish a strong confirmation of the divine character of the Christian priesthood, and of its vital importance to the hope of man as derived from the gospel of CHRIST. As *no man taketh this honour unto himself, but he that is called of* GOD, *as was Aaron,* the sanctions by which its duties are bound upon the conscience, are all of a spiritual and eternal character. *My kingdom is not of this world,* said our blessed LORD. This world, therefore, and the things that are in it, are equally excluded from the motives to undertake office in the kingdom of CHRIST, and from the sanctions by which official duty is enforced. Eternity alone can furnish the reward, or inflict the punishment, which await the faithful, or the unfaithful, steward of the mysteries of GOD. As nothing of a temporal nature enters into the derivation of the Christian ministry, nothing of worldly enjoyment or suffering is referred to, as the end to be kept in view. You watch for your souls, my reverend brothers, and for souls you must give account; not with the loss or gain of worldly honours, dignities, and emoluments, but with your own souls. There is no alternative——there is no escape from this condition, on which you hold and exercise your holy office.

If, then, these things are so, and most surely believed among us: if they are confirmed by the standard of revealed truth, and by the stream of testimony in the Church, unbroken from the apostles through a period of fifteen hundred years ; and subsequently asserted and contended for by the confessors, martyrs, and fathers of that Church through which we derive our succession ; if they form the distinctive principles of our communion, and constitute the very foundation on which we can either claim or be recognized as a true branch of the one catholic and apostolic Church in which we profess to believe ; they surely form a part of that necessary edification which the pastor owes to his flock, and without which the expectation is vain, as woful experience proves to us, that they should continue steadfast, and be enabled to resist the various artifices now resorted to, to bring these fundamental principles into contempt, as illiberal and uncharitable—as infringements upon Christian liberty, and unsupported by the word of GOD.

These are daring assertions, and though totally unfounded, and demonstrably opposed to the plainest principles of the doctrine of CHRIST, nevertheless the temerity and pertinacity with which they are announced, have given them an influence over the ignorant and prejudiced, under the operation of which, the gracious purposes of an infallible Scripture, a visible Church, and a divinely authorised ministry, in the salvation of sinners, are deprived of their appointed use ; and the various shades of infidelity are fast ripening those bitter fruits of irreligion and departure from GOD, which shall complete the predicted apostacy of this latter day.

Shall we, then, my reverend brethren, become accessory to this moral death of the immortal souls around us, by with-holding from the ignorant that instruction which they will no where else receive, and from the presumptuous, that warning without which their blood will be required at our hands ?   May GOD forbid.   Shall we sit with folded hands, and see the Church of our faith and of our affections declining around us, under the influence of an infidel liber-ality which claims the concession, and brands as unchristian and uncharitable the refusal to acknowledge the most opposite systems of faith, as equally the doctrine of CHRIST—the most forced and discordant interpretations of Scripture, as equally the truth of God's most holy word—and the multiplied and disagreeing divisions of professed Christianity, as equally true branches of the Church of Christ, equally entitled to the promises of God, and equally safe for salvation—without an effort in the fear of God, to arrest so deadly a delusion? No, my fellow labourers in the vineyard of the Lord, far be such apathy and indifference to the interests of our Zion, from our hearts and from our conduct. Let us then, take *the sword of the Spirit*, and *the shield of faith*, and go forth against this modern Baal, to which so many of our sons and our daughters have been sacrificed. These are strictly the weapons of our warfare, and they are *mighty, through God, to pull down the strong holds of Satan*. Especially are they mighty to meet this particular error, in all its various shapes; for it is from a broken and perverted Scripture only that it derives any semblance of support.

The RELATION IN WHICH THIS SACRED OFFICE STANDS TO THE MEMBERS OF THE CHURCH, comes next to be considered.

This has already been stated to be *purely spiritual*, and as such, to be of a more sacred character than the mere consent and agreement of the parties to stand in this relation to each other, could possibly give to it. A connection whose results are to be determined chiefly in another life, and with which the peace and comfort of the present life are very closely united, must undoubtedly carry along with it the highest claims to the serious consideration of every Christian people. For it is not a connexion of choice or convenience merely, but one of indispensable necessity; without which, the advantages of religious condition can neither be obtained nor continued.

Viewed in this light, which is submitted as the just and scriptural view of the subject, the first obligation which this divine appointment for the administration of the grace of the gospel to men involves, is, that men provide themselves with ministers. No body of Christian people can continue to prosper in their religious concerns, when deprived, for any length of time, of the services of the sanctuary. And experience proves, that the most flourishing congregations quickly decline from the power of religion, and dwindle into utter decay, under this privation.

The next obligation involved is, that the persons thus employed to minister to the spiritual wants of the people, be true and lawful ministers of CHRIST. And this obligation rests upon the same ground of reason and propriety, whereby all other agencies are held to be valid or void, *viz.* power and authority from the principal to act in his behalf. As in temporal affairs, no qualifications for any particular office, however great; no desire to do good, and promote the welfare of the community, however sincere; nor yet any willingness on the part of others, to reap the benefit of such qualifications; can confer the right to assume office, and bind the State to recognize acts thus performed: in like manner in things spiritual, no qualifications of natural or acquired ability, however great; no piety, however ardent; no acknowledgment or solicitation of others, however general; can authorize the assumption of office in the kingdom of CHRIST, or give any reasonable ground of assurance, as to the benefit to be derived from it; for the benefit or advantage to third persons, is as inseparably tied to the authority to perform the act in things religious, as in the affairs of civil life. And just as certainly as confusion, disorder, and ultimate dissolution of the frame and purpose of civil government, would follow the adoption of the principle that the qualifications for, or the desire to fill, an office, authorized the assumption thereof, and rendered the actings and doings of such agents obligatory upon the State; so sure it is, that the same disastrous consequences will follow the adoption of this principle in the administration of the gospel. And so obvious is this principle to common sense, and so clear the analogy by which it is supported, that it may well excite some feeling stronger than surprize, that Christians, with the Bible in their hands, should ever have given countenance to so palpable a delusion; and in particular, that episcopalians should so far have been blinded by this deceit, as to allow their prime distinction as a religious body, to be undermined, undervalued, and finally exploded, by its operation.

And notwithstanding the numbers who assert these liberal novelties—notwithstanding the reproach which attends those who denounce them as dangerous and destructive errors—I should be false to my solemn consecration vows, and to your eternal interests, my brethren of this convention, did I fail to assert, and to warn you, that the question of ministerial commission is a vital question ; that is, is a question of the essence of revealed religion, and fundamental to the hope of the gospel. For this hope cannot be separated from the sacraments of the visible Church, any more than the sacraments can be separated from the right to administer them, as things pertaining to GOD. If men can be saved without the sacraments of the Church of CHRIST, where they may be had ; wherefore were they ordained by CHRIST himself for perpetual observance, and whence their acknowledged character as means of grace to the souls of men? And if they are equally sacraments and means of grace, with and without the authority of CHRIST to administer them, wherefore the institution of a visible Church, to be entered into and continued in, no otherwise than by participation of the sacraments, rightly administered by men duly commissioned to act as STEWARDS OF THE MYSTERIES OF GOD? These are questions which bring this subject home to the reason and to the conscience of every sincere and informed Christian, and are calculated to fortify the less informed against the plausible, but unfounded, reasonings by which so many have been led away from the truth.

Nor are there wanting other grounds, on which to show the fallacy of all such innovations upon primitive truth and order. On the principle here argued against as unscriptural and dangerous to the souls of men, the unity of the Church ; the fellowship of believers in one body, by the operation of one spirit ; and the assurance of faith—all of them fundamental doctrines of CHRIST'S religion—are no longer blessed and comfortable realities in religious condition, grounded on the divine character of the Church, the Ministry, and the Sacraments, as the channels of that grace through which the heart has been renewed to GOD, and the life recovered from sin to holiness; but mere imagination and assumptions of such benefits, grounded on ministrations incapable of being verified as divine and true, and consequently not to be relied on, in the awful concern of the loss or salvation of the soul.

On this liberal principle, instead of *one body* and *one spirit, one* LORD, *one faith, one baptism*—which St. Paul asserts as the characteristic of CHRIST's religion, there must be as many of each of these, as there are existing divisions on the faith and order of the gospel.

On this modern system of general comprehension, it is not perceived possible to give any good reason why every man may not be his own priest, and minister to himself in spiritual things. For if one division from the body of CHRIST is justiable, why not one hundred, or one hundred million? If one man has a right to take the ministerial office unto himself, upon some impulse or persuasion of his own mind, why not another —why not every other, until the Church of CHRIST is scattered into the dust of individuality? And if men, rational beings, who have an eternity of misery or bliss before them, on the specified conditions of the gospel, were but as watchful as to the security of their title to spiritual privileges, as they are to that by which their temporal interests are held; no place would have been found for the entertainment of this dangerous error, nor would the sophistry wherewith it is attempted to be defended in the present day avail to continue the delusion, could Christians be roused to *compare spiritual things with spiritual*—to consider well the foundation on which they are building for eternity; and by bringing their entire religious condition to the standard of revealed truth, thence be taught the important lesson, that as the *faith* and *order* of the gospel are *equally* from GOD, *both* must combine to give assurance to that hope which the LORD JESUS CHRIST has purchased, by the sacrifice of the cross, for a world of sinners.

A third obligation, growing out of the pastoral relation, is, that the members of the Church attend regularly on his ministrations; that they make him acquainted with their spiritual condition, and consult freely with him thereupon; that they bear with reverence, and judge with candour his expositions of Christian doctrine, and his admonitions and exhortations to holiness of life ; and that they practise diligently the duties and obligations of Christian profession.

This is so plain an obligation, or rather class of obligations, and so indispensable to any reason or use in the ministerial office, that it may suffice merely to state it, with this single remark :— thus to improve the advantages of the external ordinances of Christianity, is not only a religious obligation, but it is the only ground on which any reasonable expectation can be entertained of edification and establishment in the faith.   St. Paul speaks of a class of Christians, as abounding in the latter day, who *will not endure sound doctrine, but after their own lusts they shall heap to themselves teachers, having itching ears* : and he further informs us, what the certain consequence would be, *and they shall turn away their ears from the truth,* says the Apostle, *and shall be turned unto fables.*   Now as observation confirms the truth of this prediction, so should it incline us to take heed to the warning ; nothing being better established than the fact, that those persons who are so very liberal, or so fond of variety, as to attend the services of all denominations, do rarely or never themselves make any profession of religion, or manifest any other sense of its importance, than by thus running about to hear preaching, as it is called ; and consequently they are, *ever learning, and never able to come to the knowledge of the truth,* as the same inspired apostle testifies.

A fourth obligation of the pastoral relation, is the decent and comfortable support of their Minister, in a suitable and certain provision for the temporal wants of himself and his family.

This also is so plain an obligation, and enforced by such express warrant of GOD's word, that the simple mention of it might be sufficient, were it not that a growing indifference as to this duty begins to manifest itself, and suggests the fear that our clergy may be driven away by absolute inability to provide for their necessary wants, from their salaries.

That this is in some degree to be attributed to the present pecuniary pressure upon all classes of the community, I have no doubt ; nor would I contend for any exemption of the clergy from the operation of those vicissitudes to which all human affairs are liable. In times of public distress, they ought to submit to the privations which are forced upon all; and I can answer for my reverend brothers of this diocese, that they will do it cheerfully. But where the remuneration promised is far below a reasonable compensation for their services, and affords at the best but a subsistence, it ought not to be curtailed but on the most evident necessity; and Christian parents need not surely to be told, that a clergyman feels the same anxieties for his growing family that others do——or that as his family increases and grows up, his expenses unavoidably also increase. Above all, it ought sacredly to be borne in mind, that what is contributed to the support of religion ought not to be the first, and never the sole retrenchment of expenditure among Christians.

This is a delicate subject, my brethren of the laity, both to you and to me, and therefore I forbear to extend it. But if it is taken into serious consideration, upon Christian principles, what I have said will suffice to produce a change in this respect, creditable at once to yourselves as Christians, and encouraging to your ministers——not because of the gain, but because it will manifest a more earnest and lively sense of the importance of religion, and of your attachment to the Church, which otherwise may, and will be justly questioned. Nothing my brethren, marks a dead and decaying state of religious profession more surely than backwardness and indifference to provide for the regular services of the sanctuary.

Permit, me however, to observe——what I think is loudly called for by the present pressure upon our ecclesiastical and civil condition, that you owe it to the community, both as Christians and as citizens, to set the example of retrenchment, in all those useless extravagancies of annual expenditure, which the fashion of the world hath entailed upon society, which is the real cause of the present distress, and which the retributive providence of ALMIGHTY GOD is making the instrument of a sore chastisement. Excess of apparel, fashionable decoration, and profuse living, add nothing to our real comfort or respectability, my Christian brethren; while they take much from our means of doing good, are seriously hostile to the inculcation of religious principle in the rising generation, and grievously impair the confidence entertained of the truth and sincerity of our Christian profession.

Let it therefore be put away from among us, as men and women professing godliness ; and by so doing we shall be gainers every way ; we shall speedily relieve our temporal necessities, while at the same time we promote the advancement of the Church, by giving the most convincing testimony to the purity and sincerity of our faith, and to the power and tendency of our distinctive principles to enforce that holiness without which no man, be his profession what it may, shall ever see the LORD.

A fifth obligation which I will mention, not directly the result of the pastoral religion, but growing out of your connexion with the Church, is a faithful observance of the directions and canons of your convention. This is a duty as binding upon the conscience of the churchman, as obedience to the laws of the land is, upon the conscience of the citizens. For both are enacted by representatives, chosen to consult and provide for the common good ; the only difference is, that what in the one case is enforced by the civil power of the State, in the other is entrusted to the moral principle of the man. This, if rightly considered, ought to ensure the most exact obedience of the two ; and if applied to the pecuniary affairs of the diocese, will produce hereafter a stricter attention in paying up the assessments laid upon the different congregations, whether for general or special purposes.

There is yet, however, another obligation, the combined result of the pastoral relation and of your profession as episcopalians, of such commanding influence, not only upon the advancement, but upon the very being of the Church in this diocese, that my duty calls upon me imperiously to present it to your most serious consideration—and that is, the education of your families in the faith of their fathers, in the principles of the Church, of which by their baptism, they are members.

That great laxity is exhibited by episcopalians, on this most obvious duty, is unhappily beyond dispute. And while I admit that it is in some degree the result of what may be termed necessity, from the circumstances in which our seminaries of learning are almost exclusively found, I must, nevertheless, record my fear that it proceeds in a greater degree from indifference on the subject of distinctive principles in religion.

Is it, then, consistent with our public profession, my brethren —with any vital impression of the divine truth of our religious doctrines; is it consistent with integrity of principle as parents ; to commit the tuition of the rising hope of the Church, where the most that can be hoped for is, that if no pains shall be taken to impress their religious principles deeper upon their hearts, no inroad shall be made upon them.

Who are to succeed us, my Christian brethren, when the few and fast waning years of our earthly pilgrimage shall be closed? Who are to occupy our places in the sanctuary, and transmit to posterity in the integrity of primitive adoption, the *faith once delivered to the saints*, as set forth in that *form of sound words* in which our fathers worshipped GOD, and enjoyed the comfort of his grace and heavenly benediction? If our children are not to be trained up with this view, and taught to love the Church the more, because it is the Church of their fathers ; if the principles of primitive truth and order, recovered from Romish corruption, asserted against sectarian innovation, and recorded as *the lively oracles of* GOD, in the blood of the martyrs and confessors of the British Church, our spiritual mother, are now to be abandoned to the fostering care of their professed opponents, vain are your labours and self denials, my brethren of the clergy—vain are your exertions and sacrifices, my brethren of the laity. We shall soon be gone ;—soon shall the place that now knows us, know us no more. And then, strangers shall enter upon this fair inheritance, and pull down the landmarks of its most holy faith, and prohibit the ordinances of its rational spirit-stirring worship, and lay waste the goodly proportions of its apostolic order, and scatter the assurance of its heaven-derived institutions to the wild intemperance of misguided zeal and fanatical delusion.

Pardon me, my brethren, if I seem to you to anticipate an ideal danger. I am indeed no prophet, to look into futurity, and draw from thence its hidden events. But as your watchman in chief, and charged with all the interests of the Church, I have to keep my eye upon remote as well as upon immediate consequences, and to give the warning from the quarter whence danger threatens.

Our danger, at the present time, seems to me to arise from a decline in the spirit and power of religion—from loose and erroneous views of the prescribed and covenanted character of revealed religion—from consequent indifference to our distinctive principles—and from an over conformity with the spirit of the world, which if not arrested must soon, and certainly, produce that moral death which precedes the removal of our light from the candlestick. Against this danger, what is to be our resort, my brethren? Anxiously have I cast about for the most effectual remedy, and my judgment can find that no where, under God, but in a return to first principles. These, through his blessing, may yet revive us to *the power of godliness*, and sustain us against the opposition of our enemies—yea, may turn those enemies into friends and favourers of our righteous cause, through the power of truth plainly announced, and faithfully exhibited in practice.

Pardon me, also, if I seem to any to have spoken more forcibly than the occasion called for. Alas, my brethren, that the desire to conciliate, where experience demonstrates that concession only increases demand, should have so prevailed as to enervate and neutralize the truth, by the qualified and doubting terms in which it is expressed! But a more powerful motive than the fear or the praise of men, constrains me. This may be my last address to a convention of this diocese—of which frequently recurring disease, and increasing difficulty to relieve the symptoms, give serious notice. I therefore have to speak as a dying man to those for whom he has to give account—recalling them, as Christians and churchmen, to those pure principles of primitive truth and order, which alone give to the religion of the gospel its practical importance as the prescribed institution of the wisdom of GOD for the salvation of sinners—which alone give to the visible Church, ministry, and sacraments, any definite purpose, in the economy of grace—which alone give to the faith of the gospel its covenanted character, and to the hope of eternal life through the merits of the divine Saviour the support of divine assurance. On these principles, derived from the Bible, and from the Bible alone—searched for among the various accessible denominations of Christian profession, but found, in their integrity, only in the Church—I shall go, GOD being my helper, to my account. On these principles, professed and acted on, or compromised and surrendered, will the Church, the protestant episcopal Church, flourish or decline, continue or melt away into a sect : and I commit them to this convention for the diocese, as the highest proof I can give of my deep and sincere concern for your spiritual and temporal welfare, with my earnest prayers to the great Head of the Church, that through his heavenly grace they may be considered, approved, and applied, only as they are in agreement with His revealed will.

SERMONS,

ON VARIOUS SUBJECTS.

SERMONS.

SERMON I.

BAPTISM.

JOHN iii. 5.

"JESUS answered, verily, verily, I say unto thee, except a man be born of water, and of the spirit, he cannot enter into the kingdom of GOD."

THE divisions and dissentions among Christians are at once the reproach of the gospel and the proof of its divine origin, in the fulfillment of the prophecy of its author and founder. *Think not that I am come to send peace upon the earth, I came not to send peace, but a sword.* The foresight and declaration of this perversion of the gospel of peace tends in no degree however, my brethren and hearers, to lessen the guilt and responsibility of those who separate themselves from the visible communion of that one spouse and body of CHRIST, here called the kingdom of GOD, and by which is meant that Church of CHRIST, which he purchased with his own blood—which he hath built on the foundation of the apostles and prophets, himself being the chief corner stone—with which he hath left the sacraments of his grace, and in which only are the promises of GOD, yea and amen to us, in CHRIST JESUS. *Woe unto the world because of offences. It must needs be that offences come, but woe unto that man by whom the offence cometh. Many shall come in my name, and shall say, I am CHRIST ; but believe them not, for there shall arise false CHRISTS and false prophets, and shall deceive many, but go ye not after them—behold I have told you before.* If these passages of Scripture, then, mean any thing, and are intended for our warning and instruction, it must be to teach us that it is not a matter of that indifference we are so prone to think it, in what way, or by what means we attach ourselves to the gospel in the outward communion of Christian privileges—that among such direct opposition in doctrine and practice as now obtains in the Christian world, all cannot be right—that as there may be false CHRISTS and false prophets, there may also be false hopes and unfounded expectations—and that as the consequences are eternal, every care and diligence should be adopted that we build on a foundation which cannot be shaken, and use as much caution not to be imposed upon in our spiritual concerns as we do to avoid it in temporal affairs. This, it appears to me, is so very reasonable a duty, that all must assent to the propriety of being guided by it ; and as all are furnished in the word of GOD, and in the purpose of visible ordinances in religion, when rightly considered, to make this necessary inquiry, I would hope that the principle will be remembered and acted upon by all who are seriously concerned for the salvation of their souls.

Among the existing divisions in the religious opinion and practice which prevail in the present day, there is none more pointed or more injurious in its effects than that on the doctrine of baptism, as to the subject, the mode, and the effects. As by reason of this difference many are unsettled in their minds, and not a few disposed to neglect it altogether—as the solemnity and importance of the ordinance is lessened in general estimation, and the obligations growing out of it impaired and neglected in those who use it—and as I am in the practice of admitting to the sacrament of baptism the infant or other children of those who apply to me for that purpose, and there is a denomination of Christians who consider this as unscriptural and a corruption of Christianity—for these reasons, I have considered it my duty on this occasion, to make known the foundation on which, with a good conscience, I thus act. And that what I may say on the subject may be to your edification, I shall consider,

FIRST, the ordinance itself.

SECONDLY, the subject, or description of persons entitled to its administration.

THIRDLY, the mode, or manner of administering it.

And then,

CONCLUDE with an application of the subject.

JESUS *answered, verily, verily, I say unto thee, except a man be*

born of water and of the spirit, he cannot enter into the kingdom of
GOD.

I. First the ordinance itself.

There can be no difficulty, I should suppose, as to the meaning of the expression in the text——*Being born of water*, that it recognizes and establishes in the most pointed terms the institution of water baptism in the Church of CHRIST. Neither can there be a doubt in any serious mind, I think, of the absolute necessity which all who would become Christians are under, of being thus baptized. A more solemn and express declaration is not to be found in the Scriptures, to any point of faith and practice. But if any doubt could reasonably be entertained, it must be done away when it is considered that the concluding injunction of the Author of our religion to his apostles, was *to teach all nations——baptizing them in the name of the Father, and of the Son, and of the* HOLY GHOST. And when to this solemn command was added a declaration no less express, of the awful consequences depending on the observance or rejection of this institution——*He that believeth and is baptized, shall be saved ; he that believeth not, shall be damned*——it must be a hardier mind than I possess, that can lightly esteem this sacred ordinance and initiating sacrament in the Church of CHRIST.

The obligation of the ordinance, therefore, in the outward application of water in some way, to all who would be, or even be called, Christians, being out of all reasonable dispute, I will say a few words on its nature and use.

When the terms and conditions of the covenant of mercy in the Son of GOD were made known to our first parents after their fall, the Scriptures do not inform us that any particular token or outward seal was given to them, and it is not for us to conjecture where the Scripture is silent. When the same covenant, however, was renewed with Abraham, and it pleased GOD to appoint and define the channel or course in which the promised seed of the woman should come, a special outward sign, token, and seal of the covenant was appointed by the Almighty, to designate and keep separate this channel, and to confirm to the chosen people the assurance of GOD's favour in their obedience to the terms thereof. *This is my covenant which ye shall*

VOL. I.——60

keep between me and you, and thy seed after thee, every man child among you shall be circumcised, and it shall be a token of the covenant betwixt me and you; and he that is eight days old shall be circumcised among you, every man child in your generation, and the uncircumcised man child shall be cut off from his people—he hath broken my covenant.

Hence we learn, my hearers, that circumcision as the outward sign of the covenant, was strictly in the nature of a signature to a contract, that it conferred special privileges which could no otherwise be obtained, and its use was to determine by a visible mark, who were, and who were not, parties to the covenant.

In like manner under the gospel dispensation, when it pleased God to put an end to the shadows of the law, by the offering up the body of Christ once for all, and to call all nations, as well the Gentiles as the Jews, to the hope of eternal life, by the obedience of faith, the same method was pursued by appointing a seal to the covenant of grace also, which seal is baptism, and is of the same nature and use as the previous seal of circumcision, and as certainly determines our interest in the covenant of redemption, as the former determined the interest of the seed of Abraham in the covenant of promise. As it was the same mercy founded on the original covenant, *that the seed of the woman should bruise the head of the serpent,* so those to whom it was proposed under either of its subsequent forms, could only become parties to it, and be made partakers of its benefits by personally subscribing to the terms, and conforming to the conditions on which it was tendered to them.

As the descendants of Abraham were not parties to the first covenant by their natural birth, but by the application of the seal or token annexed to it; in like manner the children of Christian parents cannot be parties to the second or new covenant otherwise than by the application of the appointed seal in the sacrament of baptism. And the reason and connexion of the appointment, with the express declarations of the word of God most undeniably teaches—that there is no revealed method of entering into covenant with God, of becoming entitled to the benefits of the death of Christ, in the forgiveness of sin, the renewal of the HOLY GHOST, and the reward of eternal life, but by the water of baptism.

I therefore do not wonder that baptism should have occupied so much the attention of Christians, even in the circumstantials belonging to it, as a rite or ceremony. All I regret is, that attention has not been rightly directed, and that in disputing about circumstantials, the end and design of it, which is newness of life, has too far been lost sight of.

That the arguments drawn from the analogy between Christian baptism and Jewish circumcision, have been objected to and considered irrelevant by those who deny to infants the privileges of baptism, is very certain, as it also is, that this objection has been pushed so far by ignorant and heated minds as to separate the New from the Old Testament altogether. But this proves only to what lengths men will go in favour of a particular notion, and that they will even risk the certainty and obligation of the Bible, rather than yield a distinguishing though untenable point. For beyond dispute, if you destroy the connexion between the Old and New Testaments, you deprive us of the whole Bible. Uncertainty or disagreement in the revelation of GOD's will deprives us of it entirely. Yet nothing is more plain and certain than that our LORD himself and his inspired apostles viewed this point very differently, and continually refer to the Old Testament, as the ground and authority of those transactions which afterwards formed the New. And St. Paul himself argues this very point on the analogy of the two ordinances, styling Christians the circumcision made without hands. And if we would only bear in mind, my friends, that in the days of our LORD and his apostles there was no such book as that which we call the New Testament, it might serve to convince us, how dangerous it is to separate the Scriptures from the unity of their purpose, and how certainly unsound and unsafe that form of doctrine must be which requires so desperate a support.

From the words of my text also, we learn the connexion of spiritual regeneration with the baptism of water ; *except a man be born of water and of the* SPIRIT. This has been a fruitful theme of opposition and even of ridicule on the subject of baptism, not only from those who are opposed to infant baptism, but even from some who practise it. Yet nothing is more clear from the express words of Scripture, than the connexion of regeneration with the sacrament of baptism. The words of my text connect them inseparably. The apostle St. Paul expressly styles baptism the washing of regeneration, and it is every where spoken of and set forth in Scripture as a new state, a new life, commenced on new principles, and actuated by new motives. Nothing is more clear from the actual condition of man, as a fallen creature, spiritually dead, than that at some time, and by some means, he must be rendered capable of spiritual growth and advancement, otherwise the gospel is preached to stocks and stones. Now this we are certified by our baptism is then done for us ; such a measure of divine grace being then imparted, as renders us once more capable of trial and improvement, if duly cultivated. To this amount the Scriptures speak, *Repent and be baptized every one of you for the remission of sins, and ye shall receive the* HOLY GHOST. Nor is there a single instance in the acts of the apostles, the case of Cornelius excepted, which was for a special purpose, where spiritual communication of any kind was obtained, except at and after baptism.

In the primitive Church, immediately after the days of the apostles, the word baptism was hardly ever used, but instead thereof some word which expressed its spiritual accompaniments—such as regeneration, re-creation, renovation, resurrection, renewal, with many others, which all expressed a communication of spiritual benefit annexed to the right administration of this ordinance. Nor is there a single denomination of Christians who have set forth the articles of their common belief, as the principle of their particular union, who do not recognise this doctrine in connection with water baptism. If there are any such I have not met with them. That the Protestant Episcopal Church recognises it in the fullest manner, you have witnessed in the service of this day ; and though attempts have been made to explain away the true meaning of the words as used in the baptismal office, they are unauthorized and indefensible from any just view of the subject.

But however certain it is, that this view of the connexion of spiritual regeneration, with the sacrament of baptism is that set forth in the articles and declarations of their faith by the great majority of reformed Christian denominations, it has within no very distant period come to be questioned, so that the faith of many is unsettled, and the ordinance itself lowered in estimation, and lessened in the use. Considering this, therefore, to be a most dangerous corruption of Christianity, inasmuch as it strikes at the only revealed and appointed means of entering into covenant with GOD, and becoming partakers of his grace ; it is my duty to show you, both the true ground on which the doctrine rests, and also the fallacy of that on which the opposite notion is supported. Now this fallacy is two fold—

First an alteration in the meaning attached to the word regeneration.

Originally as I have showed you, it was always used to express the spiritual benefit conferred by baptism in connection with the change of outward condition thereby accomplished ; and as the spiritual benefit was infinitely the most valuable, that was chiefly in view in the use and application of the word.

By degrees, however, the word has become to be generally used as synonimous with conversion, or the turning of a sinner to GOD by repentance and faith. And this change it is, which creates the chief difficulty in the question. Accustomed to use the word in a particular sense, it sounds strange when used in a different one, as I doubt not was felt by many of you to day during the baptismal service. To give thanks to GOD for the conversion of an infant, which common sense told you could not possibly be the case, must have sounded strange in your ears, and contributed to lessen your respect for the ordinance itself. But take the word regeneration in its scriptural, primitive, and only just meaning ; as the communication of that principle of a new and spiritual life, which every child of Adam must receive from GOD, to render him capable of religious attainment, and consequently of salvation; all is consistent and harmonious, and is calculated to produce a deep and lasting impression upon the mind, of the goodness of GOD, of the reasonableness of religion, and of the worth and efficacy of this sacrament.

Secondly—Those views of the doctrine of grace, which are commonly called Calvinistic.

As it is the opinion and belief of those who thus think, that the grace of GOD, when given, cannot fail, but must operate in producing holiness of life ; and as much the greater uumber of baptized persons, who live to years of discretion, not only fall into sin, but continue therein through life, therefore they cannot admit, that the grace of GOD is bestowed on every baptized person.

And had they established this doctrine, had they proved their point, that the grace of GOD is of this nature, and necessitating in its operation, the conclusion would be a just one.   But as they have not done this, and never can do it, but at the expense of all religion, the scriptural connexion of regeneration with baptism, stands firm for the confirmation of that reasonable service, which the gospel requires, for the comfort and edification of parents, in the religious education of their children, and for the encouragement of all baptized persons, to work out their salvation with care and diligence, inasmuch as they are certified by this sacrament lawfully administered, that it is GOD that worketh in them both to will and to do.

That regeneration and conversion are not the same thing, is evident from this—that regeneration, or imparting spiritual life, to a creature spiritually dead, must be previous to the conversion of such a person from a state of actual sin ; it being clear and beyond dispute, that an unregenerate person never could be converted.

That the grace of GOD does not act upon us in a manner necessitating and compulsory is shown from our condition as accountable beings, hereafter to be judged, and punished or rewarded according to the improvement or abuse of the grace given to every one of us in CHRIST JESUS, whereof baptism is the only seal and certificate.

Having thus showed you the obligation of the ordinance, together with its nature and use, as an appointment of JESUS CHRIST in his Church ;   and noticed some of the corruptions and perversions of the doctrines which prevail in the present day ; I come now to the inquiry, who are the proper subjects of this ordinance—that is, who are entitled to it.

Secondly then—Every denomination of Christians is agreed, that all who can with understanding profess their faith in CHRIST, are fit subjects of this ordinance. In other words, that believers' baptism is lawful and scriptural : on this subject there is no dispute.

Every denomination of Christians, with the exception of one, is further agreed, that the infants, and other children of believing parents, are entitled to this only seal of the covenant of grace, and are in the practice of receiving them to Church membership by baptism. And being of the number of those who thus act, I shall now lay before you the grounds on which I think myself warranted in so doing, by the word of GOD.

First—As the covenant of mercy established in the blood of CHRIST, is one and the same, under every dispensation of religion, and embraces every description of persons, (every creature under heaven, is the strong expression of St. Paul) it must embrace infants as well as adults. But as there are no revealed means of becoming parties to the Christian covenant, but by the waters of baptism, I consider infants entitled to this benefit. *For the promise is unto you and to your children.*

Secondly—As it pleased GOD, in constituting the Old Testament Church, to command the membership of infants, and to direct them to be taken into covenant with him, by receiving the seal thereof at eight days old ; I consider, that an alteration in the seal merely, without any alteration in the conditions of the covenant, does not make such a change, as to exclude those who were before admissible—I therefore receive infants to membership in the Church of CHRIST, by the now appointed seal of baptism.

Thirdly—As the covenant is an everlasting covenant, ordered in all things and sure, no change, in any thing that relates to its essence, can be made, from the very nature of the parties to it, Almighty GOD, and mortal man. As therefore, the benefits of this covenant were once extended to infants by divine appointment, and no notice of any repeal of this privilege is either known or pleaded, as a minister of CHRIST, I dare not take upon me to narrow or curtail the grace of GOD, by refusing its seal now, to those who were once clearly entitled to it, upon any presumed inconsistency, or specious reasonings of an incapacity of which I cannot judge—I therefore baptize them.

Fourthly, As it is only by the influence of the HOLY SPIRIT that we are rendered capable of any thing good and acceptable in the sight of GOD—as this help and influence is essential to our growth in grace—and as it is only to persons rightly baptized, that this grace is promised and given, according to the authority of GOD's word, which is the more sure word of prophecy—I therefore receive and baptize them, that they may receive the gift of the HOLY GHOST—that the spirit of grace may early occupy their hearts, and work in them, and with their parents and friends, in training them up in the nurture and admonition of the LORD, that they may be guided into all necessary truth, and strengthened unto all required duty.

Fifthly. As *that which is born of the flesh is flesh* as by natural birth, we have no part in the covenant of grace, but are under a sentence of condemnation, which can be removed only by the merits of CHRIST's death, applied in the appointed means, by being baptized into his death, I therefore receive them into the ark of CHRIST's Church, that they may be made partakers of the promises, and nourished up unto eternal life: for *it is not the will of your Father which is in heaven, that one of these little ones should perish.*

On these scriptural and reasonable grounds, brethren and friends, do I as a minister of CHRIST, with a good conscience administer the sacrament of baptism to the subject, and after the manner, ye have this day witnessed; and it is your part carefully to consider and apply them.

But it may reasonably enough be expected that the objections of those who are opposed to this practice should not pass without notice, more especially as it might be said, that they could not be answered, and therefore were not met: for I know by long experience, that what I have this day said in discharge of my duty, will be considered as an attack upon a favourite notion, and withstood in every way that can be devised.

As there are two main objections to the practice of infant

baptism, and chiefly made use of by those who are opposed to the practice, I shall confine myself to them ; and this the rather because they contain all of difficulty on the question.

The first objection is, that there is no warrant in Scripture, no Thus saith the LORD, for administering this ordinance to infants. And I admit that there is no such express command as, Thus saith the LORD, thou shalt baptize thy children : but in reply I observe, that it was not necessary to give any such command.

Reflect a moment my hearers, what description of persons it was to whom the gospel was first preached. Was it not to Jews ?—to descendants of Abraham, the Israel of GOD, who for nineteen hundred years had been accustomed to the church membership of infants, by express command of GOD, in the application of the outward seal of the covenant, with a severe penalty denounced against the neglect of it ? In what sense then would those Jews to whom Peter preached the gospel on the day of Pentecost receive his exhortation to repent and be baptized, that they might receive the HOLY GHOST, with his declaration that the promise of this benefit was to them and to their children ? Would they understand it as excluding their infants from the benefits of the Christian covenant and membership in the church of CHRIST, or as continuing to them the privilege they were already in possession of and accustomed to ? I think there cannot be a reasonable doubt in any mind as to what their understanding of it would be. For it was a Jew preaching to Jews, and as such, would be understood, according to the general and long accustomed impression among them, on this point ; and the reason is equally good for a like understanding and practice on our part.

But Further. Had it been in the counsel of the unchangeable GOD to alter the terms of his covenant, on the revelation of the gospel, so as to exclude infants, then would an express prohibition of the former practice have been made. No such prohibition however being to be found, and no express command being necessary to those who were already accustomed to the membership of infants, I conclude that the objection is not of that serious nature which those who rely upon it would have it thought, nor sufficient to warrant the dangerous and injurious innovation of denying the sacrament of regeneration to infants.

But further yet. Was a Thus saith the LORD indispensable to the circumstantials of a positive institution? There are many things in our common Christianity to which we attach a very high degree of reverence and sanctity, and as to which we are equally deficient of this particular kind of authority. Where, for instance, shall we find a Thus saith the LORD—a positive command to observe the first day of the week, instead of the seventh, as the day of rest and holiness to the LORD? Where is the command obliging us to attend public worship on this or any other day? Where is there a like authority for admitting females to the LORD's Supper? None of these are thus provided for in the New Testament. Are they therefore corruptions of Christianity, and to be abandoned and put down in the use and observance? GOD forbid! and yet if the objection is good in the case of infant baptism, it is good as to these also, and the opponents of the one, ought to be equally so of the others to be consistent with their principles. How then stands the authority of all these religious observances? To this I answer: on the same ground on which the Scriptures themselves stand, as the word of GOD—that is, on the testimony, authority, and practice, of the primitive Church under the unerring guidance of the inspired apostles of our LORD JESUS CHRIST, than which, I think, we need no better security for the quiet and assurance of our consciences in any religious observance.

The next objection is, That faith and repentance being necessary preparations for baptism, therefore, as infants are incapable of either, they ought not to be baptised. To this I reply: that faith and repentance are absolutely necessary, and strictly required of all who are capable of them; and I would no more baptize an adult, a person come to years of discretion, without a profession of faith than my opponents would. But where do we learn, either from Scripture or reason, that these are required of those who from the nature of things have nothing to repent of, and cannot believe? How stands the case, as respects these qualifications for the seal of the first covenant? Of Abraham and all who were capable of it, faith was required;

but of those who were incapable it was not required, nevertheless we know assuredly that they were entitled to the seal and all its benefits. Shall we then, my hearers, venture to apply the Scripture differently in a similar case, and without an express warrant, say that the words of my text require an impossibility when they declare, *that except a man be born of water and of the spirit, he cannot enter into the kingdom of* GOD.

In defence of this objection, the strong hold of the opponents of infant baptism, is a text from St. Mark's gospel——*He that believeth and is baptized shall be saved.* Believing, they say, is put before baptism, and therefore none but believers ought to be baptized. Now, my friends, to show you the weakness and fallacy of all such arguments, I will oppose my text to theirs; in that it is said, and very expressly too, *except a man be born of water and of the spirit.* Here baptism is put before spiritual influence of any kind, of course before faith and repentance, which are fruits of the spirit; and therefore, if the views of our opponents are just, there is a contradiction in the Scriptures. In this case what is to be done? The same mouth spake both passages of Scripture, and the same mouth hath told us that the Scripture cannot be broken. Shall we reject either of the texts? We dare not. Shall we prefer one to the other? They are of the same authority. Shall we, then, force them to suit some particular notion of our own? GOD forbid! No, my brethren, let us learn to treat the word of GOD with more reverence, and comparing spiritual things with spiritual, that is, the two Testaments with each other——so expound and understand our Bible, that the whole purpose of GOD in the salvation of sinners may present one unbroken chain of wisdom and mercy from beginning to end; which can no otherwise be done, than by understanding that purpose to be the same, and applied to the same objects in every dispensation of religion. And let this difficulty from the two texts, according to the objection above noticed, show you the childishness of thus treating so weighty a subject, and warn you against all partial interpretation of Scripture. It is ONE, my hearers, like its great Author, and cannot safely or without sin, be broken up into separate authorities for disagreeing doctrine.

The two main objections to the practice of infant baptism being thus shown to have no foundation in either Scripture or reason, it is the less necessary to take up your time with those of a minor order. There are two more observations, however, closely connected with Scripture authority, and applying to the objections under notice, which I will lay before you.

The first is, that for fifteen hundred years, that is, from the days of the apostles to the reformation of religion in the sixteenth century, the practice of infant baptism was unquestioned in the Church of CHRIST. Now we know that the different religious parties watched each other as closely then as they do now. We know that every attempt to corrupt the gospel was denounced by some of them. If, then, the practice of admitting infants to baptism is a corruption, a departure from apostolic precept and practice in the religion of JESUS CHRIST, how unaccountable, my hearers, that no notice should be taken of it in all that time, and that only in the last three hundred years it should have been discovered and opposed.

The second is, that in a period of sixty-five years, that is from the ascension of our LORD to the death of the apostle St. John, there is no mention made, either in the Acts or in the Epistles, of any child or children of the first converts to Christianity being baptized when they came to years of discretion. Now, they were either baptized in infancy, or at adult age, or relapsed into Heathenism. But we read nothing, as I have said, of their being baptized when they came to a proper age—and we do read of whole households being baptized at once. Therefore, I conclude, *that the root being holy, the branches are so likewise*—that the promise being to them and to their children, every parental feeling would urge Christian parents to procure for their infants, as early as possible, the GRACE OF GOD, in the baptismal seal of the new covenant.

With these remarks I leave the question of the proper subjects of this sacrament to the judgment and the feelings of every Christian father and mother present, with the word of GOD for their guide, in preference to the vain reasoning of men, in favour of their own inventions, and proceed

III. Thirdly, to consider the mode, or manner of administering baptism.

The opponents of infant baptism are also opposed to the application of water to the subject in that sacrament, in any but one mode. They consider immersion, or plunging the whole body under the water, as the only Scriptural mode ; and that the practice of applying the water by pouring or sprinkling, as used by other denominations, is such a corruption, as vitiates and renders null and of no effect the rite itself, even when applied to a proper subject.

Though I do not subscribe to this opinion, yet fortunately there is no necessity that I should take up more of your attention upon a matter of so little real consequence. The mode of any ritual performance is not a point of saving faith, though it may and ought to be, under the same reasons, a point of dutiful observance. No Christian denomination thinks it an essential part of the LORD's supper to eat it at night, or to observe a fixed posture of the body ; yet certainly we have more exact information of the mode of administering that sacrament than the other ; and had such circumstances been of the essence of the ordinance, there would have been a clear direction in the Scriptures, which there is not.

The Church of which I am a minister, however, authorizes the administration of baptism by immersion ; and I am free to administer it in this way to any who scruple to receive it by the more usual, and equally efficacious mode, of pouring or sprinkling.

On this contested point, and the more contested, perhaps, because so little depends upon it, Scripture authority is not decisive of the mode, there being as much ground to infer that they went down into the water for the purpose of more easily pouring it on the multitudes, as for the purpose of immersing them.

In the case of St. Paul's own baptism, there is no evidence that he was immersed, or that there was any convenience for it in a private house. And in the baptism of the jailer by St. Paul in the prison at midnight, together with his whole house, all the circumstances are against the conclusion that immersion was the mode, and in favour of the supposition that infants or children formed a part of those baptized by St. Paul. Indeed so very indefinite are the authorities relied upon on those points, that it is difficult to conceive how sincere men can find in them a justification for separating from the Church, and adding to the divisions which deform the Christian world.

I will, therefore, conclude what I have to say on the mode of baptism, with these two remarks—

First, whatever is said in the gospel respecting John's baptism, the baptism of our LORD in the river Jordan, or any other baptizings there mentioned, have nothing to do with Christian baptism, which was not instituted until after our Saviour's resurrection, nor administered until the day of Pentecost. So that all reasonings from one to the other are inconsequent, and all analogies unfounded.

Secondly, as it is not the quantity of wax, or the size of the seal, that makes an instrument legal and effectual, so it is not the quantity of water in baptism, but the authority by which it is applied, that gives it its effect. Oceans of water without the authority of CHRIST to administer it, signify nothing, can bring no persons into covenant with GOD through him—while the smallest quantity duly applied, is effectual to convey over all the blessed fruits of his most gracious undertaking for the salvation of sinners. Hence arises a most serious consideration, my friends, in this enquiry; whether all who venture to administer baptism to any of the subjects, or in any of the modes in which it is used, have such authority for what they do, as to render valid and worthy to be depended on, the high privileges contained in the authorized application of water, in the name of the FATHER, and of the SON, and of the HOLY GHOST.

The application of what has been said is,

I. To those who, by reason of the contentions which have grown out of this subject, have become unsettled in their minds as to the nature and necessity of the ordinance, and have therefore neglected it either as to themselves or their families. Upon such let me press the words of my text; they speak volumes in a small compass—*Except a man be born of water and of the* SPIRIT, both baptized outwardly, and renewed inwardly, *he cannot enter the kingdom of* GOD—he can neither become a member of the Church militant upon earth, or of the Church triumphant in heaven. By the express appointment of GOD, baptism with water is the seal of that covenant in which the mercies of redemption are made over to men. Let no man, therefore, deceive you with vain reasonings, lessening the obligation and and importance of this sacred ordinance. Reflect, my friends, on the awful condition of those who are without any title to the covenanted mercy of the gospel, and *come thou and all thy house into the ark.*

Next, to those who baptized in the name of the FATHER, the SON, and the HOLY GHOST, and thereby most solemnly pledged to the service of GOD, have nevertheless broken their baptismal engagements, and walking according to the course of this world, set at nought the promises and threatnings of GOD in the gospel. Alas, my brethren, are you aware of your danger, of the double guilt you are heaping upon your souls, by thus rejecting JESUS CHRIST and him crucified for you? Hear, therefore, the warning this day given you. GOD is yet merciful, and calls you to repentance, and CHRIST ever liveth to make intercession for you. While this your day of grace lasts, therefore, be zealous, and repent, that your sins may be blotted out, and your spiritual strength be renewed to escape from the snare of the devil, and from that eternal death which is the only wages of his service.

Lastly, to those who have this day pledged their children to GOD in the sacrament of baptism.

Let the solemn engagements this day entered into pervade your whole duty to your children and to yourselves. Whatever you plan and contrive for their welfare, let the affecting remembrance that you have given them to GOD, and promised to train them for his service both here and hereafter, rule over your conduct. And let the blessed assurance that in all you now undertake for their well being and advancement, either as respects the present life or that which is to come, you have the promise of Him who cannot fail you, that they are his peculiar care ; that his blessing will be upon them and upon your faithful endeavours to train them up in the nurture and admonition of the LORD ; that his good providence will so direct and order their cause through this troublesome and evil world ; that they will be an ornament to their family, a credit to their friends, useful to their country, and a comfort and support to the declining years of their parents.   And in the great day of eternity he bids you look forward to such a re-union with those who are most dear to you in this life, as shall never be interrupted or done away.   Take courage then from the word of Him, all whose promises are yea and amen to us in CHRIST JESUS. They are pledged to you this day in the covenant of his rich redeeming love, and may they strengthen you to a faithful discharge of all your duties.

And now my brethren and hearers, let me appeal both to your hearts and to your understandings, whether this solemn reception of these children to the benefits of the .Christian salvation has any thing in it that savours of folly, or is liable to ridicule—whether it is mere baby sprinkling as some profanely call it, or a most efficacions means of grace both to parents and children ? Consider what the effect upon society would be, were all parents and children really under the influence of these solemn engagements, and diligent to fulfil their vows to GOD. Consider further, who can look forward to comfort and satisfaction in his family, with the best hope—the parent who *dedicates*, or he who withholds his family from GOD ? And then look round and see what the neglect of this and of other religious duty has brought the morals of the people to, and let the awful absence of the fear of GOD every where visible, warn you to try another course, and engage you to *ask for the old paths—where is the good way, and to walk therein, that you may find rest for your souls.*   And may GOD bless this endeavour to state plainly his truth, and recall you to the right ways of the LORD, for JESUS CHRIST's sake.   AMEN.

SERMON II.

CONFIRMATION.

ACTS xv. 41.

" And he went through Syria and Cilicia, confirming the churches."

THE person here spoken of, my brethren and hearers, is the apostle St. Paul ; and the work he is represented as engaged in, must be considered as of importance to their religious advancement, and in such a sense important, as connected with the assurance of their Faith. This I trust will appear evident to you, my hearers, when you recollect that, at the time here spoken of, the Gentile Christians had no Scriptures of any kind, as a fixed standard to which to refer for the trial of their faith. More particularly they had not as yet the Scriptures of the New Testament to which to bring both their faith and hope. Every thing depended on the evidence, the ministers of CHRIST were enabled to give of the authority by which they spake and acted. Without this there could have been no claim on their obedience, nor could the guilt of unbelief and rejection of the gospel have been charged upon them.

Hence we discern the importance of St. Paul's personal ministry to these newly planted Churches, and how much depended upon the authority by which he acted, for the assurance of their faith.

To suppose, however, that the promulgation and spread of the Scriptures has done away the importance of this evidence to us, and that the Bible is a substitute for it, can proceed only from ignorance, prejudice, or interested motive ; because the ordinances of the gospel, from the very nature of the things they are connected with, derive their whole certainty, and by consequence their efficacy, from the authority by which they are administered.

Having before us then this day the performance of the like

duty, it appeared reasonable for the edification and assurance of those most interested, to take this brief notice of a point now too much overlooked in the Christian community, that they might with the greater confidence, both dedicate themselves to GOD, and expect those spiritual blessings which he has been pleased to annex, in the ordinary administrations of his grace, to the use of outward means.

The words of my text may be thought by some, remote from the particular object now before us. But whether we take the expression *confirming the churches*, in the extended sense of animating and encouraging them by his exhortations, by his counsel, by his example and authority, to steadfastness and increase in faith and holiness; or use it in the more restrained sense of administering those sacred rites and holy ordinances of CHRIST'S religion, which are by divine appointment, at one and the same time, outward and visible signs of GOD'S mercy and grace, and means or channels whereby we receive the same; we are equally furnished with the warrant of apostolic usage, for the performance of a like duty to the same gracious end. The text therefore needs no forcing to suit my purpose, more especially as I trust to show beyond all reasonable ground of objection, that the more special purpose of our assembling together at this time, formed a part of that duty which the apostle performed in this visit to the churches of Syria and Cilicia.

The subject under consideration being the ordinance or rite of confirmation, I shall discourse upon it, for your edification, under the following heads.

FIRST. The origin and authority of this ordinance as used in the Church of CHRIST from the very beginning of Christianity.

SECONDLY. The purpose or design with which it was administered in the primitive Church.

THIRDLY. Its use and propriety, as continued in the Church to this day.

FOURTHLY. I shall point out the qualifications necessary to those who would receive it with advantage.

And he went through Syria and Cilicia confirming the Churches.

First, I am to lay before you the origin and authority of this ordinance of confirmation, as used in the Church of CHRIST from the very beginning of Christianity.

For this, my brethren and hearers, as for all the other appointments of GOD's wisdom and mercy, in the redemption and salvation of sinners, we must go to the Scriptures of our faith ; whatever is not there set forth for our learning, or commanded for our obedience, cannot be essential in our practice. Nor yet on the other hand, can it be safe for us to reject or lay aside what is there set forth, as an ordinance of our religion, which has the sanction of apostolic usage, and of a reasonable and profitable application.

Coeval, then, with the administration of the ordinances of religion in the Church of CHRIST, we find it to have been the practice of his apostles to follow the sacrament of baptism, sometimes immediately, sometimes more remotely in point of time, with the imposition of their hands together with prayer, that the persons who by baptism had become the disciples of CHRIST, might in this, the ordinary and appointed mode, receive the gift of the HOLY GHOST, whether that was in the communication of those extraordinary operations which at the first evidenced the divine original of the gospel, and of the authority of those to whom it was recommitted ; or in the more ordinary, more necessary, and more frequent effects of his presence as the promised comforter, guide, and sanctifier of CHRIST's disciples. And the first instance of its administration is mentioned in the eighth chapter of the Acts of the apostles, under these circumstances.

Philip, who was ordained one of the seven deacons, or inferior ministers of the Church, driven by the persecution consequent on the death of Stephen, from Jerusalem, went down to Samaria, and preached CHRIST unto them ; and by the power of his doctrine, and the evidence of the miracles which he wrought in proof of its divine origin, converted them to the faith, and baptized them. We learn further, however, my hearers, that though they were converted and baptized, there was yet something more provided for their furtherance in the faith, which Philip, though a minister of CHRIST, and clothed with miraculous power, could not confer upon them.

Hence we read, that when the apostles, who were at Jerusalem heard that a Church was gathered at Samaria, they sent two of their body, Peter and John, who went down to them, and prayed for them, and laid their hands upon them, and then and thereby, as the appointed means, they received the HOLY GHOST.

The next instance of the exercise of this apostolic ordinance, recorded in the Scriptures, is in the nineteenth chapter of the same book, where St. Paul having baptized some of the disciples of John the baptist, afterwards laid his hands upon them, by which act they received the HOLY GHOST, and spake with tongues, and prophesied.

From these two instances then, we learn, my brethren and hearers, that a sacred and significant ordinance or religious rite, subsequent to and connected with the sacrament of baptism, has the same origin and authority with our holy religion, and is as much a part of it, as the sabbath and the sacraments. And when we are further informed, as we are by this same apostle, that this ordinance or rite, under the name of laying on of hands, is among the first principles of the doctrine of CHRIST, our regard for, and observance of it, must be greatly increased; as must also be our admiration that in so large a portion of the professing Christian world it should be so lightly esteemed, and abandoned in the use; for without any dispute, first principles in all institutions, whether civil or religious, are sacred, and can neither be departed from without danger, nor abrogated without guilt.

In the sixth chapter of St. Paul's Epistle to the Hebrews, we find that apostle, in enumerating the principles of the doctrine of CHRIST, including laying on of hands, in connexion with baptism. And in the third chapter of his Epistle to Titus, he speaks of the washing of regeneration, together with the renewing of the HOLY GHOST, as parts or principles in that salvation, which GOD *our Saviour, hath shed on us abundantly, through Jesus Christ our Saviour.* From all which, and from the practice of every apostolic Church, continued unto this day; we feel and believe that it was intended so to be continued, and that by abandoning it, we should deprive the Church of an appointed means of grace, and of a ground of assurance to all her devout members. Our hope of salvation, my brethren and friends, if it be a good hope, is so interwoven with conformity to the gospel, and the assurance of faith so dependent for its reality, on the authority by which the outward and sensible signs of invisible things, the sacraments and ordinances of the Church, are administered and received, that we dare not venture to add to, or diminish from the pattern given us in the primitive Church; or to cast off a practise, which then was, and now is, so helpful, in confirming to believers the promises of the gospel; which rests upon such clear declarations of GOD's holy word, and such safe interpretation of their meaning, as that of apostolic usage. Remember, I pray you my brethren, that it is one thing to take assurance in matters of faith, it is quite a different thing to be entitled to it.

More especially, is the continuance of this ordinance in the Church, at the present day, of the highest use and importance; by reason that in the natural and regular course of things, the sacrament of baptism, which at the first was administered chiefly, though not solely, to adults, or grown up persons, came to be administered to their children. For as the promise was to them and to their children, there can be no reasonable doubt, that as soon as there were those, in any Christian society, who could be the subjects of this grace, its benefits were applied to them. And I appeal to every Christian mother present, whether she would not just as soon withhold the breast from the infant, as the infant from the grace of GOD given in baptism duly and rightly administered.

When these infants therefore, came to years of discretion, to understand the nature and extent of the Christian obligation, and were desirous in their own persons, to make profession of their faith in CHRIST, to take upon themselves their baptismal vows, and dedicate themselves to the cause of GOD and religion, they were provided, in this apostolic ordinance, with the means of doing so, in a manner calculated both to impress and encourage them.

It is calculated to impress them with the deepest reverence, from the solemn nature of the engagements entered into, and from the preparation required, from its being transacted in public, with the Bishop or chief governor of the Church, by whom in person, could this office alone be performed.

It is calculated to encourage them, by the fullest assurance of all spiritual help given them for the performance of their Christian duties, by the prayers of the whole Church in their behalf, and by the laying on of the hands of him, to whom is committed, according to the appointment of CHRIST, the dispensing of his mysteries in the Church.

Hence it is called Confirmation, because it is a public ratifying or confirming of the joint obligation entered into at baptism, between GOD and his creature ; and because it is to every true believer, the baptism of the HOLY GHOST, certified by an appropriate sign.

With these scriptural, reasonable, and profitable claims on the observance of all Christian people, it is surely worthy of the most serious consideration, why it has been abandoned by any denomination, or how it is possible to find a substitute for it, in any of those inventions of men, who, wise in their own conceits, venture to sit in judgement on the appointment of heaven, and to alter and amend the gospel, and its ordinances, as if it were a constitution of civil government, or a regulation of civil society. We are told by way of warning, my hearers, by Him who knew to its root, the pride and presumption of our fallen natures—*that there is a way which seemeth right unto a man, but the end thereof are the ways of death.* Let us ever reverently bear in mind, my brethren and friends, that our religion in all its parts, is the appointment of heaven for our good ; that in its every office there is a purpose of divine wisdom to be answered, and that we never can be safe, (safe in such a sense as alone ought to satisfy a rational being, on the unspeakable interests of eternity,) unless we are built on the joint agreement of GOD's word and GOD's authority. These two he hath seen good to join indissolubly together, for our comfort and assurance. That which GOD hath joined therefore, let no man venture to put asunder.

Secondly, I come, now, in the second place, to point out

to you the purpose and design with which it was administered in the primitive Church.

This, as has been already showed in part, was to draw down upon the person or persons confirmed, the blessing of GOD, in the gift of the HOLY GHOST, as the seal of their covenant state, the witness to their adoption into the family of CHRIST, and the root or spring whence all holy desires, all good counsels, and all just works do proceed. This was always the chief design of this ordinance——whether the presence of the HOLY SPIRIT was manifested by those extraordinary gifts which were for signs to them that believed not, and for the spread and advancement of the gospel; or by those ordinary, but more essential operations of his power, by which the heart is sanctified to GOD, and the life devoted to his service.

But another purpose also was intended to be answered by this ordinance of confirmation——which was, to establish believers in the vital doctrine of the unity of the Church. A doctrine which our LORD laid down with the utmost plainness and precision, as decisive of the fellowship to which we are called by the gospel, and which his apostles pressed upon their converts with the utmost earnestness, but which seems now to be nearly lost sight of, in a divided Christian world. *There is one body*, says St. Paul to the Ephesians, *and one* SPIRIT, *even as ye are called with one hope of your calling.* Therefore the power to impart the gifts of the SPIRIT, whether ordinary or extraordinary, was confined after the ascension of CHRIST to his apostles, and to such as they commissioned to govern the Churches in his name. Hence we find St. Paul appealing to this, the sign or mark of an apostle of CHRIST, manifested in his person, as an argument with the Corinthian and Galatian Churches, to recover them from the heresy and schism into which they had been seduced. (Have Christians of the present day lost the meaning of these words—— or has any revelation been made by which the crime is no longer possible?) *I am jealous over you with a godly jealousy*, says he to the Corinthian Church, *lest by any means your minds should be corrupted from the simplicity that is in* CHRIST. *For if he that cometh preacheth another* JESUS, *or if ye receive another* SPIRIT, *or another gospel*, then may you reasonably dispute my claim.

But such are false apostles, deceitful workers, transforming them-
selves into the apostles of CHRIST. *For truly the signs of an*
apostle were wrought among you (by me) in all patience, in signs
and wonders, and mighty deeds.

In like manner he argues with the Galatians on the same
subject. *I marvel* (says he) *that ye are so soon removed from*
Him that called you into the GRACE OF CHRIST, *unto another*
gospel. O foolish Galatians, who hath bewitched you? This
only would I learn of you, Received ye the SPIRIT *by the works of*
the law, or by the hearing of faith? He, therefore, that ministereth
the SPIRIT *to you, and worketh miracles among you, doeth he it by*
the works of the law, or by the hearing of faith? And thus could
every individual Christian, as well as every Christian Church,
determine satisfactorily on the truth and certainty of their interest in CHRIST, by this standing witness to the Divine Authority
of those by whom the gospel was preached, and the sacraments
and ordinances of the Church administered to them. And well
would it be for Christians of the present day to consider whether
they have any other, or better, means of determining such
important questions.

At this stage of the subject, we are prepared to inquire,
whether this particular ordinance of confirmation, known in
the apostles' days by the name of laying on of hands, formed
part of the duty performed by St. Paul in this visit to the
Churches of Syria and Cilicia.

The opinion that it did, rests on the following circumstances.
An interval of seven years, at the least had passed, according
to the chronology of the Bible, from the time they had first
received the gospel until this visit from Paul and Barnabas. In
that space of time many converts were doubtless added to the
Church, who required, and were equally entitled to the benefit
and assurance of apostolic ministrations with those who preceded
them—to say nothing of those younger members of baptized
households, who must in this time have grown up in the nurture
and admonition of the LORD, and been prepared to make a
public profession of Christianity. When, therefore, we find
this ordinance under the name of laying on of hands, set forth
in the Scriptures as one of the first principles of the doctrine of

CHRIST—when we find that it was practised by the apostles, in connexion with the sacrament of baptism—that it was used by St. Paul himself : when we hear him appealing to the Corinthian and Galatian Churches, led away into heresy and schism—by this personal proof to them of his authority as a minister of CHRIST, under the name of ministering and receiving the SPIRIT—when, above all, we reflect that to apostolic hands was committed the power of communicating the SPIRIT, whether in his ordinary or extraordinary operations—you, my hearers, must judge whether the text is forced to the subject, or whether it is such a fair and reasonable inference, as it is our duty to make from the known character of the apostles and the circumstances of the case.

There was yet a further purpose, however, to which this ordinance was applied in the primitive Church, but subsequent to the times of the apostles, which I will mention.

It was believed to obviate and cure any defects, either of irregularity, or of want of authority in the administration of baptism. Hence, such persons as had been baptized in infancy either by laymen or by ministers of heretical Churches, when they came afterwards to a better mind on the subject of religion, and were desirous to join the true apostolic Church of CHRIST, had the deficiencies of their baptism remedied by the laying on of the hands of the Bishop : for it was an early decision of the Council of the Church, that as there was but one baptism, it ought not to be repeated, even where irregularity and defect of authority attended it.

Observations of this description appear strange, and of an obsolete character, to many of you I doubt not, my hearers ; but they belong to the subject—they are necessary to explain and enforce it, as a Christian ordinance, and a Christian duty ; and in their just application they belong to thousands, who are accountable for gospel privileges, for the light of life in the word of CHRIST, and for saving ordinances—but who quench them all, in the pride and poverty of human authority. Who search not the Scriptures for thus saith the LORD, but blindly follow the thus saith the sect or leader, to whom they have attached themselves—and they are mentioned on this occasion to awaken your attention to what can never prejudice your eternal interest, to wit: the ground of your hope—the foundation on which you are all building it, with this additional remark, which I beseech you to take to your most serious consideration—that the sacraments and ordinances of the gospel are of divine appointment, and can only be lawfully administered by divine authority—that Christian privileges, gospel hope, and Scriptural assurance, are all founded on covenant engagements, and are only to be enjoyed by us as we are faithful to the engagement on our part—that sincerity in error, is no excuse for it, and that all this flows from the unalterable Scripture declaration. *Other foundation can no man lay, than that is laid, which is* JESUS CHRIST.

III. Thirdly, I am to point out its use and propriety, as continued in the Church to this day.

Now whatever this was in the primitive Church, the same in its degree is it in the present day, *For* JESUS CHRIST *is the same yesterday, to-day, and for ever.*

The only difficulty on the subject grows out of the close connexion of this ordinance with miraculous gifts as used in the primitive Church. But when we know, as we do my brethren, from the word of GOD, that this was not the sole purpose of its administration, but that it was the appointed means of obtaining the HOLY SPIRIT, in those gifts and graces, which are universally necessary to salvation, the difficulty should be done away, and all stand prepared to submit themselves to the righteousness of GOD in any and every appointment of his wisdom for the communication of his grace.

The unity of the Church also, by which is meant the union, fellowship, or agreement of believers in the faith, doctrine, worship, and authority of that one spouse and body of CHRIST, which he bought with his own blood, and in communion with which only, are the promises of GOD yea and amen to us in CHRIST, is of as great importance to us now as to the primitive Christians. And though we cannot evidence our title to this distinction by miraculous powers, yet we can avouch the authority of those to whom miracles were given for the establishment of the Church, transmitted down to us by a verifiable succession for your benefit. And by the orders of the ministry, the sacraments of the Church, and this ordinance we show that we continue *in the apostles' doctrine and fellowship, and in breaking of bread, and prayers;* and we only ask those who in any of these particulars act differently, to show an equally safe and satisfactory ground of trust in matters of faith.

In the application of the sacrament of baptism to infants, however, (a practice which stands on the same ground of divine authority with the Scriptures and the Christian sabbath,) both the use and the propriety of continuing this rite in the Church is most clearly evidenced.

That those who have been dedicated to GOD in their infancy, and by the providence and permission of the great Head of the Church, have been admitted to become parties to the covenant of grace, should, on obtaining a suitable sense of the benefits conferred on them, and of the weighty obligations they have come under, manifest their thankfulness, and ratify in their own persons, the engagements entered into for them, is the dictate both of reason and religion. From the days of the apostles, therefore, it has been the rule of the Church to receive such as were baptized in infancy, to full fellowship and communion by this ordinance of confirmation, in which the person confirmed renews or ratifies, before the assembled congregation, the baptismal covenant, with a full understanding of the nature and extent of the obligations he or she comes under——enters into a most solemn engagement to fulfil the duties of the Christian life, and before many witnesses, makes that good confession of CHRIST, which is required of every believer. And the Church receiving this accession to her communion, invokes the blessing of GOD on the engagement made, and by the imposition of the hands of her chief officers, imparts that HOLY SPIRIT which was given to abide with her for ever, for the comfort, strength, and sanctification of all her members.

In the sacrament of baptism rightly administered, we receive by the HOLY GHOST, spiritual regeneration, together with remission of sins, whether original or actual. But unless we cast away from us the authority of GOD's word, and seek to be wise above what is written, it is by this divine appointment of laying on of hands, that we receive such measure of the HOLY GHOST as is required to enable us to overcome the world, to resist the devil, deny the flesh, to fight the good fight of faith, and lay hold on eternal life.

By the continuance of this ordinance in the administrations of the Church, a strong objection against the baptism of infants is removed.

It is objected that it is a mockery to administer a solemn sacrament to a creature unconscious of any thing that is done ; and that it is unjust to bind any one by the assent of another, without the privity and concurrence of the person bound. These objections, my brethren, are more specious than solid, and carry on their face the mark of this world's wisdom.

In reply, it may briefly be observed, that it is nevertheless just such a mockery as GOD commanded and countenanced in the Old Testament Church in the ordinance of circumcision, which is no where forbidden in the gospel which the apostles of CHRIST sanctioned, and which the records of the Church show to have been the practice from the days of St. John the beloved disciple. And just such a piece of injustice as is most readily allowed in temporal things for their benefit.

But whatever weight any may be disposed to give to objections of this character, must be removed by the provision made in this ordinance for their taking upon themselves with understanding and seriousness, the obligations and privileges of that sacrament. While there is abundant cause of thanksgiving to GOD, that by this mockery, as it is profanely called, these unconscious creatures have been taken care of, trained up and nurtured in the fear of the LORD, prayed for, and prepared for those fuller communications of his grace and good SPIRIT, promised to carry them onward in the divine life *unto a perfect man, unto the measure of the stature of the fulness of* CHRIST.

Having thus, my brethren and hearers, laid before you— though in a very brief and inadequate manner, the origin, authority, and use of this ordinance in the Church of CHRIST, I will now, as was proposed in the fourth place, point out the qualifications necessary to those who would receive it with advantage.

The first qualification I will mention, is knowledge, by which is meant such an acquaintance with what GOD hath revealed to us of the condition of man, of his purposes of mercy in CHRIST, of the means of grace, and of the duties and obligations of a Christian as all may attain to from reading the Scriptures, and the instructions of pious friends.

Secondly, a devout and serious spirit, or religious frame of mind. This is essential to any expectation of advantage from this or any other ordinance of religion. And if any thing can produce such a frame of mind, it surely must be present when we come forward in the face of the Church, to enter into solemn covenant with GOD in CHRIST, and in the terms and spirit of the baptismal vow, to renounce the world, the flesh, and the devil, to believe in GOD and to serve him, with the firm though humble expectation of being enabled, by his good SPIRIT, to keep this vow, unto our life's end.

Thirdly, repentance, by which is meant a hearty and sincere sorrow for all the sins, negligences, and ignorances, we have been personally guilty of against GOD and our neighbour, with real purpose of amended life. And this evidenced by humble confession of them to GOD, with prayer for pardon of them through the merits of CHRIST—by earnest endeavours to repair any wrong done or offence committed against our neighbour—and by a change or alteration in our former course of life.

The last qualification I shall mention is faith ; by which is to be understood, in this case, such a belief of what GOD hath spoken unto us by his Son, with such reliance on the promises made us through him, as to lead us to desire and earnestly to expect the fulfilment of them ; and with such trust and confidence in the means he hath appointed for the communication of his grace, as enables us cordially and joyfully to use them.

Examine yourselves then, my brethren, who now mean to ratify and confirm your baptismal engagements, whether you are thus prepared, whether you can now, with a good conscience, make that full and unreserved surrender of yourselves to GOD, which his service requires, that open confession of JESUS CHRIST as your GOD, your saviour and your king which his religion demands from all who would be his disciples indeed, and that firm determination to obey the gospel which its precepts enjoin. For confirmation is only another name for your solemn dedication of yourselves to God and his Son—an open renunciation of the world, and separation of yourselves from henceforth, from its unlawful and unhallowed pursuits.

If you are thus qualified and prepared, I can answer for the effect—the blessing awaits you, and there is help at hand to go on unto perfection. If you are not thus qualified, make not a mockery of sacred things, but let your deficiency deepen your penitence, and quicken your endeavour in preparing to meet your Saviour in the appointments of his grace upon earth, that you may thereby be prepared to meet him with joy, and not with grief in his heavenly kingdom.

Yet let none be deterred by timidity of spirit, humility of mind, or unreasonable fears, that they are not good enough to offer themselves to God ; you can surely tell whether you sincerely desire and seek the favour of God, and the life of the world to come. If you do long for this happy frame of mind, let your wants be your warrant to come to Christ, for this is a gracious ordinance : *Come unto me all ye that are weary and heavy laden, and I will give you rest—unto this man will I look saith the* Lord, *even to him that is of a contrite heart, and of an humble spirit, and that trembleth at my word.* Heaven and earth are full of encouragement to the penitent—to such *the* Spirit *and the bride say, come—and let him that heareth say, come—and let him that is athirst, come—and whosoever will, let him come, and take of the water of life freely.*

SERMON III.

NATURE AND DESIGN OF THE HOLY COMMUNION.

St. Luke xxii. 19. (last clause.)

"This do in remembrance of me."

Few things of such prime importance to our religious condition are so little understood, it is to be feared, as the nature and design of the sacraments of the Church. Of the small number, comparatively speaking, who come to them, the number is still smaller of those who rightly apprehend their purpose, and perceive distinctly, the solemn obligation entered into by their observance.

This is more especially the case with the sacrament of baptism, which has declined in the estimation of the great majority of those who bring their children to this ordinance, into a mere ceremony for giving its name to an infant, coupled perhaps with somewhat of a superstitious feeling. But it is also true, in a degree greatly to be lamented, of the higher sacrament of the body and blood of Christ, as is evidenced by the slight influence produced upon the life, in numbers who partake of it ; it being by far too common, for the credit of the Christian profession, to see in those who are communicants, as much engagement with the world as if they had not renounced it in their baptism, and solemnly undertaken, over the broken body and shed blood of their Saviour, to walk in newness of life.

If to this we add, that entire neglect and disregard of this divinely appointed ordinance, which the great majority in Christian lands manifest, it presents an awful proof of the declining state of religion among us, and calls for the united exertions of ministers and members to withstand this evil ; the one by explaining the nature and design of the institution, with the obligation to observe it, in all who would be saved—the other by showing, in the example of their lives, its influence and effect as a means of grace.

That it is a duty which no baptized person can excuseably neglect, there can be no question. *This do in remembrance of me* being as much a command of the gospel, as *Thou shalt not kill* is of the decalogue ; and let us ever bear in mind, that they proceeded from the same mouth, and will be enforced by that supreme authority which governs all things, in heaven and upon earth. And I mention this to awaken the consciences of that great multitude who, though they are partakers of the benefits of the gospel, are yet unaffected by them, and in an especial manner withhold themselves from this ordinance. Now though this unjustifiable neglect most commonly proceeds from a real and visible preference of the pleasures of sin, in some of its many and deceitful allurements ; yet in some cases, and those not infrequent, ignorance of the nature and design of the institution, and a consequent erroneous view of all that relates to it as a positive appointment of Christianity, keeps back some who might otherwise be induced to make this good confession of the LORD JESUS CHRIST as their only hope of acceptance with GOD.

This therefore I shall endeavour to remove by laying before you,

FIRST ; A brief explanation of the word Sacrament.

SECONDLY ; I shall point out the nature and design of the ordinance,

And then conclude with an enforcement of the duty.

This do in remembrance of me.

I. First, I am to lay before you a brief explanation of the word sacrament.

It may perhaps appear strange to you, my brethren and hearers, that the word sacrament is not used in the Scriptures as applied either to baptism or the LORD's Supper, and that the original word in the Latin language translated *sacrament* in our version, has little or no affinity with that in the original Greek in the New Testament, for which it has been substituted. It is nevertheless the case, while it is by no means clear, that the exchange has been advantageous.

In its most common use the original Latin word, translated sacrament, was applied to the military oath by which the Roman soldiers pledged themselves to their general, and in which, being heathens, they devoted themselves to the infernal Gods if they proved unfaithful ; whereas the Greek word for which this was substituted denotes what we express by the word mystery, that is, something of a spiritual and invisible nature, figured out by an external and visible representation. And as the word mystery was chiefly applied to the higher and more sublime superstitions of heathen religion, to which none were admitted but with proper qualifications, and under the most solemn obligations, it was naturally and properly made use of by the Apostle to express in like manner, both the obligations and the expectations contained in the most sublime appointments of the Christian religion.   The doubt expressed, that the exchange of the words has not been advantageous is grounded upon this, that by reason of this change, the obligations incurred are mainly respected, while the means of fulfilling them through the aid of divine grace, specially annexed to the sacraments of the gospel, and an integral part of their value to us is not sufficiently set forth.   Especially true is this of the sacrament of the LORD's Supper, which is not an initiating ordinance like the sacrament of baptism, to be but once performed, but a continually returning duty, involving the original obligations entered into at baptism, with the assurance thereby pledged of the spiritual help, necessary to fulfil them.

This however is only so far of importance, my brethren, as it may serve to keep your minds evenly balanced ; equally free from a low, and too familiar, view of the ordinance, as a mere memorial of the death of CHRIST, and from an inflated and enthusiastic notion of a superstitious sanctity, alike destructive of all rational performance of this, or of any other religious duty.   For the word sacrament is now understood, by all well instructed Christians, to mean, when applied to the LORD's supper, not simply the commemoration of our Saviour's passion for us, nor yet the renewal of our baptismal engagements ; nor as a fresh vow of fidelity to the captain of our salvation, as soldiers of the cross ;   nor yet as a visible pledge of heaven's mercy and favour, to all who worthily partake of it ; but as combining all these, in one sublime and sacred mystery, accompanied by visible and significant symbols, ordained by CHRIST himself, for the perpetual comfort and assurance of all his faithful disciples.

With this brief explanation of the word Sacrament, we shall be better prepared, I trust, to apprehend the nature and design of the ordinance ; which was what I proposed, in the second place, to point out to you.

II. All appointments of a ritual and ceremonious description, in religion, are rendered necessary by the corrupt and fallen condition of human nature. Through this depravation of our faculties, we naturally prefer things present and sensible, however transitory in their nature, to those which are remote and invisible, however satisfied we may be of their superiority, both in degree and duration. Of this the proof is, alas, but too easy ; there being none present, who are not fully persuaded of the infinite disproportion between things temporal and eternal, while there are many, who are in no way influenced or affected by this acknowledged difference. A religion therefore wholly spiritual, and abstracted from sensible things, would have been impracticable to creatures so continually acted upon by external objects, while their spiritual faculties were deadened and perverted by the entertainment of sin. To meet this, the actual condition of human nature, the religion GOD hath revealed to us, is most wisely and mercifully adapted. The evidence that it is divine, is so full, clear, and convincing, as to render inexcusable all who reject or neglect it, when fairly proposed to them. The doctrines it teaches are so consistent with the perfections of GOD, and so fitted to the imperfections of man, so adapted to increase his happiness in this life, and to perpetuate it in eternity, that faith and obedience are enforced by the purest and highest reason, while the external appointments of the gospel in things ritual and positive are not only orderly and decent in themselves, but calculated moreover to give vigour and effect to things moral and spiritual, of which they are a figure.

The Church, the ministry, and the sacraments therefore, are helps to faith ; resting places, as it were, and sensible objects, on which our poor earthly and grovelling minds may repose, while contemplating the substance of those shadows, as we journey onwards to eternity ; and they are therefore of divine institution, that our assurance may be full and complete. It is not however as helps to faith only, that these divine appointments are limited ; a wise and merciful GOD hath been graciously pleased to constitute them channels, or means, of that spiritual grace, or divine assistance, without which we can do nothing in working out our everlasting salvation.

With respect, therefore, to the particular ordinance under consideration, as all the benefits and advantages we derive from the mercy of GOD, are the consequences of CHRIST's undertaking for us ; and as his death upon the cross was in full satisfaction of the penalty we had incurred ; and at once, a proof of the highest love towards us, both on the part of GOD the Father, in laying upon his beloved Son *the iniquities of us all ;* and on the part of this beloved Son, in freely consenting *to bear our sins in his own body upon the tree ;* this particular circumstance, of his humiliation and sufferings in our behalf, has been consecrated into the highest and most comprehensive, the most solemn and efficacious appointment, of the religion he has established in the world.

The Sacrament of the Lord's Supper therefore, is in the nature of a memorial, or solemn religious commemoration of this great and influential event, to be perpetually celebrated by all his true disciples and worshippers, until the end of time. Of this its commemorative nature, we have an example and exposition in the institution of the passover in the Old Testament Church. For as that was to the Jews a constant annual memorial of their deliverance from Egyptian bondage, and particularly of the distinguishing mercy of GOD in sparing those households which were marked with the blood of the Paschal Lamb, when he smote the first born of the land of Egypt with death ; in like manner, and by the closest analogy, the sacrifice of CHRIST upon the cross, is to Christians the perpetual memorial of their deliverance from the bondage of sin ; and the application of his blood, who is the true Paschal Lamb, the only shield from the penalty of eternal death, denounced against every transgression of the holy law of GOD.

To limit this solemn ordinance, however, my brethren, to the nature of a mere memorial, after the manner of an anniversary commemoration of some memorable temporal event, is altogether to lose sight of its sacramental character. For it is further, in the nature of a feast upon a sacrifice, that is, a thankful and joyful religious participation of instituted emblems—or outward and visible signs of a sacrifice already offered—from the efficacy of which sacrifice, all benefits and blessings are derived to redeemed man. Thus is this ordinance every way adapted to our condition, my hearers; what is outward and visible, is appointed and intended as a remembrancer, a help to faith—while what is signified thereby, calls forth the spiritual faculties of the soul, to realize the exceeding greatness of that love, wherewith CHRIST *hath loved us, and given himself for us,* and stirs up the will, and engages the affections, to cleave to his blessed example and holy truth, and walk worthy of him who hath purchased for us, pardon, grace, and everlasting life.

In the design of this sacrament, also, we shall find the same infinite wisdom put forth to render it effectual to all the spiritual wants of our condition; and in this, as in all other, the commands of GOD, to render our obedience the source of our comfort and happiness.

The design, therefore, of the institution of this, the most solemn ordinance of CHRIST's religion, and of the command—*Do this, in remembrance of me,* is—First, to fix and imprint in our minds a deep and abiding impression of his passion and death, as the most effectual motive to universal obedience.

And what, my dear hearers, can be considered a more powerful argument, to persuade and prevail upon men to pursue the paths of peace and holiness, than a due consideration of the exemplary life, and meritorious death of our blessed Saviour. His life is so complete a pattern of all virtue, and his death so conclusive an evidence of the hatred which GOD bears towards sin, that whosoever frequently and seriously meditates upon these things, can be at no loss either for sufficient direction or for the most powerful motives, to a holy life upon the principles of the doctrine of CHRIST.

What more powerful antidote to temptation than to behold

JESUS CHRIST, and him crucified, evidently set forth among us in the sacramental elements? What more persuasive exhortation against all the deceits of sin, than the proof to be drawn from the death of CHRIST, of GOD's hatred of sin, and compassion for the sinner? And what more affecting argument for the observance of this, and all our Saviour's injunctions, than to consider that it was his dying command, dying too for our sakes, to do this in remembrance of him, as the most effectual means to fill our hearts with devout affections, and adorn our lives with fruits of righteousness. O what cords of love do the careless and thoughtless votaries of the world, who turn away from this sacrament, break through! What painfully purchased means of mercy and salvation, do they contemptuously cast from them! Alas, for those immortal souls, who will not be saved.

2. Secondly, partaking of the sacramental elements in commemoration of the death of CHRIST, is designed to impress upon our hearts, that the atonement thereby made upon the cross for sin, is to fallen man the only ground of hope, and assurance of pardon and acceptance.

The receiving this sacrament, therefore, is a continual acknowledgment, that, that pardon of sin, which GOD vouchsafes us upon the condition of unfeigned repentance, is the purchase of the death of CHRIST, and the effect of that great and eternal sacrifice, once offered as an expiation for the sins of the whole world. And sincere penitents can never, with more reasonable and well-grounded faith, hope to have applied to themselves, the benefit of the grace and forgiveness purchased for all, by that great propitiation, than when they are, with true devotion, and with full purpose of amended life, commemorating their Saviour's sufferings, in that solemn manner, which he himself has appointed. They can never with more lively hope express their full trust and humble dependance upon GOD, that *he will also give them freely all other things*, than when they are worthily and devoutly commemorating, according to our LORD's own institution—how GOD *spared not even his own Son, but delivered him up for us all.* '

One main design of this ordinance, then, my brethren and

hearers, is to encourage men to repent, and to enable them to perfect their repentance. It is not, therefore, to be confined as a privilege to confirmed believers, as some teach, and is too generally admitted.   The blood of CHRIST, in the language of Scripture, is a fountain opened for sin and for uncleanness——that is, for sin truly repented of ; and the benefit thereof is never more likely to be effectually applied, than when, with sincere resolutions of renewed obedience, we obey the injunction of my text, by partaking of these holy mysteries.

What an awful account, then, will those have to give, who are called to the knowledge of this grace ; and yet, with a careless indifference, neglect this appointment of a Saviour's dying love ?——and what excuse can be made, even for the sinner, who thus shows that he prefers to continue in sin, with eternal death as its wages, rather than to repent and be saved?

3. A third design of the sacrament of the LORD's supper, is to continue down to all generations the memory of *the love of* GOD *our Saviour, which he shed on us abundantly, through* JESUS CHRIST *our Saviour.*

And as this is what is to be understood in the more confined sense of the word memorial, when applied to this institution of religion, so observation and experience teach us, my brethren, that without some such solemn observance the memory even of this great event might have been lost among men.

To communicate, therefore, in remembrance of CHRIST, is to profess publicly our faith in his death, as that full satisfaction to the broken law, which the justice of GOD required, as the condition of forgiveness, while it is also a perpetuating or keeping up in the world, the memory of this great event, as the ground of mercy and reconciliation with GOD to every generation of sinners.   It is on our part *showing forth the* LORD's *death until he come.*

4.   Another and very important design of this institution, as a public ordinance of religion, is to give to Christians a very impressive and affecting opportunity to unite with one heart and one voice in returning thanks to GOD for his unspeakable mercy, in the gift of his only begotten Son, for the redemption of mankind; whence the whole of this service is usually called

the eucharist, that is, the solemn thanksgiving.   And if we are at all times bound to return thanks to GOD for all his mercies, for the mercies of every day, and of every hour, with how much greater earnestness ought we to express the same thankful disposition of soul, when we are commemorating that mercy, my brethren, which is not only the greatest of all others, but the fountain also and foundation of them all?

As it is an ungrateful heart which receives the blessings of GOD's fatherly providence, day by day, without one tribute of a thankful spirit offered up to the Giver of every good and perfect gift, so it must be an ice-cold, infidel disposition, which can contemplate this precious gift of GOD's love, and hear the thanksgivings of his people, without being moved to go and do likewise, and to add his voice and his heart to the eucharistical hymn, with which we conclude our sacramental service.   "We praise thee, we bless thee, we worship thee, we glorify thee, we give thanks to thee, for thy great glory, O LORD GOD, heavenly King, GOD the Father Almighty."   Yet, alas! though all are redeemed, such is the enmity of the carnal mind, that ten tongues are silent, or lifted up in blasphemy, for one that returns to give glory to the GOD of our salvation.

5. A fifth design of the sacrament of the LORD's Supper is, the confirming and renewing of the covenant with GOD, entered into at our baptism ; and thus to keep alive and fresh in our minds the obligations we have come under by being baptized into the death of CHRIST, and the promises of GOD of the succour and help of his HOLY SPIRIT, sealed to us in that sacrament, and renewed in this.

And who that considers what poor, frail, sinful, and corrupt creatures we are—who that knows how compassed about with infirmity, and exposed to temptation our whole pilgrimage is, but must admire and adore the wisdom and goodness of GOD our Saviour, in making this provision for our comfort and assurance.

As there is no man that liveth and sinneth not, as the grace given in baptism decays, by reason of sin wilfully committed— and as without repentance there is no return to GOD, and renewal of spiritual strength, and no available repentance without faith in the LORD JESUS CHRIST, therefore is this wise and effectual provision of the sacrament of the body and blood of CHRIST made, that the sincere penitent and humble believer, beholding by faith, *the Lamb of GOD which taketh away the sins of the world*, may have a visible and sensible pledge of GOD's promised mercy and favour, in the use of the means through which he hath been pleased to appoint that we are to receive them. Therefore it is of perpetual obligation and continuance in the Church, for the nourishment and sustenance of his followers, until *he shall appear the second time, without sin, unto salvation*. And what an awful thought it is, my brethren, to reflect how those will then meet him who have been baptized into his name and death, have had the light of his blessed gospel shining around them, the means of his grace freely offered and pressed upon them, and yet have made light of it, and never once confessed him before men, or acknowledged any obligation to him, as their Redeemer, by obeying this his dying command. Oh! what an aggravation of our guilt it is, to add contempt to ingratitude.

The last purpose I shall mention as designed by the institution of this ordinance, is a profession of our communion one with another, and a strong obligation to mutual love, charity, and good will.

As the death of CHRIST is the means whereby we are reconciled to GOD, so it is intended also to reconcile men to each other—that is, to enforce all those motives by which peace and union are promoted, forgiveness of injuries encouraged, and loving kindness extended. With great reason, therefore, it is, that the commemoration of his death for us all, should be accompanied, in our degree, by that temper and mind which was in CHRIST JESUS—*Beloved, if GOD so loved us, we ought also to love one another.*

That creatures of the same GOD, partakers of the same ruin, and heirs of the same hope, springing from the one only mediator between GOD and man, should be of one mind and of one doctrine in the great affair of religion, and in all things kindly affectioned one toward another, is the most reasonable of all expectations, the most natural of all duties. That it is not so, is greatly to be deplored.   It therefore behoves us my brethren, to be very careful upon Scripture principles, and under Scripture directions, that we be not of the number who violate this obligation.   Nor is the obligation of that difficult nature which many suppose ; for Christian charity involves no surrender of Christian principle, neither does it demand any accommodation with error, either in the doctrines or order of the gospel.   In its exercise it is confined exclusively to persons.   Opinions are not, neither can be the objects of its operation.   And if thus understood, and acted upon, it would fully answer the great and gracious purpose of its enactment, in maintaining peace and good will, even amidst the dissolution of that unity among Christians, which marks the latter day of the gospel dispensation.

I shall now conclude with an enforcement of the duty, enjoined in my text, *Do this in remembrance of me.*

And First, to whom are these affectionate words addressed, my hearers ? primarily to the twelve disciples, certainly, who had been with him from the beginning and were therefore the better qualified to be his witnesses, and to make known his will and intention to the rest of the world, as our LORD himself told them, *And ye also shall bear witness, because ye have been with me from the beginning.*

As these witnesses, therefore, taught and commanded, that this commemoration of the death of CHRIST was to be considered as a standing ordinance in the Church, as the primitive Christians received and practised it as of general obligation, and the canon of Scripture hath recorded it as an integral part of Christianity——these circumstances, independent of any reason or benefit to us from the ordinance itself, put all who have been and yet continue negligent of it, in the class of transgressors, not only of a plain law of the gospel, but of a law enforced by every motive which can have weight, either with a grateful or a selfish nature.   Every way therefore, they are without excuse, who from year to year hear the invitations of the ministers of CHRIST to prepare themselves for this duty, and yet turn away from it with indifference, as from something they were at perfect liberty to observe or refuse.

Secondly, as it is clearly revealed to us that there is no

VOL. I.—65

approach to GOD for us sinners, but only through the LORD JESUS CHRIST, as our saving relation to him, our new or affiliated state, in contradiction to our state by nature, is begun in the sacrament of baptism and continued in that of the eucharist, by virtue of our union with his son JESUS CHRIST our LORD, and is no otherwise even to be hoped for under the gospel: Where shall those appear who are wilfully strangers to this saving ordinance of his express appointment, when he shall arise to shake terribly the earth, and to execute his threatenings upon the ungodly? Who is then to release them from the obligations of their baptismal vow, and put in a plea to defend them from the just demands of GOD's violated law? Who is to present an atonement for them adequate to the infinite demerit of sin in the sight of GOD? Can they apply to the LORD JESUS to plead for them—alas, he then sits as their judge, not as their advocate, and must say according to truth—I never knew you, you formed no acquaintance with me, in that state of reprieve and probation my sufferings purchased for you. Can they plead for themselves either ignorance or penitence, or procrastinated good intentions cut short by death—alas! before that dread tribunal every human mouth shall be stopped by the consciousness that there can be no excuse for rejection of the means of grace, no voice shall be heard but that of the man CHRIST JESUS, nor any other sentence be passed but that of, *come ye blessed, or depart ye cursed.* O my poor fellow sinners, would ye but hear it, *Now is the accepted time, now is the day of salvation*—now your crucified LORD can plead for you and with you—now he offers you the free and full benefit of all his tears, and groans, and blood, and beseeches you by the mercies of GOD, to lay to heart the things which make for your peace, before they are forever hid from your eyes. *Turn ye, turn ye, for why will ye die.*

But you will say, perhaps, that we are unworthy to partake of so sacred an ordinance. It is invested with such an awful sanctity that we consider it unapproachable by mortals, without the danger of incurring extreme guilt. And is it really so, that any present are deterred by this erroneous estimate of a means of grace? Are any so misled as to think that a gracious GOD would appoint and command an ordinance of his religion, either dangerous or unprofitable in itself, to his creatures? Far, very far, be such an impious thought from every soul present. No, my brethren and hearers, whatever the most merciful GOD hath provided for us, and commanded to be observed, is both animating and profitable, when duly considered. We may be unworthy, and in one sense the very best of us is unworthy of the least of all GOD's mercies. But if we are unworthy in the more common use of the word it is our own fault; we can have taken no pains to prepare ourselves—we must be in the awful condition of preferring sin to GOD, the world to heaven, or at the best, our own righteousness to the righteousness of GOD, which is by faith of JESUS CHRIST.

And what ground have those who thus make faith of none effect, by resting on their own righteousness, to suppose that it will stand them in any stead in the great and dreadful day of the LORD? Has heaven spoken of any such dependence? Does the revelation GOD has made to us through his Son give countenance to such a presumptuous hope? If it does not, where do you find it unless in the whispers of the father of lies to the desperately wicked heart of the natural man? O trust not to it my hearers, for it will deceive you—trust rather to him who hath bought you with his own blood—who invites you to peace here and glory hereafter, through faith in his only saving name, and who tells you, in words which cannot fail, *No man cometh unto the Father but by me—Except ye eat the flesh of the Son of man, and drink his blood, ye have no life in you.* My dear hearers, if under the gospel men can be saved without the sacraments of the Church of CHRIST, wherefore did GOD appoint them? If the spiritual grace indispensable to the salvation of a fallen sinner is to be had, independently of the means to which it is expressly annexed by divine institution, whereto serveth the Christian dispensation, or what is the use of revealed religion? Cast away from you, therefore, this fruit of unbelief and death, and build upon that tried foundation stone, which neither the storms of time, nor the tempest of a dissolving world shall be able to shake, even JESUS CHRIST and him crucified for us.

To whom &c. &c.

SERMON IV.

THE OBLIGATION TO PARTAKE OF THE LORD'S SUPPER.

---

1 CORINTHIANS, xi. 26.

"For as often as ye eat this bread, and drink this cup, ye do show the LORD's
death till he come."

To apprehend aright the purpose and design of a religious
ordinance, is the best means to feel, as we ought to feel, the
obligation we are under to observe it, and to enable us, understandingly, and so far acceptably, to perform it. This is
rendered peculiarly necessary, my brethren, from another
consideration, which is this, that the external appointments of
Christianity, are not only duties, because of institution and
command, but means of grace; that is, channels of personal
benefit and advantage, in the communication of spiritual
blessings, and helps to faith also; that is, divinely authorized,
outward and visible representations and assurances, of things at
present invisible.

This distinctive character is derived to them altogether from
the appointment of the institutor, and this so strictly, that there
can be no rational grounds of confidence in their efficacy, when
severed from the authority of their original institution. Imagination, stretched to enthusiasm, may indeed supply this defect,
but it cannot cure it; and the persuasion of an erroneous
judgment, may altogether disregard it; but no persuasion of
mind can make that to be, which is not, or alter the fixed order
of revealed truth, or give to imitations of religious mysteries,
however exact the copy, the sanctified character of the means
of grace.

As GOD alone can appoint to what external religious
observances his grace shall be annexed, and by what marks
they are to be verified to us, as divine; it can never be a matter of
indifference to a serious mind, upon what its assurance rests,

that religious ordinances are what they profess to be. Could this view of the subject be reasonably disputed, it may be further confirmed by this ; that as in the celebration of religious ordinances, particularly of the sacraments, there is an administrator, as well as recipient of what he administers, there must be an authority, or right to act in this case, in the administrator, which is not in the recipients. And this authority, or right to act, in things divine, must surely partake of the nature of the things acted, and be itself divine.

In the very serious exercises of mind which should precede religious observances, and particularly the higher solemnities of religion, it is very important, especially to young communicants ; and, in the present circumstances of the gospel, may I not venture to say, to old communicants too—that this should form such a part of that consideration of the subject, as shall enable them to act with a rational confidence, not only, that they are duly qualified with proper dispositions of heart, but with such an understanding of the nature and design of the ordinance, and with such a full persuasion of the divine character of its administration, as is worthy of the name of faith. For faith, in the just and scriptural meaning of that word, is not any, or every persuasion of the mind, however full and strong, which a person may entertain on the subject of religion, for then would the greatest errors be the highest points of faith. But true faith is the reception of divine truth, upon divine testimony, adherence to divine direction upon divine command, and reliance upon divine promises, upon divine authority to administer the seals of the covenant of grace in the sacraments of the Church. This being once ascertained upon just and scriptural grounds, the mind is settled, and the ordinances of religion are met and engaged in, with that union of the understanding and the affections, which render them at once a reasonable and a profitable service, performed towards God.

Applying these observations to the solemn purpose we have before us this day, my brethren, will at once, I trust, confirm their soundness, and practical utility ; and impress upon all our hearts, that deep personal interest, which every individual favoured with the gospel actually has, and should feel in the event commemorated.

For as often as ye eat this bread, and drink this cup, ye do show the LORD's *death till he come.*

That these words of the apostle, present to us the death of CHRIST, as the object of our perpetual commemoration ; that they require this commemoration to be made publicly through the medium of material symbols or emblems ; and that each one of us has the highest personal interest in the effect produced by this death, upon the condition of the world ; I consider such plain and obvious inferences, as to stand in no need of any proof : but at the same time, so little heeded by the great majority for whose benefit they are revealed, and so superficially considered by many who make the commemoration, as to demand both exposition and enforcement. I shall therefore make them the subjects of our consideration and improvement on the present occasion.

FIRST, then, the death of CHRIST is here presented to us as the object of our perpetual commemoration.

This is confirmed to us by these words of the text—*Ye do show the* LORD's *death till he come*—which plainly extend its observance to the close of the Christian dispensation ; when the crucified JESUS will come in the full glory of the Godhead to inquire into the fruits of his sufferings for sinners, and to reward or punish them everlastingly, according to the effects produced upon their hearts and lives, by the truth of his doctrine, the laws of his religion, and the grace of his HOLY SPIRIT. And this is enforced by whatever is elsewhere set forth in the Scriptures, of the cause and the purpose of his death, and of the end and design of its being set apart, as a solemn ordinance of religion.

To a reasonable and profitable observance of this sacred mystery, then, it must be evident, my brethren and hearers—it is necessary that we be so far informed and instructed in the fundamental truths of revealed religion, as to apprehend, in some good degree, the connexion of CHRIST's death, with our personal condition, as respects Almighty GOD ; because, without this there can be no ground at all, either for requiring or rendering the commanded observance. And equally evident it must be, that to this information and instruction in religious truth, must be added faith, or that full and entire persuasion of the mind, which applies the truth received personally to ourselves ; and so applies it, as to overbear and cast down all objection and opposition, whether suggested by our own pride and vanity, countenanced by the course of this present evil world, or supported by interests and regards of the highest temporal concernment. The knowledge that man is a fallen, spiritually dead, creature by nature, may be obtained from the Scriptures, and credit may be given to it, as to a general and admitted truth. The same may be said of man's recovery from this fallen condition, through the satisfaction made to the Divine Justice by the sacrifice of the cross. But to make these truths profitable to our souls, and influential to the commanded commemoration of them, it is indispensable that a higher prinple than knowledge and assent, even that principle which quickens knowledge, and gives life to testimony, shall be wrought in the heart by the SPIRIT OF GOD. Now, faith, we are told from the highest authority, is at once a fruit of the SPIRIT, and an attainment of our own diligence, and earnest endeavours, in the use of the appointed means. For, *faith cometh by hearing, and hearing by the word of* GOD. And the gift of the SPIRIT, we are also told, is the fruit of prayer and supplication to GOD. *Ask and ye shall receive—seek and ye shall find—knock and it shall be opened unto you.* Hence the want of faith is never considered and spoken of in the Scriptures as a pitiable, and, therefore, pardonable infirmity, but as a wilful, and, therefore, criminal denial or neglect of revealed truth. Because GOD's public message to mankind is warrant sufficient for every man to whom it comes, to verify his actual condition by, and so to appropriate the promises and helps therein set forth for his encouragement, as to act upon them, and thereby reap the full benefit of their personal application.

But it is an inseparable quality of faith, that a course corresponding with what is professed to be believed, should mark the life ; otherwise it is mere assent to abstract truth, of no moral value whatever. Hence, the man who admits the two fundamental doctrines of Christianity, in the fall of man by sin, and his recovery by the death of CHRIST, and yet manifests no active sense, either of the danger of his fallen condition or of love of GOD, in providing for his redemption from it, through the LORD JESUS CHRIST, must stand condemned by his own heart, as an unbeliever. For so tremendous are the consequences of separation from GOD, rendered eternal by neglect of the gospel, and so infinite the value of restoration to his favour, rendered everlasting by faith in his only begotten Son—that the doctrines which involve these awful sanctions, if really believed, will be acted upon, and if truly felt in their personal application, will draw out the life in a grateful, thankful, commemoration of that surpassing mystery, the death of CHRIST—through which, the door of mercy is opened to sinful mortals. *The love of* CHRIST *constraineth us,* says St. Paul ; and the true believer, will in like manner, *show the* LORD'S *death till he come,* not only because it is a command—*Do this in remembrance of me,* but because his heart feels the benefit conferred, and longs to offer this homage to its benefactor.

SECONDLY, This commemoration is required to be made publicly through the medium of material symbols or emblems.

As often as ye eat this bread, and drink this cup, ye do show the LORD'S *death till he come.*

The elements of bread and wine were chosen and appointed by our LORD himself, as the symbol of his body broken and blood shed upon the cross for our redemption. They are, therefore, in such wise, integral parts of this religious ordinance, that without them there cannot be that special commemoration of his death which he commanded his followers to observe. Bread and wine, however, being in the number of those good things which GOD has graciously bestowed for our daily nourishment, their sacramental quality cannot be referred to their nature, but must be sought for in their solemn consecration, or setting apart to this special purpose.

That the elements used by our LORD were a part of that provision of which he had just partaken with his disciples in the paschal Supper, is very evident from the account given by all the evangelists. It was, therefore, by his particular designation of them as representations of his passion, and by the solemn offering of them to Almighty God, as figures of the sacrifice of himself upon the cross, that they were made to differ from what had previously been partaken of. This is my body, this is my blood of the New Testament, said our blessed Lord, after he had given thanks, or solemnly consecrated the bread and wine, which he took from the table. This bread which I break and distribute among you, represents my body, about to be broken upon the cross for the sins of mankind.—*Do this in remembrance of me.* In like manner this cup, or the wine in this cup, represents my blood, about to be shed upon the cross for you and for many, for the remission of sins.—*Do this as oft as ye shall drink it in remembrance of me.* To their consecration, therefore, must the sacramental character of these elements be referred. And though no change takes place in their nature, though they continue as before, bread and wine, yet a change is made in their use or purpose to us, which ought to be understood and felt by all who partake of them. Otherwise the same profanation takes place which St. Paul is reproving in the Corinthian Church— *They do not discern the* Lord's *body.* We eat, it is true, my brethren, bread, actual bread, unchanged in its nature, and we drink wine equally unchanged in its nature, as is verified to our senses, and without surrendering our senses we cannot think otherwise. But by the institution of heaven, and who shall say unto God, What doest thou? we eat and drink bread and wine, to which is annexed by its consecration, the mysterious quality of conveying to worthy partakers, the full benefit of the actual communication of the body and blood of Christ. And as this benefit consists in the forgiveness of repented and forsaken sin, and the renewal of divine grace, we learn of what great importance it is, in coming forward to this ordinance, that Christians should possess, not only suitable depositions of heart, but such just expectations also, as to free them from the weakness of of superstitious ignorance, or the rashness of a presumptuous confidence.

As the substitution, then, of other elements would change, so as to divest this ordinance of its proper character, the ground is still stronger for affirming that the substitution of any other authority than that of Christ, in their consecration and administration, must render null and void whatever belongs to the religious and spiritual nature of a sacrament. It was in his priestly character that our LORD consecrated the elements of bread and wine, and impressed upon them the sanctified quality of representing his body and blood given for us. And it is by virtue of the priestly character derived from him, through his apostles, that the same sanctified quality is still impressed, and the same benefits derived, in all ages under the gospel dispensation. Hence we learn, my brethren, how very important it is, and how conducive to their growth in grace, and to their individual comfort, that Christians should well consider all that relates to the administration of the sacraments of the gospel— that they should diligently search out and ascertain, not only their own qualifications for the participation of them, but the qualifications of those also who profess to administer them. For unless we assume, that the promises of GOD are so annexed to the outward and visible signs of his grace in the sacraments, that they pass with them, whether administered with or without his authority, we must admit, that to any such reliance upon their efficacy, as is worthy of the name of faith, there must be divine warrant. But to assume such a principle, is contrary to the whole tenor and example of the Scriptures, and to the very nature and design of positive institutions in religion. These are intended, not only as means of grace, but as helps to faith—as visible assurances of things divine and invisible. And since our obligation to observe them is derived solely from the appointment of GOD, their efficacy to us is in like manner dependent on his authority to administer them. Without this, they are not in fact sacraments, but at the best, imitations only, of holy mysteries, from which a deluded mind alone can draw either comfort or assurance.

This may be exemplified in various ways: for instance, if any number of private Christians were to meet together for a religious purpose, and it was proposed that they should commemorate the death of CHRIST, by partaking together of bread and wine, and should do so, would this constitute a sacrament, in the scriptural meaning of that word? Every well informed Christian will say no. But wherefore not? The answer will readily be given, because there was no authorized administrator—and the answer is just. But suppose some one of the number should undertake, or be requested, to consecrate and administer the bread and wine to the rest : would this at all change the character of the act, and constitute that a sacrament, which before was not a sacrament ? If the answer shall be yes, from any, as I dare say it would be be from some, I then desire to know, why every private Christian may not just as well consecrate and administer to him and herself, and the communion of saints be expunged from the Apostles' creed ? For in the case supposed, the administrator must either assume the authority, or derive it. But to assume divine authority is sacrilege ; and the acts performed under it, are not only nullities, but profanations, which no piety of intention can cure, because the ignorance which alone can excuse such a proceeding, is itself inexcusable. If the authority is considered good, because derived from others, it is still insufficient, because those from whom it professes to be derived, have it not themselves, and therefore cannot confer it upon another. If the answer shall be no, as from every well instructed Christian it must and will be, it can no otherwise be sustained as the correct one, than from defect of authority in the administrator.

But to bring the whole of this vital subject more directly under your serious consideration, my brethren, and to show the fallacy and the danger too, of the latitudinarian notions, so current, and so much favoured in this latter day, suppose we were to substitute some other article of our bodily nourishment, pulse and water, for instance, instead of bread and wine, as the outward and visible signs, in the administration of this sacrament, would the most authorized consecration of such elements impress upon them the sacred character of our LORD's body and blood, or could any Christian be prevailed upon to partake of them in commemoration of CHRIST's death, or be induced by any reasonings to expect the benefits of his passion, to be thereby transferred and made over to him ? Assuredly no such delusion could fasten upon any of your minds, my brethren. Upon what ground of scripture or reason then is it founded, that bread and wine, consecrated and administered without divine authority, are nevertheless effectual to the high and holy purposes of the sacramental commemoration of that death, which is our life? Surely, if a change in the elements would vitiate either of the sacraments, much more must defect of divine authority to consecrate and administer those which are divinely instituted, render all such administrations void and of none effect.

And these observations are addressed to you, my brethren, at this particular time, in the hope, that the occasion itself, will form a practical enforcement of the points presented to your consideration; and in connexion with the real importance of steadfastness in your religious views and opinions, and of union, both in sentiment and practice, lead to such an unprejudiced examination of the subject, as shall bring the members of the Church to be of one mind and of one heart, in all her services. With this view they are addressed to your understandings, and not to your feelings, that when weighed and tried by the only unerring standard, the word of GOD, your hearts may be established and knit together, in the one faith of the gospel, and in the one hope of your high calling, certified by the sacraments of the gospel duly and rightly administered.

THIRDLY—The words of my text present to our consideration the personal interest we all have in the effects produced by the death of CHRIST, on the condition of the world.

Of the importance of the gift of JESUS CHRIST to mankind in general, we are all without exception, in some good degree aware. But with the great majority of men under the light of the gospel, and with many of you my hearers, this is all; you carry it no further; you do not receive it as a divine and infallible communication from heaven, for your individual benefit. You do not dwell upon it in your thoughts, and apply it to your personal condition. You do not consider it in the cause which rendered it necessary, and in the effects which flow from it. Above all, the death of CHRIST is not dwelt upon, as in itself the most important and influential part of his undertaking for us; indeed that part without which all the rest would have been of no avail to make our peace with GOD. Hence it is, that sin is esteemed so slight and trivial a thing, that the wrath of GOD, revealed from heaven against it, is sported with, and the only means of escape neglected.

But my dear hearers, what can give to sinners so convincing a proof of the deadly nature of sin as the death of CHRIST? What can manifest so conclusively, GOD's infinite hatred of it, as the humiliation and sufferings of his only begotten Son, endured for us? What can enable man to realize the terrors of the LORD, equal to the consideration of that agony, whose overwhelming pressure, drew from GOD and man united in one person, the sweat of blood, abandoned him to the malice of men and devils, and to the cruel and lingering torments of the cross? Was it for a slight cause, think ye, that the love of GOD, and the power of GOD, and the wisdom of GOD, combined in one high counsel, for the salvation of sinners, saw this, the fittest method to fulfil his gracious purpose towards mankind? Alas! how we trifle with eternal death, within reach of the tree of life. How we labour to stifle the convictions of GOD's HOLY SPIRIT, the better reason of our own minds, and the better feelings of our fallen nature! How do we assent, and then retract, and yield, and then put off, and melt and give way, and then harden and lock up the heart; but, like a door turning upon its hinges, still remain in the same place! Yea, how many when driven from all their subterfuges, by the voice of divine truth, rather than surrender to the call of CHRIST, take shelter in unbelief, and sit down contented without GOD in the world.

Look around you my friends, and inquire, on which side of this awful controversy betwixt GOD and the world do you stand? On which side stand the men of name and note amongst us—those to whom GOD hath given wisdom and understanding, and riches, and honour, and influence, among their fellows—men who ought to know, because they have the means and the leisure, and who do know, because they have heard GOD's message of warning and mercy to his creatures. What sense do they in general manifest of the death of CHRIST? are they in the number of those who thankfully show it forth as their one only hope for hereafter? Alas, for the truth—the cruel heart-rending truth, *that not many wise, not many noble, not many mighty are called, because they close their ears, and harden their hearts, lest at any time they should be converted, and I should heal them,* says the Saviour.

And for what do they thus sport with destruction, and choose death, in the error of their life ? For the love of that which brought the Son of God, like a criminal to the cross—for a little more of that world which with themselves is hasting to vanish away—for an increase of that superfluity which already weighs them down with anxious days and wakeful nights, shutting out God from their thoughts, or at best postponing the chief good to some distant and uncertain period—for the follies and vanities of the day—for the revellings and banquetings, upon which God's portion for the widow and fatherless, the poor and the needy, the suffering and the distressed, the ignorant and the vicious, is squandered. Oh ! did they but think—could they but realize, the account that is to be given in for example, how many lost souls will be charged to their contempt and neglect of the great sacrifice for sin made upon the cross, to their disregard of the heart-cheering hope given to a lost world, by the resurrection of Christ—but alas ! it is hid from them. Their foolish heart is darkened—the god of this world hath blinded their minds—they will not come to the light—and even at this moment when conscience is awakened, and the understanding is convinced and fear is alarmed, and pride perhaps offended, some surrender of the world is anticipated, which gives them all to the winds.

But for your souls' sake, for Christ's sake, bethink you. If this provision of mercy and grace for sinners is rejected, is there another ground of hope for hereafter? Was sin thus visited upon him who knew no sin that we might continue in sin ? Is the pardon of the penitent no otherwise possible than through the death of Christ believed in and relied upon for the expiation for its guilt? Must the effect of that death be manifested in us by a holy and religious life, as the only evidence which God will accept, that we believe the testimony he hath given to his son, as the only name under heaven whereby we must be saved ? Owe we any thing to the love of Christ dying for us ? is there any gratitude due for so high a favour freely bestowed upon us? is there any force in the dying request of our best friend? what say our fallen corrupt hearts, under the searching application of such inquiries as these? My dear hearers, how then shall those look their Saviour in the face, in the great day of eternity, who have here, in the time of mercy, made light of these high claims upon them, who have never manifested any sense of the importance of his death for them individually, who are unknown as his disciples, and have never showed forth before the world, their faith in his atoning blood by partaking of the elements which represent and convey the benefits of his death to believers? O when they look on him whom they have pierced by their sins, and by their sinful neglect of the gospel what will be the emotions of their despairing souls—whither shall they flee from the wrath of the lamb? When they hear the awful, and as to them, literally true, words, *I never knew you*—I cannot save you—the time is past—what compensation will the world then prove in exchange for their souls? alas, it is consuming under their feet, and all its glory reduced to a cinder.

But thanks be to GOD, there is yet given to us by his mercy, a little precious though uncertain hour, in which through the intercession of this same JESUS, repentance may undo past neglect, and a new life give proof of faith unfeigned. In which preparation may be made for a happy eternity, and GOD be glorified by your professed subjection to the gospel. And shall it pass unheeded, unimproved, my friends, all given to the world and no part reserved for GOD? GOD forbid! *awake then, thou that sleepest, and arise from the dead, and* CHRIST *shall give thee light.* Come to Him who hath died for thee, and will by no means cast thee out. And let it dwell upon your hearts my brethren and hearers, that *now is the accepted time, now is the day of salvation.*

May GOD bless his truth to all present; and to his holy name in FATHER, SON, and HOLY SPIRIT, be glory and praise, now and forever.

SERMON V.

COMMUNION OF SAINTS.

1 CORINTHIANS, X. 17.

"For we being many, are one bread and one body; for we are all partakers of that one bread."

THE Communion of Saints is an article of the faith we profess, my brethren, and one of those primary and fundamental doctrines which are embodied in that form of sound words called the Apostles' Creed. It is one which we declare our belief of in the daily service of the Church, and respecting which we ought not to be ignorant. Yet it is to be feared, that the acknowledgment of the doctrine is too often made without any very clear or precise import of its meaning; or right sense of the obligations growing out of it. In its application, nevertheless, equally with all the other doctrines of our religion, it is intended for the comfort and edification of the body of CHRIST, for the perfecting of the saints, and for the advancement of the gospel in the world, by the exercise of that mutual love among Christians which is involved in this communion or fellowship.

To consider and apply this doctrine, therefore, will be a suitable improvement, I trust, of the present occasion, when we are met together to manifest our fellowship in the one faith and hope of the gospel, and mutually to refresh each other, and be refreshed in the participation of that one bread, in and by which we are constituted one body, though many members. For the religion of the gospel, my brethren, is a social principle, looking for and affording mutual assistance, consolation, and joy, to those who embrace it, in our present pilgrimage, and expecting the full measure of its enjoyment and reward, in that perfect communion and fellowship of the just, which shall be before the throne of GOD and the Lamb, for ever.   Where trial shall be ended, where no imperfection shall be found, where all tears shall be wiped from our eyes, and where increase of bliss shall occupy the sublimed and exalted faculties of glorified spirits.

For your edification herein, therefore, my brethren, I shall, in the

FIRST place, endeavour to explain the meaning of that communion or fellowship, which is referred to in the text, in the words, *we are one bread and one body.*

SECONDLY, I shall consider the origin and nature of the principle, in which that communion or fellowship consists.

THIRDLY, I will show you the nature and extent of those duties which grow out of the participation of this one, established, symbol of union among the disciples of CHRIST throughout the world; and, then,

CONCLUDE, with an improvement of the subject.

For we, being many, are one bread and one body; for we are all partakers of that one bread.

I. First, I am to explain the meaning of that communion or fellowship which is referred to in the text, in the words, *we are one bread and one body.*

The original word translated communion, in this passage, and so frequently made use of by this apostle, varies in its meaning according to the nature of that which it is used to express.

When the thing or subject referred to may be divided into parts, and distributed among many, so that each may have a share, it then means the communication and participation thereof, to and by the community or body.

Thus in the case of alms-giving or relief to the poor, as this is a distribution of a part of our substance to the necessities of others, and a religious duty; it is expressed in the original by the same word, because it is a communication of good to, and a participation of relief by them.

The same word is also applied to the gifts of the HOLY SPIRIT. As there are diversities of gifts, differences of administrations, and diversities of operations, yet all divided to man by the same SPIRIT; the bestowing these gift and operations and the use and improvement of them by men, is styled by this apostle, the communion of the SPIRIT.   And because one consecrated loaf of bread and cup of wine were originally distributed in the Church, as memorials of CHRIST's death, and of the benefits derived to men thereby ; therefore, the participation of those emblems in the eucharist, by his disciples, is styled the communion of the body and blood of CHRIST : that is, the joint participation of those emblems which represent his body broken, and blood shed upon the cross, for the salvation of sinners ; and the joint acknowledgment of those partaking of them, that they depend only on the efficacy of this sacrifice, for pardon, grace, and everlasting life.

When however the thing or subject in question is incapable of division or partial distribution, but each one must have the whole ; the word then means a fellowship or joint participation in the same thing. In this sense, Christians are said to be called by GOD, to the fellowship of his Son—to have a fellowship in his sufferings, in his death, in his resurrection, and in his glory— to be heirs together of the grace of life, heirs of GOD, and joint heirs with CHRIST ; and thus St. John expresses it where he says, *and truly, our fellowship or communion is with the Father and with the Son.*   In like manner, my brethren, the communication and joint participation of all good things in the Church militant, in connexion with those who by the same means have joined the Church triumphant, is what is meant by our professing to believe, as it is expressed in the creed, in the communion of saints.

The doctrine, therefore, referred to in my text, in the words *we are one bread and one body*, will mean this, that by our joint participation of the established symbols of CHRIST's death in the eucharist, we do in effect declare our union with CHRIST in his death, our trust and dependence on this his sacrifice and atonement, for satisfaction to the divine justice—our hope to be also partakers of his resurrection, and our union and fellowship one with another, and with all who have departed this life in the faith and hope of the gospel.   That as there is one body or Church of CHRIST—one LORD or head over that Church—one faith possessed in it—one baptism, or door of entrance to its privileges—one hope of our calling in it, and one authority for the administration of the sacraments in it ; so is there also, but one bond of love and union, and one channel of grace, from one everliving source of spiritual nourishment, growth and life, to the disciples of CHRIST throughout the world.

Hence it is said in this chapter, of the Church in the wilderness, *that they did all eat of the same spiritual meat, and did all drink of the same spiritual drink, for they drank of that spiritual rock that followed them, and that rock was* CHRIST. Hence the doctrine in my text, that all the true disciples of CHRIST, are one bread and one body, that is one body or society, because they partake of that one bread, which by virtue of its consecrated character, represents JESUS CHRIST and him crucified, and confers on the worthy receiver the inestimable benefits purchased by the passion and death of the Son of GOD. Not separate assemblies of worshipping people, differing in name, in authority, in form of worship, and in received doctrine ; but one extended Society of believers in CHRIST—professing the same faith—fed by the same spiritual food and drink—consecrated and administered by the one authority of the head of the body, and as an incontestible evidence thereof, *continuing steadfast in the apostles' doctrine and fellowship, and in breaking of bread, and in prayers.*

This, my brethren and hearers, was the root of unity to the first Christians, the ground of their assurance in working out their eternal salvation. *They were built upon the foundation of the apostles and prophets,* JESUS CHRIST *himself being the chief corner stone. From whom the whole body, fitly joined together and compacted by that which every joint supplieth, according to the effectual working of the measure of every part, maketh increase of the body unto the edifying of itself in love*—and it will be of the same vital efficacy to us also, if we entertain the same sense of the spirit, and obligation, and purpose, of this appointment of the wisdom of GOD, and bear ever in mind, that in the great concerns of religion, *other foundation can no man lay, than that is laid, which is* JESUS CHRIST.

II. Secondly, I am to consider the origin and nature of the principle in which that communion or fellowship consists.

In the undertaking of JESUS CHRIST for a lost world, there

was a double purpose to be answered, my brethren and hearers. First, to reconcile a justly offended GOD to the world of his creatures, and secondly, to unite men to each other, and all to GOD, in the living bond of brotherly love.

Of the first, the gospel is the authentic declaration to the world, that CHRIST, by the suffering of the cross, having made the required satisfaction to the justice of GOD, for the sins of mankind, a door of mercy is thereby opened, and a day of grace and repentance granted to every sinner of the race of Adam. Hence we read *that* GOD *was in* CHRIST, *reconciling the world unto himself not imputing their trespasses unto them.* And hence CHRIST is said to have *made peace by the blood of his cross, and of twain one new man.* And this not only between heaven and earth—between Jew and Gentile, but between all who embrace his doctrine, and imbibe his SPIRIT, as the only certain and allowable evidence, that the religion he came to establish in the world is so received as to bring forth its proper fruits.—*By this shall all men know that ye are my disciples, if ye have love one to another.*

Of this, the second object of his undertaking for sinners, all the institutions of the gospel, and the very foundation of gospel hope, are so constructed as not only to bear witness of the fact, but to produce it in the heart. The love of GOD manifested towards his enemies in the gift of his only begotten Son, to suffer and die—the love of CHRIST, in consenting to be thus made an offering of sin, with the HOLY GHOST sent down from heaven to renew, and strengthen, and sanctify the hearts of sinners—what, my brethren, so calculated to soften, and subdue, and engage the affections of rational beings—to lead them back to GOD, by turning them round from sin, and prepare them for that everlasting reward revealed to their faith through the Redeemer's merits? And this is the very message of the gospel, the glad tidings which have come from heaven to every one of us, without exception. This is that message of mercy which I am commissioned as an ambassador for CHRIST, to proclaim to every one of you, and to pray you in CHRIST'S stead, as though GOD did beseech you by us—Be ye reconciled to GOD. And

O that you could be prevailed upon to hear it, and lay it to heart.

And when this purpose is answered, when the gospel is embraced, when its law rules the life, when its hope fills the heart, when the breadth, and length, and depth, and height of GOD's rich redeeming love, expands all the affections, and enlarges them to feel that *if GOD so loved us, we ought also to love one another*—what more uniting principle can be thought of my brethren, to knit together in one, those who are partakers of this grace—especially when assembled round the table of our common LORD, our hearts filled with all those emotions which a deep sense of our own unworthiness, and of GOD's unspeakable mercy draw forth, we partake together of that one bread, which represents our Redeemer laying down his life for us—our sins thereby forgiven, and all other benefits of his passion conferred on the faithful in this sacrament. When we thus manifest to the world, my brethren, that this is our hope, even JESUS CHRIST and him crucified for us, what more appropriate appellation can be given to this holy union of a common benefit, and a common hope, than the communion of saints? And what more powerful obligation to cherish and strengthen the cords of Christian love, can be laid upon believers, than to be thus assured *that they are no more strangers and foreigners, but fellow citizens with the saints, and of the household of* GOD.

The origin of the principle, therefore, in which this communion or fellowship consists, must be referred to what is the foundation of the Christian character in fallen man—the communication of the SPIRIT OF GOD, renewing the heart, and transforming us in the spirit of our minds. Until this change is wrought in us by the power of the SPIRIT OF GOD, there is no room for any thing of a divine or heavenly nature to dwell in. Constitutional good temper, compassionate disposition, or judicious education, may produce the semblance of a gracious state, but it is only the semblance; and thousands are deluded thereby to think well of their state, while at the same time there is nothing of love to GOD, no sense of obligation to CHRIST, no constraining power of the spirit of the gospel pervading the whole course of their conduct. Yet, my dear hearers, we know, beyond all dispute, even by the reason of our own minds, confirmed by the word of GOD, that if a corrupt tree is ever to bring forth good fruit, the tree itself must previously be made good. Even so must it be with fallen man. By nature, he is a corrupt tree. By grace only can the tree be made good. And without this mighty change wrought in us, there can be no fellowship with GOD, with his Son, or with the children of GOD, because there is nothing common to both—nothing in which they are mutually interested—no near and dear sense of the love of GOD in CHRIST, shed abroad in the heart, and drawing out their soul in love and good will to all men, especially to them who are of the household of faith.

O who is athirst for this blessed privilege, who is desirous to burst the bonds of unbelief, to break the chains of sin, to yield to the sceptre of divine love, and experience the transforming power of divine grace ? Let him turn to the gospel, that he may learn his want, and find the remedy. There let him see that JESUS, who loved us, and gave himself for us, and redeemed us to GOD by his own blood, and learn of him, and he shall find rest to his soul—rest from the power of sin—rest from the fear that hath torment—and *rest with us when the* LORD JESUS *shall be revealed from heaven, with his mighty angels, in flaming fire, taking vengeance on them that know not* GOD, *and obey not the gospel of our* LORD JESUS CHRIST.

III. Thirdly, I am to show you the nature and extent of those duties which grow out of the participation of this one established symbol of union, among the disciples of CHRIST throughout the world.

The duties of the professing Christian, may fitly be considered as general and special ; but in neither case are they increased in number by coming forward to this sacrament, the effect of this ordinance being to enforce the obligation of existing duties, and to increase the diligence and earnestness, wherewith we apply ourselves to the performance of them ; while at the same time we are furnished in it, when worthily received with grace or spiritual help, equal to all that is required at our hands, of Christian duty.

The general duties of the Christian grow out of his relation to the Church, as a member of the visible body of CHRIST, and comprise whatever can contribute to the honour and increase of the body—to the spread of the gospel, to the promoting the influence of true religion in all around him, and through these to the advancement of the glory of GOD. To the serious Christian, adoption into the family of CHRIST, is indeed a new relation; all whose obligations and privileges, are carefully considered, and faithfully observed. They refer, therefore, to his public and visible conduct in the common affairs of life, all of which is regulated by the presiding principle which he professes. Seeking first the kingdom of GOD and his righteousness, the world, in its business and in its pleasure, is made subservient to this great end—no unlawful conformity with its sinful courses is submitted to; but it is so used as not abusing it. Called to an incorruptible inheritance, he labours to make his calling and election sure. Having openly professed himself a disciple of CHRIST, he is watchful to bring no reproach upon the gospel, but rather, to adorn the doctrine of GOD his Saviour, in all things. He is, therefore, constant and regular in his attendance on the public ministrations of religion. His heart is with it. He enjoys it, and his enjoyments increase with his diligence and faithfulness. He is forward to provide the established means of grace for others, and according to his ability, is ready and willing to distribute to the spiritual, as well as to the temporal, necessities of his brethren. Having well considered the grounds of his public stand in religion, he is steadfast to his principles—there is no indifference towards that on which he has staked his eternal interests, nor is there any uncharitableness towards those who have chosen a different way. Being ready himself to render a reason of the hope he entertains, he follows peace with all men—but he is not, therefore, carried about with divers and strange doctrines—nor yet deluded with the impossible attempt to reconcile truth and error—order and confusion. This course may, indeed, bring upon him the reproach of foolish men, but it insures him the approbation of his own conscience—and that alone can bring a man peace at the last.

The special duties of the Christian grow out of his relation to GOD, as redeemed by the blood of CHRIST—made a child of GOD by adoption and grace, and bound by the baptismal **covenant,** to the improvement of all his talents.

These, therefore, include the private, personal religion of the man—the things which are transacted between GOD and himself alone, as well as those which are not of a directly public nature—and here it is that the sincerity and truth of Christian profession are manifested. If the fear and the love of GOD lead us to our closets, and intercourse with heaven, in prayer and meditation, lift our hearts above the world, he that seeth in secret stands engaged in our behalf, and the grace of his HOLY SPIRIT is supplied for our strength and guidance in all required duty—and as the duties of religion are mixed up with the common duties of our several stations in life—the private exercises of religion best prepare us to fulfil our Christian calling.

Of those special duties which are not of a directly public nature, the most important is that which the Christian owes to his family. As that is first in his affections, there is he allowed and required to manifest the full fervour both of natural love and religious affection. His exertions for their temporal comfort are religious duties. *If any provide not for his own, specially they of his own house, he hath denied the faith, and is worse than an infidel.* How much more strongly, then, will this condemnation apply to those parents who neglect the spiritual concerns of their families? And would to GOD that professing parents could be made to see and to feel how solemnly they are bound to this duty—how inseparably it is united with their own claim to the name of Christian—how fatally they deceive themselves, if they hope to work out their own salvation, while that of those who are bone of their bone and flesh of their flesh, is neglected. With me this neglect is decisive, that in those to whom it applies, either absolutely or in a cold and careless attention to the duty, the religious principle is not present, is not yet formed—there is some delusion at the bottom—some fatal deceit, crying peace where there is no peace. For independent of natural affection—independent of the solemn stipulations entered into at their baptism—the spirit of religion, where it occupies the heart, delights in nothing so much as in communications to others, and yearns, in a manner inexpressible, to find those who are dear to us, united in the same bond of love, and partakers of the same blessed hope.

Of the same obligation, though lower in degree, are the claims of relationship and kindred upon the Christian; and it is to the praise of the gospel, and a strong proof of its divine original, that its duties and its enjoyments are all connected with, and bound up in the natural affections of our condition. Its commandment is benevolence; its law is love; love, commencing in the dear relations of family union, embracing the connexion of kindred, and branching out to friends, country and kind, and rendered still more sacred by the holy hope that though broken and interrupted here, they will again be revived, where no separation shall be permitted to break in upon their enjoyment.

But my brethren, if the common relations of life, have the duties belonging to them enforced by the sanctions of religion, much more are those which spring from fellowship in the one faith and hope of the gospel, imprinted with the sacred character of that holy relation—*ye are one body, for ye are all partakers of that one bread.* The mutual love, comfort, help, and countenance which we owe to each other in the common relations of life, are sanctified to a holier obligation by our mutual relation to CHRIST.

In this view they overstep the boundaries of time, and branch out into that unseen world, of which faith is the evidence. They are the commencement, here, in an imperfect degree, of that course of love and good will, of that complacency and delight which will be perpetuated in eternity. But it must be begun here, if we would enjoy it there; for just as sure as we entertain any hostile, malevolent, unmerciful or unforgiving tempers towards our brethren here, so sure may we be, that the spirit of love and joy and peace which presides in heaven, will reject us from that blessed abode of pure and perfect happiness.

Let us learn then, my brethren and hearers, that the religion of the gospel takes nothing from, but adds to the enjoyments of this life; that the obligations we come under by embracing the gospel, are not a hard and grievous, but a light and easy burden, growing more and more pleasurable, as we experience more and more of its gracious effect upon our hearts ; and that the duties of religion are all calculated by infinite wisdom, to increase the sum of human happiness in time, and to perpetuate it in eternity.

Under these obligations you come, my Christian brethren, by partaking of that one bread ; and may the knowledge of your duty be followed by a faithful and fruitful performance of it. Your Redeemer speaks to you in this ordinance, in the moving and affectionate language of one, who manifested his love by laying down his life for your souls, *be ye kind one to another, tender hearted, forgiving one another, even as* GOD *for* CHRIST'S *sake, hath forgiven you.* He speaks to you in this ordinance of that mystical bond, by which you are constituted one body with him, and with the blessed company of all faithful people ; and through the humiliation of his death, he would lift your faith to the communion of saints and angels at the marriage supper of the Lamb, where sin and sorrow, pain and death, shall be forever banished from the paradise of GOD.

I come now to make a short application of the subject.

The knowledge of our duty, my brethren, is one thing—the performance of it another ; and we are too often disposed to rest contented with the knowledge, while we leave the duty undone.

To a Christian congregation, all that I have said ought to be familiar, and where this is the case, the only advantage will be the refreshing your memories with admitted truths. But to profit you my brethren, the truth must be brought to bear upon your consciences. How is it with you then, in the application of this subject? Is that holy principle of love and union, which animates the mystical body of CHRIST, alive and active in your hearts? Is it manifested in compassion and relief to the suffering members of CHRIST? Is it drawn out in prayer for the prosperity of the Church, and followed by exertions, according to ability, for the advancement of CHRIST's kingdom? Is it exercised with zeal and diligence, for the eternal interests of your family? Do you long and even agonize that they may be added to the communion of saints, and increase your hope and your thankfulness, in the dear expectation, of meeting them at the right hand of God? Or are your children permitted to grow up, like the wild asses colt, untutored in the knowledge of God, of themselves, and of the Lord Jesus Christ, though carefully furnished for the course of this present evil world? And is there not to many of you my brethren, a nearer interest still, in some dear husband or wife, who are strangers yet to the hope of the gospel, for whom, the deep, continued, and fervent supplication, besieges the throne of grace, and wrestles with God for the blessing? O, ask yourselves these questions, dear brethren, and thence judge in what degree the spirit of Christian love is abiding in your hearts; that true and genuine heavenly temper which cultivates good will to all, in the faithful exercise of Christian duty to its own. This is the order which heaven has appointed, which heaven has promised to bless, which alone is practical to us. It is the only practical rule also, in the exercise of Christian charity, in a divided Christian world. To pretend to more is to deceive ourselves, and to put words for things; is to promote indifference instead of love, and to neutralize the just and commanding claims of revealed religion and instituted means of grace; is to make this blessed sacrament, my brethren, a mere ceremony, and not an effectual means of heaven's grace to our souls.

Draw near, then, with true hearts, in full assurance of faith, in the exercise of that forgiveness which mercy experienced calls for; in the exercise of that penitence which a sense of many sins and short comings must beget in your hearts; in the exercise of that lively faith which springs from this manifestation of God's truth and love, in the fulfilment of his gracious promises; in the exercise of that hope which springs from the resurrection of Christ; in the exercise of that charity which includes all for whom Christ died; and in earnest prayer that he who died for all, would be pleased to bless and sanctify this memorial of his passion and death, to the spiritual nourishment of your souls, to the increase of his love in your hearts, and to the advancement of his glory in the world; especially, that he would be gracious to those over whom your hearts yearn, until Christ be formed in them—*That the eyes of their understanding being enlightened, they may know what is the hope of his calling, and what the riches of the glory of his inheritance in the saints, and what the exceeding greatness of his power to us ward, who believe.*

Now, our LORD JESUS CHRIST *himself, and* GOD, *even our Father, which hath loved us, and hath given us everlasting consolation and good hope, through grace, comfort your hearts, and stablish you in every good word and work.*——AMEN.

SERMON VI.

UNITY OF THE CHURCH.

Ephesians iv. 4.

"There is one body."

It has come to pass, my brethren and hearers, from causes neither very remote from observation, nor difficult to be investigated, that what was once of the highest importance to the comfort and assurance of a Christian in the great concern of eternity, is now, throughout a very extended portion of the Christian world, lost sight of and rejected, as an article of the faith once delivered to the saints; and considered in those who entertain it, as the mark of an illiberal, uncharitable, and bigotted spirit. I mean the doctrine of the unity of the Church of Christ, and its use or purpose in the mighty and merciful work of bringing sinners to salvation, and preparing them for eternal glory.

That it is a prominent doctrine however, one which we profess to receive as the unerring and unchangeable word of God, can be denied only by those who are under the dominion of ignorance or prejudice. The words of my text, in connexion with the context, even were there no parallel passages of Scripture, being sufficient of themselves, to awaken and excite our attention to the subject—for in all that is revealed our benefit is intended—and it is our duty to search it out, *that we may know what is that acceptable and perfect will of God concerning us,* and apply ourselves thereto with all the earnestness, and exactness of minds truly engaged in working out their everlasting salvation with fear and trembling.

That edification on this point of Christian doctrine is much wanted, unhappily requires no other proof than the divided state of the Christian community; for it is never to be presumed, that persons seriously concerned for the salvation of their souls, would knowingly reject what the Scriptures plainly teach, and be led away from the appointments of GOD, into new and unknown paths of error and division, after inventions of men who speak without knowledge, and act without warrant.

On the present occasion then, when the thoughts are naturally drawn to the subject by the erection and opening of a building, to be set apart to the service of Almighty GOD, as a branch of that holy apostolic Church which claims and possesses a regular episcopal succession from the apostles of our LORD and Saviour JESUS CHRIST, as her warrant for administering the affairs of his kingdom upon earth, and for dispensing the word and sacraments of salvation to his members; I trust it may be allowed to one of her ministers, according to his poor ability, for the edification of all present, and for the comfort and assurance of those into whose hearts GOD hath put it, to build an house to his name, to lay before you what the Scriptures teach us on this much neglected subject of Christian obligation; and to draw from the doctrine those conclusions which are fairly and reasonably to be deduced from them. I say fairly and reasonably, for this doctrine, like every other in the religion of JESUS CHRIST, addresses itself to our understanding, to our interest, and through these to our affections, and only when thus received and applied, can be productive of any benefit to our souls. With all the other doctrines too, this is capable of being perverted and abused, and even corrupted, to suit the particular views of designing men, though we are plainly warned that thus to wrest the Scriptures is to ensure our own destruction.

In discoursing, therefore, on this subject, I shall in the

FIRST place, lay before you those passages of Scripture which declare the unity of the Church of CHRIST.

SECONDLY, I shall endeavour to show you in what that unity consists.

THIRDLY, I shall point out the purpose and design of this appointment of the wisdom of GOD, in the great work of our redemption and salvation; and, then,

CONCLUDE, with an application of the subject.

There is one body.

I. First, I am to lay before you those passages of Scripture which declare the unity of the Church of CHRIST.

The gracious design of our blessed LORD's coming in the flesh, was not merely to declare the will of GOD, to set an example of its performance, and to expiate by his death the guilt of sin, and then leave mankind to make what advantage they could of the mercy and reconciliation thus procured for them ; but beyond this, to gather together out of the world, those who received him, as St. John expresses it, and by believing in him, became entitled to all the benefits of his undertaking for sinners. Hence he is said to have suffered, *that he might gather together in one, the children of* GOD *scattered abroad.* In one, that is into one uniform visible society, actuated by the same spirit, professing the same faith, entertaining the same hope, joining in the same worship, and participating in the same spiritual food for the nourishment of their souls, in the administration of the same word and sacraments in the Church, by the stewards of these his mysteries.

In agreement with this view of the subject, the Scriptures inform us, that he came *to purchase to himself a peculiar people, zealous of good works ;* that *he purchased a Church with his own blood,* that this Church so purchased, is his body—his spouse—the bride, the Lamb's wife—and that CHRIST is the head of the body—the Church. In which we must observe that the expressions, the Church, his body, are in the singular number, and denote unity in the simplest acceptation of the word. While the figurative descriptions made use of, such as spouse, bride, wife, confirm this unity, by associations not to be mistaken. But it is from the passage of which my text forms a part, that we derive the strongest confirmation, and clearest illustration of this doctrine.

There is one body, and one spirit, even as ye are called in one hope of your calling—one LORD, *one faith, one baptism*—one GOD *and Father of all, who is above all, and through all, and in you all.* In which passage of Scripture it is impossible, I think, not to be struck with the important part here ascribed to the Church, as a visible body in the work of our salvation, not to perceive that it is in no shape or sense, the creature of human contrivance, or allowably subject to the alteration or amendment, if it must be so called, either of assumed necessity, or presuming wisdom.

In other places of Scripture, this body or Church of CHRIST is represented as a family, of which GOD is the Father, and JESUS CHRIST the elder brother, and first-born from the dead—and in which all the members of this family, in their several stations, are followers of GOD as dear children, walking in the steps of that holy example which CHRIST, their elder brother, hath set them.

It is designated as a household, in which CHRIST rules, as a son in his own house, every inhabitant deriving from him his daily supply, and rendering those services which are considered by the householder most beneficial to the general good—in which he appoints what each shall be occupied about, and wherein none can be lawfully employed but by his direction. It is spoken of as a city of which Jerusalem was the type, in which all rule and authority was derived from the appointment of the great king, in which only the true worship of the true GOD was maintained, and which is represented as builded compact together, and at unity in itself.

It is set forth as a kingdom, of which the LORD JESUS CHRIST, the king of saints and angels, is the Almighty Sovereign and gracious Ruler, from whom all power is derived, and to whom all power in heaven and upon earth is committed.

Under all these names and allusions, the Church of CHRIST is spoken of in Scripture, my hearers, and must necessarily be assimilated, in its order and government, to what is essential to the well being of each and all of those figures, by which it is represented for our easier and better comprehension. As a family and household, it must not be divided against itself, lest it come to nought. As a city and kingdom it must be under the rule and government of its proper officers, all deriving their authority from the king himself. Nothing short of this can entitle it to be considered as an orderly and regular society, commanding respect and confidence, and conferring those benefits with which it is furnished by its living Head.

This distinctive character of the Church of CHRIST is confirmed and enforced, by the unity which is constantly attributed to those who are members of it here in its visible state. They are every where in Scripture spoken of as one, in the strongest manner in which unity can be expressed. Speaking of Christians collectively, St. Paul says, *There is neither Jew nor Greek, there is neither bond nor free, there is neither male nor female—for ye are all one in* CHRIST JESUS. And the same apostle writing to the Corinthian Church on the subject of their divisions, and improper intercourse with Heathens and idolaters, tells them as an argument for union, *Now ye are the body of* CHRIST *and members in particular ; for as the body is one, and hath many members, and all the members of that one body, being many, are one body, so also is* CHRIST, *for by one* SPIRIT *are we all baptized into one body.* And this argument from the unity of that one sacrament, by which alone we can be received into his mystical body, and are made *members of his body, of his flesh, and of his bones,* as St. Paul strongly expresses it, he carries forward to our joint participation of the eucharist, as a still more conclusive demonstration of the unity of the body and the members. *The cup of blessing which we bless,* says St. Paul, *is it not the communion of the blood of* CHRIST ? *The bread which we break, is it not the communion of the body of* CHRIST ? *For we being many, are one bread and one body, for we are all partakers of that one bread.*

Thus clear, plain, and express, my brethren, is the warrant of Scripture for the unity of the Church of CHRIST—a unity not limited by time or place, but co-existing and co-extensive with the gospel—a unity which includes the Church triumphant as well as the Church militant, and from which we cannot separate or disjoin ourselves, without incurring the heinous guilt of rending the body of CHRIST, and doing what in us lies, to make void that affectionate prayer with which our blessed LORD concludes his ministry upon earth.—*Holy Father, keep through thine own name those whom thou hast given me, that they all may be one, as thou Father art in me, and I in thee ; that they also may be one in us.*

A principle so important, as to occupy the wishes and prayers of the author and finisher of our faith, at the very moment when the powers of darkness had taken possession of the hour allotted them, in which to prevail against his life, cannot surely be safely disregarded by us, my friends. I shall, therefore,

VOL. I.—69

II. Secondly, endeavour to show you in what this unity consists.

To determine this satisfactorily, we have to consider two things—First, what it was in the preaching of the apostles, that presented itself with unvarying uniformity, to the eyes and to the understandings of all descriptions of persons—and, Secondly, what it is that to the present moment, gives to the word and sacraments of the visible Church, the same character and efficacy in the most remote parts of the evangelized world.

As respects the first point, there cannot be a question that this was the divine authority, with which, as ambassadors of CHRIST, they were clothed, to confirm the truth of the doctrines they taught, and to ratify the conditions on which its sanctions were proposed to the acceptance or rejection of a rebel world.

To demonstrate this, let us reflect, my brethren, that in things which are not the objects of sense, and respecting which we can have no experience, such as those which are the subject matter of revelation, the authority of GOD, manifested in some way to our senses, is the only safe foundation either of faith or practice. The obligation we are under to receive it, depends upon this single circumstance, and not upon the reasonableness, fitness, and importance of the things themselves ; that is, a subsequent consideration, and derives its weight altogether from the prior authority of him, by whom, or in whose name it is proposed. Just as in the matter of the law of the land, it is not the justness, or expediency, or policy of the law, which gives it its force and obligation, but the legitimate authority by which it is enacted. These, indeed, increase the obligation all are under to obey the law, and perform the duty ; but they are subsequent, both in time and fact, to the authority : nor is that at all affected by them ; it remains the same, and when supreme, is independent of the quality of its enactments, as is exemplified in the clearest and strongest manner by the revelation we have.

The miracles wrought by Moses, were the conclusive evidence to the Israelites in Egypt, that GOD had sent him as their deliverer—and to Pharoah and his subjects, that heaven had commanded him to let his people go. Upon the same evidence rested the authority of their law given from Mount Sinai, and not upon the reasonableness, or fitness, or wisdom of the law itself. By the same evidence did our blessed LORD demonstrate to that people that a greater than Moses was present with them, and on this ground did he challenge their acceptance of him and his doctrine. *If I do not the works of my Father, believe me not, but if I do, though ye believe not me, believe the works.* On this also did he declare that their condemnation rested for rejecting the gospel. *If I had not come and spoken unto them, they had not had sin. If I had not done among them the works which none other man did, they had not had sin.*

By the same testimony was the glad tidings of the gospel by his apostles, evidenced, supported, and established. By mighty signs and wonders, and works of the HOLY GHOST, attendant on the persons and preaching of men of like passions with themselves, were the words and actions of the apostles and first ministers of CHRIST confirmed as the truth of GOD, and verified to the nations, as *the way, the truth, and the life,* as it is in JESUS, for the salvation of a lost world. And by this, and this only, were all who embraced the gospel certified that they were not following cunningly devised fables, or led astray by the inward assurance of a heated or deceived imagination, after inventions of men, or opinions which seemed good in their own eyes, on the unspeakably serious consideration of the loss or salvation of their souls.

And here we cannot help remarking, my friends, with what infinite wisdom this first and standing proof of the heavenly origin of the gospel is fitted to every capacity. Had it been made to depend on strength of understanding, or cultivation of mind, it must have varied with the unequal state of those qualifications, and could not have possessed that unity of character which was, and is yet, essential to its effect; while constituted as it is, it cuts off every shadow of excuse, and powerfully impels the mind to consider and apply, what is so highly and incontestably witnessed.

Of the same nature is the second consideration on this point, to wit: what it is, that to the present moment, gives to the word and sacraments of the visible Church, the same character and efficacy in the most remote parts of the evangelized world.

Perhaps, my hearers, many of you may never have asked yourselves the question. Perhaps many who profess the gospel, may never have considered what their faith and hope of its blessings rests upon. Perhaps many who are preachers of the gospel have never seriously put to themselves the question, *by what authority doest thou these things ?* Perhaps it may be considered a contentious rather than a useful inquiry, to investigate and ascertain what principle it is, that from India to America, from Iceland to the Cape of Good Hope, gives to the ministrations of CHRIST's religion the sanctified and saving character affixed to them by the author and finisher of our faith, and to the varied millions of its population, the one hope of their high and heavenly calling.

And yet, my hearers, if there is a subject on which we cannot be too sure, it must be this ; if there is a point which deserves all the attention we can give to it, it must be that which involves our connexion with that one universal Church or body of CHRIST, which has one LORD, one faith, one baptism. Much may be said on this subject, my brethren, and it deserves the most careful consideration. But the time requires me to be brief.

As the Church is but one all over the world, purchased, founded, and ordered, by its living head—a vine with but one root, though with many branches—as in that Church there is but one faith taught and professed, one GOD to worship, one LORD to serve, one SPIRIT to inhabit and abide, and one final reward of eternal life to be obtained, so is there one only appointed mode or means for admission to its privileges, and one communion of saints in it. This being so, there can be but one principle, on which all these duties can be performed, and all these privileges enjoyed ; and it can only be found, in the joint participation of the members in the word and sacraments, administered by the one authority of the Head. No other principle of unity, for the practical purposes of a visible Church, can be imagined, which can operate alike on every class and description of men ; none so readily and certainly verifiable and available to that assurance, which is the crown of Christian hope. Which assurance, while it is without any doubt, the witness of the HOLY SPIRIT, can only be relied on when its testimony is in agreement with that outward order which the same SPIRIT has revealed, to guide us into all saving truth. To suppose, or to take for granted, that the witness of the HOLY SPIRIT in the heart of man will be given in favour of any thing in opposition to the outward order and authority of the Church as founded by CHRIST, is to suppose that GOD would contradict himself. Consequently to rely upon internal impressions, however strong, which are in opposition to, or have no counterpart in the written spirit, as I may call it, or word of GOD, is, to say the least, to encourage delusion, and to cast ourselves loose from the Church and compass which GOD has mercifully provided for us to steer our course by, through the mixed and troubled sea of time, to the secure haven of his presence in the boundless ocean of eternity.

Should we count him a wise or a prudent man, who could thus act in any affair of temporal moment, who in any short voyage from one port to another, could throw away his chart and compass, unship his helm, discharge his pilot, and commit himself to the great deep, relying on some fancied assurance in his own mind, or plausible reasoning of others, that he would reach his destination securely without them ? In like manner is he an unwise and imprudent man, who discards the more sure word of prophecy, or perverts it to suit the impressions of a disordered and prejudiced imagination, who, instead of considering the word of GOD as a light shining in a dark place, trusts to some rush-light of human reason, by which he steers from the harbour instead of towards it, and is sooner or later stranded on the quick-sands of enthusiasm, or wrecked on the rocks of heresy and schism.

It appearing then, that the unity of the Church of CHRIST, as a visible society, consists in the profession of the same faith, the worship of the same GOD, the entertainment of the same hope, in the communion, fellowship, or joint participation of the same word and sacraments, as revealed means of grace, by the authority of JESUS CHRIST, the head of this body, and witnessed by the miraculous powers of the HOLY GHOST, given to his apostles personally, for this very end, and to the Church to abide with it for ever in his ordinary operations, it follows necessarily, that only as we are united to him, in this holy fellowship, can we have any sure and certain hope, that the promises of Almighty GOD, made to his Church and people, are ours; for they are made to us by covenant engagement in the Church, and not elsewhere; they are sealed to us in the sacraments of that Church, which can be lawfully administered only by the authority of CHRIST, and fulfilled in the attainment of that holiness, which alone can fit us for the general assembly and Church of the first-born—the Church triumphant in glory. All which I trust to make more manifest to you, in what I have to say on the next head of my discourse; which was,

III. Thirdly, to point out the purpose and design of this appointment of the wisdom of GOD in the great work of our redemption and salvation.

The condition of man as fallen, and the nature of religion, will best evidence the purpose and design of an outward and visible Church. The faculties of the soul being all impaired by sin, and the desires and affections of the heart perverted from their original direction, to make man a religious creature, and capable of loving and serving his maker, it was necessary to renew his spiritual strength, so far at least, as to enable him to profit by that state of reprieve and trial, which the love of GOD in CHRIST JESUS decreed to afford him. And this we have good reason to believe is so far done to every creature under heaven. But as trial and improvement are of a progressive nature, and can only be met and carried on by care and diligence on our part, it depends on ourselves so far, what the result shall be.

Religion on the other hand, being conversant mainly with things invisible and spiritual, all its sanctions being future, and what is revealed depending simply on the veracity of GOD; therefore, faith, or a fixed and firm persuasion of the being of GOD, and of the truth and certainty of the invisible things of a future state, lies at the very foundation of all religious attainment.

This faith being required of us my friends, and being the only principle which can counteract and overcome the influence and power of present and sensible things, which constitute our trial and make them yield to the higher and nobler things which are revealed to us; a gracious and merciful GOD, hath so ordered and disposed what concerns our religious condition as to strengthen and keep alive this first foundation of all.

To that end the Church, the ministry, and the sacraments are instituted, that by outward and sensible signs, we might be reminded and kept under the influence of those invisible things which are the objects of Christian faith and hope; and furthermore, that they might be means and channels for conveying grace, that is spiritual help, to our souls. This is the scriptural and only just view we can take of them, and hence we may see of what high importance the principle of unity is in those institutions, and particularly that on which the whole depends, to wit: the authority of the institutor, as the life-blood which animates and invigorates the whole system.

The Church then, or mystical body of CHRIST, is the rallying point of true believers—the appointed and visible refuge of all who would flee from the wrath to come; and is aptly and forcibly represented to us in the use, by the ark in which Noah and his family were saved from the destruction which came upon all who were out of it. In another place, by the figure of a sheep-fold, of which CHRIST is the chief shepherd and the door of the sheep, into which fold, he tells us, *whosoever enters in by him shall be saved, and go in and out and find pasture,* that is, shall walk at liberty and have all his spiritual wants supplied. It is further represented as the guardian and keeper of holy writ—of the Scriptures of our faith, and hence it is styled *the pillar and ground of the truth.* Here again we must observe, the absolute and essential nature of that principle of unity or oneness in the Church, which I have been setting before you. How else could this only rule of saving faith and right practice, have been kept pure and unadulterated, and transmitted through so many ages and oppositions, and with the sacred character of being able to save our souls; and what else but this very principle, overruled and supported by the watchful care of his living head, makes it the standard of truth to every denomination under the Christian name—the court of appeals as it were, to the Christian world. But for this standing miracle, for such in truth it is, the bush burning, but not consumed—how would every thing calling itself a Church, have pared and trimmed this sacred deposit of divine truth to suit its own views of doctrine and order, and Scripture been multiplied, until all reverence and regard for its truth and certainty would have ceased among men.

As a visible society, the Church must have its officers for the due management and administration of its affairs for the general good. And just as certainly as no man has any shadow of right to appoint servants and prescribe their duties in your family, or in mine, my hearers, no more can any such right be presumed or exercised towards the household of CHRIST; and when we consider that the affairs of this household are altogether of a a spiritual nature, and must depend for their effect, on the authority by which they are transacted, it must be the height of delusion, ignorance, or presumption, for man to meddle with them on his own warrant; hence we read, *that no man taketh his honour unto himself but he that is called of* GOD *as was Aaron;* and as the whole polity of the Jewish Church in its unity, was the shadow of better things to come under the gospel dispensation, the constitution of the Christian Church, is founded on this principle; consequently the right to minister in that Church, must be derived from its head and founder.

In perfect agreement herewith, St. Paul tells us, that when our LORD had finished his work upon earth, and was about to ascend up on high, *He gave some apostles, and some prophets, and some evangelists, and some pastors and teachers, for the perfecting of the saints, for the work of the ministry, for the edifying the body of* CHRIST, *till we all come in the unity of the faith, and of the knowledge of the Son of* GOD, *unto a perfect man, unto the measure of the stature of the fulness of* CHRIST. Here then, my brethren, we have the appointment and the purpose of the ministry fully declared to us, and all depending on this root of unity, the authority of CHRIST—they are in his name to declare to you the whole counsel of GOD, repecting your present and future condition, to call you to repentance, to faith, to holiness, as the conditions of eternal life. As ambassadors of CHRIST, they are to negotiate peace and reconciliation between GOD and his rebellious creatures, and to ratify the terms of that new and gracious covenant of mercy, and forgiveness of sins, which CHRIST by his death has purchased for all who shall believe in his only saving name.

And can such weighty and unspeakable interests be intermeddled with without warrant ? Are we so foolish as to transact an affair of this importance, without being well assured, that the person who stands forward between GOD and us, has authority from GOD to pledge his promises and to receive our submission ? And can we not perceive and understand, in this appointment of visible agents, the exceeding goodness of GOD our Saviour towards us, in so accommodating the mystery of redemption to our condition, that faith should have something to rest upon, something outward and sensible to realize itself by, and to grow and increase, as we faithfully use the means appointed ; can we not be made to feel, that as it is of the last importance for men to receive, that therefore they ought to know with certainty, where to look for the depositaries of his grace and HOLY SPIRIT, and is it not the very blindness of delusion to make no inquiry, whether those who say, CHRIST *is here, or lo, he is there*, have indeed any authority to say that he is any where.

But here it may be asked, and very properly, how are we to determine this point? To this I answer, that GOD hath not left us unprovided on so material a circumstance, would we only be guided and directed by his word. For just as this was determined in the days of the apostles, is it to be determined now—— and by evidence just as satisfactory, though not of the same kind. For what the miraculous witness of the HOLY GHOST, was to the divine commission of the apostles, *that* the ordination and authority of the Church, founded by them, and holding succession from them, is to us. For it is the authority of CHRIST running in that channel which himself appointed, and is capable of being proved or disproved with the same certainty as any other matter of fact. To say or to think otherwise, is to take for granted either that these words of CHRIST concerning his Church—*the gates of hell shall not prevail against it*——have failed, or what would be the same thing in effect, that it has become so obscured, that no reasonable search can find it. But GOD be thanked, it is not so. And thanks to his holy and merciful name, he hath not in this weighty affair left us comfortless. We can try the spirits whether they are of GOD, by that open and verifiable standard, their descent from those apostles, to whom he committed the keys of the kingdom of heaven, whom he empowered to bind and to loose ; whom he sent to convert and baptize the nations, to gather and establish his Church ; whom he empowered to commit to faithful men after them, the same precious deposit, even unto the end of the world ; and whom he fully authorized for all these glorious and gracious purposes in that plenary commission—*As my Father hath sent me, even so send I you*—*As my Father hath appointed unto me a kingdom, I also appoint unto you a kingdom.*

While the Church, and the ministry in it, are thus wisely and mercifully constituted, to help the weakness, and increase the strength of our faith, and to give to things spiritual and invisible, a body and substance as it were, united to the grossness of our sin-enfeebled faculties ; the sacraments are in a more especial manner, appropriated as the channels of that grace, without which we can do nothing, and calculated to evince in the clearest manner, the all-pervading influence of the authority of CHRIST, as the only verifiable root of unity in his Church.

By the sacrament of baptism, and by that only, can we be received into the visible Church, be made members of CHRIST, become parties to the Christian covenant, and entitled, until forfeited by personal sin, to all the benefits of CHRIST's undertaking for us. And this so strictly, that an unbaptized person has no right to the name of Christian, nor any covenant claim to revealed mercy. But let no one here represent me as saying, that persons unbaptized are, therefore, cut off from all hope of salvation. What I say is, that they have no covenanted, or promised title to it. In a matter of such moment, then, where such mighty benefits are annexed to this ordinance, the authority by which the sacrament is administered, is of the first importance, unless we entertain the monstrous notion, that the certainty and assurance arising from authorised ministrations in religion, are of no moment to the peace and comfort of believers. But can any serious person think thus of so solemn an ordinance as a sacrament? And such an ordinance too, as lies at the very root of Christian profession, at the entrance to those covenanted mercies, which were ratified in the blood of CHRIST; the seal and pledge that we shall obtain them on the conditions then entered into, and the instituted means or channel of that grace by which alone we are enabled to fulfil them.

In a temporal interest, my friends, do we enter into a contract with persons at a distance, without examining whether their representative is properly and legally authorised to bind his principal? And is not baptism a contract, with mutual engagements between GOD and man, which can no otherwise be executed or transacted but by an authorised and accredited agent? Alas! what blind delusion has seized upon men, that in what concerns their immortal souls, they are carelessly satisfied with a security on which they would not risk their estates, and are filled with rage perhaps at the friendly hand which would point out their error, while it is not too late to retrieve their mistake. But be it so, whether they will hear or whether they will forbear— the whole counsel of GOD must be declared.

The same argument applies still more powerfully to the higher sacrament of the eucharist, on which I have not time to enlarge, but which yourselves, I trust, my brethren, can carry out in its application to that ordinance, for the analogy is the same, while the extent is greater, and the consequences of a higher order.

On the one depends our entrance into, on the other our continuance in the Christian covenant of salvation by grace through faith.

The application of what has been said, addresses itself to the plain understanding of plain Christian people, on the deep interests of their condition, as respects the covenanted mercies of GOD in CHRIST JESUS—Whether they are held and hoped for, as set forth in his true and lively word, according to the conditions on which they are therein limited, or whether some unconsidered, unauthorized scheme of man's invention, recent or remote, is blindly followed and relied upon, in what is of more worth than millions of such worlds as this. This is the point, my friends, to which to bring my text, and what grows out of it. If what I have laid before you is a fair and reasonable exposition of undoubted Scripture, there can be no escape from it, but at a risk which is terrible to think of. And if the whole subject is fortified against all vain reasonings, by the circumstance, that in the Church derived from the apostles of our LORD and Saviour JESUS CHRIST, the Protestant Episcopal Church, once more reviving among you, all these advantages are to be found, with whatever of Christian edification may be promised you elsewhere, if the question is between certainty and uncertainty, between doubt and assurance—if you may gain but cannot lose—what room can there be for hesitation. *I speak as unto wise men, judge ye what I say.*

Well do I know, my hearers, the power of prejudice and early prepossession, and long had I to struggle with it. But truth is mighty, and will prevail, if allowed to speak. Well do I know the power of pride, and the fear of the world's remark, in stifling the convictions which truth of this description will force upon the mind. But it is the experience of every day, that these will yield to temporal convenience, and temporal interest. And shall they not give way in favour of our souls; shall they not yield to interests which are eternal ? Let the truth, then be counted worth a serious consideration. That it might be the simple truth, and the plain reasonings growing out of that truth, which should be laid before you this day, I have avoided all learned criticisms—all authorities for opinion, but the one irreversible authority of GOD's word.

THERE IS ONE BODY, says that word—one Church, or ark of safety for sinners to betake themselves to, to escape from the wrath of GOD. Where shall we find it, how shall we know it ? should be the earnest inquiry of every soul seeking salvation. There is *one baptism,* says the same true and unchangeable word, and *he that believeth and is baptized shall be saved.* Who shall administer to us this precious seal of covenanted mercy ? should be the careful consideration of all who look for that GRACE OF GOD *which bringeth salvation.* There is one cup of blessing, and one bread of life to be partaken of, in one communion of saints—say the Scriptures of truth. Who shall bless and consecrate, and hand over to us these lively memorials of a Saviour's dying love, these authoritative pledges of pardon, peace, and eternal life in him? should be the anxious cry of every redeemed sinner. *Beloved believe not every* SPIRIT, *but try the* SPIRITS, *whether they be of* GOD, *because many false prophets are gone out into the world.* Try them, then, my hearers, not by their own assertions or reasonings—not by any pretensions to a call from GOD, which they can neither prove, or you determine. Bring them to that test, which is the same in all ages of the Church, and capable of being proved or disproved, with a certainty which precludes imposition, to wit: the authority of CHRIST, transmitted through his apostles to the Church— GOD *is not the author of confusion, but of order.* To this test bring him who now speaks to you, both as respects his office and his doctrine—I ask no more—and may GOD give you the hearing ear, and the understanding heart.

SERMON VII.

CHRISTMAS.

St. Matthew, xi, 26.

" Come unto me, all ye that labour and are heavy laden, and I will give you rest."

THE wonderful event, which, as a Christian people, we are called upon to celebrate, by the anniversary return of this day, is replete with every consideration which can engage the attention, gladden the hearts, and elevate the hopes of a redeemed world. GOD made man, that man might be made the righteousness of GOD in him, has in its very announcement, my brethren, the most impressive application ; for there lives not, in the compass of this world, that being, whose highest interests and brightest hopes, are not bound up, and identified with the incarnation of GOD the Son. GOD in CHRIST reconciling the world unto himself, not imputing their trespasses unto them, contains such an animating discovery of the breadth and length and depth and height of his rich redeeming love, as to tune every heart, and unloose every tongue with joyful praise; for there is not found that descendant of Adam, who has not to look to GOD for the pardon or penalty of sin. The union of the divine and human nature in one CHRIST, presents that spectacle of infinite and unsearchable wisdom, which even the angels desire to look into, and which offers to every soul of man that tried foundation stone, on which to build the hope that shall not be disappointed. And these all, my friends, high, holy and infinite as they are in themselves, and in their application to us, depend for their truth and certainty, for their whole value and importance, on the birth of JESUS of Nazareth. For of this it may be said, and with equal truth, as is said of his resurrection, if CHRIST be not born, according to the Scriptures, then there is no hope for man; Christianity is a fable, and revelation a romance.

Need we then to wonder my brethren, that a season pregnant with such glad tidings and precious hopes, should be celebrated by the Church, with such appropriate offices as gives to the religion she inculcates the cheerful and happy character of a reasonable service ? Ought we not rather to admire, that any who say they are CHRIST's, should refuse this tribute of annual respect to the Saviour's birth, and withhold themselves from those high gratulations with which Christians should meet each other on this morning, and from those edifying meditations, which are prompted by the near survey of this auspicious event ? *Unto us a child is born, unto us a Son is given,* and the gracious purpose of his advent in the flesh, with the fulfilment of that purpose, in his life, death, resurrection and ascension, must ever form the most profitable source of Christian knowledge and Christian hope. His birth into our nature, my brethren, was necessary in order to our redemption from sin and eternal death ; and in like manner, our birth into his nature is equally necessary in order to our sanctification and attainment of eternal life. Grant, O GOD, that while we, and all thy whole Church, are rejoicing at the birth of thy holy child JESUS, there may be joy in heaven over one sinner that is brought to CHRIST, and born again of incorruptible seed by the living word !

To that blessed end, I meet you this joyful morning, my brethren and hearers, with the gracious invitation of the Saviour ; and that it may be a word in season to all, I shall endeavour to explain and point out.

FIRST, What that burden is, from which CHRIST offers to deliver us.

SECONDLY, The nature of the rest he promises to give those who come to him.

I shall then inform you how to come to him, and conclude with an application of the subject.

Come unto me all ye that labour and are heavy laden, and I will give you rest.

1. First—I am to explain and point out what that burden is, from which CHRIST offers to deliver us.

To form some just estimate of this part of our LORD's

undertaking, we must consider the effect of sin on the state and condition of the world ; for whatever we may choose to think or say, it is thus only, my friends, that we can learn the infinite importance of the Saviour, and be drawn by the gospel to come to him.

From the nature and perfections of God, the first effect of sin is separation and exclusion from him forever ; for he is of purer eyes than to behold iniquity, and cannot look upon sin with the least degree of allowance. From the nature and perfection also of the law of his holy government, the penalty therein denounced against the transgression of its precepts must be inflicted. *The soul that sinneth it must die—without shedding of blood there is no remission.* Hence it is evident that if a sinner, that is, a wilful transgressor of the law of God, or a race of sinners, is allowed to continue in being, it must be on some principle of substitution and satisfaction, whereby these infinite perfections are maintained and reconciled both with the letter and the spirit of their requirements. And what is the whole discovery of revelation to us, my hearers, but an exemplification of that infinite wisdom and unspeakable love, whereby God has provided for the exercise of mercy, and yet preserved inviolate the sovereignty of his righteous government ?

From the nature and condition of man as a created and accountable being, the effect of sin is spiritual death, or subjection to its power and dominion forever. As the life of the soul consists in union with God by his Spirit, the loss of this union by the wilful transgression of God's holy law delivers man over to another master, even to the law of sin in his members ; hence return to God is impossible to the sinner himself ; he is equally without inclination, as he is without the means of regaining his lost estate. The law of sin ruling his depraved and degraded faculties, his desires are earthly, sensual, devilish ; God is not in all his thoughts ; nor is there a wish, from himself, to regain the divine favour. But even were the wish possible, the means are wanting. What has the sinner to do with God ? O that the millions under the gospel, who are therefore doubly sinners, would ask themselves this question, and bring it to trial, even by the reason of their own minds.

Rebellion, disobedience, impurity, hatred ; these form the sum total of what the sinner is possessed of in himself; this is therefore all that he could offer.   But for each of these, the law demands its penalty, and justice dooms him to destruction.

On the highest interests of man, then, his spiritual and eternal welfare, the effect of sin is like the desolation of the whirlwinds, it uproots and scatters them irrecoverably.   It raises a barrier between GOD and man, which can be passed by no human fraud, or human force.   It is the flaming sword in the hands of the cherubim, which turns in every direction to guard the paradise of GOD, and the way of the tree of life, from all who are submitted to its power, and in love with its bondage.

But this my brethren and hearers, though more than sufficient to show its detestable nature to rational beings, is but a part of its deplorable effects.   To sin, as the cause, we can trace all the miseries of the present life.   Pain, sorrow, sickness, disappointment, death, break in upon every enjoyment, and cloud the happiest lot of mortality, with the sigh of regret, and the throb of anguish.   Inordinate affection, conflicting interest, pride, passion, and revenge, burst through the feeble restraints which oppose their gratification, and work the ocean of life into rage, amid the storm of their angry encounter.   What period of life, or portion of this world is exempt from its deleterious influence ?   Infancy suffers, youth is blasted, manhood withers, and old age groans, under its stroke.   Neither wisdom, nor worth, nor power, can evade its curse.   It has obtained possession, and maintains its sway.   Yet strange to tell, this public enemy, this general destroyer, is nevertheless the close companion, the intimate associate of millions in Christian lands, who, though they are warned of the danger, heed it not, but yield themselves to its deceitful and dangerous seductions.   And stranger still, though a heavenly physician has undertaken the cure, though an Almighty Saviour offers his help, though the Son of GOD hath taken upon himself the nature that sinned, though he hath paid the penalty, and purchased salvation for all that believe in his name, *yet they will not come to him that they may have life* ; and this it is, my friends, which marks its deadliest feature—it closes the ears, it stupifies the understanding, it hardens the hearts of its votaries.   Wisdom may warn—experience may teach—yea, GOD may call, but too often it is all in vain—*Like the deaf adder, they will not hear the voice of the charmer, charm he never so wisely.*

In this short and very inadequate statement of the dreadful effects of sin, we learn what that burden is from which CHRIST offers to deliver all who come to him ; and surely, if separation from GOD—exposure to his curse—suffering in the present life, and everlasting misery, in that which is to come, deserve to be considered as a burden—such is the load under which the sinner labours.   He may not indeed feel it—he may not be willing to believe that it is so—and herein is the strongest proof of its power and dominion over him ; yet as GOD is true, the guilt and the damnation of sin, is upon every soul under the gospel, who has not come to CHRIST for deliverance.   This is the solemn truth which I wish to press upon your hearts my hearers—which I wish you to consider, to examine, to weigh, as for eternity ; because it is this only which can make the invitation of my text a joyful sound, and JESUS CHRIST precious to your souls. *They that are whole*, indeed, *need not a physician ;* but where is he to be found who is free from the disease, the mortal distemper of sin ? where shall be found the man who dare venture to meet the justice of GOD, without the shield of a Saviour's merits ?   Oh ! *If the righteous scarcely be saved, where shall the ungodly and the sinner appear ?   To-day then, if you will hear his voice, harden not your hearts,* but meet this propitious season, with that deep and serious interest which a message of mercy and peace, from heaven to a world of sinners should receive from all to whom it is addressed.

II. Secondly, I am to explain and point out to you the nature of the rest, he promises to give to those who come to him.

The words *rest* and *peace* being nearly synonimous in scripture usage ; and a state of sin being a state of enmity with GOD, it is with reference to this, that the word rest is to be taken. The rest promised therefore, will respect as well the life that now is, as that which is to come.

To every rational mind the most grievous and heart-sinking condition which can be imagined is that of alienation from GOD and exposure to his wrath. But this is the condition of all mankind by nature—*All have sinned and come short of the glory of God.* To be released and delivered therefore from the terrible apprehensions of such a state of condemnation, is to obtain rest. This, the undertaking of the Son of God hath accomplished for the whole world, and converted a state of destitution and death into a state of reprieve and trial, with means commensurate to the end. And this is the foundation of those glad tidings which by the gospel, are commanded to be preached among all nations for the obedience of faith; hence we read that God *was in Christ, reconciling the world unto himself,* that Christ *is our peace, having made peace by the blood of his cross,* and hence the gracious command and commission to his ministers, *Go ye into all the world and preach the gospel to every creature—he that believeth and is baptized shall be saved, he that believeth not shall be damned.*

To an accountable being, the consciousness of guilt by reason of actual sin, and the conviction that sin shall not go unpunished, but must endure for ever the out-pourings of the wrath of God, is a burden too heavy to be borne. Yet such is the power and prevalence of sin, even under the grace of the gospel, that there lives not the descendant of Adam, whom a faithful examination of himself by the law of God, would not bring under all the fearful forebodings of the sentence denounced against sin. And from this heavy burden also, the Saviour offers rest; and to those in chief who thus labour and are heavy laden, is the invitation of my text directed. Now this rest consists in a sure and certain trust, wrought in the heart by the Holy Ghost, through the revealed word, that for what Christ hath done and suffered, the penitent sinner is forgiven, his offences blotted out, and himself received into a state of favour and acceptance with God. And this, my friends and hearers, is what is meant by experimental religion; the actual experience, by a particular sinner, of the pardon procured for all in general, by the death of Christ; a blessing of God, to the peace and comfort of his people in the present life, without which the religion of the gospel would be only a speculation of the head, a science to exercise the ingenuity of the understanding, but with which it becomes the hidden man of the heart, the moving power which re-settles the affections, and rules the life with the love of God. *We love him, my brethren, because he first loved us.* Now this rest is attained by faith, and as faith cometh by hearing, and hearing by the word of God, it is there we must look for its foundation, and thus it is found.

In the substitution of the Son of God for the sinner himself, the believer apprehends the true ground of his justification and acceptance; in the very nature that sinned, full satisfaction is made to the infinite justice of God; in the very nature that sinned, complete obedience is rendered to the holy law of God. Hence, the penitent sinner learns, and by faith realizes, *that God can be just, and the justifier of him that believeth in* Jesus. The debt being paid, the debtor is released; he walks at liberty. *Being justified by faith we have peace with* God, *through* Jesus Christ *our* Lord.

And do I look on any this morning, within whose reach this rich blessing is placed, who are yet strangers to the comfort which peace with God, brings to the heart? Do I look on any, who because they are without the experience of its power, therefore doubt, and deny its reality? Alas, my dear friends, is there then, in your view, nothing in religion, beyond the speculative knowledge of the wonders revealed to us; no influence or effect of divine truth upon the heart; no constraining power of the love of Christ upon the life? Shall sin be allowed a testimony which is denied to the grace of God? Is not the Spirit given to convince of righteousness, as well as of sin? O, think again, and ask yourselves, where is your foundation for eternity; where is your rest and your peace, when this world and its vanities shall consume away into nothing? O, think again, is sin a speculation; is death a mere phantom of the imagination; is judgment a conjecture of man, and are heaven and hell fictions and romance? For such they must all be, if that religion which is provided to overcome sin and prepare us for eternity, is without an experimental testimony of its power and its peace. O, be no longer faithless, but believing; meet the invitation of the Saviour with a willing mind; resort to the means he hath provided for you; let conscience this moment be heard and followed, and then you shall know the power, and the comfort of that grace of GOD, which bringeth salvation.

Another part of the rest which the Saviour promises to all who come to him, is deliverance from the power of sin; and this also, my hearers, is a point of experimental religion, and the abiding testimony that we belong to CHRIST.

To pay the ransom of immortal souls sold under sin; to deliver them from the condemnation due to it, and reconcile a Holy GOD to his sinful creatures, though an infinite and a priceless work, is yet but a part of his saving office. To have left us thus, would have been to have died in vain; sin would still have reigned, and man been shut out from GOD.

But he who came to redeem and save us, my brethren, came also *to put away sin by the sacrifice of himself; He came to redeem us from all iniquity, and to purify unto himself a peculiar people, zealous of good works.* To this gracious end, all the institutions of his religion, his doctrines, his precepts, the example of his sinless life, and the assistance of his HOLY SPIRIT, are adapted; these are all the purchase of his death, and among those precious gifts which he received for men, when he ascended up on high, and led captivity captive. And as moral beings, these we are required so to use and apply, as to fulfil the purpose for which they are given.

To the awakened soul, convinced by the HOLY SPIRIT of the exceeding sinfulness of sin, the sinful nature which yet remains, even in the true convert, is the most grievous of all burdens. St. Paul mourned over the corruption of his nature, I know, says he, that in my flesh dwelleth no good thing. The law in his members warring against the law of his mind, drew from him the impassioned exclamation, *Oh! wretched man that I am, who shall deliver me from the body of this death.* And as all believers agree with him in this experience of the remaining power of sin, so do they also unite in his testimony to the means by which it is met, restrained, and overcome—*The grace of GOD through JESUS CHRIST our LORD.*

In the language of Scripture, my brethren, the word grace, when applied to moral beings, means assistance; the supply of that, without which, we can do nothing. The corruption of our nature by the taint of sin, affects not our physical, but our moral ability; to this, therefore, the help of GOD is given, in working out our salvation. Hence the encouragement every where held out in the Scriptures, to those who embrace the gospel. *Sin shall not have dominion over you, for ye are not under the law, but under grace—the law of the spirit of life in* CHRIST JESUS *hath made me free from the law of sin and death—work out your own salvation with fear and trembling, for it is* GOD *that worketh in you both to will and to do of his good pleasure.*

The rest, therefore, which the Saviour promises to those who come to him, from the power and prevalence of sin, is of that nature as to require the putting forth our own exertions; and such must ever be the case, where a moral object is to be attained. Necessitating grace makes man a mere piece of mechanism, no more capable of reward or deserving of punishment, in the judgment of a moral governor, than a clock or a watch. No, my brethren and hearers, *the grace of* GOD *hath appeared to all men, teaching them that denying ungodliness and worldly lusts, they should live soberly, righteously, and godly in this present world.*

To obtain the Saviour's rest, then, from the power of sin, we must put forth the ability he hath given in resisting sin—we must watch against its stirrings and excitements—we must avoid its temptations, and guard against all its approaches—especially we must keep the body under, the lusts of the flesh, the lust of the eye, and the pride of life. St. Paul speaks of crucifying the flesh with the affections and lusts; now, this is a slow and a painful process, but it is the only one by which we can succeed. It is the only one, also, which gives at the same time encouragement to proceed. Victory over one sinful propensity, is the Saviour's witness, that greater is he that is for us, than he that is against us. Hence, the believer goes on, conquering and to conquer, till all his enemies are subdued; and the rest he obtains here, is a foretaste of that complete and never interrupted rest, which remains for the people of GOD in the life that is to come.

Well is our present state compared to a warfare, my brethren; and though it is a state of rest, when compared with that of those who will not come to CHRIST, it is chiefly in the anticipation of the issue, that this rest is to be sought and found. *In the world ye shall have tribulation*, says he who offers us rest, *but be of good cheer, I have overcome the world.* And to contrast the different conditions of those who embrace, and those who neglect the gospel—let us think for a moment of their respective dependancies in the day of GOD. What will the worldling, who has been too careless, or too busy in the present life, to heed the calls of the Saviour, then have to depend on ? Will the farms and the merchandize, the pleasures and the applause of the world, have merit in the sight of GOD to deliver his soul ? Will the neglect of the gospel stand excused, by intentions never realized ? Can any supposable case be pleaded, in extenuation even, for not coming to CHRIST ? Alas ! my dear hearers, be not deceived by the specious deceits of sin. The care of the soul is the one thing needful. And what will the humble Christian, who has obeyed the call, and come to the Saviour for life, and staked his soul on his power and willingness to save—who has striven against sin, and grown in grace—what will he have to offer to GOD in that awful day ? The Saviour's blood, the the Saviour's merits, the Saviour's righteousness—received and applied by faith.——The wedding garment of holiness, the passport to eternal life, in the kingdom of CHRIST and of GOD.

Every way, then, it is safe to come to CHRIST ; in this life, it is rest from the guilt, and the power, and the condemnation of sin ; and in the life to come, it is eternal felicity in the presence of GOD. O, who is athirst for this blessing—who is mourning under the pressure of sin—who is suffering under its present miseries, and dreading its future wages, the weary and the heavy laden with its intolerable burden ? To you is the word of this salvation sent. The Saviour calls——*Come unto me, and I will give you rest.* O, let your ears and your hearts open to the glad tidings, and make this happy season of his advent in the flesh, the anniversary of a new and heavenly birth in your souls. *Now is the accepted time—now is the day of salvation.*

On this mighty interest——to this gracious invitation——how careless and how cold are those to whom it is presented. When He who spake as never man spake, uttered these very words, it was then as it is now——they heard, but they heeded not. Yet, my dear friends, if you would hear the most joyful sound that tongue shall ever utter, addressed to you——*come ye blessed of my Father*——you must now come to CHRIST, and take his yoke upon you and learn of him.   He alone *is the way, the truth, and the life——and no man cometh unto the Father but by him.*   And with this additional claim to your attention, I will now proceed to inform you how you are to come to him.

To come to CHRIST, in Scripture language, means to embrace the gospel, to make profession of his religion, to accept of him as your Saviour, and to obey him as your king.

In fulfilling this duty, the first step is the sacrament of baptism, as the seal of that covenant wherein we give ourselves to him, and receive from him the pledge of all the blessings he hath purchased for us.   And so strictly is this the first step in coming to CHRIST, that there is no other revealed mode of becoming entitled to the promises of GOD in him.   For thus *it is* written——*He that believeth and is baptized shall be saved. Except a man be born of water and of the* SPIRIT *he cannot enter into the kingdom of* GOD——and though it has become the fashion to undervalue the ordinances of CHRIST's house, and to speak lightly of this sacrament, yet surely, my friends, what is written will stand fast, when the vain reasonings of men shall be as chaff before the storm.

This step, all present, perhaps, have already taken and so far have come to CHRIST ; but as the baptism which saves *is not the washing away the filth of the flesh, but the answer of a good conscience towards* GOD, in the fulfilment of the baptismal engagement, therefore, as all, alas, have herein failed, and have thereby forfeited the promises then made over to them, and lost the privileges then conferred upon them, the next step in coming to CHRIST is, by repentance and obedience.   These GOD hath been graciously pleased to accept from the penitent sinner when offered in the name of his only begotten Son, and in steadfast reliance on his merits, for their efficacy.   Now this repentance consists in such a godly sorrow for sin, as renders it hateful and burdensome, and creates a hearty and earnest desire to be delivered from its power.   This desire is manifested by prayer to GOD, for pardon and deliverance, and by departing from all iniquity ; and the fruit of true repentance is conversion of the heart to GOD, with renewed obedience, and confirmed faith, in his precious promises through CHRIST. The penitent is again received into favour, the HOLY SPIRIT is again renewed in his heart, and all the privileges of his baptism restored. To this repentance sinners are continually exhorted by the gospel, without this repentance they are assured that they shall perish ; and that they may be able to repent, the HOLY GHOST is sent down into the world, and so far present in every baptized person, as to convince them of sin ; speaking in their consciences, and bearing witness to the truth of the promises and threatenings of the gospel. These good motions of the SPIRIT of GOD, I hesitate not to say, every impenitent sinner now before me hath again and again experienced. Often would he have led you to CHRIST, my friends, but ye would not—often has his witness in your hearts almost persuaded you to be Christians, but you have stifled his saving convictions, and put off till a more convenient season, the one thing needful. O, let not the convictions of this day be added to the number, for GOD hath said, *my SPIRIT shall not always strive with man.* But now, even as you are, come to CHRIST ; yield not to the delusion that you are not good enough to come to him—*he came to call sinners to repentance.* If therefore you are a sinner, and sensible of it, you are the person he came to save, and he is the very Saviour you need. To the gracious invitation of my text, add the merciful declaration, *him that cometh unto me I will in no wise cast out,* and let sin and unbelief, and fear, and shame, bow down before the mercy seat, subdued by redeeming love.

Come unto me, all ye that labour and are heavy laden, and I will give you rest.

O that the application of this Scripture may be made to every heart by the spirit of GOD—that this joyful Sabbath may have rejoicing witnesses upon earth, and responding hallelujahs in heaven.

My brethren, it is the voice of affection, of deep interest in the welfare of the world he made and redeemed—O, let it be met with that fervour of faith and love in our hearts which shall unite us still closer to him and to each other. In the faith of his promise we have come to him, and should testify of his truth in giving us rest, and peace, through the atonement of his cross, and the power of his resurrection. This witness we can best give, my dear brethren in the LORD, by conforming to his example, and obeying his commands. His last command is, *love one another.* In this then, let us strive for the mastery, *and by love serve one another.* The last act of his blessed life, was an act of love in praying for his murderers ; as our lives then draw to their close, let us study to be found as he was, in peace and charity with all men.

As we rejoice over his birth, and bless GOD for the mercy and love herein showed to our souls, let us approach the sacrament of his death with hearts the more deeply penetrated with every emotion which the contemplation of this unspeakable gift is calculated to raise ; it is an overwhelming subject, my brethren, and defies the tongues of men and angels to reach its worth.

Greater love hath no man than this, that a man lay down his life for his friends—*but* GOD *commendeth his love towards us, in that while we were yet sinners,* CHRIST *died for us ;* yet the heart may feel what the tongue cannot express ; and he who looketh on the heart stands ever ready to accept the offering it brings, in humble love and holy faith. Let us draw near then, my brethren, with true hearts, in full assurance of faith, that if when we were enemies, we were reconciled to GOD, by the death of his Son—much more, being reconciled, we shall be saved by his life.

Now to GOD the Father, GOD the Son, and GOD the Holy Ghost, be ascribed, as is most justly due, all glory, honour, and praise, now, henceforth and for ever. Amen.

SERMON VIII.

NEW-YEAR'S DAY.

Psalm xxxi. 15. (First clause.)

"My times are in thy hand."

OUR condition in the present life, my brethren, is such, that if considered aright, it could hardly fail to produce that seriousness and sobriety of mind which is the inlet to all religious impression. However we may try to hide from ourselves what poor dependent creatures we are, the uncertain transitory nature of temporal things is exactly calculated to teach the salutary lesson, that here we have no continuance, no abiding interest, worth that exclusive care and passionate eagerness wherewith so many pursue the world, and the perishing portion of its vain, unsatisfying, yet ensnaring delights. And however still more unwisely we may turn away from the counsel and warning of God's revealed word, yet certain it is that no where else can we find comfort and relief in times of trouble and distress, in those trying moments when the world betrays, and its hope deceives, and disappointment casts down the tottering fabric we had built up on the sandy foundation of an earthly dependence. Thus is it ordered by the all-pervading wisdom of God, and through his tender love to us his creatures, that the frailty and weakness of our mortal state, the disappointments and sorrows of the present life, the insecurity and uncertainty of every earthly good, with all other the consequences of our fallen condition, should be present and sensible arguments to direct our views to a better hope, our trust and confidence to a more secure and permanent dependence than the promises of time, the delights of sense, or the glory and praise of this world can supply.

To produce this salutary effect upon us, many considerations are set before us, both by the light of nature, and in the page of revelation; but none of more weighty application than that presented in the words of the text—*My times are in thy hand.* A sentiment, my friends, deeply expressive of a devout and confiding spirit, of a submissive and humble heart, and truly descriptive of that Christian temper, which has learnt to trust in God, believing *that all things shall work together for good to them that love him.*

That God is, and that he is the rewarder of such as diligently seek him, is the first foundation of all, my brethren, the never to be shaken principle on which all religious dependence must be built up, the living root, from which branch out in beautiful order, the faith which works by love, the hope that maketh not ashamed, the charity that never faileth. That there is a supreme Being, infinitely good, wise, and powerful, who holds in his hands the issues of life and death, who directs and controuls, disposes, and overrules events both for general and particular good, is the only solid ground of hope and comfort, to which such poor, short-sighted, frail and transient creatures as we are, can resort, either for relief in present distress, or defence from future evil. That we are not given over to the guidance of our own misrule, to the anarchy and destruction which our own evil passions would inevitably produce, is such a proof of the love and compasssion of our heavenly Father towards his rebellious children, as should draw all our hearts to him in subjection and and obedience, and fill our souls with the deepest thankfulness, that amid the sundry and manifold changes of this mortal life, our times are in the hands of Him, who is infinite in wisdom and power, perfect in goodness and truth, and glorious in majesty and holiness.

In discoursing on these words on the present occasion, I shall use them chiefly as a lesson of caution and admonition to the careless and inconsiderate, and of comfort and support to the Christian ; with an application of the whole to the present season, and the use we should make of it.

My times are in thy hand. It may be useful to premise that by the word times as here applied, we are to understand, not barely the limit of our lives, but the whole state of our condition in the world. This is evident from the word being in the plural number. Had the expression been, My time is in thy hand, the sentiment would have been confined properly enough to the uncertain tenure of this mortal life. But being in the plural number, *My times are in thy hand,* it comprehends not only that, but also, whatever is providential in the whole course of it.

This view of the subject opens a wild field to our meditations, my brethren, and must increase the interest we all have, in deriving from it such instruction as may profit us, in running the race set before us.

Now nothing can be more conducive to this end, than to be rightly informed as to the purpose and design of Almighty God in bringing us into being under the circumstances in which we are found ; because our duties, generally speaking, are derived from our condition, and always proportioned to the means and opportunity given. What our condition in life may be, and what the extent of our means––is in the hand of another over whom we have no controul ; but what use we shall make of them, is altogether in the disposal of that moral agency, that freedom of will and choice, which alone constitutes us accountable creatures, and capable either of reward or punishment.

This may be exemplified in various ways. When we shall be born, and how long we shall live, are certainly not in our own controul. But to what we shall apply life when given, and time when bestowed upon us, must be the result of some choice made by ourselves. Again. In what circumstances we shall come into life, whether poor or rich, bond or free, whether with a bright or dull capacity is with him in whose hand our times are ; but the consequences to us depend not on the condition itself, but on the voluntary improvement or abuse we make of it. Once more. Whether we shall be born under the light of the gospel, or the darkness of Heathen superstition, is at the disposal of him whose kingdom ruleth over all ; but whether we will hear the joyful sound and embrace its saving mercy, or turn a deaf ear and oppose a hard heart to its life-giving truth, depends on ourselves. This is the true and practical distinction which it concerns us to make, my hearers, in those things for which we are accountable, and on which our present peace and future happiness altogether depend ; and may serve to show the folly and fallacy of pushing metaphysical speculations beyond what is plainly revealed, and far beyond what plain minds can possibly understand; for it is exactly what the apostle condemns, as an *intruding into things not seen, vainly puffed up by a fleshly mind.*

The deepest sense of GOD's sovereign disposal of all events, the fullest acknowledgment that we derive every power and faculty, every motive and means from him, so that, literally, *without him we can do nothing,* is in no shape at variance with that freedom of will and choice which alone renders us capable of religion; of which freedom (whatever may be said to the contrary,) we are perfectly conscious, whether in sinning or refraining; while of any constraining necessity, distinct from moral motive, compelling our actions, we are no more conscious than of what never had a being. Therefore, *let no man say when he is tempted, I am tempted of* GOD; *for* GOD *cannot be tempted with evil, neither tempteth he any man; but every man is tempted when he is drawn away of his own lust, and enticed. Then when lust hath conceived, it bringeth forth sin, and sin when it is finished bringeth forth death.* Do *not err, my beloved brethren,* our times are indeed in the hand of GOD—they are so for our good—they are so, as nevertheless to be compatible with the freest choice of the will, the deepest engagement of the heart and affections of reasonable beings; for it is just as inconsistent with the holiness of GOD, to force sinners to become holy, that they may be happy with him forever, as it is repugnant to his essential goodness to compel them to sin, that he may damn them for ever. Far different, my friends, is the view which GOD himself has given us, of his love to lost sinners, in converting the condemnation of sin into the reprieve of mercy, the curse of the law into the blessing of the gospel, the trials and sufferings of time into the glories of eternity, through JESUS CHRIST our LORD, who, *by the grace of* GOD *tasted death for every man, that he might redeem us to* GOD *by his blood*—who came into the world to save sinners, and invites even the chief of sinners to come to him for life and salvation, assuring them, that he will in no wise cast out him that cometh. Thus does GOD commend his love to us, in that, while we were enemies, CHRIST died for us; how much more then shall we be saved by his life. And thus are we cautioned against wresting the Scriptures to a sense and meaning, which if true, leaves to poor mortals no medium between presumption and despair.

Another lesson of caution, growing out of the text, is derived from the circumstances in which it shows us we are placed. If neither the limit of our days, nor the course of events, are in our own control, then is the reason unanswerably strong, for care and diligence in the employment of what we do possess, because we can never know how soon it may be taken from us. And this is evidently the purpose of Almighty GOD, in keeping this, with some other, to us, equally interesting subjects, locked up in the unrevealed counsel of his own will.

On no one point perhaps, are we more disposed to be presumptuous, my friends, than in the disposal of time; no other possession do we consider so securely our own; of no other do we commit such cruel and inexcusable waste. We know there is a bound to human life, which it cannot pass, and within that limit we see every age and condition swept away by the hand of death. We all profess to believe, and we do believe after a sort, that eternal happiness or misery waits upon it; and yet how few are wise enough, *so to number their days, as to apply their hearts unto wisdom*, while among that few who are considered to be thus wise, what remissness in redeeming the time, what coldness in religious duties, what conformity to the world, what deadness to GOD. Alas, my Christian brethren, do we indeed believe that our days are numbered, that an unseen hand holds the thread of our life, that a moment, which we can neither stop or turn aside, may realize to us the unspeakable certainties of death and judgment, and yet trifle with our souls, starving them on the corrupted manna of past experiences, grieving the SPIRIT of grace, and wearying the patience of our GOD? O, let a new year witness a new life. *Forget the things that are behind*, except to increase your repentance, and double your diligence in *reaching forth unto the things which are before, that you may the more earnestly press toward the mark, for the prize of your high calling of* GOD, *in* CHRIST JESUS.

O, that those of mature age, who have hitherto turned a deaf ear to the warnings of GOD, both in his word and by his SPIRIT, preferring the world to their souls, would now hear the voice of a departed year, calling to them to number how many are gone never to return, how few are left in the ordinary course of nature, and to consider how short they may be cut off, in the wise disposal of him, in whose hands their times are.   My friends who stand in this danger, was it to seize upon you, could you plead want of time, want of means, want of warning? You must answer, No. What then could you plead—the mercy of GOD? But where do you find an offer of mercy to the impenitent sinner? Be not deceived—wrath, burning wrath, is the portion of his cup.   But the merits of CHRIST, you will say— What! the merits of CHRIST pleaded and relied upon by those who have never become his disciples, never once confessed him before men, who have heard him preached to them for forty years perhaps, without receiving him as their Saviour and their GOD? this will never do; this is indeed to make CHRIST the minister of sin.   What then can you plead, but unbelief, unwillingness to receive the truth in the love of it, undue engagement with the world, or at best, often broken resolutions of future amendment.   But will these be accepted; are such the returns which a gracious GOD expects and requires for the precious gift of JESUS CHRIST to die for our sins, to purchase repentance for us, and make us "heirs of eternal life? No, indeed, faith in CHRIST, with the fruits of holiness, is the only passport to the kingdom of GOD.   Now then, while it is called to-day, while your sand yet runs, put away from you these refuges of lies, and flee to the cross of CHRIST; take the Redeemer's yoke upon you and learn of him, and ye shall find rest to your souls.

And O, that the young persons who now hear me would hear the caution my text gives, and remember their Creator in the days of their youth, before their affections are perverted and their feelings hardened by the deceitfulness of sin. O, that they would consider him in whose hand their times are, and early put themselves under his fatherly guidance; laying the only safe foundation on which to build with assurance, an useful and happy life, a blessed death, and a glorious immortality.

That we are here but for a season, brethren, and that uncertain too, shows the folly of so setting our affections upon temporal things, as to defeat the influence of those which are eternal upon our lives. That on this limited and uncertain being depends, whether we shall be happy or miserable for ever, is the unanswerable argument for seriousness and engagedness, in working out our everlasting salvation. And that our time and means, our power and help for this mighty work, are all in the hand of another, who measures out his grace in proportion to our improvement of it, is the awakening caution, that while this our day of life and grace lasts, we should give all diligence to make our calling and election sure. O, that these commanding motives may sink deep into all your hearts, and the blessing of him who hath the remainder of the spirit, make them fruitful in you to newness of life.

I come next to the comfort and support which the Christian draws from the doctrine of the text. I confine it to the Christian, because, though the providence of GOD embraces all creation, causing the sun to rise on the evil and on the good, and sending his rain upon the just and upon the unjust, so that not even a sparrow falls to the ground, without his notice and permission; yet it is to him only who hath the LORD for his GOD, that the faith expressed in the words of the text, is, in every trial and trouble, in every strait and extremity of life, like the shadow of a great rock in a weary land.

If we consider the present life, my brethren, without reference to another, we find it compounded of joy and grief, enjoyment and suffering, of hope and disappointment, of trouble and trial in all their shapes, of failure and success in every variety—*so that the race is not to the swift, nor the battle to the strong; neither yet bread to the wise, nor riches to men of understanding; nor yet favour to men of skill: but time and chance happeneth to them all.* But if we consider it in the light which revelation enables us to use, we see the same ingredients in the hand of a master, controlled and applied to bring good out of evil, holiness out of sin, happiness out of misery and life out of death. In this complex and unsearchable mystery, we are appointed to act a part, my brethren, and are furnished and instructed for all that is required of us; for the rest, we are commanded to depend upon the power and goodness of him, who seeth the end from the beginning, and is alone competent to sustain the weight, and direct the motions, and sway the sceptre of the universe. This fundamental truth, made still clearer by the revelation of JESUS CHRIST, the Christian receives, relies and lives upon. He sees and understands, that by reason of sin, " man that is born of a woman hath but a short time to live and is full of misery ; he cometh up and is cut down like a flower ; he fleeth also, as it were a shadow, and never continueth in one stay." In the trials and sufferings of this life, he is instructed to perceive the infinite wisdom of GOD at work, to purify and prove, to prepare and perfect sinful mortals for another and a better life. In the gift of his only Son, to atone for the guilt of the world, and redeem sinners from eternal death, he sees the unreserved love of that GOD who is not willing that any of his creatures should perish. And in the daily mercies of his good providence for the support of the perishing body, he is taught that the more important wants of his soul shall not be neglected. Thus does the just man live by faith ; his heart is fixed, trusting in the LORD. Founded on this rock, the believer is prepared to run the race set before him with patience. He knows that he is the hand of him whose faithful promise is recorded, *that all things shall work together for good to them that love* GOD ; so that whether his lot in life be prosperous or adverse, it is the good hand of his GOD upon him for good.

Does it please the Almighty to put his secret on his tabernacle—setting his family and fortunes in a flourishing state ; he thankfully acknowledges the giver of every good and perfect gift. LORD, *by thy favour, thou hast made my mountain to stand strong. Thou anointest my head with oil ; my cup runneth over. What shall I render unto the* LORD *for all his benefits*—deeply sensible of the account he must give for them, his great study is to apply them to the glory of the Giver, by promoting the welfare of all around him, dealing his bread to the hungry, and help to the poor and needy, and cloathing the naked with a garment. *Laying up a good foundation against the time to come.* Making a friend of the mammon of unrighteousness, that when earthly mansions fail, as they must do, everlasting habitations may receive him. His family, raised and trained up in the fear of the LORD, are partners with him in all his labours of love, and early learn, both by precept and example, to trust in their father's GOD, and to lay up treasure in heaven. On the other hand, does infinite wisdom see fit to prove him with adversity, to smite at the root the gourd of his creature comforts, and cast down his flourishing prospects to the ground, *It is the* LORD, says the believer, *let him do what seemeth him good—shall we receive good at the hand of* GOD, *and shall we not receive evil?* Blessed be his holy name for breaking the snare of worldly delights. Does the fear of want for himself and his children assault him? He strengthens his heart against the temptation. The LORD will provide—*never saw I the righteous forsaken, or his seed begging their bread.* Is a domestic calamity added to poverty and want, in taking away from him by the hand of death the dear partner of all his joys and sorrows, or the child of his affections and hopes—he kisses his Father's rod, and while his heart is wrung with anguish, exclaims—*The* LORD *gave and the* LORD *hath taken away—blessed be the name of the* LORD. Do friends desert him and join with his enemies to persecute and destroy him, he looks to the captain of his salvation, who was made perfect through sufferings, and glad to be counted worthy to suffer with him, he commits his cause to the LORD—*my times are in thy hand,* my trust is in thee—*I will not fear what man can do unto me—thou shalt bring forth my righteousness as the light, and my judgment as the noon day.* Is disease commissioned to consume his strength, and lay him on the bed of pain and languishing, the power of faith sustains him, and *makes all his bed in his sickness.* Does death draw near, attended with the anxious thought, that a dear wife and beloved children will be exposed to an unfriendly world, even in this extremity there is comfort for the Christian—*Leave thy fatherless children, I will preserve them alive, and let thy widow trust in me.* And in the closing scene of this world's tribulation, when all its help is in vain, and all its promises prove false—when the king of terrors claims his devoted victim—the believer meets him to triumph over him. *For we know that if our earthly house of this tabernacle were dissolved, we have a building of* GOD, *an house not made with hands*—*eternal in the heavens.   O death, where is thy sting*—*O grave, where is thy victory.* Thus, through the trials of life, and in the hour of death, does the firm persuasion that his times are in the hand of Almighty goodness, power, and wisdom, arm the believer to endure as seeing him who is invisible.   And thus do *the light afflictions of this mortal life, which are but for a moment, work for* the Christian, my brethren, *a far more exceeding and eternal weight of glory*—*while he looks not at the things which are seen, but at the things which are not seen ; for the things which are seen are temporal, but the things which are not seen are eternal.*

But not only in outward trials from the world, but in those which are inward and spiritual, does the power of faith give him the victory.

His grand enemy, the believer knows, is vanquished and held in a chain by the captain of his salvation, without leave from whom he cannot assault him ; further than he permits, he cannot tempt him.   For the trial of faith, and to prove obedience, the spiritual enemy hath a little space given him.   But in every conflict, the faithful promise, that GOD *will not suffer him to be tempted above what he is able to bear, but will, with the temptation, also make a way for his escape,* encourages the Christian to fight manfully, as a good soldier of JESUS CHRIST.   With the shield of faith he quenches all the fiery darts of the wicked—with the sword of the SPIRIT he cuts up the artful deceits of Satan transformed into an angel of light, with the hope of salvation for a helmet, he resists even unto blood, should he thereto be called, and having put on the whole armour of GOD, he is able to stand in the evil day.   But should the trial be sore, and the heart and the flesh failing, his LORD's voice—*My grace is sufficient for thee, let no one take thy crown*—renews his spiritual strength and gives him the victory.   Yea, even though the enemy prevail against him—for where is the man that liveth and sinneth not—the Christian does not yield himself a captive. He falls fighting, and with this word of faith in his mouth—*Rejoice not over me, O mine enemy.   When I fall I shall rise again.   When I sit in darkness, the* LORD *shall be a light unto me.*   In deep repentance he humbles himself before GOD—in earnest prayer he implores through

Jesus Christ the pardon of his guilt and unbelief—with groanings that cannot be uttered he waits until the Lord have mercy upon him—learning from every failure to distrust himself more and more—to lean upon the arm of the Lord more unreservedly, and to feel and say with the apostle, *when I am weak, then am I strong.*

Thus may we draw from the doctrine of the text, my brethren, the strong consolation which the promised help and favour of God should bring to our souls. Our times being in his hand, nothing can harm us without his leave; with him the very hairs of our head are all numbered; and greater is he that is for us than he that is against us. But where shall we find the Christians who thus live by faith? Alas! *when the son of man cometh shall he find faith upon the earth?* Nevertheless my brethren, it is God's gift to us, if we would only exercise it. *Unto you it is given to believe.* Let us then arise and shake ourselves from the dust of worldly cares, from the snare of its vain delights, and in the holy comfort of his protection and disposal of us, in the blessed hope of his mercy through Jesus Christ, let us renew our trust in his power and goodness; our obedience to his most holy law; our submission to his most righteous government, that in newness of life we may henceforth walk by faith and not by sight.

In the application of this subject I trust that you all anticipate me, my hearers, and each for himself feels the bearing of the subject upon the present season, and the meditations it supplies. I trust also that some of you are resolved, by the grace of God, to consider well the importance of time; that it is the great inclusive talent, upon which the value of all the rest depend; that it is the day of grace to us sinners; yea more, that it is the prelude to eternity, for on time well or ill employed depends the everlasting happiness or misery of each one of us.

Through the sparing mercy of our God, we are permitted, my brethren and friends, to see another year; but it is beyond any reasonable calculation that we shall all see the end of it. Some must go, but whether you or me, who can tell? Hope may flatter, and presumption may be confident; but both may be deceived. Our times are in the hand of another, and none

can lift the veil, which hides either his own, or the time of
another's departure. And why should we wish to know it?
The event itself is the only certainty we are possessed of, though
the time be hid from us; and to know this, is all that can be
useful to any reasonable being, because it presents motive
sufficiently powerful to urge to the·most diligent application,
without repressing exertion or encouraging delay, one or other
of which would be the certain consequence of more knowledge
on the subject.

To know that our days are numbered, that the noiseless
flood of time is sweeping us along with it into the boundless
ocean of eternity, is a startling thought. But alas! how few
entertain it, or count its worth with the risk of its uncertainty, except for some purpose of worldly advantage. How
few consider that time is a witness, the faithful unimpeachable
witness of heaven. Days and months and years pass away,
unheeded perhaps, yet loaded with the record of actions, unnoticed perhaps, yet irrevocable—until they shall once more
appear for or against us at the bar of GOD. We may waste them
in folly, or bury them in thoughtlessness and levity, but together
with our dead bodies shall they arise, and bring with them the
colour they now receive from our lives.

Was this considered in its true light my brethren, we should
not see such numbers of our fellow creatures possessed of
reasonable minds, and favoured with the light of the gospel, so
entirely taken up with business and pleasure, that the great
business of being saved, the lasting pleasure of being in favour
with GOD, is but little thought of, if not neglected altogether.
We should not see so many young people growing up around
us, trained only for the part they are to act here for a little
while, leaving the one thing needful wholly unprovided for.
Perhaps the decay of religion, the loss of that lively impression
which its vital power communicates to the soul, is in nothing more
marked, than in the neglect manifested even by proffessing
parents, for the religious education of their children. As
Christians they should know, that the world is a great pitfall for
their children's souls, of which it is their prime duty to warn
them; the insidious enemy, against whose deceitful blandish-

ments it should be their chief care to arm them. Experience must have shown them the uncertainty and insecurity of the fairest and most flattering worldly dependence, while the religion they profess must have taught them that there is but one antidote against the poison of worldly love ; one strait and narrow way to pass through the snares spread out, though concealed, under its alluring but destructive pleasures ; one shield against its enmity ; one comfort under its tribulation ; one refuge from the storm and tempest of its destruction. And can those parents be really sincere in a profession of religion, who suffer any considerations of custom or advantage or expediency, to interfere with their first and earliest duty, in pre-occupying the hearts of their children with the serious things of GOD and religion ? Can they remember their solemn baptismal covenant, renouncing for them the pomps and vanities of this wicked world, when the whole course of modern education, especially for females, serves only to foster and increase those evil natural propensities in them ? O unthinking parents, take these truths home with you, and consider how little it will profit you and them, that they should glitter and shine here for a little while, and then drop into the darkness of everlasting night.

Surely these are weighty and unanswerable arguments to induce parents, and those who have the care of youth, to stop short in the present unprofitable and ruinous course. Surely also they should be equally powerful to induce the careless and thoughtless to pause a moment in the race of vanity, and count the cost of turning a deaf ear to the warnings and invitations of the gospel, to the reason and conscience of their own hearts, to the dearest interests of their immortal souls, all suspended on the time now given to prepare for eternity, perhaps on the present year. O that they would but count up how many years are gone, loaded with sin and guilt, how few may remain to perfect that repentance, and attain that holiness, without which no man shall see the LORD. Gracious GOD, impress upon all our hearts, the solemn but neglected truth, that our limit is fixed, our sand is running, and by a decree which we cannot reverse, the hour is numbered when to each one of us time shall be no more. O that it would please thee to strengthen the hearts of thy people to be followers of GOD as dear children, walking in love, and living by faith ; that their light may shine to the glory of thy name, and thy work revive among us to the increase of pure and undefiled religion. And O that it may be given to the dissipated and thoughtless, to the careless and negligent, to the lovers of pleasure more than lovers of GOD, to discern this time, to see in the flight of another year how much is taken away from the short and uncertain period on which eternity depends. O that they may consider how many of their precious years have fled away from them, never to return—that in the patience and forbearance of GOD hitherto, they may see that goodness which should lead them to repentance ; that in the mercy which hath brought them to the promise of another year, they may learn the comfortable truth that GOD hath not appointed them to wrath, but to obtain salvation through our LORD JESUS CHRIST. O that they may consider the time past of their life more than sufficient to have wrought the will of the flesh, and this day hear the voice of the Son of GOD, calling to them by the gospel— *Awake thou that sleepest and arise from the dead, and* CHRIST *shall give thee light.*

SERMON IX.

NEW—YEAR'S DAY.

———

HEBREWS i. 12. (Last clause.)

"But thou art the same, and thy years shall not fail."

OF whom speaketh the prophet this, we may ask, my brethren, as did the pious Ethiopian, when sitting in his chariot he read the book of the prophet Isaiah. For surely the description of a being, whose properties thus transcend our experience, and in this attribute of unchangeableness, or independence of time, soars beyond the limit of created things, and remains unaffected by that which is silently, but surely bringing to an end, as well that which is seen, as that which perceives; must be calculated to awaken in our hearts a feeling of awe and reverence, and leads to such contemplations of his eternal power and godhead, as shall become the forerunners of that fear of him which is the beginning of wisdom. To this, indeed, every thing we see, should lead us my hearers, for it is the lowest result of reason to conclude, that creation must have a creator, and the most noble exercise of the faculties conferred on us, to travel through the works to the work master, and *as the heavens declare the glory of* GOD, *and the firmament showeth his handy work*—to make them praise him too, through that favoured creature to whom it is given thus to adore creation's LORD and man's Redeemer. O that this reasonable service had more of reason's sons and daughters under its influence—that the foundation being laid in the consideration, knowledge, and fear of GOD, the superstructure might grow up unto an holy temple in the LORD.

In the transition from such a glorious and unchangeable Being, to ourselves, how vast the distance, how infinite the difference, my brethren, and yet it is but a single step for the mind to take, so wonderfully are we constituted for our own good and his glory. In this transition, however, is contained the speaking application of that solemn lesson which our vanishing lives present in the close of every day, and more impressively in the termination of another of those few and fleeting years, which bound our earthly pilgrimage. And in the contrast between him who is ever the same, and whose years shall not fail, and beings who are daily drawing to their end, we might learn, my friends, *so to number our days as to apply our hearts unto wisdom.* Alas! that so few permit these first lines as it were, in religion, to occupy their thoughts. Alas! that such multitudes see nothing in the silent flight of time but the fulfilment or disappointment of the little hope that is bounded by this world, and who turn away with disgust from the awakening truth, that every hour of life is but a step towards the grave, and every year of time a more rapid flight towards the boundless ocean of eternity. Yet so it is, my brethren and friends, we meet this morning a year nearer to the close of all our worldly expectations, a year nearer to all that we hope, or fear in the world to come. The thoughtless, impenitent sinner—nearer by a whole year to the gnawings of the worm which never dies, to the torments of the fire that never shall be quenched. The believing Christian, by the same period nearer to that joy unspeakable and full of glory, which awaits the righteous. Methinks our very countenances should show something of our respective feelings and states, on so tremendous a consideration. But alas! custom and habit have so strengthened the original delusion—*Thou shalt not surely die,* that both saint and sinner have learnt to escape from the solemn warning which the flight of time conveys alike to all. But if there is truth with him who is set forth in my text as unchangeable, all these consequences, and many more of great importance to us, flow from the simple fact that we are all so much nearer to the account we have to give in to Him, as a year is greater than a day, and of course so much nearer to happiness or misery eternal. Now my dear hearers, let me ask you with all the affectionate earnestness of one truly desirous of your highest good, what advantage can there be in smothering up the awakenings which so plain a statement of your actual condition must occasion in your hearts. Will ruin be any thing else than ruin, because it comes upon you by surprise and unprovided for? Or will it not double destruction, if I may so speak, to look back, and see how often and how easily this destruction might have been escaped—with how much long-suffering and forbearance, God waited and warned—and with what carelesness and obstinacy you disregarded and resisted the counsels of his love. Let me then entreat you to make a better use of this renewed proof of God's patience. And while we congratulate each other on being yet left in reach of the means of grace, let me exhort you to go along with me in those meditations which flow from the text, and from the time, from the unchangeable nature of God, and the short, and withal, most uncertain condition of man's present life.

But thou art the same, and thy years shall not fail. There is a sublimity, my brethren, in the whole passage, and a bearing upon my present purpose, which inclines me to read it to you: *And thou* Lord, *in the beginning, hast laid the foundations of the earth, and the heavens are the work of thine hands. They shall perish, but thou remainest ; and they all shall wax old as doth a garment and as a vesture shalt thou fold them up, and they shall be changed, but thou art the same, and thy years shall not fail.* In this most devout and impressive address of the apostle, we learn from the context, that the person to whom it was offered up, was the Lord Jesus Christ, and we feel beyond the reach of cavil, that it is such an acknowledgment of his essential divinity, as causes that doctrine, and the divine inspiration and authority of the Scriptures, to stand or fall together.

The consideration of the unchangeableness of Almighty God, not only in his nature and essence, but in the appointments and administration of his government of the world, is the only foundation, on which faith can be exercised. A being who was either fickle in purpose, or weak or limited in power, could in no sense be the object of such trust and confidence as is always implied in the Scripture notion of faith. Hence the vital importance of the divinity of Christ to the faith of his followers, and the deadly hostility to the best interests of man, and the damnable guilt of those who, on any pretence endeavour to shake it ; for it is most evident to whoever reads the Scriptures with attention, that the hope of the Christian is so built on Jesus Christ, as the propitiation for the sins of the whole world—so limited on his power to save—so dependant on his grace to sanctify—that if he is not infinite in his nature, omnipotent and omnipresent, he cannot meet the requirements of faith—he cannot be an object of lawful worship—he cannot be present, and privy to the hearts of all his worshippers, in all parts of the world, this day, nor can their hope of eternal life in him be sure and steadfast, if that life be not in himself, by inherent divinity. With admirable propriety, therefore, (if indeed we ought to use such a phrase of an inspired man,) with admirable propriety does St. Paul preface his argument to his Hebrew brethren, for the superiority of the gospel over the legal dispensation, with the assertion of the divinity of its author; and this not formally, but incidentally, as it were, and in a strain of the most sublime devotional feeling of which we have any example; and thus it is with every devout Christian in the manifestation of his Saviour. He is able to say with St. Thomas, *My* LORD *and my* GOD, and with unshaken confidence to depend on the power and faithfulness of him whose love for his soul overcame the infinite distance between the Creator and creature, and brought him from heaven to earth to die for his salvation. It is this alone my brethren and hearers, which gives to Christianity the sublime character which belongs to it. Deprive it of the divinity of its author, and you divest it of its spirit, and of its power; and you cast a veil over the glory, and beauty, and efficacy of GOD, manifest in the flesh, to put away sin by the sacrifice of himself; and you send the gospel forth into the world, like Sampson shorn of his strength, to make sport for the sons and daughters of unbelief and ungodliness. This is a cardinal point, my brethren, in the faith we profess; but I fear is too often taken for granted without being considered and dwelt upon, and carried out, to all the invigorating, heart-cheering consequences which flow from it, not only to the furtherance of the power of godliness in our lives, but as a strong tower of defence, against the afflictions and sufferings which belong to the present life.

Having thus noticed, though in a cursory manner, what forms so very prominent a part of my text, I come now to those considerations which grow out of the contrast between the unchangeable, everlasting being of GOD, and the fleeting, transitory existence of man.

FIRST, no circumstance, it appears to me, is better calculated to invest the mind of man with a just sense of his condition as a mortal creature. Of this it may be thought we stand in need of no better monitor than the daily waste of human life, than the dropping into the grave, one after another, of our friends and neighbours; but experience tells us, that when we measure ourselves with others we always strike the balance in our own favour, and in nothing is it more strikingly exemplified than in the case of our common mortality. There is no escape from the fact that all are appointed to die, and while we can see, and express, clearly enough, the effect which this unalterable destiny should have upon others, we contrive, pretty generally, to elude it, as respects ourselves; in other words, we do not permit it to bear upon our individual connexion with the common fate, but think and act as if we were of a different race of beings; for remember, my friends, to admit a fact, is neither to believe or to apply it, and in a case of this kind, general admission is quite consistent with practical denial.

Now of this, cannot I draw a proof from the consciences of all present? I think I can, in this way. Another year of the limited being of young and old, is gone for ever; eternity, therefore, is so much nearer to each—but has this been the thought which the fact has presented to us; has this been the solemn certainty which has dwelt upon our minds, and led us to count the cost at which such weighty portions of our time, as years, are lightly esteemed? Have the careless and thoughtless heard, in the departure of another year, the funeral knell, as it were, of their day of grace? Have they realized the awakening summons of time, as it passes on into eternity, that they must shortly follow? But why do I ask the question? To the careless and the thoughtless there is no eternity, as yet, realized—they have never raised their thoughts to that unchangeable being who sits upon the circle of the heavens, and himself unaffected by time, beholds its mighty flood rolling them, and all sublunary things, onward to the consummation of his righteous judgment on their improvement or abuse of his wondrous love and undeserved mercy: yet by GOD's blessing it may startle them, and lead to reflection, and thus be a proof from their consciences, of the danger of resting in the mere knowledge or admission of religious truths.

Have the followers of the world heard the voice of the departed year, calling upon them to consider what agreement their pursuits and their pleasures have with that unseen world to which they are so fast hastening? Alas, time is estimated by them, only as it accelerates or retards the gain or the enjoyment of earthly things; it is the profit or loss of their estates and not of their souls, by which they measure the flight of time, and calculate the improvement of it. Yet ask them, and they admit that they are to die—but it is yet a great way off; ask them, and none can better tell you how hard it is to overtake a lost year, in worldly matters, and therefore, they are the better able to estimate how hard, and almost impossible it must be, to undo a a course of sin, and tread back the path of folly, and overtake, not a year only, but years, of grace and waiting mercy, gone, never to return, until they appear as witnesses against them, at the bar of GOD; and thus do their consciences also, speak the same language, and give them a lesson of wisdom, which I pray GOD they may hear.

Have the aged, on whose heads the hand of time has shed the garb of winter, heard this, perhaps last, messenger of GOD's mercy, calling to them in his flight, *set thine house in order, for this year thou shalt die!* Alas, my hearers, that even with such, the summons should be disregarded; for what more common in this Christian land, than old age and impiety; than carelessness and unconcern under the warnings of even seventy years, and than consciences satisfied with admission, but dead to consequences? Dead to improvement! What can it lead to, my friends, but that second death which shall never die?

Have Christians, whether old or young, opened their ears and their hearts to the passing warning of that silent monitor, who is gone to report them to their LORD. Has the season been a time of review, of recollection, of repentance, of prayer, of thankfulness, of renewed dedication to GOD? Has it been a season of spiritual refreshment and holy comfort in GOD's continued favour? Or have the common forms of Christian profession, seen only in the world, hid from them that all-seeing eye, who searches the reins and the heart? Alas my brethren, must our consciences also witness to this general neglect of so plain and pointed a monitor? Shall our salvation, which is now surely nearer than when we first believed, stir up no feeling of earnestness, anxiousness, I had almost said impatience to reap so great reward? no sense of past mercies, no faith and hope of future goodness, and send us forth to another year of duty and trial, more engaged to do the will of our heavenly Father, and adorn the doctrine of GOD our Saviour? O let not the spirit of the world quench and grieve the spirit of GOD, nor any of his mercies or warnings pass without acknowledgement and improvement. Remember that he who is unchangeable, hath said, *Unto him that hath shall be given, and he shall have more abundance ; but from him that hath not, shall be taken away even that which he hath.* And that this is spoken, primarily, of improvement, and can have no other practical meaning, let the honest witness within you, at this serious moment, be attended to, whether for encouragement or reproof, that the fruit may be peace, and the effect of peace quietness and assurance forever.

There is however one more circumstance, growing out of the consideration of our connection with time, which must not be omitted, and that is its uncertainty—a consideration which is confined to no particular description of persons, but bears alike upon all, whether believers or unbelievers, whether worldlings or Christians, whether young or old.

By this appointment of heaven's wisdom and mercy in the grant of time to creatures on trial, all the arguments and exhortations to diligence drawn from a limited duration, are infinitely increased and strengthened ; an event certain to all, but uncertain in its approach and application to any, is in itself an awakening reflection. We know not what a day, what an hour may bring forth ; how this little congregation may be disposed of in the current year, we can none of us say ; the eternal condition of all our souls may be at stake. Can there then, with this knowledge confirmed to us by experience, be the shadow of excuse for putting off till to-morrow? Is there a heart present, that feels not at this moment the force of such an appeal to its own uncertainty of continued being? Yet alas! how weak will the feeling be with too many ere one little hour is past. O let the commencement of another year of health and hope, be to us all, my hearers, the commencement of that fear of the LORD which is the beginning of wisdom; so shall we be prepared alike for the vicissitudes of time, and the unchangeable realities of eternity.

SECONDLY—Another consideration to be drawn from the unchangeable nature of GOD, extends that attribute to his purposes, as well as to his being; and with this we are more concerned, perhaps, my hearers, than with his eternity of existence, because it is in our conformity to these only, that we can derive any rational hope of his favour. Hence it follows, that whatever is in any way opposed to him, either in the holiness of his nature, or the supremacy of his government, must in fact be in a state of hostility against him; and as such, exposed to whatever vengeance the vindication of his sovereign dominion over all created things, shall require. Now as this opposition can only be manifested by rational creatures, and by them only, in the violation of the law or rule given them to keep; therefore they alone can become guilty of sin; and as sin is thus a direct opposition, at one and the same time to the holiness of GOD's nature, and the dignity of his government, it must either be atoned for, or punished, according to the conditions of the law. This we all know my hearers, both from the nature of government, which would cease to be such, could it be opposed with impunity; from the nature of GOD, who cannot look upon sin with the least degree of allowance; and from the express declaration of his revealed will, *the soul that sinneth, it shall die.* And this his purpose is just as unchangeable as his nature and essence. Yet he is a GOD of mercy as well as a GOD of justice; a GOD of love as well as a GOD of vengeance; and hath most wonderfully provided for sinful mortals a full atonement for sin, in which, it was at once punished, and forgiven; a reprieve from the sentence of death, denounced against them, and means of reconciliation and return to his favour. Of this, the gospel of CHRIST is the authentic declaration to the whole world; the warrant, for even the chief of sinners, to expect and obtain mercy upon repentance, and at the same time the most solemn confirmation of his unchangeable purpose to destroy forever, the impenitent and ungodly. Hence it follows most undeniably, that the sinner must change, or perish forever ; must be altered and amended, not only in the outward deportment of his life, but in the very source and spring of his actions, the heart. And as all this must be done in the short and uncertain period of the present life, we may from this alone, form some estimate of the importance of time ; some judgment of the danger, as well as wickedness, of delaying our repentance, and be moved forthwith to address ourselves to GOD, for pardon of our past delay, and for grace to enable us to bring forth fruit meet for repentance. In this view the past year may be our monitor, for all of us that are yet to run, in our daily shortening limit of mercy; may be made to us, by the blessing of GOD, what the death of a friend is often sanctified to, the turning point of our present and everlasting happiness. O that GOD may thus be pleased to sanctify it to every sinner present. O that his unchangeable purpose to punish sin, evidenced even by his love to sinners, in the gift of JESUS CHRIST, and of time and means to regain his favour, and eternal life, may move them to that change of life, and to seek that change of heart which he is ever ready, by his HOLY SPIRIT, to work in them. Surely the time past of this life, may suffice the youngest sinner present, to have wrought the will of the flesh, to have continued in enmity against GOD, and exposed to his wrath. Surely the sparing mercy of GOD may soften the hardest heart, and melt down the most obdurate temper. Surely the love of CHRIST may constrain the most determined sinner to submit to the sceptre of his grace, and take upon him the light yoke and easy burthen of the gospel. And surely the uncertainty of how long this may be possible, in an hourly shortening day of life and grace, may start them to escape from everlasting burnings, and seek the salvation of their immortal souls. *Awake, then, thou that sleepest and arise from the dead, and* CHRIST *shall give the light.* Now is the accepted time, now is the day of salvation—another year, another month, yea another day, may place thee beyond the reach of that mercy, which now invites, and waits to bless thy soul with the salvation of GOD.

THIRDLY, a further consideration of the unchangeableness of GOD in his nature and purpose, gives to the Christian that full assurance which enables him to meet the various trials of this life with patience, and in connexion with his own short and limited state of being, enables him to look beyond them, and to triumph over them.

Our light afflictions which are but for a moment, says St. Paul, *work out for us a far more exceeding and eternal weight of glory —while we look not at the things which are seen, but at the things which are not seen.* In which passage we find the unchangeableness of GOD, and the shortness of human life, combined together as the ground of the faith and patience of the saints. Every passing year of our life, therefore, my brethren, if rightly considered, is gain to us in two respects. It shortens the time allotted to trial, and brings us so much nearer to our reward. It abridges the period of sorrow and suffering, should such be our lot, in the wise providence of GOD, and thus lightens the burthen—and it doubles the graciousness of prosperity, while it counteracts the ensnaring character of such a state, by its uncertainty, and by the nearer approach of that glory which excelleth. Thus are all things made to work together for good to them that love GOD, to them who are the called according to his purpose. And are any present not of that number? GOD forbid that any should think so. For if the testimony of GOD is of any worth—the day and its appointments—his sparing mercy in the grant of more time—the counsel and invitation of his true and faithful word, yea our whole gospel state are witnesses, *that he hath not appointed us to wrath, but to obtain salvation by our* LORD JESUS CHRIST. Yet true it is, that though many are called, but few are chosen. And why? Because they will not enter in at the strait gate, because they prefer the broad and beaten way that leadeth to destruction, to the narrow way of life—and not because a gracious and merciful GOD either withholds his grace, or withstands their desire. No, my dear young friends, and halting, hesitating, fellow-sinners of all ages, whatever the testimony of men may be, this witness of GOD is greater.

He hath set before you an open door, which neither the force nor the fraud of man can shut against you, unless you believe men rather than GOD—unless you withstand those drawings of the Father, wherewith he would bring you to his Son—unless you break away from those cords of love with which CHRIST would bind you to himself, in the triumph of his cross, over sin, death, and hell. And every Christian present can tell you, that it was not because he could not, but because he would not, that he did not long before enter upon the joy and peace of a believing state. He can look back upon many awakenings which he stifled, and many seasons of mercy, when GOD would, but he would not—and it is his sentiment of deepest thankfulness, and highest admiration of GOD's mercy, that he was not provoked to abandon him, but strove with him by his holy and loving SPIRIT, until a better mind was renewed in him. O, my dear brethren, what miracles of grace are we debtors for . The common argument resorted to by the narrowers of GOD's grace to a sinful world—that because a sinner does not come in until a certain time, that, therefore, he could not come sooner, is, with all the art and cunning of its construction, both unscriptural and illogical—as is that still more dangerous conclusion, that because a sinner never comes, but dies impenitent—that, therefore, GOD withheld from him the means of grace, because he was a vessel appointed to wrath. These are not the doctrines of JESUS CHRIST, though we may draw them, and some support for them, by wresting the Scriptures from their true purpose. His doctrine, who gave himself a ransom for all, is, repent, believe, and be saved—his invitation is, come unto me all the ends of the earth, and be saved. His encouragement for us to come is, him that cometh unto me, I will in no wise cast out. In this language he speaks to us all, this day, my hearers ; and by the vanishing away of another of our years, tries to awaken us to the supreme importance of preparation for that day, when he shall appear in his glorious majesty—when the heavens shall flee away from his presence—when all the proud and all who have done wickedly—when those who know not GOD, and obey not his gospel, shall be fuel for those everlasting burnings, in which sin and sinners shall be shut up for ever, no more to vex the children of GOD, or spoil the beauty and mar the happiness of a new creation.

O, come that blessed day and its blessed enjoyments—but come first, in GOD's mercy, that day of power, in converting grace, turning the hearts of the disobedient to the wisdom of the just, and the hearts of his children to their Father which is in heaven. O, come first that day of the Son of man, which shall establish his kingdom in every heart, and prepare this little congregation of redeemed creatures to meet the Shepherd and Bishop of their souls with joy and not with grief.——Amen—even so come LORD JESUS, with the blessings of thy grace upon our souls, that the years which remain in thy gift may witness for us, in the great day of eternity, that warning was not thrown away upon us, and time and opportunity abused, to the dishonour of GOD, and to the destruction of those immortal souls, whom thou didst redeem, and call by thy gospel to an inheritance of glory and blessedness.

Now, to GOD the Father, GOD the Son, and GOD the HOLY GHOST, be ascribed, &c. &c.

SERMON X.

ASCENSION OF CHRIST.

St. John vi. 62.

" What and if ye shall see the Son of Man ascend up, where he was before ?"

HARD sayings in religion are exceedingly multiplied to that description of persons, whose affections and habits are determined chiefly by the gratifications and advantages of the present life. So far as the morality of the gospel is opposed to the debaucheries and profligacy of dissolute conduct it is approved of; but when the doctrines of Christianity are applied to the regulation of the heart as well as of the outward life, when the spiritual nature of its requirements are brought to bear upon the indulgencies and enjoyments which the rules of fashionable life endeavour to keep within the boundary of decency and decorum, then it is that the carnal mind is offended, and its ingenuity set to work to frame some excuse for going back from that imitation of our blessed LORD, which is required of all his true disciples. Yet these hard sayings, have in themselves no difficulty, insuperable to honest endeavour, either to apprehend or to practice them. As fundamentals of the religion we have received from heaven, they are within the reach of our assisted powers, to apply them to that attainment of renewed desires and affections which constitute our fitness for those mansions of blessedness whither our Saviour CHRIST is gone before, to prepare a place for his faithful followers. The difficulty is wholly in ourselves, and it is one which every consideration of reason, of duty, of interest, and of obligation, bind us to counteract, and to overcome.

Nor has heaven been unmindful of this ruinous propensity of our aliénated hearts. To the declarations of inspired truth, are superadded the conclusions of the plainest reason, the results of a most extended and continually recurring experience, the facts in the history of Christianity, and more directly, the facts in the personal history of the author and finisher of our faith. These all bear testimony against the delusion of neglecting the care of our souls, because of some presumed difficulty in that system of faith and obedience, by which only, their everlasting welfare can be secured.

To the fact of our Lord's ascension into heaven, in particular, is referred the refutation of an objection of this description, taken by the Jews who had become his disciples, to the doctrines which he taught. *Doth this offend you,* says our Lord, *what, and if ye shall see the Son of Man ascend up, where he was before?* What will then become of your objections to the reception of my doctrine, when you have such visible proof of its being divine and true, as my ascent into heaven, who came down from thence, to make known to you the will of God, and to prepare a new and living way for your return to your Father's house?

The inquiry put in my text, therefore, naturally directs our meditations to what forms the subject matter of that public and private instruction which the Church has provided for the edification of her members, on this day, and will form the ground work of my discourse.

First, To that class of persons who withhold themselves from any profession or practice of the duties of religion, on the assumption that there are difficulties attending it, which they are unable to overcome, the consideration of the nature and strength of the testimony hereby given, to the divine origin and truth of Christianity, is full of the most awakening reflections, and if dwelt upon with any seriousness and sincerity of mind, must put to flight all objections of this sort—for, I pray you, would the God of truth give this continuing demonstration to the truth of a system of religion, which these, for whose benefit it was contrived and revealed, could neither apprehend or practise? The supposition is impious, and ought to strike with dismay all (if indeed there are any who really entertained it,) who resort to this cover of a more hardened antipathy to the gospel; for to what else can it be attributed, but to the love of sin, if men reject the only remedy against its fatal effects, because of some supposed difficulty in the obtaining or the taking it ? When inordinate affection for the riches and pleasures of the world, when over engagement with its occupations, or pursuit of its frivolous dissipations, shelter themselves against the claims of religion, under the plea of difficulty, what else is it, but a clear demonstration of the carnal mind, which is enmity against GOD, a speaking proof that such persons prefer the gains and the business, the profits and the pleasures of the world, to the favour of GOD, and everlasting felicity in his heavenly kingdom. Certainly the wisdom of GOD puts this interpretation upon their conduct, and will deal with them accordingly.

But the objection is not merely impious—it is not altogether a pretext, and consequently the more sinful ; because, no attempt having been made by them, either to ascertain what the difficulty really amounts to, or in what way it may be overcome, it is a gratuitous objection, and as such must be classed with those strong delusions which GOD not only judicially permits, but which he sends upon those *who receive not the love of the truth that they might be saved*. In a concern so important as the salvation of the soul, nothing but endeavours, the effort of conviction, can manifest sincerity and secure success ; and as the bare possibility that the condition of eternity may be well or ill affected by the course of the present life is sufficient to convince every reasonable mind of the great importance of religion, it is equally sufficient to condemn the neglect of indifference, the evasions of artifice, and the opposition of unbelief, to those high and concerning truths, which GOD hath revealed to the world, by our LORD JESUS CHRIST.

Religion being a provision of heaven's mercy for the benefit of mankind, a contrivance of heaven's wisdom, to deliver them from the dominion of sin, and eternal death, and a proof of the love of GOD even towards his enemies ; a very malignant character is thereby stamped upon every shade of opposition to its requirements. And when in addition to this, we consider its further and more gracious purpose of preparing sinful creatures for the presence and enjoyment of GOD in everlasting glory, the folly and wickedness of all objections to its wholesome discipline, and life-giving doctrine, is enhanced beyond all power of expression.   Yet the course and condition of the Christian world is such, that the opponents of the gospel, whether direct or indirect, are by far the most numerous body, and thereby call very loudly upon professing Christians to examine carefully what occasion their lives may give to cast reproach upon religion, and thereby increase the difficulties, and strengthen the opposition of many, who might otherwise be brought to a better mind.

SECONDLY then, to professors of religion who yet so mingle the world with the outward duties of religion as to give its adversaries the advantage against the gospels, by the inconsistency of their lives, with its strict and holy requirements— to such persons the arguments derived from the ascension of the LORD JESUS CHRIST, in proof of the religion he taught and established in the world, are all strengthened and enforced by their own voluntary adoption of the conditions on which the promises of GOD in the gospel are suspended.   Hence, when professors of religion are seen as intent upon the world's reward, and as free and frequent in its vain and proscribed enjoyments as those who make no profession of the fear of GOD, the conclusion is at once, and justly, drawn, that they do not believe what nevertheless they profess ; and encouragement is hereby given to the thoughtless and the dissolute, to persevere in their iniquity while the ungodly are furnished with means to triumph against the gospel, and the name of GOD is blasphemed through those who are pledged to promote his glory.

That this is more frequently the case than it ought to be, requires no other proof than experience and observation ; and that the evils resulting from it are justly charged, is demonstrated by the increasing tendency in the religious world to lower the standard of religious duty ; and as the morality of unbelievers approaches the morality of the gospel, to assimilate the strict and holy requirements of the Christian profession, to the loose accommodating maxims of the world. By this unhallowed exchange, infidelity is the only gainer ; and therefore it is that it is so countenanced, and the smile of the world so freely bestowed on those liberal minded Christians, whose system of faith and practice is accomodated to this specious, but heartless manifestation of charity.

To the production of this great and increasing evil, many causes conspire; but chiefly the apprehended difficulties of fulfilling the requirements of religious duty. This prepares the way for one compromise after another, until little but the form of godliness is left; and when once a sufficient number can be found, to countenance each other in this course of decline from vital godliness, the delusion is increased, and the world quickly gains the ascendency in their hearts.

This may be exemplified by the duties which professing parents owe to their children, and which they have solemnly undertaken to perform, as the condition on which the favour of God is pledged to them and to their offspring. This highest parental duty requires the utmost watchfulness, self-denial, perseverance, and prayer; it is prompted by the tenderest of all feelings, and the highest of all motives; yet the difficulties which the corruption of our nature, and the temptations of the world, continually present, in too many cases overcome them all, and the woful spectacle is presented, of these very children, not only unnurtured in the fear of God, but actually trained and furnished for the love of the world, and its maxims inculcated, and its sanctions made to operate with more care and with more effect than the maxims of religion and the sanctions of eternity. Need we to be surprised then at the decline, not only of the tone and temper of religious feeling in professors themselves, but of its influence on the community at large? I think not; and that our surprise rather should be, that God hath not been provoked to withdraw from us altogether the succours of his grace. While he therefore spares us, and in various ways presents the admonitions of his wisdom and love for our good, let us consider what arguments and motives to a different course are presented by the ascension of our Lord into the heavens.

I. And, first, as the ascension of the man Christ Jesus to the right hand of God, is conclusive proof that the religion he taught and established in the world, is divine and true, the duty is imperious upon all who are called to the knowledge of this grace, to acquaint themselves with its doctrines—to believe its declarations, and to obey its precepts. In this, as there is no discretion, so can no difficulty, either real or imaginary, be pleaded as an excuse. From the goodness of GOD, we are bound to believe that nothing is required of us, either impossible in itself, or beyond the power of those faculties which constitute us moral beings, and by the aid of his promised grace, are equal to all that religion requires of us. Nor yet are we to presume that the service of GOD is inconsistent with our present happiness—rather are we bound to believe, from the benignity of his nature, that whatever has that appearance, is occasioned by erroneous views of what our present happiness consists in ; and by the surrender of our own sinful inclinations, to his wise and holy counsels, to make proof, at once of our own docility and of the truth of his holy word. Especially is this course called for in those whose woful experience has given them sensible proof, that the ways of self-will, of sin and folly, are ways of disappointment, and sorrow, and bitterness of spirit. And as the goodness of GOD has provided that sincere repentance shall renew favour, through the merits and death of JESUS CHRIST, encouragement is given, even to the chief of sinners, to return to GOD, and by a new and amended life, to reap the happy fruit of peace here, and reward hereafter ; and as the voice of reason points out the wisdom of thus turning from death unto life, so is it confirmed by the word of revelation, which declares to every sinner, that *except he repent he shall perish.*

II. Secondly, as the ascension of the man CHRIST JESUS is the great proof of the truth and divine origin of the religion he taught, so is the consideration of this fact the strongest inducement to repent, and believe the gospel.

Now, this inducement is found, not merely in the truth and divine nature of his religion, which yet is ground sufficient for every wise man to build his faith and hope upon, but in the circumstances connected with it.

His ascension into heaven, was a visible installing him into his office, as head over all things to his Church ; so that through him we now look up to GOD, address our prayers and praises, with hope of acceptance ; and through him receive those returns of mercy and favour, which for his sake are vouchsafed to a race of redeemed sinners.

His ascension into heaven was a demonstration of the triumph of human nature over the powers of darkness, thereby giving assurance of the like victory over their power and malice, to every true believer in his name.

His ascension into heaven was the prelude to those manifold gifts of grace, which he poured out upon the world in the gift of the HOLY GHOST, to abide with his Church for ever, as the comforter, enlightener, and sanctifier of his people.

This was the promise of the Father to the Son, in order to complete the great work of our salvation from sin and eternal death, by the renewal of our hearts, and the sanctification of our lives ; and the first display of our Redeemer's exaltation was the gift of the HOLY GHOST. And herein are all who have hearts to feel and tongues to utter praise, called upon to adore and magnify the riches of that grace in which all are provided, to conquer sin, to overcome death, and inherit eternity, in the heavenly mansions of love, and joy, and peace—and hereby are all bound, to whom the knowledge of this salvation is sent, forthwith to turn from the error of their ways, to embrace the gospel, and by a life and conversation conformed to its holy requirements, to follow the captain of their salvation to his heavenly kingdom —and this they are required to do, because, through the gift of the HOLY GHOST, power is conferred to fulfil their high calling. Whatever excuse, therefore, men may be disposed to make from difficulty in religion, is altogether unfounded. No more difficulty exists, than is absolutely necessary to the probation of moral beings—none that is insuperable to the renewed and assisted powers of redeemed beings—and, as on this is founded the responsibility of accountable beings, reward or punishment will surely follow, according as this state of grace and salvation is improved or neglected.

III. Thirdly, the ascension of CHRIST into heaven in that same body which suffered on the cross, is the clear and convincing proof that the mortal bodies of all who embrace the faith, obey the precepts, and follow the example of the man CHRIST JESUS, shall with him also thither ascend, and enjoy for ever the pleasures which flow from the presence of GOD, in the society of CHRIST, of the holy angels, and of the spirits of just men made perfect.

The consideration of our LORD's ascension, therefore, presents religion to our notice in a near and very interesting relation, to those endearing ties which connect us so closely in the present life. As our state hereafter will depend on our conduct here, so have we reason to believe from the circumstance of the resurrection of our bodies, that those affections and qualifications which form the nobler part of our nature in this our state of trial, will form a corresponding part of the enjoyments of a future state of being. A reflection, my brethren, which links the religion of the gospel to the sanctified ties of family and kindred, and unites the tenderest affections of our mortal natures with the holiest hopes of our immortal spirits ; and if dwelt upon and realized, as it ought to be, adds another to the many proofs we are furnished with, of that wisdom and prudence, as the apostle expresses it, wherewith a gracious GOD hath dealt with us, and fitted this dispensation of his grace, so exquisitely, to the nature of the Being for whom it is contrived, that only by the most inveterate opposition to reason, and interest, and feeling, can he fail to be moved, and drawn by cords of divine and human love to seek his own happiness and the happiness of all who are dear to him, by the performance of those duties which GOD has enjoined to this very end. And who does not see what happy effects would flow from such considerations, what union among Christians, what endearment in families, what zeal to promote religion, what comfort and consolation, amidst those inevitable privations, which are only unbearable when the hope of reunion is precluded by the absence of religion. O how cold and comfortless is the condition of the unbeliever. He looks around him perhaps on many blessings, on a flourishing family, and a prosperous worldly condition; but he must look upon them as transient things—in a few short and uncertain years to come to an end, and no more to visit his heart for ever. He cannot, therefore, feel the holy influence of that sanctified character which the same blessings impart to the heart of the believer, nor can he enjoy them with that high relish, nor resign them with that blessed hope, which religion sheds over the brightest as well as the darkest periods of our pilgrimage.

Lastly, the ascension of CHRIST into heaven, as it is conclusive proof of the truth and divine original of his religion, and of the obligation all are under, to embrace and obey the gospel—as it is demonstrative of his exaltation to supreme dominion in heaven and on earth, so is it an irrefragable testimony, that this same JESUS is he whom GOD hath ordained the judge of quick and dead.

This is a consideration, my hearers, which is cheerful and encouraging, or gloomy and alarming, according to the influence religion hath obtained over our hearts and lives. To the Christian, it is very full of comfort, that the infirmity and imperfection of his best intended services, that the short-coming of his best performed duties, and the sinfulness of his holiest affections, are to be tried before a Friend and fellow-sufferer, from the temptations of the world, and the malice of the devil—that his Judge has himself been tempted, and though without sin, knows how *to have compassion on the ignorant, and them that are out of the way*. While to the unbeliever, to the redeemed sinner, who hath turned away from his word, and derided his grace, who hath refused his love, and scorned his wrath, who hath trampled on his blood, and done despite to his holy SPIRIT, the thought that he has to meet this same JESUS as his Judge, is a heart-sinking reflection. For what plea can he then put in to move the compassion of his Judge. The season of mercy is past, the intercession of CHRIST has ceased, he is no longer a Saviour, but a Judge. The period of probation is over. No repentance can then avail, and as the unbeliever has chosen death in the error of his life, so death awaits him in all the plenitude of endless remorse and despair. O what a price to pay for the pleasures of sin, for the vanities of the world, for the vanished honour of its perishing applause. Yet thus it must be, my hearers, for GOD cannot deny himself, and make CHRIST the minister of sin, by awarding eternal happiness to those who have not prepared themselves in their day of grace for the blessed company of heaven. They must go to their own place, to the society of such as themselves, to the company of devils, and to the interminable torments of the wrath of GOD, poured out upon their ingratitude, as the just wages of sin preferred, and salvation slighted.

And is there an escape from this misery to the thousands who are exposed to it ? Yes, blessed be GOD, there is deliverance from this body of death, through JESUS CHRIST our LORD—he hath suffered for sin—he hath risen from the dead—he hath ascended into heaven—he hath led captivity captive, and given gifts unto men, even the HOLY SPIRIT, to guide them into all truth, to convince them of sin, to show them the efficacy of his death, and to sanctify them for those mansions of blessedness, whither he is gone before to prepare a place for all who believe and obey him. And shall the sinner, the helpless deathstricken sinner, remain unmoved by this display of mercy and love ? Shall sin prove stronger than salvation, and CHRIST die in vain for any present ? GOD forbid ! Let serious reflection then, lead you to desire the knowledge of GOD ; let his holy word guide you to the truth as it is in JESUS ; let his HOLY SPIRIT bring you to repentance, and the prayer of faith replenish your soul with the fear of GOD, and the love of CHRIST—then shall the hope that maketh not ashamed purify your heart from the love of sin, and inspire those holy affections which fit you for the presence of GOD, that when the end shall come, you may leave a world of sin and sinners, and ascending with CHRIST to the habitation of his holiness, sit down forever at the right hand of GOD, where there shall be no more sin, no more death, no more sorrow, no more suffering ; but all shall be love, and joy, and peace—a felicity, bounded only by the omnipotence of GOD, and the extent of eternity. To which that we may all come, GOD in his infinite mercy grant, for JESUS CHRIST'S sake. To whom, &c. &c.

SERMON XI.

───

1 Timothy iii. 16.

"And without controversy, great is the mystery of godliness; God was manifest in the flesh, justified in the Spirit, seen of angels, preached unto the Gentiles, believed on in the world, received up into glory."

WHETHER we understand godliness in its common acceptation of an habitually religious disposition and conduct, or of the means which the wisdom and love of God have contrived and appointed in order to the production of this effect, upon a race of depraved and sinful creatures; the assertion of the apostle is equally true, and equally demands our devout and serious consideration.

Godliness is a great mystery, or a deep and unsearchable operation of divine grace, manifest or made sensible to us in the one case, by the effect produced upon our own hearts, and exhibited in the other case, by that eternal purpose of mercy and salvation to fallen man, which was decreed in the counsels of heaven before the world was, is now fully made known by the revelation of the gospel, and is in operation in the world.

That the apostle here uses the word godliness to denote the plan and fulfilment of the redemption of the world by the Son of God, must be evident from the enumeration in the text, of those particulars, which constitute the mystery he refers to. And as the subject, however deep, embraces a fundamental doctrine of the faith once delivered to the saints, is practically edifying to Christians, and appropriated to the services of the day, I shall endeavour to apply it to these purposes, by laying before you,

FIRST, some considerations, calculated to obviate the objections hastily and erroneously taken up against such doctrines of religion as are mysterious in their nature, and particularly against the doctrine of the Trinity.

SECONDLY, by pointing out the confirmation given to this doctrine by the different facts mentioned in the text, and which, together, form the mystery of godliness.

THIRDLY, by showing you the connexion between the belief of this doctrine and practical religion, or personal godliness.

And without controversy, great is the mystery of godliness; GOD was manifest in the flesh, justified in the SPIRIT, seen of angels, preached unto the Gentiles, believed on in the world, received up into glory.

I. First, I am to lay before you some observations calculated to obviate the objections, hastily and erroneously taken up, against such doctrines of religion as are mysterious in their nature, and particularly against the doctrine of the Trinity.

The word mystery, in its common acceptation, means something secret and inexplicable, and is applied either to natural events, the causes of which we cannot penetrate, or to moral actions, the motions and springs to which are so concealed and impervious as to preclude discovery. Of each of these, observation and experience teach us, that there is a great variety, and might thereby prepare us, with all humility and readiness of mind, to expect, and to receive without objection, the higher and more sublime mysteries of religion.

In the religious acceptation of the word, it is applied to whatever is in such wise above or beyond human intelligence, in its own nature or mode of being, as to be known only by express revelation. Of these there are two descriptions—one, which when revealed, may in a good degree, if not altogether, be explained and understood; such as the satisfaction of CHRIST'S death for the sins of men, the operation of divine grace upon the human heart, the resurrection of our mortal bodies, with others, which might be named. The other, embracing those doctrines, the truth and certainty of which we know likewise by revelation, but cannot comprehend either their nature or the manner how they are; such as the trinity of persons in the unity of the GODHEAD, and the union of the divine and human natures in the man CHRIST JESUS. These are facts revealed to our faith, not to our understanding—they rest upon the authority of the revealer, not upon the reason of the creature, and from their very nature, warn us, that as all speculation into the manner of their being must prove abortive, it is both presumptuous and dangerous to intrude *into things not seen, vainly puffed up by a fleshly mind.*

In a communication from heaven to mankind on subjects purely spiritual, it is, *a priori,* reasonable to expect that there should be much above any power of comprehension we possess as rational beings. Mysteries in religion, therefore, ought not to excite our surprise, far less should they be resorted to, either as a ground of objection, or as an excuse for unbelief; and this we are taught by the analogies both of the natural and of the moral world. How many things palpable to our senses are yet beyond the reach of our faculties to comprehend the manner of their being, or the properties of their nature? *The wind bloweth where it listeth, and thou hearest the sound thereof, but canst not tell whence it cometh and whither it goeth*—And shall He *who bringeth the wind out of his treasures* be denied in the communications he hath made of himself to his creatures, because he is more incomprehensible than his works? Folly and enmity, even the enmity of the carnal mind, is stamped upon the presumption. If the elements in the midst of which we live, if the earth upon which we tread, and the food which nourishes our bodies, all contain secrets as to their nature and properties, which the wisdom that is in man cannot search out, shall not the pride that is offended, and rejects the mysteries of the divine mind, revealed for our good, stand rebuked for its impiety, and humble itself to receive the invisible things of GOD, just as He *in whom is no darkness at all, who is perfect in knowledge,* hath prepared and fitted them to our actual condition? Surely, if that boasted reason, to which the appeal is so confidently and constantly made, in support of this objection to revealed religion, be not itself a fallacy, it must see and acknowledge, that in things wholly beyond its observation and experience, GOD himself is the only source of knowledge. All that regards his nature, his properties, his mode of being, his will as to us, and his purposes concerning us, must come from him. If then, GOD hath spoken, let all the earth be silent before him, and casting away their unbelief, submit themselves to *receive with meekness the engrafted word, which is able to save their souls.*

This being undeniably the duty of every reasonable being, as to religion in general, it is equally so as to any particular doctrine of religion.   In truth, and I mention it as a general caution, and as the very first point which should be settled by every individual, in regard to religion ; the previous question as to the parts, as well as to the whole of religion, is, hath GOD revealed it ? If he hath, there ought to be no question as to the fitness or reasonableness of any particular doctrine, as the ground of our reception of it.   Faith springs not from, neither rests upon reason, but from, and upon divine authority ; and whatever in religion is not built upon this foundation, is built upon the sand. Reason may examine the fact of a revelation, or not, which is its proper province—reason may strive within its proper and guarded limits, to apprehend the deep things of GOD, and to apply them to the attainment of clearer views of his glorious perfections, which is its noblest exercise—and reason may enforce the obligation and the interest of its possessor, to embrace the truth of GOD, as GOD hath revealed it, as the only light of the soul, which constitutes reason the high and distinguishing privilege of our nature. But with the mysteries of religion, with *the secret things which belong to the* LORD *our* GOD, reason meddles, at its highest peril, and risks making shipwreck of the faith.   For they are therefore mysteries, because they are above our reason, beyond any possible enlargement or exercise of that faculty, in our present state of being, are to be discerned by faith only, and comprehended by a higher and different grade of intellectual progression.

To bring the mysteries of godliness to this tribunal, then, is a daring presumption of the carnal mind, and effectually shuts men out from that knowledge of them, which is practical and profitable to the entrance and increase of true religion in the heart.   And as this is experimentally true, as respects this abuse of religious mysteries in general, those who give into it remaining dead to GOD, and strangers to his renewing grace ; so is it emphatically true of those unhappy persons who are seduced with *great swelling words of vanity,* to reject the doctrine of the trinity in unity, as the mode of being in the divine nature, because it is contrary to reason, say some, because it is incomprehensible, say others. But when reason can develope the mysteries of the natural world, which it knowingly acts upon, though uncomprehended, and thereby both receives and gives the proof that they are not contrary to reason, let it take up this objection to the high mystery of the manner of subsistence in the godhead of Jehovah, our revealed Almighty Cause of all other being.— When reason can comprehend its own mode of being, how soul, body, and spirit yet form but one man, let it venture to question upon any grounds the mode of subsistence in its Creator, as revealed by himself, and let the broad and palpable atheism of the objection banish it for ever from the realms of Christian light. For without controversy, if its being incomprehensible to reason, is a good objection to the belief of GOD, as subsisting under a particular mode of being, it is equally good against his subsisting at all, it being just as impossible for reason to comprehend an eternal, underived, spiritual essence, in the mode, or manner of his subsistence, whatever that may be. The mode of Being in Deity, therefore, must of necessity be matter of direct revelation—and to this let reason in man submit itself—not replying against GOD.

II. Secondly, I am to point out to you the confirmation given to the doctrine of the trinity, by the different facts mentioned in the text, and which together form the mystery of godliness.

GOD *was manifest in the flesh.* That the apostle here refers to the incarnation of the second person in the trinity of the godhead, as revealed and set forth in the gospel, must be evident from those various passages of Scripture which refer to the same event. The original promise to fallen man was, that *the seed of the woman should bruise the serpent's head.* To this, as its leading object, the providence of GOD in the government of the world, and the whole system of revelation and prophecy in the Old Testament Church was directed. Jacob prophecied that Shiloh should come, and that unto him should be the gathering of the people. Moses prophecied to the children of Israel, *a prophet shall the* LORD *your* GOD *raise up unto you of your brethren, like unto me, him shall ye hear.* Isaiah gave notice, *Behold a virgin shall conceive and bear a son, and shall call his name Immanuel,* which St. Matthew interprets to mean GOD *with us,* or in our nature. *Yea, and all the prophets, as many as have spoken, have testified of him.*

In fulfilment of these predictions, the inspired writers of the New Testament unite in declaring, *that when the fulness of the time was come,* GOD *sent forth his Son, made of a woman, that he who was in the form of* GOD, *and thought it not robbery to be equal with* GOD, *was found in the likeness of man—that He who is over all,* GOD *blessed forever as concerning the flesh, came of the seed of David—that the word which was in the beginning with* GOD, *which was* GOD, *the same was made flesh and dwelt among us.* This is such clear and decisive testimony as to what was in the mind of the apostle when he made the declaration in my text, that GOD *was manifest in the flesh,* that no reasonable doubt can be entertained, that he meant to assert that a divine person took our nature upon him, and appeared in the world, according to the predictions going before concerning him, and consequently that St. Paul, inspired by the SPIRIT OF GOD, believed and taught a plurality of persons in the unity of the godhead. In further confirmation of this point, I would direct your attention to some declarations of our LORD himself, which on any other supposition than that of his divinity, are irreconcilable with the truth and integrity of his character.

In order to give his immediate disciples a clear view of his person and office, he told them, *I came forth from the father, and am come into the world*—again, *I leave the world and go to the Father ;* which is in perfect agreement with the pre-existence of CHRIST, and with the fact, as predicted and fulfilled in the mission of the Son of GOD. Again, in the affecting prayer which he uttered before he went into the garden to encounter his passion, he made this petition—*And now O Father, glorify thou me with thine own self, with the glory which I had with thee before the world was.* Now here is a pre-existent state of glory with GOD the Father Almighty, asserted to exist before the creation of things, and that by a plurality of persons, which is not conceivable of any created being, without a force of construction which defeats all certainty of meaning in the use of language. Once more, *Philip saith unto him, Lord, show us the Father, and it sufficeth us. Jesus saith unto him, He that hath seen me hath seen the Father*—which could not be true in the sense in which Philip put the question, unless in very truth, He who was thus manifest in the flesh, was very God. And here again we have a plurality of persons asserted in the godhead. And again, *I and my Father are one*, says the Saviour. Now, the context informs us, that this declaration was made, of equality of power with the Father. The question between our Lord and the Jews at the time was, as to his being the Christ, the expected Messiah. Of this he told them they had sufficient proof, but would not believe, because they were not of his sheep. *My sheep hear my voice*, says he, *and I give unto them eternal life —neither shall any man pluck them out of my hand.—My Father which gave them me is greater than all : and no man is able to pluck them out of my Father's hand.—I and my Father are one.* But equality of power must include equality of nature, and by consequence, a plurality of persons in the subsistence of Deity.

God was justified in the spirit. The expression is technical, and means that the person here spoken of, was authoritatively declared and certified, as to his nature and office, by the visible testimony of the Holy Ghost, according to that expression of John the Baptist, *he that hath the bride is the bridegroom.* The person thus justified, and here declared to be God, was undoubtedly our Lord Jesus Christ, and this justification consisted, in his miraculous conception by the Holy Ghost ; in the visible descent of the Spirit upon him at his baptism ; in the miracles wherewith he attested his mission ; in his resurrection from the dead ; and in the effusion of the Holy Ghost on his disciples, on the day of Pentecost ; by all which, the man Christ Jesus was declared *to be the Son of God with power ;* that is, certified to be a divine person, even God *manifest in the flesh.* Many individuals in this world, have in like manner been justified by the Spirit, as the messenger of God, to their fellow sinners ; but neither in measure or in manner, as was Jesus of Nazareth. In them it was limited and controlled, by the power which bestowed the gift ; in the man Christ Jesus, the fulness of the godhead dwelt bodily, and the Spirit without measure. They spake and acted in the name of him who sent them.   JESUS of Nazareth spake and acted in his own name, as one having authority, absolute and irresistible, over both the natural and the spiritual world ; and as the SPIRIT, by which the prophets and apostles were actuated, and justified to men, is expressly called the SPIRIT of CHRIST, and was derived from him to them, the SPIRIT by which CHRIST is here said to be justified by GOD, must be inherent, underived, and his property as a member of the godhead.

GOD *was seen of angels.   No man hath seen* GOD *at any time.*   From the nature and properties of the Supreme Being, he is and must be invisible to the highest created intelligences. He who filleth immensity and all space, cannot be circumscribed by a visible form or shape.   The blessed angels do indeed behold the face of our Heavenly Father, as it is expressed in Scripture, but this denotes neither shape nor similitude, but their nearness to that glory and brightness of his presence, in which they contemplate and adore his perfections, and from which they derive those supplies of unspeakable bliss, which constitute the happiness of Heaven.   In what sense then, was GOD *seen of angels?*   In that sense, and no other, in which, by taking our nature upon him, he became visible to angels and to men ; and he is here said to be seen of angels particularly, because, as they had a higher perception of *the divine nature,* so had they a clearer insight into the mystery of the incarnation. But what divine person took our nature upon him ?   The only begotten Son, who left the bosom of his Father, emptied himself of his essential glory for us men, and for our salvation came down from Heaven, and *was found in fashion as a man.*   GOD, then, was seen of angels, in the manger of the infant JESUS at Bethlehem ; at the close of his temptation in the wilderness ; during his passion in Gethsemane ;   they witnessed his triumphant resurrection, and accompanied his glorious ascension into his heavenly dominions.   The person thus seen of angels, is declared by St. Paul to be GOD ; but JESUS CHRIST, and none other was thus seen of angels.   JESUS CHRIST therefore is GOD.

GOD *was preached unto the gentiles.* The history of the gospel, and our own condition, my brethren, is sufficient proof of the fact. But it is declared to be a mystery, how this became possible, consistent with the honour of GOD; and this mystery can be cleared up no otherwise than by referring to the satisfaction made by the death of CHRIST, for the sins of the whole world, to the reconciliation thereby effected beween GOD and man, and to the offers of pardon and grace, commanded to be made to all nations, on the conditions of the covenant ratified in his blood. Hence we read that, GOD *was in* CHRIST *reconciling the world to himself, not imputing their trespasses unto them;* and the offers of the gospel, being made to men by the authority of CHRIST, being limited on the condition of faith in the name of CHRIST, and witnessed and made effectual by the SPIRIT of CHRIST, as the Church is the body of CHRIST, and believers the members of CHRIST, the whole dispensation is called the kingdom of CHRIST; and hence the preaching of the gospel, and preaching CHRIST, are expressions of the same import in Scripture. Thus we read, that *Philip went down to Samaria, and preached* CHRIST *unto them*—that St. Paul determined to know nothing among the Corinthians, *but* JESUS CHRIST *and him crucified.* Hence he calls the gospel *the unsearchable riches of* CHRIST, *the grace of our* LORD JESUS CHRIST, *the grace of* GOD *which bringeth salvation.* And as the whole history of the gospel proves that CHRIST was and is the sum and substance of all sound preaching, therefore, as CHRIST was what *was preached unto the gentiles,* CHRIST is GOD, by a testimony as wide as the spread of the gospel.

GOD *was believed on in the world.* The triumphs of the name of CHRIST over the gods of superstition, and the establishment of the gospel upon the ruin of the profane religions of the world, is the standing demonstration of his divine power, who said to his first ministers, *Lo, I am with you always, even unto the end of the world.* That a self-denying religion, at war with the lusts of the flesh, and the vanities of the world, with invisible rewards and visible sufferings, should have been embraced and followed by the darkness and depravity to which it was preached, is a mystery which can be solved only by the deity of its Author.

The reception of CHRIST as GOD, exalted his doctrine above the morality of the schools, and gave power to his word superior to all the wisdom of the world. The testimony of the HOLY GHOST to this truth, in the preaching of his ministers, confirmed their doctrine as from GOD, and the fruits of faith in the lives of believers, spread over the world the knowledge and the power of that *name which is above every name*. *Believe in the* LORD JESUS CHRIST *and thou shalt be saved*, was the message of life and hope to awakened sinners, and as CHRIST was preached to them as *the only name under heaven* by which this could be effected, he was believed on and trusted in as the GOD of their salvation ; and wherever the gospel has been established, this doctrine has been received as a fundamental truth of our holy religion, that the same CHRIST which was preached unto the Gentiles, and believed on in the world, is GOD *over all, blessed for ever.*

GOD *was received up into glory*—but he must first have left or surrendered his glory, otherwise he could not have been received again to it ; and as this is true only of our LORD JESUS CHRIST, it is an unanswerable declaration of the inherent divinity of his nature—for thus this same apostle argues in another place, from our LORD's ascension : *Now that he ascended, what is it but that he also descended first into the lower parts of the earth ? He that descended is the same also that ascended up far above all heavens, that he might fill all things.* He who had glory with the father, before the world was, came into the world, and having finished the work of our redemption, again ascended up where he was before ; circumstances, which as they can be affirmed of no created being, but are literally true of the LORD JESUS CHRIST, so are they conclusive as to the divinity ascribed to his nature, and are asserted by himself as proofs of this doctrine, in his conversation with Nicodemus : *And no man hath ascended up to heaven, but he that came down from heaven, even the Son of man which is in heaven.*

Each separate fact then, mentioned in the text, being thus clear and conclusive for our LORD's divine nature, the amount of the whole taken together, presents such a confirmation of the catholic faith, as to this fundamental doctrine, as cannot sincerely and honestly be withstood.

III. Thirdly, I am to show you the connexion between the belief of this doctrine and practical religion, or personal godliness.

The belief of the doctrine of the trinity has a favourable influence on personal religion, inasmuch as it involves the divinity of the Saviour, and the assistance of the HOLY GHOST. If sin is of that malignant nature that nothing less than the death of the Son of GOD could expiate its guilt, and obtain remission for sinners, the strongest of all arguments is hereby presented against continuing under its power, and the highest of all inducements held out, in the love of GOD and the merits of CHRIST, to bring sinners to repentance and amended life. And if the infection of our nature, by the poison of sin, is so deep and radical that nothing short of divine power can extract it, and nothing lower than divine assistance enable us to contend with its deceits, and overcome its influence, the encouragement derived from the HOLY GHOST to this very end, is beyond all expression. Indeed so ample, so suitable, and so effectual, is the provision made for our recovery to GOD, under the Christian system, of acceptance by the Father, through atonement by the Son, and sanctification by the HOLY SPIRIT, as persons concerned jointly and separately in bringing us to salvation, that it must be wholly our own fault if we fail of the grace of GOD.

Again, if we are to be judged hereafter, and rewarded or punished according to our works, it is a most consoling thought, even to the holiest of men, that he who is appointed the judge of quick and dead, is the same who, in the truth of our nature, encountered all its temptations—who therefore has a feeling of our infirmities, and who knows how to have compassion on the ignorant, and on them that were out of the way. To take him as our Saviour, secures his mercy as our judge. And if holiness is indispensable to happiness with GOD, the blessed assurance, that the HOLY GHOST is given to change and renew the heart—to shed abroad the love of GOD in our souls, and transform us into the divine image and nature, is calculated to stir up every faculty of soul and body, to be workers together with GOD for

the prize of our high calling.   To believe a work to be possible
is the first step to exertion—to have the means of performing it
provided, encourages to begin—and to be sure of success, if we
faithfully apply the means, leads to diligence in duty.   Now all
this is found in the belief of the doctrine of a trinity of persons
in the unity of the godhead, engaged in carrying on the plan
of our salvation, and no where else can it be found.   Discard
this doctrine and sin immediately loses the malignity of its nature, man is no longer the fallen, sinful creature who has no
hope in himself ; atonement is needless and grace superfluous—
reason can perform the office of the HOLY SPIRIT, and man's
righteousness abide the scrutiny of GOD's judgment.   Heaven
is the reward not of grace, but of debt, and eternal life the
retribution of justice, not the gift of GOD, through JESUS
CHRIST our LORD.

As the provisions of GOD's wisdom and love are only sought
and valued by men in proportion as they believe and feel the
want and misery of their state by nature, you can all judge,
my hearers, of the effect likely to be produced on the heart of
man by opposite systems of doctrine ; one of which presents to
his faith and hope, the love and the might of omnipotence in
the trinity of the GODHEAD, engaged for his recovery and salvation, through a divine atonement for the guilt of sin, and supernatural assistance to overcome its powers ; and the other,
which leaves him with human means only to perfect himself for
the presence of GOD, and claim eternal life upon his own merits,
without a Saviour, who is GOD as well as man, without a sanctifier, who is GOD the HOLY GHOST.   From which of these,
then, the righteousness of faith is most likely to spring, and personal godliness, that holiness without which no man shall see
the LORD, to be sought and attained, sinners—judge ye.

Now to GOD the Father, GOD the Son, and GOD the HOLY
GHOST, three persons in one GOD, be ascribed glory, honour,
and salvation, now and ever, world without end.   Amen.

SERMON XII.

ORDINATION, OR INSTITUTION.

1 Thessalonians v. 25.

" Brethren pray for us."

If an inspired apostle found it profitable to request the prayers of the Churches which he had planted, much more must it be needful to the Christian ministry at this day, that prayer should be offered up to God, by the congregations to whom they minister, that their labours be not in vain.

Much more is it required of us, who are deprived of those extraordinary displays of the power of the Holy Spirit with which the apostles were favoured, earnestly to pray, that his ordinary and continual assistance may be granted us, both to speak and to hear, to edification. And how much the more ought your poor servant—when taking upon himself the charge of your spiritual concerns—to address you in the words of the apostle—*Brethren pray for us.*

Arduous is the task, to stand between the living and the dead —to check and stay the plague of sin—to watch over the welfare of immortal souls—to conflict with the powers of darkness —with all the varied and multiplied arts of the crafty enemy of God and man—with spiritual wickedness in high places—and with what I believe to be more difficult than all, the inherent depravity of the human heart.

How needful, then, my brethren, that both minister and people should so feel the deep importance of the ministerial offices, as to be drawn out in frequent and fervent prayer to Almighty God, for that blessing upon his word preached, which shall make it profitable to their immortal souls. Paul may plant and Apollos may water, but without help from God there can be no increase—and the very appointment and privilege of prayer, involves the duty of its exercise, if we would obtain spiritual benefit, for prayer is the expression of desire to GOD. If therefore, there be no private intercession with GOD, on the part of a Christian congregation, for guidance and direction from the HOLY SPIRIT, for their minister, and for his blessed influences on their own hearts, in favour of divine truth, it is surely too plain evidence, that no sincere desire is felt for religious attainment. And hence it comes to pass, that the word preached doth not profit them, as we see so awfully exemplified in the existing condition of the Christian world—wherein many are hearers of the word, while but few indeed are doers thereof. Now, whether indifference on the subject of religion be the cause or the effect of the neglect of the duty of prayer in general, and of this particular exercise of supplication to GOD, the event is the same ; for in things moral and spiritual, the concurrence of our own will and desire, as well as the exertions of our respective abilities, must accompany the operations of divine grace. GOD, indeed, worketh in us, both to will and to do, and for that very reason requires us to work out our own salvation ; and as the ministerial office is a prominent appointment of the wisdom of GOD to this great end, it should ever be the subject of fervent intercession with GOD, by every serious Christian, on the joint consideration of duty and interest. For your own spiritual advantage, then, and for my help in the charge to which you have called me—for the revival of religion, and for the increase of the Redeemer's kingdom, I beseech you, my brethren, *pray for us*.

But, as the understanding, as well as the spirit is required in the office of prayer, grant me your attention, while I endeavour to lay before you some of those high and solemn duties which peculiarly belong to the gospel ministry : variously described, and under differing, though very apposite emblems, pointed out to us in the Scriptures.

While man continued in that holy and happy state in which he was placed at his creation, we read of no offices of devotion, no sacrifices, no oblations ; the whole man, both soul and body, being pure and holy, was an acceptable offering—a living sacrifice—a perfect oblation, to his Maker. But when this blessed condition was forfeited through disobedience, immediately we find sacrifice and offering, and with them the offices of devotion appointed. We read, however, of no priesthood, none specially set apart to minister in holy things, and to act as the medium of communication between God and his creatures ; neither do we hear of assemblies for the public worship of Jehovah : but there is good reason to believe, that every family composed its own Church, and the head thereof officiated as priest. This state of things, as regarded religion, continued before and after the deluge, for a period of twenty-four hundred years.

But when it pleased God, in fulfilment of his promise to our first parents, to select Abraham as the stock from which, in the fulness of time, Messiah, the Prince, should spring—and when, after many very wonderful displays of his power and providence, the posterity of Abraham, delivered from Egyptian bondage, were gathered together in the wilderness—then do we first read of the altar, and the continual burnt offering of the ark of the covenant, and the mercy seat above it, with all the splendid, yet typical furniture of the tabernacle, or place of public worship. Then, also, do we first read of a particular family, selected from the tribes to minister in the sanctuary, in their different orders, and favoured with Urim and Thummim—that is, with light and perfection, set apart to burn the incense of morning and evening supplication, to declare the will of heaven to the congregation, and make daily atonement for the sins of the people.

And when it further pleased him, as the time drew near for the fulfilment of his promise, to send his servants, the prophets, to warn his chosen people, to reprove their backslidings, and rebuke their rebellions, to make clearer discoveries of the gospel dispensation, obscurely shadowed out in the ceremonial law, and the services of the temple, then begins to open upon us, with clearer light, the high responsibility and sacred nature of the ministerial service of God.

Hear the appointment of the prophet Ezekiel—*Son of man, I have made thee a watchman unto the house of Israel, therefore hear the word at my mouth, and give them warning from me—when I say unto the wicked, thou shalt surely die, and thou givest him not warning, nor speakest to warn the wicked from his wicked way to save his life ; the same wicked man shall die in his iniquity ;*

but his blood will I require at thy hand. Yet if thou warn the wicked, and he turn not from his wickedness, nor from his wicked way, he shall die in his iniquity, but thou hast delivered thy soul. Again when a righteous man doth turn from his righteousness, and commit iniquity, and I lay a stumbling block before him, he shall die; because thou hast not given him warning, he shall die in his sin, and his righteousness which he hath done, shall not be remembered: but his blood will I require at thy hand. Nevertheless, if thou warn the righteous man, that the righteous sin not, and he doth not sin, he shall surely live, because he is warned; also, thou hast delivered thy soul. Awful appointment indeed. Well may we exclaim, who is sufficient for these things? And earnestly do we beseech you brethren, to join us in prayer, that a full measure of the grace of God may be afforded us.

Hear also the evangelical watchman, Isaiah. Inquiry is made respecting his office—Watchman, what of the night? Watchman, what of the night? Hear also his reply. The morning cometh, and also the night; if ye will inquire, inquire ye; return; come. The very message, my hearers, yea almost the very words of the gospel. The morning of the resurrection is fast approaching; the night of despair and darkness also cometh. Inquire, search diligently; return to the Lord, and he will have mercy upon you. Come unto me and be saved all ye ends of the earth. He that hath ears to hear let him hear. Hear the warning voice of your watchman this day, and pray for him, that he may always be found at his post, vigilant, ready, and profitable to his hearers.

But it is to the New Testament dispensation, that we must more particularly look, for the designations of the Christian ministry. Accordingly in the very first discourse of our blessed Lord to his disciples, he addresses them as the salt of the earth, as the light of the world.

The salt of the earth—As having those doctrines committed to their charge, by which the corruptions of our fallen nature may be arrested, the health of the soul restored, man renewed after the image of him who created him, and fitted for that state of never ending happiness, prepared for the righteous in the kingdom of God. The light of the world—As commissioned to declare to those who sat in darkness and the shadow of death, the terms of the new covenant of peace and reconciliation. In subsequent communications he addresses them as stewards, as shepherds, and last of all as preachers and teachers. To each of these designations appropriate duties and obligations are annexed.

As *stewards*——In this branch of our office, it is required that we shall have an intimate knowledge of the supplies provided in the spiritual treasury of GOD's word, for the support and comfort of the household and family of CHRIST. Infinite almost, is the variety of condition, both in sinful debasement and spiritual attainment, among mankind ; equally varied and extensive are the stores of instruction and rebuke, of exhortation and edification, contained in the sacred scriptures of our faith. To the unbelieving, impenitent, and ungodly, the terrors of the LORD are to be denounced ; to the humble, contrite, broken hearted sinner, the comforts of the gospel, of the grace of GOD, are to be administered ; and to the obedient persevering believer, the assurances of glory and immortality and eternal life, are to be held full in view. *It is moreover required of stewards*, even in temporal things, *that a man be found faithful* ; how much more then in those to whose care are committed the unsearchable riches of CHRIST, must faithfulness abound. Pray for us dear brethren, that as good stewards of the manifold grace of GOD, we may so fulfil our trust, that when called to render an account of our stewardship, we may do it with joy and not with grief.

As *shepherds*——Perhaps no comparison is more frequent in the scriptures (I am sure none can be more descriptive) than this, of the people of GOD, to a flock of sheep ; and that flock scattered by the violence of an enemy ; wandering, weary and fainting, without a guide to direct them back to the fold. Peculiarly applicable was it to that period of time, when our blessed LORD declared himself the shepherd of the sheep. And as it was prophesied, that he should *feed his flock like a shepherd, gathering the lambs with his arms, carrying them in his bosom, and gently leading those that are with young ;* so in event was it fulfilled by him. who came *to seek and to save that which was lost ; who went about doing good ; seeking the lost sheep of the house of Israel.* With this designation of our office, he hath left us the bright example of his labour, patience, and unwearied diligence in the discharge of duty. We are exhorted accordingly by his apostles, particularly by the apostle Peter, to *feed the flock of* GOD *which is among us, taking the oversight thereof ; not by constraint, but willingly, not for filthy lucre, but of a ready mind ; neither as being lords over* GOD's *heritage, but being ensamples to the flock.* And with strict propriety does this exhortation come from him, to whom was thrice emphatically committed the charge of feeding the lambs and sheep of his divine master. *Pray for us* then dear brethren, that in the labour of love, patience of hope, and diligence of duty we may be unwearied, ever abounding in the work of our LORD and master ; feeding his lambs with the sincere milk of the word, and his sheep with the nourishing food of the bread of life. *Pray for us,* that those who have strayed from the fold, may hear the voice which calleth them to return to the shepherd and bishop of their souls. That there may be one fold and one shepherd, one flock and one acclamation of praise and thanksgiving, to him that sitteth on the throne and to the Lamb forever.

As *preachers and teachers*—Hear the words of our commission. *All power is given unto me in heaven and in earth,* saith our blessed LORD. *Go ye therefore into all the world, and preach the gospel to every creature ; teaching them to observe all things, whatsoever I have commanded you.* My hearers, can a commission be couched in more comprehensive terms ? Can human ingenuity devise language more inclusive and general in its expression ? I think not ; and understanding it as I do, unclogged with any secret degree of preterition, or absolute reprobation, it is not only my duty but my delight, to offer the grace and mercy of the gospel to all men ; and to obey the gracious commandment, that repentance and remission of sins should be preached among all nations, in his name, *who by the grace of* GOD *tasted Death for every man.* This is the true gospel of JESUS CHRIST, the *glad tidings of great joy, which shall be to all people.*

With this message of love committed to us, how diligent ought we to be, in following the bright example of our divine master, who early and late, in public and in private, in the temple, in the synagogue, on the mountain, on the plain, and journeying by the way, was ever intent on his Fathers business. Anointed as he was in a peculiar manner, *to preach the gospel to the poor, to heal the broken-hearted, to preach deliverance to the captives, and recovering of sight to the blind, to set at liberty them that are bruised, to preach the acceptable year of the* LORD *;* so to his ministers in all ages is this holy trust committed. *As my Father hath sent me, even so send I you, and he breathed on them and saith unto them, receive ye the* HOLY GHOST *; whosoever sins ye remit they are remitted unto them, and whosoever sins ye retain they are retained ; and lo, I am with you always, unto the end of the world.* Sacred deposit, awful authority, blessed promise—*But we have this treasure in earthen vessels.* Pray for us dear brethren that we may be strengthened from above *to preach the word, to be instant, in season, out of season, reproving, rebuking, exhorting with all long-suffering and doctrine.* Pray for us, that we may be so taught of the spirit of wisdom as to *speak the things that become sound doctrine, showing ourselves approved unto* GOD, *workmen that need not to be ashamed, rightly dividing the word of truth.* Pray for us, that the spirit of meekness, gentleness, patience, long-suffering, faith, and charity, may so dwell in us, and abound, that GOD may be glorified by the shining of our light before men : and that as ensamples to the flock, we may with a good conscience say to them, *be ye followers of me even as I also am of* CHRIST.

There is, however, one more designation of our sacred office, which, was I to fail to point out to you, would argue on my part too limited an acquaintance with its duties to warrant my occupying any station in the ministry of reconciliation. *Now then* (says the apostle Paul) *we are ambassadors for* CHRIST, *as though* GOD *did beseech you by us ; we pray you in* CHRIST'S *stead, be ye reconciled to* GOD.

Surely, brethren and friends, this proof of the condescending mercy of GOD ought to humble us in the dust before him. What ! shall the king eternal, immortal, invisible, the only wise GOD, propose terms of peace, of pardon and reconciliation to his rebellious creatures—shall he, who has no need of the sinful man, condescend, as it were, to beseech us to throw down the arms of our rebellion and return to our allegiance—shall the proof of his merciful intentions towards the creatures of his power, evidenced by long suffering patience, by continued preservation, by a rich and varied provision for all our wants, and to crown the whole, by the gift of his only, his beloved Son, produce no softening effect upon our hard and stony hearts? GOD forbid, my hearers, for *how shall we escape if we neglect so great salvation?*

But as ambassadors we have our credentials to you, and our instructions for you; we come not in our own name or authority, or as ministers plenipotentiary, with discretionary powers, authorised to cut, and carve, and trim the terms of the new covenant, according to the whim and caprice of shortsighted, thoughtless, sinful mortals. No indeed—but with the commission of CHRIST, with directions full, plain, and precise. Hear a few of them, from this sacred storehouse of divine wisdom: *say ye to the righteous, that it shall be well with him; for they shall eat the fruit of their doings; woe unto the wicked, it shall be ill with him, for the reward of his hands shall be given him. When the wicked man turneth away from his wickedness that he hath committed, and doeth that which is lawful and right, he shall save his soul alive. Let the wicked forsake his way, and the unrighteous man his thoughts, and let him return unto the* LORD *and he will have mercy upon him, and to our* GOD, *for he will abundantly pardon.* GOD *so loved the world that he gave his only begotten Son, that whosoever believeth on him should not perish, but have everlasting life.* GOD *now commandeth all men every where to repent; because he hath appointed a day in which he will judge the world in righteousness by that man whom he hath ordained; whereof he hath given assurance unto all men in that he hath raised him from the dead. Tribulation and anguish upon every soul of man that doeth evil; but glory, honour, and peace to every man that worketh good. For the wrath of* GOD *is revealed from heaven, against all ungodliness and unrighteousness of men.* It were an easy matter to multiply quotations of this kind; enough, I think, is produced to prove that our line is marked out; and I would hope to excite a desire in you to search the Scriptures for the terms of that reconciliation purchased by JESUS CHRIST, for a ruined world.

Men and brethren, hear the soul-reviving, heart-cheering truth—GOD is reconciled, for what CHRIST hath done and suffered for us ; and the great embassy on which the ministers of CHRIST are still sent, is to persuade, nay to pray you, be ye on your part reconciled to GOD. Come, then, my fellow sinner ; let not unbelief of this precious truth keep thee at a distance from the mercies of the gospel. Come unto him who is *our peace, and suffered that he might reconcile both unto* GOD, *in one body, by the cross, having slain the enmity thereby. For it pleased the Father that in him should all fulness dwell ; and, (having made peace by the blood of his cross) by him to reconcile all things to himself; and you,* my Christian brethren, *that were sometime alienated, and enemies in your mind by wicked works, yet now hath he reconciled, in the body of his flesh, through death.*

Thus argues the apostle Paul, in his epistles to the Ephesians and Colossians ; in those to the Corinthians the same doctrine is maintained, and in that to the Romans, it is placed even beyond the reach of a cavil. *But* GOD (saith the apostle,) com*mendeth his love towards us, in that while we were yet sinners* CHRIST *died for us. Much more then, being now justified by his blood, we shall be saved from wrath through him. For if when we were enemies, we were reconciled to* GOD *by the death of his Son, much more, being reconciled, we shall be saved by his life.* Merciful GOD, open the hearts of this people to receive and apply the word of reconciliation, that they may have peace with thee, through JESUS CHRIST our LORD !

And *pray for us,* dear brethren, that in all the varied offices of the ministry, whether as watchmen, as stewards, as shepherds, as preachers, teachers, and ambassadors, we may hold fast the faithful word—*looking unto Him who is head over all things to the Church, and who is the author and finisher of our faith.*

Pray also for yourselves. O that I could impress on your very souls the necessity of earnest, fervent, persevering prayer, both in public and in private. Nearly in vain shall we preach, and worse than in vain will you hear, if prayer, mighty prayer, bring not down upon us the refreshing dew of GOD's blessing.

At no time, and under no circumstances, can your assembling yourselves together for the worship of GOD be indifferent or neutral in its consequences—of necessity you must be benefitted or injured, and that for eternity. *Take heed then how ye hear— for whosoever hath, to him shall be given, and whosoever hath not, from him shall be taken even that which he seemeth to have.* Surely, my friends, the tremendous alternatives of death and judgment might be expected to take some hold on even the most giddy and thoughtless. But alas for man—poor fallen man! How seldom do the world, the flesh, and the devil, permit a serious thought to enter the mind, at least to be entertained there. The old deception, *Ye shall not surely die,* is yet listened to. And to this day, thousands reject the counsel of GOD against their own souls, and are called into eternity without an interest in—yea, without even knowing the terms of that reconciling mercy, purchased by the sufferings and death of GOD's dear Son. GOD forbid, dear friends, that any of us should listen to the syren song of the destroyer. What deep damnation shall we of this favoured land deserve, if we continue to slight the warning voice of the gospel, if we prefer the darkness of our own foolish hearts and vain imaginations to that clear light which once again shines to conduct us to our everlasting happiness. GOD *hath not appointed us to wrath, but to obtain salvation through our LORD JESUS CHRIST.* Behold the proof in the light of the gospel, to guide you to your everlasting peace, in the appointment of a ministry, to instruct, to reason with, to persuade, yea, to beseech you by all the unutterable consequences, suspended on this our probationary state, to look to the end, to weigh in the balances of the sanctuary, the favour of GOD, with the utmost supposeable advantage and enjoyment which this world can bestow. O that you could, O that you would feel for yourselves, for your immortal souls, what every true minister of the LORD JESUS feels for you; that you would but believe them to be actuated by a heartfelt desire to promote your eternal welfare, that in all the varied offices of ministerial duty, this one sentiment is paramount, as most effectually promoting the glory of GOD in the salvation of sinners.

I speak as unto wise men, judge ye what I say. Is there an assignable motive, other than an imperious sense of duty, a burning love for souls, to press men into this service? Is it the road to advancement in temporal dignities, honours, and emoluments? Does it hold out the enticement of an indolent, sinecure enjoyment of life? Does it even contribute to the vapour-like acquisition of the praise of men? In no wise. Surely the meed of sincerity may be allowed to us—assuredly might we expect to be heard with interest; and when a faithful discharge of duty called for animadversion or reproof, with attention and charitable regard; *we seek not yours, but you.* Shut not your ears against us, and the message wherewith we are intrusted; it is at the peril of our souls if we fail to warn the wicked of his way, it is to our everlasting reproach, if we prophecy smooth things, crying *Peace, where there is no peace,* daubing up with *untempered mortar,* the chasms and the breaches which the assaults of the enemy have made in the temple of the LORD. And it will be to your everlasting loss, if *not enduring sound doctrine, but heaping to yourselves teachers, having itching ears, ye turn away from the truth, and are turned unto fables; if forsaking the fountain of living waters, you hew out to yourselves cisterns, broken cisterns, which can hold no water.*

My hearers, especially you my brethren of the Church, I would bespeak your favour for myself and for my brothers in the ministry. Israel is conflicting with Amalek, the Church of the living GOD is at issue with the world; which would ye should prevail? Your unbiassed judgment I know, speaks in behalf of the religion of the gospel. Be faithful then to that judgment, and as Aaron and Hur supported the arms of Moses, when lifted up in prayer, that Israel after the flesh might prevail in the conflict; so do ye support the hands, and strengthen the spirit of your aged pastor, that victory in the spiritual contest may crown his efforts. Let him not be to you as the prophet Ezekiel was to the Jews—*a very lovely song of one that hath a pleasant voice, and can play well on an instrument.* It was the reproach of Israel of old, (I beseech you let it not be yours also,) that to the prophets sent among them—*with their mouth they showed much love, but their heart went after their covetousness.* O while it is called to-day, while the day of grace and salvation is within your reach, harden not your hearts, but let the morning mercies and evening favours of a gracious GOD lead you to repentance. Hard indeed must that heart be, and deeply rooted that depravity, which stands aloof from GOD's reconciling love—heareth not the voice of the charmer, charm he never so wisely—neither listens to the voice of the law written in the heart by the HOLY SPIRIT, sent to convince of sin, of righteousness, of judgment.

To that awful judgment, brethren and friends, we are all fast hastening. With what emotions do we entertain the solemn thought? Do we desire or do we dread that day, which, removing this veil of flesh and blood, shall display alike the glories and the horrors of the invisible world—shall summon you and your pastor, and your poor servant, and all who have spoken to you the words of this life, as witnesses for and against each other; even this day's warning, light as some may make of it, shall not pass unnoticed; it must so far clear or condemn me, must benefit or injure you. Examine yourselves, dear friends, by every test; you cannot be too sure—take this as one. In serious, solemn retirement, put the awful question to yourselves, "Soon as from earth I go what will become of me." And may the GOD of mercy, the GOD and Father of our LORD JESUS CHRIST, enable you to come at the true answer.

Now to Him who is able, and mighty, and willing to save us; to the only wise GOD and our Saviour, be glory, and honour, and praise, world without end. AMEN.

SERMON XIII.

AN ORDINATION SERMON.

2 Corinthians, iv. 5.

"For we preach not ourselves, but Christ Jesus the Lord, and ourselves your servants, for Jesus' sake."

The grounds and motives for undertaking the ministerial office, and the principle which should preside over all other considerations in the performance of it, are both set before us in the words of my text; and coupled with the apostolic example give us readily to perceive both the weight of the duty, and the arduous nature of the undertaking.

It presents also, to those for whose benefit the ministry is instituted, those considerations which render the appointment of a distinct order of men to minister in sacred things, profitable at once to edification and assurance on those high and holy interests which form the ultimate expectation of immortal beings.

The purpose before us then, my reverend and lay brethren, being one of common concern and common advantage, I shall endeavour so to frame the enlargement I propose to make of the text, as to contribute to our joint benefit. To this end, I shall

First, consider what we are to understand as the apostle's meaning in the first clause of the text—*We preach not ourselves.*

Secondly, I will endeavour to explain what it is in the Scripture sense, to preach Christ.

Thirdly, I will make some remarks on the motives which should govern, in undertaking the ministerial office.

Fourthly, On the duties involved in this office both to ministers and people; and, then,

Conclude with a short application of the subject.

For we preach not ourselves, but CHRIST JESUS *the* LORD *; and ourselves your servants, for* JESUS' *sake.*

I. First, I am to consider what we are to understand as the apostle's meaning in the first clause of the text——*We preach not ourselves.*

The method by which St. Paul and the other apostles of our LORD were qualified and commissioned to preach the gospel, and the manner in which they performed this duty, are a sufficient comment on this passage of Scripture, and instruct us, that as St. Paul received it not from man, so neither did he preach it as the attainment of any knowledge or wisdom of his own, but as a direct revelation from the LORD JESUS CHRIST. As such, he proposed it in its original plainness and simplicity to Jew and Gentile, as the doctrine of life and salvation ; and stood prepared to demonstrate it to be such, both by arguments of reason and miraculous proofs of divine attestation.

By not preaching ourselves, then, we are to understand in the first and highest sense, the keeping present in our own minds, and pressing upon the consciences of our hearers, that the truths preached to them are not systems of human contrivance, or inventions of human wisdom, or yet the profitable conclusions of moral science, for present advantage to the world ; but *the true sayings of* GOD, *the wisdom of* GOD *in a mystery, now made manifest, and commanded to be preached among all nations for the obedience of faith.* This is the only ground, my friends, upon which we can preach, or you can hear to edification. Upon any other principle, the gospel degenerates into a mere system of ethics, and ministers of religion, instead of being, and being regarded as *Stewards of the mysteries of* GOD, descend into the comparatively insignificant station of teachers of morality. The connexion between morals and religion is indeed very close, yet is there this never to be forgotten distinction betwixt them, a distinction peculiarly required to be inculcated in the present day. True religion necessarily includes the highest attainments in morals, whereas no advancement in morality, as such, necessarily includes any religious attainment at all.

That the ministers of CHRIST then assume this ground, and hold it as the very essence of their calling and office, is indispensible both to themselves and their hearers. Without this en graven on their own hearts, and manifested in the tenour of their lives, and pressed upon the hearts, and exhorted to in the lives of their hearers, they will soon cease to respect themselves, and their hearers to respect them, through their sacred office.

Another and very important sense in which we are to understand the apostle's meaning in these words, is, that we do not preach the gospel from unworthy and improper motives.

To preach for popularity, is in the truest sense, to preach *ourselves* ; to fit our public or private duties to the wishes, rather than to the wants of our hearers, is literally to *speak unto them smooth things, to prophecy deceits* ; to frame our discourses rather to tickle the itching ears, than to search the sinful hearts of our charge, is to surrender the fidelity we owe to GOD to the fear or the favour of man ; to seek for opportunities of displaying particular talents, to be ambitious of shining and attracting notice, betrays a degree of pride and vanity, and of confidence in our own powers, which has forgotten that our sufficiency is of GOD; and to preach the gospel for the sake of the emoluments of the gospel, for filthy lucre, as St. Peter calls it, is truly to serve mammon and not GOD. All these in their different degrees, come under the description of preaching ourselves, and ought to have no place either in the motives which prompt us to desire the sacred office, or which govern us in performing it.

That St. Paul was superior to all such considerations, is demonstrated by his whole history. His foundation was, that the gospel is from GOD ; as such he believed, and as such he preached it in the plainness and simplicity of its convincing and saving truth. In natural and acquired abilities, inferior to none, and inspired withal, he yet tells the Corinthians, that his *speech and his preaching was not with the enticing words of man's wisdom.* Nor could the taunts and scoffs of his adversaries, the false teachers, draw him away from that great plainness of speech which he used. His desire was to win souls to CHRIST, not to acquire the praise of men for himself. His ambition was to shine as a Christian, not as an orator or philosopher. As he had personally experienced the efficacy of CHRIST as a Saviour, he determined to know nothing in his preaching, *but* JESUS

VOL. I.—80

CHRIST, *and him crucified*—and he gives as his reason, *that your faith should not stand in the wisdom of men, but in the power of* GOD. And, as it is the same gospel which we have to preach, as the same gracious purpose is yet to be answered by it, so are the same means to be used, and the same motives to govern the hearts of all who undertake this holy office. The ministers of CHRIST are not now, indeed, inspired men ; nor do they receive the gospel by direct revelation. These are supplied, and sufficiently supplied, by the recorded Scriptures, by learning and study, and by the ordinary influences of the HOLY SPIRIT. These, in the wisdom of GOD, are the substitutes for those miraculous endowments which transformed illiterate fishermen into able ministers of the New Testament ; and as such are to be diligently applied by us. Nor is there wanting an equally satisfactory attestation of the commission to preach and baptize, with that furnished to the first Christians, by the miracles of the apostles. As in every age of the world this is needed to give assurance to faith, in the infinite interests of eternity, GOD hath been pleased to provide it for every age, in the transmission of the original commission to them, by succession from them, through the bishops of the Church. Nor is it conceived upon what other possible, and at the same time rational, principle, one set of men can venture to preach the gospel as a revelation from heaven, and the rest of mankind become *guilty before* GOD, for refusing to believe and obey the gospel. For, of necessity, and upon every known principle of equity, if the obligation to believe and obey the gospel now be just as strong and binding as at the first, the means of ascertaining that it is the gospel, and performing with full assurance, the duties required by the gospel, must either be the same as at the first, or equivalent in moral obligation. But, this being undeniably the case, the ministers of CHRIST in this day are as much bound by apostolic example as Christians in general are by apostolic authority. Ministers are not to *preach themselves, but* CHRIST JESUS *the* LORD. Private Christians are to *receive with meekness the engrafted word which is able to save their souls.*

II. Secondly, I am to explain what it is, in the Scripture sense, to preach CHRIST—*we preach not ourselves, but* CHRIST JESUS *the* LORD.

As we can hardly open the Scriptures of our faith, my brethren and hearers, without being presented with something which relates to our LORD JESUS CHRIST, so neither can a Christian minister frame an admonition, or an exhortation, a reproof of sin, or an encouragement to virtue, a source of comfort in time, or hope in eternity—which does not begin, continue, and end in him. Abstracted from CHRIST, he has neither a motive, or an argument, or a hope, or a help, or a promise, for himself or others. Being without GOD in the world, there is nothing sure to man but death and fear. As a minister of religion, moreover, he must speak in the name of CHRIST, he must speak in the words of CHRIST—he must act by the authority of CHRIST—he must speak to the redeemed of CHRIST, to those who shall be judged by CHRIST, and who, without CHRIST can do nothing acceptable to GOD, or profitable to themselves.

But to be more particular.

To preach CHRIST with effect, men must first be showed their need of him—in what it is that he is so all-important to their welfare—to their peace with GOD here, to their hope hereafter. As the sick only require the physician, men must have their disease pointed out and brought home to them before they will seek the remedy for it.

The fallen condition of human nature, then, the curse of GOD weighing it down to eternal death, and the entire loss of all spiritual capacity in the natural man, must be laid as the foundation, and this foundation must be laid both wide and deep, and entire—no otherwise can the building of GOD be raised in its due proportions, and to its proper hight, and to its happy issue, in a recovered and sanctified creature. To treat this fundamental doctrine lightly, then, to take it for granted, and, therefore, only now and then allude to it—to skim it over and avoid its pointed application to every soul that liveth, is to bury the gospel and all its glad tidings to a world of sinners, in the grave of revealed religion. For of what worth is salvation to him who is not lost ? Wherefore should he accept deliverance, who is unconscious of his captivity, and in love with his fetters ? And what form or comeliness is there in Jesus Christ to men, who have not learnt the depth of their own undoing in the first Adam, and the absolute impossibility of recovery to God, through themselves ?   Here, then, my reverend brethren, we must take our stand ; on this doctrine, wide as the world, universal as its population, and absolute as death, must the gospel be preached. It is God's gracious discovery, confirmed by all we know of ourselves and others, and witnessed to every heart in the fear and anxieties which render death terrible, and haunt our forebodings of eternity with despair.

This foundation being laid—to preach Christ with effect the stewards of the mysteries of God must open up from the faithful word, the fulness and sufficiency of Christ in all his offices, and the duty of redeemed creatures.   Under this display of the love of God to sinners, St. Paul calls it *the unsearchable riches of* Christ, and so full was he of its unspeakable value, that he never approaches towards the mention of it, in any argument or exhortation, that he does not seem transported, as it were, and stops, or steps aside to refresh himself at this perpetual feast.

The building however, to be secure, must proceed in order, with recovery by Christ ; men must be taught the necessity of renewal by his Spirit—of that deep and radical *change of the inner man, of the heart and affections, of the will and desires* which constitute the new creature—that birth from above—that being born of the Spirit, which alone qualifies the new creature for his new duties.   And this also is a fundamental doctrine to be pressed upon the attainment of all who would be joint heirs with Christ of a heavenly inheritance.   *Except a man be born of the* Spirit, *he cannot enter into the kingdom of God.* To treat this doctrine lightly then, or to content ourselves with merely telling men that they must be born again, is literally *shutting up the kingdom of heaven against men.*   No my brethren, the minister of Christ must not only declare the doctrine, but instruct also how to apply it—must show the steps to be taken, and the exertions to be made, and the source to be applied to, in order to obtain this blessing.   Here particularly, he must show that he is a *scribe instructed unto the kingdom of hea-*

ven, which bringeth forth out of his treasure things new and old. And here caution and experience are indispensable, *lest the hurt of the daughter of my people be healed slightly.* As there are degrees of sin and guilt, so are there also of conviction; as there are diversities of operations by the same SPIRIT, so are there also of manifestations. The ordinary and the extraordinary are not to be confounded, but the seasonable counsel of the word is to be dealt out to each as need shall require. In one thing, however, both ordinary and extraordinary unite, and that is, newness of life. This is the true and unerring standard to which to bring the reality of every conversion by the SPIRIT of GOD. This is his unvarying testimony, nor can it be disputed. The wind indeed bloweth where it listeth—it may be a storm, or it may be a refreshing gale, or it may be a gentle breeze. It is however the same agent, visible only in its effects; *so also is every one that is born of the* SPIRIT.

In connexion, however, with this practical application of re-vealed truth, through the primary doctrine of man's fallen state, all that JESUS CHRIST is to his recovery and salvation, is brought into view, is brought near, and bound up as it were with every step, from darkness to light, and from the power of Satan to GOD. Conviction of sin, the first step to conversion, is the work of the spirit of GOD, purchased to this very end, by the undertaking of the Son of GOD for fallen men. Repentance from dead works to serve the living GOD is the work of the same SPIRIT, rendered available to the pardon of past and forsaken sin only through the satisfaction made to the divine justice by the death of CHRIST; and the pardon of sin, repented and forsaken, is no otherwise to be had than through the atonement made by his blood shed upon the cross for the sins of the whole world. These operations of the HOLY GHOST upon men, though now sensible and visible only in their effects, are nevertheless vital realities, revealed to faith and by faith received. They are to be preached therefore, that they may be known and expected, that they may be sought for and obtained, and as faith in the LORD JESUS CHRIST includes these benefits, therefore they are virtually expressed in the frequent exhortation, *Believe in the* LORD JESUS CHRIST, *and thou shalt be saved.*

In preaching these doctrines, therefore, we preach CHRIST JESUS, the LORD; for only as they are kept in connexion with his undertaking for sinners, and relied upon for acceptance through faith in his name are they effectual to us. Conviction of sin overtakes every sinner, when his sin finds him out. Repentance for sin necessarily and unavoidably takes place when the consequences of sin are to be encountered; but this is devoid of any spiritual or saving character: it is the mere sorrow of the world. It might be admitted, perhaps, in a code purely moral; but can have no place in the higher and purer code of religion. Morality respects only the present life; religion looks beyond it, even to life eternal, in the presence of GOD.

Hence I think we may understand why it was that St. Paul confined himself to this one point in preaching; and may learn, that by preaching CHRIST JESUS the LORD, and *determining to know nothing among the Corinthians but JESUS CHRIST and him crucified,* he did not mean that the name of CHRIST, or the sufferings of CHRIST, or faith in his name, or reliance upon his merits were to form the subject matter of public preaching exclusively—but rather, that as his undertaking for us gave worth and efficacy to any endeavours of ours to propitiate GOD, and regain his favour, that therefore they were not to be separated, but that Christians should be continually instructed to look to him, and the atonement of his cross, as the ground of their acceptance with GOD.

In like manner also, in building up believers in their most holy faith, the Christian minister preaches continually CHRIST JESUS the LORD. He preaches him as the pattern and example of every divine perfection in righteousness and true holiness—of cheerful submission to the will of GOD—of patience under affliction—of compassion for the sufferings, and active benevolence in relieving the wants of all around him—of love, even to his enemies, and forgiveness of his very murderers. And he preaches him as the source of supply for all spiritual grace, to the attainment *of the mind that was in* CHRIST by all his followers. *Whatsoever ye do, in word or deed, do all in the name of the* LORD JESUS, is the constant exhortation of the faithful ministers; and in every strait, in every trial, in the season of sickness and suffering, and at the approach of death, *look unto* JESUS, *the author and finisher of your faith, who, for the joy that was set before him, endured the cross, despising the shame, and is set down at the right hand of the throne of* GOD, is the animating encouragement he holds out *to fight the good fight of faith, and lay hold on eternal life.* Thus is CHRIST JESUS the LORD, *the alpha and omega, the first and the last,* with the faithful minister who watches for souls, as one who for souls must give account. Even when his subject does not directly require that it be mentioned, there is yet a seasoning and a savour of CHRIST to be perceived, which marks the mainspring of all his exertions—which gives point and impression to his doctrine, startling the sinner from his security, and carrying hope and comfort to the heart of the believer. With CHRIST in his heart, and CHRIST upon his lips, the Christian minister *preaches to edification, to exhortation, to comfort*—he preaches *not himself but* CHRIST JESUS *the* LORD, *and himself your servant for* JESUS' *sake.*

III. Thirdly, I am to make some remarks on the motives which should govern, in undertaking the ministerial office.

These, I am fully persuaded, should be purely spiritual in their origin, pressed upon the heart by the well considered conviction, that it is a duty specially required by Almighty GOD, and only in this way to be fulfilled; nothing less than this, it appears to me, can enable a candidate for the ministry to answer the solemn question—" Do you trust that you are inwardly moved by the HOLY GHOST to take upon you this office and ministration ?" with a good conscience. As this however is a point of experience, it must in a great degree be left to the determination of him who alone can read the heart. I say in a great degree, because there are cases in which there can be no difficulty in determining the point both affirmatively and negatively. For instance, where the requisite qualifications of natural or acquired ability are accompanied by known and tried piety ; and such a person professes to be moved by the HOLY GHOST to take upon him the ministerial office ; all the assurance is given that the nature of the case either demands or admits of ; but if either piety or the requisite qualifications of natural or acquired ability be wanting, there is equally satisfactory assurance, that the person thus professing, labours under some delusion of mind, or comes forward to deceive ; because, as without piety the HOLY GHOST cannot be presumed to call any man, so neither is it to be allowed, since miraculous endowments have ceased, that he will call one unqualified : the most that can possibly be conceded to such instances, being, that the call remain unacted upon until suitable qualifications be obtained, by reading and study, to enable him to answer the call.

In subordination to this, as supreme, all other motives good in themselves, and allowable to the Christian ministry—the respect attached to the office in Christian lands, the advantage he may be of to others, the credit, he may humbly hope, he will confer on the cause of religion—these, as they naturally tend to diligence and circumspection, are not to be denied to the ministers of CHRIST, or denounced as inconsistent with the inward motions of the HOLY SPIRIT ; what we have to guard against is, that they be not mistaken or allowed for the first and highest motive of all. Neither are we to consider the necessary accommodations of this life as unlawful, among the subordinate motives which govern our choice of this calling. As GOD hath appointed that they *who preach the gospel should live of the gospel*, they have not only a claim in common with all other professions, to reasonable compensation for their services, but they have this claim sanctioned by divine warrant, and may lawfully require such support as shall free them from worldly care and anxiety, and enable them to apply wholly to their great work. And did Christians duly consider the dignity of the office, its infinite importance to their own comfort, or the credit of religion in general, there would not be such just ground for complaint, and reproach too, as there really is. Nothing marks a cold and declining state of religion more distinctly than indifference and reluctance to the comfortable support of those who minister to their spiritual wants. And if the public estimation in which any liberal profession is held, is justly measured by the remuneration awarded its practice, religion must be placed at the bottom of the scale, perhaps even lower than many merely mechanical callings. And this I speak of religion in general, believing that it is a subject upon which all de-

nominations need edification, and also because it is one on which
individual clergymen feel a delicacy in speaking. But it might
surely be considered that, though clergymen, they are yet men;
that generally, they have families to educate and provide for,
and are cut off from all secular means to enable them to
meet this want. Christian fathers and mothers might find, in
their own anxieties on this near subject, wherewithal to measure
the anxiety of the clergy, and to prompt them to aid in
relieving it.

IV. Fourthly, on the duties involved in this office, both to
ministers and people.

To the public duties of leading the devotions of the congregation, and preaching pure doctrine to the edification of his charge,
the minister of CHRIST owes it to the usefulness of his office, to
devote a part of his time to private communication with his
charge, that he may learn more nearly their spiritual state, and
be better enabled to adapt both his public and private instructions to their immediate wants. But to do this with effect, it is
absolutely necessary, that free and unreserved interchange of
sentiment be established between them; that it be considered a
matter of duty, when the minister makes his appearance, that
the conversation take the serious turn, which belongs to the
occasion, and the object be to impart and to receive some spiritual benefit. It is in these more private interviews that the
advantage derived from the public ministrations is confirmed—
because it is in this way that doubts can be proposed and resolved, points of experience examined, reproof and encouragement
more fitly administered, and any error detected before it become
established into habit.

But however evidently beneficial to both parties, on no point
of duty is there greater difficulty to a clergyman than on this.
His appearance is generally the signal for a dead silence; and
if he prevails to break it by any general remark, so soon as he
leads the subject to his purpose, he has it all to himself—hence
there is neither pleasure nor profit to either, and it soon ceases
to be attended to. This is exactly my own experience, with a
very few exceptions, and I find it pretty much the same throughout. Even in visiting the sick and the dying, there is a strange

VOL. I.—81

reluctance to open up the state of their minds, and, consequently, very great difficulty in suiting our services to their wants. But, my Christian brethren, the loss is yours, the public services of your minister are the least valuable. It is in your families, and in the counsel and admonition of private intercourse, that his knowledge, experience, and spiritual attainments will be most profitable ; and that they be thus profitable, the state of your own hearts must be noticed and borne in mind—the difficulties you meet with in subduing temptation, and the progress you make in the divine life, should be subjects of constant attention ; so that the counsel of an experienced guide, who hath passed through the same exercises, may comfort and strengthen you in your course, and guard you against either the *deceits of your own heart*, or the snares of the enemy of souls. These things in their minuteness and variety cannot enter into the public instruction of the pulpit so as to suit every case, but they can well be attended to in this more private kind of preaching, in which ministers and people, and private Christians among themselves, can be so profitable to each other.

Another duty involved in the office of a Christian minister is, attention to the lambs of the flock, in devoting a part of his time to instructing and catechising the children. But in this also, unless he is assisted by the parents, but little can be done ; yet nothing of greater importance to religion, to society, to the Church, to time, and to eternity, can be mentioned. Unless the the foundation be laid in early life, small is the hope that the influence of religion will be the ornament of mature age—unless the good seed of the kingdom be sown in the heart, before the thorns and the briers of the world have taken hold of its affections, the expectation is vain, ordinarily speaking, that the fruit will be unto holiness. It may indeed be, but let it never be forgotten, that what may be may also not be, and that our best security for the event is, to follow as near as possible, the directions of divine wisdom—*Train up a child in the way he should go, and when he is old he will not depart from it.*

These, with the additional duties of visiting the sick, and administering consolation to the afflicted ; of watching the bed of death, and pointing the departing soul to CHRIST JESUS the

LORD; with the labour of study and preparation, and the paramount duty of personal religion——for ministers of religion have their own souls to save, as well as the souls of those who hear them——show what a laborious, and anxious, and arduous, and deeply responsible calling is the office of a minister of CHRIST; and this faint delineation of its duties, may serve to convince Christians how much depends upon them for the comfort and usefulness of their pastors. It is a joint interest, my brethren—— an interest which oversteps the boundary of time——an interest which will flourish or fade in your descendants, according to the pains now bestowed upon it; and will reward your diligence or punish your neglect by an eternal re-union with those now so dear to you, in everlasting blessedness or endless misery.

V. I come now to conclude with a short application of the subject.

To you, my brethren, who are about to assume the full responsibility of this sacred office, all I have said, has long, I trust, been familiar. But as it is safe, as it is profitable to be reminded, on such deeply accountable duty, carry along with you into this undertaking, a higher impression than I have been able to express of its infinite importance to yourselves and others. If the consequences were limited to the present life only——well might caution exert itself in solemn warning and direction. But when they extend into eternity, when no calculation can limit the thousands, whose everlasting condition may take its unchangeable colour from the faithfulness or the negligence with which the trust this day committed to you is fulfilled, language is exhausted of expression, and the heart only can be appealed to, in those unutterable workings of the deep and realizing sense of the account to be given to GOD for souls, redeemed at the priceless ransom of the blood of his only begotten Son. Well did St. Paul say, *Who is sufficient for these things?* And well did he say, *Necessity is laid upon me, yea, woe is me, if I preach not the gospel.* For who that could refuse it with a good conscience, would undertake this pre-eminence of toil and labour, and privation and responsibility? O it is a solemn trust, and, but for the constraining power of *the love of* CHRIST, could be undertaken by none. Yet the same blessed apostle hath told us,

Our sufficiency is of GOD——*My grace is sufficient for thee,* says CHRIST JESUS the LORD, to all his faithful ministers and members. To that grace then I remit you, my brethren, with this exhortation, DETERMINE TO KNOW NOTHING BUT JESUS CHRIST, AND HIM CRUCIFIED——PREACH CHRIST THE WISDOM OF GOD AND THE POWER OF GOD TO EVERY ONE THAT BELIEVETH—— UNFURL THE BANNER OF THE CROSS, AND, POINTING TO HIM WHO WAS LIFTED UP UPON IT, PROCLAIM HIM A PRINCE AND A SAVIOUR, EXALTED TO GIVE REPENTANCE AND REMISSION OF SINS TO HIS PEOPLE——PROCLAIM HIM AS THE ONLY NAME UNDER HEAVEN GIVEN, WHEREBY WE MAY BE SAVED, AND AS ABLE TO SAVE TO THE UTTERMOST ALL WHO COME UNTO GOD BY HIM.

And may he who is head over all things to his Church, look with favour on our work, and add that blessing which shall cause it to redound to his glory, the good of his Church, the safety, honour, and welfare of his people, in the increase of pure and undefiled religion in this congregation.

Now unto GOD the Father, &c.

SERMON XIV.

CONSECRATION.

PSALM, xciii. 5, (last clause.)

"Holiness becometh thine house, O LORD, for ever."

WE are not as much aware as we should be, my brethren and hearers, of the importance of applying to the words of any author, that meaning in which they were used by him—nor are we generally aware how much a change in the original meaning of a particular word will affect the belief and the practice of the system to which it belongs. It is a matter of experience also, that in the course of time, words do change, and sometimes even lose their original signification, and that great confusion of mind, as well as very serious difficulty in arriving at truth, grows out of this cause.

This is true of all sciences. They have each particular or leading words, to which a fixed and appropriate meaning is attached, and which can only be correctly understood, and advantageously applied, as that particular meaning is continued in use. But it is more especially true of religion, and is proportionally important as that science excels all others in the magnitude of its discoveries, and in the excellency of its knowledge.

This may be made more familiar to you, my hearers, by an example. The words regeneration and conversion, are used in the Scripture to express two things, as different from each other as cause and effect. Yet it has come to pass, that in popular acceptation, the word regeneration is applied, and almost exclusively, to what was originally expressed by the word conversion. Hence, also, it has come to pass, that Christians generally, have nearly lost sight both of the idea and of the thing intended in Scripture by the word regeneration; while nothing of force or of elucidation has thereby been added to the idea or to the thing intended in Scripture, by the word conversion. On the contrary, both confusion of mind, as to the two doctrines, and injury to religion, as a reasonable and practical service, has been the consequence, as is known to all who, without explanation, have witnessed the administration of baptism according to the primitive method which is pursued in the Episcopal Church.   When the minister pronounces the child which has just been baptized, regenerate, and calls upon the congregation to give thanks to Almighty GOD, that it hath pleased him to regenerate this infant with his HOLY SPIRIT, persons who are not aware of the distinction between the two words are bewildered, while the more ignorant and conceited are prepared to sneer and scoff at the notion of an infant being converted.

Thus one vital and fundamental doctrine of CHRIST's religion is thrown entirely out of sight ; another, no less essential, is embarrassed with a difficulty which cannot be surmounted, and a holy sacrament, instituted by CHRIST himself, is lowered in estimation, and degraded in the use.   Yet, my Christian hearers, while the word of CHRIST stands, the sacrament of baptism will be the only sign and seal of our regeneration to GOD.   While common sense stands, spiritually dead creatures, such as fallen but redeemed men must, in some way and at some time, be restored to spiritual capacity, before it can be reasonable either to require them to lead religious lives, to exhort those who do not, to repentance, or possibly to produce their conversion. Regeneration, as originally understood, being the root of all religious capacity and obligation in redeemed man, must be previous in point of time, and independent of any qualification in man, but the necessity arising from original sin ; whereas, conversion in its original and proper meaning, being the actual change of heart and life in the wilful sinner, must be subsequent not only to regeneration but to sin actually committed, and must be preceded by conviction of and sorrow for his sins, as offences against GOD, and be followed by a new life.

Infants, as such, may be and are regenerated by the HOLY SPIRIT ; practical sinners only, previously regenerated, can and must be converted.   Repentance and faith are not necessary to regeneration ; to conversion they are indispensable.

Something of the same kind has taken place as to the meaning of many other leading words in the Christian system of faith and practice, amongst which the leading word in my text, holiness, is one ; and requires to be noticed, not only on account of its connexion with the solemn ceremony which you have this day witnessed, but also for general edification. The original and proper meaning of the word holiness, in Scripture, when spoken of men, invariably includes their separation to God, by the external appointments of religion, as well as the moral effect of the means of grace exhibited in the deportment of the life. Whereas the modern notion of holiness is applied altogether to the latter or moral effect, without any regard being had to whether the means of grace appointed by Almighty God, have been duly used, or altogether neglected. In the following discourse, therefore, I shall

First, explain the word holiness ; and, .

Secondly, apply it to the various relations in which it is connected with religious condition.

Holiness becometh thine house, O Lord, for ever.

I. First to explain the word holiness.

This word, as used in the Scriptures, hath both an absolute and a relative signification. In the absolute and unqualified sense it belongs and is applied exclusively to Almighty God, who is essentially and underivedly pure, holy, and perfect beyond the comprehension of any created intelligence. In the relative or derived sense, the word holiness is applied to angels and men, to things inanimate, and even to places, as is instanced in my text.

In this relative signification, and as applied to our condition, my hearers, the word holiness denotes—First, Separation to God, by his calling and appointment, evidenced by some external mark or religious rite by him appointed, to denote the condition. By this external separation individual persons, nations, things, and places, become, in a peculiar manner, the property of Almighty God, who is accordingly said to sanctify them to and for himself. Thus the prophet Jeremiah and John the baptist were sanctified from the womb, to their respective offices. Thus the nation of the Jews was separated from the rest of the world by the calling of God, and made holy to the Lord by the rite of circumcision ; and all Christian nations, by obeying the call of the gospel, and receiving the ordinance of baptism, are sanctified to God as his peculiar people.　　Thus the tabernacle and the temple, their furniture and implements for the daily sacrifice, with the priests and Levites who ministered therein, under the Old Testament dispensation, were holy to the Lord ; and the Christian Church, with its buildings, its worship, its sacraments, and its ministry, under the New Testament dispensation, are sanctified and set apart to their respective uses, in the appointed service of Almighty God.　　This is sometimes called a legal holiness, and as such undervalued, and even by some derided ; but not with understanding.　　For while religion shall continue to be the duty of redeemed man, the holiness which is derived from the express appointment and institution of the author and finisher of our faith, must lie at the root of all rational comfort from its public ministrations, of all reasonable expectation of growth in grace, and of any good hope of its promised reward.

II.　Secondly—The word holiness, as applied to moral beings, denotes separation from the love and practice of sin ; union with God through Christ, by the renewal of the Holy Ghost ; and conformity to the nature and will of God, in the conduct of the life.　　This is the holiness which it is the declared purpose of religion to produce and extend in a sinful world ; for the furtherance of which all its institutions, appointments, and ordinances are devised and adapted to the restored competency of moral beings, by the wisdom of God ; to the attainment of which all Christians pledge themselves, and without which divine truth assures them, there is no salvation.

Now my dear friends, as no man can sanctify himself in either meaning of the word, holiness ; as it is the office of the Holy Ghost to prescribe the means, to provide the instruments, and to give effect to the work of grace, by renewing the heart, and maintaining the soul in holiness ; it must be a most dangerous error, to expect the end, either without the means which God hath prescribed, or with a part of them only, or in the use of other means, or of the means unlawfully administered. Yet to all this, the common notion and use of the word holiness, most certainly tends ; as it is evident, from the disregard, and even neglect of the sacraments in general, and from the indifference with which the ministerial commission, or authority to administer them, is regarded by the majority of professing Christians amongst us. Yet while the world continues, must it ever be a previous question, my brethren, with every serious person—am I in covenant with GOD? The answer to which, can no otherwise be obtained than from actual conformity with those requirements, both external and internal, both legal and moral, which GOD hath instituted, to give certainty and assurance to his people, on this cardinal point. And while GOD shall continue holy and unchangeable, all excusable mistake is provided against, in the clear delineation given us in the scriptures of what holiness consists in, and in the solemn declaration that without it, *no man shall see the* LORD.

I come in the next place, to apply the word, thus explained, to the various relations in which it is connected with religious condition.

I. And first to the people of GOD. Holiness becometh them.

All men are the creatures of GOD ; but all men are not the people of GOD, in the scriptural meaning of that expression. This is a distinction which Almighty GOD confers, according to the good pleasure of his own will, as is manifest by the present condition of the world, by far the greater part of which is yet under the dominion of darkness, alike ignorant of GOD, and of his revealed mercies in CHRIST JESUS.

Who then are to be considered as the people of GOD ? To this the scriptures teach us to answer—first, those whom GOD hath called to the knowledge of his grace by the gospel, are thereby, and therefore, designated as his people. This is the most usual sense in which the expression, the people of GOD, is applied in the scriptures. Secondly, in a more scriptural sense, the people of GOD are those, who, out of the body of this community, make a profession of religion, and conform to its laws and regulations. These, with their children, form, properly speaking, the visible Church of CHRIST. But, as under the Old Testament dispensation, *they were not all Israel which were of Israel ;* therefore, under the gospel in like manner, the people of God, are, thirdly, and in the highest sense, those who are truly what they profess to be, by a real intrinsic sanctity of heart and deportment.

But though this difference of character has always been found among the people of God, it has never deprived them of their denomination. On the contrary, it is the standing argument of the prophets under the law, and of the apostles under the gospel, to exhort and encourage them to faithfulness and diligence in working out their everlasting salvation. Tares are indeed sown among the wheat, and they must grow together until the harvest, when the Omnipotent Judge will himself make the just and final separation.

This is the view which the Scriptures give us of this appellation, the people of God. All nations, therefore, where the gospel is received, and the religion it teaches acknowledged and established, among which, praised be God, we are numbered, are entitled to this high distinction ; nor is there any escape from the obligations and duties annexed to this privilege, but with the eternal perdition of our immortal souls. It is not in your choice, my hearers, whether you will be the people of God. But it is in your choice, as moral beings, whether you will profit by this distinction of the providence of your heavenly Father, to attain eternal life, or increase your *condemnation,* by casting away from you the rich mercies of redemption, purchased by the blood of Christ.

Now what becomes a people thus favoured? What return should all be engaged in making to him who hath thus preferred them to millions of his creatures, in themselves equally deserving? Is not every tongue ready to answer, holiness, *in the* fullest sense of the word, becometh such a people. Yes, my hearers; reason and conscience both unite in confirming this to be the duty, the first and highest duty, of every soul, under the grace of the gospel. As God hath separated you from the world that lieth in wickedness, and given you the light of life in his holy word, it is your part to come to the light, and to separate yourselves to his service, by denying ungodliness and worldly lusts. As he hath furnished you with the means of grace, in the word and sacraments, in the privilege of prayer, both public and private, in the clear declaration of his will, and in the glorious hope of eternal life, through the merits and death of his only begotten Son, no duty can be so urgent as that of informing yourselves of the will of GOD, and setting yourselves earnestly to perform it: nor can a stronger argument be devised to enforce this upon rational beings, than to set before them the high privileges conferred upon them in this distinction, and the strong assurance thence to be derived, that if they are but faithful to their own best interest, the victory that confers immortal glory will be attained. For what higher evidence can be given to any people, that GOD *hath not appointed them to wrath, but to obtain salvation by our* LORD JESUS CHRIST, than thus calling them to be his people, and furnishing them with the means of salvation? What higher or more affecting motive can be presented to the sinner, yea, even to the chief of sinners, to break off his sins by repentance, and his iniquities by righteousness, than the manifestation of the love of GOD in the gift of JESUS CHRIST, *that whosoever believeth in him should not perish, but have everlasting life.*

And who is there now before me, who knows not of this precious gift? And do you not know it exclusively because you are the people of GOD? Have those who are not his people—the Heathen, for instance—have they the knowledge of this surpassing favour, have they any revelation to direct them how to come to GOD? Have they any prescribed means of grace to prepare them for eternal life in his kingdom? No. They have not the knowledge of his ways, they have not the bright and blessed hope which shines upon Christian lands. Awake, then, my hearers, to that holiness which becometh a people thus favoured. Awake to that separation of yourselves from the world and its wickedness, from the flesh and its lusts, from sin and all its deceits, which is the first step to the holiness to which you are called. Awake to the hope which the gospel sets before every one of you, and purify yourselves, even as He who hath purchased it for you is pure. Set about it without delay, as a thing possible, indispensable, and without which you are lost for ever.

God hath called you to holiness, and furnished you to become holy, not only by external separation from the viciousness of sin, but by real and intrinsic transformation of the soul. But my dear friends, this is to be sought for as the one thing needful, by having recourse to the means of grace, in the holy word, in prayer, in the duties of the holy Sabbath, in the sacraments of the Church, and in forsaking all sin. These evidences on your part, of a sincere desire to obey and please him, God hath promised to bless, and to make effectual to you by the operation of the HOLY GHOST, who is the SPIRIT of holiness, the Giver of all spiritual grace, and the author of everlasting life. Awake, then, my dear hearers, to the high privileges to which you are called as the people of God. Burst the bonds which sin hath coiled around you, and in the strength of God's blessed invitation, come to JESUS, that merciful Saviour, who hath also promised, *Him that cometh to me I will in no wise cast out.*

II. Secondly, to the ministers of God—holiness becometh them.

All Christians are the servants of God, but all Christians are not the ministers of God. The holiness which becometh, or is required of them, therefore, must partake of this distinction, and be measured by the nature and purpose of their office.

As the ministerial office, then, relates solely to spiritual things, and is instituted to dispense the *mysteries of religion,* to the comfort and edification of the body of CHRIST, we are accordingly instructed, that *no man taketh this honour unto himself, but he that is called of God, as was Aaron.* And as the ministry of the word and sacraments of religion is for the benefit of third persons, and a representative office, all reasonable assurance should be had, that the ministrations from which Christians derive the comforts and the hopes of the gospel, are performed by the authority of CHRIST. Hence the holiness which becometh the ministers of religion, consists, First, in being inwardly moved and called by the HOLY GHOST to the office ; and, also, in being duly and really commissioned by those who have lawful and verifiable authority from CHRIST thereto. Without both of these qualifications, the holiness of a minister of CHRIST is imperfect, either as respects God, or as respects the people of GOD, and consequently is not such as becometh the high concerns he is entrusted with, and the mighty interests dependent on their being authoritatively performed. In this respect the Church of CHRIST as a visible society is governed by the same principles which prevail in every other society, and the same reasoning must be applied to it.

A man may be every way qualified for the office of a magistrate, and truly desirous to benefit the community by his services ; but it his commission only that makes his judicial acts either of force or value to those amongst whom he officiates. If then he is not commissioned at all, yet undertakes to act on the impulse of his strong desire to do good ; or is commissioned by those who have no authority thereto—in either case, as the state is not a party to his acts, however wise and beneficial, it is not bound by them, either legally or morally, and they are consequently of no worth, as a dependence for those whose interests are at stake. In like manner of a minister of religion ; and were men as watchful and earnest in their spiritual as in their temporal concerns there would not be the cause to fear that there now is, for the awful insecurity in which the religious hope of thousands is placed by the indifference manifested to this branch of ministerial holiness.

The holiness which becometh the ministers of religion consists, in the next place, in their being truly spiritual-minded men, filled with the love of CHRIST, devoted to the service of GOD, and faithfully engaged in the great work of turning sinners from darkness to light, and in preparing the souls committed to their charge for eternal glory. This is the great work to which the ministers of CHRIST are called, and for which, they must be furnished with all those qualifications which an experimental knowledge of divine things, and a diligent study of the learning immediately connected with revealed religion, can confer upon them. Without these, they will be either insufficient or unsafe instructors of others, and liable to be deluded, and drawn aside into some specious error, under the pretence of improvement or reform.

The minister of CHRIST is to be an instructor of righteousness, and an ensample of what he teaches, to his flock. His holiness, therefore, must be such as the flock can observe and imitate. It is not in the pulpit only, that he is to manifest his separation from the world; but in his daily deportment and in his more private conversation he is to show that holiness to the LORD is inscribed on himself, on his family, and on all his occupations. *Be ye followers of me, even as I also am of* CHRIST, was the challenge of St. Paul to the Corinthians; and happy that minister of CHRIST who with equal fidelity strives to be able to speak the same language to his charge—and happy that flock who are favoured with a pastor who thus unites a holy calling, a true commission, a cultivated understanding, and a godly conversation.

III. Thirdly, To the house of GOD, *Holiness becometh thine house, O* LORD, *forever.*

As GOD is infinitely removed from all impurity and pollution, whatever is appropriated to his service requires to be separated from all common and profane uses. The houses, therefore, in which the public offices of religion are to be performed, where Christians are to meet to present their united prayers and praises to their common Father, and where the holy sacraments are to be administered, should have some mark to distinguish them from common buildings, and appropriate to the holy uses to which they are applied. Now this mark can in no way so well be given them as by a solemn dedication unto GOD, and a public separation of them from all other and common uses, for ever thereafter, as his especial property. This you have seen performed to-day, after the manner and form prescribed by the Episcopal Church; and by this we have conferred upon this building, that relative holiness which becometh the place where GOD hath put his name, and promised to meet his people.

GOD, indeed, *dwelleth not in temples made with hands,* yet as the public exercises of religion require suitable accomodations, it hath been the grateful duty of Christians, in every period of the Church, to provide such as were answerable to their ability, and to dedicate them solemnly, and exclusively, to the service of GOD. And in doing this, they consulted not only their duty, but their interest; for surely, a more reverend and religious feeling must be impressed upon the heart on entering a convenient and suitable building thus consecrated to holy uses, than on entering those miserable hovels, which through the week are the receptacles of brute animals, and on the LORD's day are too dark and dirty to afford comfort to human beings.

It is said, and truly said, my hearers, that the religious character of a people may be safely estimated by the appearance of the houses provided for public worship among them. A truly pious people, who are alive to GOD, and to the great things he hath done for them, will not be content to dwell in houses of cedar, while the ark of GOD abideth under curtains only ; and much has yet to be done e'er this reproach is wiped away from our land. Let us hope, however, that the delusion which expects the abiding blessing of GOD upon a people where his name and worship are not honoured with those requisites which his holy service demands, is passing away, that a better mind is beginning to manifest itself, and that Scripture, and reason derived from Scripture, will at length triumph over the corruptions which erroneous views of religious truth have engendered ; and that the good example given in the erection and consecration of this building, will rouse the dormant spirit of reverence for GOD, of concern for the souls of their fellow creatures, and stir up the hearts of others, to go and do likewise. It is a charity of the highest order, and of the most lasting nature—a good work in the best acceptation of the term, and to be surpassed only by that zeal for the glory of GOD which shall provide for the regular performance of those holy offices to which it is now set apart. HOLINESS BECOMETH THINE HOUSE, O LORD, FOR EVER.

May this truth be impressed upon every heart, in the full meaning of the expression ; and a holy people, a holy ministry, and a holy house, in the true Scripture sense of separation and Godliness conjoined, be speedily raised up in every destitute portion of our Zion, prepared to sanctify and adorn that holy day, which GOD hath given us as his peculiar people; and may they ever be found here united, to the glory and praise of his holy name, and to the increase of his kingdom of righteousness, peace, and joy in the HOLY GHOST.

Now, to GOD the Father, GOD the Son, and GOD the HOLY GHOST, be, &c. &c.

SERMON XV.

THE OLD PATHS:—A CONSECRATION SERMON PREACHED IN VIRGINIA AND NORTH-CAROLINA.

JEREMIAH vi. 16.

" Thus saith the LORD, stand ye in the ways and see, and ask for the old paths, where is the good way, and walk therein, and ye shall find rest to your souls."*

IN selecting this passage of Scripture for the edification of the day, I am actuated, my brethren, with an earnest desire for your establishment in the right ways of the LORD ; and I think that its plain application to the present religious condition of the country will enable me to make such an improvement of it as shall tend to confirm you in the good way, and be profitable also to all others who are disposed to weigh truth and reason in the balances of the sanctuary, rather than in the scales of prejudice and passion.

A short view of the circumstances under which the exhortation in my text was delivered, will enable us the better to appre-

---

* Amongst the manuscripts of the Bishop, there were found two sermons upon this text, both having his mark of assent to their publication. The first appears to have been composed in 1822, and to have been preached at the opening of Mount Laurel Church, Halifax County, Va. The second sermon is substantially the same with the first, being evidently a transcript from it, and was preached at Warrenton, N. C. in 1824, and afterwards at several other places. The sermons being the same as to division, course of argument, style of illustration, and almost the whole of the phraseology, it was deemed expedient to print only the last. How they could have escaped the notice of the lamented author; or why, if he knowingly left them both in the parcel of sermons designed for publication, he should not have placed upon them some discriminating mark to show which had his preference, or have declared, if he wished a collation of the two, in order to give the very few passages in which they differ, cannot now be explained. Possibly the manuscripts were revised at different intervals during his sickness, and the fact that one had received his "imprimatur" (for upon all the manuscripts revised by him and designed for publication, was written in his own hand "imprimatur, J. S. R.") escaped his memory, when he examined the last. The most recent, and that which had been most frequently preached, is the one here presented to the reader, in conformity with what in all probability would have been the author's decision.

hend the nature and necessity of the awakening appeal herein made by the Almighty to his people, and through them to the Christian world.

Nothing could be more convincing and satisfactory than those evidences on which the nation of the Jews received and held their religion in all its appointments, as the express and positive direction of the wisdom of GOD ; neither is any thing more clear than that, notwithstanding this certainty, they had forsaken the *fountain of living waters,* and in the pride and vanity of their minds, *had hewed out to themselves cisterns, but they were broken cisterns, which could hold no water.* By this figure, the prophet would denote to us their departure from the law and the testimony —their abandoning the prescribed service of the sanctuary, and those means of grace in that form of worship to which the blessing was expressly limited. Tired, we may suppose, of the uniformity, the sameness of their mode of worship, and vainly thinking to amend and improve what Jehovah himself had minutely enacted, and commanded to be observed, the charm of novelty gave strength to the spirit of innovation, until confusion and every evil work abounded, and corruption filled up its measure in the idolatrous worship of the work of their own hands— *Saying to a stock, thou art my father, and to a stone, thou hast brought me forth.* Even the ministry became corrupt. *The prophets prophesied falsely, and the people loved to have it so. The priests said not, where is the* LORD ! *The pastors also transgressed against me, and the prophets prophesied by Baal, and walked after things which do not profit.*

Yet there is a place of repentance for nations as well as individuals, my hearers. In this extremity GOD remembered his mercy and truth to Israel, and sent his servant Jeremiah to show them their folly and wickedness, to warn them of their danger, and to call them back to that appointed duty and service *which was given to Jacob for a law, and to Israel for a testimony. Thus saith the* LORD, *stand ye in the ways and see, and ask for the old paths, where is the good way, and walk therein, and ye shall find rest to your souls.* The point pressed upon their attention in this message, was consideration, comparison of their state with the standard of GOD's word, with the spirit and letter of their institutions from him, and according thereto, to return to that from which they were departed, as the only safe ground of comfort and assurance ; and as the same principle applies equally to us under the gospel, a similar examination, comparison and agreement with its requirements, is the only true source of peace to our souls.

In discoursing on these words, therefore, on this occasion, I shall, in the

FIRST place, take a view of the present state of religion among us.

SECONDLY, I shall inquire into, and endeavour to point out, the causes of that decline in the profession and practice of Christianity, which must be obvious to all ; and,

CONCLUDE with an application of the subject.

I. First, As to the present state of religion among us.

As it will necessarily be helpful to our understanding the subject properly, to settle some definite meaning of the word religion, I shall preface what I have to say on these heads of discourse with this inquiry. Indeed, so many and so various are the notions now entertained, both of the word and of the thing, that its original meaning is nearly sunk into obscurity, and there are numbers of Christians who have never asked themselves the meaning either of the word or the thing which they profess.

The word religion, in its highest sense, *means the moral quality* of conformity to the divine nature in the dispositions and desires of the heart ; the life of GOD in the soul of man, communicated through the grace of the gospel. In a lower sense, it means that method which GOD himself has appointed for the attainment of this great end in sinful mortals. In this practical definition of the word, we are furnished with a *safe standard* to which to bring every religious notion, by which to try all religious conduct. The right or the wrong in doctrine and practice, is not made to depend on the fallible and varying ground of human opinion, but is bounded and determined by the unerring wisdom and unchangeable nature of revealed truth. And to us in particular, who are blessed with the clear light of revelation, is this standard given, to which, as to a light shining in a dark place, we would do well to take heed. To this light must

I bring the examination before me, and by this, my brethren and hearers, must you not only examine yourselves now, but be examined and judged too in the great day of eternity.

In a concern of such infinite importance as the salvation of our immortal souls, it is reasonable I think to presume, that where all are provided with the means, all would be earnestly engaged in the attainment of the end.

Now, my hearers, is it thus with us, either collectively or individually? Is the public countenance given to the gospel, such as denominates us a Christian nation, or is it that of mere acknowledgment and sufferance? Is the way the truth and the life as it is in JESUS, the strait and the narrow way that leadeth unto life for this people, as much regarded and cared for as the way to market? Alas, my friends, we do not barely suffer and tolerate what we esteem and love, we do not usually neglect what we consider necessary and profitable. And the power being in the hands of the people, the character of all public acts, whether positive or negative, must be referred to them, and taken as indicating their special intention. May GOD then be merciful to us as a nation, for if heaven were to search our public records I know not where the proofs would be found of our regard for the Redeemer's kingdom. I know not what more could be produced than jealousy of a hurtful, or permission of a harmless thing.

But while I thus unburden my conscience in the performance of my duty towards your souls, I am not required to expose myself either to misapprehension or misrepresentation, more especially as from my official station, the reproach would extend beyond myself. Let no man therefore draw from this honest exposure of public neglect on the dearest interest of man, the unfounded inference that I am an advocate for a public establishment of religion, in some of its many forms, and preferably, in that which I myself profess, for it is unwarranted, either from the words I have used, or from the fact, as declared with sincerity and solemnity. No, my friends, far, for ever distant from my heart, my head, and my hands, and from the hearts, and heads, and hands of those who think with me in religion, be the unscriptural and injurious desire and design of

an establishment of the Church by the State.   For ever removed from us, be the base suggestion of throwing a political
disqualification over any shade of Christian opinion, and thereby enticing men to become hypocrites.   No, my brethren, *the
weapons of our warfare are not carnal but spiritual.*   Force, of
any kind, is unknown to religion, is indeed impossible, in its application to any thing moral and spiritual, and wherever attempted has proved injurious.   No, my hearers, I would not meet
the wildest fanatic among us, with an arm of power in any shape,
but with the sword of the SPIRIT, the weapons of reason, *the
armour of righteousness, on the right hand and on the left.* These
the wisdom of GOD hath provided for the support and defence
of his cause in the world, and no other do I wish to wield ;
they are mighty through GOD, to the putting down the strong
holds both of sin and error, and must prevail.

But it does not follow, that because an establishment is injurious, and renounced, Christian states are under no obligation,
and have no other means compatible with religious freedom to
provide for the religious instruction of the people, and thus
manifest public regard for the gospel—for it is not so.   It is
amply within their reach—and I for one think it their first duty,
even in a political view ; but the plan is no part of this days
work.

Let us next inquire into our religious condition as *individuals,*
whether public neglect is compensated by the personal regard
manifested for the gospel.

To this, there is unhappily an answer before me in this congregation which is awfully conclusive.   What proportion of
those now present are known to any profession of religion ?
How many are able to rise up and say, *I have sought the LORD
and he heard me,* I have obtained a good hope through grace.
O that I were put to silence by a general burst from every
heart, *I know that my Redeemer liveth,* for I have experienced
the power of his resurrection.

But this may be a singular case—how stands it then at large ?
What are the prevailing pursuits of all classes among us ? Do
they savour of heaven or of earth, of GOD or of Mammon ? Let
the profanation of the Sabbath, in every possible way, bear wit-

ness—let the neglect of the public worship of GOD bear witness —let the absence, in many neighbourhoods, of all provision for that worship, and for religious instruction bear witness—let the general abandonment of family religion, and the consequent ignorance of GOD, and of his saving mercy, in which young people now grow up, bear witness—and let its decline in the families of professing Christians, bear witness. Need we be surprised, my brethren, at the growth of profaneness, intemperance, and covetousness—at the prevalence of the world and the flesh—at the unfeeling rapacity with which the unfortunate and necessitous are ground to powder, on the nether millstone of a human heart, untouched by the influence of religion ? No indeed, such are its proper but bitter fruits. *Men do not gather grapes from thorns, nor figs from thistles.* Neither ought we, my friends, to expect religion to bear sway over the conduct of those who are brought up without religious instruction and example. Alas, we too often see it yield, and give way to these temptations, in those who profess its power.

If such, then, are the miserable effects of the neglect of the gospel, if such is the dangerous precipice to which the road we have followed has brought us, shall we persevere and leap over into perdition ? or shall we hear the words of my text, as those of a friend in extremity, and stop short, and stand in the ways and see if there be not a better, and inquire out that good way in which only there is rest for our souls ? As a nation, GOD hath done great things for us, and not the least in causing the light of the glorious gospel to shine unto us. As individuals, he hath done us good, and not evil, all the days of our life. Stand forth the man with whom GOD hath not dealt more mercifully than his own conscience tells him he might most justly have done ; and let the hard heart melt to penitence under the goodness of GOD our Saviour. Let us not renew the sin of Israel, my brethren and friends, and have it said of us as of them, *Hear O heavens, and give ear O earth, for the* LORD *hath spoken—I have nourished and brought up children and they have rebelled against me. The ox knoweth his owner, and the ass his master's crib ; but Israel doth not know, my people doth not consider.*

II. Secondly, I am to inquire into, and endeavour to point

out the causes of that decline in the profession and practice of religion, which must be obvious to all.

On this head of my discourse, it might perhaps be sufficient to assume the general principle of unbelief, as in itself productive of all the vice and immorality that can be imagined ; because where the sense of accountability is dismissed, or smothered up, where this life is practically the boundary of our expectations, and the object of our exertions, its profits and its pleasures become the GOD whom we worship ; its applause or its reproach the object of our hopes and of our fears, and its enjoyments and gratifications, the reward which we covet.

But even unbelief itself, though the natural fruit of the carnal mind, is matured and ripened into infidelity, by causes acting from without, and even by causes operating by intention for its removal.   For as faith cometh by hearing, so likewise doth infidelity find nourishment, both by hearing and by refusing to hear.   By ascertaining those causes then, and by making some fair and reasonable estimate of their influence on the human mind, we shall so meet this inquiry, as to find a remedy against it.

The First, and that to which all the others may, in a good degree be referred, is the neglect on the part of the government of any and all provision for public instruction in religion ; and whether we consider this as the result of *design,* or rather as the unfortunate consequence of a combination of fortuitous circumstances, whose bearing was new, and could not be calculated, the effect is nevertheless the same.   Example will descend, whether in governments or in individuals.

That a country professing Christianity, all whose institutions are bottomed on its divine original, should thus lose sight *of an* object of such vital importance, is an anomaly without a parallel.   That on the issue of a plausible but untried theory, should be staked all that can encourage virtue and repress vice—all that can give to hope its encouragement, and to fear its effect, the very basis of governing power, and required submission in civil society, was an experiment hazardous in the extreme, and will, I fear, be found injurious in the issue, and destructive of that form of government in whose favour it was made.   It seems not to have been considered, that to fallen man religion is a forced state, not the natural production of the soil; and although enforced by the most tremendous sanctions which can be applied to intelligent beings, yet without careful instruction and diligent cultivation, it cannot even exist, much less grow and flourish. And that the effect has been deleterious, and is increasing in its evil influence, must be acknowledged by all who have eyes to see, and ears to hear, the immorality and profaneness of high and low, rich and poor. In the fact, my friends, there can be no mistake, whatever there may be thought to be, in the cause to which it is here in part ascribed ; and it is surely deserving the attention of all classes, in what way an evil of so great magnitude, and which threatens to sweep before it all that is dear and valuable in social life may be arrested, and the miseries which must follow, both in time and in eternity, be averted.

The external appearance of a people may be fair and flourishing my brethren, every thing may smile upon them, and their comparative condition be the theme of exultation to them, and of desire to others ; yet if the fear of GOD is not cultivated, if his worship, both public and private, is neglected, if the mass of the community sit loose, to the claims of the gospel upon a Christian people, and the influence of religion is owned and felt, but by here one, and there another, there is a worm at the root of this flourishing tree, which will blast its greenness, blight its blossoms, wither its fruit, and in the end lay it low and leafless on the ground. If we would avert this ruin then, if we would say to our country, be thou perpetual ; if we would leave to our children the fair and fruitful, and free and peaceful inheritance our fathers left us, we must turn and ask for the old paths, for the good way of GOD's holy fear, reverence of his sacred name, encouragement of his commanded worship, and trust in his redeeming love. Then will the banner of his Almighty protection be over us; we shall find rest here from the turmoils and confusions of an agitated world, and rest to our souls forever, in the security and safety of that kingdom which shall know no end.

A second cause, to which I would ascribe the decline of

religion among us, is the divisions among those who profess and call themselves by the Christian name.

This, though an evil unavoidable in the present condition of man, and pronounced such by the author of our religion himself, is nevertheless not therefore excusable in those who divide. *Woe unto the world because of offences. It must needs be that offences come ; but woe unto that man by whom the offence cometh.* That the word offence here used by our LORD, means stumbling block, something that perverts from the truth, an occasion of difference and division in religion, is plain from the context. Indeed this is the true meaning of the word throughout the New Testament. It therefore presents an awful lesson to all beginners of new systems in religion, and in proportion *to all* who are induced to follow them.

By divisions in religion, its unity is broken, its evidences weakened, its effects counteracted. This was well known to the author and finisher of our faith, and therefore so expressly denounced. It was also well known to the enemy of GOD and man, and therefore so perseveringly prompted by every temptation which could lead to such an end, not only through the more sinful passions of our nature, but even through piety itself. Unity being the indelible nature of divine truth, it is utterly impossible that it should be such, either in variation from or opposition to itself. And as it is divine truth to us, only *by or through* the authority of GOD for its announcement, whatever separates or divides it from this, defeats its character of unity, weakens the evidence of its claim, and destroys its influence, not perhaps as truth, but as divine truth ; truth in which our souls are concerned.

That this is the effect produced in the present day, is witnessed to us, not only by the serious confession of many, that it operates against the reality of religion in their minds, in such wise as to paralyze all its other proofs, but also, by producing such confusion of mind, as to which of the many divisions is the true kingdom of the Saviour, that the investigation is abandoned in despair, and thereafter, with all its mighty realities, committed to chance. And this I am persuaded would prove to be the fact, with nine out of ten of those, who take no concern with the gospel, were they seriously asked, and would as seriously answer, why they remain, either opposed or indifferent, to so lively a hope as is therein given to man. Sin, though the element of fallen man, is yet a troublesome companion, my friends, at the first. Conscience will speak, and, if not listened to, must be silenced in some way, and what readier, or more generally attempted way, than to get clear, some how, of GOD's revelation against it ; and what more convenient a resort than the disagreement of Christians, as an argument against religion ?

There is another mode, however, in which the divisions among Christians operate to the decline of religion in the world, and this, under the specious pretence of advancing its interests.

Well disposed men, seeing many pious and estimable persons of every denomination, have hastily concluded, that there was no difference, but in the mere name ; others again have gone so far as to insist, in the very teeth of scripture, that a variety in religious belief was just as pleasing to GOD, and as much his design, as the other varieties visible in his works. Hence the modern doctrine of liberality as to opinions, and modes of faith ; and hence, as a natural consequence, total indifference to religion in any shape ; for I believe the fact is without contradiction, that these holders of liberal opinions always stand aloof from religion, in any tangible shape. Nor can it well be otherwise. The man who can think all right, in the sense of being true, in the mass of discordant religious opinion professed in the world, cannot possibly respect any particular one, so much, as really to embrace it. Yet experience and observation tell us, my brethren, that it is a captivating doctrine, and a growing opinion. All denominations wish to be thought right and true, but as this is beyond the reach of any credulity, without the help of this soul killing deceit of liberality, therefore it is hailed and applauded, pretty much in proportion to the consciousness of their need of it. But, my brethren, it is a most fatal deceit, the very Moloch of truth, and to be shunned at every hazard ; for fire does not more certainly consume the stubble, than those pestilent notions eat out the very life of religion in the soul.

It has also become common to blend the Christian doctrine

of charity with this modern notion of liberality of opinion. They have, however, in truth, no more connexion than light and darkness.   Christian charity, whether considered as a frame of mind, or as an active duty, has no application to opinions, no connexion with them—it applies solely to persons. With an erroneous or unscriptural doctrine in religion, the Christian is to have no connexion—on the contrary, he is bound to oppose it. But with the person holding it, he is bound, at the peril of his own soul, to be in charity, that is, not only to wish, but to do him good; any other view of this doctrine is erroneous—defeats, and renders it impossible as a Christian duty; but thus understood and applied, it is equal to all the great things spoken of it, and is the only principle that can maintain *peace in the* divisions among Christians, without sacrificing religion.   This is the old path, in which the primitive professors of charity walked, and it is the good way, into which we should do well to return, from the broad but deceitful road of a spurious liberality.

A third most fruitful cause of the decline of religion, must be referred to the character and qualifications of those acting as its ministers.

To keep up in the minds of men the reverence due to religion, and thus to gain their attention to its outward ministrations, it is essential that those who appear as its ministers should command respect, not only from their sacred office, *from their piety* and zeal, but from their acquirements in learning, and ability to fill the post of public instructors.   To see the gospel of our salvation in the hands of an incompetent ministry, is the readiest and surest way to defeat the influence of divine truth in the religion of CHRIST.   It is not in the nature of things, that persons of information—men of cultivated minds—should listen *with* any expectation of profit, or even with patience, to the unconnected effusions of ignorant men, however well intentioned they may be; and this may serve to account for the melancholy fact, that nearly all of this description of persons, have withdrawn themselves from ministrations in which neither their understandings, or their feelings, could take any part; and the awful consequence has been, not only an accession to the ranks of infidelity and irreligion, of these men themselves, but of others also, after their example, who had not the same excuse, if it may be so considered.

But incompetent men cannot long keep their hold, even upon the ignorant and uninformed, without some delusion of a fanatical character. Hence the claim of supernatural inspiration for their preachers, which some of the denominations set up, and which is insinuated and asserted by some of the preachers for themselves, in a variety of ways; while no pains is taken, by the body to which they belong, either to correct the delusion or to repress the practice. This is the charm which draws out crowds after men, who possess no single qualification, good intention perhaps excepted, for this most responsible office; and thus ignorance and delusion are extended and increased. The imagination, that spiritual power, in a preternatural sense, is lodged in particular men, produces its proper fruit, and heated minds are excited to give witness to this delusion, by yielding to its operations upon themselves.

In aid of this claim, the arguments and example of primitive times are boldly assumed. Nothing more common than this defence, of this every way indefensible delusion. They will tell you triumphantly, that GOD *hath chosen the weak things of the world to confound the strong, and the foolish things of the world to confound the wise.* They will appeal to the uneducated ignorance of our LORD's apostles, and tell you that they were poor fishermen and tradesmen. And so indeed they were, and for the very purpose, *that the excellency of the power might be of* GOD, *and not of men,* in the spread and establishment of the gospel. But they forget, or overlook, that these poor and ignorant fishermen, to qualify them to preach the gospel, were miraculously educated— that they became linguists, philosophers, and divines, in the school of the HOLY GHOST—that by one pentecostal out-pouring of the HOLY SPIRIT they were enlightened to understand and apply the Scriptures unerringly, to speak to every people in their own language, and to convince gainsayers, by those miraculous powers which were the proper evidence, that the gospel was the truth of GOD, and themselves his only ambassadors to this world of sinners. They forget that all these wonders were for a special purpose, and were not to continue—*Whether there be tongues, they shall cease,* and that the purpose being answered in the establishment of the gospel, miracles were withdrawn from the Church. And they are wilfully ignorant that under an established gospel, an authentic Scripture, a visible Church, and instituted means of grace, the ordinary influences of the HOLY SPIRIT are all that we are to look for, whether for private or public usefulness in the Church—as also, that it is true beyond the possibility of contradiction, that the HOLY GHOST calls no man to the ministry, who is not qualified with the necessary knowledge, or who possesses not the means and the desire to obtain it.

While this delusion, therefore, is countenanced, even with a tacit avowal of its fallacy on the part of better informed Christians, it will operate with great force against the religion it is intended to support. It must increase infidelity, because it contradicts our senses. Our ears—our eyes—our understandings, all concur in denying the truth of this claim, by whomsoever now made, and it leaves a fearful taint of unbelief on the mind against that religion whose public minister is thus found either deceived himself or trying to deceive others. It is impossible that religion should be respected in such hands, and if not respected, it will soon be thrown aside.

A fourth cause, of the decline of religion, and with which I shall conclude, is transient and occasional *preaching.*

The object of a preached gospel, is instruction in righteousness, impression upon the heart, and direction in the way of life ; and the object of a fixed ministry in the Church, is to watch for the souls given in charge, to provide food for each in due season, and suitable to the condition ; and by personal intercourse to be examples to the flock. None of which are ! compatible with a transient wandering ministry. No interest is felt like that of a pastor for his flock, by the man who is here to-day and gone to-morrow ; his object is too general, too diffuse, to occupy his heart with a special object of care and inspection. Nor can any of that close connexion exist between the flock and their pastor, which is so pleasant and so profitable to both. *The good shepherd calleth his own sheep by name, and he goeth before them, and the sheep follow him.* Yes, and he feedeth the lambs of the flock—all which is impossible to the transient preacher.

Occasional preaching also leaves many intervals in which there is no supply. In these cases the effect dies away, instruction is forgotten, the spirit declines, and the work is to do over. Thus like a door turning upon its hinges, they veer to this side and to that, but never move out of the place.

As a necessary consequence of transient and occasional preaching, disagreement in doctrine, and opposition in practice, among the preachers of the different denominations, will be sure to follow, as will also the effect in minds confused, bewildered, and unsettled, on the truths of religion, until unbelief steps in, and sweeps them all into equal contempt and oblivion.

To expect then, my brethren and hearers, under such a state of things, a flourishing state of religion, of rational, scriptural religion, would be the folly of looking for an effect without its cause, or that a cause should operate different from its nature. Whether those which I have pointed out, are sufficient to account for that decline in religion, which we must all deplore, is for you to judge, as it also is for you to consider, how far you are bound in the value of your souls, to strive for its correction. I can but show the evil, and exhort you to apply the remedy, the only remedy—*stand ye in the ways and see, and ask for the old paths, where is the good way, and walk therein, and ye shall find rest to your souls.*

As an application of what has been said, I appeal to the experience of all present, for the truth of that decline in religion which I have stated, and ask them, is it not an alarming fact, and one in which they are most deeply interested, both as citizens and Christians? And I appeal to the knowledge and observation of all present, for the sufficiency of the causes I have assigned, and ask, are they to continue to operate against your own souls, and the souls of your children? Oh what a fearful delusion has come upon us, and how contented we are under its death doing mischief. Oh what an awful prospect is there before the rising generation ; and yet we take no alarm. And shall no watchman in Zion take the trumpet, and give warning? Yes, there shall be one, who for the love of immortal souls, will set at nought misrepresentation and reproach, and blow an awakening note throughout her borders.

But it may be said, *Physician heal thyself.* Where is the remedy? My hearers, will you apply to it, will you take it if I present it? Behold it then in my text. Let us return to first principles, to the right ways of the LORD. It is an axiom we have consecrated in political science, it is the only remedy for a wrong road in the wanderings of this life. It is the only cure of religious errors; and it is put to you this day as the admonition of the LORD.

In exhorting you thus to turn to the LORD, from ways which have not profited, it glads my heart, my brethren, to be able to say, that the Church of your fathers, the old and good way in which they found rest to their souls, stands ready to receive you, and, as a nursing mother, to nourish you with sound doctrine, and feed your souls with the bread of life. That you may hear her counsel, she calls upon you to consider what you have gained by casting her off; what advance you have made in religion and morals, while you have been living without her ministry, her service, her ordinances, her instruction—she would meekly ask you, what have you profited, as to your souls, by the new ways in religion which have been proposed and pressed upon you? O let truth be heard without prejudice; let reason judge upon information; let experience teach by *observation;* let Scripture, the word of GOD, utter its warning to willing ears; let not example be thrown away. But as GOD hath put it into the hearts of the contributors to this building, to erect a Church to his name, let it encourage you to believe, that he is yet waiting to be gracious. It is indeed but a little one—Jacob is small, but Jacob's GOD can make of a little one a great nation. It is indeed the Church in the wilderness, but his blessing can turn the wilderness into a fruitful field. Yet he works by instruments; your exertions, as well as your prayers, are called for. Ye have well done in that ye have built an house to his name. But to be profitable to you, and honourable to him, it must be occupied, and attended upon. Transient, occasional preaching you have all had sufficient experience of, to know that it ends in listlessness and carelessness, indifference to religion, and deadness to GOD.

Put forth an effort then, in your own behalf and in behalf of all around; let not faith fail and GOD be dishonoured, through indolence or despair, and he will put it in the hearts of the ability, as to this world's good, which abounds around you, to supply this mighty void in your otherwise favoured condition. They are in the like necessity, and we cannot think they mean to continue thus. They will see their interest, they will see their duty, and give themselves to the glorious work of renovating the moral condition of all around them, and making a wilderness of sin and death, of ignorance and error, to bud and blossom as the rose, the desert, and the solitary place, to become vocal with the praises of GOD; and pure and undefiled religion, will be the rich legacy they bequeath to their children, with rest to their own souls in the kingdom and glory of our LORD JESUS CHRIST; to whom, &c. &c. .

THE END.

CPSIA information can be obtained
at www.ICGtesting.com
Printed in the USA
BVHW081538230819
556656BV00007B/226/P